CRACKS IN THE CLASSROOM WALL

CRACKS IN THE CLASSROOM WALL

Thomas G. Robischon
Antioch College West

Jerome Rabow
University of California at Los Angeles

Janet Schmidt
Santa Monica College

Goodyear Publishing Company, Inc.,
Pacific Palisades, California

Library of Congress Cataloging in Publication Data

Cracks in the classroom wall.

1. Education—Addresses, essays, lectures.
I. Robischon, Thomas Gregory. II. Rabow, Jerome.
III. Schmidt, Janet.
LB41.C9   370'.973   74-18728
ISBN 0-87620-177-X

Copyright © 1975 by Goodyear Publishing Company, Inc.,
Pacific Palisades, California

Library of Congress Catalog Card Number: 74-3721

ISBN: 0-87620-177-X

Y-177X-5

Current Printing: (last number)
10 9 8 7 6 5 4 3 2 1

Printed in the United States of America

Many helped to produce this book. There is the anonymous typing pool at UCLA who labors and works without recognition. We are grateful for their efforts and diligence. In the Sociology Department at UCLA Nadine Napier and Mary Takami took on our deadlines and transcribed academic handwriting into legible copy. The people at Goodyear have been most professional: David Grady with his special knowledge and Al Goodyear who stands behind quality. There are also the more emotional supports as well as the general hopes that each of us wants to personally cite and point toward.

To the colleges and universities where I have taught—Amherst, American International, Vassar, Elmira, Tuskegee, UCLA, and Antioch-West—which have unfailingly nurtured in me the conviction that there has to be another way for American education.

T.G.R.

This book is especially dedicated to the children in my life.

Josh and David are the children I know the best and love the most. Others whom I know and care for and who have touched me are: Josh A., Josh A. (Yes, two of them), Evie C., Jay G., Tracy G., Cara H., Emmanuel H., Hillary L., Phil N., Andrea N., Shawn R., Leigh S., Jonathan S., Alex W., Mandy W., Paul Z., and Rachel Z.

During my sabbatical the adolescents in the Area D Alternative School in Los Angeles taught me about the Sturm and Drang of adolescence in the 1970s while the fourth graders at the Overland Public School helped train and develop my patience. The adults, those special teachers, whose work with younger children includes the heart as well as the mind are Jill Josephson, Jill Krash, and Thelma Kaplan. Barbara Avedon works for children all over the earth and she has been a special neighbor and friend. Debra L. Schneiders' friendship and support have meant so much as to be extra special.

J.R.

To Victor & Heidi for their love and support, and to those persons and groups also engaged in struggle against the conditions of our oppression.

J.S.

CONTENTS

PREFACE

It no longer needs to be documented that American education or the American school system is in trouble. The cries and complaints come from students, academics, philosophers, educators, parents of middle-class, minority, and working-class youths, and from the teachers. What is not so clear or widely accepted is an understanding of how and why the schools became that way, and what alternatives to them are available to us.

As we have come to accept the unhappy idea that all is not well with our schools, there has spread among many the belief that reform is no longer the answer. There are still a few—but only a few—who believe that a new curriculum, an innovative text, some programmed learning, new groupings, a free classroom, team teaching, or more money can seriously change the structure and function of an entire school, let alone a system of schools. The growing assessment is that we need serious alternatives to the schools, and that we need them soon.

While many are firmly convinced that they do not want what we now have in the schools and that educational alternatives are the only answer, at the same time there seems to be little understanding or agreement as to the origin of these alternatives, their characteristics, and perhaps most especially, their authenticity—whether they are indeed alternatives or just more of the palliatives and tokens which have so often characterized school reform in the past.

The readings in this book have been brought together with the idea that in them can be found what we like to call the foundations of educational alternatives. Those who have embarked on the development of educational alternatives have discovered, sometimes to their dismay, that while it is easy to agree on what we don't want in our schools, we seem worlds apart when we try to agree on what we do want. This lack of agreement has characterized the free school movement in this country. More importantly, the lack of consensus was often accompanied by an explicit refusal to analyze schools and education, to develop explicit criteria, and to do the hard thinking that is necessary if we are to separate myth and reality. It was enough, so the belief went, to see that the public schools were abominable, that kids needed to be liberated, and that bringing together the like-spirited would result in reforms being made.

Many alternatives, public and private, have been devised. Some have flourished, but most have floundered. The possible danger in the recent attempts is that educational alternatives will become a fad; that the kind of piecemeal and pragmatic school reform of the past will be mistaken for genuine alternatives. We hope that these writings will help prevent such possibilities from happening. If we are to have alternatives that are not just new tokens that siphon off the discontent, they need to be grounded in historical, sociological, and philosophical analyses of schools and education. We attempt to provide such alternatives here.

This book is dedicated to our students, past and present, who have contributed much to our education. A percentage of royalties from this book will be given to needy students in the departments with which each of us are affiliated.

Ah Love! could you and I with Him conspire
To grasp this sorry Scheme of Things entire,
Would not we shatter it to bits—and then
Re-mold it nearer to the Heart's Desire!

Rubaiyat of Omar Khayyam

chapter one

THE NEED FOR
A NEW ANALYSIS

It is often noted that Americans are very ahistorical. Certainly this charge can be leveled at all citizens, but perhaps the young are most guilty on this count. The vigor and freshness of youth, with its zeal for its own ideas and virtues, is attractive and appealing. Yet it is clear from a careful reading of reform movements in social welfare, education, and government that reformers, young and old, often neglect the past and proceed on the basis of an inadequate or incorrect analysis.[1] It is probably safe to apply this latter statement to the educational reformer of the past ten to twenty years.

Schools, like prisons, like Congress, like welfare, and taxes are badly in need of reform and revision. But it is clear that none of the reform movements of today are new. The goal in this first chapter is to provide some historical perspective on the public school system in the United States. Without a clearer understanding of how the schools have failed to liberate, emancipate, or democratize individuals, how they have failed to provide mobility to the disadvantaged or the working class, and how they have failed to instill a democratic ideology and ethos in their constituents, the reformers and radicals, change agents and innovators are bound to repeat the errors of their forebears.

We do not view the struggle between reformers of education as the struggle between good people and bad people, between idealism and materialism, between people who care about children and those who care about money. The major reason for rejecting such a notion is its simplicity. For example, community control advocates might have some appeal for us, but what if the advocates of such control are bigots, or racists? How then do we respond to the idea of community control? And what of the people who vote against the school bonds? Are they shortsighted and materialistic, or are they responding to some deeper concerns about the quality of education, the senselessness of much schooling and the unequal costs of sharing public education?

The major contention of this first chapter is that public school education in America has survived, without basic changes, in part, because of the insufficient analysis by critics of the *myths,* the *assumptions,* and the *ideology* that have cloaked the public school. This chapter seeks to explode the myths, challenge the assumptions, put aside the ideology, and document the realities of public education. To change the realities of public schools, the myths and incorrect assumptions supporting them must be removed.

Myths, assumptions and ideology are not arbitrary. They occur in specific

---

1. Anatole Shaeffer describes the phenomenon with regard to grass roots medical care and the undermining of local democracy by state and federal officials. See "The Cincinnati Unit Social Experiment: 1917-19," *Social Service Review,* 45, No. 2 (June 1971). Also reprinted in Jerome Rabow, ed., *Sociology, Students and Society,* (Pacific Palisades, Ca.: Goodyear Publishing Co., 1972).

cultural and structural contexts. They are used by those in power to sustain the status quo. Louis Wirth said that the most important facts about a society are those that are seldom debated and generally regarded as settled. The particular assumptions, myths and facts needed to perpetuate American society were and are still related to an industrial and capitalistic order. This generality will be documented throughout the book.

One assumption that most Americans have held has to do with the exclusiveness of the public school model as *the* model of education. In part, this assumption comes from the "who cares about history" attitude noted earlier. We call this assumption: "The way it is is the way it had to be." Recent historians argue against the assertion that we have never had alternative models for education. In the first part of this chapter we describe some of these alternative models from our not too distant past. Accordingly, we assert now that:

"THE WAY IT IS IS NOT THE WAY IT HAS TO BE!"

Public schooling is taken for granted in America. Indeed, it is often thought of as The American Way to the American Dream. Yet the public school as we know it is less than 100 years old. That it is only 100 years old is not as important as that it has persisted without basic changes for these past 100 years. Yet in the 1850s there were four alternative models of schooling competing for acceptance in this country. By 1880 the debates had ended and American education assumed the structural characteristics that remain to this day. Anyone interested in understanding and reforming the school system should first understand how that system developed.

Historically and contemporaneously, the view of the clash between reformers as a clash between good folks and bad folks, or radicals and conservatives, is too narrow a view. As Michael D. Katz reminds us in his pioneering work, there were four different proposals or models of organizing education that were rivals in this country at one time.[2] Each of them, while having some overlap in reality, rested upon a different set of social values. The merits of these models were debated vigorously much in the way the recent Ocean Hill-Brownsville case was debated.[3] The acceptance of what Katz calls the incipient bureaucracy model, the model we know all too well today, is the reality that those who want educational alternatives are confronted with today. The questions about this model that must be asked include: Why has this structure remained so resistant to change? What is the possibility for genuine educational alternatives in the face of this resistance? Must structural change precede educational change? And, perhaps most importantly, how far can we hope to go with alternatives in education if we do not at some time develop alternatives to the other institutions in our society which reflect and are reflected in our schools? These questions provide the basic structure of this textbook.

We begin not at the beginning of educational alternatives but at a time when

---

2. From *CLASS, BUREAUCRACY AND SCHOOLS: The Illusion of Educational Change in America*, by Michael B. Katz. Copyright 1971 by Praeger Publishers, Inc., New York. Excerpted and reprinted by permission (fns. 4-8).

3. Marilyn Gittell and Maurice Berube, *Confrontation at Ocean Hill-Brownsville*. This book documents the modern version of community control and the conflict that developed between teachers and the community (New York: Praeger, 1969).

different models of education were striving for acceptance in America, with brief descriptions of the models that Katz illuminates for us. They are called "Paternalistic Voluntarism," "Democratic Localism," "Corporate Voluntarism," and "Incipient Bureaucracy." We shall return later to the questions of what we can learn from these models and the staying power of the incipient bureaucracy which is with us today.

PATERNALISTIC VOLUNTARISM

The Paternalistic Voluntarism model had as its major purpose the extension of education to poor children who were not provided for by any religious society. The adherents advocated free schools only for the very poor. Because of problems of misappropriated funds and acrimonious debates between several religious societies, the members of the New York Public School Society reversed their position about free school being only for the poor. In 1825 they became responsible for public education in the City of New York. Voluntarism meant there was an unpaid board of citizens desirous of "serving mankind," of being benevolent and acting as servants of the people. These men had leisure, wanted to avoid politics and benefit mankind. Voluntarism was an American form of noblesse oblige. It rested upon a belief in the devotion and talent of the amateur, scorned large overall administrative units and was disdainful of professionals. The society taught thousands of children at a minimal cost, and with financial integrity. It was, however, a class system of education. One class was responsible for civilizing another to insure that society would remain tolerable, orderly and safe. The parents of the poor were seen as intemperate and not interested in their offspring, who would become urchins and then burdens and pests. The parents and the children were told to practice temperance, industry, piety, frugality and cleanliness. Discipline was strict in the enormous one-room schools. Several hundred students coexisted with one headmaster. Education was reduced to drill, and norms of docility, sobriety, cleanliness and obedience were inculcated. Solitary study was nil and children were disciplined by shame rather than pain. The system was designed not for one's own children or for the children of your friends, but rather, as Katz says, "to ensure social order through the socialization of the poor in cheap, mass, schooling factories."[4]

The critics of the paternalistic model stressed three shortcomings. First, a private group of citizens was engaging in an important government function and yet had no immediate responsibility to the people. Thus it was considered undemocratic. Second, the New York Public School Society was not truly voluntary. The Society did not permit the parents of the children to participate in the course of studies or education of their children. The children were turned over to strangers who were not accountable to parents. Finally, paternalistic voluntarism ignored the tremendous variety in American life and imposed a cultural hegemony upon the clientele.

DEMOCRATIC LOCALISM

The first alternative to paternalistic voluntarism was democratic localism. The

---

4. Michael Katz, *Class, Bureaucracy and Schools* (New York: Praeger, 1972) p. 11.

goal of this model was to adapt to the city the organizational form that was currently in use in rural areas, the district or community school. The democratic localists fought against the paternalistic voluntarism and against bureaucracy or centralization. The attack on voluntarism stressed the variety and difference in urban life, while the attack on centralization rested upon antiprofessionalism and upon the imposed social change of outsiders on the local community. The democrats' position reflected a belief in the wisdom of the people, i.e., that the people are intelligent enough to act for themselves, and also the belief that forced schooling would not be accepted by the people. The democrats felt that if the system were voluntary, free choice and grass roots action would help people develop affection and belief in their school system.

Democratic localism was trying to deal with the rapid social change of the 1830s and '40s. Unfortunately it rested upon a vision of the small rural town. At its best it was a construct for the cure of powerlessness and alienation. At its worst it could be the tyranny of the local majority whose ambition was control in terms as biased as those of the voluntaristic model. It was, however, a noble vision not suited to the realities of the urban poor or of urban life.

CORPORATE VOLUNTARISM

The third model was corporate voluntarism. By this is meant the conduct of "single institutions or individual corporations which are operated by self-perpetuating boards of trustees and financed either wholly through endowment or through a combination of endowment and tuition."[5] This model applied to secondary and higher education, to academies and the colleges, and was a serious challenge to the other models. It seemed likely to become the general model for secondary education.

The basic argument behind this model was that autonomous competing corporations that were *aided* by the state best served the public interest. This was considered true of finance, transportation and manufacturing, so why not education? Academies were, of course, considered *educational corporations*. Corporate voluntarism, like democratic localism, stressed the idea that education ought to be suited to the character and condition of its clientele. Its clientele, however, was not the working class. Its obvious elitist recruitment prevented this model from being successful. Academies could not be considered *public* schools.

INCIPIENT BUREAUCRACY

The triumphant model and the model we still have today is called Incipient Bureaucracy. This model is associated with some of the great figures in educational reform. Horace Mann and Henry Barnard were two pivotal characters who concentrated their attack on democratic localism. Over and over they would argue that 51 percent of the "local" parents could, under the democratic model, dictate the religious, moral and political ideas to the children of 49 percent of the community. Over and over the argument was made against the multiplicity of peculiar doctrines that would be taught if the community con-

5. Katz, p. 22.

trolled their education. Democratic localism was not only seen by its detractors as inefficient but also as being unsuited to the complexities of modern urban life. Barnard argued for the schools to act as agencies which would uplift the quality of urban life. The rhetoric of incipient bureaucracy condemned the poverty, the crime and the immorality that accompanied urban and industrial development. The moral condemnation was backed by a fear about the potential class conflict that such conditions breed. A class gulf would ensue if the working masses were not cleansed of idleness, rude manners, profane language, and ignorance. To change this hotbed of potential revolution, school reformers had to remove the child from the parent. Away from the parent and under the direction of a surrogate mother (a female teacher), the child would become virtuous, clean, refined, even-tempered, and gentle. The focus of schooling was clearly not intellectual. After the age of twelve a child could be further educated in the practical business of earning a living. School attendance was not to be taken lightly. Truancy was, said Barnard, the "crime of neglected childhood." The above emphasis indicated the choice of heart over head, of character development over intellectual development, of morality over mind or skill, of morals over subject matter. These preferences and choices still exist in the contemporary scene of education. The school was considered a training arena for commerce and industry. Good work and discipline had to be instilled in the working class and knowledge was going to be second to morality.

When democratic localism was rejected, plans were swiftly presented for a system of schools complete with architectural details, curricula, and an overall attempt to *standardize* and systematize the structure and conduct of public education.

The plans of Mann, Barnard and their contemporaries were concerned with centralization. By means of centralization, the locus of power and decision making, the school district, the bastion of democratic localism, could be eliminated. Towns under centralization would not run their own schools. Rather, a central board of education would manage the several schools in a town or in several towns. This was an administrative device to remove power from the local scene and put it into the hands of administrators and professionals.

The first public high school was established in Boston in 1820. By 1865 Massachusetts had 103 high schools, or about one high school to every three towns and cities. By 1856 San Francisco had its first high school. The laws requiring towns of a certain size to maintain high schools also were accompanied by laws requiring attendance. Supervision and professional expertise were now introduced as components of the administrative domain. Education had become within a few years a difficult and complex undertaking which required well-trained persons with special knowledge, special skills, and special experience. Whereas the localists had been suspicious of and hostile towards professionals, the bureaucrats announced and heralded the day of the pedagogue.

The challenge to the new system was great. Part of the challenge lay in converting a preindustrial proletariat into a modern work force with transformed attitudes towards work, time and discipline. A commitment to competence in narrow terms was to replace the well defined roles and social structure of preindustrial society. But the content of education could not be imposed willy nilly upon the masses. Minority and lower class sensibilities could not be offended. To ward off the cries of assimilation and absorption and intrusion upon cultural differences, the schoolmen proclaimed the schools to be politically and religiously neutral. But neutral they were not. The Catholics were well aware of the nonneutrality of the schools. Schools, administrators and teachers were predominantly Protestant, and the public school tone and focus exuded a Protestant tone. Nor were schools without their class bias. The mid-Victorian emphasis on self-denial and sublimation permeated textbooks and the educational objectives of education. Self-denial was something all children must learn, for it was through self-denial that future good was to be obtained. One's present suffering and toil were to be rewarded eventually through enjoyment. The schools' goal of sublimation or the desexualization of the working class was developed as a mirror image of Victorian sensibility and propriety. Schoolmen did not recognize their own biases in these matters, though there is evidence that their views were based upon a fear of the great cultural variety and the ethnic and religious differences that existed in the urban environment. This was a version of the melting pot rhetoric. The terms *difference* and *inferior* abound in the discussions and arguments of the day.

The evidence on the success of the public high schools in the nineteenth century is scanty. Again, we quote Katz.[6]

> What little evidence exists of an actual connection between high school attendance and middle-class employment in the mid-nineteenth century seems to indicate that the schools did offer some advantages to boys in search of white-collar work. Unquestionably, they served girls in search of teaching jobs, and female students generally far outnumbered male. However, contrary to popular belief, in its early history the high school was not popular with the working class, which frequently viewed it as a class institution irrelevant to its own aspirations and impossible to utilize when the earnings of adolescents were needed to keep the family alive. Nor, in its early history, did the high school actively promote social mobility, social harmony, or egalitarianism. Very few poor children attended; indeed, only a very small minority of the community's children even began high school, and most of them left before graduation.

We have then inherited a model of public education that is tinged with religious aspects, politically biased in its link with modern industrial capitalism, discriminatory towards the working class, unappreciative of cultural variety, racist by implication, and more concerned with character development than intellectual development. It has taken about 100 years to make these biases explicit and to make these contradictions apparent.

The idea that American education has not changed as much as we might have thought heretofore, that, indeed, it has changed very little over the past 100 years, seems to be emerging at the same time there is a growing awareness that American education has not been the basically beneficient institution so many of us have thought it to be. This awareness is reflected in the new analysis or approaches to understanding education in America represented by the selections in this chapter. It will continue to be reflected in many of the selections in subsequent chapters.

Katz, from whom the descriptions of the models were taken, expresses this new awareness without equivocation:

6. Katz, pp. 42-43.

This is a realization to which the young came first and older reformers more slowly. The creation of a counterculture and the attempt to find alternatives to public schooling express the same impulse and the same truth. There is only one way to grow up in America if one wants to eat regularly, to be warm, and not to be harassed by the police. For the vast majority there is only one place to go to school, and that place is the same nearly everywhere.[7]

Later he puts it succinctly and bluntly: The features of American education that became fixed so firmly by the late nineteenth century, remaining with it ever since, were that it was "universal, tax-supported, free, compulsory, bureaucratically arranged, class-biased, and racist."[8]

The foregoing analysis should lay asunder the notion that "schools are the way they had to be." We have presented descriptions of alternative models of schooling not merely to correct the ahistorical perspective on education and schooling but to show the connection between modern versions of those older models.

The paternalistic voluntarism model finds its modern derivative in the suggestion that school boards should be composed of a small body of citizens appointed by a mayor. The assumption in this proposal is that politics can be divorced from education. As Anthony M. Platt has shown in his studies of riot commissions, it is naive to assume that there exists a body of disinterested and wise citizens who are devoid of political values and personal motives and who are capable of identifying the public interest.[9]

Corporate voluntarism has its modern counterpart in the voucher system of education. Christopher Jencks has proposed the replacement of the public monopoly of schooling with competing private groups who would operate their own educational system. This proposal rests on the assumption that competition among schools will raise the quality of education since the clients of schools will be able to choose a better product from the different varieties of types of schooling being offered.

Democratic localism is popularized today by the proponents of community control. Today's advocates of community control, like the Irish Catholics in New York City in the 1840s, distrust professionals, emphasize the radical decentralization of school systems into small districts governed by local community organizations and in general want to gain power and wrest control from the bureaucratic administrator and professionals who currently run the school system.

The model we know so well, the model of incipient bureaucracy, also has its modern proponents. It would be more correct, however, to call this model incipient technocracy. In this view, the problems of modern public school education are solvable through machines and technology. The most visible symbols are the teaching machine or computer-aided instructions. Efficiency is again stressed, size is no problem and professionalism is very critical to the proponents. Whether this incipient bureaucratic model will continue in a reformed manner is unclear. What is clear is that the staying power of the bureaucratic model is enormous and that support for that model comes from professors of education who see position and power being perpetuated in this

7. Ibid., p. 3.
8. Ibid, p. 106.
9. Anthony Platt, *The Politics of Riot Commissions* (New York: Collier Books, 1971).

model and see power being eroded in the community control model. Another source of support from this model comes from those who advocate integration and see large educational parks as a way to overcome de facto segregation.

The debates over these modern variants will continue. What we hope we have made clear is the value preference in each model. We ourselves differ about some eminent issues. Will community control improve the content of education? Does professionalism result in improved learning in the classroom? Will corporate industries produce mere technocrats who will examine issues in terms of efficiency? While these questions are not clearly answerable now, what is clear is that now is the time for viewing alternative models in terms of their value preference. These values must be made explicit or else we shall continue with the incipient bureaucratic model, and the illusion of the "way it is is the way it had to be" will be perpetuated.

We turn now to the second assumption, namely that schools are value-free. The myth is that schools do not teach values. We have already noted some of the value differences in explicating the four models; values of local control versus efficiency, values of standardization versus difference, values of vocational skills over matters of the mind and the heart. It could be argued that these are *implicit* values resulting from the form or patterns of social organization. Our position is that the schools explicitly teach values. We will for the moment put aside the major values of sexism and racism, but again return to history for some careful documentation of the value dimensions encouraged by early public school education. Accordingly we assert that:

SCHOOLS TEACH VALUES

While there are many values that we could focus on in this chapter, values regarding nature or time, we shall concentrate instead on the economic values and individualistic values stressed by the public school system of education. We want to tie the emphasis upon values to the period described earlier when the four competing models of educational alternatives were being argued within American society.

Shortly after the Civil War in 1873, America, the "land of opportunity" entered a depression that lasted for six years. This depression took a deadly toll of the working class. Only 20 percent of the working class retained regular employment throughout that six-year period.[10] Forty percent of the working class worked only six to seven months per year during the depression. Yet vast fortunes were being made!

In 1870 Standard Oil was organized and John D. Rockefeller was on his way to becoming "the most feared and hated man in America."[11] Commodore Vanderbilt had assets of one million dollars prior to the Civil War. By 1877, when he died, he left an estate of over 100 million. This railroad king of the seventies had done very well in the land of opportunity. In 1877, however, his company, the New York Central, announced wage cuts and the United States had its first major railroad strike. The strike spread from West Virginia to Canada and to

10. Phillips Foner, *History of the Labor Movement in the United States* (New York: International Publishers, 1955).
11. Stewart A. Holbrook, *The Age of the Moguls* (New York: Doubleday, 1953).

California. Governors throughout the land called out the militia and violence developed across the face of the nation. In one pitched battle in Pittsburgh, 26 workers were killed and an angry mob destroyed 5 million dollars worth of railroad property.[12]

Riots were unknown to the American people, and although the end of the depression quelled much of the disquiet and uneasiness, some fears still lingered among the wealthy and affluent. If the American worker lost his belief in America as the land of opportunity, then the workers might resort to radicalism and violence. How could the faith be maintained? One of the ways to perpetuate the belief that America was still the land of opportunity despite depression and industrial warfare was to promulgate the idea that there was room at the top, that one could gain fame, fortune, and success. What form could such urgings take? There were the tried and successful success manuals.

America had started out with a success manual (Benjamin Franklin in 1757 published *The Way to Wealth*),[13] and by 1900 the numbers of success manuals proliferated greatly. More manuals were published in the period between 1880 and 1885 than in any other five-year period. It is not coincidental that these manuals came at the end of the depression. Desperate workers might just as easily turn to the success manuals as to Karl Marx.

Most millionaires had neither the time nor the talent to write their own biographies, and so journalists supplied the bulk of the biographical data on the rich men of America. What were the secrets of success? What were the moral suggestions urged on the masses by these manuals? What wisdom could one glean from these successful Americans?

Genius was not required! Indeed, genius was often an obstacle to success since very bright people were thought to be vain, lazy, forgetful of time and undisciplined. In deprecating genius, the authors of the success manuals made clear that practically anybody who wasn't a genius could be a success. Being less than brilliant was a necessary condition, but not the sole requisite.

Another necessary conditon for bringing about success turned out to be *poverty*. In struggling against poverty one developed the personal qualities necessary for success. If you were born in a rural area, that alone gave you a decided advantage on the path to success. A rural life meant a healthy body and a moral character that was strengthened by the rigors of country chores and fresh air.

So, if you were born poor and in the country, you had two of the necessary conditions for success. What else was required? What was the final sufficient condition for success? One needed moral virtue! Moral virtue was demonstrated with qualities of industry, thrift, and perseverance. Idleness could not be justified. Perseverance was the great thing. Frugality was not only a way to insure your personal fortune, but with the gaining of private fortune you could also become a *public* benefactor. The young adults who were reading the success manuals had probably heard the latter idea before—in their school books. The most famous of all the textbooks were *The McGuffey Readers.*[14] In 1870-1880 over

12. Henry J. Perkinson, *The Imperfect Panacea: American Faith in Education 1865-1965* (New York: Random House, 1968) p. 105.
13. Benjamin Franklin, *The Way to Wealth* (Dijon, printed by P. Causse, 1975). This was first printed in *Poor Richard's Almanac* in 1758.
14. See Richard D. Mosier for his analysis of the *McGuffey's Readers--Making the American Mind; Social and Moral Ideas in the McGuffey Readers* (New York: King's Crown Press, 1947).

60 million copies were sold. What did these textbooks instill in public school children?

From the first to the sixth grades American children were encouraged to be industrious and persevering, thrifty, and loyal. Obedience was stressed over and over. Disobedience invariably brings about disaster. The stories demonstrated how virtue is always rewarded with material success. The texts showed how a young man fights poverty to save his widowed mother from starvation or shovels snow to get money to buy his school books. By the 1880s Americans who were weaned on McGuffey's Readers were ready for the Horatio Alger novels. Starting with *Ragged Dick,*[15] in 1867, in 106 books for boys the same sure-fire formula is used. The typical Alger hero is poor, and through pluck and a little luck rises to the top. He is never a genius. He is manly and self-reliant and embodies thrift, perseverance, and honesty. The novels were on YMCA shelves and often bestowed on children as prizes. The names of the novels perhaps are indicative of what Americans dreamed of. *Only an Irish Boy, The Chicago Newsboy, Luck and Pluck, Phil the Fiddler, Slow and Sure, The Store Boy, Strong and Steady, Tom the Bootblack, Try and Trust,* are among the titles devoured by thousands. There were, of course, some Americans who doubted this version of America. America *had* changed, and *that* reality was being described by a few.[16] The Horatio Alger hero had absolutely no connection to mining, construction, transportation, or manufacturing, the industries that were reshaping America into an industrial giant.

So while America was changing, the success stories—the McGuffey Readers and the Alger novels—and the schools had not caught up with the structural and economic shifts.

Our contention is that much of the values described in the success stories, McGuffey Readers, and Alger novels are still with us *today.* An ethic of individual competition is rampant in our textbooks and schools. Competition is still presented as a natural or inborn aspect of human nature. The rural benefits of life, up until ten years ago, were being reiterated. The importance of perseverance not as a quality one could or could not elect but as evidence of moral virtue is still encouraged today. Most importantly, the notion of obedience and a place in the world is instilled very soon and very quickly in our children. As Miriam Wasserman argues so eloquently in her book *The School Fix, N.Y.C., USA,*[17] the classroom experience, the day-to-day interactions teach the child, regardless of class and race, to submit to authority, to submit to established procedures and to accept classroom rituals.

The last assumption we wish to address ourselves to is the assumption that education is synonymous with schooling. We assert:

EDUCATION DOES NOT EQUAL SCHOOLING

It is incorrectly assumed that one receives an education simply by going to school. The argument is made in different ways, "If you don't go to school

15. Horatio Alger, *Ragged Dick* (New York: Collier Books, 1962).
16. Eric Goldman describes the disenchantment of Americans in the eighties. See *Rendezvous with Destiny* (New York: Alfred A. Knopf, 1952) and also Chester A. Destler, *American Radicalism* (New London: Octagon, 1946).
17. Miriam Wasserman, *The School Fix* (New York: Simon & Schuster, 1971 A Clarion Book).

you cannot be educated": "To improve education or improve your education you improve schools or get more school." Whether one has a progressive view (Dewey),[18] a traditionalist view (Rickover),[19] or a contemporary educational reformer's view (Bruner),[20] all agree that better education requires better schooling. But as Peter Schrag points out in our first selection, one of the reasons that the impossible dream has ended is that educational alternatives have been shut down. The farm, the shop, apprenticeships, and small entrepreneurs are no longer viable alternatives. The school has become the major, or even exclusive, legitimate way to educate young people. Peter Schrag, in our first selection, describes how the dreams and hopes for our schools have crashed around us and have become nightmares instead of dreams.

END OF THE IMPOSSIBLE DREAM

Peter Schrag

It is ten years later, and the great dream has come to an end. We thought we had solutions to everything—poverty, racism, injustice, ignorance; it was supposed to be only a matter of time, of money, of proper programs, of massive assaults. Perhaps nothing was ever tried without restraint or dilution, perhaps we were never willing to exert enough effort or spend enough money, but it is now clear that the confidence is gone, that many of the things we *knew* no longer seem sure or even probable. What we believed about schools and society and the possibilities of socially manageable perfection has been reduced to belying statistics and to open conflict in the street and the classroom.

Twenty years ago we took as fact the idea that American public schools— that *the school system*—could be reformed, first to make the education enterprise more intellectually rigorous and selective, and then to make it more democratic. Thus we had our decade with the Rickovers, the Bestors, the Conants, and the Zachariases; men who believed that students did not know enough physics or French or English, and that through new programs, or a return to "the fundamentals," or through adjustments in teacher training, students could become superior academic operators and, above all, better qualified candidates for the university. And then, beginning in about 1960, we had our decade with the democrats, the integrationists, and the apostles of universal opportunity:

18. John Dewey, *The Child and the Curriculum,* and *The School and Society* (Chicago: University of Chicago Press, 1902, 1900).
19. Hyman G. Rickover, *Education and Freedom* (New York: Dutton, 1960).
20. Jerome S. Bruner, *The Process of Education* (New York: Vintage, 1960).

Kenneth B. Clark, Thomas Pettigrew, Francis Keppel, and John Gardner, who believed that by changing teacher attitudes, or through busing, or through fiscal and geographical rezoning, all children could have equal educational opportunities.

In the first instance the reformers represented the aspirations of the enfranchised, the suburban parents of affluence who once sent their children to Harvard by right of birth and now had to do it by right of achievement. In the second, the reformers demanded for the deprived what they thought the advantaged were getting, believing in the magic of the good school and accepting the rhetoric of individual accomplishment. Now, suddenly, the optimism is gone, and the declining faith in educational institutions is threatening the idea of education itself.

If we want to understand why the schools have "failed," we have only to state the criteria of success. The schools achieved their reputation when they did not have to succeed, when there were educational alternatives—the farm, the shop, the apprenticeship—and when there were other routes to economic and social advancement. Every poor little boy who became a doctor represented a victory. Poor little boys who became ditch diggers disappeared from the record. As soon as we demanded success for everyone—once there were no alternatives—failure was inevitable, not only because the demands were too great, but because they were repressive and contradictory. No other nation, wrote Henry Steele Commager in a representative flight of self-congratulation, "ever demanded so much of schools and of education . . . none other was ever so well served by its schools and its educators." We expected the schools to teach order, discipline, and democracy, the virtues of thrift, cleanliness, and hard work, the evils of alcohol, tobacco, and later of sex and communism; we wanted them to acculturate the immigrants, to provide vocational skills, to foster patriotism and tolerance, and, above all, to produce a high standard of literacy throughout the population. All this they sometimes did and still do.

The impossible demand was enshrined in the mythology of the American dream itself: that the schools constitute the ultimate promise of equality and opportunity; that they enable American society to remain somehow immune from the economic inequities and social afflictions that plague the rest of mankind; that they, in short, guarantee an open society. In 1848, Horace Mann, in one of his annual reports as secretary of the Massachusetts Board of Education, described his vision of the common school—the school for children of all classes and backgrounds—as "a great equalizer of the conditions of men, the balance wheel of the social machinery. . . . It does better than disarm the poor of their hostility toward the rich: It prevents being poor. . . ." The school is our answer to Karl Marx—and to everything else. With the closing of the frontier, which once was regarded as a safety valve and from which the schools inherited many of their mythological functions (if you're not born rich you can go west, can, that is, go to school), and with the rise of a certificated, schooled meritocracy, the educational system has become the central institution of the American dream. Education, it has often been said, is the American religion. Thus, if the school system fails, so does the promise of equality, so does the dream of the classless society, so does our security against the inequalities of society. The school system has failed.

Evidence? Is it necessary again to cite statistics, dropout rates, figures on black and white children who go to college (or finish high school), comparisons of academic success between rich and poor kids, college attendance figures for slums and suburbs? The most comprehensive data on hand indicate that, in the final analysis, nothing in school makes as much difference as the economic background of the student and the social and economic backgrounds of his peers. There is no evidence that increasing educational expenditures in a particular district will produce greater achievement, and a fair amount of evidence that it will not. But this sort of argument is still misleading and, in the final analysis, rather useless, because it presumes that we agree on what constitutes success. Failure to complete high school is regarded as some sort of cosmic failure, a form of personal and social death. Dropout becomes synonymous with delinquent. Yet the evidence indicates that in some school systems the smart ones drop out and the dumb ones continue. Self-educated men used to be heroes; now they are prejudged unfit, or, more likely, they just don't appear in the social telescope at all.

Then why have the schools failed? Why boycotts and strikes, why the high school SDS, why the battles over long hair, underground newspapers, and expressions of independent student opinion? Why are there cops in the corridors and marijuana in the gym lockers? Why is it that most students panic when they're invited to work on their own, to study independently? Why is it that most students are more interested in what the teacher wants or what's going to be on the test than they are in understanding the subject that's ostensibly under study? Why bells, monitors, grades, credits, and requirements? Why do most students learn to cheat long before they learn how to learn? Yes, there are exceptions—there are teachers who ask real questions and schools that honor real intellectual distinction and practice real democracy. But a system that requires all children (except the very rich who can buy their way out) to attend a particular school for a specified period—that, in other words, sentences everyone to twelve years of schooling—such a system can and must be judged by its failures.

Everything that we could not, or would not, do somewhere else we expected to be done in the schools. And in the process we thought we saw what in fact does not exist. The greatest failure of American educational journalism in the last decade is that its practitioners refused to believe what they saw, and reported instead what they were supposed to see. Thus we have been inundated with millions of words about the new math, the new physics, the compensatory this and advanced that, about BSCS and PSSC, about IPI and SMSG, about individual progress and head start, upward bound, and forward march. And thus also we have read, with increasing incomprehension, about student uprisings, protests and boycotts and strikes. But few of us ever described the boredom, the emptiness, the brutality, the stupidity, the sheer waste of the average classroom.

What choices does a fifteen-year-old have in the average high school? Choices as to courses, teacher, or physical presence? What does he do most of the day? He sits—and maybe listens. Follow him, not for a few minutes, but for six hours a day, 180 days a year. What goes on in the class? What is it about, what questions are asked? Is it about the real world? Is it about an intellectually honest discipline? Is it about the feelings, passions, interests, hopes, and fears of those who are present? No. It is a world all of its own. It is mostly about nothing.

It worked as long as the promise of schooling itself appeared credible, that is, as long as the proffered reward looked more like a rainbow and less like a mirage, before the end of the road was crowded with people reporting back that the trip wasn't worth it. It is not necessary again to describe the travesties of the average classroom or the average school. But it is important to point out the nothingness of schooling because nothingness (or conformity and repressions and boredom) is necessary to the system. Which is not to suggest an Establishment conspiracy to keep children docile so they will become satisfactory candidates for the military-industrial complex. No one planned schools this way, nor have teachers and principals betrayed them: The schools do what they do out of a structural necessity, because we don't know enough about learning, and because mythology permits very little else.

Any single, universal public institution—and especially one as sensitive as the public school—is the product of a social quotient verdict. It elevates the lowest common denominator of desires, pressures, and demands into the highest public virtue. It cannot afford to offend any sizable community group, be it the American Legion, the B'nai B'rith, or the NAACP. Nor can it become a subversive enterprise that is designed to encourage children to ask real questions about race or sex or social justice or the emptiness and joys of life. Occasionally, of course, it does do these things, but rarely in a significant and consistent manner. Students who ask real questions tend to be threatening to teachers, parents, and the system. They destroy the orderliness of the management procedure, upset routines, and question prejudices. The textbook, the syllabus, the lesson plan are required not only because most teachers are lost without them, but because they represent an inventory for the community, can be inspected to ascertain the purity of the goods delivered. Open-ended programs, responsive to the choices and interests of students, are dangerous not only because all real questions are dangerous, but because they cannot be preinspected or certified for safety. The schools are not unresponsive to the immediate demands of the society. They are doing precisely what most Americans expect.

Earlier, I spoke about contradictory objectives. One is the objective of "equality of educational opportunity"; the other is to reinforce and legitimize distinctions. For many years, these objectives were, in fact, consistent. They share certain behavioral values that are honored and enforced in the average classroom: discipline, order, certain kinds of manners, styles of speech and dress, punctuality, cleanliness, and so on. Kids who do not meet these standards are ridiculed, punished, and demeaned. The two sets of values also share a declared commitment to certain skills: reading, writing, the skills of the average intelligence test—and a disdain for other attributes: originality, curiosity, diversity. They share, in other words, a linear standard of success and failure. Slow and bright, average and retarded, all fall on one scale, one straight line that runs from zero to one hundred, from A to F. Any teacher in any school can tell any other teacher in any other school about his good, average, and slow students, about his difficult students, and about his cooperative ones, and both will know precisely who and what is being described. (Occasionally, of course, some school or teacher honors a "difficult" child, or a genuinely curious one, or one who has skills—in music or dance, for example—which are outside the normal scale of classroom success. But those are rare instances.)

About a decade ago, something began to change. Until then "equality of educational opportunity" was understood in simple (and misleading) terms. It was the equality inherited from social Darwinism: Everyone in the jungle (or in society, or in school) was to be treated equally: one standard, one set of books, one fiscal formula for children everywhere, regardless of race, creed, or color. Success went to the resourceful, the ambitious, the bright, the strong. Those who failed were stupid or shiftless, but whatever the reason, failure was the responsibility of the individual (or perhaps of his parents, poor fellow), but certainly not that of the school or the society. It was this premise that fired the drive for school integration. Negro schools, we believed, were older, more poorly equipped, badly financed. By equalizing resources, and perhaps throwing in a little compensation to offset differences deriving from "cultural disadvantage," everybody would be competing in the same race. Thus Head Start and "counterpoise" and "early enrichment." Every program launched in the past decade assumed a linear standard of success; each took for granted that schooling was a competitive enterprise and that life was a jungle where only the fit survive. Integration was, more than anything else, a political attempt to win white hostages to black education: Where white kids went to school with black there would be better resources and teachers. Apparently it never occurred to anyone that as long as we operated by a linear standard (bright, average, slow, or whatever) the system would, by definition, have to fail at least some kids. Every race has a loser. Failure is structured into the American system of public education. Losers are essential to the success of the winners.

In the process of compensating and adjusting, of head starting and upward bounding, the burden of responsibility shifted subtly from the individual to the school and the society. Failure used to be the kid's fault; now, increasingly, it seems, at least in part, to be the fault of the system. And thus all was thrown into confusion. Do we measure equality by what goes in or what comes out? That is, do we measure it in terms of resources provided, efforts made, or by achievement? Assuming some form of cultural pluralism (not yet proved or even argued)—assuming, for example that certain groups in the society are not merely "disadvantaged" but culturally distinct, and that those distinctions are valuable—assuming these things, what does equality mean when it comes to education? Equality before the law, yes; equality in medical treatment, yes; equality in the hiring of plumbers and mechanics, yes. But equality in education? James Coleman, who directed the huge federal study called "Equality of Educational Opportunity," subsequently wrestled with the question (in an article in *Public Interest*) and concluded that "equality of educational opportunity implies not merely 'equal' schools but equally effective schools, whose influences will overcome the differences in starting point of children from different social groups." This is the statement of a homogenizer, hardly different from that of the DAR lady who, sixty years ago, gave the schools a similar mission. "What kind of American consciousness can grow," she asked, "in the atmosphere of sauerkraut and limburger cheese?" The differences, in these views, should be equalized away: All comers should be transformed into mainstream, middle-class competitors (or consumers?) who are equally able to run the race.

There was nothing insidious or sinister about these things; they are as American as the flag. Our dream, as a society, was in the possibilities of transformation: frogs into princes, immigrants into Americans, poor children into affluent adults. And now, with other options closed, the schools, which always have received a major share of the credit for such accomplishments, are expected to do it all. But the schools never did what they were praised for doing; many immigrant groups, for example, did not achieve economic and social success through the public school, but through an open market for unskilled and semi-skilled labor, through sweatshops and factories, through political organizations and civil service jobs. There are more poor whites in America than poor blacks, and if the schools can be credited with the success of those who made it, they also have to be blamed for the failure of those who did not. But to say all this is not to say very much, because in the definition of making it, in a competitive race with one set of criteria, one man's success is defined by another's failure.

Then what do the schools actually do? More than anything else they certify and legitimize success and failure. "Equality of educational opportunity," even if it has no meaning, is necessary because it says to the lóser, "You had your chance." Therefore equality remains a significant political and moral imperative, a tune that has to be sung by politicians, guidance counselors, and other apologists of the status quo. (Increasingly it also becomes a rallying cry of liberal intellectuals, who now ascribe their personal triumphs in the brain business to the same ego-flattering virtues as the self-made entrepreneurs of another age: opportunity, hard work, ingenuity. I have made it, son, and so can you.) But there is, as Mr. Conant once said in another context, social dynamite in this propaganda.

The common school, quite simply, no longer exists, except as public rhetoric. With the large-scale movement to the suburbs after World War II, much of the American middle class seceded from the common school by physically removing its children to what it regarded as a more salubrious educational environment. For the successful in the suburbs the schools became contractual partners in a bargain that trades economic support (higher taxes, teacher salaries, bond issues) for academic credentials and some guarantee of advancement in the form of college admission. They went there seeking not equality but advantage, a head start for the rich. And who can blame them? We all "want the best for our children." Education, and especially higher education, is regarded as the sine qua non of position and power in this society. The "new class" of managers and technicians, as David Bazelon has said, is not based on birth or social standing but on educational skills (or at least on credentials). Cash and power, in other words, can be converted into degrees, then reconverted into more cash and power. The suburban school, the current demands for community control, and the concomitant failure of integration are all massive testimonials to the end of the common school.

What is being ignored is that the suburban schools don't actually do anything for most kids, other than bore them. Their prime function (aside from baby sitting) is to certify skills and reinforce characteristics and attitudes that are produced somewhere else. The money, in other words, did not buy much learning. But it did buy exclusiveness. They come in at this end, bright and shiny, and come out at that one, ready for Harvard or Cornell. The schools are, in brief, selective mechanisms, and through their selections they appear to justify (and are, in turn, justified by) the distinctions the society wants to make.

This is why we are fighting about schools and why we are in such serious trouble. Part of the fight—in the cities at least—is over a share of political power, over jobs and patronage and control. But the ideology that gives that battle energy, the ideas that help rally the troops, is the belief in the schools and in what remains of the dream of opportunity. But if *the* school system is the only mode of access to social and economic salvation, and if there is only one officially honored definition of such salvation (house in the suburbs, job at IBM, life insurance, and a certain set of manners), and if the school excludes any sizable minority from such salvation, then we have obviously defined ourselves into a choice between revolution and repression. The great dream of universal opportunity originated in an era of social alternatives, when schooling was one of several options for advancement; the school therefore could demand certain kinds of conformity. Individuality and pluralism could take refuge and sustenance elsewhere. But for the moment all advancement (we are told, are indeed required, to believe) begins in school, and we are, for this reason if for no other, no longer an open society. By definition, no society with but one avenue of approved entry into the mainstream of dignity can be fully open. When that single instrument of entry is charged with selecting people out, and when there are no honorable alternatives for those who are selected out, we are promising to all men things that we cannot deliver.

Inevitably, there are questions about the demands of a technological society and the necessity for universal literacy. Haven't many schools succeeded; don't we have one of the highest standards of literacy in the world? Don't schools make selections according to the demands that the technology and the culture impose? The answer is complicated, but there is nothing in it that makes the existing system of schooling imperative or even desirable, except—as always—the maintenance of the status quo. Which is to say that the system is necessary if the system is to be preserved.

Obviously, the society, as organized, makes certain demands—sometimes irrelevant, but often not—for employment and acceptability. Computers impose a rigid discipline on programmers, and heart transplants are better performed by people who have learned what they are doing. A dishwasher with the soul of a poet (or even the skills of a poet) may be more valuable than one without, but he is still a dishwasher. But for every flight of romantic nonsense there are a hundred statements about the rigors and demands of technology and about the complexities of this world. We have hitched the deities of complexity and technology to the rhetoric of success. Technology is not the curriculum (nor, needless to say, is complexity); it is the liturgy of motivation.

Even if the school system were proficient in training people to deal with a world defined as technological (which it is not), it would still be guilty of the worst sort of parochialism and idolatry. Part of the significance of technology, we are told, is to free man from all those boring, menial tasks, maybe even to free him from the necessity of working at all. To prepare for this, the school system imposes boring, menial tasks. The very propaganda of technology would suggest other worlds, other options, time for other concerns. It suggests more, not less, pluralism, more leisure time, more lonely moments, and the necessity for more personal resources for recreation, satisfaction, and human encounter. But what actually happens is that by deifying technology, or by joining the rest of us in so doing, the schools are reinforcing the existing linear standards of judgment and selection—are, in other words, employing the rhetoric of the brave new world to coerce kids and parents rather than to free them.

What the technology argument does is to lock the schools into one definition of complexity, one version of education, and hence only one honorable way of becoming a full human being. It perpetuates and updates an essentially vocational view of schooling. Technological complexity, yes; inner, human complexity, no. We are always—all of us—asked to understand the world by studying the transistor and the laser. All arguments to the contrary notwithstanding, the message comes out backwards: Technology is given; people are dependent variables who must be trained to use and control it.

Mathematics and history and literature thus become tokens of acquiescence rather than instruments of liberation. They are used by teachers to maintain order, reinforce distinctions, and intimidate or embarrass students. Complexity becomes a club and technology a prison. We are training a generation of people who regard the disciplines of the intellect as instruments of oppression.

One of the things we learned in the past decade is that we don't know very much. We don't know much about kids, about learning, or about motivation. One of the more fundamental assumptions of ten years ago was that curriculum planners sitting in some university, a foundation, or a central school office could invent programs (for teachers and students) and thereby engineer pedagogical success. What we discovered is that most of the time it couldn't be done, which may well be a good thing. If our pedagogical instruments were really powerful, we would have in hand one of the most totalitarian instruments imaginable. It is by now patently clear that not only history and politics but the very way that people think can be loaded with cultural and social presumptions, and that "reason" itself is often, if not always, political. Teaching inevitably assumes a form of control; it may be directed toward independence, but there is no assurance of it: The more centralized our school systems and our social agencies become, the greater the danger of creating pressures for the production of socially and technologically acceptable people. Fortunately, we don't yet know how to do these things.

What we do know is that children are different, and that different people learn different things in different ways, that some people think better in numbers than in words, that certain groups perceive and understand mathematical relationships more easily than verbal relationships, and that still others are particularly skillful in manipulating spatial problems but relatively incompetent with literature. Most of all, we know that personalities, backgrounds, and interests differ. It may well be that certain levels of literacy and ability in arithmetic constitute "fundamentals" for survival in America or anywhere in the Western world. But it does not follow that learning these things can be achieved by a single set of techniques, or that any teacher can be trained to them. More defensible is the assumption that, while drill, order, and tight discipline may be suitable for some students and teachers, they may be destructive for others; that "permissive" classes or Deweyan practices may work well with certain personalities but not with everyone. It is even possible to assume that the "fundamentals" should not always precede music or auto mechanics, but may, in many cases, grow naturally from other activities and from curiosity stimulated in other ways. We know that illiterate adults, properly motivated, have learned to read and write in a few months, and that recruits who almost failed Selective Service intelligence tests can be trained to operate computers and maintain radar equipment.

More important, we should have learned in the last decade that there is no magic in the single school system or in any set of curricular prescriptions, and that the most successful motivating device may simply be the sense that one has chosen what one wants to learn and under what conditions. In urban areas there is no reason why children in one neighborhood should be forced to attend one particular school for a specified period of time; why there should not be choice as to place, subject, style of teaching, and hours; why, for all children, French and history and algebra should have absolutely equal value; why, for some, art or dance or music should not be given more time than history; why reading a book is more of a humanistic activity than making a film or playing an instrument; why children should not be allowed to choose between permissive and highly structured situations (many would choose the latter); why parents and children should not have the economic power to punish unsuccessful schools (by leaving them) and reward effective ones; or why single, self-serving bureaucracies should continue to hold monopoly power in what is probably the most crucial, and certainly the most universal, public enterprise in America. Wealthy children and middle-class parents have some options about schools: lower-class children have none.

What I am arguing for, obviously, is a restoration of multiple options and, as much as possible, multiple values. Christopher Jencks and others have proposed a system whereby parents are given educational vouchers that they can spend in any school or educational activity of their choice. The voucher would be roughly equal in cash value to the amount that the local school system spends each year on the education of one child, and it could be spent in any school that does not charge more in tuition than the voucher is worth. With support from the Office of Economic Opportunity, Jencks will try the system over a period of eight years in a place yet to be chosen. No one claims that this is the only way of restoring choice, options, and multiple values. It is conceivable that single public school systems might, on their own initiative, introduce the kind of pluralism that the voucher system is designed to achieve. Clearly, many have become more "flexible" and more cognizant of individual choice. And yet the pressure within a single system is likely to be the other way; it is likely, always, to demand a certain caution. Separate schools, accountable not to public vote and citizen support but only to their clients, may be immune to such pressure; they will have to make their way on the basis of performance. Ideally, moreover, vouchers would be usable in apprenticeships, in community-operated schools, in projects of independent study, travel (for older kids), or simply for learning resources to be used at home.

There is, obviously, no certainty that changes in the structure or financing of public education will generate a situation in which individuality is honored and where the system does not impose the fearful price it now extracts from the young in the name of "growing up." But such changes may, at least, remove some obstacles. They may, if nothing else, represent a social declaration by the system—by the state and the citizen—that education is not simply the acceptance of impersonality and conformity, and that schooling is not merely the training and selection of candidates for corporate life. The practice of encouraging, through a new structure, the idea that personal fulfillment is the first responsibility of an educational system, and that human dignity is not founded on a single standard, may do more than anything else to mitigate the alienation and hostility of the angry young. What the ideal system would do—not in rhetoric nor with slogans from the principal, but in practice—would be to declare itself unequivocally to be the ally of difference, of individuals, and of the tolerant against the invidious; it would recognize its own limitations in choosing for people and recognize their ability to choose for themselves, and it would, in all cases, stand at their side against the imperious collective demands of crowds, machines, and bureaucrats. All of that may be a vain hope, but given the impossible and possibly destructive hopes of social engineering that we entertained in the Sixties, it is, at least, a hope worth hoping.

Peter Schrag

One of the myths supporting the dreams we held about school is also well analyzed by Everette Reimer.[21] Reimer points out that once schooling became equated with education and once public education became institutionalized into the bureaucratic model we have described, bureaucrats—educators and administrators—could now control the product (they could package, label, describe and evaluate it) and control access or usage of the product. The growing complex of education sought to have *its* definition of education (education = schooling) accepted among the needy and then sought to exclude part of the needy from having access to the package.

The early settlers of America had never conceived of the idea that education and schooling were synonymous. Vocational instruction necessary for adult life was provided by the family.

The forms of education assumed by the first generation of settlers in America were a direct inheritance from the medieval past. Serving the needs of a homogeneous, slowly changing rural society, they were largely instinctive and traditional, little articulated and little formalized. The most important agency in the transfer of culture was not formal institutions of instruction or public instruments of communication, but the family . . . the family's educational role was not restricted to elementary socialization. Within these kinship groupings, skills that provided at least the first step in vocational training were taught and practiced. In a great many cases, as among the agricultural laboring population and small tradesmen who together comprised the overwhelming majority of the population, all the vocational instruction necessary for mature life was provided by the family. . . .

What the family left undone by way of informal education the local community most often completed. It did so in entirely natural ways, for so elaborate was the architecture of family organization and so deeply founded was it in the soil of stable, slowly changing village and town communities in which intermarriage among the same groups had taken place generation after generation that it was at times difficult for the child to know where the family left off and the greater society began. . . .

More explicit in its educational function than either family or community was the church. . . It furthered the introduction of the child to the society by instructing him in the system of thought and imagery which underlay the culture's values and aims. . . .

Family, community, and church together accounted for the greater part of the mechanism by which English culture transferred itself across the generations. The instruments of deliberate pedagogy, of explicit, literate education, accounted for a smaller, though indispensable, portion of the process. . . . The cultural burdens it bore were relatively slight.[22]

21. Everette Reimer, *School is Dead* (New York: A Doubleday Anchor Book, 1972).
22. B. Bailyn, *Education in the Forming of American Society: Needs and Opportunities for Study* (1960), pp. 15-19, cited in Fred M. Newman and Donald W. Oliver, "Education and Community," *Harvard Educational Review*, 37, No. 1 (Winter 1967), pp. 61-106.

No longer do Americans believe that the community, the family, or the church can perform educational functions, for education is equated with schooling. Education (i.e., going to school) was for preparing for life, for being useful and productive, for voting intelligently, for raising our children wisely, and for serving our country well. We have, then, up until recently, the belief and faith that through our educational establishment we, individually and collectively, shall achieve much. But this is of course being challenged. Peter Schrag described the growing awareness or disenchantment with the public school. In the first selection, he noted that the belief that American public schools could be reformed is no longer taken as fact, as it was twenty years ago. He speaks here of the "end of the impossible dream," meaning an end to the dream that the schools would be the path to equality, opportunity, and the open society for all.

But it may be more than an end of a dream. Such views as Schrag's strike close to the heart of what might be called America's great secular religion, the faith in its educational system. To confront the probability that American education has not been beneficent for all Americans, that it has even been maleficent for significant numbers of people in this country, may be for many as difficult an experience as a loss of one's faith in the existence of God. So deep has been our faith in education that parents almost from the beginning have been forced to send their children to public schools, or, if they chose to send them to private schools, these schools had to adhere to the same educational code that governed the public schools.

The size of the educational establishment that has resulted from this faith testifies to the strength and pervasiveness of that faith. Over sixty million Americans are engaged full-time in some aspect of education. It is one of our largest businesses—may critics liken it to an industry—with expenditures of over 70 billion dollars, something like thirty percent of this country's capital. Not only have we required children to attend school, even when it was against their will, but we have also extended the amount of time they spend in school. As a result, more than one writer has noted, we have transformed the nature of childhood and adolescence in America. The state, through its monopoly of compulsory schooling, now monopolizes the lives of our children. As a result, and serving to maintain that monopoly, we have no other place for children to go but school. The thought of closing these schools, or seriously attenuating attendance at them, must be deeply disturbing to many. Were we to awaken in the morning with no schools to go to, we would very likely proceed to build institutions very much like them.

In subsequent readings we will return to these themes. Peter Schrag's description of how the "dream" has come to an end, and how, at least for some in our midst, it may have been more nightmare than dream, poses the issue of change and reform. Our next selection addresses this issue.

Some analysts of American education see the schools so inextricably intertwined with the rest of American society—especially with the American economy —that they reject the idea that there can be meaningful reform of the schools without meaningful reform of the rest of society, and again, especially its economic system. And for people in this group—sometimes called "neo-Marxists" —meaningful reform means revolution, the "total transformation of the economic, political, and legal structure of a given society, establishing in power a class which was previously suppressed and exploited."

These are the words of the author of our second selection who, in after describing what he means by revolution, and drawing an analogy between it and gestation, goes on to confront the likelihood, though not the necessity, that such a revolution would be violent. In "A Case Against Capitalism," Richard Lichtman, a philosopher, looks at American education, particularly the student uprisings of the 1960s.

A CASE AGAINST CAPITALISM

Richard Lichtman

The idea of revolution is modern. Ancient and medieval social systems experienced revolts and rebellions and underwent substantial and often violent change, but the idea of revolution was unknown.

Rebellion is essentially negative; in involves the removal of a grievance, the overcoming of a specific evil. Revolution, on the other hand, involves the idea of a total transformation of the economic, political, and legal structure of a given society, establishing in power a class which was previously suppressed and exploited. In modern times it has been assumed that the transformation of public power would also lead to a transformation of social relations and of human nature itself. But as yet this hope can be neither verified nor denied.

Revolution involves a total seizure of power. It aims to control the future. Ancient utopias, on the contrary, looked backward; they were attempts to reinstate a previous condition (or one that, according to myth and ritual, was believed to have existed). Revolution is a normative term, to be distinguished from restoration, for revolution implies a belief in progress, the growth of rationality, human autonomy, and control over nature and human society itself. The precondition of revolution is therefore the growth of an apparatus of control technology—and the precondition of this apparatus itself is capitalism, which supplies the material motive for transforming material and human nature.

Revolution implies the fulfilling of previously blocked and frustrated human possibilities. There cannot be a progressive restoration any more than there can be a reactionary revolution. There can of course be a reactionary seizure of power but this is not a revolution. It does not result in a total transformation carried out by a dominated social class.

Some nominal revolutions are not strictly revolutionary at all. Or, to put it another way, the locus of the revolutionary process, the actual subject of the revolutionary movement is misplaced. The Industrial Revolution provides an example. There is no doubt about the profound transformation which occurred in England between 1770 and 1830, but the source of this change was not industry. Industry was the result, not the cause of the transformation. Nor was the state of technological understanding existing in England at the time the cause of change. The French were probably superior in this regard. The fundamental source of the transformation in the British system of production was

Reprinted with permission from The Center Magazine, a publication of the Center for the Study of Democratic Institutions.

the development of technology in the content of a capitalist mercantile empire driven to the expansion of commodity exchange and the accumulation of profit. The so-called Industrial Revolution was therefore a phase in the evolution of capitalism. But a "revolution" which produced capitalism out of precapitalist society was itself an evolution, not a revolution. The great revolutions of modern times—the French, Russian, Chinese, and Cuban revolutions—all required a period of gestation reaching back at least a century. This has been clearly noted by the leaders of these revolutions.

Gestation is a useful analogy. The act of birth is a revolutionary change in the relation of fetus to mother. A previously dependent organism, drawing on another, is thrust into separateness. Its organs have evolved slowly but inexorably and cumulatively over time. Finally, a radical break occurs which makes it possible for them to function independently. Both slow growth and sudden rupture are integrally connected in any revolutionary process.

It is not part of the definition of revolution that it be violent, but in the contemporary world it is far from accidental. In the contemporary world the state becomes more and more critical to the functioning of the socio-economic system, highly self-conscious, and armed with the technologies of military violence and ideological persuasion. It utilizes the latter device when possible and the former when necessary. Generally it employs both in combination. American capitalism attempts domination in Vietnam today through massive brutalization; it attempts hegemony in the United States through consumer pacification and political alienation. Since its material affluence is dependent on imperialist exploitation and domestic inequality, violence is a tactic which, if not actually exercised, always remains close to the surface of social reality.

The contemporary capitalist state is the executive of the capitalist ruling class. This aspect of Marx's analysis remains true although the specific function of the state has changed considerably since the time of Marx's writing. When Marx suggested that England and the United States might avoid violent transition to socialism he cited as the reason for this the absence of a massive military or bureaucratic apparatus. Obviously, the present condition is different from that in which Marx made his suggestion.

American capitalism cannot exist without a military force and a bureaucratic structure. Both are necessitated by the development of modern multinational corporate capitalism. They are evidence of the political will and economic exploitation by the capitalist class. All the available evidence is that this class will concede reforms as long as its fundamental power—its control over corporate property—remains intact. But when the source or legitimacy of its rule is challenged, it will react with as much violence as it deems necessary. "You can peel an onion skin by skin, but you cannot disarm a tiger claw by claw."

Capitalism continually transforms its technological foundation. It is driven to this by its relentless search for profit and need to reduce cost and expand markets. Its promise is a society of material well-being, equality, freedom, and human fulfillment. This is the liberal credo. It is built into the historical origin of capitalism. In contrast to ancient slave society or medieval society, capitalism is required to elaborate the ideal of freedom and equality. It was through this ideology that it gathered the whole dissenting mass of small artisans, merchants, peasant tenants, rising industrial powers, and independent professionals against the power of landed aristocracy. Capitalism is founded on the illusion of market equality between producer and consumer, and most crucially between capitalist and laborer. The illusion of equality is part of the reality of capitalist exploitation.

In capitalism the laborer is "voluntarily" compelled to labor for the capitalist class. This is not a contradiction but a social mystification. Its demystification lies in grasping the fact that freedom under capitalism is defined by the terms of capitalist property and power.

The more thoroughly capitalism develops its material abundance, the more the level of its affluence rises, the more glaring become the contradictions between the reality of inequality and exploitation and the liberal myth of equality and freedom. Those segments of society which have either not been admitted into American affluence or have achieved material comfort and realized the price that must be paid in terms of the loss of dignity, creativity, and fellowship rise in rebellion. The state replies with an arsenal of distractions, ideological seductions, and brute force. The critical question is whether the growing violence, distress, and anguish of social life can crystallize into a revolutionary movement or whether it will continue to rise and fall in periodic challenges to power which are repressed and eventually dissipated.

The conditions of social life under capitalism produce discontent and apathy, rebellion and cynicism, disintegration of authority, and rootless surrender. This ambivalence is already present in Marx's writings. On numerous occasions he wrote as though the proletariat would surely develop the revolutionary class consciousness it required to constitute itself a class and overthrow capitalism in favor of socialism. But Marx often struck a more pessimistic note. In *Das Kapital* he held that "the advance of capitalist production develops a working class, which by education, tradition, habit looks upon the conditions of that mode of production as self-evident laws of nature."

Contemporary capitalism is impregnated with the movement of rebellion and the countermovement of the state toward containment and suppression. The contradiction between reality and ideal provides the key to this dialectic. It will be helpful to illustrate this particular source of rebellion with a specific example—the student uprisings of the nineteen-sixties.

The rise of a student movement in the past decade is an expression of the contradictions in capitalist society. These contradictions are both external and internal to student life in the university; they exist in the realm of American imperialism and domestic exploitation, on the one hand, and in the state of the university, on the other. These two are of course integrally related. The same social system which produces the barbarism of American foreign policy and the alienation of everyday life also produces the transformations of the American university which have trivialized and perverted student life.

In the nineteen-sixties the internal and external antagonisms of student life— the objective and subjective deformities in American society—reinforced and focused each other. The rhetoric and the reality of American life became violently discrepant. Put another way, capitalism—the system of concentrated exploitative power based on the control of private property—revealed itself as grossly incompatible with its own ideal self-justification, liberalism, the social theory which endorses the values of individualism, equality, freedom, justice, and universal self-determination.

The liberal ethos pictures the United States as the champion of world freecom, opponent of imperialist exploitation, and protector of independence for once-colonial nations. In an era in which the United States struggled to undermine the world power of other capitalist nations, this ideology was useful. Not that American practice was ever compatible with its own stated ideals. American expansion brutalized ethnic minorities at home and extended itself inexorably beyond the continent to establish America as a predominant world power. But through the nineteenth and early twentieth centuries the hypocrisy of American apologetics was more readily disguised.

The Second World War ravaged the productive capacity of America's capitalist competitors. Alone among capitalist nations, the United States emerged with its industrial system intact and efficiently organized through the stimulus of a military economy. The United States emerged as the central power in the world capitalist system, and in this context it became predominantly responsible for maintaining the international system of imperialism. It began to perpetrate more openly and forcefully those same acts of international violence for which it had previously condemned its capitalist rivals. John F. Kennedy, then a senator, could excoriate France for a policy in Algeria which he would soon duplicate in Vietnam. In short, the price of America's ascension to leadership of the world capitalist empire was the stripping away of the veil which had previously hidden the true character of American foreign expansion and consequent domestic affluence.

The United States rose to the position of leadership in the world capitalist system during an era of permanent revolution. Socialist and nationalist movements have arisen in this century to challenge capitalist domination. This is the objective factor which has unmasked America's pious rhetoric of devotion to self-determination. Given this fact and the polarization of world power between socialist and capitalist forces in an era of advanced technology, "the American century" reveals the United States in its ultimate power as a massive barbarism toward which its entire previous history had been tending. American "success" illuminates the depth of America's failure.

A parallel demystification has occurred in American domestic life, where the rhetoric of equality, justice, freedom, and social welfare has been confronted with the reality of racism, poverty, economic domination, brutalization of nature, and a pervasive banality and alienization of social life. This society is rapidly losing any power it may have once possessed to inspire devotion and a commitment to preserve it. This is particularly important in understanding the rise of the student movement, for students are being trained to enter a society in slow and steady decay. Students find themselves being prepared to fill roles in a society which inspires in them a feeling somewhere between boredom and revulsion.

But the corruption of American society both in its domestic and foreign policy would not in itself have generated the student protest movement unless it had also permeated the American educational system at the historical moment it was expanding rapidly under the pervasive influence of state support. This confluence—objective social corruption replicated within the system of education

—is crucial for the understanding of the situation against which the student movement has rebelled and the possibility of its having the capacity to rebel. Students are being trained to supply the sophisticated labor power which continually reproduces American brutalization; but they experience a move toward rebellion because their preparation is imposed within an institution which offers them a direct encounter with alienation, the capacity to grasp its nature, and the need to transcend it.

This juxtaposition of objective and subjective evidence was dramatically focused in the events of spring, 1970—the Cambodian invasion and the murders at Kent State. Students did not react to the escalated violence of American foreign policy until the irrationality of American society was focused in these killings. The murders at Kent State were a terrible witness to the powerlessness of students and the willingness of the capitalist system to employ force against internal dissent when it threatens the system of state power. The murder of innocent students at Kent State and Jackson State further unmasked the hypocrisy of American pretensions to democratic self-determination.

The dehumanization of American life does not merely face the student as he or she moves to protest the iniquities of the larger society, however. It permeates the very institution in which student consciousness is formed and malformed. For the primary function of the university is to equip students with the skills and attitudes necessary to manipulate nature, theoretical systems, other human beings, and even themselves for the sake of continually expanding capitalist exploitation. But like all the other institutions of American life, the educational system is torn by the contradictions between its rhetorical purpose and its actual function; on the one hand, the pretense that the university is a neutral marketplace of ideas in which the student is offered the opportunity to investigate a variety of substantially different alternatives so that he or she may choose freely that social and personal existence which best accords with reason and self-realization, and, on the other, the reality of university education as training for the acquisition of fragmented skills which separate "learning" from active self-determination by subordinating knowledge to corporate power. The university produces the expertise and attitudes which are useful to the practice of American capitalism. The university does not transcend in theory what capitalism requires in practice. Yet, against its will, it produces a student movement directed toward transcending these limits.

Students are trained to increase the productivity of capitalism in a context in which they live by the decisions of others. They are periodically apathetic, bored, cynical, rebellious, and escapist. For students have some recognition of their own powerlessness and the uses for which they are being "programmed," but they have no deep conviction that they can successfully challenge the social system which deforms them in the present and threatens to alienate them in the future. They tend to vacillate, therefore, between sporadic disruption and a pervasive sense of defeat and futility. Our American society however is not invincible, and the American university system is the locus of a series of contradictions which a critically self-conscious student movement can seize upon and exacerbate. It is crucial to understand that the university is vital to capitalist society as the supplier of sophisticated technical, social, and ideological labor power and is simultaneously permeated by contradictions which focus the general irrationality of social life.

These contradictions manifest themselves in a series of antagonisms:

■ Between the need for a student population which can master ever more complicated technological and social systems and the structure of corporate power which cannot permit this developing intelligence and creativity to challenge the irrational foundations of social power. Students must be made sufficiently intelligent to service the capitalist system which will employ them but not knowledgeable and critical enough to challenge the right of this system to alienate their power to determine their own social existence.

■ Between the ideology of knowledge for its own sake, and the entire instrumental apparatus of units, grades, and exams whose basic justification is the occupational placement of students in accordance with the necessities of capitalist development.

■ Between the liberal rhetoric of the freedom and equality of all human beings, and the elitist, hierarchical structure of the very university in which these values are transmitted.

■ Between capitalist culture which permeates the consciousness of youth with the virtue of immediate gratification—a result of the shift in capitalism from a concern with production to a concern with consumption—and a continuing emphasis on discipline and the standardized performance of routine and intrinsically meaningless intellectual tasks which are still necessary to the productive functioning of the corporate-bureaucratic economy.

■ Between the high ideals of American liberal culture—Paine, Jefferson, the Declaration of Independence, etc.—and the banality and terror of actual American life. The response of the university cadres to this antagonism is to stress the process of education as sheer contemplation. The university is said to function as a respite from social life. It is denied any responsibility for the evils that flourish there. The university is held to be a place where the universe is contemplated, not affected in action. Education provides the foundation upon which future responsible action is to be constructed. This view would be worthy of consideration if the university provided knowledge which could be used at some future time to transform social life. But the same capitalist state which dominates mass education also renders powerless the student population, which is enjoined to suspend action in the immediate present for the sake of that wisdom which will make future action more meaningful.

In fact, the university does not dispense knowledge relevant to the self-determination of men and women. It manipulates consciousness to provide the skills useful to a system of continued alienation. And the society into which the student moves does not permit equal participation in its basic decisions; it separates technical skills serviceable to the prevailing institutions from the capacity to direct the ultimate use and meaning of these skills. The university is at once an ivory tower and a service station, excessively relevant to the system of corporate capitalism and irrelevant to human needs.

■ Between the social genesis and fruitful functioning of reason and its private appropriation by an educational system whose ultimate structure is shaped by the needs of the capitalist state.

These contradictions are the result of the basic fact that human reason is deformed under capitalism. It is alienated from the actual lives of men and women and objectified in a system of exploitation which utilizes the sensibilities and creativity of human beings to further the expropriation of their efforts at self-fulfillment. The university carries this pattern of domination both in its structure and its content—in the way it organizes the process of learning and in the substantive content of what it teaches. The content and method reinforce and validate each other. The teaching of reified apologetics in departments like sociology and political science, for example, is inseparable from the structure of authority, departmental fragmentation, the homogenization of knowledge through standard units, and the competitive setting of students against each other as it is enforced in the very structure of the university system.

The university is able to teach alienated ideological subject matter because it reproduces this exploitation in its structure. The alienation of content is reinforced and grounded in the alienation of intellectual life. The student becomes an active, competitive participant in his or her own stultification. This is why student life is frantic and yet suspended and unreal, at the same time. The student is actively engaged in re-creating his or her own passive subordination.

These in brief are the factors leading to the rise of the student movement. Of itself this movement cannot become revolutionary. A revolution in contemporary capitalist society requires a revolutionary theory—a common perspective which can unite the enormously diversified segments of the contemporary proletariat. For American laborers are divided into critically distinct areas of social life. The sense of isolation and antagonism is powerful; the sense of common purpose weak. Those in poverty, those who have rejected affluence for counterculture, and those striving comfortably for additional commodities do not make likely political allies. Nor do those who labor in the state bureaucracies, those who work in the competitive sector of the economy, or those who are members of the giant unions which are integral to monopoly corporations.

All these groups are frustrated and dehumanized by capitalism. But they are defeated in very different ways. They not only fail to see each other as allies, they are often made into antagonists. In fact, they become their own antagonists. The building-trades worker who votes for continued high-rise expansion is providing himself with employment while he destroys his environment. The alternatives under capitalism are truncated and abortive. Only a socialist society offers the possibility of humane development for all those human beings who are presently coming necessarily to feel the boredom, vacuity, and destructiveness of contemporary capitalism. But before a socialist society can be built, a socialist movement will have to develop based on a common historical understanding and commitment. Only in such circumstances is contemporary socialist revolution at all conceivable.

Richard Lichtman

We have argued that the beliefs about the virtues of American education do not stand up under a structural, historical analysis. Public education has not propelled the poor and the nonwhite into the occupational and professional roles that have high status, prestige and income. Nor have the schools been value-free or educational. The analysis of the mechanisms and processes by which the schools have operated to fulfill the needs of the capitalistic, and now the corporate, orders will be the task of this book.

We turn first, however, to an historical analysis of alternatives in Western society. To understand where we are today we must know where we have come from. This analysis will be the goal of Chapter 2. The reader will be able to trace our contemporary dilemmas and questions to issues that have plagued society and educators since the rise of Western civilization.

chapter two

ALTERNATIVES FROM THE PAST: HISTORICAL ANALYSIS OF EDUCATIONAL IDEOLOGY AND PRACTICE

"Someone said, 'The dead writers are remote from us because we know so much more than they do.' Precisely, and they are that which we know."
T. S. Eliot

"And how will you inquire, Socrates, into that of which you are totally ignorant? What sort of thing, among those things which you know not, will you put forth as the object of your seeking? And even if you should chance upon it, how will you ever know that it is the thing which you did not know?"

"I know, Meno, what you are trying to say. Just see what a specious argument you are introducing, that a man cannot inquire either about that which he knows or about that which he does not know. For he cannot inquire about what he knows, inasmuch as he already knows it and he has no need to inquire, nor can he inquire concerning that which he knows not, since then he does not know about what he is to inquire."[1]

The dialectic method of Socrates led him to seek the answers to questions such as: What is truth? What is knowledge? What is virtue? These questions led to his death at the hands of Athenian democracy.

Where does the dialectic of Socrates lead us?

In taking up a search for new educational alternatives, at some point we invariably ask, where did what we have come from? How did the system of schooling take on the shape and pattern it maintains today? A complete response to this inquiry leads us back in history to changing modes of production and productive relations and societies resulting therefrom to the beginnings of written language, urbanization, political institutionalization, and most particularly to the fifth century B.C., when Greek thinkers began the basis for Western thought. During this period, new conceptions of the nature of man and of his world were debated, and the first written conscious investigations into socially organized learning took place. The fundamental premises on which the present educational system is based are strikingly similar to those which evolved as a result of the practice of early Greek life. The principles underlying

---

1. Plato, *Meno*, trans. by B. Jowett, ed. by A. Sesonske, and N. Fleming (Belmont, Calif.: Wadsworth Publishing Co., 1965), p. 16.

today's educational ideology and practices, and those systems from which they sprang, clearly show the influence of Greek thinkers, for whom the problem of education was of intense political significance and about which they wrote profusely. The guiding philosophical tenets of their educational outlook have influenced us most notably in the following ways.

1. They held the belief in Reason above all, as the principle which explained the universe and everything in it. Reason alone reduced chaos to order. Information obtained from sense perception was totally untrustworthy, mere opinion, and only through the intellect could true knowledge be arrived at—the concept of the mind as separate from the body. Therefore, education was designed to emphasize thought and contemplation, and minimize practice, experience and doing. The world of ideas and words was separate from and more worthy than the world of practice and experience. Logic and language were considered the perfect instruments of intellectual analysis and expression, in contrast to reports from the senses.

2. They believed in a permanent reality, of ideal forms in which things participated, of absolutes, ultimate and eternal Truth, Good, Virtue, Right, Justice, which could be sought after through Reason and found. Even if true knowledge could not be acquired, the Greeks held that a better opinion could be substituted for an inferior one. There was an objective standard derived from the Truth by which the well-being of the community and its parts could and must be measured.

3. The Greek thinkers recognized the problem of the relationship of the individual to the State, but saw it as an opposing dualism, with the decision that what was best for the State was best for the individual, since the highest end was the prosperity of the State. Man was a social creature, satisfying his destiny through the social world.

4. They considered formal education as the means of social reform, as a way of deliberately molding human character in accordance with an ideal. Thus a select few who had been trained in conceptions of the absolute were to be the teachers of moral and intellectual excellences.

5. Concern with political and civic virtues was considered to be of prime importance. These concerns existed dormant in all men and could be activated by formal means, the primary function of education being to fit the young to become efficient members of society.

6. In ancient Greece the great concern of education was with the formation of an elite class, trained through formal and conscious means to govern the lesser citizenry. This concept became the basis of a pyramidical hierarchy of human values and social control, and of the modern university.

7. They assumed there was a perfect harmony between power and worth.

GREECE

The Greek philosophers of the fifth and fourth centuries B.C., arising from a tradition-bound, aristocratic and militaristic society, where communal groups had given way to a division of labor based on privilege and property, began the process of speculative thinking in an attempt to explain the universe in terms of man and not the supernatural. In recognizing the problems confronting an individual within his society and within an unexplained environment, they developed a rational explanation of reality which offered a guide to conduct and would serve to direct persons on the course of a harmonious life. Their ideas were considered radical at a period of time when a nonintellectual, nonrational, religious and military spirit under strict State control were the existing features of society. The changes they proposed would undermine and forever alter traditional value systems and practices; thus, it was not without controversy and struggle that their "new" education came to be accepted.

The "old" Greek education (until the middle of the fifth century B.C.), as epitomized by the Spartan method of education, was determined and strictly controlled by the city-state, which had grown into being through the amalgamation of families and tribes into village communities and then into cities. As in most societies of this period, ties were by blood and by possession of land. Nobility was confined at first to heads of families, but in time developed to include less of those with merely wealth and noble birth and more of those who possessed certain traits of character, primarily men of physical valor (warriors) and wise speech (orators). The "old" education existed during the Homeric Period (850 B.C.), with Achilles (*The Iliad*) and Odysseus (*The Odyssey*) representing the ideal types. Plutarch's *Life of Lycurgus* gives a full description of the aims and processes of the "old" education, organized primarily for an aristocracy of warriors. Although largely informal and concerned with practice, the beginnings of formal instruction can be seen, as well as the division of education into two aspects, the physical (gymnastics) and the intellectual (music).

The changes in education after the middle of the fifth century B.C. came about as a result of changes in social and economic conditions, as Athens became an imperial power and expanded both politically and commercially.

Tribal groupings gave way to class groupings of families, with the rise of private property, exchange between individuals in a new money economy, and the transformation of products into commodities for exchange rather than just use. There followed the division of labor between the different branches of production—agriculture, handicrafts, trade, shipping—each new group with its own common interests. In order to look after these interests, a public force was created in the form of the state.

Along with industrial growth came an influx of foreign men and ideas, breaking up further the previous self-contained life and old kinship organizations. A new type of political ability was needed, as leadership was gained and held by intellectual superiority rather than military strength. Greater wealth allowed for more artistic and intellectual activities. No longer operating on a survival level, citizens developed an interest in pursuing civic careers and achieving some power over their lives. Growing skepticism developed towards old religious traditions, ethical ideas and myths; and philosophers searched for a new understanding and interpretation of man.

The Clouds of Aristophanes reflects these changes and presents the conflict from the conservative or "old" point of view, holding the "new" education to account as a corruptive element which was destroying the fundamental stability of society.

Selections from THE CLOUDS

Aristophanes

(SCENE–the interior of a sleeping apartment; STREPSIADES, PHIDIPPIDES, and two servants are seen in their beds; a small house is seen at a distance. Time–midnight.)
Strepsiades, formerly a wealthy country gentleman, without culture, has married out of his station to a luxury-loving Athenian woman. Their son, Phidippides, has squandered much of his father's fortune in horse racing and other extravagances. Anxiety concerning some of these debts, now due, causes the father a sleepless night. The son dreams of his racing and in his sleep talks of his sporting friends. The comedy opens with the lamentations of the father and the broken mutterings of the son.

*   *   *   *   *   *   *   *

Strep. I have discovered one path for my course extraordinarily excellent; to which if I persuade this youth, I shall be saved. But first I wish to awake him. How then can I awake him in the most agreeable manner?–How? Phidippides, my little Phidippides?

Phid. What, father?

Strep. Kiss me, and give me your right hand!

Phid. There. What's the matter?

Strep. Tell me, do you love me?

Phid. Yes, by this Equestrian Neptune.[1]

Strep. Nay, do not by any means mention *this Equestrian* to me, for this god is the author of my misfortunes. But, if you really love me from your heart, my son, obey me.

Phid. In what, then, pray, shall I obey you?

Strep. Reform your habits as quickly as possible; and go and learn what I advise.

Phid. Tell me now, what do you prescribe?

Strep. And will you obey me at all?

Phid. By Bacchus, I will obey you.

Strep. Look this way, then! Do you see this little door and little house?

Phid. I see it. What then, pray, is this, father?

Strep. This is a thinking-shop[2] of wise spirits. There dwell men who in speaking of the heavens persuade people that it is an oven, and that it encompasses us, and that we are the embers. These men teach, if one give them money, to conquer in speaking, right or wrong.

Phid. Who are they?

Strep. I do not know the name accurately. They are minute-philosophers, noble and excellent.

Aristophanes, *The Clouds*, in Paul Monroe, *Source Book of the History of Education* (London: The Macmillan Company, 1906), pp. 66-72.

1. Patron god of his favorite sport. Probably represented in the bed chamber by a statue.
2. Or subtlety-shop.

Phid. Bah! they are rogues; I know them. You mean the quacks, the pale-faced wretches, the bare-footed fellows, of whose number are the miserable Socrates and Charephon.[3]

Strep. Hold! hold! be silent! Do not say anything foolish. But, if you have any concern for your father's patrimony, become one of them, having given up your horsemanship.

Phid. I would not, by Bacchus, if even you were to give me the pheasants[4] which Leogoras rears!

Strep. Go, I entreat you, dearest of men, go and be taught.

Phid. Why, what shall I learn?

Strep. They say, that among them are both the two causes,—the better cause, whichever that is, and the worse: they say, that the one of these two causes, the worse, prevails, though it speaks on the unjust side. If therefore you learn for me this unjust cause, I would not pay to any one not even an obolous of these debts, which I owe at present on your account.

Phid. I cannot comply; for I should not dare to look upon the Knights, having lost all my colour.

Strep. Then, by Ceres, you shall not eat any of my goods! neither you, nor your draught-horse, nor your blood-horse; but I will drive you out of my house to the crows.

Phid. My uncle Megacles will not permit me to be without a horse. But I'll go in, and pay no heed to you.

[Exit PHIDIPPIDES.]

Strep. Though fallen, still I will not lie prostrate: but having prayed to the gods, I will go myself to the thinking-shop and get taught. How then, being an old man, and having a bad memory, and dull of comprehension, shall I learn the subtleties of refined disquisitions?—I must go. Why thus do I loiter and not knock at the door? *[Knocks at the door.]* Boy! little boy!

Disciple. *[from within].* Go to the devil! Who is it that knocked at the door?

Strep. Strepsiades, the son of Phidon, of Cicynna.[5]

Dis. You are a stupid fellow, by Jove! who have kicked against the door so very carelessly, and have caused the mis-carriage[6] of an idea which I had conceived.

Strep. Pardon me; for I dwell afar in the country. But tell me the thing which has been made to miscarry.

Dis. It is not lawful to mention it, except to disciples.

Strep. Tell it, then, to me without fear; for I here am come as a disciple to the thinking-shop.

Dis. I will tell you; but you must regard these as mysteries. Socrates lately asked Chaerephon about a flea, how many of its own feet it jumped; for after

---

3. "A hanger-on of the philosopher, and appears to have been laughed at even by his fellow-scholars for the mad extremes to which he carried his reverential attachment."—WALSH.

4. Reference to another extravagant taste of wealthy Athenians. Leogoras is known for the luxury and dissipation in which he wasted his property.

5. Strepsiades gives name, paternity, and deme (native place), as was required in judicial proceedings, thus adding to the serio-comic aspect.

6. Referring to Socrates' characterization of himself as an intellectual mid-wife.

having bit the eyebrow of Chaerephon, it leapt away on to the head of Socrates.

Strep. How, then, did he measure this?

Dis. Most cleverly. He melted some wax, and then took the flea and dipped its feet in the wax; and then a pair of Persian slippers[7] stuck to it when cooled. Having gently loosened these, he measured back the distance.

Strep. O king Jupiter! what subtlety of thought![8] . . . Open, open quickly the thinking-shop, and show to me Socrates as quickly as possible. For I desire to be a disciple. Come, open the door.—*[The door of the Thinking-shop opens, and the pupils of SOCRATES are seen, all with their heads fixed on the ground, while SOCRATES himself is seen suspended in the air in a basket.]* O Hercules, from what country are these wild beasts?

Dis. What do you wonder at? To what do they seem to you to be like?

Strep. To the Spartans, who were taken at Pylos.[9] But why in the world do these look upon the ground?

Dis. They are in search of the things below the earth.

Strep. Then they are searching for roots. Do not, then, trouble yourselves about this; for I know where there are large and fine ones. Why, what are these doing, who are bent down so much?

Dis. These are groping about in darkness under Tartarus.[10] . . . *[Turning to the pupils.]* But go in, lest he meet with us.

Strep. Not yet, not yet: but let them remain, that I may communicate to them a little matter of my own.

Dis. It is not permitted to them to remain without in the open air for a very long time.[11] *[The pupils retire.]*

Strep. *[discovering a variety of mathematical instruments].* Why, what is this, in the name of heaven? Tell me.

Dis. This is Astronomy.

Strep. But what is this?

Dis. Geometry.

Strep. What then is the use of this?

Dis. To measure out the land.

Strep. What belongs to an allotment?

Dis. No, but the whole earth.

Strep. You tell me a clever notion; for the contrivance is democratic and useful.

Dis. *[pointing to a map].* See, here's a map of the whole earth. Do you see? this is Athens.

Strep. What say you? I don't believe you; for I do not see the Dicasts[12] sitting.

Dis. *Be assured* that this is truly the Attic territory.

Strep. Why, where are my fellow-tribesmen of Cicynna?

Dis. Here they are. And Euboea here, as you see, is stretched out a long way by the side of it to a great distance.

7. Close-fitting shoes.
   8. Here follow a number of such incidents, designed to ridicule the practice of the Sophists and the "new" educators.
   9. Refers to their lean and haggard appearance after their long imprisonment.
   10. Beneath Tartarus there was nothing.
   11. They would lose their scholarly pallor.
   12. Popular quiries or courts. Every year six thousand citizens were jurymen.

Strep. I know that; for it was stretched by us and Pericles.[13] But where is Lacedaemon?

Dis. Where is it? Here it is.

Strep. How near it is to us! Pay great attention to this, to remove it very far from us.

Dis. By Jupiter, it is not possible.

Strep. Then you will weep for it. *[Looking up and discovering SOCRATES.]* Come, who is this man who is in the basket?

Dis. Himself.[14]

Strep. Who's "Himself"?

Dis. Socrates.

Strep. O Socrates! Come, you sir, call upon him loudly for me.

Dis. Nay, rather, call him yourself; for I have no leisure.

[Exit DISCIPLE.]

Strep. Socrates! my little Socrates!

Soc. Why callest thou me, thou creature of a day?

Strep. First tell me, I beseech you, what you are doing.

Soc. I am walking in the air, and speculating about the sun.

Strep. And so you look down upon the gods[15] from your basket, and not from the earth? if, indeed, it is so.

Soc. For I should never have rightly discovered things celestial, if I had not suspended the intellect, and mixed the thought in a subtle form with its kindred air. But if, being on the ground, I speculated from below on things above, I should never have discovered them. For the earth forcibly attracts to itself the meditative moisture. Watercresses also suffer the very same thing.[16]

Strep. What do you say? Does meditation attract the moisture to the watercresses? Come then, my little Socrates, descend to me, that you may teach me those things, for the sake of which I have come.

[SOCRATES lowers himself and gets out of the basket.]

Soc. And for what did you come?

Strep. Wishing to learn to speak; for, by reason of usury, and most ill-natured creditors, I am pillaged and plundered, and have my goods seized for debt.

Soc. How did you get in debt without observing it?

Strep. A horse-disease[17] consumed me,—terrible at eating. But teach me the other one of your two causes, that which pays nothing; and I will swear by the gods, I will pay down to you whatever reward you exact of me.

Soc. By what gods will you swear? for, in the first place, gods are not a current coin with us.

Strep. By what do you swear? By iron money, as in Byzantium?[18]

---

13. Subdued by the Athenians under Pericles, twenty years previous to the presentation of the play.

14. The usual designation of a teacher by a pupil or of a master by a slave.

15. Strepsiades understands Socrates to mean the sun-god.

16. In ridicule of Socrates' habit of drawing his illustrations from the affairs of common life.

17. A cancerous ulcer.

18. A Dorian colony at that time.

Soc. Do you wish to know clearly celestial matters, what they rightly are?

Strep. Yes, by Jupiter, if it be possible!

Soc. And to hold converse with the Clouds, our divinities?

Strep. By all means.

Soc. *[with great solemnity]*. Seat yourself, then, upon the sacred couch.

Strep. Well, I am seated!

Soc. Take, then, this chaplet.

Strep. For what purpose a chaplet?[19]—Ah me! Socrates, see that you do not sacrifice me like Athamas![20]

Soc. No; we do all these to those who get initiated.

Strep. Then, what shall I gain, pray?

Soc. You shall become in oratory a tricky knave, a thorough rattle, a subtle speaker.—But keep quiet.

Strep. By Jupiter, you will not deceive me; for if I am besprinkled,[21] I shall become fine flour.

Soc. It becomes the old man to speak words of good omen, and to hearken to my prayer.—O sovereign King, immeasurable Air, who keepest the earth suspended, and thou bright AEther, and ye august goddesses, the Clouds[22] sending thunder and lightning, arise, appear in the air, O mistresses, to your deep thinker.

Strep. Not yet, not yet, till I wrap this around me, lest I be wet through. To think of my having come from home without even a cap, unlucky man! . . .

[The CHORUS representing the clouds appears.]

Strep. Tell me, O Socrates, I beseech you by Jupiter, who are these that have uttered this grand song? Are they some heroines?

Soc. By no means; but heavenly Clouds, great divinities to idle men;[23] who supply us with thought and argument, and intelligence, and humbug and circumlocution, and ability to hoax, and comprehension.

Strep. On this account therefore my soul, having heard their voice, flutters, and already seeks to discourse subtilely, and to quibble about smoke, and having pricked a maxim with a little notion; to refute the opposite argument . . .

19. It was the custom to crown with a chaplet the head of the victim for sacrifice.
20. Recently reproduced on the stage. Athamas had been crowned by sacrifice to Zeus, but was saved by Heracles.
21. The head of the sacrificial victim was sprinkled with meal.
22. The transition to monotheism, with the early Greek philosophers, was usually by a combination of the three related deities, Air, AEther, Clouds.
23. Referring to the Sophists, who took no part in public affairs.

Aristophanes

The realization of the need for skills of state, organization, oratory, diplomacy, and other political abilities led to the rise of itinerant teachers. They are difficult to describe as a group, for they varied greatly from each other in aim, premises, curriculum, and educational practice—from the teaching of "civic virtue," to "wisdom," to "morality" and "ethics," to "pure rhetorical style." Most of them contracted with parents and taught for money wherever there were pupils.

These first professional educators, who thought of teaching as their distinctive occupation and worked out theories about who should be taught and how, were classified together as "Sophists," which at one time had meant "wise" or "expert." They represented a radical change in education in several ways.

1. They popularized intellectual inquiry as more valuable than physical activity, and contributed to democratic political aims, as opposed to rule by an aristocratic class characterized by high birth and wealth. Success became defined in terms of an individual's ability to influence the course of his life by political participation.
2. They placed great value on rhetoric, oratory, and the ability to persuade, and made people conscious of the power of language and the skills of manipulation.
3. They extended formal education late into young manhood.
4. In their social consciousness, they shunned superstition and encouraged individual thought.
5. They credited man with the power to improve his condition.

They had no organization in common, such as a school. However, several Sophists later came to organize their own schools. Socrates and Plato, although considered essentially to be Sophists, saw themselves as different, and indeed, differed considerably in philosophical orientation and practice from other Sophists.

The very earliest philosophers of the fifth century B.C. were chiefly concerned with the material composition of the universe, with being and nonbeing, with whether things in nature were permanently fixed or in constant flux. The theories of Heracleitus (constant change) and Parmenides (permanence) exemplify this latter metaphysical concern and conflict. Heracleitus argued:

> This ordered universe, the same for all, has been created by no one, either god or man, but was always and is and shall be everliving Fire, kindled in measure and quenched in measure.

> Everything is on the move; that is, particular existence as we know it is on the move. Nothing, not even the most stable-seeming and solid substance, is really at rest. Life is like a River; we cannot step twice into the same water. . . .

> The existing arrangement is maintained by the strife or tension of the Opposites. War is the father of all and the king of all. It is, by a paradox, the producer of harmony, since the fairest harmony is made out of differing elements. A kind of balance is preserved between them.[2]

The world is in perpetual flux; true knowledge, therefore, is an impossibility. (This view is similar to that of the Chinese philosopher, Lao-Tzu, 479 B.C.) Parmenides, on the other hand, argued:

---

2. Heracleitus, in Kathleen Freeman, *The Pre-Socratic Philosophers* 3rd. ed. (Cambridge, Mass.: Harvard University Press, 1959).

The mind cannot conceive Not-Being; therefore, Not-Being does not exist. Being is the only possible object of thought. Being does not pass away, is whole, and is motionless. It stays fixed in one place. This is the Way of Truth. . . . The Way of Opinion is that of sense-perception, the validity of which is doubtful. To be and to think are the same. The sensory world is illusory, since the senses manifestly report change; only what exists in the mind is real.[3]

True knowledge is possible, and thus we can escape from uncertainty.

The early premises of the Sophists were made against this background of philosophical alternatives. Some of the writings of the Sophists were directed towards this ontological conflict; their main thrust, however, was directed towards practical success in life and conduct. Their concern was not with the heavens and earth, but with man, society, and language, turning from metaphysics as futile and needlessly upsetting, to a conscious ideal of "culture." As a group, they espoused the relativistic theory of values and skeptically regarded absolute truths as unknowable. They claimed the ability to teach a young man virtually anything he or his father thought desirable, most particularly rhetoric and those virtues which would enable him to become successful in public life. The methods of the Sophists varied with each to some extent, but in general they taught through public debate and discourse or continuous speech by one person. Socrates, however, taught through conversation and the dialectic method of directed questioning.

The idea that there is more than one side to every question seems not very profound, but such an idea has always threatened the established or conservative element in society. Debates had always existed among the Greeks, but the Sophists brought the spirit of argumentation out of the war councils and diplomacy of heads of state into the everyday life of the citizenry. To learn to challenge others' opinions, to lay verbal traps for one's opponents, to argue against authority, to orate eloquently—these were the instruments of influence and ambition, and such excellences were presumed to be teachable.

Little remains of what the Sophists themselves wrote and taught; most of our understanding of them comes from secondary sources, most particularly from a reading of the dialogues of Plato, who was primarily concerned with refuting their doctrines. Our knowledge of Socrates, too, comes from the writings of two of his students, Plato and Xenophon.

Most respected among the Sophists were Protagoras, Gorgias, Hippias, and Isocrates.

Protagoras is noted for his views on the gods:

About the gods, I am not able to know whether they exist or do not exist, nor what they are like in form; for the factors preventing knowledge are many: the obscurity of the subject and the shortness of human life. (*On The Gods*)[4]

Life is and man is, and such knowledge seems unattainable.

The most important of Protagorean ideas is the idea that knowledge is perception and that each man is the truth unto himself, as far as the way things

3. Ibid., pp. 147, 149.
4. Ibid., p. 347.

'really" are. This reduced all knowledge to sensation, and did away with any possibility of stable knowledge.

> Of all things the measure is Man, of the things that are, that they are, and of things that are not, that they are not.[5]

The idea of the relativity of reality and knowledge is in direct opposition to the absolutist ideas of Plato and Socrates; Plato spent much of his time disparaging the notion that so important a concept as virtue could be left to the judgment of individuals. The Sophists recognized that man is not merely the measure of things, but also the inventor of much of what was attributed to the gods, but they never investigated why such creations took a particular form. The type of education espoused by the Sophists was practical in emphasis and secular in outlook, with little patience for those who did not live the present life, but prepared with great diligence as if they were going to live another one.

However, in their belief that through formally structured education social reform would come, and in the assumption that virtue was teachable (whatever "virtue" was to be defined as), the Sophists were similar to Plato and Socrates, and they strike a modern note.

Gorgias the Sophist was primarily known for his ornate rhetorical style and for his writings on skepticism with respect to metaphysics and the unknowability of being.

> 1. Nothing exists.
> 2. If anything exists, it is incomprehensible.
> 3. If it is comprehensible, it is incommunicable.

> For if the existent things are objects, externally existing, of vision and of hearing and of the senses in general, and of these the visible things are apprehensible by sight and the audible by hearing, and not conversely, how, in this case, can these things be indicated to another person? For the means by which we indicate is speech, and speech is not the real and existent things.[6]

This endeavor was intended to show that the whole metaphysical enterprise of philosophers such as Plato was futile and doomed to disappointment: pure mind is a myth.

Hippias was the one Sophist whom Plato thoroughly despised, and he is portrayed in his dialogues as pompous and insensitive. How much of the presentation is due to personal prejudice against Hippias's general outlook and profession, and how much is truth is impossible to discern.

> But what, Socrates, do you conceive to be all this, taken together? They are the parings and snippings, . . . of reasonings, separated into little bits. But that is a thing both beautiful and of great worth, to be able to put together well and beautifully a speech before a court of justice, or the Council-Hall, or any other official tribunal, before whom the speech may be

---

5. Protagoras, in Plato, *Theaetetus,* in *Plato: Selections,* ed. by Raphael Demos (New York: Charles Scribner's Sons, 1927), p. 309.
6. Gorgias, in James Jarrett, *The Educational Theories of the Sophists* (New York: Teachers College Press, Columbia University, 1969), pp. 68, 70.

addressed; and after producing conviction, to depart, carrying off not the least, but the greatest, of prizes, in the preservation of oneself and one's own property, and that of one's friends. These then you ought to lay hold of, and to bid adieu to such petty disputes, in order that you may not seem to be a simpleton, by taking, as just now, trifles and inanities in hand.[7]

In the *Protagoras,* Hippias is credited with expressing the view that Nature and Law are opposed; that Law is a tyrant over mankind and forces men in many ways contrary to nature.

Isocrates was a later and well respected Sophist. From his point of view, there were unworthy members who had emerged in his craft; those who professed to impart absolute knowledge which would enable others to direct their conduct under all circumstances (including Socrates and Plato), those who claimed to be able to make anyone a good speaker regardless of his natural abilities, those who were greedy for money but taught little, and those who professed to write on rhetoric but confined themselves to political discourses.

For Isocrates, philosophy was a synonym for "paideia" or culture, and the discourse he dealt with in his school had to do with society and the political arena, relations which human values bear to each other, not merely rhetoric as an abstract exercise. In his quarrel with Plato, he felt "It is much better to form probable opinions about useful things than to have exact knowledge of useless things."[8]

Thus, the fundamental difference between general sophistic belief and that of Plato is that Plato searched after absolute truth, or at least sought to reduce the arguments to clear and precise order. The Sophists saw this activity as trivial, a private amusement. Their prized arena was the court of law and the assembly; they dealt with litigation, defense or prosecution of persons, war or peace, poverty or prosperity, freedom or banishment, culture and political affairs; they sought applause from the masses, not admiration from associates for a well-drawn distinction. This was an early form of the conflicts which extend throughout the entire history of philosophy, between materialism (emphasis on nature and social practice) and idealism (emphasis on thought and consciousness), and between static, absolute conceptualizations and dialectical, changing methodologies.

To the Sophists, Socrates and Plato appeared as foolish visionaries, lacking public spirit, corrupters and misguiders of youth, wasting time on unknowables. Plato in return led the attack on the Sophists and on empirical knowledge as revealed by the senses. He saw the Sophists as deceptive flatterers, selfish and incapable of seeking the Truth. They did not reject the old society and attempt to set up a radically new one, a "better" one, but instead prepared for success in a corrupt one. To the conservative public, as represented by Aristophanes, both appeared as corruptive and disruptive influences. "Sophist" had become a term of abuse hurled at each other by rival schools. The urge to reaffirm ancient loyalties led to attacks on the Sophists, and eventually to death for Socrates for his allegedly impious teaching.

In his various dialogues, Plato presents his alternative to the Sophistic views, through the voice of Socrates.

7. Plato, "Greater Hippias," in Jarrett, *Educational Theories of the Sophists,* pp. 81-82.
8. Isocrates, "Encomium on Helen," in Jarrett, *Educational Theories of the Sophists,* p. 103.

It is Socrates whom we credit with having established the dialectic method of teaching through questioning. He used questions to expose ignorance of eternal truths—what is virtue, what is knowledge, can it be taught through education, can any man become virtuous? His concern was with man's moral and intellectual nature. In the final analysis, Socrates adopted the position that virtue is knowledge; it is given by divine favor; it is inherent in every human being, to be uncovered through thought and intelligent questioning—through "anamnesis" or recollection from one's memory, based on one's past life and the immortality of one's soul. If virtue is knowledge and knowledge is teachable, then virtue is teachable. In Plato's *Meno,* the epistemological puzzle is pursued. In the end, Socrates taught that the furthest we could go in being wise was to know what we didn't know—and persist in loving "wisdom."

The importance of this position to Socrates and Plato was that it countered the sophistic theory of knowledge as empirically determined from the senses. Socrates and Plato stressed a theory of ideas as absolute, universal truths which could be discovered by Reason. In *Phaedo,* Socrates' conversations on the last day of his life are recounted, summing up the basic issues with which he was concerned: that the world of opinion, the senses, experience, was merely a deception, and the world of knowledge, truth, and virtue could only be gained by thought and reason; that the body was separate from the mind or soul; and that the soul was immortal.

The Socrates whom Xenophon, his other well-known student, presents, is most concerned with getting men to live virtuously by showing them what is right and wrong. Xenophon was not a philosopher in the sense of Plato, but rather was interested in the practical aspects of social life. For him, education was purely civic and political; the intellectual aspect was almost eliminated, and the system he proposed was predominantly like that of old Sparta. His understanding of Socrates is presented in *Memorabilia:* the following communication between Socrates and Hippias the Sophist points up their differences.

Selections from MEMORABILIA

Xenophon

. . . I assert that what is "lawful" is "just and righteous."

Do you mean to assert (he asked) that lawful and just are synonymous terms?

Socrates. I do.

Xenophon, *Memorabilia,* trans. H. Dakyus, (London: Macmillan and Co., Ltd., 1897). pp. 156-59.

I ask (Hippias added), for I do not perceive what you mean by *lawful,* nor what you mean by *just.*

Soc. You understand what is meant by laws of a city or state?

Yes (he answered).

Soc. What do you take them to be?

Hipp. The several enactments drawn up by the citizens or members of a state in agreement as to what things should be done or left undone.

Then I presume (Socrates continued) that a member of a state who regulates his life in accordance with these enactments will be law-abiding, while the transgressor of the same will be law-less?

Certainly (he answered).

Soc. And I presume the law-loving citizen will do what is just and right, while the lawless man will do what is unjust and wrong?

Hipp. Certainly.

Soc. And I presume that he who does what is just is just, and he who does what is unjust is unjust?

Hipp. Of course.

Soc. It would appear, then, that the *law-loving* man is *just,* and the *lawless unjust?*

Then Hippias: Well, but *laws,* Socrates, how should any one regard as a serious matter either the laws themselves, or obedience to them, which laws the very people who made them are perpetually rejecting and altering?

Which is also true of war (Socrates replied); cities are perpetually undertaking war and then making peace again.

Most true (he answered)

Soc. If so, what is the difference between depreciating obedience to law because laws will be repealed, and depreciating good discipline in war because peace will one day be made? But perhaps you object to enthusiasm displayed in defence of one's home and fatherland in war?

No, indeed I do not! I heartily approve of it (he answered).

Soc. Then have you laid to heart the lesson taught by Lycurgus to the Lacedaemonians, and do you understand that if he succeeded in giving Sparta a distinction above other states, it was only by instilling into her, beyond all else, a spirit of obedience to the laws? And among magistrates and rulers in the different states, you would scarcely refuse the palm of superiority to those who best contribute to make their fellow-citizens obedient to the laws? And you would admit that any particular state in which obedience to the laws is the paramount distinction of the citizens flourishes most in peace time, and in time of war is irresistible? But, indeed, of all the blessings which a state may enjoy, none stands higher than the blessing of unanimity. "Concord among citizens"— that is the constant theme of exhortation emphasized in the councils of elders and by the choice spirits of the community; at all times and everywhere through the length and breadth of Hellas it is an established law that the citizens be bound together by an oath of concord; everywhere they do actually swear this oath: not of course as implying that citizens shall all vote for the same choruses, or give their plaudits to the same flute-players, or choose the same poets, or limit themselves to the same pleasures, but simply that they shall pay obedience to the laws, since in the end that state will prove most powerful and most prosperous in which the citizens abide by these; but without concord neither can a state be well administered nor a household well organized.

And if we turn to private life, what better protection can a man have than obedience to the laws? This shall be his safeguard against penalties, his guarantee of honors at the hands of the community; it shall be a clue to thread his way through the mazes of the law courts unbewildered, secure against defeat, assured of victory. It is to him, the law-loving citizen, that men will turn in confidence when seeking a guardian of the most sacred deposits, be it of money or be it their sons or daughters. He, in the eyes of the state collectively, is trustworthy —he and no other; who alone may be depended on to render to all alike their dues—to parents and kinsmen and servants, to friends and fellow-citizens and foreigners. This is he whom the enemy will soonest trust to arrange an armistice, or a truce, or a treaty of peace. They would like to become the allies of this man, and to fight on his side. This is he to whom the allies of his country will most confidently entrust the command of their forces, or of a garrison, or their states themselves. This, again, is he who may be counted on to recompense kindness with gratitude, and who, therefore, is more sure of kindly treatment than another whose sense of gratitude is duller. The most desirable among friends, the enemy of all others to be avoided, clearly he is not the person whom a foreign state would choose to go to war with; encompassed by a host of friends and exempt from foes, his very character has a charm to compel friendship and alliance, and before him hatred and hostility melt away.

And now, Hippias, I have done my part; that is my proof and demonstration that the "lawful" and "law-observant" are synonymous with the "upright" and the "just."

Xenophon

Plato did attempt to reconcile the early metaphysical conflicts between the world of essences or universal truths and the world of changing and partially unreal sense experience, determined by individual perception. Plato said that there *were* two worlds, that of flux or opinion and that of permanence or true knowledge; opinion comprised particular objects, true knowledge comprised universals—there are beautiful landscapes and there is the sheer essence of beauty. Two convictions determined Plato's thinking: one, that the philosopher seeks and finds what is absolute and permanent behind appearances; the second, that because he grasps the absolute, the philosopher should be at the head of affairs in the community. Plato perfects the Classical point of view, that logical analysis and clear thinking and not experience, are the gateways to wisdom.

Plato was not merely a theorist; he was also concerned with political problems and how to train expert political advisers. In the *Republic,* Plato presents his ideal utopian state, including a complete educational theory in order to achieve this social order.

Concerning education, Plato's position was that it must be considered as preparation for efficient life as a citizen, and that what was essential was "virtue" or "character," which could be produced by the proper training but was not perfected until habits gave way to insight. The human soul may either be fed or starved, poisoned or nourished. Development is from within; the function of the educator is not to put knowledge into the soul but to develop the best that is latent within it by surrounding it with the right kind of environment. The existence of an individual is to be judged in terms of how useful a member he is of the community. Plato saw the establishment of "justice" or the best life as coming into being through the exercise of pure reason in order to attain a higher state of consciousness, which was that of philosophical insight. In Book VII of *The Republic,* Plato presents an allegorical look at humanity as prisoners inside a deep cave, existing at the level of mere sense perception. The principal problem of education is to bring those "guardians" who can attain the highest state of philosophy and who should properly guide the rest, into the world of reality, to enable them to see the "sun," the Good, or the ultimate Truth. When reason awakes, the prisoner breaks his chains and goes into the daylight, sees the true objects themselves instead of shadows. Upon his return to the cave he is received with jeers from those still confined below, who have not as yet attained his understanding. Also inherent in the allegory is a warning against plunging untrained minds into an intent discussion of moral problems; Plato designed a ten-year course in pure mathematics in order to habituate the intellect to abstract reasoning before moral ideas could be called into question.

Selections from

THE ALLEGORY OF THE CAVE

Plato

Next, said I, here is a parable to illustrate the degrees in which our nature may be enlightened or unenlightened. Imagine the condition of men living in a sort of cavernous chamber underground, with an entrance open to the light and a long passage all down the cave.[1] Here they have been from childhood, chained by the leg and also by the neck, so that they cannot move and can see only what is in front of them, because the chains will not let them turn their heads. At some distance higher up is the light of a fire burning behind them; and between the prisoners and the fire is a track[2] with a parapet built along it, like the screen at a puppet-show, which hides the performers while they show their puppets over the top.

I see, said he.

Now behind this parapet imagine persons carrying along various artificial objects, including figures of men and animals in wood or stone or other materials,

Plato, *The Republic,* trans. F. Cornford (New York: Oxford University Press, 1945), pp. 227-35, by permission of The Clarendon Press, Oxford.

1. The *length* of the 'way in' (*eisodos*) to the chamber where the prisoners sit is an essential feature, explaining why no daylight reaches them.
2. The track crosses the passage into the cave at right angles, and is *above* the parapet built along it.

which project above the parapet. Naturally, some of these persons will be talking, others silent.[3]

It is a strange picture, he said, and a strange sort of prisoners.

Like ourselves, I replied; for in the first place prisoners so confined would have seen nothing of themselves or of one another, except the shadows thrown by the fire-light on the wall of the Cave facing them, would they?

Not if all their lives they had been prevented from moving their heads.

And they would have seen as little of the objects carried past.

Of course.

Now, if they could talk to one another, would they not suppose that their words referred only to those passing shadows which they saw?[4]

Necessarily.

And suppose their prison had an echo from the wall facing them? When one of the people crossing behind them spoke, they could only suppose that the sound came from the shadow passing before their eyes.

No doubt.

In every way, then, such prisoners would recognize as reality nothing but the shadows of those artificial objects.[5]

Inevitably.

Now consider what would happen if their release from the chains and the healing of their unwisdom should come about in this way. Suppose one of them set free and forced suddenly to stand up, turn his head, and walk with eyes lifted to the light; all these movements would be painful, and he would be too dazzled to make out the objects whose shadows he had been used to see. What do you think he would say, if someone told him that what he had formerly seen was meaningless illusion, but now, being somewhat nearer to reality and turned towards more real objects, he was getting a truer view? Suppose further that he were shown the various objects being carried by and were made to say, in reply to questions, what each of them was. Would he not be perplexed and believe the objects now shown him to be not so real as what he formerly saw?[6]

Yes, not nearly so real.

And if he were forced to look at the fire-light itself, would not his eyes ache, so that he would try to escape and turn back to the things which he could see distinctly, convinced that they really were clearer than these other objects now being shown to him?

Yes.

And suppose someone were to drag him away forcibly up the steep and rugged ascent and not let him go until he had hauled him out into the sunlight, would he not suffer pain and vexation at such treatment, and, when he had

3. A modern Plato would compare his Cave to an underground cinema, where the audience watches the play of shadows thrown by the film passing before a light at their backs. The film itself is only an image of 'real' things and events in the world outside the cinema. For the film Plato has to substitute the clumsier apparatus of a procession of artificial objects carried on their heads by persons who are merely part of the machinery, providing for the movement of the objects and the sounds whose echo the prisoners hear. The parapet prevents these persons' shadows from being cast on the wall of the Cave.

4. Adam's text and interpretation. The prisoners, having seen nothing but shadows, cannot think their words refer to the objects carried past behind their backs. For them shadows (images) are the only realities.

5. The state of mind called *eikasia* in the previous chapter.

6. The first effect of Socratic questioning is perplexity. . . .

come out into the light, find his eyes so full of its radiance that he could not see a single one of the things that he was now told were real?

Certainly he would not see them all at once.

He would need, then, to grow accustomed before he could see things in that upper world.[7] At first it would be easiest to make out shadows, and then the images of men and things reflected in water, and later on the things themselves. After that, it would be easier to watch the heavenly bodies and the sky itself by night, looking at the light of the moon and stars rather than the Sun and the Sun's light in the day-time.

Yes, surely.

Last of all, he would be able to look at the Sun and contemplate its nature, not as it appears when reflected in water or any alien medium, but as it is in itself in its own domain.

No doubt.

And now he would begin to draw the conclusion that it is the Sun that produces the seasons and the course of the year and controls everything in the visible world, and moreover is in a way, the cause of all that and his companions used to see.

Clearly he would come at last to that conclusion.

Then if he called to mind his fellow prisoners and what passed for wisdom in his former dwelling-place, he would surely think himself happy in the change and be sorry for them. They may have had a practice of honoring and commending one another, with prizes for the man who had the keenest eye for the passing shadows and the best memory for the order in which they followed or accompanied one another, so that he could make a good guess as to which was going to come next.[8] Would our released prisoner be likely to covet those prizes or to envy the men exalted to honor and power in the Cave? Would he not feel like Homer's Achilles, that he would far sooner "be on earth as a hired servant in the house of a landless man"[9] or endure anything rather than go back to his old beliefs and live in the old way?

Yes, he would prefer any fate to such a life.

Now imagine what would happen if he went down again to take his former seat in the Cave. Coming suddenly out of the sunlight, his eyes would be filled with darkness. He might be required once more to deliver his opinion on those shadows, in competition with the prisoners who had never been released, while his eyesight was still dim and unsteady; and it might take some time to become used to the darkness. They would laugh at him and say that he had gone up only to come back with his sight ruined; it was worth no one's while even to attempt the ascent. If they could lay hands on the man who was trying to set them free and lead them up, they would kill him.[10]

Yes, they would.

---

7. Here is the moral—the need of habituation by mathematical study before discussing moral ideas and ascending through them to the Form of the Good.

8. The empirical politician, with no philosophic insight, but only a "knack of remembering what usually happens" (*Gorg.* 501 A). He has *eikasia* = conjecture as to what is likely (*eikos*).

9. This verse being spoken by the ghost of Achilles, suggests that the Cave is comparable with Hades.

10. An allusion to the fate of Socrates.

Every feature in this parable, my dear Glaucon, is meant to fit our earlier analysis. The prison dwelling corresponds to the region revealed to us through the sense of sight, and the fire-light within it to the power of the Sun. The ascent to see the things in the upper world you may take as standing for the upward journey of the soul into the region of the intelligible; then you will be in possession of what I surmise, since that is what you wish to be told. Heaven knows whether it is true; but this, at any rate, is how it appears to me. In the world of knowledge, the last thing to be perceived and only with great difficulty is the essential Form of Goodness. Once it is perceived, the conclusion must follow that, for all things, this is the cause of whatever is right and good; in the visible world it gives birth to light and to the lord of light, while it is itself sovereign in the intelligible world and the parent of intelligence and truth. Without having had a vision of this Form no one can act with wisdom, either in his own life or in matters of state.

So far as I can understand, I share your belief.

Then you may also agree that it is no wonder if those who have reached this height are reluctant to manage the affairs of men. Their souls long to spend all their time in that upper world—naturally enough, if here once more our parable holds true. Nor, again, is it at all strange that one who comes from the contemplation of divine things to the miseries of human life should appear awkward and ridiculous when, with eyes still dazed and not yet accustomed to the darkness, he is compelled, in a law-court or elsewhere, to dispute about the shadows of justice or the images that cast those shadows, and to wrangle over the notions of what is right in the minds of men who have never beheld Justice itself.[11]

It is not at all strange.

No; a sensible man will remember that the eyes may be confused in two ways—by a change from light to darkness or from darkness to light; and he will recognize that the same thing happens to the soul. When he sees it troubled and unable to discern anything clearly, instead of laughing thoughtlessly, he will ask whether, coming from a brighter existence, its unaccustomed vision is obscured by the darkness, in which case he will think its condition enviable and its life a happy one; or whether, emerging from the depths of ignorance, it is dazzled by excess of light. If so, he will rather feel sorry for it; or, if he were inclined to laugh, that would be less ridiculous than to laugh at the soul which has come down from the light.

That is a fair statement.

If this is true, then, we must conclude that education is not what it is said to be by some, who profess to put knowledge into a soul which does not possess it, as if they could put sight into blind eyes. On the contrary, our own account signifies that the soul of every man does possess the power of learning the truth and the organ to see it with; and that, just as one might have to turn the whole body around in order that the eye should see light instead of darkness, so the entire soul must be turned away from this changing world, until its eye can bear to contemplate reality and that supreme splendor which we have called the Good. Hence there may well be an art whose aim would be to effect this very thing, the conversion of the soul, in the readiest way; not to put the power of sight

---

11. In the *Gorgias* 486 A, Callicles, forecasting the trial of Socrates, taunts him with the philosopher's inability to defend himself in a court.

into the soul's eye, which already has it, but to ensure that, instead of looking in the wrong direction, it is turned the way it ought to be.

Yes, it may well be so.

It looks, then, as though wisdom were different from those ordinary virtues, as they are called, which are not far removed from bodily qualities, in that they can be produced by habituation and exercise in a soul which has not possessed them from the first. Wisdom, it seems, is certainly the virtue of some diviner faculty, which never loses its power, though its use for good or harm depends on the direction towards which it is turned. You must have noticed in dishonest men with a reputation for sagacity the shrewd glance of a narrow intelligence piercing the objects to which it is directed. There is nothing wrong with their power of vision, but it has been forced into the service of evil, so that the keener its sight, the more harm it works.

Quite true.

And yet if the growth of a nature like this had been pruned from earliest childhood, cleared of those clinging overgrowths which come of gluttony and all luxurious pleasure and, like leaden weights charged with affinity to this mortal world, hang upon the soul, bending its vision downwards; if, freed from these, the soul were turned around towards true reality, then this same power in these very men would see the truth as keenly as the objects it is turned to now.

Yes very likely.

Is it not also likely, or indeed certain after what has been said, that a state can never be properly governed either by the uneducated who know nothing of truth or by men who are allowed to spend all their days in the pursuit of culture? The ignorant have no single mark before their eyes at which they must aim in all the conduct of their own lives and of affairs of state; and the others will not engage in action if they can help it, dreaming that, while still alive, they have been translated to the Islands of the Blest.

Quite true.

It is for us, then, as founders of a commonwealth, to bring compulsion to bear on the noblest natures. They must be made to climb the ascent to the vision of Goodness, which we called the highest object of knowledge; and, when they have looked upon it long enough, they must not be allowed, as they now are, to remain on the heights, refusing to come down again to the prisoners or to take any part in their labors and rewards, however much or little these may be worth.

Shall we not be doing them an injustice, if we force on them a worse life than they might have?

You have forgotten again, my friend, that the law is not concerned to make any one class specially happy, but to ensure the welfare of the commonwealth as a whole. By persuasion or constraint it will unite the citizens in harmony, making them share whatever benefits each class can contribute to the common good; and its purpose in forming men of that spirit was not that each should be left to go his own way, but that they should be instrumental in binding the community into one.

True, I had forgotten.

You will see, then, Glaucon, that there will be no real injustice in compelling our philosophers to watch over and care for the other citizens. We can fairly tell them that their compeers in other states may quite reasonably refuse to collaborate: there they have sprung up, like a self-sown plant, in despite of their country's institutions; no one has fostered their growth, and they cannot be expected to show gratitude for a care they have never received. "But," we shall say, "it is not so with you. We have brought you into existence for your country's sake as well as for your own, to be like leaders and king-bees in a hive; you have been better and more thoroughly educated than those others and hence you are more capable of playing your part both as men of thought and as men of action. You must go down, then, each in his turn, to live with the rest and let your eyes grow accustomed to the darkness. You will then see a thousand times better than those who live there always; you will recognize every image for what it is and know what it represents, because you have seen justice, beauty, and goodness in their reality; and so you and we shall find life in our commonwealth no mere dream, as it is in most existing states, where men live fighting one another about shadows and quarrelling for power, as if that were a great prize; whereas in truth government can be at its best and free from dissension only where the destined rulers are least desirous of holding office."

Quite true.

Then will our pupils refuse to listen and to take their turns at sharing in the work of the community, though they may live together for most of their time in a purer air?

No; it is a fair demand, and they are fair-minded men. No doubt, unlike any ruler of the present day, they will think of holding power as an unavoidable necessity.

Yes, my friend; for the truth is that you can have a well-governed society only if you can discover for your future rulers a better way of life than being in office; then only will power be in the hands of men who are rich, not in gold, but in the wealth that brings happiness, a good and wise life. All goes wrong when, starved for lack of anything good in their own lives, men turn to public affairs hoping to snatch from thence the happiness they hunger for. They set about fighting for power, and this internecine conflict ruins them and their country. The life of true philosophy is the only one that looks down upon offices of state; and access to power must be confined to men who are not in love with it; otherwise rivals will start fighting. So whom else can you compel to undertake the guardianship of the commonwealth, if not those who, besides understanding best the principles of government, enjoy a nobler life than the politician's and look for rewards of a different kind?

There is indeed no other choice.

Plato

Plato believed that true knowledge or insight could only be attained by a few persons; thus, his utopian state was divided into three classes: the common people or artisans who would provide the material necessities of existence; the guardians or military who would safeguard the community; the rulers or philosophers responsible for the theory and practice of government. Politics was an art and a science, and the average person had neither the knowledge nor the native intelligence to govern. Plato's aristocracy of intellect would not become exploitative, for the interests of the group were their first concern, and of course, such men would only be interested in philosophical ideals and not material gain, being secure in absolute knowledge. He agreed in theory with the idea that every citizen had a right to participate in government, but this was adjusted to correspond to the individual's capacity, upon which his future status in life depended.

> You are, all of you in this land, brothers. But when God fashioned you, he added gold in the composition of those of you who are qualified to be Rulers (which is why their prestige is greatest); he put silver in the Auxiliaries, and iron and bronze in the farmers and the rest. Now since you are all of the same stock, though children will commonly resemble their parents, occasionally a silver child will be born of golden parents, or a golden child of silver parents, and so on. Therefore the first and most important of God's commandments to the Rulers is that they must exercise their function as Guardians with particular care in watching the mixture of metals in the characters of the children. If one of their own children has bronze or iron in its makeup, they must harden their hearts, and degrade it to the ranks of the industrial and agricultural class where it properly belongs: similarly, if a child of this class is born with gold or silver in its nature, they will promote it appropriately to be a Guardian or an Auxiliary. For they know that there is a prophecy that the State will be ruined when it has Guardians of silver or bronze.[9]

In *The Republic,* Plato was reacting to some extent against Athenian direct "democracy" which had allowed Socrates to be condemned to death. He argued for many features of the old Spartan system. The ideal State was to be organized on a communistic basis where family life was to be eliminated. All children belonged to the State, and all would be brought up by State nurses.

Plato differentiated his plan of education into three stages. The first was intended for all citizens and was the same conventional Athenian education—music for the mind and gymnastics for the body. (Music included literary skills such as reading, writing and poetry, and the study of customs and laws.)

The age at which studies were to begin, as mentioned in *Laws,* was ten. Children would go to school and spend three years learning to read and write, and three more years studying music. Boys and girls would be educated together. Because careful attention must be paid to their surroundings, children must see and hear nothing ugly or mean; thus, Plato believed in censorship of traditional poems showing imperfections of gods and heroes, and that the State should invent new myths which were moral and substitute these myths for those which were rejected and censored.

At age 17 mental studies were to be completely broken off and a severe, systematic military and physical training begun, until age 20.

By this stage, the common people would have passed out of the system and those who were worthy would spend the next 10 years in the study of sciences: arithmetic, astronomy, geometry. All of these studies would gradually develop the intellect until at age 30, a still smaller number was to be selected for the study of the dialectic or philosophy, which continued for five years. At 35, then, a man who had passed through this trying course was fit for the highest position in public life and must, as a public servant, devote his energies to the good of the community until the age of 50, when he must face the final trial and lift his mind to see the Good itself. For the rest of his life, he would spend

9. Plato, *The Republic,* trans. by H. Lee (Great Britain: Penguin Books, Ltd., 1955). pp. 160-161.

his time in philosophy, doing his duty in politics, bringing up successors like himself.

When Plato was 40 years old, he established his school, the Academy, and devoted himself to teaching and writing.

Plato's position held, then, that a life of knowing is superior to a life of doing. An allegorical example of his thinking would be found in an examination of the participants at a sporting event—lowest are those who sell refreshments, second are the athletes who compete, and highest of all are the spectators.

What is the final truth? The history of philosophy shows a continuous recurrence of certain well-defined points of view (empiricism, nominalism, materialism, idealism, realism, rationalism, humanism, mysticism, etc.), each of which has had its devotees and each of which purports to represent a final insight into the nature of things, the nature of man, the relationship of man to knowledge, of men to one another, and of man to the universe. Indeed, it has been said that "The safest general characterization of the European philosophical tradition is that it consists of a series of footnotes to Plato."[10]

The designers and advocates of the "new" Greek philosophical and educational alternatives do not appear "radical" to us today, for their concern was still, like ours, with the moral order of society, with functional images of man in society, of rational man with a higher duty to the State than to himself, of a hierarchy of social control, all based on externally derived values supposedly not man-made, but man-received. Any sense of "individualism" was to be gained through participation in social activities, by following recognized and approved standards, under the dominance of a rigid public opinion upholding a traditional social morality. Only from some of the Sophists does there come a hint of the idea that life may involve much more than this.

The last significant contribution to Greek educational theory was made by Aristotle (384-322 B.C.), whose works sum up and form the culmination of the philosophical and educational movement begun by the Sophists. His influence on future generations was immense, for his works contain the first statement of many technical distinctions, definitions and convictions on which later philosophies and science were based. Authorities in centuries to come would interpret and give new meanings to his extensive work in order to support their various theories and doctrines.

Under the instruction of Plato in his early life, he approached many of the same problems in a different way. Upon Plato's death, he left Athens and traveled for twelve years, devoting himself to study and investigation and to the education of Alexander the Great of Macedonia. When Alexander became King, Aristotle returned to Athens and established the Lyceum, his own school, dedicated to research and to the organization and production of an encyclopedia of all the "sciences," a compilation of all human knowledge.

Aristotle's method was objective and "scientific" or empirical, as opposed to the philosophical or introspective method of Plato. The commonly-made distinction between Plato and Aristotle is that Plato sought truth through the vision of reason in a world of ideas and changeless things, while Aristotle sought truth primarily in the world of nature and the regularities of social life. This dualism may be only a partly adequate conception, for Aristotle also believed

10. Alfred Whitehead, quoted in Alvin Gouldner, *Enter Plato* (New York: Harper & Row, 1966), p. 8.

in truths and the unchanging aspects of human existence. Using the dialectic method of Socrates, Plato searched the regions of the mind for formal value. Aristotle searched in experience and developed as his methods the inductive and deductive processes of reasoning. Plato introduced the ideal of intellectual culture into his system of educational thought. This ideal was reconciled with efficient citizenship, which was the main thrust of education. Aristotle, on the other hand, took culture as the ultimate aim and showed that efficiency was necessary in the attainment of that end. Both appear, however, to arrive at similar results. Both were concerned only with elites.

Where Aristotle differed sharply from Plato was in his belief that true knowledge had no separate existence, but rather, that it was formed by generalizations arrived at by discovering something common to various phenomena, like the "laws" of modern science. An idea was a name for something held in common by like objects, instead of being a thing in itself.

To all the Greeks, education was recognized as an integral part of politics, and was a practical and not a theoretical science. Aristotle's views on education are expressed in his book on *Politics*. While Plato's ideal state was an aristocracy, Aristotle held that a monarchical form was best. However, he advocated the republican form, since that was least open to abuse, and it is for this form of government that he expounded his scheme of education. The system still retained a heavy aristocratic bias, for any involvement by an individual in economic activity precluded him from being a free citizen and participating.

In his specific treatment of education, Aristotle did not offer fundamental alternatives to Plato's scheme. He did reject Plato's plan for a communistic upbringing of children, and retained the family form. He believed, like Plato, that a child's morals were to be well-guarded by his exclusion from public life and by special care taken by pedagogues. The ideal state could only be realized through education; thus, its aim was again training children in "right" courses of action or virtue. Like Plato, Aristotle's curriculum consisted of gymnastics, reading, writing and music. He distinguished two great periods of intellectual education, elementary and higher, preceded by a period of home education and separated by an interval devoted to severe forms of physical training. The industrial and commercial classes, as well as the slaves, were excluded from citizenship. Only those relieved of the necessity of all manual labor could hope to become educated and politically and intellectually aware. Those engaged in practical or industrial activities were to be educated by participation in occupations, or appreticeship.

Insofar as education was concerned, Aristotle made no major changes in the system described by Plato. Both agreed that the training of character and intellect was primary, but that educators had to keep in mind the practical requirements of the community. However, the highest cultural function of education went far beyond the practical life of the state. Both presented views opposite to those of the Sophists, who advocated individual success in the political realm as the prime concern.

The ultimate aims of Aristotle were the welfare of the state and also the "happiness" of the individuals within it. Aristotle, like Plato and Socrates, presumed that happiness could be found only in the "highest" life, that of contemplation, and in the performance of intrinsically excellent activities for the State. Happiness was the highest good. Virtue was those activities of a rational being which led to happiness. Education was instruction in those virtues. The realization of happiness for the individual citizen was the same as the realization of the happiness of the state because it involved his activity in performing his own proper function within it.

Concern with happiness led Aristotle to discuss the "right" use of leisure, which would culminate in the highest life of speculative insight into the reason which pervades the universe. The high life, the good life, the ultimate happiness of contemplation could only be achieved by those who had wealth, social position, health, good looks and luck, and were therefore able to use their leisure time in the "right" ways. A life of labor allowed the mind no time for leisure or profound thought.

In his *Politics*, Aristotle discusses which of two basic educational alternatives the schools should concentrate on, a liberal and noble education or a practical and useful one. The former was most essential if the state was to create citizens who were capable of attaining the highest life, and in the end intellect and truth-seeking were victorious over practical political concerns.

Selections from POLITICS

Aristotle

*   *   *

(2) Again, since the state as a whole has a single end, it is plain that the education of all must be one and the same, and that the supervision of this education must be public and not private, as it is in the present system, under which everyone looks after his own children privately and gives them any private instruction he thinks proper. Public training is wanted in all things that are of public interest. Besides, it is wrong for any citizen to think that he belongs to himself. All must be regarded as belonging to the state: for each man is a part of the state, and the treatment of the part is naturally determined by that of the whole. This is a thing for which the Lacedaemonians deserve all praise; they are thoroughly in earnest about their children, and that as a community.

(3) We now see that we shall have to legislate on the subject of education, and that education must be public; but we must not overlook the question of the character and method of this education. As it is, there is a dispute about subjects. There is no agreement as to what the young should learn, either with a view to the production of goodness or the best life, nor is it settled whether

Aristotle, *Politics*, trans. John Burnet. (Great Britain: Cambridge University Press, 1913), pp. 106-111.

we ought to keep the intellect or the character chiefly in view. If we start from the education we see around us, the inquiry is perplexing, and there is no certainty as to whether education should be a training in what is useful for life or in what tends to promote goodness or in more out-of-the-way subjects. Each of these views finds some supporters; but there is not even any agreement as to what tends to promote goodness. To begin with, all people do not appreciate the same kind of goodness, so it is only to be expected that they should differ about the required training.

It is, of course, obvious that we shall have to teach our children such useful knowledge as is indispensable for them; but it is equally plain that all useful knowledge is not suitable for education. There is a distinction between liberal and illiberal subjects, and it is clear that only such knowledge as does not make the learner mechanical should enter into education. By mechanical subjects we must understand all arts and studies that make the body, soul, or intellect of freemen unserviceable for the use and exercise of goodness. That is why we call such pursuits as produce an inferior condition of body mechanical, and all wage-earning occupations. They allow the mind no leisure, and they drag it down to a lower level. There are even some liberal arts, the acquisition of which up to a certain point is not unworthy of freemen, but which, if studied with excessive devotion or minuteness are open to the charge of being injurious in the manner described. The object with which we engage in or study them also makes a great difference; if it is for our own sakes or that of our friends, or to produce goodness, they are not illiberal, while a man engaging in the very same pursuits to please strangers would in many cases be regarded as following the occupation of a slave or a serf.

Now the subjects most widely disseminated at present show a double face, as was remarked above. There are, speaking broadly, four which usually enter into education, (1) Reading and writing, (2) Gymnastics and (3) Music, to which some add (4) Drawing. Reading and writing is taught on the ground that it is of the highest utility for practical life, and gymnastics as tending to promote courage; but, when, we come to music, we may feel at a loss. At the present day, most people take it up with idea that its object is pleasure; but the ancients gave it its place in education because Nature herself, as we have often oberved, seeks not only to be rightly busy, but also the power of using leisure aright. That is the root of the whole matter, if we may recur to the point once more. Both are wanted, but leisure is more worth having and more of an end than business, so we must find out how we are to employ our leisure. Not, surely, in playing games; for that would imply that amusement is the end of life. That it cannot be, and it is rather in our busy times that we should have recourse to games. It is the hardworked man that needs rest, and the object of play is rest, and we find that it is business that involves hard work and strain. So, when we introduce games, we should do so with a due regard to times and seasons, applying them medicinally; for motion of this character is a relaxation of the soul, and from its pleasantness gives it rest. Leisure, on the other hand, we regard as containing pleasure—nay, happiness and the blessed life—in itself. That is not a thing that we find in busy people, but only in people at leisure. The busy man is busy for some end,—which implies that he has not got it,—while happiness is itself the end and by universal consent involves not pain but pleasure. To be sure, when we come to the question "What pleasure?" we no longer find a universal agreement. Each man determines it in his own way, the best man choosing the best and that which has the fairest source.

It is clear, then, that there are subjects which ought to form part of education solely with a view to the right employment of leisure, and that this education and those studies exist for their own sake, while those that have business in view are studied as being necessary and for the sake of something else. That is why our predecessors gave music a place in education, not as a necessary thing, —there is nothing necessary about it,—nor yet as a useful thing, as reading and writing are useful for making money and the management of property and many political occupations. Even drawing is supposed to be useful in enabling us to judge the work of craftsmen better. Nor again is music useful like gymnastics for health and the production of military prowess; we see no such result accruing from it. There is no object left for it, then, but the right employment of our time in leisure, and, as a matter of fact, it is just in this way that the ancients do introduce it; for it is in what they regard as the right way for free men to enjoy leisure that they give it a place. That is why Homer made the verses beginning "Tis meet alone to bid to the bounteous feast," and, after mentioning some others adds "who bid the minstrel to delight them all." And in another place Odysseus says that the best way of spending time is when men are merry and "the banqueters throughout the hall give ear to the minstrel, all seated in a row."

We conclude, then, that there is such a thing as a subject in which we must educate our sons, not because it is necessary, but because it is fine and worthy of free men. Whether there is only one such or a larger number we shall have to discuss later on. At present, from our consideration of the received subjects, we have gained this point, that we can quote the evidence of the ancients in favor of our view. The case of music shows that. Further we have found that our children must be educated even in some of the "useful" subjects, as for instance in reading and writing, not merely for their utility, but because they enable us to acquire many other subjects. Drawing is to be taught, not merely to save us from making blunders in our private purchases, to secure us against being cheated in the buying and selling of furniture, but still more because it enables us to see bodily beauty. To seek utility everywhere is by no means the way of free men with a sense of their own dignity.

Aristotle

The Greeks conceived of the state as an organism, the parts important because of the functions they performed in maintaining the system and in the attainment of its goals. From this belief followed the necessity for differentiation and specialization of the parts. Inequalities among parts were not imperfections or injustices, but natural and necessary differences. Some parts shared more in the whole because they contributed more than the others, were more clever, knew more, thought more, did more of the most important things. In this conceptualization lies the basis for limiting the rights of citizenship to those who knew and aimed at the "real" ends of the state. Here lies the basis for a hierarchy of human values, for social control and the aristocratic and the later meritocratic systems. Greek education in its final form aimed to produce persons of such character and intellect as would act to maintain the form of society as it existed, and the class in power intact.

It was in the generation following Aristotle and Alexander the Great that Greek culture, and the system of education in which it is reflected, finally assumed its definitive classical form. This is known as the Hellenistic era. Greek civilization had shifted even more from a rural folk warrior society to an urban political setting. While education retained some of its moral character, it became more and more dependent on books, and music and art yielded to literature. Schools developed an institutional character, taking the place of spontaneous and enthusiastic bands of men and boys such as those who had gathered around Socrates in face-to-face interaction.

The ideal of human existence became the man of culture and not the man of action. The aim of education did not involve techniques of equipping the child for a place in society, but of realizing the human intellectual ideal. This was called 'paideia,' the spirit and mind of man as formed by the study of classical literature (in direct line from Isocrates). Classical education in its final form was aesthetic, artistic and literary, with general instruction in all subjects. It was neither scientific, political nor social. Geometry, for example, was an abstract sequence of theorems, not a problem for engineers or surveyors; arithmetic was the theory of numbers, not a matter for accountants or statisticians. For a time mathematics was considered part of the curriculum of secondary education, until it was eliminated by the classicists with their emphasis on literature. The Hellenistic effort was directed towards forming the perfect individual who would be ready for anything but had no particular professional competency. But political, economic and technical conditions of the period did not provide for anything to do with this well-rounded human material. The Greeks did not develop administrative and professional organizations or political groups which might have given their society more stability.

In this Hellenistic era, schools became of concern and interest to the municipality, and received some support from it. However, the city's economic structure had neither the resources nor the administrative apparatus which would have enabled it to take direct charge of public education. Thus, most schools remained private, where the teachers received fees from the pupils or where wealthy individuals provided the necessary funds. Only the "ephebia" (schools established primarily for military training, but which also dealt with some civic, moral and religious training in preparation for citizenship) were public institutions.

Successors to the Sophists, Socrates, Plato and Aristotle began to demand regular fees, thus giving their schools a definite student body (sometimes consisting of 2,000 pupils). Their schools acquired specific names and locations, much like the Academy and the Lyceum, and developed a basic system of organization and continuity of administration. These scholars attempted only to set forth the ideas of the founders of their schools and of philosophers before them; they did not aspire towards investigation, research, or discussion of new topics. The successors of Plato and Aristotle, together with the leaders of two newer schools of philosophy, the Stoics (who gave emphasis to virtue and morality through ethical teachings) and the Epicureans (who were oriented towards a materialistic, scientific interpretation of the universe and the power of pleasure) joined with the ephebic schools and formed the University of Athens. The old military state training had become a literary university training. The University of Athens of this period bears a great resemblance to the medieval universities of the 12th century. However, the University of Athens as a center of classical learning aroused the opposition of the Christian Church as it grew in power, and it was finally closed in 529 A.D. by the Emperor Justinian.

ROME

Though dominated by the same institution, the city-state, upon which their civilization was based, the Romans took a course of development somewhat different from that of the Greeks. Roman interests centered on the practical. They aimed to accomplish concrete purposes outside of an individual's own realm of thought, and measured things against a standard of usefulness and effectiveness in both social and institutional life. Their genius lay in devising the social institutions and systematic organization necessary for realizing their ideals. For the Greeks, the highest life was one which was an ideal model of virtue, happiness, intellect, and some form of personal satisfaction. For the Romans, the highest conception of life was one spent performing some duty, with its corresponding rights and obligations—i.e., life in terms of law or principle. Through their development and organization of law, the Romans established the system of management and morality which serves to a great extent as the basis of modern social life.

Education was the preparation for life's practical duties and was primarily concerned with the formation of moral character. Roman schools had a minor place in the scheme of socialization. Above all, the institution of the home and the power and personal influence of the father were magnified in importance, as children were inducted into the customs of the group. The rights of a father were the strongest rights of a Roman, involving power over the life and death of his children and the right of enforcing all laws upon them.

The fundamental Roman ideal was respect for tradition. The young Roman had specific duties of citizenship which he was expected to perform, including taking legal care of his property, serving on various public committees, and engaging in military duties as a soldier. The Romans, unlike the Greeks, were not adverse to industrial life, since it was developed to greater extent and importance, and business training and training in the management of estates and farms became an important element of schooling. The duties of a father included the responsibility for training his children in the appropriate abilities, particularly in piety and obedience to the gods, to his parents and to the state. The most important method of Roman education was imitation, of one's father and also of heroic characters embodied in old legends and histories. A radical difference from Greek education was the rejection of gymnastics, dancing and music as effeminate. The Romans valued "manliness" and instilled it on the martial field and in military camps. The training of older youths was accomplished either by apprenticeship or by actual participation in the activities to be required of them later as citizens. Instead of instruction in cultural ideals and virtues and the liberal education of the Greeks, education was primarily in the practical duties of a Roman citizen.

Part of the Roman youth's education consisted of memorizing, understanding and following the *Laws of the Twelve Tables*. These fundamental laws of Roman society, adopted in 450 B.C., constituted the framework and embodied the ideals of life, and gave shape and direction to Roman education.

For example, Table IV discussed the duties and obligations of a father.

TABLE IV

The Rights of the Father.

I.   Provision as to the immediate destruction of monstrous or deformed offspring.

II. Provision relating to the control of the father over his children, the right existing during their whole life to imprison, scourge, keep to rustic labour in chains, to sell or slay, even though they may be in the enjoyment of high state offices.

III. "Three consecutive sales of the son by the father releases the former from the *patria potestas.*"

IV. Provision relating to the duration of gestation: no child born more than ten months after the decease of his reputed father to be held legitimate. . . .[11]

The following comment by Cicero illustrates the high regard in which these Laws were held.

FROM THE DE ORATORE OF CICERO
Book I., Chapter XLIV

Though all the world exclaim against me, I will say what I think: that single little book of the Twelve Tables if any one look at the fountains and sources of laws, seems to me, assuredly, to surpass the libraries of all the philosophers, both in weight of authority, and in plenitude of utility. And if our country has our love, as it ought to have in the highest degree,—our country, I say, of which the force and natural attraction is so strong, that one of the wisest of mankind preferred his Ithaca, fixed, like a little nest, among the roughest of rocks, to immortality itself,—with what affection ought we to be warmed toward such a country as ours, which, preeminently above all other countries, is the seat of virtue, empire, and dignity? Its spirit, customs, and discipline ought to be our first objects of study, both because our country is the parent of us all, and because as much wisdom must be thought to have been employed in framing such laws, as in establishing so vast and powerful an empire. You will receive also this pleasure and delight from the study of the law, that you will then most readily comprehend how far our ancestors excelled other nations in wisdom, if you compare our laws with those of their Lycurgus, Draco, and Solon. It is indeed incredible how undigested and almost ridiculous is all civil law, except our own; on which subject I am accustomed to say much in my daily conversation, when I am praising the wisdom of our countrymen above that of all other men, and especially of the Greeks. For these reasons have I declared, Scaevola, that the knowledge of the civil law is indispensable to those who would become accomplished orators.[12]

---

11. "Laws of the Twelve Tables," in Monroe, *Source Book of the History of Education,* p. 337.
12. Cicero, "De Oratore, (The Orator)" in Monroe, *Source Book of the History of Education,* p. 345.

In 146 B.C. Macedonia was conquered and Greece became a Roman province. Greek scholars, literature and libraries were transferred to Rome, and Hellenistic customs, ideas and educational practices began to infuse Roman society, which had by then grown into a republic. Greek influences resulted in the Hellenizing and institutionalizing of Roman education. A system of schools was established, corresponding to elementary, secondary and higher education. "Paideia" became the model of this later Roman education.

A small number of elementary schools had previously existed to supplement the education of the home. These were known as "ludi," and in them basic reading, writing and arithmetic had been taught. They had been private schools and had served a nonessential function well below that of the home in importance. Two other types of schools now began to emerge. The first, grammar schools, based their studies on the *Odyssey,* which had been translated into Latin. The second were schools of rhetoric, furnishing instruction in oratory and debate. Many charges were brought against these new schools by conservatives who felt that the only proper education was that received in the home. Their charges were similar to those brought against the Sophists when they first appeared in Athens.

The Romans, in effect, appropriated Greek culture by adopting its educational institutions and perfecting them into an organized system. This was a major factor in the preservation and dispersion of Greek thought.

In this second period of Roman education, the whole aim of higher education became oratory. The system of observation and imitation of father and master was supplanted by formal measures, and schools began to instruct in rhetoric and dialectical discussion. The Romans incorporated what later came to be known as the "seven liberal arts" into their program: grammar and literature, rhetoric, dialectic, arithmetic, geometry, music and astronomy. Gymnastics, however, were never introduced in the schools. The pursuits of the Roman mind continued to be of a legal, practical, systematizing character, and education remained oriented towards the practical affairs of life. In time, music and the other arts receded in importance, and oratory (grammer, literature, rhetoric) provided for the practical application of higher learning. The orator was esteemed more than the philosopher, for he was effective in public service, whereas the philosopher withdrew into himself. Greek educational ideas and practices had been modified by the Romans, and the creative character of education was diminishing.

The work of the grammar schools began with the teacher and pupils reading a selection from poets and historians, of which Homer, Virgil and Horace were standards. Comment was made on the substance and literary form, and special attention paid to oral reading as a preliminary to oratorical training. Exercises in paragraphing, composition and the writing of verse then followed. The objective was to acquire mastery of the language and correctness of expression in speaking, reading and writing.

The work of the higher schools of rhetoric consisted of declamation and debate. Such themes as "Was Hannibal justified in his delay before the walls of Rome?" and "If a stranger buys a prospective catch of fishes and the fisherman draws up a casket of jewels, does the stranger own the jewels?" were the subjects of discussion.[13] Problems such as these, relating to historical subjects and fine

13. Paul Monroe, *A Textbook in the History of Education* (New York: The MacMillan Company, 1928), p. 202.

distinctions in law and moral principle, were the means of sharpening rhetorical wit. Latin rhetoric remained very closely connected with Greek rhetoric; thus Isocrates and not Plato succeeded in this respect in having his educational ideas accepted by posterity.

Following the lead of Isocrates, Cicero, in *De Oratore* (55 B.C.), provided the final conception of the orator, the highest type of public figure, who was to be given a broad general background in the liberal arts in order to apply intelligence to the problems of the world.

The *Institutes of Oratory* (96 A.D.) by Quintilian, the foremost Roman teacher, contains the most systematic summary of Roman educational theory. Quintilian enumerated the qualities of an orator, the finished product of the rhetorical schools:

> . . . a knowledge of things gained through a mastery of literature; a good vocabulary and an ability to make careful choice of words; a knowledge of human emotions and the power of arousing them; a gracefulness and urbanity of manners; a knowledge of history and also of law; a good delivery; a good memory.[14]

The education described by Quintilian was a formally organized process, and as such was best given in the schools and not in the home. Quintilian argued that public education was to be preferred to private tutoring. This was probably due to the fact that in this way the state could retain greater control over the kinds of citizens which were created.

Selections from **INSTITUTES OF ORATORY**

Quintilian

CHAPTER II

1. But let us suppose that the child now gradually increases in size, and leaves the lap, and applies himself to learning in earnest. In this place, accordingly, must be considered the question, whether it be more advantageous to confine the learner at home, and within the walls of a private house, or to commit him

Quintillian, *Institutes of Oratory* in Paul Monroe, *Source Book of the History of Education* (London: The Macmillan Company, 1906) pp. 459-64.

14. Ibid., p. 203.

to the large numbers of a school, and, as it were, to public teachers. 2. The latter mode, I observe, has had the sanction of those by whom the polity of the most eminent states were settled, as well as that of the most illustrious authors.

Yet it is not to be concealed, that there are some who, from certain notions of their own, disapprove of this almost public mode of instruction. These persons appear to be swayed chiefly by two reasons: one, that they take better precautions for the morals of the young, by avoiding a concourse of human beings of that age which is most prone to vice (from which cause I wish it were falsely asserted that provocations to immoral conduct arise); the other, that whoever may be the teacher, he is likely to bestow his time more liberally on one pupil, than if he has to divide it among several. 3. The first reason indeed deserves great consideration; for if it were certain that schools, though advantageous to studies, are pernicious to morals, a virtuous course of life would seem to me preferable to one even of the most distinguished eloquence. But in my opinion, the two are combined and inseparable; for I am convinced that no one can be an orator who is not a good man; and, even if any one could, I should be unwilling that he should be. On this point, therefore, I shall speak first.

4. People think that morals are corrupted in schools; for indeed they are at times corrupted; but such may be the case even at home. Many proofs of this fact may be adduced; proofs of character having been vitiated, as well as preserved with the utmost purity, under both modes of education. It is the disposition of the individual pupil, and the care taken of him, that make the whole difference. Suppose that his mind be prone to vice, suppose that there be neglect in forming and guarding his morals in early youth, seclusion would afford no less opportunity for immorality than publicity; for the private tutor may be himself of bad character; nor is intercourse with vicious slaves at all safer than that with immodest free-born youths. 5. But if his disposition be good, and if there be not a blind and indolent negligence on the part of his parents, it will be possible for them to select a tutor of irreproachable character, (a matter to which the utmost attention is paid by sensible parents,) and to fix on a course of instruction of the very strictest kind; while they may at the same time place at the elbow of their son some influential friend or faithful freedman, whose constant attendance may improve even those of whom apprehensions may be entertained.

6. The remedy for this object of fear is easy. Would that we ourselves did not corrupt the morals of our children! We enervate their very infancy with luxuries. That delicacy of education, which we call fondness, weakens all the powers, both of body and mind. What luxury will he not covet in his manhood, who crawls about on purple! He cannot yet articulate his first words, when he already distinguishs scarlet, and wants his purple. 7. We form the palate of children before we form their pronunciation. They grow up in sedan chairs; if they touch the ground, they hang by the hands of attendants supporting them on each side. We are delighted if they utter anything immodest. Expressions which would not be tolerated even from the effeminate youths of Alexandria, we hear from them with a smile and a kiss. Nor is this wonderful; we have taught them; they have heard such language from ourselves. 8. They see our mistresses, our male objects of affection; every dining room rings with impure songs; things shameful to be told are objects of sight. From such practices springs habit, and afterwards nature. The unfortunate children learn these vices

before they know that they are vices; and hence, rendered effeminate and luxurious, they do not imbibe immorality from schools, but carry it themselves into schools. 9. But, it is said, one tutor will have more time for one pupil. First of all, however, nothing prevents that one pupil, whoever he may be, from being the same with him who is taught in the school. But if the two objects cannot be united, I should still prefer the daylight of an honorable seminary to darkness and solitude; for every eminent teacher delights in a large concourse of pupils, and thinks himself worthy of a still more numerous auditory. 10. But inferior teachers, from a consciousness of their inability, do not disdain to fasten on single pupils, and to discharge the duty as it were of *paedagogi*. 11. But supposing that either interest, or friendship, or money, should secure to any parent a domestic tutor of the highest learning, and in every respect unrivalled, will he however spend the whole day on one pupil? Or can the application of any pupil be so constant as not to be sometimes wearied, like the sight of the eyes, by continued direction to one object, especially as study requires the far greater portion of time to be solitary? 12. For the tutor does not stand by the pupil while he is writing, or learning by heart, or thinking; and when he is engaged in any of those exercises, the company of any person whatsoever is a hindrance to him. Nor does every kind of reading require at all times a praelector or interpreter; for when, if such were the case, would the knowledge of so many authors be gained? The time, therefore, during which the work as it were for the whole day may be laid out, is but short. 13. Thus the instructions which are to be given to each may reach to many. Most of them, indeed, are of such a nature that they may be communicated to all at once with the same exertion of the voice. I say nothing of the topics and declamations of the rhetoricians, at which, certainly, whatever be the number of the audience, each will still carry off the whole. 14. For the voice of the teacher is not like a meal, which will not suffice for more than a certain number, but like the sun, which diffuses the same portion of light and heat to all. If a grammarian, too, discourses on the art of speaking, solves questions, explains matters of history, or illustrates poems, as many as shall hear him will profit by his instructions. 15. But, it may be said, number is an obstacle to correction and explanation. Suppose that this be a disadvantage in a number (for what in general satisfies us in every respect?) we will soon compare that disadvantage with other advantages.

Yet I would not wish a boy to be sent to a place where he will be neglected. Nor should a good master encumber himself with a greater number of scholars than he can manage; and it is to be a chief object with us, also, that the master may be in every way our kind friend, and may have regard in his teaching, not so much to duty, as to affection. Thus we shall never be confounded with the multitude. 16. Nor will any master, who is in the slightest degree tinctured with literature, fail particularly to cherish that pupil in whom he shall observe application and genius, even for his own honor. But even if great schools ought to be avoided (a position to which I cannot assent, if numbers flock to a master on account of his merit), the rule is not to be carried so far that schools should be avoided altogether. It is one thing to shun schools, another to choose from them. 17. If I have now refuted the objections which are made to schools, let me next state what opinions I myself entertain. 18. First of all, let him who is to be an orator, and who must live amidst the greatest publicity, and in the full daylight of public affairs, accustom himself, from his boyhood, not to be abashed at the sight of men, nor pine in a solitary and as it were recluse way of life. The mind requires to be constantly excited and roused, while in such retirement it either languishes, and contracts rust, as it were, in the shade, or on the other hand, becomes swollen with empty conceit, since he who compares himself to no one else, will necessarily attribute too much to his own powers. 19. Besides, when his acquirements are to be displayed in public, he is blinded at the light of the sun, and stumbles at every new object, as having learned in solitude that which is to be done in public. 20. I say nothing of friendships formed at school, which remain in full force even to old age, as if cemented with a certain religious obligation; for to have been initiated in the same studies is a not less sacred bond than to have been initiated in the same sacred rites. That sense, too, which is called common sense, where shall a young man learn when he has separated himself from society, which is natural not to men only, but even to dumb animals? 21. Add to this, that, at home, he can learn only what is taught himself; at school, even what is taught others. 22. He will daily hear many things commended, many things corrected; the idleness of a fellow student, when reproved, will be a warning to him; the industry of any one, when commended, will be a stimulus; emulation will be excited by praise; and he will think it a disgrace to yield to his equals in age, and an honor to surpass his seniors. All these matters excite the mind; and though ambition itself be a vice, yet it is often the parent of virtues.

23. I remember a practice that was observed by my masters, not without advantage. Having divided the boys into classes, they assigned them their order in speaking in conformity to the abilities of each; and thus each stood in the higher place to declaim according as he appeared to excel in proficiency. 24. Judgments were pronounced on the performances; and great was the strife among us for distinction; but to take the lead of the class was by far the greatest honor. Nor was sentence given on our merits only once; the thirtieth day brought the vanquished an opportunity of contending again. Thus he who was most successful, did not relax his efforts, while uneasiness incited the unsuccessful to retrieve his honor. 25. I should be inclined to maintain, as far as I can form a judgment from what I conceive in my own mind, that this method furnished stronger incitements to the study of eloquence, than the exhortations of preceptors, the watchfulness of *paedagogi* or the wishes of parents.

26. But as emulation is of use to those who have made some advancement in learning, so, to those who are but beginning, and are still of tender age, to imitate their school-fellows is more pleasant than to imitate their master, for the very reason that it is more easy; for they who are learning the first rudiments will scarcely dare to exalt themselves to the hope of attaining that eloquence which they regard as the highest; they will rather fix on what is nearest to them, as vines attached to tree gain the top by taking hold of the lower branches first. 27. This is an observation of such truth, that it is the care even of the master himself, when he has to instruct minds that are still unformed, not (if he prefer at least the useful to the showy) to overburden the weakness of his scholars, but to moderate his strength, and to let himself down to the capacity of the learner. 28. For as narrow-necked vessels reject a great quantity of the liquid that is poured upon them, but are filled by that which flows or is poured into them by degrees, so it is for us to ascertain how much the minds of boys can receive, since what is too much for their grasp of intellect will not enter their minds, as

not being sufficiently expanded to admit it. 29. It is of advantage therefore for a boy to have school-fellows whom he may first imitate, and afterwards try to surpass. Thus will he gradually conceive hope of higher excellence.

To these observations I shall add, that masters themselves, when they have but one pupil at a time with them, cannot feel the same degree of energy and spirit in addressing him, as when they are excited by a large number of hearers. 30. Eloquence depends in a great degree on the state of the mind, which must conceive images of objects, and transform itself, so to speak, to the nature of the things of which we discourse. Besides, the more noble and lofty a mind is, by the more powerful springs, as it were, is it moved, and accordingly is both strengthened by praise, and enlarged by effort, and is filled with joy at achieving something great. 31. But a certain secret disdain is felt at lowering the power of eloquence, acquired by so much labor, to one auditor; and the teacher is ashamed to raise his style above the level of ordinary conversation. Let any one imagine, indeed, the air of a man haranguing, or the voice of one entreating, the gesture, the pronunciation, the agitation of mind and body, the exertion, and, to mention nothing else, the fatigue, while he has but one auditor; would not he seem to be affected with something like madness? There would be no eloquence in the world, if we were to speak only with one person at a time.

Quintilian

It is surprising at first to realize that as Rome became an empire, and as its society began to disorganize and disintegrate, schools became more prolific and teachers more important. The empire, through both municipal and imperial governments, pursued a policy of interest and financial support for public schools. Economic privileges, such as reduced taxation, and political honors, such as consulates and governorships and exclusion from some of the unpleasant duties of citizenship, were granted to teachers. However, higher and lower education became a privilege of only the favored few, as the formation of the empire gave rise to an aristocratic class. Autonomy of local governments disappeared as the emperors centralized more and more power into their own hands. The army and the Senate engaged in intrigue and counterintrigue, leading to a chaotic political situation. Society took the form of a great pyramid, with the emperor, his family and followers, army officers and high religious and state officials at the top, catered to by merchants and speculators, all resting upon the work of the masses, who had little province for political participation.

From about 50 A.D. to 500 A.D., abuses of power on the part of the aristocracy, military, and corrupt, highly centralized official bureaucracy, and struggles which emerged between patricians (old landed nobility) and plebians (newer landed and commercial groups), led to the political and economic decline of the empire. Being a citizen ceased to be an honor and became little more than governmental servitude, under a tremendous burden of taxation. Eventually, the emperor could summon no support or enthusiasm from the people to support his policies or ward off disaster. The spurt of interest in education by the leaders of the empire can be interpreted as an effort to combat the tendencies towards disintegration.

Oratory lost its originality and inspiration as opportunities for its application in the political sphere disappeared. It became formal and artificial, to the point of becoming a form of display or entertainment. Schools of rhetoric no longer dealt with questions of public policy relevant to actual experience, but with imaginary and improbable events. Higher education modeled itself more and more on Hellenistic ideals of culture and intellect, and political eloquence became aesthetic eloquence focused in the art of lecturing. Education withdrew into and became an end in itself. Studies became more and more divorced from the realities of Roman society. Now a student merely learned the complex system of rules and then practiced using them in speeches memorized and delivered.

The original contribution of Rome to education had been its judicial system and schools of law, which went beyond the previous folk reliance on family, kinship, and communal rules for decision-making. The Romans began the whole system of precedents whereby cases and analogies from the past could be used to support cases in the present. However, these schools, too, began to degenerate into formalism.

It is questionable as to whether the literary education of the rhetorical schools, even if it had been more widespread among the various social classes, would have enabled the Romans to surmount the problems facing their civilization. The "liberal" education did not really liberate.

Having become a system of education which did not benefit or interest the people at large, the Roman schools were altered with the Christianization of the empire and, finally, extinguished with its conquest by the Germanic tribes in the sixth century.

MEDIEVAL TIMES

The Christian Faith

The emergence of Christianity as a world power and the conquest of Rome by the Germanic tribes gave rise to the meeting of the factors which combined to be most influential in modern Western culture: Greek intellectual and aesthetic concerns, Roman legal and political institutions, Eastern Hebraic traditions as interpreted through Christianity, and the vigor and explosiveness of various Germanic tribes. At this point in history, all of these diverse forces in the ancient world came together and began to undergo mutation almost instantly.

The period of time from 500 to 1500 A.D. is known historically as the Middle Ages, the term which was introduced by leaders of the Renaissance, who considered everything between the classical age (Greco-Roman culture) and their own times as "middle." The first few centuries became known as the "Dark Ages," barbarous and chaotic times. However, this definition does not fit uniformly throughout Europe, nor were the Middle Ages simply a period when time passed and societies, culture and order completely disappeared until the world was reawakened during the Renaissance with new and novel thought.

Development during this period consists largely of the conquests by the Germanic peoples, their adoption of Christianity, its systematization and organization into complete doctrine, the mingling of the Germans with the population of the old Roman empire, the establishment of the social and economic pattern and ideals known as feudalism and chivalry, and the rise of kingdoms which laid the foundation for the modern European states.

An analysis of education and social order from this point on depends upon understanding the forces of Christianity and the Germanic invasions.

The Romans had, through their conquests, broken up the old kinship groups and latinized most of Europe—Spain, Gaul (France), Italy, Britain, the Greek East, and parts of North Africa—and in so doing, spread the cultural ideals and institutions which they had adopted and adapted from the Greeks. By the fourth century, Christianity, which had been merely one of many small religious sects in the Eastern Roman Empire, had become the major political force throughout the Empire. In the Western Roman Empire, the old classical culture retained adherents only among some of the aristocrats, the teachers of philosophy, and those who lived in the remote countryside. In the Eastern Roman Empire, classicism never really ended, and the premises and ideals of what became the Byzantine Empire, although profoundly Christian, remained loyal to classical standards, and the ideal educated man remained classical. (In 1453, conquest by the Turks broke this tradition and the Eastern Empire found itself in the same situation as the West had 1,000 years earlier.)

Along with the rest of the eastern Mediterranean world, the Hebrews had come under the influence of Greek culture, so that by the time of Christ, the language of the most educated was Greek, and culturally all were tied to Greece. Under Roman rule, Greek culture still prevailed. When Roman civilization began to crumble under the weight of its socio-economic contradictions, the Hebraic-Christian sect began to dominate the empire with its ideals. Christianity was the one institution which directed itself to the deprived masses. Its basic activities were missionary work and local organization. There were no religious schools, and training in Christian morality came from the family and the clergy.

As it took power, the Church denounced classical culture as paganism and heresy, having suffered much persecution under its domination. Yet Christianity arose in Hellenistic Palestine and developed in the midst of Greco-Roman civilization. It did not come into being brand-new. It, too, was a synthesis, an adaptation to and from preexisting cultures, and as such could not escape the permeation of the civilizations in which it grew up. The early Church fathers themselves had been educated in Roman schools, and in their writings ancient learning still lived. Without realizing it, the Church became the main institution for the preservation and transmission of the learning of the classical world. After the Roman Empire collapsed, the Church became the central organizing authority as all learning passed into its hands.

Christianity offered its solution to the problematic character of the individual and society in the emotional realm, and appealed to classes totally neglected by earlier aristocratic societies. People had to have some hope, either that men could create a better world or that God would care for them and improve life. For centuries to come, God was given the vote of confidence rather than man. In Christian doctrine, there was no ideal of individual happiness or activity of a rational and inquiring nature, but rather a statement of faith in a supreme authority with salvation and understanding in a world after this.

The problems identified by the Church, Plato and Aristotle are the same. The unknown God can be seen as a symbol for the same unknown Truth for which Greek thinkers had been groping. The dualistic view which separated the universe into pure, good spirit (reason, control of impulse) and evil, impure matter (flesh, body) was inherent in Christianity and Greek philosophy. Plato and Socrates had themselves argued against worldliness and materialism and for contemplation and spiritual development. However, the Christians were wholly indifferent to the intellectual and aesthetic elements of the Greek ideal and followed more of the pragmatic Roman interests.

Christianity directed its attention to morality, and attempted to influence conduct through ethical teachings, a feature it had in common with Stoic philosophy. However, the Stoics had believed in the use of reason in order to obtain virtue, whereas Christians found virtue through faith. The virtue of the Stoics could only be achieved by an elite group in whom the intellect was developed; the virtue of the Christians could be achieved by everyone. This limitation of Stoicism was a limitation of all classical philosophy.

Christians placed primary emphasis on the family as the institution responsible for the development of the Christian soul. The Church, however, could not afford to ignore schools completely if its doctrine was to persist and spread, since a certain amount of literary knowledge was necessary in order to read the Scriptures. Knowing that the early Christians were opposed to ancient beliefs, we would expect them to establish their own type of religious schools separately from the classical Roman schools. But this they did not do. They simply added their own kind of religious training to the existing classical teaching, which might indicate there were no essential contradictions between them. Because the young also received a religious upbringing in the home and Church, they would be properly enlightened and able to discriminate between classical evils and Christian ideals. A comparison of the exercise books of a Christian schoolboy in 400 A.D. and that of a Hellenistic book seven centuries earlier would show little difference except for the sign of the cross added to the top of the first page. The early Christians accepted the fundamental qualities of the Hellenistic literary type of education. The curriculum of the schools was still composed of the seven liberal arts, divided into the Trivium and Quadrivium. The Trivium contained grammar, rhetoric, and dialectic; the Quadrivium included arithmetic, geometry, astronomy and music. After these had been completed, some advanced schools added courses in philosophy and theology.

The Church did not introduce into the schools any teaching of its own; education and instruction in religious matters were not combined with purely academic work. The Church itself, through specially appointed delegates, instructed its new converts through the catechetical system of schools organized by individual churches. These schools taught the Scriptures and hymns, and met one or two hours per week. The only instruction received by the faithful was by way of simple catechism, preaching and exhortation, and example. The clergy learned through private lessons and personal contact with the bishop and older priests.

Opinion concerning the relationship between Greek and Christian culture divided the early Churchmen into two groups—one holding that ancient learning was valuable to use in Christianity's search for understanding; and the other holding that there could be no compromise between "truth" and the seductions of the world, and that classical learning could teach only impure thoughts and was hostile to the purposes of Christianity. Two areas of human knowledge were considered irrelevant, insignificant, and even harmful: the practical sciences (architecture, engineering, medicine, mechanics, law), which dealt with controlling the physical environment; and the natural sciences, deemed injurious to the developing theology of the Church. In the East, the view more friendly to classic learning prevailed. In the West, the other view was accepted: the Church wished to acquire and maintain a hold on its people; if other ways of thinking were allowed, it would diminish their power. Also, the Church was concerned with its message of spiritual salvation and morality; thus, learning and other mundane world affairs were trivial by comparison. The Church had its greatest success with the lower, uneducated social classes which had been ignored by the aristocratic, intellectually oriented classical cultures. It found greater opposition from the classes aware of Greek and Latin literature.

The leading intellectual leader of the early Church was St. Augustine. He had received a Roman upbringing and schooling, and completed his education in rhetoric, which he later taught at Carthage and Rome. At the age of 32, after a life of conflicting loyalties and values and a search for understanding, he came to read part of the New Testament. This had a powerful impact upon him, and he decided to convert to Christianity. St. Augustine recounted his personal history in a nine-volume autobiography, the *Confessions*. His writings, which gave the Church a systematic philosophical and political base, attempted to assimilate classical with Christian learning. Augustine felt that the classic authors, selectively and in moderation, could aid Christian purposes.

In his treatise *On the Teacher,* Augustine inquired into the nature of ideas much as Plato had done, and agreed with him that education was not an accumulation of facts, but an illumination of the soul from within.

> We think that an interchange of ideas takes place between the teacher and the pupil, but we are mistaken. There is only an interchange of words. The true function of language is not to bring ideas into our minds but to stimulate and awaken those that are already there . . . If by teaching we mean the transference of the teacher's ideas to the pupil, then no teaching has taken place. In reality, the teacher has stimulated the pupil to employ experiences and ideas which were already in his mind to form a new idea through the reflection on experiences he had previously had . . . In no sense is it the role of the teacher to impart knowledge; in fact, this is impossible. Ideas are not introduced into the mind through communication. The latter may serve as a stimulus for thought, but ideas are the result of the activity of the mind itself which by reflection upon what is given in experience or by communication, grasps the truth by a flash of intellectual insight and realizes its universality and necessity.[15]

The spirit of investigation which was found in early Greece had never reappeared in Rome and was further weakened by the Church, which turned away from classical works even more. In its growing distaste for secular learning, disdain for criticism, and primary concern with disseminating its own doctrine, dogma and morality, the Church became authoritative and completely opposed to philosophical speculation in patterns other than those which it prescribed. The Christian alternative was the security found in absolute certainty, the peace of mind and resolution of obedience to unquestionable authority. Whatever remained of the classical heritage was used to enable the educated elite to read the Scriptures and religious commentaries and administer the business of the Church.

15. St. Augustine, "De Magistro, (On the Teacher)" in S. Curtis and M. Boultwood, *A Short History of Educational Ideas* (London: University Tutorial Press, Ltd., 1953). pp. 79, 80, 86.

Cassiodorus, a scholar and monk of the seventh century, integrated much secular and religious material into a form usable by the Church, establishing the clear definition of the "seven liberal arts." Latin became the universal medium of communication among educated persons, and grammar was the most important subject taught in the schools. Education was highly bookish in character, and submissiveness and obedience were qualities the schools hoped to instill in their pupils. The practical goal of the schools was the ability to read Latin; the method was memorization of books.

The Germanic Tribes

The final element to be added to the blend of cultures was the conquest of this intercultural mixture by the various Germanic tribes from the North, which had theretofore lived a primitive existence. These tribal societies were characterized by communal ownership of land and property and communal relations of production, division of labor by sex, the gens (kinship) as the basic social unit, undifferentiated institutions, and an informal and practical system of education for self-preservation and the perpetuation of tradition. They had no body of formally organized knowledge or a written literature. From the sixth to the ninth centuries, the old classical schools disappeared, along with what remained of the Roman political and economic institutions. The only form of education and intellectual life which continued was that which had been taken over by the Christian Church, or was carried on in the homes of wealthy gentlemen or small secular town schools in a few areas. Some scholarly lines of communication did remain, providing a tenuous link between the West and Byzantium, Carthage and the East.

The invading tribes brought with them war, destruction, and a vigorous spirit. They found themselves amid remnants of a highly developed and widespread civilization with a complete system of ideals and institutions, which they adopted as a model for themselves. In order to govern what they had conquered, they created state organs similar to those of the Roman state. They found in the Catholic Church an organized and authoritative voice which provided a moral basis of divine sanction for the social order. In time, they came to adopt Christianity and its attendant forms. It has been suggested that the tremendous social flux had created such emotional deprivation, insecurity, and alienation that people were grateful for a faith which was secure in truth and demanded deep commitment.

The confusion and disorder which followed the complete economic, social, and political breakup of the Roman Empire led to the development of a multitude of flimsy, small, unstable kingdoms under the leadership of such tribes as the Ostrogoths (Italy), Visigoths (Spain), Franks (Gaul, Rhineland, Holland), Lombards (Italy), Huns (Hungary), Anglo-Saxons (Britain), and Vandals (North Africa). Military leaders became kings. The feudal system of social order arose from the need of free peasants to band together for protection. Men began to align themselves with the Church and with some comparatively powerful lord, transfering to him their rights of property in land and placing themselves under his protection in exchange for services to be performed. One lord would owe allegiance to a higher lord, who in turn was the "vassal" of a still more powerful leader. A king was often at the top of this pyramidal structure of power. The foundation of the feudal relationship was the "fief," which was usually land but could also be an office or a right. Europe became covered by a network of fiefs rising in graded rank. After 400 years, class structures still remained, and the masses of people had no greater power than before. This corresponds to the fact that there had also been no changes in the level of agricultural and industrial production.

Feudalism became cemented by customs and traditions, such as those of loyalty and specific services and duties to be performed by both sides of the relationship. The political and economic institutions of feudalism came from former Roman ones; of Germanic inspriation was the social institution of chivalry, an ideal of knightly association, devotion, and personal service. Chivalry represented the social values of the secular society and an attempt to realize them through definitely established forms. The only type of secular education was that which sought to impart knightly traits of character. It was again education only for the aristocracy. Knighthood was not merely inherited as was nobility; there was a long period of training. The ideal knight was a "gentleman," possessed of heroic traits such as courage, pride, respect, and honor, whose duties of life could be summed up under obligations to God (religion), lord (warfare), and lady (courtesy). For a formerly rough and wild people, chivalry made a life of gallantry, service, obedience, and restraint the ideal, and kept them more easily under the influence of the Church.

The education of a knight was divided into three periods: training at home by his mother (1-7 years old), as a page (7-14 years old), and as a squire (14-21 years old). Training was given in a definitely organized household or court. A page performed simple services about the house or castle, waited on the table, attended the ladies, learned to play the harp and pipe, to read and write verse, to ride, run, wrestle and box. A squire, in addition to these tasks, performed a variety of personal services at home, on the battlefield or in the tournament for the lord or knight. He learned to ride, hunt and fight. The page and squire were to learn the rudiments of love from service to the ladies, war from jousting tournaments, hunting and hawking, and religion through Church ceremonies sanctioning these and other activities. At age 21, the young man was inducted into knighthood, taking oaths of allegiance to his overlord and to the Church. He would then become a "vassal," and in return receive some land or other means of subsistence as a fief. Little emphasis was placed on intellectual development.

Chivalry in this world did much to balance the otherworldly occupation of the Church. Chivalric education made participation in political, economic, and cultural life possible. Chivalry gave rise to a distinctive written literature in the vernacular of French, Italian, English, Spanish, and German. This literature was based upon oral folk traditions. It included such poems as the *Song of Roland*, the numerous stories of King Arthur, the Anglo-Saxon *Beowulf*, and other works incorporating myths, fables and folk tales of the people. The development of this vernacular literature foreshadowed the eventual demand that schools teach in the vernacular as well as in Latin.

Chivalry was to secular life what monasticism was to religious life. In the fourth century there appeared a type of Christian school which had none of the features of classical education. This was the monastery. Until the eleventh century, these monasteries were the principal literary, artistic, intellectual, and educational centers. The basic premise of monasticism was asceticism—rising to spiritual excellence and insight through the mortification of all natural and material desires and renunciation of the secular world. In the West, St. Benedict, an Italian monk of the sixth century, organized a community of monks at Monte Cassino under a set of rules which became of universal significance and which all other monasteries came to follow. Under these rules, priority was given to manual labor and to reading—to work was to pray. The basic ideals were: discipline of one's physical being, through fasting, discomfort and uncleanliness; chastity, including condemnation of the family and of all human relationships, whose place would be taken by a religious relationship; poverty of material interests, including disavowal of concern with economic provision for the present and future; and absolute obedience to the will of one's superior, which entailed giving up allegiance to any other institution such as the state or any other political body. Although monasticism negated many important aspects of social life, it became an important educational force as it entered into the reorganization of feudalistic society.

Although monastic education was designed to create monks, in a broad sense it furnished an education to the people. Monasteries were rural institutions that had to be largely self-supporting. Thus, the monks trained the peasants in agriculture, introduced new processes for craftsmanship in wood, metal, leather and cloth, gave new ideas to architecture, and encouraged the draining of swamps and clearing of forests.

Along with intense regard for manual labor, the Benedictine rules were highly concerned with reading. The purpose of study in the monasteries was never as an end in itself, but as a means of discipline and occupation for otherwise idle moments. Were study to have become a pleasure, its very purpose would have been negated. Any study of ancient literature was still considered a temptation leading to eternal damnation, for it might cause doubt as to the truth, and doubt was in itself an evil. Truth was to be ascertained not through rational principles or plausibility, but from its agreement with religious dogma. The preservation and copying of ancient manuscripts became an important function, under the rule of constant industry, and not out of a desire to understand. Although the monks did not value what they preserved in the monastery libraries, their activities furnished whatever remains today of classical learning, other than that recovered from Arab civilizations. The monasteries were the only safe places during the long period of conflict and instability. And therefore, even though the classical authors had fallen into disrepute, classical knowledge had not disappeared. It remained, condensed and dry, and known as the seven liberal arts: grammar, dialectic, rhetoric, geometry, arithmetic, astronomy, and music.

During this period, the one important event concerning education which was not wholly monastic was the revival of learning under Charles the Great (Charlemagne). In 800 A.D., he attempted to unify the Germanic and Roman elements under one strong centralized government. He transferred those political and legal foundations of social organization which were typically Roman to the Frankish kingdom (a confederation of Germanic tribes, which had established a somewhat permanent kingdom to be later divided into France and Germany), thus establishing what was known as the Holy Roman Empire. In order to help accomplish this, Charles organized the Palace School at which he and his family were taught. With the help of Alcuin from a monastery in England, he also developed both religious and secular teaching in the monasteries. He directed that every monastery have a school where boys could be taught the Scriptures, psalms, music, reading, grammar, and arithmetic, under the belief that intellectual training and practical competence in Latin scholarship were as essential to social welfare as were purely religious and moral training. He required the clergy to improve their own ability to read and write, recognizing the need for a supply of trained personnel for the administration of his empire. For several generations, there was a revival of educational interest, and most monasteries supported and fostered schools and gathered libraries together. However, because of weakness of Charles' successors, new attacks by the Northmen, and the state of civil disorder, the enthusiasm for learning faded, the Holy Roman Empire became weak and inadequate, and society fell back into feudalism. Charles' attempt to graft political and cultural forms onto a productive system whose means and modes of production had not changed, had necessarily to fail.

The medieval Christian alternatives for the "educated man" were different in many ways from the classical ideals. The Greek hero possessed civic virtues, intellectual skills, and an investigative and contemplative spirit, and a reliance on reason in order to "know." The medieval secular hero was romantic and chivalrous, loyal to his lord, concerned with duty and service to king and kingdom, and unwavering in devotion to a supreme uncontested authority, God. The medieval religious ideal was ascetic, withdrawn from public life into one of work and prayer, concerned with the spiritual realm and salvation in another world, and relying on faith and revelation in order to "know." Critical inquiry, individual judgment and other Greek characteristics were essences which had vanished.

THE LATE MIDDLE AGES

In the eleventh century, changes began to occur in modes of commodity production, trade, and social relationships. A type of intellectual life reappeared which led to fresh interest in knowledge. By this time, the Church had maintained a climate of absolute obedience to its doctrines for more than six centuries, and had become the unquestioned authority possessed of all final truth which had come to it by divine revelation. However, men were becoming aware of questions which could not be ignored. Initiative and intellectual skills were beginning to be required. The study of only those parts of classical knowledge which bolstered Church doctrine was no longer so easily acceptable. Studies in law, medicine, natural science, mathematics, philosophy, logic, and rhetoric seemed more attractive than the literature of the Church Fathers. An attempt to rework the knowledge of the past became the order of the day. The cathedral school, and later the university, replaced the monastery as the citadel of higher learning. Trade and commerce were stimulated by the Crusades; towns grew in importance, agricultural techniques improved, and interest in secular affairs increased along with this urbanization and economic stimulation. Contact with Islam through the Crusades brought the West once more into contact with the East, with vital and creative civilizations. Moslem scholars had learned from the Byzantines, the Persians, the Jews, and the Hindus, as they had come into contact with these civilizations. Greek philosophy had been absorbed with the tenents of Islam, Arab scholars preferring Greek science and philosophy to Greek literature, unlike the Romans. There were great centers of scholarship at Cordoba, Alexandria, Cairo, Damascus, Jerusalem, and Bagdad. Elementary schools taught Arabic reading and writing; secondary schools taught grammar, poetry, the sciences, law, and history. Museums, theological centers and research institutes existed for the most advanced learning in medicine, mathematics, chemistry, astronomy, and law. Westerners sought eagerly after this new knowledge, and for all they could find out about the Hellenic past, which had been lost to the West after Roman times. They found it in translation from the Greek to the Arabic, added to by Arab scholars.

The central problem presented to the Church was to reconcile religious values with the new secular growth of political, economic, and educational institutions, and to defend itself against the challenges of urbanization, national sovereignty, and demands for autonomy from emperors, kings, towns, guilds, and universities. Intellectually, the Church had to reconcile the conflict between the classically inspired claims of reason and the Christian claims of faith, and it was towards this end that the work of the Scholastics was directed. Scholasticism was the method whereby the Church tried to integrate logical questioning (particularly that of Aristotle) with faith. Its intent was to show the basic harmony between the forces of reason and religion, and to develop a systematic, complete and final dogma of Church belief. The fusion of faith and knowledge was primarily based on the writings of Aristotle in the *Organon,* regarding the process of deductive logic.

St. Anselm believed that all reasoning and discussion had to be preceded by faith in revealed truth. "We must believe in order to understand." Opposing him, Peter Abelard believed that through human reason truth would be arrived at. "We must understand in order to believe."[16] To arrive at a truth, one had to begin with individual objects, observe how they worked, and arrive inductively at generalizations. In *Sic et Non,* Abelard stated approximately 150 religious theories in the form of questions and then quoted authorities from the Scriptures and Church Fathers to support both sides. He argued that if the authorities contradicted each other, it was the business of the scholar to use reason in arriving at the answer.

> Should human faith be based upon reason, or no? Is God a substance, or no? Is God the author of evil, or no? Can God be resisted, or no? Do we sometimes sin unwillingly, or no? Does God punish the same sin both here and in the hereafter, or no?[17]

Abelard became one of the most prominent teachers at the University of Paris. He was famous for the teaching of logic and dialectic as instruments for probing into the relationship between man and God and into metaphysical problems of the universe. However, because he persisted in criticizing unquestioned acceptance of the Church's authority, he was personally condemned and regarded as a heretic, and forced to leave Paris.

---

16. R. F. Butts, *The Education of the West* (New York: McGraw-Hill, 1947), p. 169.

17. Peter Abelard, "Sic et Non (Yes and No)," in Monroe, *Textbook in the History of Education,* p. 301.

St. Thomas Aquinas attempted to strike a balance in his synthesis of faith and reason. He did this by differentiating between natural philosophy and supernatural theology. Philosophy dealt with phenomena of the natural world, including everything open to human argument and reason. Theology dealt with revealed truth and involved eternal and ultimate reality not subject to change by human reason. There was no contradiction between revealed truth and scientific truth, for God was the author of both. Science (reason) and religion handled the same facts and ideas, but looked at them from different sides. Science and reason began with the particular thing and worked up to generalizations. Religion started with God and worked down to the individual. Thus, the science and logic of Aristotle were reconciled with and made to serve the higher ends of theology.

Selections from SUMMA CONTRA GENTILES

St. Thomas Acquinas

CHAPTER 79

That Lower Intellectual Substances are Ruled by Higher Ones

(1) Since certain intellectual creatures are higher than others, as is clear from the foregoing, the lower ones of an intellectual nature must be governed by the higher ones.

(2) Again, more universal powers are able to move particular powers, as we said. But the higher intellectual natures have more universal forms, as was shown above. Therefore, they are capable of ruling the lower intellectual natures.

(3) Besides, an intellectual potency that is nearer to the principle is always capable of ruling an intellectual power that is more removed from the principle. This is evident in both speculative and active sciences; for a speculative science which derives its principles of demonstration from another science is said to be subalternated to that other; and an active science which is nearer the end, which is the principle in matters of operation, is architectonic in regard to a more distant one. Therefore, since some intellectual substances are nearer the first

St. Thomas Aquinas, *Summa Contra Gentiles (On the Truth of the Catholic Faith)*, trans. A. Regis. (New York: Image Books, 1955), p. 263. Copyright © 1957 by Doubleday & Co., Inc.

principle, namely God, as was shown in Book Two, they will be capable of ruling others.

(4) Moreover, superior intellectual substances receive the influence of divine wisdom into themselves more perfectly, because each being receives something according to the being's own mode. Now, all things are governed by divine wisdom. And so, things that participate more in divine wisdom must be capable of governing those that participate less. Therefore, the lower intellectual substances are governed by the higher ones.

(5) On the same basis there is also found an order among men themselves. Indeed, those who excel in understanding naturally gain control, whereas those who have defective understanding, but a strong body, seem to be naturally fitted for service, as Aristotle says in his *Politics*. The view of Solomon is also in accord with this, for he says: "The fool shall serve the wise" (Prov. 11:29); and again: "Provide out of all the people wise men such as fear God . . . who may judge the people at all times" (Exod. 18:21-22).

St. Thomas Aquinas

Whatever the point of view, those involved in education felt that the newly found treasures of classical learning had to be assimilated and brought into line with Christianity. It was the literary side of classic thought which was victorious. The level of production was not yet ready for science.

Later scholars tended to regard the Scholastics' efforts with derision, criticizing their complete reliance on Aristotle as the supreme authority in support of established custom. Francis Bacon wrote in the seventeenth century, denouncing their pretensions to knowledge:

> This kind of degenerate learning did chiefly reign amongst the Schoolmen: who having sharp and strong wits, and abundance of leisure, and small variety of reading, but their wits being shut up in the cells of a few authors (chiefly Aristotle their dictator) as their persons were shut up in the cells of monasteries and colleges, and knowing little history, either of nature or time, did out of no great quantity of matter and infinite agitation of wit spin out unto us those laborious webs of learning which are extant in their books. For the wit and mind of man, if it work upon matter, which is the contemplation of the creatures of God, worketh according to the stuff, and is limited thereby; but if it work upon itself, as the spider worketh his web, then it is endless and brings forth indeed cobwebs of learning, admirable for the fineness of thread and work, but of no substance or profit.[18]

Although the criticisms of Scholasticism are true in that their writings possessed no relation to reality, to the concrete, political world, or to open inquiry concerning the validity of what they were dealing with, their investigations did serve to legitimize intellectual interest to the point of stimulating development of the cathedral schools of professional competence and the universities.

18. Francis Bacon, quoted in Monroe, *Textbook in the History of Education,* pp. 307-308.

The cathedral schools were oriented to urban life and the professions such as law, medicine, and business, rather than to strictly religious study. The liberal arts came to be seen as preparatory to these advanced professional studies. Thus, there grew up a new class of professional men. The cathedral school at Bologna became famous for its canon (Church) and civil law; Salerno for the skill of its physicians. In addition, various cathedral schools transmitted knowledge of Greek natural philosophy, Latin and theology. The latter was the keynote of all university study.

As the Middle Ages progressed, interest in intellectual expression increased, stimulated by the recovery of classical knowledge, the increase of commercial enterprise, greater urbanization, changes in the means and mode of production, and the growth of merchant and craft guilds which influenced the development of municipal government. The merchant class grew in wealth and power until it became the new middle class, winning increased privileges of political and economic participation. European isolation had broken down, new ideas and recovered classical knowledge infiltrated, and in the twelfth century, under charter from the emperor or pope, universities arose throughout Europe, the earliest being at Bologna, Paris, and Oxford. Large groups of students and teachers existing previously under monastery or Church control, developed into universities. Students and masters organized themselves into guilds, on the basis of national identity. Upon these groups, charters containing privileges were granted. By the sixteenth century, 75 or 80 universities existed. Privileges granted universities, as independent corporations which could issue licenses to teach and subject-matter degrees, reduced Church control over the method and content of teaching. This authority was invested in the self-governing universities. Students were subject to university law rather than the law of the land. Universities had the right to strike against a city over grievances they might have, or even move to another city. When a student could demonstrate an ability to defend some thesis against members who already possessed a degree, he was given the degree, authorizing him to teach publicly and admitting him into the guild or faculty. Doctoral degrees were granted in Law, Medicine, and Philosophy. Universities were encouraged by popes and kings who hoped to benefit from their work in a spirit of nationalism. Universities also took shape in response to the need to decide important questions of theology and settle political disputes. The curriculum consisted primarily of Law, Medicine, Theology, and Arts (the seven liberal). All instruction was in Latin; the method of instruction was lecture, student repetition, commentation and explanation, and disputation, although conclusions were generally pre-assumed. The study of logic consumed most of the time, and until the middle of the fifteenth century, Aristotle's deduction remained the main method of inquiry. Education in the early universities was related exclusively to books, which were believed to contain absolute and ultimate truth.

The university was the first organization offering some form of democratic control to its officials; however, their sympathies rested with the privileged classes. Universities had the right to a voice in the government and a seat in parliament.

The dominant conception of education remained the same: the individual would develop the intellectual power of logic and possess the ability to state, interpret, define and argue about abstract conceptions. Intellectual interests became highly regarded and schools of all kinds became prolific. Input from the well-developed Arab cultures encountered during the Crusades stimulated education and led to the substitution of Hindu notation (now called Arabic) for the cumbersome Roman method, the knowledge of algebra and other advanced arithmetical processes, and the increase of knowledge in medicine, surgery, pharmacy, astronomy, physiology, and physics.

The feudal system was breaking up, creating great numbers of displaced persons. Students migrated from school to school without remaining long in one community, joining such other wanderers as pilgrims, merchants, craftsmen, knights, and friars. Since they had become a relatively privileged group, they received help from rich philanthropists or took up the custom of begging which had acquired some dignity because of the greater frequency of, and new sanctions for, religious pilgrimage and wandering. (Chaucer's *Canterbury Tales* provides a description of the wayfaring life.) As the number of masters increased to exceed the demand for university instruction, wandering masters became numerous, as well as wandering students. To all of these were attached younger boys, often six or seven years old, who accompanied them from city to city, supposedly to acquire knowledge, but in actuality to attend them as servants, beg for them, and perhaps sing for money.

Monastic and cathedral schools lost their dominance as secular influences began to pervade education. Chantry schools became common. These were foundations and grants of property from wealthy families to priests in exchange for their teaching the children of the community, as well as conducting religious services. Another common type of school was that supported by merchant and craft guilds. As guilds merged with municipal government, these schools fell under the control of secular authorities and the content of the schoolwork represented the economic interests and demands of the citizens. Lay teachers became more numerous. With the rise of towns and trade, apprenticeship as a means of preparing youth for a skilled occupation replaced the direct handing down of skills from father to son. The stage was being set during the late Middle Ages for the changes to come.

THE RENAISSANCE

During the fifteenth and sixteenth centuries, reaction continued to form against the rigidity and absolute authority of the Scholastic period and the ecclesiastical tradition which dominated it. Society had begun to change even more. Feudal relationships and strict religious dogma were becoming more and more incompatible with newly developing productive forces. Cities grew up around the political authority of monarchies and became nation-states. Kings attacked the Church in attempts to extend their political authority. Commercial enterprise became more complex, increasing the development of diverse economic interests and the need for a trained professional class and broadening the structure of social participation. Feudalism was giving way to the capitalistic system of "free" labor, trade, banking, and manufacturing. More and more, the universities came to replace the aescetic religious education which had not provided for the application of man's knowledge and power in the business of life and the life of business. The invention of gunpowder gave the common man power to challenge the elite; the invention of the printing press made it possible to extend intellectual thought to greater numbers of people. A wider spectrum of social groups began to gain a voice in political and economic affairs of the nation-states. For the rural gentry and new urban middle classes, education was a way to achieve respectability, and they expended great sums in support of existing schools and helped to found new ones. The merchant classes demanded schools with greater emphasis on the vernacular languages and on practical and vocational training for occupations in business, commerce, and agriculture. The middle classes used their growing political power to pass laws creating schools supported at public expense to disseminate their ideology and increase their numbers. A series of technological inventions and discovery of new world markets further accelerated trade in goods and ideas and enlarged and transformed industrial enterprises from individual to large-scale manufacturing and trade. The conditions of feudalism were no longer compatible with the new productive forces. Nor was intellectual knowledge at the time compatible with the changes taking place. It, too, had to change its character, in response to new material conditions.

At the beginning of the Renaissance, the early Greek trend toward greater valuation of the individual was renewed. This is compatible with new emphasis on individual competition in the market place. Renaissance intellectuals recovered many Greek and Roman manuscripts and delved once again into issues which had been the concern of Plato and Aristotle. Trends of thought revived during this period form the basis of various conceptions of education found in later centuries.

One philosophical trend (Platonic) formed around individualism and social development. All knowledge was inside man. Man was an individual part, functioning in the organic, ordered whole of society. Political and civic responsibility were of great importance.

A second trend formed around an understanding of the natural world (Aristotelian), which led to the later development of science. This is compatible with the development of new modes of production and the ever-increasing need for new technology. Demand for the "real" and concrete as opposed to the abstract and metaphysical led to direct observation and experimentation, to astronomical discovery (beginning with Copernicus and on to Galileo), and to extensive geographical exploration and new markets and resources.

A third trend centered around Latin literature, particularly that of Cicero. This became known as "humanism," which was not a new philosophical system of thought, but "the general tendency of the age to attach the greatest importance to classical studies and to consider classical antiquity as the common standard and model by which to guide all cultural activities."[19] "Humanistic" education was used in the same general sense as the term "liberal" education had been used in Hellenistic Greece and ancient Rome. It was felt that the classics contained all the knowledge of vital importance to mankind. This is compatible with the reproduction of a new elite class, and the maintenance of a new hierarchy of social class and social control.

The historically recognized Renaissance began in Italy, with the recovery, internalization and imitation of classical literature. The humanists of the Renaissance felt that they were creating an abrupt and fundamental break with medieval tradition, which they felt was stifling and degenerate. They saw their time as a period of new life and creative activity through the "rebirth" of an earlier culture. The period was not a "new" birth, therefore, but a revival of the same

19. Butts, *Education of the West,* p. 201.

alternatives presented during classical times. Greek and Christian ethics were maintained, as was the aim of education to produce the perfect man fit for participation in the activities of the dominant social institutions. The transition from Middle Ages to Renaissance was, however, not as sudden nor as severe a break with the past as Renaissance writers liked to believe. It was certainly no revolution, and introduced no alternative description of the world which had not been offered before. Its system of education, too, retained cultural continuity with previous generations.

Humanistic writers and artists were an elite group who lived on the patronage of the great and often reflected their arrogance. They looked down on those who did not know Cicero and on those who spoke contemporary and not classical Latin. Representative of these times are such men as Dante Alighieri, Leonardo da Vinci, Michelangelo, Boccacio, and Francesco Petrarch, who was the first to break with Scholasticism and chose Cicero as master instead of Aristotle, rhetoric instead of logic. Early Renaissance interest in nature and in individual personal development soon faded, and the study of classical literature and language began to dominate the schools. As it did, it also began to decline into formalism, much as it had in ancient Rome. Humanism, which had been a means, came to be considered an end in itself. Substituting Ciceronian Latin for simple, everyday medieval Latin led only to the death of Latin itself. The Renaissance movement shifted north of the Alps to France, England and Germany.

In Italy, the Renaissance had been aristocratic; in the north, it emerged as a religious movement through the efforts of social and religious reformers. Thus, humanism became fused with the Protestant Reformation, and the new view was that study of classical literature could promote piety. Desiderius Erasmus of Holland is representative of this idea. His aim was to remove ignorance, root out gross evils of church and state, and condemn the greed, selfishness and hypocrisy of those who used their offices for personal gain. The Renaissance of the North became more specifically concerned with education, since it was believed that all social injustices were based on ignorance and that true reform would come with the better education of the young. This social and moral aim was also expressed by Jacob Wimpfeling of Germany: "What profits all our learning if our characters be not correspondingly noble, all of our industry without piety, all of our knowledge without love of our neighbor, all of our wisdom without humility, all of our studying if we are not kind and charitable?"[20]

However, within a short time, education in the North, too, became restrictive and limited in scope. Through emphasis on moral and religious training, restraints came to be placed upon individual judgment and intellect. Erasmus fought against the tendency to narrow the conception of education. But after his death the spirit of criticism of authority, of tolerance of personal opinion, of investigation and research into ideas, practices and the processes of nature, degenerated once again into intellectual formalism as it had in Italy. This time the formalism was founded in literary and linguistic studies instead of the logical formalism of the Scholastic period—quite similar to the course Greek logic and dialectic had taken when transferred to Roman society.

20. Jacob Wimpfeling, *A Guide to the German Youth,* quoted in Monroe, *Textbook in the History of Education,* p. 378.

In *The Ciceronians,* Erasmus satirized the prevailing conception of education in order to show the extreme and ridiculous form humanistic education was taking. For a summary of the Christian faith:

Jesus Christ, the word and the Son of the Eternal Father, according to prophecy, came into the world, and, having become man, voluntarily surrendered himself to death, and so redeemed his Church, and delivered us from the penalty of the law, and reconciled us to God, in order that, justified by grace through faith, and freed from the bondage of sin, we might be received into his Church, and preserved in its communion, might, after this life, be admitted into the kingdom of heaven.

the Ciceronian would substitute:

The interpreter and son of Jupiter Optimus Maximus our Saviour and our sovereign, according to the responses of the oracles, came down to the earth from Olympus, and, having assumed human shape, of his own free will sacrificed himself for the safety of the republic to the Dii Manes, and so restored it to its lost liberty, and, having turned aside from us the angry thunderbolts of Jupiter, won for us his favor, in order that, through our acknowledgment of his bounty having recovered our innocence, and having been relieved from the servitude of flattery, we might be made citizens of his republic, and having sustained our arts with honor, might, when the fates should summon us away from this life, enjoy supreme felicity in the friendship of the immortal Gods.[21]

Under humanistic influence, schools returned to the teaching of rhetoric and Latin, and schoolwork became drill work in Latin grammar, study of selected Latin texts, and study of the Scriptures. A child was considered a miniature man, with interests differing from adults in degree and not in kind.

The universities had for some time resisted the early spirit of Renaissance revival, and the formalism of their work was never radically changed. The basic modifications from Scholastic times were the addition of literary and linguistic subjects, such as Greek, and the substitution of classical for medieval Latin.

During this period the German 'gymnasien' were established, which were typical humanistic schools (Christian teachings combined with study of the classics) that became the model secondary schools for all Western nations. The word "gymnasium" came to indicate schools of the new classical discipline. Work was divided into ten grades or years, and gauged for age and stage of advancement of the student. The subject matter was chosen from the Latin classics, with some Greek works and the New Testament. The curriculum of the gymnasium at Strassburg in 1537 (which often had over 1,000 pupils) is representative of the education of the times:

Tenth Class: The Alphabet, reading, writing, Latin declensions and conjugations; catechism in Latin or German.

Ninth Class: Declensions and conjugations; Latin vocabulary of terms of everyday life; irregular Latin forms.

21. Desiderius Erasmus, *The Ciceronians,* in Paul Monroe, *Textbook in the History of Education,* pp. 373-74.

Eighth Class: Continuation of above; composition of Latin phrases; some letters of Cicero; exercises in style.

Seventh Class: Syntax in connection with Cicero's *Letters;* composition; translation of catechism, etc., into Latin.

Sixth Class: Translation of Cicero, Latin poets, catechism, and *Letters* of Jerome with grammatical exercises; Greek begun.

Fifth Class: Latin versification, mythology; Cicero; Virgil's *Eclogues;* Greek; exercise in style; double translations; Paul's *Epistles.*

Fourth Class: Same as fifth class, with wide reading of Latin authors.

Third Class: Rhetoric; *Orations* of Cicero and of Demosthenes; double translations of orations; composition of letters; presentation of comedies of Plautus and Terence in this and higher classes.

Second Class: Greek orators and poets; dialectic and rhetoric in connection with Cicero and Demosthenes; presentation of selected dramas of Aristophanes, Euripides, and Sophocles, in addition to Plautus and Terence.

First Class: Dialectic and rhetoric; Virgil, Horace, Homer, Thucydides, Sallust, Epistles of St. Paul.[22]

The work of the schools was determined by its purpose—the development of the ability to speak and write the Latin of Cicero. The orators and comedians were especially studied for the command they gave of the spoken language. The aim of education can be summed up as piety (knowledge of catechism, reverence for religion and participation in Church services), knowledge (Latin language and literature), and eloquence (the ability to use that language in practical life). With gradual reduction of the classical element and the addition of modern language, history, mathematics and to some extent the natural sciences, this represents the curriculum of the secondary schools throughout Europe until the nineteenth century.

THE REFORMATION

At the beginning of the Renaissance, a critical spirit of reason had redeveloped, which came to be applied to matters of religion. This movement culminated in the Protestant Reformation of the sixteenth century. It began with an effort to reform the abuses within the Catholic Church, and not as a break with it. But the Church resisted any change of doctrine or ritual, and change finally came about by force. The conflict centered around religion as revealed truth completed in the authority of the Church, to be obediently accepted without question (Catholic), and religion as truth divine in origin but complete only with the growth and development of the spirit of the individual through progressive interpretation of the original teachings (Protestant). Martin Luther was the great protagonist of the Reformation; it was said that he hatched the egg which Erasmus had laid. Luther was primarily concerned with delivering education from the confining domination of the Catholic Church. He urged wider dissemination of opportunities and felt that schooling should be integrally related to social life. Against the Church schools, he wrote as follows.

22. Ibid., pp. 391-92.

Solomon was a right royal schoolmaster. He does not forbid children from mingling with the world, or from enjoying themselves, as the monks do their scholars; for they will thus become clods and blockheads, as Anselm likewise perceived. Said this one: "a young man, thus hedged about, and cut off from society, is like a young tree, whose nature it is to grow and bear fruit, planted in a small and narrow pot." For the monks have imprisoned the youth whom they have had in charge, as men put birds in dark cages, so that they could neither see nor converse with anyone. But it is dangerous for youth to be thus alone, thus debarred from social intercourse. Wherefore, we ought to permit young people to see, and hear, and know what is taking place around them in the world, yet so that you hold them under discipline, and teach them self-respect. Your monkish strictness is never productive of any good fruit. It is an excellent thing for a young man to be frequently in the society of others; yet he must be honorably trained to adhere to the principles of integrity and to virtue, and to shun the contamination of vice. This monkish tyranny is, moreover, an absolute injury to the young; for they stand in quite as much need of pleasure and recreation as of eating and drinking; their health, too, will be firmer and the more vigorous by this means.[23]

Luther felt that education should be sponsored by the state for religious purposes, and also for the prosperity of the State. For him, social life and religious life were the same; therefore, schools were just as much an arm of religion as they had been under the Catholics. It was the beginning of religion in a covert role within the State, determining the value orientation nevertheless. Note that Luther, for all his concern that the young enjoy and participate in life's activities, still encouraged external control over the individual, by the training in discipline, virtue and integrity. Unintentionally, Protestant doctrine thus opened the way later for arguments regarding complete separation of church and state.

The Reformation called for the establishment of state schools dedicated to the ideal of universal education, since it was part of the doctrine that the welfare of every individual depended upon the application of his own reason to the revelation contained in the Scriptures. It was thus necessary to train the people's rational powers to some extent. The doctrine also included the political belief that the welfare of the state depended on the education of every citizen. Schools were to be maintained at public expense for everyone, rich and poor, boys and girls. As time progressed, however, and the Protestant leaders became successful, their dogma of reliance upon reason hardened into a fresh distrust of any individualism. When fighting the pope, Luther had declared "that reason is the chief of all things, and among all that belongs to this life, the best, yea, a something divine." Later on, once his own doctrines and opinions were well fixed, he declared "the more subtle and acute reason is, the more poisonous a beast it is, with many dragons' heads; it is against God and all his works."[24] The Reformation gave way to the return of narrow authoritarian systems and definitions, and petty, bitter quarrels between the various Protestant sects, each of which was as intolerant of any opposing doctrine as the Catholic Church had been. Education and intellectual life became bound within the narrow limits defined by each

23. Martin Luther, in Paul Monroe, Ibid., p. 411.
24. Martin Luther, quoted in Frank Graves, *A History of Education* (New York: The MacMillan Company, 1922), p. 204.

particular sect, with education merely a new version of Scholasticism instead of a real alternative.

The Catholic Church had begun to take effective counter-Reformation measures (the Inquisition, the Council of Trent, the Jesuit Society) in order to crush heresy, and was successful in maintaining the long-held conception that education was properly a function of the Church and should therefore be religious. In this, Protestants had never disagreed. They had argued only about the specific doctrines to be taught and the relative role of church and state. "Religious freedom" was far from realized. As for the Reformation doctrine advocating universal education for all, this did not mean equal education for all. Class structure was still firmly embedded in society. Education became a two-track system: a vernacular elementary education for the lower classes and a humanistic secondary education for the upper classes, both heavily religious in spirit. The humanistic Renaissance effort had been to reform the content and orientation of an aristocratic literary education; the Protestant effort had also aimed primarily at teaching literacy, so that the common man could read the Bible for himself. The process of education had not changed.

In effect, the Reformation resulted in little reform. Despite disagreements between Catholics and Protestants, neither departed much from the conception of the universe created by God, wherein man played a role assigned to him by God. For both groups, man's purpose was the salvation of his immortal soul. Both believed that knowledge of the spiritual world was more important than knowledge of the physical world, joining together against the world view of empirical science. (Luther condemned science as "That silly little fool, that Devil's bride, Dame Reason, God's worst enemy.")[25] Catholics and Protestants agreed that the primary aim of education was to arrive at a true knowledge of God's laws and commandments. The "reformers," therefore, maintained strong ties with medieval tradition. As for the child, he was no longer merely a small adult. His nature was evil and the work of education was to eradicate it and replace it with "true religious goodness." Socrates and Plato would have disagreed with this conception of good and bad, for they did not believe that the soul of man was evil.

> But if there is no one who desires to be miserable, there is no one, Meno, who desires evil; for what is misery but the desire and possession of evil."[26]

> "No wise man, as I believe, will allow that any human being errs voluntarily, or voluntarily does evil and dishonorable actions; but they are very well aware that all who do evil and dishonorable things do them against their will.[27]

However, their conceptualizations led to the same outcome. Plato and Socrates stressed the role of ignorance; men suffered from their lack of knowledge of the true morality, which could be supplied by those who knew it.

---

25. Butts, *Education of the West*, p. 210.
26. Plato, *Meno*, p. 13.
27. Plato, quoted in Gouldner, *Enter Plato*, p. 40.

THE REALISTS

Once again, during the late sixteenth and seventeenth centuries, a protest movement against prevailing narrow formalism and authoritarian definitions developed. This became known as Realism, and it posed the philosophy of empirical science as an alternative. Theorists began to emphasize a materialist view of learning through sense experience rather than learning from books. They argued that learning was to be applied in practical affairs instead of to religious devotion and elaborate speech. New technologies were needed for growing industries, which supported and led to the idea that perhaps all the doctrines were wrong and that a new way to truth might be found. If the answer to man's behavior and his education did not lie in the classical humanities or in religious creeds, it might very well lie in the natural world, as portrayed by the underlying concepts of modern science. The secrets of nature could be revealed by an accumulation of facts, obtained by direct study and objective verification of these facts, followed by mathematical analysis. No longer were reading and memorization to be the basis of schoolwork; rather, the scientific method of learning through the senses by acquaintance with actual things (realia), and observation and generalization from the simple to the complex, would become the method of education. Education was to be designed in order to create the scientific spirit and encourage original investigation, foster critical attitudes, and free the individual from preconceived beliefs and fixed ideas. Representative of this realistic education were Francois Rabelais, Michel de Montaigne, Francis Bacon, and John Amos Comenius.

The importance of Rabelais to education comes from the effect his tales about good and wise giants had on educational theorists. In these tales, he ridiculed traditional ideas and practices (especially formalism in the schools) and attacked corrupt representatives of medieval institutions—monks, judges, lawyers. Through satire and exaggeration, he affirmed man's right to enjoy life, to be exuberant, to think for himself. While he advocated study of classical knowledge, he related this to nature and to social life. The senses, as well as the intellect, were to be trained; the body as well as the mind. His first book, *Gargantua* (1532) begins with a mocking account of the young giant's medieval schooling which makes a dunce of him, and goes on to relate how later humanistic schooling makes him a real person. Rabelais' second book, *Pantagruel,* describes the adventures of Gargantua's son and his encounters with corruption and hypocrisy. It includes a letter written by Gargantua to Pantagruel, indicating his beliefs regarding a proper education.

> I intend, and will have it so, that thou learn the languages perfectly. First of all, the Greek, as Quintilian will have it; secondly the Latin; and then the Hebrew, for the holy Scripture's sake. And then the Chaldee and Arabic likewise. And that thou frame thy style in Greek, in imitation of Plato; and for the Latin, after Cicero. Let there be no history which thou shalt not have ready in thy memory; and to help thee therein, the books of cosmography will be very conducible. Of the liberal arts of geometry, arithmetic, and music, I gave thee some taste when thou wert yet little, and not above five or six years old; proceed further in them and learn the remainder if thou canst. As for astronomy, study all the rules thereof; let pass nevertheless the divining and judicial astrology, and the art of Lullius, as being nothing

else but plain cheats and vanities. As for the civil law, of that I would thee to know the texts by heart, and then to compare them with philosophy.

Now in matter of the knowledge of the works of nature, I would have thee to study that exactly; so that there be no sea, river, or fountain, of which thou dost not know the fishes; all the fowls of the air; all the several kinds of shrubs and trees, whether in forest or orchard; all the sorts of herbs and flowers that grow upon the ground; all the various metals that are hid within the bowels of the earth; together with all the diversity of precious stones that are to be seen in the Orient and south parts of the world; let nothing of all these be hidden from thee. Then fail not most carefully to peruse the books of the great Arabian and Latin physicians; not despising the Talmudists and Cabalists; and by frequent anatomies get thee the perfect knowledge of the microcosm, which is man. And at some hours of the day apply thy mind to the study of the holy Scriptures: first in Greek, the New Testament with the Epistles of the Apostles; and then the Old Testament, in Hebrew. In brief, let me see thee an abyss and bottomless pit of knowledge: for from henceforward, as thou growest great and becomest a man, thou must part from this tranquility and rest of study; thou must learn chivalry, warfare, and the exercise of the field, the better thereby to defend our house and our friends and to succour and protect them at all their needs against the invasion and assaults of evil-doers. Furthermore, I will that very shortly thou try how much thou has profited, which thou canst not better do than by maintaining publicly theses and conclusions in all arts, against all persons whatsoever, and by haunting the company of learned men, both at Paris and otherwhere.[28]

The trend towards realism and individualism continued with de Montaigne, who saw education as direct preparation for a successful and pleasurable career in life.

If the mind be not better disposed by education, if the judgment be not better settled, I had much rather my scholar had spent his time at tennis . . . Do but observe him when he comes back from school, after fifteen or sixteen years that he has been there; there is nothing so awkward and maladroit, so unfit for company and employment; and all that you shall find he has got is, that his Latin and Greek have only made him a greater and more conceited coxcomb than when he went from home.[29]

The most important phase of a youth's education was a period of extensive travel which he would undertake in order to gain experience, become familiar with men and customs, and acquire practical knowledge by dealing with people.

That he may whet and sharpen his wits by rubbing them upon those of others, I would have a boy sent abroad very young . . . This great world, which some multiply as several species under one genus, is the true mirror wherein we must look in order to know ourselves, as we should. In short I would have this to be the book my young gentleman should study with most attention. Many strange humours, many sects, many judgments, opinions, laws, and customs, teach us to judge rightly of our own actions, to

28. Francois Rabelais, *Pantagruel*, in *Our Heritage of World Literature*, ed. by S. Thompson and J. Glassner (New York: Henry Holt and Co., Inc., 1938), p. 681.
29. Michel De Montaigne, *Essays*, in Monroe, *Textbook in the History of Education*, p. 452.

correct our faults, and to inform our understanding which is no trivial lesson
... In these examples a man shall learn what it is to know, and what it is to
be ignorant; what ought to be the end and design of study; what valour,
temperance, and justice are; what difference there is between ambition and
avarice, bondage and freedom, license and liberty; by what token a man may
know true and solid content; to what extent one may fear and apprehend
death, pain, or disgrace, "Et quo quemque modo fugiasque ferasque laborem.
(And how one may avoid or endure each hardship.)" He shall also learn
what secret springs move us, and the reason of our various irresolutions; for,
I think, the first doctrines with which one seasons his understanding ought
to be those that rule his manners and direct his sense; that teach him to know
himself, how to live and how to die well. Among the liberal studies let us
begin with those which make us free; not that they do not all serve in some
measure to the instruction and use of life, as do all other things, but let us
make choice of those which directly and professedly serve to that end. If we
were once able to restrain the offices of human life within their just and
natural limits, we should find that most of the subjects now taught are of no
great use to us; and even in those that are useful there are many points it
would be better to leave alone, and, following Socrates' direction, limit our
studies to those of real utility.[30]

For Montaigne, studies were means to an end, subordinate to character and
the practice of life. By studying diverse cultures firsthand, all of man's contradictions would emerge, teaching that mankind could not be forced into a single
mold, nor could one rigid dogma be imposed on everyone. Montaigne advocated
tolerance, intellectual detachment and constant investigation, and stressed contact with other men and the study of history. In his *Essays,* he discussed the
methodology to be used in the schools.

'Tis the custom of pedagogues to be eternally thundering in their pupils'
ears, as they were pouring into a funnel, while the business of the pupil is
only to repeat what the others have said: now I would have a tutor to correct this error, and, that at the very first, he should, according to the capacity
he has to deal with, put it to the test, permitting his pupil himself to taste
things, and of himself to discern and choose them, sometimes opening the
way to him, and sometimes leaving him to open it for himself; that is, I
would not have him alone to invent and speak, but that he should also hear
his pupil speak in turn. Socrates ... made first (his) scholars speak, and
then (he) spoke to them ...

Let the master not only examine him about the grammatical construction
of the bare words of his lesson, but about the sense and substance of them,
and let him judge of the profit he has made, not by the testimony of his
memory, but by that of his life. Let him make him put what he has learned
into a hundred several forms, and accommodate it to so many several subjects, to see if he yet rightly comprehends it, and has made it his own, taking
instruction of his progress by the pedagogic institutions of Plato. 'Tis a sign
of crudity and indigestion to disgorge what we eat in the same condition it
was swallowed; the stomach has not performed it office unless it has altered
the form and condition of what was committed to it to concoct.

Whoever asked his pupil what he thought of grammar or rhetoric, and of such
and such a sentence of Cicero? Our masters stick them, full feathered, in o'

30. Ibid., pp. 453-54.

memories, and there establish them like oracles, of which the letters and syllables are of the substance of the thing. To know by rote, is no knowledge, and signifies no more but only to retain what one has entrusted to our memory. That which a man rightly knows and understands, he is the free disposer of at his own full liberty, without any regard to the author from whence he had it or fumbling over the leaves of his book. A mere bookish learning is a poor, paltry learning; it may serve for ornament, but there is yet no foundation for any superstructure to be built upon it, according to the opinion of Plato . . .[31]

In sum, Montaigne felt that "For though we may become learned by other men's reading, a man can never be wise but by his own wisdom."[32]

During the seventeenth century, this belief that knowledge came primarily through the senses and that nature was the source of truth became very prevalent. Science became a more viable way of knowing than the way of the ancients. Laws and principles upon which education should be based were also presumed discoverable in nature, and exclusive emphasis on literature and linguistic materials was replaced by material from the natural sciences and contemporary life. This turning to science was caused partly by disappointment at the failure of both reform in religion and recovery of classical learning to bring about any great changes regarding the general improvement of mankind, the social betterment of life, and the perfection of human nature. It was the beginning of analysis as to the structural reasons why such reform efforts had failed. The English philosopher Francis Bacon clearly formulated the thesis that the natural environment should form the foundation of learning, which came to be described more and more in technical, scientific, and practical terms, in contrast to former humanistic ones. This became part of what was known as the "pansophic" ideal. (Another important part of "pansophism" was its intended universality.)

The method of the Scholastics for attaining knowledge and truth, based upon their impressions and understanding of Aristotle, had been deductive logic (reasoning from an assumed or demonstrated truth to specifics and implications). Bacon's alternative method was inductive logic (reasoning from questions or particulars to general ideas), and in his *Novum Organum* (opposed to Aristotle's *Organon*) he described his method for the investigation of phenomena.

There are and can be only two ways of searching into and discovering truth. The one flies from the senses and particulars to the most general axioms, and from these principles, the truth of which it takes for settled and immovable, proceeds to judgment and the discovery of middle axioms. And this way is now in fashion. The other derives axioms from the senses and particulars, rising by a gradual and unbroken ascent, so that it arrives at the most general axioms last of all. This is the true way, but as yet untried.[33]

The deductive method entered the process only as a secondary factor when the principle was to be applied to a practical problem, resulting in an invention. The scientific method thus consisted of both kinds of reasoning.

31. De Montaigne in *Our Heritage of World Literature*, pp. 682-83.
32. De Montaigne in Monroe, *Textbook*, p. 457.
33. Francis Bacon, *Novum Organon (New Method)*, in Graves, *A History of Education*, 263.

Bacon termed the difficulties which stood in the way of the proper application of his method "idols." There were "idols of the tribe," those found in human nature itself and in the race of man; "idols of the den," personal biases of the individual; "idols of the market place," those arising from manners and customs of social interaction; and "idols of the theater," those formed from dogma and traditional doctrines. Bacon's plan was that after the mind was rid of these "idols" or preconceptions, lists of all the facts of nature could be gathered and tabulated (much as Aristotle had wanted to do) through the cooperative effort of scientists and inventors. He described such a scientific organization in his utopian fable, *The New Atlantis,* which foreshadowed the way in which scientific departments of governments and universities would work. Education was to be based on imparting the accumulated knowledge of nature to all pupils at every stage of their development. Education was the means to an end, which was the dominance of human power. Bacon saw ideas as blocking the way. If new ideas could replace these, man could advance. He did not see ideas as shaped by certain material conditions. The realists observed natural objects and processes in isolation and repose.

The process of induction (as well as deduction) had been formulated by Aristotle in his discussion of the reasoning process, but this had been missed by or unavailable to most of the Scholastics. Thus, Bacon's method was not a totally new alternative. Peter Abelard had urged its application toward understanding reality, truth and religious doctrine during the Scholastic period. However, it was the first time that critical reasoning and a scientific way of viewing reality began to be emphasized and applied in any systematic way in society. The alternative of investigating the phenomena of nature, and only secondarily the phonomena of man and God, represents the culmination of the social reaction which had been growing throughout the Renaissance and Reformation. Bacon did not apply his method of scientific investigation specifically to a system of education. It was a Czech, John Amos Comenius, who made this connection.

Comenius, a bishop and teacher, objected like many others of his time to the fact that study was confined to Latin language and literature, that languages were taught as words and not as things through grammar and form with little emphasis on meaning, that physical force was used to compel attention and punish failure, that there was no order of natural progress in the presentation of material, that schools were places of repression and not of interest, activity, and growth. He endeavored to reform the schools through the formulation of psychological principles and the construction of an organized and sequential curriculum. Comenius saw great possibilities of social reform and universal peace through pansophism, teaching all knowledge to all children. He presented his educational theory in *The Great Didactic.* Education was divided into four periods of six years each up to the age of 24, with special schools provided for each period: infancy, childhood, boyhood, and youth. In the infants' school, up to age six, Comenius would train the senses and bring about moral, religious and physical development through play, games, fairy tales, rhymes, music, and manual activity. In the vernacular school for children of ages six to twelve he would teach reading, writing, arithmetic, singing, religion, morals, economics, politics, history, and the mechanical arts. The classical school for adolescents of ages twelve to eighteen would teach German, Latin, Greek, Hebrew, grammar, rhetoric, logic, mathematics, science, and art. The university for youth eighteen to twenty-four would extend the latter. At all levels the subject matter would be organized into classes and graded to the pupil's ability. Small children would receive instruction in simpler versions of topics to be treated in more detail as they became older. The seeds of learning were implanted in everyone by nature and, like Rousseau later, Comenius believed that society and the schools had been so bad that the seeds hadn't had a chance to grow.

Comenius designed a universal system of education which included the key elements of Renaissance humanism, Reformation religion and realistic science (a formulation which fits our modern system, although religion enters in a covert role today). In any teaching situation, he felt the child should be approached through his sense experience, through pictures and representations of things. Comenius had, however, little effect on schools in his own generation except for introducing a more scientific mehtod of teaching languages as embodied in the textbooks which he wrote. The textbook *Janua Linguarum Reserata* or *Gate of Languages Unlocked* embodied the pansophic ideal and illustrates the new subject matter of education. Using several thousand of the most common Latin words referring to familiar objects, the plan was to arrange them into sentences, beginning with the simplest and becoming progressively more complex, in such a manner that a series of related subjects would be presented, the whole presenting a brief encyclopedic survey of knowledge as well as offering a vocabulary and working knowledge of simple Latin. The one hundred different chapter headings included: Origin of the World, the Elements, the Firmament, Fire, Meteors, Water, Earth, Stones, Metals, Trees and Fruit, Herbs and Shrubs, Animals, Man, His Body, External Members, Internal Members, Qualities of the Body, Diseases, Ulcers and Wounds, External Senses, Internal Senses, Mind, The Mechanic Arts, the Home and its Parts, Marriage, the Family, State and Civic Economy, Grammar, Rhetoric, Dialectic, Ethics, Games, Death, Burial, Providence of God, the Angels.[34] Each page gave in parallel columns the Latin sentence and the equivalent in the vernacular.[35] The method of leading by induction to generalized knowledge was consistently carried out (see p. 91).

The alternatives presented by the Realists had their greatest impact at the secondary school level; for, unlike the thirteenth century when the great intellectual leaders were university men, none of the new philosophers or scientists was closely tied with the universities. The conservative universities had been slow to take up the classics at the beginning of the Renaissance: now they were unwilling to change again and make room for the sciences. The theological-classical humanists controlled the universities until the eighteenth century, when new universities began to be formed in protest. Slowly, it became the custom to use the vernacular in the lecture rooms; and slowly, the teaching of the natural sciences also spread.

The Greeks raised the major issues regarding the nature of the universe and human activity. It remained for the philosophers of following generations to sift through Greek thought, excerpt and weave together select parts of the various ideologies—Sophistic, Platonic and Aristotelian—and come up with a series of combinations and amalgamations as consciousness changed with changes in the material conditions of life. However, these turned out to be modifications

34. John Comenius, *Janua Linguarum Reserata* (Gate of Languages Unlocked), in Monroe, *Textbook*, pp. 490-91.
35. Ibid., p. 492.

A School. C. *Schola.*

A School, 1.	*Schola,* 1.
is a Shop, in which	eſt Officina, in quâ
Young Wits	*Novelli Animi*
are faſhion'd to Virtue, and	formantur ad virtutem,
it is diſtinguiſh'd into Forms.	& diſtinguitur in *Claſſes.*
The Maſter, 2,	*Præceptor,* 2.
fitteth in a Chair, 3.	ſedet in *Cathedra,* 3.
the Scholars, 4.	*Diſcipuli,* 4.
in Forms, 5.	in *Subſelliis,* 5.
he teacheth, they learn.	ille docet, hi diſcunt.
Some things	Quædam
are writ down before them	præſcribuntur illis
with Chalk *on a* Table, 6,	*Cretâ* in *Tabella,* 6.
Some ſit	Quidam ſedent
at a Table, and write, 7.	ad Menſam, & ſcribunt, 7.
he mendeth their Faults, 8,	ipſe corrigit, 8. Mendas,
Some ſtand and rehearſe things	Quidam ſtant, & recitant
committed to memory, 9,	mandata memoriæ, 9.
Some talk together, 10, *and*	Quidam confabulantur, 10,
behave themſelves wantonly	ac gerunt ſe petulantes,
and careleſly;	& negligentes;
	theſe

rather than innovations, variations on the same theme. Though the composition of class structures had changed, the stratification of society into classes of privileged elites and the common masses remained.

Sophistic concern with rhetoric, literature, and social and political activity had been adopted, but Sophistic beliefs as to the dialectical flow of life, the relativity of perception and the impossibility of knowing absolute truths were ignored. Platonic idealistic conceptualizations of the world in absolute, abstract and static terms, and his concern for providing the state with citizens of high moral and intellectual character, ordered on a hierarchy of human abilities and values and able to function in their proper roles, had been embraced, while Plato's interest in individual judgment and self-development and a communistic upbringing, was largely ignored. Aristotelian logic and literature became the fundamental basis of intellectual activity, but that philosopher's interest in the method of science, the natural world, and human happiness was not emphasized until very late.

By the end of the seventeenth century, education, following the pattern of Western practice and thought, was oriented towards:

1. the production of an elite class of competent adults, able to lead, and the rest able to perform their functional role within society's network of activities, ordered on a pyramidal hierarchy of values predetermined and controlled by the economically and politically powerful;
2. control of environmental conditions through systematic knowledge of orderly and permanent truths;
3. the development of character and morality according to supposedly shared conceptions and religious definitions of good and bad, right and wrong, and other either/or dichotomies recognized as absolutes;
4. the use of reason, rather than individual feelings and sense experience leading to knowledge through practice;
5. control of man's dark and malevolent nature;
6. subordination of individual ends to those of the society;
7. literacy as the core of the educational structure.

Literacy was to be a means of acculturation, of bestowing social status, social mobility, and salvation (religious and intellectual) through the study of great books. Under the guise of creating mental liberation, critical thought, and intellectual independence, literacy actually became a means of ideological control and manipulation, a way of forming "good" citizens obedient to church and state who would accept a system of exploitation of the many by a few. Because of reverence for the written word, the importance of sensory experience was lost.

8. a methodology based upon idealist interpretations of the social world as opposed to a dialectical and materialist methodology. Ideas, reason, and the consciousness of men were seen as the origin and driving forces of historical social action. There was no investigation of what was behind these ideas, which shaped them in a particular form as they filtered through the mind.

THE EIGHTEENTH CENTURY: FROM TRADITIONAL TO MODERN

From 1500 to 1700, Europeans searched the world for new markets and raw materials for their new industries, and establishing trading posts, military bases, colonies and Christian missions. Exploration was stimulated by their desire to reestablish contact with the East, after it had been cut off by unfriendly Chinese rulers and by the Moslem Turks. Merchants and national rules sought ever-increasing economic gain. From the eighteenth century on, European development was greatly affected by the world overseas, as was the rest of the world affected by European development. Western Europe became the center of world movement, instead of the Middle East. In this way, the West began its political and economic domination over much of the rest of the world. The expansion of horizons and markets through exploration and discovery laid the groundwork for the change from traditional to modern society, just as the new scientific view of the universe formed the intellectual and ideological framework. The increased means of production, commodities, and exchange, the flow of ideas, the increased movement of peoples, the confrontation between different customs, values and institutions, all led to swifter social change. Wherever the Europeans went, they carried their system of education, a mixture of humanistic, Christian, and to a lesser degree, scientific "knowledge," which helped to establish their hegemony in the new lands.

In Europe, the classical humanities remained firmly fixed at the top of the educational hierarchy, supported by humanistic, religious and ruling groups. A movement in opposition continued, as economic changes brought new groups to greater power, and this was manifested by the stirring of feelings and aspirations of the masses, who were stimulated by increased economic and political participation and promises of a better life through the application of scientific knowledge.

However, society retained its basic class structure. Schools continued to provide a two-track system of education, with the lower classes channeled into a system which could not lead to higher education or to high status in society. Realists continued to argue for the addition of math and sciences to the curriculum. Economic and political reformers called for vocational and commercial education and the teaching of trades to the poor. There was a call for greater use of the vernacular in teaching. But the close connection between religion and humanism and their support by established authority kept the schools from adapting readily to new methods.

In the eighteenth and nineteenth centuries, Western civilization underwent further transformation from "traditional" to "modern" societies. These two systems are not mutually exclusive, but rather, the continuation of a historical process whereby traditions become modified but remain part of the new society. Modern society, in contrast to "folk" society, has been defined in several ways:

1. the degree to which a society's social structure reflects the use of inanimate sources of power rather than human or animal energy;[36]
2. a society which looks for objectifiable evidence for proof of phenomena as opposed to faith or tradition as the basis of proof;[37]
3. a civilization which consists of a centralized national authority, intellectual and scientific creativeness, industrial and technological advancement, urbanization, democratic aspirations, and secularization;[38]
4. a society where status is an achieved rather than an ascribed condition, impersonal rather than personal;[39]

36. Marion Levy, in Butts, *Education of the West*, p. 297.
37. Ibid., p. 297.
38. Ibid., pp. 295-299.
39. Sir Henry Maine, *Ancient Law*, in *Sociology, Students, and Society*, ed. by Jerome Rabow, (Pacific Palisades, Ca.: Goodyear Publishing Co., 1972), p. 474.

5. a society in which people are tied by complex networks of market relations which develop from self-interest, as opposed to those where people are linked by emotional ties of kinship and affection;[40]

6. a society in which social ties and relationships result from independent roles or roles which complement each other, rather than solidarity based on a common consciousness where people coalesce around similar values and standards.[41]

7. a society characterized by class antagonisms between those who own the means of production (capitalists) and those who labor for wages (proletariat), wherein production is concentrated in large-scale industrial enterprises rather than as the production of individuals.

In the eighteenth century, the nation became the unit of political authority. Political institutions grew in their capacity to cope with an increasing range and complexity of affairs, rationally and effectively, through the development of bureaucracies for the conduct of public business. Education became important for the professional training of bureaucrats for governmental service, and for supplying trained personnel for the new businesses and industrial and economic needs of the nation. Education was seen as the primary agent for developing citizens, creating an industrial labor force, strengthening nationalistic identification, loyalty and pride, and for maintaining the conditions of the new status quo.

The Enlightenment

The eighteenth century is known as the period of the Enlightenment, and was a further reaction against the traditional forces which had reasserted themselves by reacting against realism and the shifts of power it represented. The Enlightenment was a protest against religious authoritarianism, superstition and ignorance, hypocrisy in morality, an unscientific world view, and the doctrine of original sin. This was the "age of reason," which preached that through rational thought man could reform his institutions and create a better world. The world of man and nature could not only be understood by acquiring knowledge, but it could be controlled, managed and improved. This was an era of new discoveries and conceptualizations in scientific knowledge, with Newton in the areas of physics and astronomy, Leibnitz in mathematics, Malthus in economics, Pasteur and Darwin in biology, Voltaire in history, de Tocqueville in political science, Locke, Kant and Hegel in philosophy, and Rousseau in education. Science gained tremendous prestige and authority, and came to have several meanings:

1. all bodies of organized knowledge, that developed systematic and consistent statements of tested beliefs;

2. the experimental method for discovery and refinement of knowledge (careful observation, formulation of hypotheses, elaboration of consequences, testing and verifying hypotheses under controlled and measureable conditions);

40. Ferdinand Tonnies, *Gemeinschaft und Gesellschaft (Community and Society)* (New York: Harper & Row, 1963).
41. Emile Durkheim, *The Division of Labor in Society*, trans. by G. Simpson (Glencoe, Ill.: The Free Press, 1933).

3. a general philosophy or world view, according to which natural phenomena and human events both followed orderly regularities that could be observed by the senses, measured accurately, and expressed in quantitative terms.

Under the scientific view, the world was seen as a great machine operating according to "natural law" rather than according to the whims of a personal God.

As masses of material were added to traditional bodies of knowledge, many new subjects were added to education, and older subjects became subdivided into specializations. Scholars and specialists were organized into various professional associations, and the success of the scientific method within the conditions of its existence was soon apparent. The same dichotomy of opinion as to the proper use of knowledge continued. One view was still the humanistic, believing that knowledge was primarily for its own sake, expressing the purest form of culture and human sentiment. This view exalted scholarship whether in the humanities or the sciences. The other view was that knowledge had a social function to perform. This view took several forms: 1) an emphasis on nationalism; 2) the desire to increase the productive capacity of the nation through business and industry, including the idea that an individual could advance himself on the social and economic scale; and 3) the belief that knowledge should be devoted to the welfare of the majority in a democratic manner. The Enlightenment created an alliance between theoretical and practical knowledge which encouraged the organization of knowledge for practical purposes and led to the development of new technology.

The rationalistic movement in the early eighteenth century was a revolt of the intellect against repression. The movement in the second half of the eighteenth century, called the naturalistic movement, was a revolt of the masses demanding the rights of the common man. Thus were added to the rationalists' grievnaces (which were primarily against the Church) those against a rigidly stratified society and a closed economic system. Both movements composed "the Enlightenment."

The Enlightenment is said to have begun with John Locke in England. Locke's view of education held that it was the process of learning to reason rather than the thing learned which was most important. Certain subjects, such as mathematics and classical languages, were the most significant, for they developed the "powers of the mind" in and of themselves, regardless of whether they had any relation to the student's life. Locke believed that at birth the mind of a child was a blank slate, ready to be acted upon by the environment; and he rejected the belief that ideas were inherent within a child and that education was a process of illumination from within. His philosophy of education was an extension of Bacon's belief, that all knowledge came from perception of the senses, from experience. Bacon and Comenius, however, held that it was what was learned which was significant. For Locke, education was a disciplinary process, whose primary aim was the formation of character. The secret of education was to control one's natural desires and instincts and form the habit of controlling them. Moral education was a hardening process, the subordination of desires to the control of reason.

As the strength of the Body lies chiefly in being able to endure Hardships, so also does that of the Mind, and the great Principle and Foundation of all

Virtue and Worth is placed in this: That a Man is able to deny himself his own desires, cross his own inclinations and purely follow what Reason directs as best, tho' the appetite lean the other way. . . . It seems plain to me that the Principle of all Virtue and Excellency lies in the Power of denying ourselves the Satisfaction of our own Desires, where Reason does not authorize them. This Power is to be got and improved by Custom made easy and familiar by an early Practice. If, therefore, I might be heard, I would advise that contrary to the ordinary way, children should be used to submit their Desires and go without their Longings, even from their very Cradles. The first thing they should learn to know should be that they were not to have anything because it pleased them, but because it was thought fit for them.

*   *   *

But since the great Foundation of Fear in Children is Pain, the way to harden and fortify Children against Fear and Danger is to accustom them to suffer Pain. This 'tis possible will be thought, by kind Parents, a very unnatural thing towards their Children; and by most, unreasonable, to endeavour to reconcile any one to the Sense of Pain, by bringing it upon him. 'Twill be said: "It may perhaps give the Child an Aversion for him that makes him suffer; but can never recommend to him Suffering itself. This is a strange Method. You will not have Children whipp'd and punish'd for their Faults, but you would have them tormented for doing well, or for tormenting sake." I doubt not but such Objections as these will be made, and I shall be thought inconsistent with myself, or fantastical, in proposing it. I confess it is a thing to be managed with great Discretion, and therefore it falls not out amiss, that it will not be receiv'd or relish'd, but by those who consider well, and look into the Reason of Things. I would not have Children much beaten for their Faults, because I would not have them think bodily Pain the greatest Punishment: And I would have them, when they do well, be sometimes put in Pain, for the same Reason, that they might be accustom'd to bear it, without looking on it as the greatest Evil. How much Education may reconcile young People to Pain and Sufferance, the Examples of Sparta do sufficiently shew: And they who have once brought themselves not to think bodily Pain the greatest of Evils, or that which they ought to stand most in fear of, have made no small Advance towards Virtue. But I am not so foolish to purpose the *Lacedaemonian* Discipline in our Age or Constitution. But yet I do say, that inuring Children gently to suffer some Degrees of Pain without shrinking, is a way to gain Firmness to their Minds, and lay a Foundation for Courage and Resolution in the future Part of their Lives." 42

Locke was primarily concerned with the education of a gentleman's sons, and played a major role in rationalizing the English gentlemanly ideal of a liberal education: the teaching of virtue (sound moral habits), wisdom (acting with foresight and prudence in managing one's affairs), breeding (correct behavior and manners), and learning (achievement of intellectual power through mental training). Education as an intellectual discipline was more than the prevailing linguistic and grammatical grind which was then taught in the schools. It was not merely to be designed so that pupils would acquire more and more knowledge, but for acquiring more and more "power" by looking into all sorts of knowledge.

42. John Locke, *Thoughts Concerning Education,* in Monroe, *Textbook,* pp. 515-17.

As for the subject matter through which to acquire power:

> Nothing does this better than mathematics, which therefore I think should be taught all those who have the time and opportunity, *not so much to make them mathematicians, as to make them reasonable creatures;* for though we call ourselves so, because we are born to it if we please, yet we may truly say nature gives us but the seeds of it. We are born to be, if we please, rational creatures, but it is use and exercise that makes us so, and we are indeed so no further than industry and application has carried us. . . . I have mentioned mathematics as a way to settle in the mind a habit of reasoning closely . . . not that I think it necessary that all men should be deep mathematicians, but that having got the way of reasoning, which that study necessarily brings the mind to, they might be able to transfer it to other parts of knowledge as they shall have occasion. [43]

Locke's disciplinary conception of education accepted the validity of authority external to the individual. He replaced the righteousness of God with the righteousness of the State. Locke supposedly replaced authority with reason, but he found much that was reasonable in authority.

Philosophers of the Enlightenment rejected the hypocrisy and superstition of the Church, and many became atheistic. Francois Voltaire is representative of those writers and philosophers of the Enlightenment known as the "philosophes" or "encyclopedists." Their efforts were directed primarily against the Catholic Church, its harshness, violence, tyranny, and persecution as it tried to suppress all differences of opinion. They believed in the exercise of individual judgment through the use of reason. The Church became "the Infamy." The philosophes advocated tolerance, humanitarianism and free inquiry in all directions, and other social and political institutions which perpetrated the same evils as the Church also came under attack. They put themselves forward as representing the whole of suffering humanity. However, the movement was aristocratic, by those aristocrats who were attempting to secure the free use of individual reason for those classes which controlled society. They would substitute a new aristocracy of intelligence and wealth for the old aristocracy of Church, family and position. They didn't believe that the lower classes were amenable to reason or to education. They opposed the Church because it was irrational, but felt that it might have a mission with the dull and uneducated masses. The movement developed into formalism and artificiality, which, although rational, had lost touch with life and the people. Rationalists came to regard simplicity as a sign of vulgarity and naturalness as a sign of irrationality. After the French Revolution, atheistic intellectuals who had argued for the supremacy of reason were guillotined, because, as Robespierre said, "Atheism is aristocratic. The idea of a Supreme Being who watches over oppressed innocence and punishes triumphant crime is essentially the idea of the people." [44]

43. Ibid., p. 519.
44. Maximilien Robespierre, quoted in H. G. Wells, *The Outline of History* (New York: Doubleday & Co., Inc., 1971), p. 765.

Rousseau: An Educational Alternative

During the eighteenth century the rationalists concentrated their attack primarily against the Church; in the latter half of the century, criticism also grew against other social and political institutions and against the rationalists themselves. Reason had come to be as tyrannical as established authority. A new belief emerged, which was that the emotions or inner feelings were the best guide to "right" conduct, rather than the cold calculations of reason. The leading exponent of the idea that human nature was basically good and that society had made it evil, was Jean Jacques Rousseau. Rousseau was guided by his sympathy for the common people, poor and exploited, to whose plight the aristocratic rationalists and upper classes were indifferent. Rousseau and the naturalists rejected both the old orthodoxy and superstition of the Catholic Church and the skepticism of the rationalists towards all religion. They popularized their own "natural religion" based upon the fundamentals of Christianity (its ethics) and the "laws" of nature. They felt that religion was an essential part of human society because it was an essential part of the human experience. Doctrines of liberation of the common man (such as our Declaration of Independence and Constitution), and doctines on the liberation of the child, have their origin in the beliefs of Rousseau. Human happiness and welfare were the natural rights of every individual, not the special possession of a favored class or a favored age. That government and those institutions which prevented this human realization were to be objects for destruction. In Rousseau's writing is found the negation of the Renaissance and the literary, rational philosophy which flowed from it. In an essay on the question, "Has the restoration of the sciences and the arts contributed to corrupt or to purify morals?," Rousseau wrote his first emotional attack upon reason and knowledge, which he felt had made governments more powerful, crushed individual liberty, and replaced simple virtues and honest speech with the hypocrisies of present manners and morals.

> Sincere friendship, real esteem, and perfect confidence are banished from among men. Jealousy, suspicion, fear, coldness, reserve, hate and fraud lie constantly concealed under that uniform and deceitful veil of politeness, that boasted candor and urbanity, for which we are indebted to the light and leading of this age. . . . Let the arts and sciences claim the share they have had in this salutary work!

He concluded that:

> . . . luxury, profligacy, and slavery have been in all ages the scourge of the efforts of our pride to emerge from that happy state of ignorance in which the wisdom of Providence has placed us. . . . Let men learn for once that nature would have preserved them from science as a mother snatches a dangerous weapon from the hands of her child. [45]

Rousseau condemned the "advancement" of learning as the force which had corrupted the character of mankind and led him to fall from a paradise of innocence and bliss.

45. Jean Jacques Rousseau, *Discourse on the Arts and Sciences,* in Will and Ariel Durant, *Rousseau and Revolution,* (New York: Simon and Schuster, 1967), pp. 21-22. Copyright © 1967, by Will and Ariel Durant. Reprinted by permission of Simon and Schuster.

The greater part of our ills are of our own making, and we might have avoided them, nearly all, by adhering to that simple, uniform, and solitary manner of life which nature prescribed. If she destined man to be healthy, I venture to declare that a state of reflection is a state contrary to nature, and that a thinking man is a depraved animal. When we think of the good constitution of the savages—at least of those whom we have not ruined with our spirituous liquors—and reflect that they are troubled with hardly any disorders save wounds and old age, we are tempted to believe that in following the history of civil society we shall be telling that of human sickness. [46]

In *On the Origin of Inequality Among Men,* Rousseau described his ideal society of primitive men, wherein the only physical or intellectual inequality was that established by nature, which under natural conditions of life hardly revealed itself. Sympathy, the one primitive virtue, took the place of laws, manners and customs. Primarily through the rise of private property, social inequalities arose. In order to perpetuate these inequalities, political power grew and states were created.

The first man who, having enclosed a piece of ground, bethought himself of saying, *This is mine,* and found people simple enough to believe him, was the real founder of civil society. From how many crimes, wars, and murders, from how many horrors and misfortunes, might not anyone have saved mankind, by pulling up the stakes, or filling up the ditch, and crying to his fellows, "Beware of listening to this impostor; you are undone if you once forget that the fruits of the earth belong to us all, and the earth itself to nobody.[47]

While he revered the natural, primitive state of mankind, his analysis of it was abstract. He did not base his understanding on an examination of the structural conditions of social and productive relations among earlier groups which had made them so "pure." Nor did he follow these ideas with an investigation of specific conditions of power within the existing society. His analysis was subjective, in that he saw the subject (man) as having created the social and material conditions of existence, rather than a materialist analysis, which would have seen social relationships as the necessary outcome of a historical evolutionary process of changes in the forces and relations of production.

In *The Social Contract,* Rousseau modified his conception of the ideal state as primitive society, and presented life in the ideal society organized under the rule of the people, where the tastes and desires of the masses dominated. Rousseau modeled this system on the city-state of Geneva, which he felt best exemplified his ideal political system. Government was a result of a contract between people, by which some persons were given delegated power to rule. The ruled did not pledge to obey the rulers, but individuals agreed to subordinate their judgments, rights and needs to the community as a whole, and accepted the protection of the communal laws. Power lay in the "general will" of the community, which was delegated, but never surrendered. In *The Social Contract,* Rousseau no longer idealized the natural primitive state, but advocated control of instincts in order to make society possible, in a seeming contradiction to his

46. Ibid., p. 29.
47. Ibid., p. 30

earlier idolization of nature. In any event, man could no longer return to that
natural state and must therefore do his best with this one.

> The passage from the state of nature to the civil state produces a very re-
> markable change in man, by substituting law for instinct in his conduct, and
> giving his actions the morality they had formerly lacked. . . . Although, in
> this civil state he deprives himself of some advantages which he had from
> nature, he gains in return others so great, his faculties are so stimulated and
> developed, his ideas so extended, and his whole soul so uplifted, that, did
> not the abuses of his new condition often degrade him below that which he
> left, he would be bound to bless continually the happy moment which took
> him from it forever, and instead of a stupid and unimaginative animal, made
> him an intelligent being and a man.[48]

Here Rousseau sounds more like Voltaire and the rationalists, moving from
liberty to order. He labeled his ideal political system "elective aristocracy," and
we would label it today "representative democracy," government by officials
popularly chosen for their supposedly superior fitness. Direct rule by all the
people seemed to Rousseau an impossibility.

> If we take the term in the strict sense, there never has been a real democracy,
> and there never will be. It is against the natural order for the many to govern
> and the few to be governed. It is unimaginable that the people should re-
> main continually assembled to devote their time to public affairs, and it is
> clear that they cannot set up commissions for that purpose without chang-
> ing the form of administration. . .
>
> Besides, how many conditions difficult to unite are presupposed by such a
> government? First, a very small state, where the people can be readily
> assembled, and where each citizen can with ease know all the rest; secondly,
> great simplicity of manners, to prevent business from multiplying and raising
> thorny problems; next, a large measure of equality in rank and fortune,
> without which equality of rights and authority cannot long subsist; and
> lastly, little or no luxury, for luxury corrupts at once the rich and the poor—
> the rich by possession and the poor by covetousness. . . . This is why a fam-
> ous writer (Montesquieu) has made virtue the fundamental principle of
> republics, for all these conditions could not exist without virtue. . . . If there
> were a people of gods, their government would be democratic, but so perfect
> a government is not for men.[49]

Rousseau also believed that representatives would soon come to legislate for
their own interest rather than the public good, and that therefore, representatives should be elected to administrative and judicial offices, but that legislation
should be created by the people in general assembly. The ideal state should be
small enough to allow people to assemble frequently. One purpose of the social
contract was that men who were unequal in strength or intelligence would become equal in social and legal rights. However, Rousseau ignored the fact that
some had more power than others to determine the shape of the contract, and
also that most people adapted themselves to social relations unconsciously and
did not conceive of the social system in an integral, definite form.

48. Ibid., p. 173.
49. Ibid., pp. 173-174.

Rousseau did not advise revolt against civilization or a return to the woods. His "natural man" was man governed by the laws of his own nature. He advocated the practice of Christian ethics, natural sympathy for one's fellow men, and the sloughing off of artificialities and hypocrisies and the complications of modern life in exchange for rural simplicity. Although he blamed private property for nearly all evils, he believed that its maintenance was necessary because the poison of civilization was already in man's blood. To end private property would be to create a chaos worse than civilization. (A contradiction to his belief in man's natural goodness was also manifested in the fact that he wondered whether after a revolution, the nature of man would be such that he would reproduce the same old institutions and servitudes under new names.) "None but the greatest dangers can counterbalance that of changing the public order; and the sacred power of the laws should never be arrested save when the existence of the country is at stake."[50] However, Rousseau's was the most revolutionary voice of the times, and he did argue that a government which persistently ignored the "general will" could justly be overthrown. He foresaw the democratic revolutions of the late eighteenth century:

> It is impossible that the great kingdoms of Europe should last much longer. Each of them has had its period of splendor, after which it must inevitably decline. The crisis is approaching: we are on the edge of a revolution.[51]

Rousseau's thoughts led him to explore the role of education in preserving man's natural goodness. He preferred a system of public education by the state, but as public education was then directed by the Church, he prescribed private instruction by a tutor, who was paid to devote many years of his life to his pupil. The educational theories of Rousseau are expressed in *Emile* (1762). In it, he offered the first real educational alternative since the Sophists and Plato clashed in ancient Greece. Rousseau's theories were genuinely innovative and not modifications of themes which had originated in earlier generations. His was the first acknowledgment of natural goodness in a child, the first time faith was centered in individual instincts, feelings and emotions. It was his novel suggestion that in effect, no education was the best education, and experience the only teacher. Rousseau offered experience and doing, rather than thought and contemplation, as the ideal forms of human endeavor. For the first time since Plato, a life of doing was better than a life of knowing. For the first time education was not to be directed towards the conscious production of an aristocratic class, but was the same for everyone.

Rousseau's scheme of education was divided into three periods: 12 years of childhood, 8 years of youth, and an undetermined period in preparation for marriage and parenthood, economic and social life.

In the first period, education was primarily physical and moral. The child was to be given as much freedom as safety would allow. He was best brought up in the country, where life was healthy and natural, and encouraged to love nature, simplicity and natural foods.

50. Ibid., p. 176.
51. Ibid., pp. 176-177.

Men are not made to be crowded together in anthills, but scattered over the earth to till it. The more they are massed together, the more corrupt they become. Disease and vice are the sure results of overcrowded cities. . . . Man's breath is fatal to his fellows. . . . Man is devoured by our towns. In a few generations the race dies out or becomes degenerate; it needs renewal, and is always renewed from the country. Send your children out to renew themselves; send them to regain in the open field the strength lost in the foul air of our crowded cities.

. . . The indifference of children toward meat is one proof that the taste for meat is unnatural. Their preference is for vegetable foods, milk, pastry, fruit, etc. Beware of changing this natural taste and making your children flesh-eaters. Do this, if not for their health, then for the sake of their character. How can we explain away the fact that great meat-eaters are usually fiercer and more cruel than other men?[52]

Rousseau believed that the child should run and jump as he pleased, learning by action instead of by books or even by "teaching." He should merely be given materials and tools, problems and tasks, through which to explore his environment. Nature was the best guide; a child could not be trained through reason.

Let us lay it down as an incontrovertible rule that the first impulses of nature are always right. There is no original sin in the human heart. . . . Never punish your pupil, for he does not know what it means to do wrong. Never make him say, "Forgive me." . . . Wholly unmoral in his actions, he can do nothing morally wrong, and he deserves neither punishment nor reproof . . . . First leave the germ of his character free to show itself; do not constrain him in anything; so you will better see him as he really is.[53]

Rousseau felt that childhood existed for its own sake. "Nature desires that children should be children before they are men."[54] The child need not be taught to read, although he will probably pick it up on his own. Education was a training of the senses, wherein, through experience, a child would learn to measure, weigh, count, compare, draw conclusions, test inferences and discover principles. No "molding of the mind" need or should be attempted.

Intellectual education was to begin at the age of 12, after moral character was formed. The transition from nature to literature was to take place via the reading of *Robinson Crusoe,* for that was the story of life according to nature, of self-help, of the uselessness of most so-called knowledge and social forms. The goal to be attained by the age of 20 was not to have read many books, but to have learned sufficient skill in some trade, in order to be able to earn a living later in life. The purpose of learning a trade was primarily in order to overcome the social prejudices against manual and industrial activities.

When a child was eighteen, religious training could begin.

I am aware that many of my readers will be surprised to find me tracing the course of my scholar through his early years without speaking to him of religion. At fifteen he will not even know that he has a soul; at eighteen

52. Ibid., p. 180.
53. Ibid., p. 181.
54. Rousseau, in Monroe, *Textbook,* p. 561.

he may not yet be ready to learn about it. . . . If I had to depict the most heartbreaking stupidity I would paint a pedant teaching children the catechism; if I wanted to drive a child crazy I would set him to explain what he learned in his catechism. . . . No doubt there is not a moment to be lost if we must deserve eternal salvation; but if the repetition of certain words suffices to obtain it, I do not see why we should not people heaven with starlings and magpies as well as with children.[55]

Rousseau, however, defended faith and advocated a return to religion, aiming his words at rationalists such as Voltaire. He believed that despite their crimes, religions made men more virtuous and hopeful and less cruel than they might otherwise have been. "Granted that we cannot prove the existence of heaven, how cruel it is to take from the people this hope that solaces them in their grief and sustains them in their defeat."[56] Rousseau did not please the Church, however, and *Emile* shocked Christian leaders as irreligious and destructive. They suspected that most young men brought up with no religion would not adopt one later.

As for sex education, Rousseau proposed that Emile be told about sex when he asked about it, and should be told the truth, but that sexual impulses should be restrained.

Never leave the young man night or day, and at least share his room. Never let him go to bed till he is sleepy, and let him rise as soon as he awakes. . . . If once he acquires this dangerous habit he is ruined. From that time forward body and soul will be enervated; he will carry to the grave the effects of . . . the most fatal habit which a young man can acquire.[57]

Women fared much differently from Emile. They were to be educated in the home by their mothers, learning the arts of homemaking, and learning to accept their husband as master and their place as the home. Girls were to be taught religion as early as possible in order to develop modesty, virtue and obedience. Their minds were to be kept active through dancing, games, sports, and theater-going, under proper supervision of course. The proper study of woman was man. Here Rousseau violated his own principle that each person was to be educated for himself (generic use of the term) and guided by his own natural inner being. "A woman of culture is the plague of her husband, her children, her family, her servants—everybody."[58]

Rousseau did not intend that the educational system he proposed in *Emile* be put into actual practice. He hoped that later philosophers and educators would consider his scheme much as they had done with Plato's, as a model to be debated about and experimented with, which it was.

At Strasbourg in 1765 an enthusiast came to him bursting with compliments: "You see, sir, a man who brings up his sons on the principles which he had the happiness to learn from your *Emile.*" "So much the worse, sir, for you and your son!" growled Rousseau. Later, Rousseau explained, "I made clear

55. Durant, *Rousseau and Revolution*, p. 182.
56. Ibid., p. 184.
57. Ibid., p. 185.
58. Rousseau, in *Textbook*, p. 566.

in the preface . . . that my concern was rather to offer the plan of a new system of education for the consideration of sages, and not a method for fathers and mothers." Like Plato, he "laid up in heaven a pattern" of a perfect state or method, so that "he who desires may behold it, and beholding, may govern himself accordingly."[59]

Education had always focused on the making over of the child by society through literature, religion, reason, and other means, into a being much different from the natural creature he was. Opposing this well-established effort, Rousseau's alternative proposed the human being on his own. Previous educators had seen the child only as a small adult, valueless unless he could mimic adult ways. Rousseau saw only the child.

The line of educational development in the nineteenth century was greatly influenced by Rousseau's attempts to understand the experience of childhood, to allow the free development of natural instincts, to have sympathy with the child. Later educators tried to put his theories into practice in the schools. A psychological interpretation of Rousseau's doctrine of nature led to concern with education as a natural process, starting from each individual, and guided by principles derived from the study of the development and functioning of the mind. A second interpretation of Rousseau's doctrine led to education as an inquiry into nature's laws through association with nature itself, rather than from books about nature. A third interpretation led to preparation of the individual to be able to contribute by his own labor to his own support. Learning a trade or occupation as a component part of education was now considered a virtue. It was now necessary for more individuals to participate in the new industrial order.

In England, Rousseau's literary discourses and social ideas had great influence, but his educational theories received little practical support. England lacked a system of schools, and education was up to private sources. Locke's ideas recommended themselves much more strongly than Rousseau's, being closer to the conventional wisdom and structure of the time. Whereas the French Revolution stimulated support in France and Germany for a state system of schools, in England it stimulated the formation of charity organizations to help the underprivileged and provide enough education to satisfy the people at as small a cost as possible. Elementary education did not become a right instead of a charity until the late nineteenth century. Even then, the British system remained a dual one: elementary schools for the working classes and secondary schools for the middle and upper classes.

In Germany, Rousseau's theories fared much better, and several educators managed to effect changes in the nature of instruction towards Rousseau's "method of experience." Education became more child-oriented, including the development of a new literature for children. Under the influence of Johann Basedow, institutions known as "philanthropinum" sprang up throughout the Germanic countries, attempting to impart an "education according to nature." Languages were taught through conversation instead of grammar; physical exercise had an important place in the curriculum; early training was connected with motion and noise since these were the attributes of children; each child was

59. Durant, *Rousseau and Revolution,* p. 188.

taught a handicraft; the vernacular instead of Latin constituted the chief subject-matter; instruction was directed towards the world of nature instead of words. These institutions hoped to educate the rich and poor together, to give the former a natural education for leadership, and to prepare the latter to teach. Great interest developed in the training of teachers. These institutions, however, were short-lived, and their doctrines did not invade the well-entrenched classical secondary schools. The ideals of Rousseau were later worked out more explicitly in practice by Pestalozzi, Herbart and Froebel.

In France, the old regime was so rigidly set in that change could come about only through violent revolution. Robespierre, one of the leaders of the revolution, was inspired and supported by the teachings of his prophet, Rousseau. Royalty and nobility were swept away and the middle classes, the new capitalist merchants, industrialists, and manufacturers, came into power, and production became socialized in large-scale enterprises. Within ten years, although many things which had oppressed the poor were gone, they were still oppressed and had no power. A new class was created, which had nothing left but to labor for wages in the new factories. The new social relationships began to look like the old, with a new rich people and a new private ownership instead of the old, a new peasantry and working class working harder than the old had worked, and a new foreign policy just like the old. France set out after its revolution to liberate and teach republicanism to the world; it proceeded to exploit the resources of the lands which it "liberated," and revolutionary idealism faded before practical necessities.

In the seventeenth and eighteenth centuries, each nation had its own protests and assaults upon the established feudal aristocratic orders, the French Revolution being the most extreme and violent. The democratic revolution was in effect the expression of the new manufacturing and industrial bourgeoisie (middle-class) which was taking power, and was a single revolutionary movement which broke in different parts of the West at the end of the eighteenth century. In the United States, which had never experienced a feudal order, industrial changes and the accompanying "democratic revolution" broadened the base of education and led to greater economic and political participation, which led to faster productive development than in England or France.

THE NINETEENTH CENTURY

Industrialization and The Rising Bourgeoisie

During the nineteenth century, the industrial revolution continued the transformation of productive powers towards even greater concentration of wealth and advances in technology and natural science. It took men away from the home and traditional agricultural pursuits and moved them to the factory and the industrial city. Machine production created a new form of discipline over people's time and skills, and economic control passed completely from the hands of guilds and craftsmen into those of merchants and manufacturers. Political power was centered in the cities. Economic development became specialized and rationalized (technicalized), and there was a deliberate effort to apply science and scientific experimentation to the process of production. Instead of inventions being devised by skillful artisans tinkering with machines and tools, invention was taken over by engineers and technologists. Social organizations, such as stock companies, corporations and banks, developed, with enough capital amassed to invest in large-scale productive and commercial enterprises. Traditional family units gave way to the nuclear family; middle-level positions were assigned on the basis of achievement rather than ascription; greater stress was put on a managerial elite oriented towards scientific and practical knowledge rather than towards humanistic and literary knowledge. Universal education was essential to the existence of a modern capitalist urban society, in order to create a populace which could run the new businesses and work in its industries. Several characteristics distinguish this modern industrial trend in education (our present system):

1. There is large-scale participation by larger numbers for longer periods of time.
2. Emphasis is on the secular and the scientific.
3. Education is practical and professional, in direct preparation for occupational work. Faith in the power of knowledge has resulted in the establishment of research enterprises designed to produce new knowledge, where formerly interest was only in the transmission of knowledge.
4. Education is increasingly specialized and diversified, under the control of large bureaucracies. Education is an industry in itself, with the training of teachers a primary focus. Selective institutions serve differentiated functions.
5. Underlying modern educational systems is the myth that mass education will insure that both society and the individual will achieve their purposes. To guarantee that this will happen, education has attempted to adapt itself to the wide range of industrial and technological needs.

By the middle of the nineteenth century, modern education in a few European countries and the United States contrasted greatly with traditional education patterns which had changed little in unurbanized and nonindustrialized parts of Europe and outside the West.

In nineteenth century England, the great "public" schools (which were actually great private schools open only to the upper class) set the standards for other types of secondary schools. The classical humanities retained their central role, as did religion, manners and behavior. The English universities also continued to favor the classics, logic and scholastic philosophy, and not until the middle of the century were the traditional universities opened up to the middle classes.

In France after the revolution, educational reformers presented their alternatives: remove the Church from its domination; extend education to the people; make it free, universal and compulsory; remove the method of memorization from books; reduce the classics and substitute practical studies, science and democratic ethics. The most extensive plan was that developed by Marie Jean Condorcet. His plan was that for every village of 400 people there should be a primary school within walking distance for all pupils, that in every medium-sized town there should be higher schools providing vocational and technical education for the people, that there should be 100 secondary schools located in the largest towns to provide education in a wide variety of subjects, that there should be nine lycées to provide higher and professional education. Several attempts were made by the revolutionary government to establish a state system of education such as Condorcet had outlined. The schools which they set up, however, lasted only a short time, and except for the technical institutes, were nullified by the return of the Church to education under Napoleon and the restoration of the monarchy. Napoleon was concerned only with the secondary schools which he expected to use to train a loyal and efficient corps of officials, and therefore left lower education up to the Church. Politically, France in the nineteenth century was characterized by several shifts of power between liberals and conservatives. France, too, maintained a two-track system of elementary education for the lower classes and secondary education for the upper classes, with no chance of transfer from one to the other. The secondary education led to the university; the elementary did not. The country where the most extreme form of democratic revolution occurred came to develop the most rigid, standardized and centralized system of education for the training of an educated elite. It is also an anomaly that France, which produced Rousseau and his child-centered education, was the last country to recognize the learner in its educational concerns.

Germany

Germany in the eighteenth century consisted of hundreds of separate medieval political units. Some of the states, notably Prussia, began to consolidate neighboring territories into larger state systems. Through this process, the middle classes found careers as bureaucrats and civil servants for the new institutions. Germany underwent modernization initiated from the top by rulers known as the "enlightened despots," who professed philanthropic motives towards their subjects, but had no intentions of extending any real power to the populace. Frederick the Great hoped to save their souls, make them better workers, and shape them into loyal subjects. He and other Germanic rulers, in their desire to establish national control over productive and political processes, recognized the fact that education could become the basis for developing economic prosperity and political power, and they organized central systems of education with emphasis on realistic studies, science and technology. Schooling became compulsory for all children almost a century before any other country took similar action. A school code was drawn up which took the supervision of schools out of the hands of the clergy and laid the foundation for full state authority over schools. State education under state control for authoritarian purposes was thus established.

At the end of the eighteenth century, Germany was not ready to join in active revolution; it experienced a revolution in theory but not in practice. This was the beginning of the period of Kant and Hegel, Goethe and Schiller, Marx and Engels. It was a period when rulers hoped to modernize their realms with the help of bureaucrats, the middle classes and the university intellectuals, against the opposition of the privileged aristocracy and the established church. The universities became centers of radical thought, as long as thought did not result in economic or political change. In the early nineteenth century, German education tended to be broad and liberal. Teachers studied new learner-oriented methods being developed by Heinrich Pestalozzi in Switzerland.

Pestalozzi aligned himself with Rousseau and liberal groups; however, he saw traditional religious and moral instruction as the most important aims of education. It was Rousseau balanced with Plato. Pestalozzi advocated social reform, but saw it as something to be achieved by helping the individual to help himself through education. He emphasized the practical activities of children, beginning with motor skills and leading to vocational competence. He saw the child as a unity made up of moral, physical and intellectual powers, all of which were to be developed by the teacher. His theories have formed the foundation of modern educational theory and methodology. His school at Yverdun, Switzerland, came to be regarded by all of Europe as the educational Mecca of the day.

For Pestalozzi, the whole problem of education was to be considered from the point of view of the developing mind of the child. The motivation for learning was to come from the child's natural instincts and not from external prodding. Sensory perception of actual objects formed the basis of his method of instruction, as opposed to the reading of books, memorizing and reciting. (He was not the first to propose this viewpoint, but rather, the first to instill it successfully within the system.) Pestalozzi emphasized proceeding from the particular to the general and from the concrete to the abstract. Instruction was to be adapted to each individual child according to his natural stage of development. This was the beginning of learner-centered education within the classroom, and much of it sounds like a present-day course in teacher-training. Although the conservatives of his day saw Pestalozzi as a radical to be suppressed, he was not at all the radical Rousseau was. His theories relied on direction and control of the individual by an external force which was necessary to "guide his development properly." The teacher was now to induct the child into society covertly and seductively instead of overtly and harshly.

Pestalozzi's conception of the primary school was in the tradition of Comenius and Locke, and he helped introduce many of their principles and activities into the schools. Moral instruction as a means of developing national loyalty became an important element in German elementary schools. History and literature extolling the virtues of Germany were introduced into the curriculum, and physical education became the foundation for military training. Traditional and conservative elements began to supersede liberal trends, for the rulers had never intended education to change the social system. The two-track system became firmly established, with elementary schools for 90 percent of the people and secondary education for the upper class 10 percent elite. The basic curriculum in the nineteenth century was shaped by religion and nationalism, designed to produce obedient, humble subjects. Instruction came to emphasize discipline, the authority of the teacher, and the authority of the textbook. The German universities were able to maintain some degree of autonomy, and became models for graduate and professional schools everywhere, primarily in the training of the research specialist.

Throughout the nineteenth century, attempts to liberalize German education alternated with attempts by religious leaders and the king to maintain the schools for their own purposes. They considered instruction in theory and methodology of education dangerous, and moved to limit instruction to safe subjects. There was no university instruction for elementary school teachers.

Any innovations in the German educational system were, like other efforts towards modernization, part of the conservative changes passed down from the government, and not a revolution initiated by the lower classes to reform society and take over political power. A powerful bureaucracy was created, based on loyalty to the king and devotion to performance of the duties of office. The military became a means of keeping the landed aristocracy in line by providing them with an outlet for expressing their feelings of class superiority. It also provided the middle classes with the law and order necessary for expanded industrialization and commerce. German education stressed managerial and administrative skills, the scientific and technological, and the practical and professional. Vocational and continuation schools became popular as a means of training skilled workers for industry. Technical schools, which soon acquired university level status, were created for advanced study of the sciences, mathematics, medicine, engineering, economics, commerce and public administration. But the educational system, with its emphasis on pure knowledge and its application of science to technology, did nothing to counteract the established imperial order and nothing to establish some democratic forms. The educational effort was paternal and cautious. It did not seek to make students critical and independent, but to make them orderly, vocationally efficient, satisfied with conditions of life, and submissive to the authorities.

German schools became highly differentiated and specialized. The classical "gymnasium" was the prestige secondary school and the route to the bureaucracy, the army, public office, church and university. New types of secondary schools arose: the "realgymnasium," where some Latin was taught but more time given to science and modern languages, and the "oberrealschule," considered to be very radical, which eliminated classical study and shaped its curriculum around the sciences, mathematics, modern languages and social studies. A child's place in life was decided at the age of ten, when he was channeled to one or the other of these schools. Until the 1930s, the German universities were regarded as providing the highest levels of teaching and research and were thus the best in the world. Our own university system is adapted from the German model. The ideal of research became a basic ingredient in modern higher education, under the German example of specialization and "Wissenschaft."

> The very notion of "Wissenschaft" had overtones of meaning utterly missing in its English counterpart, "science." The German term signified a dedicated, sanctified pursuit. It signified not merely the goal of rational understanding, but the goal of self-fulfillment; not merely the study of the exact sciences, but of everything taught by the university; not the study of things for their immediate utilities, but the morally imperative study of things for themselves and for their ultimate meanings.[60]

The Enlightenment in Germany during the nineteenth century produced a prestigious and influential group of philosophers whose thinking came to inspire the rest of the Western world. They sought a basic compromise once again between reason and religion. Following Rousseau rather than Voltaire, the German intellectuals recognized the appeal of religion to the emotions in man and supported religion as an aid to moral development. Although writers such as Schiller and Goethe accepted religion as morality, they resented it as a rigid

60. Butts, *Education of the West*, p. 388.

system of dogmas based upon sin, punishment and repression. Goethe acknowledged that the ultimate nature of reality was beyond human comprehension, but he recommended ignoring the unknowable and concentrating on the perceived world.

> I willingly concede that it is not nature in itself that we perceive, but that nature is comprehended by us merely according to certain forms and faculties of our mind . . . But the adjustment of our organic natures to the outer world indicates a determination from without, a relation toward things. Many people resist acknowledging reality, only because they would collapse if they accepted it.[61]

In his *Faust* he wrote:

> I've now alas! Philosophy,
> Med'cine and Jurisprudence too,
> And to my cost Theology,
> With ardent labour studied through.
> And here I stand, with all my lore,
> Poor fool, no wiser than before.
> Master, ay doctor styl'd, indeed,
> Already these ten years I lead,
> Up, down, across, and to and fro,
> My pupils by the nose, and learn,
> That we in truth can nothing know![62]

In Goethe's interpretation of nature and the meaning of life lies the beginning of a philosophy of pragmatism. "That alone is true which is fruitful," and "we find truth in action rather than in thought."[63]

Immanuel Kant wrote no treatise specifically on education, but influenced that institution primarily through the effect of his thoughts on later educational philosophers, regarding the ways in which man comes to know. His *Critique of Pure Reason* attempted to study the origin, operation and limits of reason. The external world existed, but in its ultimate reality was unknowable. We cannot prove by reason that the soul is immortal, that the will is free, or that God exists. But neither can we by pure reason disprove these beliefs. There is something within us which is deeper than reason, our consciousness, which is not content to think of the world as a senseless sequence of evolution and dissolution without moral significance. In seeking to justify religious beliefs, Kant said that they provided men with some guidance in the interpretation of phenomena, as well as sanity and peace. He argued that such belief was indispensable to morality and to prevent existence from becoming a meaningless absurdity.

> If moral character and social order are not to depend entirely on fear of the law, we must support religious belief, if only as a regulative principle; we

61. Johann Wolfgang Goethe, in Durant, *Rousseau and Revolution,* p. 618.
62. Johann Wolfgang Goethe, *Faust,* trans. by Swanwick, (New York: Thomas Y. Crowell & Co., 1882), p. 33.
63. Durant, *Rousseau and Revolution,* p. 618.

must act *as if* we knew that there is a God, that our souls are immortal, that our wills are free.[64]

Kant's *Critique* supported and undermined both theologians and agnostics. God became a useful fiction developed by the human mind. Because of his attacks on organized religion, Kant was ordered to cease writing or be imprisoned. Kant's philosophy was, in effect, an attempt to reconcile idealism (thought) with materialism (being).

Kant accepted the idea of growth as the unfolding of human nature, as a process, but maintained that the process could not be left to nature alone. Without the guidance of skilled teachers, the child would drift into lawlessness. Man's innate moral good must be developed by moral instruction and strict discipline, stressing the concept of duty. Kant felt that once the principles governing human nature were discovered, rules could be derived which would make the cultivation of character and intellect more certain.

The theories of Georg Hegel, which contradicted those of Kant and stated that all things *could* be known through reason, set the stage for later philosophical thinking of the nineteenth century. Hegel suggested that ultimate reality lay in the Absolute Idea, or the dialectical process. The world was in constant motion, change, transformation, development. Out of conflict, higher forms emerge, the process being repeated until it terminates in the Absolute Idea. All of reality is thus ultimately knowable, through thought and reason. Hegel's theories served as a catalyst for intellectual thought, arousing reactions of antagonism in some and spurring others on to rearrange and extend his theories in new perspectives. Hegelian philosophy greatly influenced the thinking of Karl Marx, Auguste Comte, Sören Kierkegaard and John Stuart Mill. Educational theorists were in turn influenced by the general philosophical discussions of the time. The most important alternative theory to the musings of Kant, Hegel and other German pilosophers was the system of thought developed by Karl Marx. While earlier philosophers conceived of human activity in the realm of abstract categories, pure spirit, pure thought, or essences as things in themselves, Marx placed his analysis of phenomena directly within the social structure, and sought to understand social institutions and interaction from a historical and materialist base. The term "materialist" was for Marx an expression of the material conditions of life, the economic and social relations of production, the fundamental and primary conditions of human existence seen as a process of economic and social development. Marx made no mention of forces other than man, whose destiny was based in the socio-economic conditions which existed at a given time and which underwent changes over time. In opposition to Hegelian thought, Marx posited that "it is not the consciousness of men (thought processes or ideas) which determines their being, but on the contrary, their social being which determines their consciousness."[65] Knowledge was the result of practice within a particular mode of production, the organization of relationships linking human labor to the natural environment. The goal of human development was the same for Marx as for the earlier humanists, from Erasmus to Goethe. However,

---

64. Immanuel Kant, *Critique of Pure Reason* in Durant, *Rousseau and Revolution,* p. 539.
65. Karl Marx, quoted in T. B. Bottomore, *Karl Marx: Selected Writings,* (New York: McGraw-Hill, 1956), p. 24.

The humanists of earlier centuries, whether within or outside the Church, believed that man could be transformed by the power of religious teaching and education alone; in addition some believed that political changes would be required, particularly the substitution of democracy for the feudal and absolutist state. Marx, on the other hand, was convinced that no amount of education can help realize the ideals of humanism unless the *practice* of life is changed in such a way that it is conducive to the development of the full individuality of man. The conditions for such development were seen by Marx in the system of socialism, in which the freely cooperating citizens would direct a planned and rational economic system, the aim of which was not profit but use. Such a system would form the material basis for personal freedom and independence, but it would not be a system in which maximal and ever-increasing consumption would be the aim.[66]

As for the Hegelian dialectic, or struggle of opposites, Marx demystified this concept by placing it too within the social realm, as analogous to the conflict between the classes. Marx saw society in terms of dialectical movement, conflict, power, change—in opposition to the earlier Platonic philosophy, which thought of society as an abstract system whose parts were functional for its maintenance. In educational theory and practice, however, both in Europe and later in the United States, Marxist alternatives were ignored, and educational discussion and methodology remained centered around the point of view of those who gained and held the reigns of power, the bourgeoisie. Educational philosophy focused on idealism and abstractions, isolated from the realities of historical and material conditions.

Following Heinrich Pestalozzi, the most significant German theorists who dealt directly with education were Johann Herbart and Friedrich Froebel. Herbart built upon the work of Pestalozzi, approaching education as a science. The ultimate goal for Herbart, too, was ethics and morality. One of his more lasting contributions to educational theory was the concept of interest as an inner power of the mind which a teacher might manipulate in order to control the experiences of the child. Herbart agreed with Locke that at birth the child's mind was a blank slate. Herbart's theory of learning implied that the pupil had no innate abilities to be fostered by a teacher. The teacher's task was first to decide what must be taught and learned in order to produce the "moral man." Then the teacher had to consult the findings of psychology in order to learn how best to manipulate these ideas and set the mental processes working with the greatest speed and efficiency. Schools had to deal with a mass of "presentations" coming from a child's contact with nature and society which had been accumulated since he was born. Education would determine which further "presentations" the mind would receive. There were three stages of instruction: presentational, analytical and synthetic. These instructional steps were determined not by the character of the material, but by the way in which the human mind works. The function of instruction was to furnish the mind with ideas, establish their proper relationships, and then connect them with good will and sympathy leading to moral action. Herbart's "science" of education required the development of an educational psychology for his methodology, and he helped to transform psychology into a science in its own right. His attempts to apply mathematics to

66. Ibid, XIV.

psychology led to the development of experimental, associational and physio-logical psychology, turning psychology from a metaphysical into an empirical enterprise.

Friedrich Froebel also provided the practical application of the theories of Pestalozzi. Where Herbart was analytical and objective, Froebel was expressive and subjective, and saw education as an art. Whereas Herbart emphasized the teaching process and perfecting instructional techniques, Froebel emphasized the interests, experiences and activities of the child. Like Rousseau, Froebel saw man as a human plant to be nurtured towards self-awareness. His predomi-nant interest was in preschool education, and he established the first Kindergar-ten. He placed greater stress on instruction to build up habits, skills and powers than on building up knowledge. The child was to learn by doing. Emphasis was placed on creativity and its relation to self-realization. Children were seen as creative rather than receptive creatures, and all educational work was to be based upon this natural tendency of children to express themselves in action. The ac-tivities within the school were to be directly related to life and were to follow a generic order of development unfolding from the child's basic nature. Froebel emphasized language and drawing in the kindergarten, and recognized the value of play and self-motivated activity.

The theories of Froebel, Herbart and Pestalozzi contain the major elements of the forms which the educational application of the schemes of Rousseau actu-ally took. Concern with instruction and methodology, concern that the school should be related to real life, the ideology that the child might discover his own individuality in school, concern with cooperation leading to morality and citizen-ship, stress on activity rather than passivity, emphasis on interest and self-moti-vation—all of these are part of the eclectic shape of today's educational system. Thus were the theories of Rousseau channeled but corrupted, for education was seen as an indispensable aid to nature, to guide it to "higher" ends than might be reached were it left unaided. Ends held by the teacher were much superior to any which nature or the child might hold. Nature was good, but just not good enough. Development had to be "produced," not merely allowed to happen, and the unchecked individualism of Rousseau was thus contained by social for-ces. As Herbart put it, it was "mere folly to leave man to nature." [67] As Pest-alozzi put it, "Here you must not trust nature; you must do all in your power to supply the place of her guidance by the wisdom of experience." [68] The impo-sition within the structure of teacher-direction and given, approved ends to be attained did not allow for individuals to develop in a variety of directions which may not have fitted in with the ultimate plans. The outlook of Pestalozzi and his followers became part of a psychological perspective on education, which took precedence, and which centered around the importance of instructional method in accordance with psychical properties and developmental processes of the individual. The psychological view was fused with a social view, that of ed-ucation as the means for perpetuating and bettering society. The production of functioning individuals within the social system, in order to secure its continuity, was seen as a major task of the schools. It was an attempt to harmonize individ-

67. Johann Herbart, *Science of Education,* in Curtis and Boultwood, *A Short History of Educational Ideas,* p. 362.
68. Ibid., p. 339.

uality with social needs. However, the two views, education as spontaneous, natural individual growth, and education as controlled preparation for citizenship, are antagonistic ideologies which apparently cannot be achieved at the same time by the same institution.

THE UNITED STATES AND THE TWENTIETH CENTURY

The educational systems of Europe were transported to the New World in the eighteenth century by the colonists. This transplantation gradually modified itself to the needs and circumstances of the new environment. However, the institutional base, conception and ideologies which were fundamental to European systems of education accompanied the travelers, and thus, the educational system in the United States became a further variant of earlier systems rather than a completely new institution. The same issues persisted: the problem of the relationship between the state's need for educated and functioning citizens and an individual-centered pedagogy; the problem of what the curriculm and instructional methodology should consist of; and a continuing conflict regarding the place of religious and secular values in the schools. Education remained, as it does to this day, an adjunct to national power.

Education during the colonial period consisted of almost every type of school which had previously existed: parochial, missionary, private, neighborhood, town, and district elementary schools; medieval, humanistic (classical) and realist secondary schools; schools and apprenticeships for vocational preparation; and some colleges and universities. To maintain these institutions, various kinds of administrative devices were employed, along with various forms of financial support and ways of securing public interest. After the revolutionary war and with the establishment of a federal government, education was used to promote national unity and citizenship. The Northwest Ordinance of 1787 included a charter for public education: "Religion, morality and knowledge being necessary for good government and the happiness of mankind, schools and the means of education shall be encouraged." [69] Advocated by Benjamin Franklin, John Adams, Thomas Jefferson, James Madison and various other early political figures, schooling came to be seen as a necessary tool for creating an intelligent populace to maintain a democratic form of government.

> If a nation expects to be ignorant and free, in a state of civilization, it expects what never was and never will be.
>
> Thomas Jefferson
>
> A people who mean to be their own Governors must arm themselves with the power which knowledge gives.
>
> James Madison
>
> The whole people must take upon themselves the education of the whole people and must be willing to bear the expense of it.
>
> John Adams[70]

69. H. G. Good, *A History of Western Education* (New York: The MacMillan Company, 1950), p. 402.
70. Butts, *Education of the West,* p. 407.

Educational needs became even greater with the rise of industry, the growth of cities, the influx of immigrants, and the move westward. Universal public education gradually gained favor, under the leadership and prodding of such individuals as Horace Mann and Henry Barnard, who believed that "The more schoolhouses we build, the fewer jails we shall need."[71] Education was to be a tool for developing the vast resources of the country, which could only be accomplished by trained men. Ideally, free public education was to be the great equalizer, a mechanism for cultural assimilation and selection of the meritorious. In actuality, education was the mechanism for maintaining the position of those who had already achieved wealth and power and for creating an industrial force willing to work for them. Educational ideology was the antidote for emerging socialist thought which questioned the validity of very few Americans owning most of the wealth of the country. Education became an instrument for reinforcing class distinctions. If one failed to succeed, it was not the fault of society, but of the individual, who could be cited as lacking intelligence, aptitude, aspiration, motivation, persistence, and other such virtues determined by the powerful and elite.

Emphasis in the early schools focused on society's expectations of achievement on the part of the products of its educational system. The ideals of achievement were summed up in the selections of the McGuffey's graded readers, published in the 1830s: ". . . industry, sobriety, thrift, propriety, modesty, punctuality, conformity—these were the essential virtues, and those who practiced them were sure of success . . . a job, a farm, money in hand or in the bank. Failure was, just as clearly, the consequence of laziness or self-indulgence, and deserved, therefore, little sympathy."[72] An American textbook, "First Lessons in Political Economy," by the Reverend John McVickar, Professor at Columbia College, pointed out:

> If he has good health and is industrious, even the poorest boy in our country has something to trade upon; and if he be besides well-educated and have skill in any kind of work, and add to this, moral habits and religious principles, so that his employers may trust him and place confidence in him, he may then be said to set out in life with a handsome capital, and certainly has as good a chance of becoming independent and respectable, and perhaps *rich*, as any man in the country. "Every man is the maker of his own fortune." All depends upon setting out on the right principles, and they are these:
> 1. Be Industrious—time and skill are your capital.
> 2. Be Saving—whatever it be, live within your income.
> 3. Be Prudent—buy not what you can do without.
> 4. Be Resolute—let your economy be always of today, not tomorrow.
> 5. Be Contented and Thankful—a cheerful spirit makes labor light, and sleep sweet, and all around *happy*, all of which is much better than being *only rich*."[73]

Until the end of the nineteenth century, as in Europe, American schools gave little attention to learner-centered educational theories, and even when they began to incorporate these ideas, the issues which the socialists had raised

71. Horace Mann, quoted in Good, *A History of Western Education*, p. 415.
72. Butts, *Education of the West*, p. 426.
73. Ibid., p. 427.

were ignored in educational thinking. Education was seen in isolation from its larger economic and political context. Educators concentrated on pedagogy. The influence of Pestalozzi and his disciples was felt primarily in the principles that the teacher should understand and gain the affection of the child, and that instruction should be in concrete and objective terms so that the child would recognize what he was being asked to learn. The grading of schools was instituted and the system of an eight-year elementary school leading to a four-year free public high school was also beginning to take form. By the end of the nineteenth century, the ends of the ladder, kindergarten and state universities for liberal and professional higher education and land-grant colleges for agriculture, engineering and the newer professions and vocations, completed the system. Compulsory attendance in publicly supported schools became law.

European education developed into two-track systems, but the American system came to consist of a single track or ladder. However, it can be pointed out that the European system was an overtly dualistic system, while the American system was and is covertly dualistic. Financial, regional, racial, class and other subcultural variations have produced de facto differential education for the wealthy and the poor.

The philosophical school of thought recognized as "distinctly American" is that known as pragmatism, brought to world attention by William James. Pragmatism was a rejection of the philosophical view of the universe as static, complete, permanent, logical and orderly, waiting to be discovered by men. The pragmatists saw life as a process, and embraced a doctrine of free will and individual effort. James emphasized the utilitarian aspects of reality. The meaning of a thing lay only in its practical consequences for an individual or a group, if one or the other alternative was true. The following illustrations from James's writing indicates the basic precepts of a pragmatic philosophy, as he recalls an experience he had while on a camping trip with friends.

What Pragmatism Means

Some years ago, being with a camping party in the mountains, I returned from a solitary ramble to find every one engaged in a ferocious, metaphysical dispute. The *corpus* of the dispute was a squirrel—a live squirrel supposed to be clinging to one side of a tree trunk; while over against the tree's opposite side a human being was imagined to stand. This human witness tries to get sight of the squirrel by moving rapidly round the tree, but no matter how fast he goes, the squirrel moves as fast in the opposite direction, and always keeps the tree between himself and the man, so that never a glimpse of him is caught. The resultant metaphysical problem now is this: *Does the man go round the squirrel or not?* He goes round the tree, sure enough, and the squirrel is on the tree; but does he go round the squirrel? In the unlimited leisure of the wilderness, discussions had been worn threadbare. Everyone had taken sides, and was obstinate; and the numbers on both sides were even. Each side, when I appeared therefore appealed to me to make it a majority. Mindful of the scholastic adage that whenever you meet a contradiction you must make a distinction, I immediately sought and found one, as follows: "Which party is right," I said, "depends on what you *practically mean* by 'going round' the squirrel. If you mean passing from the north of him to the east, then to the south, then to the west, and then to the north of him again, obviously the man does go around him, for he occupies these successive positions. But if on the contrary you mean being first in front of him, then on the right of him, then behind him, then on his left, and finally in front again, it is quite as obvious that the man fails to go round him, for by the compensating movements the squirrel makes, he keeps his belly turned towards the man all the time, and his back turned away. Make the distinction, and there is no occasion for any further dispute. You are both right and both wrong according as you conceive the verb 'to go round' in one practical fashion or the other."

Although one or two of the hotter disputants called my speech a shuffling evasion, saying they wanted no quibbling or scholastic hair-splitting, but meant just plain honest English "round," the majority seemed to think that the distinction had assuaged the dispute.

I tell this trivial anecdote because it is a peculiarly simple example of what I wish now to speak of as *the pragmatic method.* The pragmatic method is primarily a method of settling metaphysical disputes that otherwise might be interminable. Is the world one or many?—fated or free?—material or spiritual?—here are notions either of which may or may not hold good of the world; and disputes over such notions are unending. The pragmatic method in such cases is to try to interpret each notion by tracing its respective practical consequences. What difference would it practically make to any one if this notion rather than that notion were true? If no practical difference whatever can be traced, then the alternatives mean practically the same thing, and all dispute is idle. Whenever a dispute is serious, we ought to be able to show some practical difference that must follow from one side or the other's being right.[74]

There is no truth, for what is true depends upon the perspective (time, place, circumstances, and material conditions), from which an object or event is viewed. And yet they theorized in idealistic and ahistorical vacuums. The pragmatists have been characterized as relativists, in the tradition of Heracleitus, Protagoras and Rousseau. The pragmatic method of problem-solving is the inductive method of Francis Bacon. The pragmatic movement grew from the conviction that there was a strong relationship between thinking and doing, but that doing and being came from thinking. The most important effect of pragmatism upon educational theory was the institutionalization of child-study (from Pestalozzi) and the furthering of the belief that education could be a science, involving it in a close relationship with psychology (from Herbart). William James saw education as "the organization of acquired habits of conduct and tendencies to behavior."[75] The teacher's task was to supervise the acquiring process. James advised teachers to "begin with the child's interest, and starting with objects that are related to the interest, move into the unfamiliar at a rate that will allow the child to assimilate all that the teacher wants him to learn . . . your pupils, whatever else they are, are at any rate little pieces of associating machinery."[76]

John Dewey applied the principles of pragmatism to educational theory with his philosophy known as "instrumentalism." This became the cornerstone for the later "progressive" education movement. The "instrumental" theory of truth was that all knowledge is personal and is made by each individual for

74. William James, *Pragmatism,* in James Jarrett, *Philosophy for the Study of Education* (Boston: Houghton Mifflin Company, 1969), p. 380.
75. William James, quoted in Carlton Bowyer, *Philosophical Perspectives for Education* (Chicago, Ill.: Scott, Foresman and Company, 1970), p. 279.
76. Ibid., p. 280.

himself for the purpose of adapting himself to new situations. There can be no absolute truth because the meaning of a concept depends on its relationship to the individual. The process of thought was most important, for through inquiry, the adjustment between the person and his environment is brought about. The beliefs, thoughts and efforts which may constitute a person's inquiry are not true or false, they are satisfactory or unsatisfactory. What is satisfactory at one point in time may be unsatisfactory at another. The pragmatists' concern for the consequences of a belief led philosopher Bertrand Russell to comment as follows.

> Generalizing, we may say that Dr. Dewey, like everyone else, divides beliefs into two classes, of which one is good and the other bad. He holds, however, that a belief may be good at one time and bad at another. A belief about some event in the past is to be classified as "good" or "bad," not according to whether the event really took place, but according to the future effects of the belief. The results are curious. Suppose somebody says to me: "Did you have coffee with your breakfast this morning?" If I am an ordinary person, I shall try to remember. But if I am a disciple of Dr. Dewey I shall say: "Wait a while; I must try two experiments before I can tell you." I shall, then, first make myself believe that I had coffee, and observe the consequences, if any; I shall then make myself believe that I did not have coffee, and again observe the consequences, if any. I shall then compare the two sets of consequences, to see which I found the more satisfactory. If there is a balance on one side I shall decide for that answer. If there is not, I shall have to confess that I cannot answer the question.
>
> But this is not the end of our trouble. How am I to know the consequences of believing that I had coffee for breakfast? If I say "the consequences are such-and-such," this in turn will have to be tested by its consequences before I can know whether what I have said was a "good" or a "bad" statement. And even if this difficulty were overcome, how am I to judge which set of consequences is the more satisfactory? One decision as to whether I had coffee may fill me with contentment, the other with determination to further the war effort. Each of these may be considered good, but until I have decided which is better I cannot tell whether I had coffee for breakfast.[77]

Dewey was influenced by the developing science of psychology, primarily a functional psychology based on learning through natural instincts as experiences are accumulated. He felt that the task of the teacher was to guide the young through the complex experiences of life and "produce" a group of young people able to cope with future conditions of life. Dewey saw the school as a testing place for new ideas. Ideally, his view of education was "child-centered" as opposed to those who were "subject-matter" centered, seeing the curriculum as one to be drawn from the fund of past human experience, interpreted by the teacher and suited to the needs of different groups. (In effect, however, Dewey's view was teacher-centered, for the teacher had certain goals and things which she wanted the child to learn.) Dewey felt that the growth of the individual through his present experiences was most important, for the future was unknown.

77. Bertrand Russell, *A History of Western Philosophy,* in *Bertrand Russell's Best,* ed. R. Egner (New York: The New American Library, Inc., 1958), p. 78. Reprinted by permission of George Allen and Unwin Ltd.

With the advent of democracy and modern industrial conditions, it is impossible to foretell definitely just what civilization will be twenty years from now. Hence it is impossible to prepare the child for any precise set of conditions. To prepare him for the future life means to give him command of himself; it means so to train him that he will have the full and ready use of all his capacities.[78]

The "growth" of an individual was defined as the development of his self-awareness and the realization of his individual capacities, but always within the societal context, for "all activity takes place in a medium, in a situation, and with reference to its conditions." However, Dewey's "society" was always an abstract entity, which consisted of abstract subjects. The conditions of existence were seen as given, rather than as the result of historical processes and socio-economic relationships.

Society had undergone a radical change under the impact of industrialization and urbanization. Traditional agrarian life, wherein each family educated its children to share in meaningful activity and acquire the cultural tradition, no longer existed. Since society had undergone a transformation, education, too, would have to change. The schools would have to take on all of the educational functions previously performed by the family or neighborhood.

Dewey saw the school as a form of community life, a miniature society, which functioned to transmit the cultural heritage and develop the child's abilities to social ends. Learning would take place through directed living, for a democratic system depended on individuals with a concern for society at large and habits of thought which would maintain the orderly reconstruction of society. The human contacts of everyday life would provide unlimited dynamic learning situations. The school would be an agency for resolving social and intellectual conflicts, much in the Hegelian tradition. Dewey's conception of democracy and education is expressed in the following statement.

The devotion of democracy to education is a familiar fact. The superficial explanation is that a government resting upon popular suffrage cannot be successful unless those who elect and who obey their governors are educated. Since a democratic society repudiates the principle of external authority, it must find a substitute in voluntary disposition and interest; these can be created only by education. But there is a deeper explanation. A democracy is more than a form of government; it is primarily a mode of associated living, of conjoint communicated experience. The extension in space of the number of individuals who participate in an interest so that each has to refer his own action to that of others, and to consider the action of others to give point and direction to his own, is equivalent to the breaking down of those barriers of class, race, and national territory which kept men from perceiving the full import of their activity. . . . A society which is mobile, which is full of channels for the distribution of a change occurring anywhere, must see to it that its members are educated to personal initiative and adaptability. Otherwise, they will be overwhelmed by the changes in which they are caught and whose significance or connections they do not perceive.[79]

---

78. John Dewey, quoted in Bowyer, *Philosophical Perspectives for Education,* p. 292.
79. John Dewey, *Democracy and Education,* in Lawrence Cremin, *The Transformation of the School* (New York: Alfred A. Knopf, 1961), pp. 121-22.

In 1896, Dewey established an experimental laboratory school at the University of Chicago. It was based upon the principle that the school should be a community and that learning should be an active and cooperative process involving investigation, construction and artistic creation. This laboratory school became the impetus for what came to be known as "progressive" education. In an account of this University Elementary School, Dewey spoke of his debt to Froebel.

> One of the traditions of the school is the story of a visitor who, in its early days, called to see the kindergarten. On being told that the school had not as yet established one, she asked if there were not singing, drawing, manual training, plays and dramatizations, and attention to the children's social relations. When her questions were answered in the affirmative she remarked both triumphantly and indignantly that that was what she understood by a kindergarten, and she did not know what was meant by saying that the school had no kindergarten. The remark was perhaps justified in spirit, if not in letter. At all events, it suggests that in a certain sense the school endeavors throughout its whole course—now including children between four and thirteen—to carry into effect certain principles which Froebel was perhaps the first consciously to set forth. Speaking still in general, these principles are:
>
> 1. That the primary business of the school is to train children in cooperative and mutually helpful living.
> 2. That the primary root of all educative activity is in the instructive, impulsive attitudes and activities of the child, and not in the presentation and appreciation of external material. . . .
> 3. That these individual tendencies and activities are organized and directed through the uses made of them in keeping up the cooperative living already spoken of, taking advantage of them to reproduce on the child's plane the typical doings and occupation of the larger, maturer society into which he is finally to go forth; and that it is through production and creative use that valuable knowledge is secured and clinched.
>
> So far as these statements correctly represent Froebel's educational philosophy, the school should be regarded as its exponent.[80]

The curriculum of the experimental school centered around the occupations of common life and industry, beginning at age six with home activities and simple industrial arts. Similar schools were established elsewhere, most of which were also based on the doctrines of Froebel. However, some were radical alternatives, more closely resembling the plans of Rousseau: no tables, desks, chairs, no reading or writing before the age of nine, no recitation or assigned lessons, no examinations, grades, failures or promotions. These schools were based on the idea that children should be outdoors in the midst of nature, but to "study" it was taboo. Interest, spontaneity, and joy, but not knowledge or skills, were the goals. (Much like the well-known Summerhill.) The radical schemes came to be considered left-wing progressive education. Such schools were disliked by more conservative progressives, who saw these efforts as a threat to social cohesion, continuity, and the need to supply society with its next generation of workers.

In 1919, the Progressive Education Association was organized by a group of educators and citizens for the purpose of uniting those who were experiment-

80. John Dewey, *The Elementary School Record,* in Good, *A History of Western Education,* p. 486.

ing with the "new" schools and wanted to secure greater public interest and support. The first president was Charles Eliot, President of Harvard University, who was succeeded in office by John Dewey. Just as Horace Mann, fifty years earlier, had viewed the schools as an instrument of public policy (". . . the true business of the schoolroom connects itself, and becomes identical, with the great interests of society"),[81] the "progressive" educators saw education politically, as a means of social reform, as a constructive agency for improving society, as the center of the struggle for a better life. However, it was assumed that all humanity was struggling for a better life, and not conceived of in terms of a class struggle. Progressive education was part of the broader program for social and political reform known as the Progressive Movement. (However, it has become apparent today that education is more an agency reflecting and affected by external social change than it is an agency effecting social change.)

The new ideology disseminated was "liberalism" based on the understanding that the state must intervene into economic life in order to reconcile and regulate social and industrial conflicts. Older ideologies, formulated during the period of early competitive capitalism, based on the separation of the state from economic affairs, were superceded, as capitalism became dominated by large corporations and monopolies. Educators in schools and universities went to work producing new ideological categories and understandings necessary to support and justify the new socio-economic relationships. Thus we can understand the shift in emphasis from the highly individualistic ethic of Rousseau when competitive capitalism was coming into being, to the social ethic of Dewey as corporate capitalism began to emerge and take precedence. The ideal educated man was no longer the cultured intellect and philosopher, the literary orator skilled in debate and civic affairs, the ascetic monk, the chivalrous gentleman, or the individualistic, "inner-directed" moral man of business. He had become the efficient and scientific corporate manager, in the service of furthering the interests of monopoly capitalism.

After World War II, the Progressive Education movement came under heavy attack by more conservative elements who disputed the emphasis on individual interest and development in favor of emphasis on the demands of society and the problems and needs of American life (not recognizing that in many respects Progressive Education did just that). It seemed to them that the lack of discipline, "inability" of many children to read and write effectively, and deficiencies in mathematics and science were all caused by "progressive" schools, which they felt had avoided intellectual training. Certainly, one of the things which the pragmatists advocated and included in their educational program was intellectual understanding, emerging directly from problematical situations. Inquiry and the processes and organization of thought were major factors in their theoretical scheme. They did not want to avoid "intellectual training," but saw it as an outcome of interaction and experience rather than as things to be practiced and memorized. But the progressive educational movement was in effect a movement of moderates. The real radicals of the time, the socialists, did not see change and reform through education. They directed their efforts towards structural change in a drive for political power. Education was a marginal issue to economic inequality. The progressives were moralists, basically conservative,

---

81. Horace Mann, in *Prologue to Teaching,* ed. by M. Smiley, and J. Diekhoff (New York: Oxford University Press, 1959), p. 284.

who themselves defended and believed much of the rhetoric and ideology of the society they wished to change. John Dewey himself had at an early point repudiated the experiments of some "progressive" educators:

> Some teachers seem to be afraid even to make suggestions to the members of a group as to what they should do. I have heard of cases in which children are surrounded with objects and materials and then left entirely to themselves, the teacher being loath to suggest even what might be done with the materials lest freedom be infringed upon. Why, then, supply materials?[82]

Today's educational system is the legatee of its personal history. Earlier ideology, structures, organization, values and conflicts have left their imprint, not easily swept away. The Western tradition is to seek absolutes, permanence, order and equilibrium, to believe in eternal verities and in its own social constructions. With an idealist rather than materialist viewpoint, it is immensely difficult to come to terms with eradicating basic structural forms, and much more acceptable to attempt modification within the structure. Without a new base, however, a superstructure cannot hope to look any different from the old, well-known, well-mythologized and safe forms. And even if the substructure changes, there is still the danger of reproducing the same kind of society if the same institutions are recreated which deal with people in the same ways. If no alternatives are developed to schools (as well as hospitals, prisons, police . . .) as we know them, and they continue to operate bureaucratically in the service of the industrial order, then, too, very little will change.

Although American education has been eulogized as a new and innovative program, it is obvious that it is not. It has avoided dealing with the real issues of inequality and poverty. It has taken nowhere near the radical shape suggested by Rousseau. It does not embody the value system which comprised schools such as that run by Tolstoy in Russia from 1859 to 1910. Dewey's experimental school was basically a conservative societal institution. Tolstoy's experimental school at Yasnaya Polyana *was* a radical departure from other public school forms. The element of coercion was missing, as a self-defeating and aggressive act. Tolstoy's answer to the question, "Who has the right to educate?," was "Nobody."

> There are no rights of education. I do not acknowledge such, nor have they ever been by the young generation under education . . . The right to educate is not yet vested in anybody.[83]

Tolstoy felt that adults must never be permitted to impose their conception of correct instruction on the young, for that would be to cheat them of their self-development and to grant unlimited political power to shape and exploit. State-controlled education would inevitably be bound to society's priorities and not to the child's. He has been proven correct.

---

82. John Dewey, *Experience and Education,* in Curtis and Boultwood *A Short History of Educational Ideas,* p. 477.
83. Leo Tolstoy, quoted in Theodore Roszak, "Tolstoy: 'The School was all my Life,' " *Times, London,* Educational Supplement, March 24, 1972, p. 16.

Schools which are established from above and by force are not a shepherd for the flock, but a flock for the shepherd.[84]

"Progressive" educators never questioned the conventional wisdom, but took its values as their own: *mass* production, intellectual *force,* brain *power.* Can we picture a public school with a sign saying, "Enter and Leave Freely" such as Tolstoy had over the door of his school? Can we say, as he did, "The pupils bring nothing to the classroom but their impressionable natures and their conviction that school will be as much fun today as it was yesterday.'"?

Educational thinkers have argued the relative merits of a classical or scientific, liberal or practical, individual, or social education. They have avoided consideration of the historical process and material conditions from which educational institutions and their ideology sprang. They have avoided the fact that structures and conceptualizations of education have been class based, and that theorists from Plato on dealt only with elites and not with the people. Knowledge has been seen as either rational or experiential, but few went beyond this conceptualization to the point of seeing the relationship between them. Knowledge does originate in the material conditions of existence, in experience, from perception of the external world. What is perceived passes through the mind and develops into rational knowledge. But it does not end here, for it is by directing rational knowledge back to social practice, that knowing and doing become united. It is through practice that Socrates' original puzzle about the nature of knowledge is solved. It has always been to the advantage of the ruling classes to perpetuate idealism, whereby thought is seen as the catalyst for social action. History is taught as a series of accidental events and "great men" with "great thoughts" as the origin of social change. A dialectical materialist view would inevitably direct attention to real social relationships and lead to the power to change the conditions of existence.

Everett Reimer has provided a concise statement as to why schools have grown so fast. "To the masses, and their leaders, they have held out unprecedented hope of social justice. To the elite they have been an unparalleled instrument, appearing to give what they do not, while convincing all that they get what they deserve. Only the great religions provide an analogy, with their promise of universal brotherhood always betrayed."[85]

FURTHER REFERENCES

The Greek and Roman Periods

1. *The Collected Dialogues of Plato,* ed. by E. Hamilton and H. Cairns, (New York: Bollingen Foundation, 1961).
2. *The Dialogues of Plato,* (4 vols.) trans. by B. Jouelet, (New York: Random House, 1937) particularly:
    Republic
    Meno
    Phaedo
    Lesser Hippias

84. Ibid.
85. Everett Reimer, *School is Dead* (New York: Doubleday & Co., Inc., 1971), p. 41.

Gorgias
Protagoras
Theaetetus
Parmenides
Sophist
Greater Hippias
Euthydemus
Laws

3. James Drever, *Greek Education*, (London: Cambridge University Press, 1912).
4. *Aristotle on Education*, trans. and ed., by John Burnet, (London: Cambridge University Press, 1913).
5. *The Basic Works of Aristotle*, ed. by Richard McKeon, (New York: Random House, 1941). particularly:
Ethics
Politics
Organon

6. Plutarch, *Life of Lycurgus* (early Greek education), in *Plutarch's Lives*, trans. by B. Perrin, (New York: G. P. Putnam's Sons, 1914), p. 205-303.
7. Isocrates, *Against the Sophists* and *Antidosis*, in James Jarrett, *The Educational Theories of the Sophists*, (New York: Teachers College Press, Columbia University, 1969).
8. J. F. Dobson, *Our Debt to Greece and Rome*, (New York: Cooper Square Publishing Co., Inc., 1963).
9. Werner Jaeger, *Paideia: The Ideals of Greek Culture*, (New York: Oxford University Press, 1965).
10. F. Beck, *Greek Education*, (London: Methuen and Company, Ltd., 1964).
11. H. I. Marrou, *A History of Education in Antiquity*, trans. by G. Lamb, (New York: The New American Library, 1956).
12. Aristophanes, *The Clouds*, trans. by H. Easterling and P. Easterling, (Great Britain: Cambridge: W. Heffer and Sons, Ltd., 1961).
13. F. Engels, *The Origin of the Family, Private Property, and the State*, (New York: International Publishers, 1941).

chapter three

THE SCHOOL AND POLITICS

THE SCHOOLS AS POLITICAL INDOCTRINATORS

Americans have always been ambivalent about their politics and their schools. On the one hand we have from our earliest days pursued and supported a system of universal, utilitarian education and considered it important enough to make it compulsory. On the other hand we feared—and continue to fear—what might happen should this system become "political." So while we expected the schools to serve purposes which clearly were political we rarely acknowledged the political aspects and consequences of schooling. We have not given attention to the political consequences of schools in part because the ends or goals of schooling were linked to the partisan nature or biases of the society. A current examination of these relationships, or even earlier evaluations done by outsiders to the political system would uncover and reveal the political purposes and consequences to education. It is the intent of this chapter to explicitly show how America's schools have, from their origin, served political purposes.

The theorized relationship between schools and politics was and is similar to that of schools and religion. The schools, we insist, must be free of religion. Religious sectarianism, like political partisanship, was so feared that a whole ideology and set of myths about the religious and political neutrality of our schools grew up along with our school system. To this day most Americans would agree with the view that our schools are and ought to be politically neutral without recognizing that political neutrality is a biased position. We have thus always in our public educational system been biased against socialism. We maintain this illusion of neutrality by allowing into our schools only the lowest common denominator of religious and political belief, like Christmas celebrations and flag salutes. What we failed to see—and continue to fail to see—is that for significant numbers of Americans this was not religious and political neutrality. Those who have sought to include atheism and communism in public school curriculums, for example, have discovered how nonneutral the schools were in such matters. And this is also the case in higher education. When attempts were made in 1970 to turn universities and colleges away from complicity in the war in Vietnam, this was viewed as "politicization" by those who were opposed to such attempts, and it was said that "the university should never be politicized." The last report of the Carnegie Commission on Higher Education reiterated the position that higher education should remain apolitical. But what is called "politicization" is, at least from another perspective, not a case of bringing politics into the university as it is an attempt to change the politics that already operate and are there (the Carnegie Commission, notwithstanding). How and why do we come to this conclusion? The articles and our analysis will allow you, the reader, to examine our arguments.

But first, let us return to our origins. Henry Parkinson points out in *The Imperfect Panacea; America's Faith in Education*[1] that the first purpose of education in the society arose from the fear that the "civilization" brought to these shores would succumb to the barbarism of the New World unless the young were educated. This, for us, was a political judgment designed to emasculate the native populations. With the winning of our independence, education took on still another political function, that of serving the needs of the newly formed republican government. Benjamin Rush argued for a general and uniform system of education to make the masses more homogeneous and thereby fit for a uniform and peaceable government. Noah Webster wanted to inculcate patriotism through common textbooks and uniform spelling and pronunciation. "Our political harmony," he said, "is therefore concerned in a uniformity of language"[2] Webster would have us begin with infants: "Let their first word be 'Washington,' " he urged. Another founding father, Thomas Jefferson, spoke for many of the founding fathers when he referred to that "natural aristocracy of talents and virtues" which would emerge from our schools, "twenty of the best geniuses . . . raked from the rubbish annually."[3]

Though the American Constitution is silent about education, this may testify more to the fear of a strong central government in control of a national system of education than to the idea that education should not have political purposes. The fathers did not include education when they wrote the first amendment to the Constitution to protect speech and religion. And education in this country, despite the myth of neutrality, continued to serve the political interests of various groups. Implicit in the politics of the founding fathers, and the politics of other groups down to this day, has been the view that schooling was to perform the selecting and sorting function that would determine who would govern. Even when Jacksonians in the early 1800s, and later egalitarians, turned against this elitism and proclaimed the schools as equalizers rather than selectors, the schools were being put to work for political purposes.

We have never had a national system of education like France and Germany. When we borrowed ideas like compulsory schooling and the Normal Schools from them, our fears of a national system of education controlled by the federal government were expressed. Thus our laws concerning education today are state laws. Our schools are organized around school districts rather than political structures like wards. Our school board elections are city- or district-wide in the hope that they will also be politically nonpartisan. But if we do not have a national system of education *de jure,* the readings in this chapter will document that we have such a system *de facto.* No matter where in this country a youngster goes to school, he can move into a school in any other part of the country with little or no need to convert or translate his earlier schooling into his later schooling.[4]

It has been in the interests of professional educators to keep politics out of the schools so that they could carry out their educational policies free from the intrusions and demands of outsiders. Part of what it means to be a professional

1. Henry Parkinson, *The Imperfect Panacea; America's Faith in Education* (New York: Random House, 1968).

2. Noah Webster, *Dissertations on the English Language* (Boston: 1789).

3. Thomas Jefferson, *Bill for the More General Diffusion of Knowledge.* Presented to Virginia Assembly, 1779.

4. Parkinson, *"Imperfect Panacea,"* Chapter III.

is to have control over your profession and its clients. Among other things, freedom from this brand of politics has meant that our schools have been unresponsive to important groups in the community who have not shared the dominant values of those who ran the schools. And professional educators continue to insist that they are and ought be be apolitical, so much so that it is difficult to get them to see the implicit or unconscious political orientations in their curricular, pedagogical and organizational decisions. Their expertise and teaching, they claim, are value-free, politically neutral and technically competent skills which are utilized in selecting the best means for ends or goals that are laid out for the schools by others. The technicians choose the means, the citizens choose the ends. Education and politics are thus supposedly split. But by what criteria do the experts make their choices? It is our contention that the decisions made by those who control and operate our schools, administrators and teachers alike, regardless of what else they may be, are political. In what way they are political and to what political purposes our schools have been and continue to be directed, is the theme of this chapter.

But the title of this chapter, and a major theme throughout this book, makes a larger claim about politics and the schools. We not only claim that the schools are political in a deep and meaningful and perhaps unavoidable way, we also claim they are politically indoctrinating. In later chapters we try to document a similar claim about schools and values and the economy.

The question of what indoctrination is, and how it differs from education, is a topic for an entire book by itself. Indoctrination is often distinguished from conditioning because of the presence of ideas, ideologies or doctrines in the former. It is often likened to conditioning in its outcome: an unthinking, more or less automatic response. But some people argue that since a principal and necessary function of the school is socialization, conditioning and indoctrination are unavoidable; that the whole business of growing up and becoming acculturated in a society involves processes of conditioning and indoctrination. If this is true, then we should acknowledge it and be aware of it when we do it. The claim we make here, that the schools act as political indoctrinators, contrasts with three opposing views: 1) that schools are politically (and religiously and economically) neutral; 2) that schools do not reflect and inculcate the values and politics of special interest groups; and 3) that school board members, administrators and teachers are and should be apolitical. But it is you, the reader, who must decide in the end whether this is valid.

When selecting writings on education and politics, it is often difficult to draw a line between politics in education and economics. There will be times in the readings that follow when economics and other realms of value are being discussed as much as politics. In a sense, every human action is political in that it represents some allocation and use of power. But in our school system there is an exercise of power that is based on presuppositions, assumptions and explicit views about race, social class, social ends, and the kind of human being that is to enter and leave the school system. Inevitably, such views reach into almost all dimensions of human experience. Thus we begin with this chapter on schools and politics, and move on in later chapters to schools and the economy and schools and values, all of which are very much interrelated.

To find out how the school system really works is to uncover the politics inside the system, and the connections between that and the politics of the larger society. We begin our readings with an article by Joel Spring.

Joel Spring is numbered among a contemporary group of historians who are known for their revisions of past histories of our society. Often these "revisionist" historians not only view their subjects differently from earlier historians, but also less favorably, and sometimes quite critically. In almost every reading in this book, the reader is asked to take a second look at what may be a familiar aspect of American education. But more than that, he is being told that things in American education are not the way they may seem; and that they may not be as worthy of our choice (or sufferance) as we have been led (or indoctrinated) to believe. In reading the following article by Spring you will probably review your own experiences with student government, football contests and chess clubs.

The first half of Joel Spring's article, "Education And The Rise of the Corporate State," will be found in chapter 4. Education and the Economy (such are the consequences of our arbitrary separation of politics and economics!). In that article Spring deals with the rise of vocational guidance in public education as a response to the needs of large-scale corporate capitalism.

But who would think that such things as student newspapers, clubs, athletics and assemblies have larger connections and purposes beyond the school? In the following article Spring sees the development of these "organization techniques" as an important step toward the public school becoming "the central instrument for corporate control and the primary instrument for socialization in the United States."

EDUCATION AND THE RISE OF THE CORPORATE STATE (PART 1)

Joel Spring

Specialization in the schools threatened the goal of socialization. In providing different courses of studies the school created the same problem of social isolation that had faced other institutions. Educators believed that like the factory worker on the assembly line, the student in separate courses of study was losing a sense of unity and interdependence. A differentiated course of study directly threatened the whole goal of training a self-sacrificing and cooperative individual. Specialization in the schools could not be abandoned for socialization because they were both integral to the development of corporate capitalist society. Educating an individual to do his part for society required both forms of education.

Joel Spring, "Education And The Rise of the Corporate State," *Socialist Revolution,* Vol. 2, No. 2, March-April, 1972.

The ideal was an educational institution that balanced the two. For this reason suggestions for separate trade schools were usually rejected. The generally accepted solution to the problem was the comprehensive high school.

The basic principle of the comprehensive high school was the maintenance of a differentiated program within one institution with unity and socialization being achieved through extra-curricular activities. Since unity was not inherent within a differentiated educational program, it had to be imposed. The methods paralleled markedly the factory activities of clubs, outings, assemblies, magazines, and the other means used to create a corporate spirit in industrial firms. In the American high school it was clubs, athletics, assemblies, student government, and school newspapers. These, in fact, became the symbols of what a high school in the United States was all about.

The classic statement for the comprehensive high school was the Cardinal Principles of Secondary Education issued by a special committee of the National Education Association in 1918. The report, which was widely distributed and discussed, was written during a period when demands were being made for highly differentiated curricula. These demands ranged from provisions for separate trade schools to differentiation based on social and economic backgrounds. For instance, Charles Hughes Johnston of the University of Illinois argued that differentiated curriculums should be planned and based "upon social rather than necessarily vague psychological considerations."[1] When the Cardinal Principles report appeared, it was criticized by educators like David Snedden for proposing a school that could give only an imitation of vocational education. Snedden believed that real vocational training required specialized schools.[2] Considering the strong pressures for differentiation the report was, as Edward Krug has shown, rather mild and compromising.[3]

The report proposed that "differentiation should be, in the broad sense of the term, vocational . . . such as agricultural, business, clerical, industrial, fine-arts, and household-arts curriculums." It supported the idea of a junior high school but limited its functions to exploration of vocations and pre-vocational guidance. This meant that systematic and organized differentiation of students would not take place in the junior high school but would be postponed to the senior high school. The junior high was defined as a period of exploration while the senior high was one of training. Both the junior and senior high school were to be comprehensive, the junior high because it would aid "the pupil through a wide variety of contacts and experiences to obtain a basis for intelligent choice of his educational and vocational career," and the senior high because it would assure the choice of a curriculum best suited to the student's needs. The committee reasoned that specialized schools might introduce distracting influences such as location, athletic teams, and friends. These influences, rather than consideration of curriculum, might determine which school the student attended. The comprehensive high school, in the opinion of the committee, would eliminate these factors from consideration. Everyone would attend the same school regardless of his or her course of study.

The comprehensive high school also allowed for what the committee called the two components of democracy, specialization and unification. The report stated, "The purpose of democracy is so to organize society that each member may develop his personality primarily through activities designed for the well-being of his fellow members and of society as a whole." The specialized and differentiated curriculum of the school was to train the individual to perform some task that would be for the good of society. This definition of democracy and education was similar to the one that permeated the vocational guidance and junior high school movements. Democracy was viewed primarily as a means of social organization that allowed everyone to do what he or she was best able to do. Education was to fit the individual for a social position that would allow for his or her maximum contribution to society. In bold type the report stated, "education in a democracy . . . should develop in each individual the knowledge, interests, ideals, habits, and powers whereby he will find his place and use that place to shape both himself and society toward ever nobler ends."

Unification was that part of the ideal of democracy that brought people together and gave them "common ideas, common ideals, and common modes of thought, feeling, and action that made for cooperation, social cohesion, and social solidarity." The report argued that in other countries social solidarity was achieved through common heredity, a centralized government, and an established religion. In America with its diverse religious and ethnic backgrounds "the members of different vocations often fail to recognize the interests that they have in common with others." The one major agency in the United States to achieve this purpose, using an argument that went back to the founding fathers, was the school. In terms of the then current concepts of childhood the unifying force had to be the secondary school and not the elementary school, for only during adolescence did the social instincts begin forming. The report stated, "In this process the secondary school with its immature pupils cannot alone develop the common knowledge, common ideals, and common interests essential to American democracy."

To compensate for the separation caused by the different courses of study the committee proposed three means of creating a sense of unity. The first, which was directed toward the immigrant, emphasized the need for teaching the "mother tongue" and social studies. The other two were organizational techniques. One was "social mingling of pupils through the organization and administration of the school." The last was directly related to this proposal. The committee called for the "participation of pupils in common activities . . . such as athletic games, social activities, and the government of the school."[4]

The two organization techniques of creating social solidarity became popularly known in the 1920s as extracurricular activities. The various phases of school life that came under this term were in existence long before the issuance of the Cardinal Principles Report. But during the 1920s extracurricular activities developed into an educational cult. Courses in organizing extracurricular activities were offered in teacher training institutions. Textbooks and books of readings on the topic were published. In 1926 the *Twenty-Fifth Yearbook of the National Society for the Study of Education* was devoted to the topic of education. Like any educational movement certain figures emerged as leaders. One in particular was Elbert K. Fretwell of Teachers College. Fretwell organized summer courses at Teachers College for school administrators so that they could perfect their extracurricular programs. Between 1923 and 1926 Fretwell flooded the *Teachers College Record* with long bibliographies of material on assemblies, clubs, student government, and home rooms.[5]

One of the sources of inspiration for the extra-curricular activity movement was Dewey's idea that the school should be a community with a real social life. Through the years this idea was reduced to mean that the school had to provide a social activities program. One aspect of this idea was that the child would learn by doing. In other words the social activities program provided concrete situations for the development of social skills and a working set of ethics. Underlying this argument was the assumption responcible for the education of the whole child. This idea had been developed by American schools at the turn of the century with the extension of school activities. In an often-quoted speech , William Bishop Owen, dean of the University of Chicago High School, in 1906 expressed this sentiment before a group of high school and academy administrators. He told them, "It is the whole pupil who goes to school. This can be made true only on condition that the school cares for all the interests which govern the child's life while he is under the influence of the school." One interesting and extremely perceptive parallel made by Owen was between the school and the factory. Owen stated, "Gradually it is coming to be recognized that it is the whole man who goes into the factory in the morning and out in the evening; that merely to serve the selfish purpose of the employer it is necessary to provide for the whole man, physical, intellectual, moral, aesthetic, and social."[6]

The basic goal of learning by doing and educating the whole person was to produce a unified, cooperative populace with common ideals and goals. As in the Cardinal Principles, the concept of democracy included personal sacrifice to the state, and social organization that facilitated the most efficient use of individual talents. Educators put forward this concept of democracy to justify activities ranging from student government to assemblies. Student government, for instance, was to be the new training ground for democracy. "Through school assemblies and organizations," in the words of the Cardinal Principles report, students would "acquire common ideas."[7]

Extracurricular activities were also intended to turn the school into an "ideal" democratic community. One very popular statement of the period was that the school must become a democracy. The Cardinal Principles report went one step further and stated flatly that "the comprehensive school is the prototype of a democracy in which various groups must have a degree of self-consciousness as groups and yet be federated into a larger whole through the recognition of common interests and ideals."[8] Statements of this nature reveal the emergence among educators of a pluralist concept of democracy.

The central extracurricular activity was student government, which resulted from activities of urban reform groups in New York City in the 1890s. At the time student government was hailed as the salvation of the democratic process. The early leader of the movement, Wilson Gill, a Columbus, Ohio, industrialist, decided sometime between 1874 and 1889 to devote his life to reforming municipal politics. The decision was occasioned by the defeat of a proposal to introduce industrial training into the schools. Gill claimed that the "project was defeated at the polls by the vote of ignorant men, under the direction of ward heelers."[9] His early educational attempts to correct this evil were devoted to forming the Sons of the American Revolution in 1889. Gill claimed the distinction of writing the constitutions for both the Sons and Daughters of the American Revolution.[10] These two groups were formed originally as Americanization organizations that attempted to solve the problem of the "ward-heeler" through patriotic education. One of the stated objectives of the Sons of the American Revolution was the encouragement of "such education as will best prepare our children for the discharge of the important duties of American citizenship."[11]

The meaning of this objective was made clear at the Second Annual Congress of the SAR in 1891 when the president of the New York chapter stated to the gathered delegates, "We want the immigrant of yesterday to say with the descendant of the soldier of the Revolution, 'My pride and inspiration . . . is George Washington.' "[12] Along with his work in these patriotic groups Gill campaigned for other educational programs. In 1888 he claimed that he secured for educational purposes an "act of Congress requiring that the name of the person represented by a portrait on paper money and other government documents shall be printed with the portrait." Later this included postage stamps.[13]

Gill became a crusader for student government when he abandoned the Sons and Daughters of the Revolution in 1891 because they did not spend enough time working with the public schools. He then formed the American Patriotic League, whose membership included such illustrious people as Rutherford B. Hayes, William McKinley, Theodore Roosevelt, Josiah Strong, Leonard Wood, and John R. Commons. As president of the organization, Gill developed an extensive Americanization program in the pages of *Our Country* magazine. During its early years the magazine was designed to provide the reader with a three-year course in American citizenship. Later this goal was abandoned and the last issue was devoted exclusively to student government. The educational program of *Our Country* reflected the close relationship that existed between student government and proposals to reform the administration of urban government. The original plan called for a chapter of a serialized book to appear each month. Topics ranged from citizenship and history to economics and sociology. The articles were not purely flag-waving statements. Frederic W. Speirs, professor of political economy at the Drexel Institute, wrote a series of articles that were highly critical of laissez-faire capitalism. He criticized the system for creating unemployment, turning the worker into an automation, and exploiting child labor. Articles by John R. Commons called for reform of municipal government and the institution of proportional representation. Other reform statements included: Edward Everett Hale on the need for an international supreme court; Theodore Roosevelt on civil service reform; and one whole issue devoted to George E. Waring and his war against dirty streets in New York and Cuba.

After several years as editor, Wilson Gill decided that printed arguments were not effective, and that this was why the public schools were not turning out good citizens. There was a great deal of talk about democracy within school walls but little practice. Writing in the last issue of *Our Country* in 1899 Gill asked, "What is the matter with Americans whose brains have been cultivated?" His reply to his own question was, "As long as one remains in school, he is subject to school government, which is monarchical in form and effect."[14] He decided the real answer to the problem of the "ward-heeler" and corrupt urban politics was training youth in democracy, later called a democratic apprenticeship program. Gill began his campaign for student self-government in 1897 when, after several visits to the classroom of a school teacher member of the American Patriotic League, he organized a "school city." The classroom was located in a school described as so unruly that Police Commissioner Theodore Roosevelt had to detail policemen to patrol it. The teacher of the classroom later stated in a book published in 1907 that while he had developed a system of self-government in his classroom it did not take on a meaningful form until Gill became interested.[15]

Gill's original plan called for the organization of the school along the lines of a model city government. Later plans were based on federal and state governments. Under the school city plan the pupils were granted a charter which gave them the power to elect a mayor, a president of the council, a city council, and clerk of the court. The mayor was to appoint commissioners of health, public works, and police. Gill wanted this plan to serve as a training ground for a democracy organized along reformist lines. In the final issue of *Our Country* he suggested that the initiative, the referendum, proportional representation, and primary reform be included in all school city organizations. He also suggested that those establishing a school city consult John R. Commons' *Proportional Representation*.[16] The New York reform mayor, William Strong, took an interest in the school city project and appointed Alfred Beebe, the assistant director of Diagnosis Bacteriological Laboratory of the New York City Board of Health, to develop a school city health department. The plan called for providing information on health practices and student supervision and control of the sanitary conditions of the schools. Each school city was to appoint food sanitary inspectors who would check on the health and cleanliness of fellow students, and the condition and quality of all food entering the schools.[17]

When *Our Country* ceased publication, Gill began to devote his time to school city projects. At the turn of the century he was assigned by the War Department to organize the schools of Cuba into School Republics. After his Cuban adventure he was hired by the Department of Interior as a commissioner-at-large to organize student governments in Indian schools.[18] By then, the idea of student government as a cure for the ills of democracy was spreading through other sources.

The real beginning of an organized national campaign for student government was in 1904 when Richard Welling, another New York reformer, organized the National Self-Government Committee, which eventually included Nicholas Murray Butler, John Dewey, Alfred Smith, William McAndrew, Harry Emerson Fosdick, and Stephen S. Wise as members. The organization campaigned vigorously into the 1940s for student government not only in the public schools but also in colleges and universities. Welling's reasons for founding the Committee were similar to the ones that had led Gill to devote his life to organizing student governments. Up to 1903 Welling had spent many frustrating years working for urban reform in New York City. After graduating in 1880 from Harvard where he had been a classmate of Theodore Roosevelt and had taught Sunday school with him, Welling studied for a law degree and returned to New York. In 1882, along with Roosevelt and others, Welling formed the City Reform Club to wage war against Tammany Hall. Welling devoted a great deal of his time both to the Reform Club and to the political campaigns of reform mayors like William Strong and Seth Low. In 1894 he participated in the founding of the National Municipal League. Through much of his work he shared common political interests and contacts with Gill and the American Patriotic League.[19]

Welling claimed that in 1903 he finally realized that education was the key to civic reform. He lamented that merely "telling the voters that their taxes were too high did not lead to action at the polls."[20] The best method, he decided, was to give the citizen an opportunity to exercise his political rights intelligently. Having reached this conclusion he contacted Charles Eliot, the president of the National Education Association, and asked permission to address its annual convention. Before the convention he made a ringing appeal for instituting student government to help cure corrupt government. He told the gathered educators, "The New generation must be imbued with a new spirit of civic patriotism . . . you must teach the machinery of the government by means of some form of applied civics. . . ." The applied civics he suggested was the "noble effort making in the School City . . . designed to bring about the very contact [between student and government] by converting the school itself into a municipality."[21]

Student governments were instituted by American schools at a phenomenal rate. By 1950 there were very few junior or senior high schools that did not have some form of governmental organization. Through the course of this development there was never any serious suggestion that the students be given real power. The purpose was to provide applied civics, not to run the school. A typical attitude was that of William McAndrew, one-time superintendent of the New York Public Schools. Writing in 1897 on a proposed student government plan he stated, "I believe the plan of delegating any of the executive powers of that officer (principal) to those so irresponsible as students must be would be unwise."[22] There was general agreement, at least among educators during this period, that, as one writer stated, "any plan that gives pupils full control of the government of a school, a school city, or a school democracy, without the advice and aid of teachers will necessarily lead to an ignominious failure.[23]

Student government, therefore, never provided training in the exercise of power but only in the mechanical details. During student elections the pupil learned the details and methods of political conventions, campaigning, balloting, and vote counting. In student councils and courts he learned procedures and parliamentary rules. But through the course of all these activities the student never had real contact with power. All student government activities took place in a vacuum without real issues. The student learned the procedural methods of democracy, not that democracy involved a constant struggle. Some educators actually worried that if the students found out they had no real power, the whole student government as "the government of pupils by pupils under the invisible direction of teachers." He then went on to wonder if student government didn't often fail "because the teachers are not skillful enough to keep their direction of affairs invisible."[24]

Student government was also attractive because it provided what was often called a democratic form of discipline. This meant control through assent to school rules or judgments made by peers. But since the pupil never had power over school policies, this made his assent a subtle form of control. One article on student government stated in 1918 that the basic reason for the reform was discipline. The article described discipline as "a matter of internal adjustment, spontaneous internal control and [it] does not properly get its significance when it is obtained by means of force or by any suppressive measures."[25] This argument was fairly typical. Meaningful discipline was impossible if it had to be achieved by force. But if it were accepted by agreement to school rules, then it became internalized and, consequently, more effective.

If student government was to be the heart of the typical democratic community, meaning the American high school, it suggests that democracy was primarily thought of as a way to maintain social order. New York urban reformers were interested in making adjustments in the political system so that it included but limited the participation of lower social and economic groups. Their major concern was that these groups learn to operate the machinery of government properly. The same thing was true of student government. The pupils were given the chance to concur in the executive power of the school. Democracy in this sense was a positive way of maintaining allegiance to the laws. This concept was similar to the one suggested by vocational guidance and the junior high school. The image of democracy in those cases was of a social system that allowed everyone the opportunity to exercise his or her best talents for the good of predetermined interests.

The other organizations that made up the extracurricular activities program had less colorful histories and were not as directly related to political reform. But they were also justified by their contribution to unifying the student body and preparing students for a cooperative democracy. In most plans the student government or student association was to work in cooperation with the faculty in the administration of programs. The other activities usually included a student newspaper, clubs, athletics, and assemblies. One principal stated in 1917 that an organized program of this nature would "assist in making the spirit of democracy, 'all for each and each for all,' pervade the entire school."[26]

The school newspaper served a variety of functions. It was a means of teaching English, and it taught team work and created a spirit of unity in the school. Publication of a paper, like any school club activity, was viewed as a means of teaching people how to work effectively in groups, while it also helped establish a sense of unity by providing each student with news about school events. One supporter of school newspapers wrote, "The Press Association . . . meets an important demand. It is a unifying organization, and is therefore a wholesome factor if properly directed. Its purpose is to edit a school paper through which a school spirit may be awakened and nourished."[27] The school newspaper through a combination of gossip and pep talk was to fill a role very much like that of factory publications. As one writer stated, "The school paper . . . will create school patriotism and an increased interest in all the activities of the school, educational, athletic, and social."[28]

Clubs in school programs eventually ranged over a variety of areas including academic, athletic, and vocational. Most high schools and academies in the nineteenth century had some social organizations, usually literary and debating societies. The difference at the early part of the twentieth century was not only the broad range of clubs that developed, but also the fact that they were justified in terms of teaching people how to cooperate. This argument was usually made in terms of the developing interests and social instincts of adolescents. After 1918 the Cardinal Principles report the argument that clubs served as preparation for worthy use of leisure frequently appeared. This was similar to the factory owner's concern about his workers' activities after working hours. One of the suggested purposes of education in the Cardinal Principles Report had been the development of meaningful leisure time activities. It was stated in one article on club activities in 1921, "A school's service to the future makers of America does not end with preparing them for working hours which occupy only a third of the day. It must also provide specifically for the worthy use of leisure."[29] The school's responsibility was to turn out not only efficient workers and citizens but also people who played efficiently and cooperatively.

It was argued that athletics could contribute to training for a democratic community in two ways. As part of a general health program athletics would assure individual physical efficiency. The Cardinal Principles, in language that suggested that the individual was a unit of national resource, stressed health. Good physical training would produce a strong and well functioning laborer. In addition athletics taught the student how to cooperate and work with a team. This was one reason for the rapid growth of football in the public schools. As a team game it represented all the coordination and cooperation needed in a corporate organization. A principal of a Seattle, Washington, high school told the National Education Association in 1915, "In the boy's mind, the football team is not only an aggregation of individuals organized to play, but a social instrument with common needs, working along common lines, and embodying a common purpose."[30] A great deal of the time in these programs was directed to some form of competitive group game. The reason for this, as given by two members of the Skokie, Illinois, school system, was "to stimulate greater interest on the part of the children and at the same time to stress the elements of cooperation or team work essential for successful competitive activity."[31]

The spirit generated by athletic games between schools united the student body, and also served the public relations function of uniting the entire community around the school. Every boy's dad would be willing to attend the local football game. The problem as seen by one professor of physical education in 1914 was maintaining a balance between the individual efficiency aspect of athletics and the entertainment of spectators. He felt very confident at this time that the balance could be achieved. Fifteen years ago, he wrote, high school athletes were "accustomed to playing a game unrestrained and without cooperation. All sorts of tricks were used to win a contest, such as importing players, choosing biased officials, and resorting to unfair tactics in general. . . . Today our athletes from the high schools represent the best sportsmanship possible."[32] The success of football in uniting the community and generating spirit eventually unbalanced these two purposes. In 1923 a high school teacher complained, "Rivalry between certain schools has become so intense that players meet in a spirit of hatred and revenge, and special policing is necessary to guard against outbreaks of hostility between rival rooters." The writer reported that athletics had become so important that in Ohio many athletes "attend school periodically and only for special sports. They are never ineligible, and some of them have been in high school athletics for a long term of years, shifting from school to school in order to conform to the letter of the rules."[33]

The extracurricular activity that educators hoped would fully unify the school was the assembly. Historically the assembly probably descended from the school chapel. By the 1920s it was hailed as the great unifier of the comprehensive junior and senior high schools. One of the early assembly programs, and one often discussed by educators, was the morning exercise of the Francis W. Parker School in Chicago. During the 1880s Francis Parker would begin each day at the Cook County Normal School by reading to the entire faculty and staff a short passage from the Bible or a book of poetry. Following a reading a group of students would present an exercise that was usually the outcome of classwork. The practice was continued after the Francis Parker School was founded in 1901.[34] The 1913 yearbook of the school referred to the exercise as "the family altar of the school to which each brings his offerings—the fruits of his observations and studies."[35] Before the family altar the child had the opportunity to become aware of the entire school. Through the years the important function of the exercise was to counteract the feelings of separation caused by the students being divided into different grades. The 1913 yearbook of the school stated, "The morning exercise is one means of impressing upon the children the unity of the whole school and of counteracting some of the undesirable effects of the separation into grades."[36]

This was precisely why the Cardinal Principles report recommended the assembly as a school unifier. The common argument given was that as the school was divided into separate grades, courses of studies, and ability groups, some means had to be found to create a corporate feeling. An associate superintendent of schools of Pittsburgh, Pennsylvania, wrote in 1925, "Students are divided into classes according to their academic advancement, further divided by their curricula. . . . Blocking the pathway to unity is an almost infinite variety of individual differences. The assembly is the one agency at hand capable of checking these tendencies."[37] Assemblies were one of the great events in the American junior and senior high schools. Books, programs, and articles flooded the educational market with suggestions for auditorium exercises. Band concerts, vocational talks, drama productions, class projects, and patriotic celebrations all became part of the public school paraphernalia. The theme of the assembly unifying a diverse educational program continued through the 1920s. At the very opening of the book *Assemblies for Junior and Senior High Schools,* published in 1929, was stated, "Junior and senior high schools daily accept the challenge to prepare students for life in a democracy. . . . Specialized organization and complex activities necessitate unification through athletics, the school newspaper, and the assembly. Because of its frequency and provision for universal participation, the assembly may be considered the foremost integrating factor."[38]

The desire to create a cooperative and unified spirit reflected the nature of the democratic aspirations of educators. The *Fifth Yearbook of the Department of Secondary-School Principals* in 1921 stated with regard to extracurricular activities, "What we wish the state to be the school must be. The character of our citizens is determined by the character of our pupils and the development of character in this broadest sense must be the goal of education."[39] The socialized classroom and school activities had as their goal a cooperative man willing to subordinate his individual interests to the "larger" social goals.

The parallels that can be drawn between the socialization programs of the factory and school are not accidental. Both faced the problem of internal fragmentation and both required cooperative individuals organized around predetermined goals.

CONCLUSION

The shaping of the schools to meet the needs of the corporate state did not go unnoticed by some radicals and union leaders. These few realized that the school system was becoming the central institution for control by corporate capitalism, and in the early 1900s attempted to establish an alternative system of schools to break the hold of the public schools over the minds of the working class. One example was the Modern School in Stelton, New Jersey, founded in 1915, which produced its own educational journal and attempted to be a model for other radical groups. Harry Kelly, chairman of the first board of management of the school, wrote ten years after its establishment, "We saw then and we see now, that the public school system is a powerful instrument for the perpetuation of the present social order. . . . The child . . . is trained to submit to authority, to do the will of others as a matter of course, with the result that habits of mind are formed which in adult life are all to the advantage of the ruling class."[40] Similarly, in the labor movement there was an attempt to establish a system of labor schools and colleges. George Counts, writing in the 1920s, stated with regard to the development of labor schools, "Labor today stands with Thomas Hodgskin when in the early part of the Nineteenth century he wrote: 'It would be better for men to be deprived of education than to receive their education from their masters; for education, in that sense, is no better than the training of cattle that are broken to the yoke.' "[41]

Yet, by the middle of the twentieth century the one-sided contest had apparently ended and the public school was unchallenged as the central instrument for corporate control and the primary instrument for socialization in the United States. As Ivan Illich has suggested, the modern school is the new Church and like the Church of the Middle Ages is pervasive and dominating. In recent years this situation has again come to be challenged, mostly spontaneously and by the students in the public high schools and colleges themselves. Not surprisingly, the initial form of the challenge has been unselfconscious and entirely negative, a modern form of the Luddite movement, striking out blindly and destructively at the modern machinery of control and oppression. Although still unformed and unclear of its goals this new movement is much more widespread and organic than the early opposition to corporate control of education. Its successful development will require not only the disestablishment of the public school system as we know it, but also the construction of a humane alternative.

NOTES

1. Quoted in Edward A. Krug, *The Shaping of the American High School* (New York, 1964), p. 320.
2. Ibid., p. 397.
3. Ibid., particularly chapters 11-15.
4. *Cardinal Principles of Secondary Education,* Bureau of Education Bulletin (1918), p. 35.
5. For instance, Elbert K. Fretwell, "Extra-Curricular Activities of Secondary Schools," *Teachers College Record,* January 1923; January 1924; May 1926; June 1926; June 1927.
6. William Bishop Owen, "Social Education through the School," *School Review,* January 1907, pp. 11-26.
7. *Cardinal Principles,* p. 20.
8. Ibid., p. 20.
9. Wilson L. Gill, *A New Citizenship* (Hanover, Pa., 1913), p. 49.
10. Wilson Gill is listed as one of the twenty-one members of the first SAR convention and also as assistant-secretary. No mention is ever made of the author of the constitution. See John St. Paul, *The History of the National Society of the Sons of the American Revolution* (New Orleans, 1962), p. 12. I cannot find any mention of Wilson Gill in relation to the DAR. But inasmuch as the SAR was involved in its organization he probably was involved.
11. William S. Webb, *National Society of the Sons of the American Revolution* (New York, 1890), p. 7.
12. Chauncey M. Depew, "Oration of Chauncey M. Depew," *Proceedings of the Second Annual Congress of the Sons of the American Revolution* (New York, 1891), p. 64.
13. Wilson L. Gill, *Manual of the School Republic* (Madison, Wis., 1912), p. 7.
14. "What Is the Matter with Americans Whose Brains Have Been Cultivated?" *Our Country,* (October 1899), p. 1.

15. See Gill, *A New Citizenship*, p. 52; Bernard Cronson, *Pupil Self-Government* (New York, 1907), pp. 3-5; and "A Summer Work of the Patriotic League," *Our Country*, September 1897, p. 1.

16. Delos F. Wilcox and Wilson F. Gill, "An Outline of American Government for Use in City and Country Schools in Connection with the Gill School City and Other Organizations for Self-Government," *Our Country*, October 1899, pp. 3-109.

17. Alfred L. Beebe, "The Gill City Health Department," *Our Country*, June 1898, pp. 177-86.

18. Gill, *A New Citizenship*, pp. 198-204.

19. Richard Welling, *As the Twig is Bent* (New York, 1942).

20. Ibid., p. 91.

21. Reprinted in Richard Welling, *Self Government Miscellanies*.

22. William A. McAndrew, *School Review*, September 1897, pp. 456-60.

23. Walter I. Phillips, "Pupil Cooperation in Self-Government," *Education*, April 1902, p. 543.

24. R. R. Smith, "Three Experiments in Pupil Self-Government," *Education*, December 1916, p. 230.

25. A. O. Bowden, "Student Self-Government," *School and Society*, 17 July 1918, p. 97.

26. Edward Rynearson, "Supervised Student Activities in the School Program," *First Yearbook, National Association of Secondary School Principals (1917)*, pp. 47-50.

27. D. E. Cloyd, "Student Organizations in City High Schools," *Education*, September 1910, pp. 17-20.

28. Frank K. Phillips, "The School Paper," *Industrial Arts Magazine*, July 1917, pp. 268-71. Reprinted in Joseph Roemer and Charles F. Allen, eds., *Readings in Extra-Curricular Activities* (New York, 1929), pp. 462-67.

29. Mary A. Sheehan, "Clubs—A Regular Social Activity," *High School Journal*, October 1921, pp. 132-35. Reprinted in Roemer and Allen, p. 304.

30. V. K. Froula, "Extra-Curricular Activities: Their Relation to the Curricular Work of the School," *National Educational Association Proceedings (1915)*, pp. 738-39.

31. Harry P. Clarke and Willard Beatty, "Physical Training in the Junior High School," *School Review*, vol. 33 (1925), pp. 532-40.

32. James Naismith, "High School Athletics and Gymnastics as an Expression of the Corporate Life of the High School," in Johnston, *The Modern High School*, p. 440.

33. C. M. Howe, "The High-School Teacher and Athletics," *School Review*, December 1923, pp. 781-82.

34. "The Morning Exercise as a Socializing Influence," *Francis W. Parker School Year Book* (Chicago, 1913), pp. 7-10.

35. Ibid., p. 11.

36. Ibid., p. 11.

37. Charles R. Foster, *Extra-Curricular Activities in the High School* (Richmond, Va., 1925), pp. 108-9.

38. Eileen H. Galvin and M. Eugenia Walker, *Assemblies for Junior and Senior High Schools* (New York, 1929), p. 1.

39. Francis H. J. Paul, "The Growth of Character through Participation in Extra-Curricular Activities," *The Fifth Yearbook of the Department of Secondary School Principals* (1921), vo. 2, pp. 54-60.

40. Harry Kelly, "The Modern School in Retrospect," in *The Modern School of Stelton* (Stelton, 1925), p. 116.

41. George S. Counts, *The Social Composition of Boards of Education* (Chicago, 1927), p. 87.

Joel Spring

Continuing our claim that the decisions and actions of the people who operate and control our schools have connections with and are part of the interests of political groups in our society, Neil Postman asks us to look again at another familiar part of American education: reading. He notes that the decision, indeed our demand, that every student learn and continue to improve his or her reading, is a political demand. Postman discovers something sinister in this demand. He goes on to portray what schools might be like if we were to change our emphasis and insistence upon reading. Postman concludes his article with an age-old question for all teachers and specialists in reading. His argument is designed to convince those with a reading bias of the political bias and consequences of their emphasis.

THE POLITICS OF READING

Neil Postman

Teachers of reading comprise a most sinister political group, whose continued presence and strength are more a cause for alarm than celebration. I offer this thought as a defensible proposition, all the more worthy of consideration because so few people will take it seriously.

My argument rests on a fundamental and, I think, unassailable assumption about education: namely, that all educational practices are profoundly political in the sense that they are designed to produce one sort of human being rather than another—which is to say, an educational system always proceeds from some model of what a human being *ought* to be like. In the broadest sense, a political ideology is a conglomerate of systems for promoting certain modes of thinking and behavior. And there is no system I can think of that more directly tries to do this than the schools. There is not one thing that is done to, for, with, or against a student in school that is not rooted in a political bias, ideology, or notion. This includes everything from the arrangement of seats in a classroom, to the rituals practiced in the auditorium, to the textbooks used in lessons, to the dress required of both teachers and students, to the tests given, to the subjects that are taught, and most emphatically, to the intellectual skills that are promoted. And what is called reading, it seems to me, just about heads the list. For to teach reading, or even to promote vigorously the teaching of reading, is to take a definite political position on how people should behave and on what they ought to value. Now, teachers, I have found, respond in one of three ways to such an assertion. Some of them deny it. Some of them concede it but without guilt or defensiveness of any kind. And some of them don't know what it means. I want to address myself to the latter, because in responding to them I can include all the arguments I would use in dealing with the others.

Neil Postman, "The Politics of Reading," *Harvard Educational Review*, 40, May 1970, pp. 244-252, Copyright © 1970 by President and Fellows of Harvard College. An earlier version of this article was presented as the keynote address at the Lehigh University Reading Conference, January 24, 1970.

In asserting that the teaching of reading is essentially a political enterprise, the most obvious question I am asking is, "What is reading good for?" When I ask this question of reading teachers, I am supplied with a wide range of answers. Those who take the low ground will usually say that skill in reading is necessary in order for a youngster to do well in school. The elementary teacher is preparing the youngster for the junior high teacher, who prepares him for the senior high teacher, who, in turn, prepares him for the college teacher, and so on. Now, this answer is true but hardly satisfactory. In fact, it amounts to a description of the *rules* of the school game but says nothing about the purpose of these rules. So, when teachers are pushed a little further, they sometimes answer that the school system, at all levels, makes reading skill a precondition to success because unless one can read well, he is denied access to gainful and interesting employment as an adult. This answer raises at least a half-dozen political questions, the most interesting of which is whether or not one's childhood education ought to be concerned with one's future employment. I am aware that most people take it as axiomatic that the schooling process should prepare youth for a tranquil entry into our economy, but this is a political view that I think deserves some challenge. For instance, when one considers that the second most common cause of death among adolescents in the U.S. is suicide, or that more people are hospitalized for mental illness than all other illnesses combined, or that one out of every 22 murders in the United States is committed by a parent against his own child, or that more than half of all high school students have already taken habit-forming, hallucinogenic, or potentially addictive narcotics, or that by the end of this year, there will be more than one-million school drop-outs around, one can easily prepare a case which insists that the schooling process be designed for purposes other than vocational training. If it is legitimate at all for schools to claim a concern for the adult life of students, then why not pervasive and compulsory programs in mental health, sex, or marriage and the family? Besides, the number of jobs that require reading skill much beyond what teachers call a "fifth-grade level" is probably quite small and scarcely justifies the massive, compulsory, unrelenting reading programs that characterize most schools.

But most reading teachers would probably deny that their major purpose is to prepare students to satisfy far-off vocational requirements. Instead, they would take the high ground and insist that the basic purpose of reading instruction is to open the student's mind to the wonders and riches of the written word, to give him access to great fiction and poetry, to permit him to function as an informed citizen, to have him experience the sheer pleasure of reading. Now, this is a satisfactory answer indeed but, in my opinion, it is almost totally untrue.

And to the extent that it is true, it is true in a way quite different from anything one might expect. For instance, it is probably true that in a highly complex society, one cannot be governed unless he can read forms, regulations, notices, catalogues, road signs, and the like. Thus, some minimal reading skill is necessary if you are to be a "good citizen," but "good citizen" here means one who can follow the instructions of those who govern him. If you cannot read, you cannot be an obedient citizen. You are also a good citizen if you are an enthusiastic consumer. And so, some minimal reading competence is required if you are going to develop a keen interest in all the products that it is necessary for you to buy. If you do not read, you will be a relatively poor market. In order to be a good and loyal citizen, it is also necessary for you to believe in the myths and superstitions of your society. Therefore, a certain minimal reading skill is needed so that you can learn what these are, or have them reinforced. Imagine what would happen in a school if a Social Studies text were introduced that described the growth of American civilization as being characterized by four major developments: 1) insurrection against a legally constituted government, in order to achieve a political identity; 2) genocide against the indigenous population, in order to get land; 3) keeping human beings as slaves, in order to achieve an economic base; and 4) the importation of "coolie" labor, in order to build the railroads. Whether this view of American history is true or not is beside the point. It is at least as true or false as the conventional view *and* it would scarcely be allowed to appear unchallenged in a school-book intended for youth. What I am saying here is that an important function of the teaching of reading is to make students accessible to political and historical myth. It is entirely possible that the main reason middle-class whites are so concerned to get lower-class blacks to read is that blacks will remain relatively inaccessible to standard-brand beliefs unless and until they are minimally literate. It just may be too dangerous, politically, for any substantial minority of our population *not* to believe that our flags are sacred, our history is noble, our government is representative, our laws are just, and our institutions are viable. A reading public is a responsible public, by which is meant that it believes most or all of these superstitions, and which is probably why we still have literacy tests for voting.

One of the standard beliefs about the reading process is that it is more or less neutral. Reading, the argument goes, is just a skill. What people read is their own business, and the reading teacher merely helps to increase a student's options. If one wants to read about America, one may read DeToqueville or *The Daily News;* if one wants to read literature, one may go to Melville or Jacqueline Susann. In theory, this argument is compelling. In practice, it is pure romantic nonsense. *The New York Daily News* is the most widely read newspaper in America. Most of our students will go to the grave not having read, of their own choosing, a paragraph of DeToqueville or Thoreau or John Stuart Mill or, if you exclude the Gettysburg Address, even Abraham Lincoln. As between Jacqueline Susann and Herman Melville—well, the less said, the better. To put it bluntly, among every 100 students who learn to read, my guess is that no more than one will employ the process toward any of the lofty goals which are customarily held before us. The rest will use the process to increase their knowledge of trivia, to maintain themselves at a relatively low level of emotional maturity, and to keep themselves simplistically uninformed about the social and political turmoil around them.

Now, there are teachers who feel that, even if what I say is true, the point is nonetheless irrelevant. After all, they say, the world is not perfect. If people do not have enough time to read deeply, if people do not have sensibilities refined enough to read great literature, if people do not have interests broad enough to be stimulated by the unfamiliar, the fault is not in our symbols, but in ourselves. But there is a point of view that proposes that the "fault," in fact, *does* lie in our symbols. Marshall McLuhan is saying that each medium of communication contains a unique metaphysic—that each medium makes special kinds of claims on our senses, and therefore, on our behavior. McLuhan himself tells us that he is by no means the first person to have noticed this. Socrates took a very dim view of the written word, on the grounds that it diminishes man's capacity to memorize, and that it forces one to follow an argument rather than to participate in it. He also objected to the fact that once something has been written down, it may easily come to the attention of persons for whom it was not intended. One can well imagine what Socrates would think about wire-tapping and other electronic bugging devices. St. Ambrose, a prolific book writer and reader, once complained to St. Jerome, another prolific writer and reader, that whatever else its virtues, reading was the most anti-social behavior yet devised by man. Other people have made observations about the effects of communications media on the psychology of a culture, but it is quite remarkable how little has been said about this subject. Most criticism of print, or any other medium, has dealt with the content of the medium; and it is only in recent years that we have begun to understand that each medium, *by its very structure,* makes us do things with our bodies, our senses, and our minds that in the long run are probably more important than any other messages communicated by the medium.

Now that it is coming to an end, we are just beginning to wonder about the powerful biases forced upon us by the Age of the Printed Word. McLuhan is telling us that print is a "hot" medium, by which he means that it induces passivity and anesthetizes almost all our senses except the visual. He is also telling us that electronic media, like the LP record and television, are reordering our entire sensorium, restoring some of our sleeping senses, and, in the process, making all of us seek more active participation in life. I think McLuhan is wrong in connecting the *causes* of passivity and activity so directly to the structure of media. I find it sufficient to say that whenever a new medium—a new communications technology—enters a culture, *no matter what its structure,* it gives us a new way of experiencing the world, and consequently, releases tremendous energies and causes people to seek new ways of organizing their institutions. When Gutenberg announced that he could manufacture books, as he put it, "without the help of reed, stylus, or pen but by wondrous agreement, proportion, and harmony of punches and types," he could scarcely imagine that he was about to become the most important political and social revolutionary of the Second Milennium. And yet, that is what happened. Four hundred and fifty years ago, the printed word, far from being a medium that induced passivity, generated cataclysmic change. From the time Martin Luther posted his theses in 1517, the printing press disseminated the most controversial, inflammatory, and wrenching ideas imaginable. The Protestant Reformation would probably not have occurred if not for the printing press. The development of both capitalism and nationalism were obviously linked to the printing press. So were new literary forms, such as the novel and the essay. So were new conceptions of education, such as written examinations. And, of course, so was the concept of scientific methodology, whose ground rules were established by Descartes in his *Discourse on Reason.* Even today in recently illiterate cultures, such as Cuba, print is a medium capable of generating intense involvement, radicalism, artistic innovation, and institutional upheaval. But in those countries where the printed word has been pre-eminent for over 400 years, print retains very few of these capabilities. Print is not dead, it's just old—and old technologies do not generate new patterns of behavior. For us, print is the technology of convention. We have accommodated our sense to it. We have routinized and even ritualized our responses to it. We have devoted our institutions, which are now venerable, to its service. By maintaining the printed word as the keystone of education, we are therefore opting for political and social stasis.

It is 128 years since Professor Morse transmitted a message electronically for the first time in the history of the planet. Surely it is not too soon for educators to give serious thought to the message he sent: "What hath God wrought?" We are very far from knowing the answers to that question, but we do know that electronic media have released unprecedented energies. It's worth saying that the gurus of the peace movement—Bob Dylan, Pete Seeger, Joan Baez, Phil Ochs, for instance—were known to their constituency mostly as voices on LP records. It's worth saying that Viet Nam, being our first television war, is also the most unpopular war in our history. It's worth saying that Lyndon Johnson was the first president ever to have resigned because of a "credibility gap." It's worth saying that it is now common-place for post-TV college sophomores to usurp the authority of college presidents and for young parish priests to instruct their bishops in the ways of *both* man and God. And it's also worth saying that black people, after 350 years of bondage, want their freedom—now. Post-television blacks are indeed, our true *now* generation.

Electronic media are predictably working to unloose disruptive social and political ideas, along with new forms of sensibility and expression. Whether this is being achieved by the structure of the media, or by their content, or by some combination of both, we cannot be sure. But like Gutenberg's infernal machine of 450 years ago, the electric plug is causing all hell to break loose. Meanwhile, the schools are still pushing the old technology; and, in fact, pushing it with almost hysterical vigor. Everyone's going to learn to read, even if we have to kill them to do it. It is as if the schools were the last bastion of the old culture, and if it has to go, why let's take as many down with us as we can.

For instance, the schools are still the principal source of the idea that literacy is equated with intelligence. Why, the schools even promote the idea that *spelling* is related to intelligence! Of course, if any of this were true, reading teachers would be the smartest people around. One doesn't mean to be unkind, but if that indeed is the case, no one has noticed it. In any event, it is an outrage that children who do not read well, or at all, are treated as if they are stupid. It is also masochistic, since the number of non-readers will obviously continue to increase and, thereby, the schools will condemn themselves, by their own definition of intelligence, to an increasing number of stupid children. In this way, we will soon have remedial reading-readiness classes, along with remedial classes for those not yet ready for their remedial reading-readiness class.

The schools are also still promoting the idea that literacy is the richest source of aesthetic experience. This, in the face of the fact that kids are spending a billion dollars a year to buy LP records and see films. The schools are still promoting the idea that the main source of wisdom is to be found in libraries, from which most schools, incidentally, carefully exclude the most interesting books. The schools are still promoting the idea that the non-literate person is somehow not fully human, an idea that will surely endear us to the non-literate peoples of the world. (It is similar to the idea that salvation is obtainable only through Christianity—which is to say, it is untrue, bigoted, reactionary, and based on untenable premises, to boot.)

Worst of all, the schools are using these ideas to keep non-conforming youth —blacks, the politically disaffected, and the economically disadvantaged, among others—in their place. By taking this tack, the schools have become a major force for political conservatism at a time when everything else in the culture screams for rapid reorientation and change.

What would happen if our schools took the drastic political step of trying to make the new technology the keystone of education? The thought will seem less romatic if you remember that the start of the Third Millennium is only 28 years away. No one knows, of course, what would happen, but I'd like to make a few guesses. In the first place, the physical environment would be entirely different from what it is now. The school would look something like an electric circus—arranged to accommodate TV cameras and monitors, film projectors, computers, audio- and video-tape machines, radio, and photographic and stereophonic equipment. As he is now provided with textbooks, each student would be provided with his own still-camera, 8 mm. camera, and tape casette. The school library would contain books, of course, but at least as many films, records, video-tapes, audio-tapes, and computer programs. The major effort of the school would be to assist students in achieving what has been called "multi-media literacy." Therefore, speaking, filmmaking, picture-taking, televising, computer-programming, listening, perhaps even music playing, drawing, and dancing would be completely acceptable means of expressing intellectual interest and competence. They would certainly be given weight at least equal to reading and writing.

Since intelligence would be defined in a new way, a student's ability to create an idea would be at least as important as his ability to classify and remember the ideas of others. New evaluation procedures would come into being, and standardized tests—the final, desperate refuge of the print-bound bureaucrat—would disappear. Entirely new methods of instruction would evolve. In fact, schools might abandon the notion of teacher instruction altogether. Whatever disciplines lent themselves to packaged, lineal, and segmented presentation would be offered through a computerized and individualized program. And students could choose from a wide variety of such programs whatever they wished to learn about. This means, among other things, that teachers would have to stop acting like teachers and find something useful to do, like, for instance, helping young people to resolve some of their more wrenching emotional problems.

In fact, a school that put electric circuitry at its center would have to be prepared for some serious damage to all of its bureaucratic and hierarchical arrangements. Keep in mind that hierarchies derive their authority from the notion of unequal access to information. Those at the top have access to more information than those at the bottom. That is in fact why they are at the top and the others, at the bottom. But today those who are at the bottom of the school hierarchy, namely, the students, have access to at least as much information about most subjects as those at the top. At present, the only way those at the top can maintain control over them is by carefully discriminating against what the students know—that is, by labelling what the students know as unimportant. But suppose cinematography was made a "major" subject instead of English literature? Suppose chemotherapy was made a "major" subject? or space technology? or ecology? or mass communication? or popular music? or photography? or race relations? or urban life? Even an elementary school might then find itself in a situation where the faculty were at the bottom and its students at the top. Certainly, it would be hard to know who are the teachers and who the learners.

And then perhaps a school would become a place where *everybody,* including the adults, is trying to learn something. Such a school would obviously be problem-centered, *and* future-centered, *and* change-centered; and, as such, would be an instrument of cultural and political radicalism. In the process we might find that our youth would also learn to read without pain and with a degree of success and economy not presently known.

I want to close on this thought: teachers of reading represent an important political pressure group. They may not agree with me that they are a sinister political group. But I should think that they would want to ask at least a few questions *before* turning to consider the *techniques* of teaching reading. These questions would be: What is reading good for? What is it better or worse than? What are my motives in promoting it? And the ultimate political question of all,

"Whose side am I on?"

Neil Postman

There is another political function which schools perform, that of instilling in new members the prevailing perspectives and conceptualizations of the society. Every society has and needs its beliefs and understandings. These are not necessarily false, but they can in time become useless and false. Then myth and reality clash. Some critics say this is happening right now. One contemporary critic, Everett Reimer, argues that the myths of modern society are so outgrown that the schools are hard-pressed to bridge the gap between these old myths and the new realities.[5]

Reimer discusses four myths or ideologies that are currently being challenged by reality. The first myth is that of freedom—that all persons have certain inalienable rights, which include the right of assembly and petition for redress of grievances; the right to counsel; to not bear witness against themselves and the right to be free from unreasonable search and seizure. These rights are diminishing in capitalist and communist countries. Reimer notes that over half of the countries in the capitalist world that were democracies 20 years ago now have military regimes. In our own country Reimer says that people's rights are increasingly being reduced by police and guardsmen. He points out that rituals of democratic process in schools and society help individuals live with the discrepancy between assumptions of freedom and facts of domination. These same processes undermine the basis for the reliance which Jefferson placed upon periodic revolution.

The second myth is the myth of progress; the assumption is that our human situation is improving and will continue to improve. This is countered by the worldwide problems of water, land and air pollution, and the widening gaps between poor and rich, and between underdeveloped and industrial nations. The limits of human patience are being reached. The facts about the lack of progress are obscured by the ritual of research. New knowledge and techniques are still seen to be the answer. We avoid facing reality squarely and directly.

The myth of efficiency is probably closest to being destroyed. This says that man has solved his production problems by means of efficient organization, and that most remaining problems can be solved in a similar way. This myth ignores the dubious value of various goods sold and tasks performed in our society. This myth is maintained through unquestioned ritualized activity, or "busy work."

The fourth myth is that of equal opportunity. It ignores the fact that advancement for one is at the expense of others. It ignores the real advantages of higher social class. It makes success dependent upon personal qualities rather than on social structure. And it is maintained by ritual progression up the ladder, a few steps for everyone, to create the illusion of equal movement for all.

5. Everett Reimer, *School is Dead; Alternatives in Education* (Long Island City, N.Y.: 1972), Chapter 4.

Americans have accepted the premise that people are unequal, in talent, job, income, good looks, wit, cleverness. Yet equality is extremely powerful in the democratic rhetoric. Americans have dealt with this contradiction by choosing to pursue equality of opportunity instead. This can be understood as a common right to achieve an unequal result. In the sphere of education, investigation of the conditions for equality of opportunity have shown how strong and pervasive is the influence of social class upon individual life chances. Equality of opportunity would only become a reality in a society without classes or elites. Under such conditions, there would be no use or meaning in speaking of the need for "equality of opportunity."

We explore this issue in greater detail in Chapters 4 and 5. In concluding this chapter on the political nature of schooling, we link the ideology of equal opportunity with the method of legitimizing inequality, the IQ.

Increasing numbers of people have been pointing to IQ as an element in the "natural" inequality among people. Schools have organized a great deal of their practices, overt and covert, around the IQ, IQ tests, and what the authors of the nest reading call "the IQ ideology." The claim that high intelligence is a necessary condition for economic and other forms of success plays an important part in this "IQ ideology," which states that the poor are poor because they are intellectually incompetent. This claim also forms the basis for the ideology of the "meritocracy", which would ideally create an aristocracy of talent in opposition to an aristocracy of wealth. The hierarchy is still there, as is inequality. And studies have always shown how closely related one's destiny is with one's economic class. In the final analysis, wealth becomes the determining factor in defining and uncovering "talent," as well as intelligence.

I.Q. IN THE U.S. CLASS STRUCTURE

Samuel Bowles and Herbert Gintis

I. INTRODUCTION

The 1960s and early 1970s have witnessed a sustained political assault against economic inequality in the United States. Blacks, women, welfare recipients, and young rank-and-file workers have brought the issue of inequality into the streets, forced it onto the front pages, and thrown it into the legislature and the courts. The dominant response of the privileged has been concern, tempered by a hardy optimism that social programs could be devised to reduce inequality, alleviate social distress and bring the nation back from the brink of chaos. This optimism has been at once a reflection of and rooted in a pervasive body of liberal social thought, as codified in modern mainstream economics and sociology. At the core of this conventional wisdom in the social sciences is the conviction that in the advanced capitalist system of the United States, significant progress

Samuel Bowles and Herbert Gintis, "I.Q. in the U.S. Class Structure," *Social Policy*, Vol. 3, No. 4, 5, November/December, 1972 and January/February, 1973, pp. 1-27.

toward equality of economic opportunity can be achieved through a combination of enlightened persuasion and social reforms, particularly in the sphere of education and vocational training.

The disappointing results of the War on Poverty, the apparent lack of impact of compensatory education, and in a larger sense the persistence of poverty and racism in the United States have dented the optimism of the liberal social scientist and the liberal policy maker alike. The massive and well-documented failure of the social reformers of the 1960s invited a conservative reaction, most notably in the resurgence of the genetic interpretation of I.Q. Sensing the opportunity afforded by the liberal debacle, Arthur Jensen began his celebrated article on the heritability of I.Q. with "Compensatory education has been tried, and apparently it has failed." In the debate that has ensued, an interpretation of the role of I.Q. in the class structure has been elaborated: the poor are poor because they are intellectually incompetent; their incompetence is particularly intractable because it is rooted in the genetic structure inherited from their poor and also intellectually deficient parents.[1] An explanation of the intergenerational reproduction of the class structure is thus found in the heritability of I.Q. The idea is not new: an earlier wave of genetic interpretations of economic and ethnic inequality followed in the wake of the purportedly egalitarian but largely unsuccessful educational reforms of the Progressive Era.[2]

The revival of the debate on the genetic interpretation of economic inequality is thus firmly rooted in the fundamental social stuggles of the past decade. Yet the debate has been curiously superficial. "The most important thing. . . that we can know about a man," says Louis Wirth, "is what he takes for granted, and the most elemental and important facts about a society are those that are seldom debated and generally regarded as settled."[3] This essay questions the undisputed assumption underlying both sides of the recently revised I.Q. controversy: that I.Q. is of basic importance to economic success.

Amid a hundred-page statistical barrage relating to the genetic and environmental components of intelligence, the initiator of the most recent exchange[4] saw fit to devote only three sparse and ambiguous pages to this issue. Later advocates of the "genetic school"[5] have considered this "elemental fact," if anything, less necessary of support. Nor has their choice of battleground proved injudicious: to our knowledge not one of their environmentalist critics has taken the economic importance of I.Q. any less for granted.[6]

We shall begin this essay with a brief review of the I.Q. controversy itself, paying special attention to the social consequences of intelligence differentials among races and social classes. This review inspires one highly perplexing question: why have American social scientists so consistently refused to question the actual role of intelligence in occupational success and income determination, in spite of the fact that the empirical data necessary for such an endeavor are well known?

In the third section we shall summarize the results of several years of empirical research into the economic importance of I.Q.[7] Our findings, based for the most part on widely available published data, document the fact that I.Q. is not an important cause of economic success; nor is the inheritance of I.Q. the reason why rich kinds grow up to be rich and poor kids tend to stay poor. The intense debate on the heritability of I.Q. is thus largely irrelevant to an understanding of poverty, wealth, and inequality of opportunity in the United States.

These results give rise to a host of novel questions—novel in the sense that

they would never be asked were the importance of I.Q. "taken for granted."
We shall deal with some of these in succeeding sections of this essay. First, if
the social function of I.Q. distinctions is not status attainment or transmission,
what *is* their function? We shall argue in section four that the emphasis on intelligence as the basis for economic success serves to legitimize an authoritarian,
hierarchical, stratified, and unequal economic system of production, and to reconcile the individual to his or her objective position within this system. Legitimation is enhanced merely when people *believe* in the intrinsic importance of
I.Q. This belief is facilitated by the strong associations among all the economically desirable attributes—social class, education, cognitive skills, occupational
status, and income—and is integrated into a pervasive ideological perspective.
Second, if I.Q. is not a major determinant of social class structure, what is?
What are the criteria for admission to a particular social stratum, and what are
the sources of intergenerational status transmission? We shall argue in section
five that access to an occupational status is contingent upon a pattern of non-
cognitve personality traits (motivation, orientation to authority, discipline, internalization of work norms), as well as a complex of personal attributes including sex, race, age, and educational credentials through which the individual aids
in legitimating and stabilizing the structure of authority in the modern enterprise itself. Thus, primarily because of the central economic role of the school
system, the generation of adequate cognitive skills becomes a spin-off, a by-product of a stratification mechanism grounded in the supply, demand, production,
and certification of these noncognitive personal attributes.

Finally we shall comment on the implications of our perspective on the stratification process for political action and social change.

II. THE I.Q. CONTROVERSY

The argument that differences in genetic endowments are of central and increasing importance in the stratification systems of advanced technological societies
has been advanced, in similar forms, by a number of contemporary researchers.[8]
At the heart of this argument lies the venerable thesis that I.Q., as measured by
tests such as the Stanford-Binet, is largely inherited via genetic transmission,
rather than molded through environmental influences.*

This thesis bears a short elucidation. That I.Q. is highly heritable is merely
to say that individuals with similar genes will exhibit similar I.Q.'s *independent*
of differences in the social environments they might experience during their
mental development. The main support of the genetic school is several studies
of individuals with precisely the same genes (identical twins) raised in different
environments (i.e., separated at birth and reared in families with different social
statuses). Their I.Q.'s tend to be fairly similar.[9] In addition, there are studies of
individuals with no common genes (unrelated individuals) raised in the same
environment (e.g., the same family) as well as studies of individuals with varying
genetic similarities (e.g., fraternal twins, siblings, fathers and sons, aunts and
nieces) and varying environments (e.g., siblings raised apart, cousins raised in

---

* By I.Q. we mean—here and throughout this essay—those cognitive capacities that are
measured on I.Q. tests. We have avoided the use of the word "intelligence" as in its common usage it ordinarily connotes a broader range of capacities.

their respective homes). The difference in I.Q.s for these groups is roughly conformable to the genetic inheritance model suggested by the identical twin and unrelated individual studies.[10]

As Eysenck suggests, while geneticists will quibble over the exact magnitude of heritability of I.Q., nearly all will agree heritability exists and is significant.[11] Environmentalists, while emphasizing the paucity and unrepresentativeness of the data, have presented rather weak evidence for their own position and have made little dent in the genetic position.[12] Unable to attack the central proposition of the genetic school, environmentalists have emphasized that it bears no important social implications. They have claimed that, although raised in the context of the economic and educational deprivation of Blacks in the United States, the genetic theory says nothing about the "necessary" degree of racial inequality or the limits of compensatory education. First, environmentalists deny that there is any evidence that the I.Q. difference between Blacks and whites (amounting to about fifteen I.Q. points) is genetic in origin,* and second, they deny that any estimate of heritability tells us much about the capacity of "enriched environments" to lessen I.Q. differentials, either within or between racial groups.†

---

*   Does the fact that a large component of the differences in I.Q. among whites is genetic mean that a similar component of the differences in I.Q. between Blacks and whites is determined by the former's inferior gene pool? Clearly not. First of all, the degree of heritability is an *average,* even among whites. For any two individuals, and a *fortiori,* any two groups of individuals, observed I.Q. differences may be due to any proportion of genes and environment—it is required only that they average properly over the entire population. For instance, *all* of the difference in I.Q. between identical twins is environmental, and presumably a great deal of the difference between adopted brothers is genetic. Similarly we cannot say whether the average difference in I.Q. between Irish and Puerto Ricans is genetic or environmental. In the case of Blacks, however, the genetic school's inference is even more tenuous. Richard J. Light and Paul V. Smith ("Social Allocation Models of Intelligence: A Methodological Inquiry," *Harvard Educational Review,* 39, no. 3 [August 1969]), have shown that even accepting Jensen's estimates of the heritability of I.Q., the Black-white I.Q. difference could easily be explained by the average environmental differences between the races. Recourse to further experimental investigations will not resolve this issue, for the "conceptual experiments" that would determine the genetic component of Black-white differences cannot be performed. Could we take a pair of Black identical twins and place them in random environments? Clearly not. Placing a Black child in a white home in an overtly racist society will not provide the same "environment" as placing a white child in that house. Similarly looking at the difference in I.Q.'s of unrelated Black and white children raised in the same home (whether Black or white, or mixed) will not tell us the extent of genetic differences, since such children cannot be treated equally, and environmental differences must continue to persist (of course, if in these cases, differences in I.Q. disappear, the environmentalist case would be supported. But if they do not, no inference can be made).

†   Most environmentalists do not dispute Jensen's assertion that existing large-scale compensatory programs have produced dismal results. (See Jensen, "How Much Can We Boost I.Q.," and, for example, Harvey Averch et al., *How Effective is Schooling? A Critical Review and Synthesis of Research Findings* (Santa Monica: The RAND Corporation, 1972). But this does not bear on the genetic hypothesis. As Jensen himself notes, the degree of genetic transmission of any trait depends on the various alternative environments that individuals experience. Jensen's estimates of heritability rest *squarely* on the existing array of educational processes and technologies. Any introduction of new social processes of mental development will change the average unstandardized level of I.Q., as well as its degree of heritability. For instance, the almost perfect heritability of height is well documented. Yet the average heights of Americans have risen dramatically over the years, due clearly to change in the overall environment. Similarly, whatever the heritability of I.Q., the average unstandardized test scores rose 83 percent between 1917 and 1943. See Jencks, *Inequality. (cont'd)*

But the environmentalists' defense strategy has been costly. First, plausible, if not logical, inference now lies on the side of the genetic school, and it's up to environmentalists to "put up or shut up" as to feasible environmental enrichment programs. Second, in their egalitarian zeal vis-à-vis racial differences, the environmentalists have sacrificed the modern liberal interpretation of social stratification. The modern liberal approach is to attribute social class differences to "unequal opportunity." That is, while the criteria for economic success are objective and achievement-oriented, the failures and successes of parents are passed onto their children via distinct learning and cultural environments. Thus the achievement of a more equal society merely requires that all youth be afforded the educational and other social conditions of the best and most successful.[13] But by focusing on the environmental differences *between* races, they implicitly accept that intelligence differences among whites of differing social class background are rooted in differences in genetic endowments. Indeed the genetic school's data comes precisely from observed differences in the I.Q. of whites across socioeconomic levels! The fundamental tenet of modern liberal social policy—that "progressive social welfare measures" can gradually reduce and eliminate social class differences, cultures of poverty and affluence, and inequalities of opportunity—seems to be undercut. Thus the "classical liberal" attitude,[14] which emphasizes that social classes sort themselves out on the basis of innate individual capacity to cope successfully in the social environment, and hence tend to reproduce themselves from generation to generation, is restored.[15]

The vigor of reaction in face of Jensen's argument indicates the liberals' agreement that I.Q. is a basic social determinant (at least ideally) of occupational status and intergenerational mobility. In Jensen's words, "psychologists' concept of the 'intelligence demands' of an occupation . . . is very much like the general public's concept of the prestige or 'social standing' of an occupation, and both are closely related to an independent measure of . . . occupational status."[16] Jensen continues, quoting O. D. Duncan: ". . . 'intelligence' . . . is not essentially different from that of achievement or status in the occupational sphere . . . what we now *mean* by intelligence is something like the probability of acceptable performance (given the opportunity) in occupations varying in social status."[17] Moreover, Jensen argues that the purported trend toward intelligence's being an increasing requirement for occupational status will continue.[18] This emphasis on the role of intelligence in explaining social stratification is set even more clearly by Carl Bereiter in the same issue of the *Harvard Educational Review:* "The prospect is of a meritocratic caste system, based . . . on the natural conse-

---

But compensatory programs are obviously an attempt to change the total array of environments open to children through "educational innovation." While existing large-scale programs appear to have failed to produce significant gains in scholastic achievement, many more innovative small-scale programs have succeeded. See Carl Bereiter, "The Future of Individual Differences," *Harvard Educational Review,* Reprint Series no. 2, 1969, pp. 162-170; Charles E. Silberman, *Crisis in the Classroom* (New York: Random House, 1970); Averch, *How Effective Is Schooling?* Moreover, even accepting the genetic position should not hinder us from seeking new environmental innovation—indeed it should spur us to further creative activities in this direction. Thus the initial thrust of the genetic school can be at least partially repulsed: there is no reliable evidence either that long-term contact of Blacks with existing white environments would not close the Black-white I.Q. gap, or that innovative compensatory programs (i.e., programs unlike existing white childrearing or education environments) might not attenuate or eliminate I.Q. differences that are indeed genetic.

quences of inherited differences in intellectual potential. . . . It would tend to persist even though everyone at all levels of the hierarchy considered it a bad thing."[19] Something like death and taxes.

Jensen et al. cannot be accused of employing an overly complicated social theory. Jensen's reason for the "inevitable" association of status and intelligence is that society "rewards talent and merit," and Herrnstein adds that society recognizes "the importance and scarcity of intellectual ability."[20] Moreover, the association of intelligence and social class is due to the "screening process,"[21] via education and occupation, whereby each generation is further refined into social strata on the basis of I.Q. Finally, adds Herrnstein, "new gains of wealth . . . will increase the I.Q. gap between upper and lower classes, making the social ladder even steeper for those left at the bottom."[22] Herrnstein celebrates the genetic school's crowning achievement by turning liberal social policy directly against itself, noting that the heritability of intelligence and hence the increasing pervasiveness of social stratification will increase, the more "progressive" our social policies: "the growth of a virtually hereditary meritocracy will arise out of the successful realization of contemporary political and social goals . . . as the environment becomes more favorable for the development of intelligence, its heritability will increase. . . ."[23] Similarly, the more we break down discriminatory and ascriptive criteria for hiring, the stronger will become the link between I.Q. and occupational success, and the development of modern technology can only quicken the process.[24]

Few will be surprised that such statements are made by the "conservative" genetic school. But why, amid a spirited liberal counterattack in which the minutest details of the genetic hypothesis are contested and scathingly criticized, is the validity of the genetic school's description of the social function of intelligence blandly accepted? The widespread agreement among participants in the debate that I.Q. is an important determinant of economic success can hardly be explained by compelling empirical evidence adduced in support of the position. Quite the contrary. As we will show in the next section, the available data point strongly to the unimportance of I.Q. in getting ahead economically. In Section IV we shall argue that the actual function of I.Q. testing and its associated ideology is that of legitimizing the stratification system, rather than generating it. The treatment of I.Q. in many strands of liberal sociology and economics merely reflects its actual function in social life: the legitimization and rationalization of the existing social relations of production.

III. THE IMPORTANCE OF I.Q.

The most immediate support for the I.Q. theory of social stratification—which we will call I.Q.-ism—flows from the strong association of I.Q. and economic success. This is illustrated in Table 1, which exhibits the probability of achieving any particular decile in the economic success distribution for an individual whose adult I.Q. lies in a specified decile.*

---

* In Table 1, as throughout this paper, "adult I.Q." is measured by scores on a form of the Armed Forces Qualification Test. This measure is strongly affected both by early I.Q. (in this paper measured by Stanford-Binet or its equivalent at age six to eight) and years of schooling, and hence can be considered a measure of adult cognitive achievement. Economic success is measured throughout as the average of an individual's income and the social pres-

TABLE 1*
Probability of Attainment of Different Levels of
Economic Success for Individuals of Differing Levels
of Adult I.Q., by Deciles†

Adult I.Q. by Deciles

	x 10	9	8	7	6	5	4	3	2	1
y										
10	30.9	19.8	14.4	10.9	8.2	6.1	4.4	3.0	1.7	0.6
9	19.2	16.9	14.5	12.4	10.5	8.7	7.0	5.4	3.6	1.7
8	13.8	14.5	13.7	12.6	11.4	10.1	8.7	7.1	5.3	2.8
7	10.3	12.4	12.6	12.3	11.7	11.0	10.0	8.7	7.0	4.1
6	7.7	10.4	11.4	11.7	11.8	11.5	11.0	10.1	8.7	5.7
5	5.7	8.7	10.1	11.0	11.5	11.8	11.7	11.4	10.4	7.7
4	4.1	7.0	8.7	10.0	11.0	11.7	12.3	12.6	12.4	10.3
3	2.8	5.3	7.1	8.7	10.1	11.4	12.6	13.7	14.5	13.8
2	1.7	3.6	5.4	7.0	8.7	10.5	12.4	14.5	16.9	19.2
1	0.6	1.7	3.0	4.4	6.1	8.2	10.9	14.4	19.8	30.9

Economic Success by Deciles (row axis label)

*Table 1 corresponds to a correlation coefficient r = .52. Example of use:
For an individual in the 85th percentile in Adult I.Q. (x = 9), the probability of
attaining between the 20th and 30th percentile in Economic Success is 5.3 percent (the entry in column 9, row 3).

The data, most of which was collected by the U.S. Census Current Population
Survey in 1962, refer to "non-Negro" males, aged 25 to 34, from nonfarm background in the experienced labor force. We have chosen this population because
it represents the dominant labor force and the group into which minority groups
and women would have to integrate to realize the liberal ideal of equal opportunity, and hence to whose statistical associations these groups would become

---

tige of his occupation as measured on the Duncan occupational status index, each scaled to
have standard deviation equal to one. See Duncan, "Properties and Characteristics of the
Socioeconomic Index." For a description of the independent behavior of income and status,
see Bowles, "The Genetic Inheritance of I.Q. and the Intergenerational Reproduction of
Economic Inequality." We have chosen a weighted average for simplicity of exposition, and
in recognition of their joint importance in a reasonable specification of economic success.
† A further word is in order on Tables 1 through 7. Most popular discussions of the relation of I.Q. and economic success (e.g., Jensen, *"How Much Can We Boost IQ"*; Herrnstein,
"IQ"; Jencks, *Inequality*) present statistical material in terms of "correlation coefficients"
and "contribution to explained variance." We believe that these technical expressions convey little information to the reader not thoroughly initiated in their use and interpretation.
The concept of differential probability embodied in Tables 1 through 7, we feel, is opera-
tionally more accessible to the reader, and dramatically reveals the patterns of mobility and
causality only implicit in summary statistics of the correlation variety.
    Let us repeat, Tables 1 through 7 have *not* been constructed by directly observing the
decile position of individuals on each of the various variables and recording the percentages
in each cell of the relevant table. This approach is impossible for two reasons. First such
statistics are simply unavailable on the individual level. As we have noted, our statistical base

subject. The data relating to childhood I.Q. and adult I.Q. are from a 1966 survey of veterans by the National Opinion Research Center and the California Guidance Study.[25] The quality of the data preclude any claims to absolute precision in our estimation. Yet our main propositions remain supported, even making allowance for substantive degrees of error. We must emphasize, however, that the validity of our basic propositions does not depend on our particular data set. While we believe our data base to be the most representative and careful construction from available sources, we have checked our results against several other data bases, including Jencks, Hauser, Lutterman, and Sewell, Conlisk, Griliches and Mason, and Duncan and Featherman.[26] When corrections are made for measurement error and restriction of range (see Bowles[27] and Jencks), statistical analysis of each of these data bases strongly supports all of our major propositions.

The interpretation of Table 1 is straightforward. The entries in the table are calculated directly from the simple correlation coefficient between our variables Adult I.Q. and Economic Success. In addition to reporting the correlation coefficient, we have described these data in tabular form as in Table 1 to illustrate the meaning of the correlation coefficient in terms of the differing probability of economic success for people at various positions in the distribution of I.Q.'s. We cannot stress too strongly that while the correlation coefficients in this and later tables are estimated from the indicated data, the entries in the table represent nothing more than a simple translation of their correlations, using assumptions that—through virtually universally employed in this kind of research—substantially simplify the complexity of the actual data. Now, turning to the table, we can see, for example, that a correlation between these two variables of .52 implies that an individual whose adult I.Q. lies in the top 10 percent of the population has a probability of 30.9 percent of ending up in the top tenth of the population in economic success, and a probability of 0.6 percent of ending up in the bottom tenth. Since an individual chosen at random will have a probability of 10 percent of ending up in any decile of economic success, we can conclude that being in the top decile in I.Q. renders an individual (white male) 3.09 times as likely to be in the top economic success decile, and .06 times as likely to end up in the bottom, as would be predicted by chance. Each of the remaining entries in Table 1 can be interpreted correspondingly.

Yet Tables 2 and 3, which exhibit the corresponding probabilities of economic success given number of years of schooling and level of socioeconomic

---

embraces the findings of several distinct data sources, no single one of which includes all the variables used in our analysis. Second, for certain technical reasons (e.g., errors in variables and restrictions of range), correction factors must be applied to the raw data before they can be used for analysis. These general issues are discussed in Jencks *Inequality*, and with respect to our data, in Bowles, "The Genetic Inheritance of IQ and the Intergenerational Reproduction of Economic Inequality," and Gintis, "Education and the Characteristics of Worker Productivity."

Tables 1 through 7 are constructed by making explicit certain assumptions that are only implicit, but absolutely necessary to the correlational arguments of Jensen and others. These assumptions include the linearity of the relations among all variables and the approximate normality of their joint probability distribution. Our statistical technique, then, is standard linear regression analysis, with correlations, regression coefficients, and path coefficients represented in their (mathematically equivalent) tabular form.

TABLE 2*
Probability of Attainment of Different Levels óf
Economic Success for Individuals of Differing Levels
of Education, by Deciles

Years of Schooling by Deciles

x	10	9	8	7	6	5	4	3	2	1
y										
10	37.6	22.3	14.6	9.8	6.6	4.3	2.6	1.4	0.6	0.1
9	20.9	19.5	16.2	13.1	10.3	7.9	5.7	3.8	2.1	0.6
8	13.5	16.1	15.3	13.8	12.0	10.1	8.0	5.9	3.7	1.4
7	9.1	13.0	13.8	13.6	12.8	11.6	10.0	8.0	5.6	2.5
6	6.1	10.2	12.0	12.8	12.9	12.5	11.6	10.1	7.8	4.0
5	4.0	7.8	10.1	11.6	12.5	12.9	12.8	12.0	10.2	6.1
4	2.5	5.6	8.0	10.0	11.6	12.8	13.6	13.8	13.0	9.1
3	1.4	3.7	5.9	8.0	10.1	12.0	13.8	15.3	16.1	13.5
2	0.6	2.1	3.8	5.7	7.9	10.3	13.1	16.2	19.5	20.9
1	0.1	0.6	1.4	2.6	4.3	6.6	9.8	14.6	22.3	37.6

Economic Success by Deciles (left vertical axis label)

*Table 2 corresponds to a correlation coefficient $r = .63$. Example of use:
For an individual in the 85th percentile in Education ($x = 9$), the probability of
attaining between the 20th and 30th percentiles in Economic Success ($y = 3$) is
3.7 percent (the entry in column 9, row 3).

background,† show that this statistical support is surely misleading: even stronger
associations appear between years of schooling and economic success, as well as
between social background and economic success. For example, being in the top
decile in years of schooling renders an individual 3.76 times as likely to be at the
top of the economic heap, and .01 times as likely to be at the bottom, while the
corresponding ratios are 3.26 and .04 for social background. It is thus quite
possible to draw from aggregate statistics, equally cogently, both an "educational
attainment theory" of social stratification and a "socioeconomic background"
theory. Clearly there are logical errors in all such facile inferences.

Of course, the I.Q. proponent will argue that there is no real problem here:
the association of social class background and economic success follows from the
importance of I.Q. to economic success, and the fact that individuals of higher
class background have higher I.Q. Similarly one may argue that the association
of education and economic success follows from the fact that education simply
picks out and develops the talents of intelligent individuals. The problem is that
equally cogent argumcnts can be given for the primacy of either education or
social class, and the corresponding subordinateness of the others. The above
figures are equally compatible with all three interpretations.

† In Table 3, as throughout this paper, socioeconomic background is measured as a weighted
sum of parental income, father's occupational status, and father's income, where the weights
are chosen so as to produce the maximum multiple correlation with economic success.

TABLE 3*

Probability of Attainment of Different Levels of
Economic Success for Individuals of Differing Levels
of Social Class Background

Social Class Background by Deciles

	x 10	9	8	7	6	5	4	3	2	1
y										
10	32.6	20.4	14.5	10.7	7.8	5.7	3.9	2.5	1.4	0.4
9	19.7	17.5	14.9	12.6	10.5	8.5	6.7	5.0	3.2	1.3
8	13.8	14.9	14.1	12.9	11.6	10.1	8.6	6.9	4.9	2.4
7	10.0	12.5	12.9	12.6	12.0	11.1	10.0	8.5	6.7	3.7
6	7.3	10.4	11.5	12.0	12.0	11.7	11.1	10.1	8.5	5.3
5	5.3	8.5	10.1	11.1	11.7	12.0	12.0	11.5	10.4	7.3
4	3.7	6.7	8.5	10.0	11.1	12.0	12.6	12.9	12.5	10.0
3	2.4	4.9	6.9	8.6	10.1	11.6	12.9	14.1	14.9	13.8
2	1.3	3.2	5.0	6.7	8.5	10.5	12.6	14.9	17.5	19.7
1	0.4	1.4	2.5	3.9	5.7	7.8	10.7	14.5	20.4	32.6

Economic Success by Deciles (row axis label)

*Table 3 corresponds to a correlation coefficient r = .55. Example of use:
For an individual in the 85th percentile in Social Class (x = 9), the probability of
attaining between the 20th and the 30th percentile in Economic Success (y = 3)
is 4.9 percent (the entry in column 9, row 3).

In this section we shall show that all three factors (I.Q., social class background, and education) contribute independently to economic success, but that
I.Q. is by far the least important. Specifically we will demonstrate the truth of
the following three propositions, which constitute the empirical basis of our
thesis concerning the unimportance of I.Q. in generating the class structure.

*First, although higher I.Q.'s and economic success tend to go together, higher
I.Q.'s are not an important cause of economic success.* The statistical association
between adult I.Q. and economic success, while substantial, derives largely from
the common association of both of these variables with social class background
and level of schooling. Thus to appraise the economic importance of I.Q., we
must focus attention on family and school.

*Second, although higher levels of schooling and economic success likewise
tend to go together, the intellectual abilities developed or certified in school
make little causal contribution to getting ahead economically.* Thus only a minor
portion of the substantial statistical association between schooling and economic
success can be accounted for by the schools' role in producing or screening
cognitive skills. The predominant economic function of schools must therefore
involve the accreditation of individuals, as well as the production and selection
of personality traits and other personal attributes rewarded by the economic
system. Our third proposition asserts a parallel result with respect to the effect
of social class background.

TABLE 4*
Differential Probabilities of Attaining Economic Success for Individuals of Equal Levels of Education and Social Class Background, but Differing Levels of Adult I.Q.

Adult I.Q. by Deciles

Economic Success by Deciles

y \ x	10	9	8	7	6	5	4	3	2	1
10	14.1	12.3	11.4	10.7	10.1	9.6	9.0	8.5	7.8	6.6
9	12.4	11.4	10.9	10.5	10.2	9.8	9.5	9.1	8.6	7.7
8	11.4	10.9	10.6	10.4	10.2	9.9	9.7	9.4	9.1	8.4
7	10.7	10.5	10.4	10.3	10.1	10.0	9.9	9.7	9.5	9.0
6	10.1	10.2	10.2	10.1	10.1	10.1	10.0	9.9	9.8	9.5
5	9.5	9.8	9.9	10.0	10.1	10.1	10.1	10.2	10.2	10.1
4	9.0	9.5	9.7	9.9	10.0	10.1	10.3	10.4	10.5	10.7
3	8.4	9.1	9.4	9.7	9.9	10.2	10.4	10.6	10.9	11.4
2	7.7	8.6	9.1	9.5	9.8	10.2	10.5	10.9	11.4	12.4
1	6.6	7.8	8.5	9.0	9.6	10.1	10.7	11.4	12.3	14.1

*Table 4 corresponds to a standardized regression coefficient $\beta = .13$.
Example of use: Suppose two individuals have the same levels of Education and Social Class Background, but one is in the 85th percentile in Adult I.Q. (x = 9), while the other is in the 15th decile in Adult I.Q. (x = 2). Then the first individual is 10.9/9.1 = 1.2 times as likely as the second to attain the 8th decile in Economic Success (column 9, row 8, divided by column 2, row 8).

Third, the fact that economic success tends to run in the family arises almost completely independently from any genetic inheritance of I.Q. Thus, while one's economic status tends to resemble that of one's parents, only a minor portion of this association can be attributed to social class differences in childhood I.Q., and a virtually negligible portion to social class differences in genetic endowments, even accepting the Jensen estimates of heritability. Thus a perfect equalization of I.Q.'s across social classes would reduce the intergenerational transmission of economic status by a negligible amount. We conclude that a family's position in the class structure is reproduced primarily by mechanisms operating independently of the inheritance, production, and certification of intellectual skills.

Our statistical technique for the demonstration of these propositions will be that of linear regression analysis. This technique allows us to derive numerical estimates of the independent contribution of each of the separate but correlated influences (social class background, childhood I.Q., years of schooling, adult I.Q.) on economic success, by answering the question: what is the magnitude of the association between any one of these influences among individuals who are equal on some or all the others? Equivalently it answers the question: what are the probabilities of attaining particular deciles in economic success among individuals who are in the same decile in some or all of the above influences but one, and in varying deciles in this one variable alone?

The I.Q. argument is based on the assumption that social background and education are related to economic success *because* they are associated with higher adult cognitive skills. Table 4 shows this to be essentially incorrect. This table, by exhibiting the relation between adult I.Q. and economic success among individuals with the same social class background and level of schooling, shows that the I.Q.-economic success association exhibited in Table 1 is largely a by-product of these more basic social influences. That is, for a given level of social background and schooling, differences in adult I.Q. add very little to our ability to predict eventual economic success. Thus, for example, an individual with an average number of years of schooling and an average socioeconomic family background, but with a level of cognitive skill to place him in the top decile of the I.Q. distribution, has a probability of 14.1 percent of attaining the highest economic success decile. This figure may be compared with 10 percent, the analogous probability for an individual with average levels of I.Q. as well as schooling and social background. Our first proposition—that the relation between I.Q. and economic success is not causal, but rather operates largely through the effects of the correlated variables, years of schooling and social class background—is thus strongly supported.* We are thus led to focus directly on the role of social class background and schooling in promoting economic success.

Turning first to schooling, the argument of the I.Q. proponents is that the strong association between level of schooling and economic success exhibited in Table 2 is due to the fact that economic success depends on cognitive capacities, and schooling both selects individuals with high intellectual ability for further training and then develops this ability into concrete adult cognitive skills. Table 5 shows this view to be false. This table exhibits the effect of schooling on chances for economic success, for individuals who have the same adult I.Q. Comparing Table 5 with Table 2, we see that cognitive differences account for a negligible part of schooling's influence on economic success: individuals with similar levels of adult I.Q. but differing levels of schooling have substantially different chances of economic success. Indeed the similarity of Tables 2 and 5 demonstrates the validity of our second proposition—that schooling affects chances of economic success predominantly by the non-cognitive traits which it generates, or on the basis of which it selects individuals for higher education.[28]

The next step in our argument is to show that the relationship between social background and economic success operates almost entirely independently of individual differences in I.Q. Whereas Table 3 exhibits the total effect of social class on an individual's economic success, Table 6 exhibits the same effect among individuals with the same childhood I.Q. Clearly these tables are nearly identical. That is, even were all social class differences in I.Q. eliminated, a similar pattern of social class intergenerational immobility would result.[29] Our third proposition is thus supported: the intergenerational transmission of social and economic status operates primarily via noncognitive mechanisms, despite the fact that the school system rewards higher I.Q.—an attribute significantly associated with higher social class background.

---

* This is not to say that I.Q. is never an important criteria of success. We do not contend that extremely low or high I.Q.'s are irrelevant to economic failure or success. Nor do we deny that for some individuals or for some jobs, cognitive skills are economically important. Rather, we assert that for the vast majority of workers and jobs, selection, assessed job adequacy, and promotion are based on attributes other than I.Q.

TABLE 5*
Differential Probabilities of Attaining Economic Success for Individuals of Equal Adult I.Q. but Differing Levels of Education

Years of Schooling by Deciles

Economic Success by Deciles y \ x	10	9	8	7	6	5	4	3	2	1
10	33.2	20.6	14.6	10.6	7.7	5.5	3.8	2.4	1.3	0.4
9	19.9	17.8	15.1	12.7	10.5	8.5	6.6	4.8	3.1	1.2
8	13.8	15.0	14.2	13.0	11.6	10.1	8.5	6.8	4.8	2.3
7	9.9	12.6	13.0	12.7	12.1	11.2	10.0	8.5	6.6	3.5
6	7.2	10.4	11.6	12.1	12.1	11.8	11.2	10.1	8.4	5.1
5	5.1	8.4	10.1	11.2	11.8	12.1	12.1	11.6	10.4	7.2
4	3.5	6.6	8.5	10.0	11.2	12.1	12.7	13.0	12.6	9.9
3	2.3	4.8	6.8	8.5	10.1	11.6	13.0	14.2	15.0	13.8
2	1.2	3.1	4.8	6.6	8.5	10.5	12.7	15.1	17.8	19.9
1	0.4	1.3	2.4	3.8	5.5	7.7	10.6	14.6	20.6	33.2

*Table 5 corresponds to a standardized regression coefficient $\beta = .56$. Example of use: Suppose two individuals have the same Adult I.Q., but one is in the 9th decile in Level of Education (x = 9), while the other is in the 2nd decile (x = 2). Then the first individual is 15.0/4.8 = 3.12 times as likely as the second to attain the 8th decile in Economic Success (column 9, row 8, divided by column 2, row 8).

The unimportance of the specifically genetic mechanism operating via I.Q. in the intergenerational reproduction of economic inequality is even more striking. Table 7 exhibits the degree of association between social class background and economic success that can be attributed to the genetic inheritance of I.Q. alone. This table assumes that all direct influences of socioeconomic background upon economic success have been eliminated, and that the noncognitive components of schooling's contribution to economic success are eliminated as well (the perfect meritocracy based on intellectual ability). On the other hand, it assumes Jensen's estimate for the degree of heritability of I.Q. A glance at Table 7 shows that the resulting level of intergenerational inequality in this highly hypothetical example would be negligible.

The unimportance of I.Q. in explaining the relation between social class background and economic success, and the unimportance of cognitive achievement in explaining the contribution of schooling to economic success, together with our previously derived observation that most of the association between I.Q. and economic success can be accounted for by the common association of these variables with education and social class, support our major assertion: I.Q. is not an important intrinsic criterion for economic success. Our data thus hardly lend credence to Duncan's assertion that " 'intelligence' . . . is not essentially different from that of achievement or status in the occupational sphere,"[30]

TABLE 6*
Differential Probabilities of Attaining Economic-
Success for Individuals of Equal Early I.Q. but
Differing Levels of Social Class Background

Social Class Background by Deciles

	x 10	9	8	7	6	5	4	3	2	1
y										
10	27.7	18.5	14.1	11.1	8.8	6.9	5.3	3.9	2.5	1.1
9	18.2	15.8	13.8	12.1	10.5	9.0	7.6	6.1	4.5	2.4
8	13.7	13.8	13.0	12.1	11.1	10.1	8.9	7.6	6.1	3.7
7	10.7	12.0	12.1	11.8	11.3	10.7	9.9	8.9	7.5	5.0
6	8.4	10.5	11.1	11.3	11.3	11.1	10.7	10.0	9.0	6.6
5	6.6	9.0	10.0	10.7	11.1	11.3	11.3	11.1	10.5	8.4
4	5.0	7.5	8.9	9.9	10.7	11.3	11.8	12.1	12.0	10.7
3	3.7	6.1	7.6	8.9	10.1	11.1	12.1	13.0	13.8	13.7
2	2.4	4.5	6.1	7.6	9.0	10.5	12.1	13.8	15.8	18.2
1	1.1	2.5	3.9	5.3	6.9	8.8	11.1	14.1	18.5	27.7

Economic Success by Deciles (row label, vertical at left)

*Table 6 corresponds to a standardized regression coefficient β = .46.
Example of use: Suppose two individuals have the same Childhood I.Q., but one
is in the 9th decile in Social Background, while the other is in the 2nd decile.
Then the first is 18.5/2.5 = 7.4 times as likely as the second to attain the top
decile in Economic Success (column 9, row 10, divided by column 2, row 10).

nor to Jensen's belief in the "inevitable" association of status and intelligence,
based on society's "rewarding talent and merit,"[31] nor to Herrnstein's dismal
prognostication of a "virtually hereditary meritocracy" as the fruit of successful
liberal reform in an advanced industrial society.[32]

IV. I.Q. AND THE LEGITIMATION OF THE HIERARCHICAL DIVISION OF LABOR

A Preview

We have disputed the view that I.Q. is an important causal antecedent of economic success. Yet I.Q. clearly plays an important role in the U.S. stratification
system. In this section we shall argue that the set of beliefs surrounding I.Q.
betrays its true function—that of legitimating the social institutions underpinning
the stratification system itself.
      Were the I.Q. ideology correct, understanding the ramifications of cognitive
differences would require our focusing on the technical relations of production
in an advanced technological economy. Its failure, however, bids us scrutinize a
different aspect of production—its social relations. By the "social relations of

TABLE 7*
The Genetic Component of Intergenerational Status
Transmission, Assuming the Jensen Heritability
Coefficient, and Assuming Education Operates Via
Cognitive Mechanisms Alone

Social Class Background by Deciles

y \ x	10	9	8	7	6	5	4	3	2	1
10	10.6	10.3	10.2	10.1	10.0	10.0	9.9	9.8	9.7	9.4
9	10.4	10.2	10.1	10.1	10.0	10.0	9.9	9.9	9.8	9.6
8	10.2	10.1	10.1	10.1	10.0	10.0	9.9	9.9	9.9	9.8
7	10.1	10.1	10.1	10.0	10.0	10.0	10.0	9.9	9.9	9.9
6	10.0	10.0	10.0	10.0	10.0	10.0	10.0	10.0	10.0	10.0
5	10.0	10.0	10.0	10.0	10.0	10.0	10.0	10.0	10.0	10.0
4	9.9	9.9	9.9	10.0	10.0	10.0	10.0	10.1	10.1	10.1
3	9.8	9.9	9.9	9.9	10.0	10.0	10.1	10.1	10.1	10.2
2	9.6	9.8	9.9	9.9	10.0	10.0	10.1	10.1	10.2	10.4
1	9.4	9.7	9.8	9.9	10.0	10.0	10.1	10.2	10.3	10.6

Economic Success by Deciles (vertical axis label)

*Table 7 corresponds to .02 standard deviations difference in Economic Success per standard deviation difference in Social Class Background, in a causal model assuming Social Class Background affects Early I.Q. only via genetic transmission, and assuming Economic Success is directly affected only by cognitive variables. Example of use: For an individual in the 85th percentile in Social Class Background (x = 9), the probability of attaining between the 20th and 30th percentiles in Economic Success (y = 3), assuming only genetic and cognitive mechanisms, is 10.1 percent (the entry in column 9, row 8.

production" we mean the system of rights and responsibilities, duties and rewards, that governs the interaction of all individuals involved in organized productive activity.[33] In the following section we shall argue that the social relations of production determine the major attributes of the U.S. stratification system.[34] Here, however, we shall confine ourselves to the proposition that the I.Q. ideology is a major factor in legitimating these social relations in the consciousness of workers.

The social relations of production in different societies are quite diverse; they lay the basis for such divergent stratification systems as communal-reciprocity, caste, feudal serf, slave, community-collective, and wage labor of capitalist and state socialist varieties. In advanced capitalist society the stratification system is based on what we term the hierarchical division of labor, characterized by power and control emanating from the top downward through a finely graded bureaucratic order.[35] The distribution of economic reward and social privilege in the United States is an expression of the hierarchical division of labor within the enterprise.

In this section, then, we shall show that the I.Q. ideology serves to legitimate the hierarchical division of labor. First, we argue that such legitimation is necessary because capitalist production is "totalitarian" in a way only vaguely adumbrated in other social spheres—family, interpersonal relations, law, and politics. Indeed history exhibits periodic onslaughts upon the hierarchical division of labor and its acceptance is always problematic. Second, we argue that the I.Q. ideology is conducive to a general technocratic and meritocratic view of the stratification system that tends to legitimate these social relations, as well as its characteristic means of allocating individuals to various levels of the hierarchy. Third, we argue that the I.Q. ideology operates to reconcile workers to their eventual economic positions primarily via the schooling experience, with its putative objectivity, meritocratic orientation, and technical efficiency in supplying the cognitive needs of the labor force. Fourth, we shall argue that the use of both formal education and the I.Q. ideology was not merely a historical accident, but arose through the conscious policies of capitalists and their intellectual servants to perform the functions indicated above.

The Need for Legitimacy

If one takes for granted the basic economic organization of society, its members need only be equipped with adequate cognitive and operational skills to fulfill work requirements, and provided with a reward structure motivating individuals to acquire and supply these skills. U.S. capitalism accomplishes the first of these requirements through family, school, and on-the-job training, and the second through a wage structure patterned after the job hierarchy.

But the social relations of production cannot be taken for granted. The bedrock of the capitalist economy is the legally sanctioned power of the directors of an enterprise to organize production, to determine the rules that regulate worker's productive activities, and to hire and fire accordingly, with only moderate restriction by workers' organizations and government regulations. But this power cannot be taken for granted, and can be exercised forcefully against violent opposition only sporadically. Violence alone, observe Lassevell and Kaplan, is inadequate as a stable basis for the possession and exercise of power, and they appropriately quote Rousseau: "The strongest man is never strong enough to be always master, unless he transforms his power into right, and obedience into duty." Where the assent of the less favored cannot be secured by power alone, it must be part of a total process whereby the existing structure of work roles and their allocation among individuals are seen as ethically acceptable and even technically necessary.

In some social systems the norms that govern the economic system are quite similar to those governing other major social spheres. Thus in feudal society the authority of the lord of the manor is not essentially different from that of the political monarch, the church hierarchy, or the family patriarch, and the ideology of "natural estates" suffuses all social activity. No special normative order is required for the economic system. But in capitalist society, to make the hierarchical division of labor appear just is no easy task, for the totalitarian organization of the enterprise clashes sharply with the ideals of equality, democracy, and participation that pervade the political and legal spheres. Thus the economic enterprise as a political dictatorship and a social caste system requires special legitimation, and the mechanisms used to place individuals in unequal (and unequally rewarding) positions require special justification.

Indeed the history of U.S. labor is studded with revolts against the hierarchical division of labor, particularly prior to the full development of formal education and the I.Q. ideology in the early twentieth century.[36]

In 1844 the Lynn, Mass., shoe workers, losing control over their craft and their labor in the face of the rising factory system, wrote in their "Declaration of Independence":

> Whereas, our employers have robbed us of certain rights . . . we feel bound to rise unitedly in our strength and burst asunder as Freemen ought the shackles and fetters with which they have long been chaining and binding us, by an unjust and unchristian use of power . . . which the possession of capital and superior knowledge furnishes.[37]

The ideology of the dispossessed farmer in the 1880s and 1890s or of the bankrupted small shopkeeper after the turn of the century is little different. That these radical thrusts against the hierarchical division of labor have by and large been deflected into more manageable wage or status demands bespeaks the power of the capitalist system to legitimize its changing structure, but in no way suggests that the perpetuation of the capitalist relations of production was ever a foregone conclusion.[38]

The contribution of I.Q.-ism to the legitimation of these social relations is based on a view of society that asserts the efficiency and technological necessity of modern industrial organization, and is buttressed by evidence of the similarity of production and work in such otherwise divergent social systems as the United States and the Soviet Union. In this view large-scale production is a requirement of advanced technology, and the hierarchical division of labor is the only effective means of coordinating the highly complex and interdependent parts of the large-scale productive system. Thus bureaucratic order is awarded the status of an "evolutionary universal"; in the words of Talcott Parsons: "Bureaucracy . . . is the most effective large-scale administrative organization that man has invented, and there is no direct substitute for it."[39]

The hallmark of the "technocratic perspective" is its reduction of a complex web of social relations in production to a few rules of technological efficacy— whence its easy integration with the similarly technocratic view of social stratification inherent in the I.Q. ideology. In this view the hierarchical division of labor arises from its natural superiority in the coordination of collective activity and in the nurturing of expertise in the control of complex production processes. In order to motivate the most able individuals to undertake the necessary training and preparation for high level occupational roles, salaries and status must be closely associated with one's level in the work hierarchy. Thus Davis and Moore, in their highly influential "functional theory of stratification," locate the "determinants of differential reward" in "differential functional importance" and "differential scarcity of personnel." "Social inequality," they conclude, "is thus an unconsciously evolved device by which societies insure that the most important positions are conscientiously filled by the most qualified persons."[40] Herrnstein is a little more concrete: "If virtually anyone is smart enough to be a ditch digger, and only half the people are smart enough to be engineers, then society is, in effect, husbanding its intellectual resources by holding engineers in greater esteem and paying them more."[41]

This perspective, technocratic in its justification of the hierarchical division of labor, leads smoothly to a meritocratic view of the process of matching individuals to jobs. An efficient and impersonal bureaucracy assesses the individual purely in terms of his or her expected contribution to production. The main determinants of an individual's expected job fitness are seen as those cognitive and psycho-motor capacities relevant to the worker's technical ability to do the job. The technocratic view of production and the meritocratic view of job allocation yield an important corollary, to which we will later return. Namely, there is always a strong tendency in an efficient industrial order to abjure caste, class, sex, color, and ethnic origins in occupational placement. This tendency will be particularly strong in a capitalist economy, where competitive pressures constrain employers to hire on the basis of strict efficiency criteria.[42]

The technocratic view of production, along with the meritocratic view of hiring, provides the strongest form of legitimation of work organization and social stratification in capitalist society. Not only is the notion that the hierarchical division of labor is "technically necessary" (albeit politically totalitarian) strongly reinforced, but also the view that job allocation is just and egalitarian (albeit severely unequal) is ultimately justified as objective, efficient, and necessary. Moreover, the individual's reconciliation with his or her own position in the hierarchy of production appears all but complete: the legitimacy of the authority of superiors no less than that of the individual's own objective position flows not from social contrivance but from Science and Reason.

That this view does not strain the credulity of well-paid intellectuals is perhaps not surprising.[43] Nor would the technocratic/meritocratic perspective be of much use in legitimizing the hierarchical division of labor were its adherents to be counted only among the university elite and the technical and professional experts. But such is not the case. Despite the extensive evidence that I.Q. is not an important determinant of individual occupational achievement (Section II), and despite the fact that few occupations place cognitive requirements on job entry, the crucial importance of I.Q. in personal success has captured the public mind. Numerous attitude surveys exhibit this fact. In a national sample of high school students, for example, "intelligence" ranks second only to "good health" in importance as a desirable personal attribute.[44] Similarly a large majority chose "intelligence" along with "hard work" as the most important requirements of success in life. The public concern over the Coleman Report findings about scholastic achievement and the furor over the I.Q. debate are merely indications of the pervasiveness of the I.Q. ideology.

This popular acceptance, we shall argue, is due to the unique role of the educational system.

Education and Legitimation

To understand the widespread acceptance of the view that economic success is predicated on intellectual achievement we must look beyond the workplace, for the I.Q. ideology does not conform to most workers' everyday experience on the job. Rather, the strength of this view derives in large measure from the interaction between schooling, cognitive achievement, and economic success. I.Q-ism legitimates the hierarchical division of labor not directly, but primarily through its relationship with the educational system.

We can summarize the relationship as follows. First, the distribution of rewards by the school is seen as being based on objectively measured cognitive achievement, and is therefore fair.* Second, schools are seen as being primarily oriented toward the production of cognitive skills. Third, higher levels of schooling are seen as a major, perhaps the strongest, determinant of economic success, and quite reasonably so, given the strong association of these two variables exhibited in Table 2. It is concluded, thus, that high I.Q.'s are acquired in a fair and open competition in school and in addition are a major determinant of success. The conclusion is based on the belief that the relationship between level of schooling and degree of economic success derives largely from the contribution of school to an individual's cognitive skills. Given the organization and stated objectives of schools it is easy to see how people would come to accept this belief. We have shown in Tables 2 and 5 that it is largely without empirical support.

The linking of intelligence to economic success indirectly via the educational system strengthens rather than weakens the legitimation process. First, the day-to-day contact of parents and children with the competitive, cognitively oriented school environment, with clear connections to the economy, buttresses in a very immediate and concrete way the technocratic perspective on economic organization, to a degree that a sporadic and impersonal testing process divorced from the school environment could not aspire. Second, by rendering the outcome (educational attainment) dependent not only on ability but also on motivation, drive to achieve, perseverance, and sacrifice, the status allocation mechanism acquires heightened legitimacy. Moreover, personal attributes are tested and developed over a long period of time, thus enhancing the apparent objectivity and achievement orientation of the stratification system. Third, by gradually "cooling out" individuals at different educational levels, the student's aspirations are relatively painlessly brought into line with his probable occupational status. By the time most students terminate schooling they have validated for themselves their inability or unwillingness to be a success at the next highest level. Through competition, success, and defeat in the classroom, the individual is reconciled to his or her social position.[45]

The statistical results of the previous section fit in well with our description of the role of education in the legitimation process. The I.Q. ideology better legitimates the hierarchical division of labor the stronger are the statistical associations of I.Q. with level of schooling and economic success, and the weaker are

---

* Recent studies, such as Hauser, Heyns, and Jencks, indeed indicate a lack of social class or racial bias in school grades: given a student's cognitive attainment, his or her grades seem not to be significantly affected by class or racial origins, at least on the high school level. See Robert Hauser, "Schools and the Stratification Process," *American Journal of Sociology*, '74 (May 1969): 587-611; Barbara Heyns, "Curriculum Assignment and Tracking Policies in Forty-Eight Urban Public High Schools," Ph.D. diss., University of Chicago, 1971; Jencks, *Inequality*. On the other hand, school grades are by no means based on cognitive achievement alone. An array of behavior and personality traits are rewarded as well—particularly those relevant to the student's future participation in the production system. For a statistical treatment of this question, see Gintis, "Education and the Characteristics of Worker Productivity."

the causal relations.* Weak causal relationships are also necessary for the efficient operation of the job allocation process. I.Q. is in fact *not* a crucial determinant of job adequacy; the placement of workers solely, or even largely, on the basis of cognitive abilities would seriously inhibit the efficient allocation of workers to occupational slots. Thus there must be a strong statistical association of I.Q. with economic success, but little economic reward for having a higher I.Q. in the absence of other traits normally associated with high I.Q.[46] Similarly there must be a strong statistical association between I.Q. and school success (grades), but enough individual variation to render "hard work" or good behavior important.[47] Again there must be a strong statistical association between school success and final level of education attainment, but enough individual variation to allow any "sufficiently motivated" student to achieve higher educational levels. Lastly there must be a strong association between level of education and economic success, but enough individual variation to reward "achievement motivation" and to allow for the multitude of personal attributes of differential value in educational and occupational performance.[48] All of these conditions appear to be satisfied.

The History of Legitimation: I.Q., Education, and Eugenics

The relationship between schooling, I.Q., and the stratification system is therefore by no means technologically determined within the framework of capitalist economic institutions. Nor did it arise accidentally. Rather, a growing body of historical research indicates that it grew out of a more or less conscious and coordinated attempt to generate a disciplined industrial labor force and to legitimate the rapid hierarchization of the division of labor around the turn of the century.[49]

This research strongly contests the dominant "liberal-technocratic" analysis of education. This "technocratic" view of schooling, economic success, and the requisites of job functioning supplies an elegant and logically coherent (if not empirically accurate) explanation of the historical rise of mass education in the process of industrial development. Because modern industry, irrespective of its political and institutional framework, consists in the application of increasingly complex and cognitively demanding operational technologies, these cognitive demands require an increasing level of cognitive competence on the part of the labor force as a whole. Thus the expansion of educational opportunity becomes a requisite of modern economic growth.[50] Formal education, by extending to the masses what had been throughout history the privilege of the few, opens the superior levels in the production hierarchy to all with the ability and willingness to attain such competencies. Hence the observed association between education and economic success reflects the achievement of a fundamentally egalitarian school system in promoting cognitive development.

Quite apart from the erroneous view that the determinants of job adequacy in modern industry are primarily cognitive, this interpretation of the rise of universal education in the United States finds little support in the historical

---

* By "statistical association" we refer to the simple correlation coefficient between the two variables. By "causal relation" we mean the partial derivative of one variable with respect to another, namely, the effect of a change in one variable on another, holding constant all other relevant variables.

record. Mass education made its beginning in cities and towns where the dominant industries required little skill—and far less cognitive ability—among the work force. The towns in which the skill-using industries located were the followers, not the leaders, in the process of mid-nineteenth-century educational reform and expansion.[51] Likewise in the late nineteenth-century rural West and South the expansion of schooling was associated, not with the application of modern technology or mechanization to farming, but with the extension of the wage labor system to agricultural employment.[52] Even the rise of the land-grant colleges— those institutions that in the popular wisdom were most finely attuned to producing the technical skills required in the modernizing agricultural sectors—cannot be explained by the cognitive needs of the economy, for during their first thirty or so years of operation they offered hardly any instruction in agricultural sciences.[53]

Thus the growth of the modern educational system did not originate with the rising cognitive requirements of the economy. Rather, the birth and early development of universal education was sparked by the critical need of a burgeoning capitalist order for a stable work force and citizenry reconciled, if not inured, to the wage labor system. Order, docility, discipline, sobriety, and humility—attributes required by the new social relation of production—were admitted by all concerned as the social benefits of schooling.[54] The popular view of the economy as a technical system would await Frederick Taylor and his scientific management movement; the Social Darwinist emphasis on intelligence appeared only in the "scientific genetics" of Binet and Terman. The integration of the I.Q. ideology into educational theory and practice had to await basic turn-of-the-century developments in the industrial order itself.

The most important of these developments was the birth of the modern corporation, with its relentless pressure toward uniformity and objectivity in the staffing of ever more finely graded hierarchical positions. The rationalistic efficiency orientation of bureaucratic order was quickly taken over by a growing educational system.[55] Taylorism in the classroom meant competition, hierarchy, uniformity, and, above all, individual accountability by means of objective testing.

A second related source of educational change emanating from the economy was the changing nature of the work force. Work on the family farm or in the artisan shop continued to give way to employment in large-scale enterprises. And millions of immigrants swelled the ranks of the new working class. The un-American, undomesticated character of this transformed work force was quickly revealed in a new labor militancy (of which Sacco and Vanzetti are merely the shadow in folk history) and a skyrocketing public welfare burden.

The accommodation of the educational system to these new economic realities was by no means a placid process. Modern education was constructed on the rapidly disintegrating and chaotic foundations of the old common school. Geared to the small town, serving native American Protestant stock, and based on the proliferation of the one-room schoolhouse, the common school was scarcely up to supplying the exploding labor needs of the new corporate order. Dramatic was its failure to deal effectively with the seething urban agglomeration of European immigrants of rural and peasant origin.[56] As large numbers of working-class and particularly immigrant children began attending high schools, the older democratic ideology of the common school—that the same curriculum should be offered to all children—gave way to the "Progressive" insistence that education should be tailored to the "needs of the child."* In the interests of providing an education relevant to the later life of the students, vocational schools and tracks were developed for the children of working families.† The academic curriculum was preserved for those who would later have the opportunity to make use of book learning either in college or in white-collar employment.

The frankness with which students were channeled into curriculum tracks on the basis of their race, ethnicity, or social class background raised serious doubts concerning the "openness" of the social class structure. The relation between social class and a child's chances of promotion or tracking assignments was disguised—though not mitigated much—by another "progressive" reform: "objective" educational testing. Particularly after World War I the increased use of intelligence and scholastic achievement testing offered an ostensibly unbiased means of measuring the product of schooling and stratifying students.[57] The complementary growth of the guidance counseling profession allowed much of the channeling to proceed from the students own well counseled choices, thus adding an apparent element of voluntarism to the system.

If the rhetoric of the educational response to the economic changes after the turn of the century was "progressive," much of its content and consciousness was supplied by the new science of "evolutionary genetics," in the form of the prestigious and influential Eugenics Movement.[58] Of course, as Karier notes, "the nativism, racism, elitism and social class bias which were so much a part of the testing and Eugenics Movement in America were, in a broader sense, part of the *Zeitgeist* which was America." Yet its solid grounding in Mendel's Law, Darwin, and the sophisticated statistical methodologies of Pearson, Thurstone, and Thorndike lent it the air of scientific rigor previously accorded only to the Newtonian sciences.

The leitmotiv of the testing movement was the uniting constitutional character of human excellence, as rooted in genetic endowment. Moral character, intelligence, and social worth were inextricably connected and biologically rooted. In the words of the eminent psychologist Edward L. Thorndike, "to him that a superior intellect is given also on the average a superior character."[59]

---

*   The superintendent of the Boston schools summed up the change in 1908:
        Until very recently (the schools) have offered equal opportunity for all to receive *one kind* of education, but what will make them democratic is to provide opportunity for all to receive such education as will fit them *equally well* for their particular life work.
In Boston, Documents of the School Committee, 1908, no. 7, p. 53, quoted in David K. Cohen and Marvin Lazerson, "Education and the Corporate Order," *Socialist Revolution,* March 1972.
†   Sol Cohen, "The Industrial Education Movement, 1906-1917," *American Quarterly,* 20 (Spring 1970) describes this process. Typical of the arguments then given for vocational education is the following, by the superintendent of schools in Cleveland:
        It is obvious that the educational needs of children in a district where the streets are well paved and clean, where the homes are spacious and surrounded by lawns and trees, where the language of the child's playfellows is pure, and where life in general is permeated with the spirit and ideal of America—it is obvious that the educational needs of such a child are radically different from those of the child who lives in a foreign and tenement section.
In William H. Elson and Frank P. Bachman, "Different Course for Elementary School," *Educational Review,* 39 (April 1910). See also Lawrence Cremin, *The Transformation of the School* (New York: Alfred A. Knopf, 1964); and Cohen and Lazerson, "Education and the Corporate Order."

A glance at the new immigrant communities, the Black rural ghettos, and the "breeding" of the upper classes could not but confirm this opinion in the popular mind. Statistical information came quickly from that architect of the still popular Stanford-Binet intelligence test—Lewis M. Terman—who confirmed the association of I.Q. and occupational status. Study after study, moreover, exhibited the low intelligence of "wards of the state" and social deviants.

That a school system geared toward moral development and toward domesticating a labor force for the rising corporate order might readily embrace standardization and testing—to the benefit of the leaders as well as the led—goes without saying. Thus it is not surprising that, while the idealistic Progressives worked in vain for a humanistic, more egalitarian education,[60] the bureaucratization and test orientation of the school system proceeded smoothly, well-oiled by seed money from the Carnegie Corporation and other large private foundations, articulated by social scientists at prestigious schools of education[61] and readily implemented by business-controlled local school boards.[62]

The success of the "cult of efficiency" in education, while obviously secured through the political power of private and public corporate elites, would have appeared unthinkable outside the framework of a burgeoning corporate order within which the "system problem" of a stable labor force demanded new and creative institutional mechanisms. Only a strong labor movement dedicated to construction of a qualitatively different social order could have prevented this, or a functionally equivalent, outcome.

We conclude that the present relation of schooling, I.Q., and economic success originated quite consciously as part of an attempt to administer and legitimate a new economic order based on the hierarchical division of labor. We reject the notion that the school system does or has ever functioned primarily to produce cognitive skills made scarce and hence valuable by the continuing modernization of the economy.

Our analysis of the contemporary structure of labor rewards, as well as our historical analysis, suggests that cognitive ability is not a particularly scarce good, and hence bears little independent reward. This conclusion will hardly be news to employers: a cotton manufacturer wrote to Horace Mann, then Secretary of the Massachusetts Board of Education, in 1841:

> I have never considered mere knowledge . . . as the only advantage derived from a good Common School education. . . . (Workers with more education possess) a higher and better state of morals, are more orderly and respectful in their deportment, and more ready to comply with the wholesome and necessary regulations of an establishment. . . . In times of agitation, on account of some change in regulations or wages, I have always looked to the most intelligent, best educated and most moral for support. The ignorant and uneducated I have generally found the most turbulent and troublesome, acting under the impulse of excited passion and jealousy.[63]

Adequate cognitive skills, we conclude, are generated as a by-product of the current structure of family life and schooling.

The Thrust of Legitimation: I.Q., Technocracy, and Meritocracy

We may isolate several related aspects of the social relations of production that are legitimized in part by the I.Q. ideology. To begin there are the overall characteristics of work in advanced U.S. capitalism: bureaucratic organization, hierarchical lines of authority, job fragmentation, and unequal reward. It is highly essential that the individual accept, and indeed come to see as natural, these undemocratic and unequal aspects of the workaday world.

Moreover, the mode of allocating individuals to these various positions in U.S. capitalism is characterized by intense competition in the educational system followed by individual assessment and choice by employers. Here again the major problem is that this "allocation mechanism" must appear egalitarian in process and just in outcome, parallel to the formal principle of "equality of all before the law" in a democratic juridical system based on freedom of contract.

While these two areas refer to the legitimation of capitalism as a social system, they have their counterpart in the individual's personal life. Thus, just as individuals must come to accept the overall social relations of production, workers must respect the authority and competence of their own "superiors" to direct their activities, and justify their own authority (however extensive) over others. Similarly, just as the overall system of role allocation must be legitimized, so individuals must assent to the justness of their own personal position, and the mechanisms through which this position has been attained. That workers be resigned to their position in production is perhaps adequate; that they be reconciled is even preferable. This highly functional mechanism for the production and stratification of labor has acquired its present form in the pursuit of objectives quite remote from the production of intellectual skills. We turn now to a more searching consideration of its workings.

V. THE REPRODUCTION OF THE HIERARCHICAL DIVISION OF LABOR

A Preview

We have argued that I.Q. plays an important role in legitimating the stratification system, but that individual differences in I.Q. are not an important source of differences in levels of economic success. What, then, does determine an individual's chances of rising to the top? Why is it that economically successful parents tend to have economically successful children? In this section we seek to explain how social class background interacts with schooling to influence an individual's chances of economic success and in so doing to reproduce a family's position in the hierarchical division of labor.

The argument may be briefly summarized at the outset. To get a job at any particular level in the hierarchy of production one has to meet two tests: first, one must be able and willing to do the work; and second, one must be of appropriate race, sex, age, education, and demeanor so that his or her assignment to the job will contribute to the sense that the social order of the firm is just. Thus criteria of worker adequacy reflect more than the employer's desire that workers be hardworking and capable. They reflect as well the need for acquiescence to the employer's monopolization of power. Thus the perpetuation and legitimation of the hierarchical division of labor within the enterprise is an important additional objective of employers in the selection and placement of workers. The smooth exercise of control from the top of the enterprise rests on the daily reconfirmation of the employee's sense of the just claim of his or her superiors, co-workers, and subordinates to their particular jobs. The ability to operate well at a particular level in the hierarchy and the legitimate claim to one's place in the authority structure and to the rewards associated with it depend to a large extent on experiences in the home and at school. The enterprise is by no means a full-blown socialization agency capable of shaping worker consciousness and behavior to its needs; its control over recruitment and internal organization can but *reinforce* patterns of consciousness developed in the larger society. That is, the particular structure of authority within the firm that will be seen as legitimate—whether based on distinctions of race, sex, educational credentials, age, manners of speech, or whatever—is an expression of broader social values and prejudices. And these too are both reflected in and dependent upon the structure of family life and schooling. Specifically we argue that a work force that is both competent to do the job and consistent with the perpetuation of the hierarchical division of labor is generated in large measure through a correspondence between the social relations of production, on the one hand, and the social relations of schooling and of family life, on the other. At the same time the corresponding relations of family life, schooling, and work tend to reproduce economic status differences among families from generation to generation.

The Criteria of Hireability

We begin with an obvious point: in capitalist society the income and social position of the vast majority of individuals derive predominately from the sale of their labor services to employers. An adequate explanation of the stratification process thus requires understanding (1) the criteria used by employers in hiring, tenure, promotion, and pay; (2) the processes whereby these criteria come to be seen as fair and legitimate; and (3) the process whereby individuals come to acquire those attributes relevant to employers' criteria.

The *prima facie* dimensions of job-relevant individual attributes are vast indeed. They include (at least) such features as ownership of physical implements (e.g., the medieval knight owned his horse, armor, and retinue), membership (e.g., the feudal guild master), ascription (e.g., sex, race, social class, age, caste, religion), and personal attributes (e.g., skills, motivation, attitudes, personality, credentials). In capitalist society it is the last of these along with a few important ascriptive traits—sex, race, and age—that come to the fore. Indeed even the relationship between social class background and economic success operates in large measure through differences in personal characteristics associated with differential family status. Employers never ask about social background.*

Thus our inquiry into the stratification process must focus on the supply, demand, and production of those personal attributes and ascriptive traits that are relevant to getting ahead in the world of work. We may begin with the demand for personal attributes by employers. While employers may have certain

---

* Warner et al., in their extensive empirical studies of stratification, place much emphasis on social class ascription. See W. Lloyd Warner et al., *Who Shall Be Educated?* (New York: Harper, 1944). Compare Warner and Paul S. Lunt, *The Social Life of a Modern Community* (New Haven: Yale University Press, 1941). But this seems characteristic only of the "small-town" economic community, rapidly becoming past history.

restrictions in their hiring practices (child labor and antidiscrimination laws, union regulations, social pressures), by and large their sole objective in hiring is to insure the ability of individuals to perform adequately in the work role in question. The requirements of job adequacy in any job, of course, depend on the entire structure of work roles, that is, on the social relations of production within the enterprise. Thus we must first inquire into the criteria by which work is organized. What determines the structure of work roles—in capitalist society characterized by hierarchy, job fragmentation, bureaucracy, and control from the top of the organization?

One objective of capitalists—both as a class and as individuals—is to perpetuate their class standing. Thus work roles must be organized so as to reproduce the position of capitalists and allied high level management in the social relations of production. A closely related second objective is securing adequate long-term profits, without which the enterprise would cease to exist. Thus profits are sought both as an instrument in maintaining the class status of the directors of the firm and as their major source of income.*

In the joint pursuit of profits and the perpetuation of their class standing, the directors of an enterprise seek to meet three immediate objectives—sometimes complementary, sometimes in conflict: technical efficiency, control, and legitimacy. Technical efficiency requires that the structure of work roles be organized so that for a given set of inputs—labor, raw materials, equipment, etc. —the maximum possible output will be produced. The second objective, control over the production process, requires both the retention of decision-making power at the top and the maintenance of labor costs in line with those prevailing in the economy as a whole. Both forms of control are highly problematic. First, as we have emphasized, the political organization of the enterprise is totalitarian, while the external political process is formally democratic. Where possible, workers demand control over the decision making about working conditions toward the improvement of their condition. Organizing production hierarchically and fragmenting tasks, by dividing workers on different levels against one another and reducing the independent range of control of each, both weaken the solidarity (and hence limit the group power) of workers and serve to convince them, through their day-to-day activities, of their personal incapacity to control—and even of its technical infeasibility. Thus hiring criteria and the structuring of work roles are based on the principle of "divide and conquer."[64] That the satisfaction of this control objective often conflicts with technical efficiency is illustrated by the many studies documenting significant increases in productivity and worker satisfaction associated with shifts toward worker participation in decision making, greater job breadth, and the use of work teams.[65] But efficiency and profitability are, of course, different things.

A third objective is that work roles be organized so as to legitimize the authority relations in the firm. That is, relations among superiors, subordinates, and peers must not violate the norms of the larger society, and the right of the

---

* Indeed under conditions of perfect competition the maximization of profits is a necessary condition for the reproduction of the capitalists' class position. We need not here enter into the complicated debate on whether firms do indeed seek to maximize profits. For a survey see Edwards, "Alienation and Inequality." We conclude that the relevant behavioral implication of the theories that posit other objectives (sales or employment maximization, for example) are, in the context of the by and large competitive milieu of the U.S. economy, virtually indistinguishable from those of profit maximization.

superior to direct as well as the duty of the subordinate to submit must draw on
general cultural values. It is for this reason that a superior must always have a
higher salary than a subordinate, whatever the conditions of relative supply of
the two types of labor. It is also for this reason that in a racist and sexist society
Blacks and women cannot in general be placed above whites or men in the line
of hierarchical authority. Employers ordinarily structure work roles so that
young people will not boss older people. In terms of personal attributes, modes
of self-presentation are also important; however well they actually function
technically, individuals must seem fit for their position and must actively protect
their prerogatives and the structure of work roles (especially their own).[66] Educational *credentials* enter here as well: it is desirable to associate hierarchical
authority with level of education, not only because higher levels of schooling
may enable an employee to better do the work at hand or because the more
educated seem more fit by their demeanor to hold authority, but also simply
because educational achievement, as symbolized by one sort of sheepskin or
another, legitimates authority according to prevailing social values. Indeed this
fact lies at the root of the I.Q. ideology described above.

From this analysis of the capitalist objectives governing the organization of
work roles in the enterprise, we may derive some insight into the employers'
demand for particular worker attributes. Our analysis suggests five important
sets of worker characteristics. First, we have noted the emphasis of the "technocratic perspective" on cognitive attributes—such as scholastic achievement—
to which we may add concrete technical and operational skills (e.g., knowing
how to do typing, accounting, chemical engineering, or carpentry). Second,
there are, parallel to cognitive attributes, a set of personality traits (such as
motivation, perseverance, docility, dominance, flexibility, or tact) that enable
the individual to operate effectively in a work role. Third, there are traits that
we may call modes of self-presentation[67] such as manner of speech and dress,
patterns of peer identification, and perceived "social distance" from individuals
and groups of different social position. These traits do not necessarily contribute to the worker's execution of tasks, but may be valuable to employers in their
effort to stabilize, validate, and legitimize the particular structure of work roles
in the organization as a whole. Similar in function are our fourth set of traits:
ascriptive characteristics such as race, sex, and age. Finally we may add to our
list of attributes credentials, such as level and prestige of education, which, like
modes of self-presentation and the ascriptive traits, are a resource used by employers to add to the overall legitimacy of the organization.

The analytical problem, of course, is to determine the precise content of
these five factors, and how each affects the stratification process. This problem
is particularly difficult in that all five tend to occur together in a single individual. Thus an individual with more cognitive achievement and skills will also, on
the average, be more capable personality-wise of operating on higher occupational levels, will speak, dress, and exhibit a pattern of loyalties befitting the
corresponding social class, and will have proper credentials to boot (though she
may be a woman!). But since there is still a great deal of variation among individuals in their relative possession of these various attributes, analysis is not
impossible. Indeed a major statistically supported assertion of this essay is that
cognitive attributes are not central to the determination of social stratification,
and hence the association of cognitive level and access to higher level occupations must be largely a by-product of selection on the basis of others.

We believe that all four of the remaining types of personal attributes—personality traits relevant to the work task, modes of self-presentation, ascriptive traits, and credentials—are integral to the stratification process. Indeed we shall argue that all four are systematically used by employers to affect the reproduction of the hierarchical division of labor, and, as such, their importance in the determination of economic success is not an expression of irrational and uninformed employment policies, subject to correction by "enlightened" employment practices and social legislation. Instead, we shall argue in our concluding section that the link between the social relations of production and the stratification process is so intimate that any qualitative change in the latter is contingent upon the transformation of the hierarchical division of labor as the archetype of productive activity.*

We do not yet understand precisely how these four noncognitive types of worker traits interact, or the extent to which each contributes to the stratification process. The strong association between education and economic success, plus the relative unimportance of cognitive achievement as a criterion of job placement, nevertheless convinces us of their overall decisive impact. We shall present evidence for the importance of each in turn, beginning with the job-relevant personality traits.

The personality traits required of "efficient" workers must correspond by and large to the requirements of harmonious integration into the bureaucratic order of the enterprise. This order exhibits four essential characteristics. First, the duties, responsibilities, and privileges of individuals are determined neither according to individual preference nor flexible cooperative decision by workers, but rather by a system of rules that precedes the individual's participation and sets limits on his or her actions. Second, the relations among individuals are characterized, according to the rules of the organization, by hierarchical authority and interdependence. An individual's actions are closely tied to the wills of his or her superiors, and the results of his or her actions have repercussions on large numbers of other workers. Third, while control from the top is manifested in rules, the principle of hierarchical authority implies that large numbers of workers have essential, though circumscribed, areas of decision and choice. Fourth, the formal nature of the organization and the fact that work roles are determined on the basis of profitability and compatibility with control from the apex of the pyramidal organization imply that workers cannot be adequately motivated by the intrinsic rewards of the work process.[68]

These characteristics of the hierarchical division of labor determine the personality traits required of workers. Some of these are general traits valuable to the employer at all levels of hierarchy and status. All workers must be dependable (i.e., follow rules) because of the strong emphasis on rules and the complex interrelations among tasks that define the enterprise. Similarly all workers must be properly subordinate to authority—diligent in carrying out

---

* We would like to show further that the hierarchical division of labor, far from flowing naturally from the exigencies of productive efficiency, has taken its present form in response to the continuous struggles of capitalists for hegemony in the control of economic activity. From this perspective the stratification system can be seen as the product of the class struggle between capitalists and workers. Given our present understanding of these issues, however, no brief survey of the evidence could do justice to the argument, to which we hope to return in a later paper. For extended historical and contemporary treatments that we find persuasive, see Marglin, "What Do Bosses Do?" and Edwards, "Alienation and Inequality."

orders as opposed to merely obeying rules. Further all workers, insofar as they have areas of personal initiative and choice, must internalize the values of the organization, using its criteria as a basis for decision. Lastly all workers must respond adequately to the external incentives of the organization—the crudest being threat of dismissal, and the more subtle including the possibility of promotion to higher status, authority, or pay. Thus the worker must work equally efficiently independent from personal feelings about the particular task at hand.

While these requirements hold for all workers, there are important qualitative differences among levels. These tend to follow directly from differences in the scope of independent decision making, which increases with hierarchical status. Thus the lowest level of worker must simply refrain from breaking rules. On the highest level it becomes crucial that the worker internalize the values of the organization, act out of personal initiative, and know when not to go by the book. In between, workers must be methodical, predictable, and persevering, and at a somewhat higher level, must respond flexibly to their superiors, whose directives acquire a complexity transcending the relatively few rules that apply directly to their tasks. Thus we would expect the crucial determinants of job adequacy to pass from rule following to dependability-predictability to subordinateness to internalized values, all with an overlap of motivation according to external incentives and penalties (doubtless with penalties playing a larger role at the lower levels, and incentives at the higher).

Much of this description of functional personal attributes of job performance is based on the work of Richard Edwards, and has been supported by his empirical research.[69] Edwards argues that supervisor ratings of employees—as the basic determinant of hirings, firings, and promotions—are the best measure of job adequacy and are the implements of the organization's stratification mechanism. Thus Edwards compared supervisor ratings on these workers with a set of thirty-two personality ratings by the workers' peers. In a large sample of Boston-area workers, he finds that a cluster of three personality traits—which he summarizes as respect for rules, dependability, and internalization of the norms of the firm—predicts strongly* supervisor ratings of workers in the same work group, while such attributes as age, sex, social class background, education, and intelligence have little additional predictive value. In addition, Edwards noted that respect for rules was most important at the lower occupational levels, dependability appearing strongly for middle levels, and internalization of the norms of the firm predicting best at the higher levels.

When we pass to the literature documenting the importance of self-presentation as attributes relevant to the allocation of individuals to status positions, we are faced with a difficult problem of assessment. Numerous studies have shown these personal attributes to be definite (albeit often covert) criteria for hiring and promotion.[70] Being descriptive and analytical rather than statistical, however, they defy comparison with other data on personal attributes as to importance in the stratification process. We must content ourselves with a simple presentation of the arguments.

"A status," says Goffman, ". . . is not a material thing; it is a pattern of appropriate conduct, coherent, embellished, and well articulated."[71] That is, apart from the "reality" of task performance, role fulfillment requires the "contrivance" of legitimation—legitimation of the role itself as well as the individual's

* R^2 = 38%, uncorrected for errors in measurement and reliability.

personal right to fill it. Thus the doctor not only must cure but also must exude the aura of infallibility and dedication fitting for one whose critical acts intervene between life and death. Similarly, the supervisor not only must supervise but also must exhibit his inevitable distance from and superiority to his inferiors, and his ideal suitability for his position. Thus role fulfillment requires a dramatic "theatrical" performance—an impulse toward idealization of role—on a routinized and internalized basis. Goffman documents the importance of self-presentation in a vast array of social positions—those of doctors, nurses, waitresses, dentists, military personnel, mental patients, funeral directors, eighteenth-century noblemen, Indian castes, Chinese mandarins, junk peddlers, unionized workers, teachers, pharmacists, as well as in the relations between men and women and Blacks and whites.[72]

Central to Goffman's analysis of self-presentation is his concept of the "front" of a performance, defined as "that part of the individual's performance which regularly functions in a general and fixed fashion to define the situation for those who view the performance,"[73] This front consists of personal behavior ("insignia of office or rank; clothing, sex, age, and racial characteristics; size and looks; posture; speech patterns; facial expressions; bodily gestures; and the like") as well as physical setting. Moreover, argues Goffman, these fronts are not merely personal and idiosyncratic, but are socially regularized and channeled, so there is "a tendency for a large number of different acts to be presented behind a small number of fronts."[74] Thus, on the one hand, "modes of self-presentation" take on a social class character, and, on the other, physical settings are allocated not to individuals but to hierarchical levels.

The role of self-presentation in social stratification arises from a similar social treatment of "personal fronts." Social class differences in family and childhood socialization, as well as the informal organization of peer groups along social class lines,[75] are likely to reinforce social class lines from generation to generation by providing stable reproduction of modes of self-presentation. Similarly social class differences in levels of schooling are likely to develop career identities, symbols and ideologies, organization loyalties, and aspirations apposite to particular levels in the hierarchy of production.

But does self-presentation play a role akin to I.Q. in the stratification process (i.e., is it by and large a by-product of allocation and socialization mechanisms based on other criteria), or does its importance compare with and perhaps even eclipse job-relevant personality traits? The answer awaits future research.

We may now consider the importance of our last two sets of employability traits: ascriptive characteristics (race, age, sex) and acquired credentials (e.g., educational degrees, seniority). We have argued that the legitimation of the hierarchical division of labor, as well as the smooth day-to-day control over the work process, requires that the authority structure of the enterprise—with its corresponding structure of pay and privilege—respects the wider society's ascriptive and symbolic distinctions. In particular, socially acceptable relations of domination and subordination must be respected: white over Black; male over female; old (but not aged) over young; and schooled over unschooled.

We make no claim that these social prejudices originated as a capitalist contrivance, although a strong case could probably be made that the form and strength of both sexism and racism here derive in large measure from the particular historical development of capitalist institutions in the United States and Europe. Save credentialist distinctions, all predate the modern capitalist era.

"Rational business practice" has reinforced and extended them, while consigning less useful prejudices to the proverbial trash bin of history.* The credentialist mentality, as we have argued, was indeed contrived to perpetuate the concept of social rank in a society increasingly eschewing distinctions of birth.

The individual employer, acting singly, normally takes societal values and beliefs as data, and will violate them only where his long-term financial benefits are secure. The broader prejudices of society are thus used as a resource by bosses in their effort to control labor. In this way the pursuit of profits and security of class position reinforces the racist, sexist, and credentialist mentality. Thus Black workers are paid less than whites with equivalent schooling and cognitive achievement,[76] and similarly for women relative to men.[77] Likewise those with more schooling are given preference for supervisory jobs, in the absence of compelling evidence of the superior performance of those less educated.[78] Lastly pay and authority increase over most of a person's working life, out of all proportion to any conceivable on-the-job learning of increased skills.

How Worker Characteristics Are Acquired: The Correspondence Principles

Having surveyed the reasoning and evidence indicating the importance of our four sets of noncognitive worker traits—work-related personality characteristics, modes of self-presentation, ascriptive characteristics, and credentials—we turn now to our last question: how are these determinants of one's place in the stratification system acquired? The ascriptive traits are, of course, acquired at birth, or in the case of age, inescapably as life progresses, so little need be said of them. The acquisition of credentials requires survival in the school system, and is an arduous, but not particularly complex, process. The way in which workers come to have a particular set of work-relevant personality characteristics or modes of self-presentation requires a more searching analysis.

We find the answer to this question in two correspondence principles, which may be stated succinctly as follows: the social relations of schooling and of family life correspond to the social relations of production.

We have suggested above that the social relations of schooling are structured similarly to the social relations of production in several essential respects.[79] The school is a bureaucratic order with hierarchical authority, rule orientation, stratification by "ability" (tracking) as well as by age (grades), role differentiation by sex (physical education, home economics, shop), and a system of external incentives (marks, promise of promotion, and threat of failure) much like pay and status in the sphere of work. Thus schools are likely to develop in students traits corresponding to those required on the job. One of us,[80] in a review of the educational literature, has shown that students are graded for personality traits associated with subordinacy, discipline, and rule following quite independently of the level of cognitive achievement. Several studies of vocational training by Gene Smith[81] exhibit the same pattern of reward, and our colleague Peter Meyer[82]

---

* At the same time, of course, the extension and development of capitalist wage labor tends to destroy class distinctions based on precapitalist social relations of production (such as nepotism, direct social class discrimination in hiring, slave status, caste, and nobility), as these are incompatible with the hierarchical division of labor. Similarly capitalist development is destructive of the ideological underpinnings of all ascriptive norms—even those that are "respected" in the above sense in the day-to-day operation of the enterprise. We shall discuss this contradiction in Section VI.

has replicated Edwards's results, using the same personality measures, in predicting not "supervision ratings," but "grade point average" in a New York high school. Lastly Edwards's analysis of data on high school records and data work supervision ratings collected by Brenner[83] indicate that variables measuring teacher's evaluation of student conduct are far more important than the student's grade point average in predicting the individual's work adequacy as perceived by the supervisor.* While more work in this area remains to be done, there are clear indications that the educational system does articulate with the economy in large part via these effective selection and generation mechanisms.

But recall that the work-related personality traits required of employees differ according to the work role in question, those at the base of the hierarchy requiring a heavy emphasis on obedience and rules and those at the top, where the discretionary scope is considerable, requiring a greater ability to make decisions on the basis of well-internalized norms. This pattern is closely replicated in the social relations of schooling. Note the wide range of choice over curriculum, life style, and allocation of time afforded to college students, compared with the obedience and respect for authority expected in high school. Differentiation occurs also within each level of schooling. One needs only to compare the social relations of a junior college with those of an elite four-year college,[84] or those of a working class high school with those of a wealthy suburban high school, for verification of this point.†

The differential socialization patterns in schools attended by students of different social classes, and even within the same school, do not arise by accident. Rather, they stem from the fact that the educational objectives and expectations of administrators, teachers, and parents, and the responsiveness of students to various patterns of teaching and control, differ for students of different social classes.‡ Further, class inequalities in school socialization patterns are reinforced by inequalities in financial resources. The paucity of financial support for the education of children from working-class families leaves more resources to be devoted to the children of those with commanding roles in the economy; it also forces upon the teachers and school administrators in the working-class schools a type of social relations that fairly closely mirrors that of the factory. Thus financial considerations in poorly supported working-class schools militate against small intimate classes, against a multiplicity of elective courses and specialized teachers (except disciplinary personnel), and preclude the amounts of free time for the teachers and free space required for a more open, flexible educational environment. The lack of financial support all by requires that students be treated as raw materials on a production line; it places a high premium on

---

* This is a particularly strong finding in view of the fact that the grades themselves are evidently determined in important measure by the teacher's evaluation of the student's conduct. For a discussion of these data, see Edwards, "Alienation and Inequality."
† Edgar Z. Friedenberg, *Coming of Age in America* (New York: Random House, 1965). It is consistent with this pattern that the play-oriented, child-centered pedagogy of the progressive movement found little acceptance outside of private schools in wealthy communities. See Cohen and Lazerson, "Education and the Corporate Order," and Neil Friedman, "Inequality, Social Control, and the History of Educational Reform," unpublished manuscript, School of Social Welfare, State University of New York at Stony Brook, 1972.
‡ That working-class parents seem to favor more authoritarian educational methods is perhaps a reflection of their own work experiences that have demonstrated that submission to authority is an essential ingredient in one's ability to get and hold a steady, well-paying job.

obedience and punctuality; there are few opportunities for independent, creative work or individualized attention by teachers. The well-financed schools attended by the children of the rich can offer much greater opportunities for the development of the capacity for sustained independent work and the other characteristics required for adequate job performance in the upper levels of the occupational hierarchy.

The correspondence between the social relations of production and the social relations of childhood socialization itself is not, however, confined to schooling. There is strong evidence for a similar correspondence in the structure of family life. The male-dominated family, with its structure of power and privilege, further articulated according to age, replicates many of the aspects of the hierarchy of production in the firm. Yet more relevant for our immediate concerns here is the evidence on social class, parental values, and childrearing practices. Most clearly directed to our formulation is Melvin Kohn's massive ten-year study, under the sponsorship of the National Institute for Mental Health.[85] Kohn's major results are that "middle class parents . . . are more likely to emphasize children's self-direction, and working class parents to emphasize their *conformity to external authority. . . .* The essential difference between the terms, as we use them, is that self-direction focuses on *internal* standards of direction for behavior; conformity focuses on *externally* imposed rules." Thus parents of lower status children value obedience, neatness, and honesty in their children, while higher status parents emphasize curiosity, self-control, and happiness. Kohn concludes: "In this exceptionally diverse society—deeply marked by racial and religious division, highly varied in economy, geography, and even degree of urbanization —social class stands out as more important for men's values than does any other line of demarcation, unaffected by all the rest of them, and apparently more important than all of them together."[86]

To refine the relation between social class, values, and child-rearing, Kohn classifies his test subjects (fourteen hundred in number) according to the amount of "occupational self-direction" inherent in their jobs—using as indices whether the worker is closely supervised, whether the worker deals with things, data, or people, and whether the job is complex or repetitive. His analysis indicates that the "relationship of social class to parents' valuation of self-direction or conformity for children is largely attributable to class-correlated variation in men's exercise of self-direction in work."[87] And he concludes:

Whether consciously or not, parents tend to impart to their children lessons derived from the conditions of life of their own social class—and thus help prepare their children for a similar class position. . . . Class differences in parental values and child rearing practices influence the development of the capacities that children will someday need. . . . The family, then, functions as a mechanism for perpetuating inequality.

Such differential patterns of childrearing do affect more than the worker's personality and aspiration level. They also determine his or her style of self-presentation: patterns of class loyalties and modes of speech, dress, and interpersonal behavior. While such traits are by no means fixed into adulthood, their stability over the life cycle appears sufficient to account for the observed degree of intergenerational status transmission.

VI. THE FAILURE OF LIBERAL SOCIAL REFORM
AND THE FUTURE OF THE STRATIFICATION SYSTEM

Social Reform in the 1960s:
An Action Critique of Liberal Theory

In 1847 Karl Marx and Friedrich Engels wrote, "Wherever the bourgeoisie has risen to power, it has destroyed all feudal, patriarchal, and idyllic relationships . . . it has left no other bond betwixt man and man but crude self-interest and unfeeling cash payment."[88] Ironically the positive aspect of this historic pronouncement lies at the base of the liberal theory of stratification. Thus John Gardner, president of the Carnegie Corporation, later to become Secretary of the U.S. Department of Health, Education, and Welfare, could confidently state: "Most human societies have been beautifully organized to keep good men down. . . . Birth determined occupation and status. . . . Such societies were doomed by the Industrial Revolution."[89]

But by the early 1960s it was painfully evident that the heralded natural trend toward equality had not fared well. Despite phenomenal economic growth, a vast expansion (and equalization) of the educational system, and the introduction of the "progressive" income tax, Social Security, and other welfare state programs, inequality of income has remained essentially unchanged.[90] The introduction of taxes on inheritance has done little to alter the distribution of wealth: the top one-half of one percent of wealth holders hold about a quarter of all wealth; the top one percent hold about three-quarters of all corporate stock.[91] Woman's suffrage and a more liberal attitude toward "the woman's place" in the home and on the job did not prevent a decline in the economic situation of women relative to men.[92] The attenuation of racial prejudice— attested to in numerous recent surveys—and the dramatic educational gains made by Blacks have not resulted in occupational or income gains for Blacks relative to whites.[93] Finally the extension of public elementary and secondary education and the growth of state supported higher education have not been accompanied by a reduction in the extent to which one's family's social status determines one's own education opportunities.[94] Similarly the correlation between the occupational status of individuals and their parents has not been reduced.[95]

Viewing this panorama of persistent inequality, the liberal community of the 1960s grew to emphasize ever more heavily the age-old distinction between inequality of *opportunity* and inequality of *outcome*. According to this perspective, inequality of outcome (income, wealth, status, and job desirability) is necessitated by the very structure of industrial society[96] whose harshest effects can be no more than ameliorated through enlightened social welfare practices. The vital progressive thrust of liberal social policy, according to the same perspective, must grow from the sobering necessity of limiting our aspirations as to equality of outcome, while setting our highest sights on providing all with a fair shot at unequal economic reward. According to this view, the justness of the social order can then be assessed by the extent to which it has eliminated discrimination based on social background, caste, or color.

In this liberal perspective the capitalist economy, finally shorn of anachronistic prejudices, can become the true meritocracy. The "performance orientation" and "organizational rationality" of employers, the impersonality of labor markets, and the "structural differentiation of the economic sub-system" all conspire to eliminate sexual, racial, and social class discriminations. Intergenerational status transmission, in this view, thus comes to depend integrally on inherited (whether through nature or nurture) differences in ability and willingness to perform. Thus Gardner can confidently assert, in the same breath, that "when a society gives up hereditary stratification . . . dramatic differences in ability and performance . . . emerge . . . and may lead to peaks and valleys of status as dramatic as those produced by hereditary stratification."[97]

Thus the decade of the 1960s was marked by the commitment to bring social policy to bear on the equalization of opportunity. In fulfilling this commitment, liberal social policy has drawn on liberal social theory in three essential respects. First, it has harbored an abiding optimism, flowing from the theorists' separation of equality of opportunity and equality of outcome. The hierarchical division of labor could be maintained while the atavistic remains of bigotry and unequal social resources could be swept away via additional legislation and more effective propaganda. Second, the technocratic orientation of liberal theory indicated that the crucial policy variables were those related to differences in cognitive and psycho-motor performance-related skills—hence the emphasis on education and training. This, then, provided the focus of the reforms of the 1960s. Third, the limits of social reform in this area, so the theory predicts, are dictated by genetic differences in ability.

A less auspicious set of assumptions could scarcely have been chosen, for the cognitive abilities central to the theory have turned out to be far less socially malleable than the liberals had hoped. By 1970 the hubris of the War on Poverty, in the face of persistent failure, had vanished. In the area of educational policy, the "empirical finding" that differing levels of resources did not significantly promote scholastic achievement[98] was quickly buttressed by a host of dismal assessments of the performance of the major compensatory educational programs—Title I, Head Start, Follow Through, and others.[99]

These failures, of course, softened the liberal position for the inevitable conservative counterattack. This counterattack has been based on both pillars of the liberal theory of stratification: *willingness* and *ability* to perform in the impersonal industrial marketplace. The voguish "culture of poverty" school locates the blame for poverty in deeply rooted deficiencies of the poor themselves, limiting their willingness to perform.[100] Progressive social theory has been unable to defend itself against this thrust, as it lacks a firm understanding of the structural relations between the cultural subsystems in the workplace and in the larger society.[101] The assault of the "genetic school" discussed in this paper is based on the purported *inability* of the poor to perform. The proponents of liberal social policy cannot defend themselves against the massive attack of the geneticists without reversing in midstream; for it had consistently posited "ability" and "performance" as the ideal criteria of employability and economic reward. This perspective has manifested itself particularly strongly in the more policy-related social science disciplines, especially in the economics and sociology of education. Thus the economic returns to schooling have been "corrected for ability differences,"[102] student quality has been measured by I.Q., and school quality by contribution to cognitive achievement,[103] and cognitive indices have been taken as the basic output variables in educational production functions.[104] In the area of social policy the findings of the Coleman report,[105] relying only on measures of cognitive achievement, were conceived, and are still consistently referred to, as basic to the solution to problems of poverty and inequality. Thus

Moynihan and Mosteller, in the introduction to their massive reanalysis of the Coleman data, refer to the report as a "revolutionary document" whose crowning achievement lies in its taking "educational output, not input alone . . . (as) the central issue."[106] Adding the critics of Jensen and Herrnstein to this list, we are faced with a degree of unanimity perhaps unparalleled in social science.

In earlier sections we argued that the liberal perspective on stratification is incorrect. Hence we are not surprised that social policy based on its premises has failed. Nor are we surprised at the success of the counterattack. The theoretical fallacy at the heart of liberal stratification theory, stated in policy-oriented terms, is the assertion that equality of opportunity is compatible with equality of outcomes. We have argued that neither "ability" nor "willingness" can be understood outside a total perspective in which social, racial, ethnic, and sexual differentiations and differential patterns of socialization interact with the hierarchical division of labor. Individuals, as well as their social subcultures, develop according to their relationship to the social division of labor. Our argument holds that the social relations of production are mirrored—via the correspondence principles—in the basic socialization agencies of family, community, and school. Thus inequality of opportunity is a by-product of the organization of production itself, and cannot be attached either to "dysfunctional" attributes of the underclasses or the self-interested malfeasance and unfeeling perversity of unprogressive social policy. In addition to performance-related individual capacities normally developed on a class basis, beneath the surface of rationality, meritocracy, and performance-oriented efficiency, the capitalist economic system operates on a subtle network of ascriptions and symbolic differentiations, quite as well-articulated as the most complex caste system. Moreover, this "open caste system" is essential to the legitimation and operation of the hierarchical division of labor itself. Any particular element may be eliminated (e.g., racism), but new modes of status differentiation must arise to take its place. Such is the logic of our argument.

Contradictory Development and the Future of the Class Structure

We have described the stratification system in the United States as a reflection of the hierarchical division of labor. Moreover, we have exhibited a strong tendency for the social system to draw on abiding status and caste distinctions (including race, sex, ethnicity, and personal demeanor) in the legitimation of the capitalist social relations of production, while creating other distinctions (e.g., I.Q. educational credentials) when necessary toward these same ends. Yet our analysis must be incomplete in one essential respect: it seems to propose that the system has little difficulty in fulfilling these preconditions for its own reproduction. Yet the political and social upheavals of the 1960s—including the Black and women's movements, radical student revolts, rank-and-file unrest in the labor movement, the rise of the counterculture and a new mood of equality among youth—have ushered in a growing consciousness directed against the stratification system, and even the hierarchical division of labor itself.[107] Clearly our analysis has been one-sided.

The problem? We have treated only the way in which the U.S. capitalist system reproduces itself, without dealing with the contradictions that inevitably arise out of the system's own successes—contradictions that lead to social dislocation and require structural change in the social relations of production for the further development of the social system.[108] The present seems to represent one of these crucial periods of contradiction.[109] We can do no more here than list some of these central contradictions.

First, the legitimacy of the capitalist system has been historically based in no small part on its ability to "deliver the goods." The ever increasing mass of consumer goods and services seemed to promise constant improvement in levels of well-being for all. Yet the very success of the process has undermined the urgency of consumer wants; other needs—for community, for security, for a more integral and self-initiated work and social life—are coming to the fore. And these needs are unified by a common characteristic: they cannot be met simply by producing more consumer goods and services. On the contrary, the economic foundations of capital accumulation are set firmly in the destruction of the social basis for the satisfaction of these needs. Thus through "economic development" itself, needs are generated that the advanced capitalist system is not geared to satisfy.[110] Thus the legitimacy of the capitalist order must increasingly be handled by other social mechanisms, of which the meritocracy is a major element. It is not clear that the latter can bear this strain.

Second, the concentration of capital and the continuing separation of workers —white collar and professional as well as manual—from control over the production process has reduced the natural defenders of the capitalist order to a small minority.[111] Two hundred years ago over three-fourths of white families owned land, tools, or other productive property; this fraction has fallen to about a third, and even among this group, a tiny minority owns the lion's share of all productive property. Similarly two hundred years ago about all white male workers were their own boss. The demise of the family farm, the artisan shop and the small store, and the rise of the modern corporation, has reduced the figure to less than 10 percent.[112] For most Americans the capitalist system has come to mean someone *else's* right to profits, someone *else's* right to work unbossed and in pursuit of one's own objectives. The decline of groups outside the wage labor system—farmer, artisan, entrepreneur, and independent professional—has eliminated a ballast of capitalist support, leaving the legitimation system alone to divide strata among the working class against one another.

Third, developments in technology and work organization have begun to undermine the main line of ideological defense of the capitalist system, namely, the idea that the capitalist relations of production—private property and the hierarchical organization of work—are the most conducive to the rapid expansion of productivity.[113] Repeated experiments have shown that in those complex work tasks that increasingly dominate modern production, participatory control by workers is a more productive form of work organization.[114] The boredom and stultification of the production line and the steno pool, the shackled creativity of technical workers and teachers, the personal frustration of the bureaucratic office routine, increasingly lose their claim as the price of material comfort. The ensuing attacks on bureaucratic oppression go hand in hand with demystification of the meritocracy ideology as discussed in this paper. Support for capitalist institutions—once firmly rooted in their claim to superiority in meeting urgent consumption needs and squarely based on a broad mass of property-owning independent workers—is thus weakened by the process of capitalist development itself. At the same time powerful anticapitalist forces are brought into being. The accumulation of capital—the engine of growth under capitalism—has as its necessary companion the proletarianization of labor. The continuing integration of new groups into the worldwide wage labor system has not brought about the international working-class consciousness that many Marxists had predicted. But the process has introduced serious strains into the capitalist order. These may be summarized as a fourth and fifth set of contradictions.

Fourth, the international expansion of capital has fueled nationalist and anticapitalist movements in many of the poor countries. The strains associated with the worldwide integration of the capitalist system are manifested in the resistance of the people of Vietnam, in the rise of the Chilean left, in the socialist revolution in China and Cuba, and in political instability and guerrilla movements elsewhere in Asia, Africa, and Latin America. The U.S. role in opposition to wars of national liberation—particularly in Vietnam— has brought part of the struggle back home and exacerbated many of the domestic contradictions of advanced capitalism.[115]

Fifth, and cutting across all of the above, with the return to comparatively smooth capitalist development in the United States in the mid-1950s after the tumultuous decades of the 1930s and 1940s, the impact of far-reaching cumulative changes in the class structure is increasingly reflected in crises of public consciousness. The corporatization of agriculture and reduction of the farm population has particularly affected Blacks, who are subjected to the painful process of forceful integration into the urban wage labor system. The resulting political instabilities are not unlike those following the vast wave of immigrants in the early decades of the century. Changes in the technology of household production and the vast increase in female labor in the service industries also portend a radically altered economic position of women. Finally the large corporation and the state bureaucracies have replaced entrepreneurial, elite white-collar, and independent professional jobs as the locus of middle-class economic activity, and the effective proletarianization of white-collar labor marks the already advanced integration of these groups into the wage labor system.[116] In each case contradictions have arisen between the traditional consciousness of these groups and their new objective economic situations. This has provided much of the impetus for radical movements among Blacks, women, students, and counter culture youth.

While searching for long-range structural accommodations to these contradictions, defenders of the capitalist order will likely be forced to place increasing reliance on the general legitimation mechanisms associated with the meritocratic-technocratic ideology. As a result it appears likely that the future will reveal increasing reliance on the "meritocratic" stratification mechanisms and the associated legitimating ideologies: I.Q.-ism and educational credentialism. Efforts and resources will doubtless multiply toward the "full equalization of opportunity," but the results, if our arguments are correct, will be limited as long as the hierarchical division of labor perpetuates itself.

The credentialist and I.Q. ideology upon which the "meritocratic ligitimation mechanisms depend is thus already under attack. Blacks reject the racism implicit in much of the recent work on I.Q.; they are not mystified by the elaborate empirical substantiation of the geneticist position, nor by the assertions of meritocracy by functionalist sociologists. Their daily experience gives them insights that seem to have escaped many social scientists. Likewise women—indeed many poor people of both sexes—know that their exclusion from jobs is not based on any deficiency of educational credentials.

We have here attempted to speed up the process of demystification by showing that the purportedly "scientific" empirical basis of credentialism and I.Q.-ism is false. In addition, we have attempted to facilitate linkages between these groups and workers' movements within the dominant white male labor force by showing that the *same* mechanisms are used to divide strata against one another so as to maintain the inferior status of "minority" groups.

The assault on economic inequality and hierarchical control of work appears likely to intensify. Along with other social strains endemic to advanced capitalism, the growing tension between people's needs for self-realization in work and the needs of capitalists and managers for secure top-down control of economic activity opens up the possibility of powerful social movements dedicated to the elimination of the hierarchical division of labor. We hope our paper will contribute to this outcome.

NOTES

1. The most explicit statement of the genetic interpretation of intergenerational immobility is Richard Herrnstein, "IQ," *Atlantic Monthly,* September 1971, pp. 43-64.

2. Michael Katz notes the historical tendency of genetic interpretations of social inequality to gain popularity following the failure of educational reform movements. Michael Katz, *The Irony of Early School Reform* (Cambridge: Harvard University Press, 1968). On the rise of the genetic interpretation of inequality toward the end of the Progressive Era, see Clarence J. Karier, "Testing for Order and Control in the Corporate Liberal State," *Educational Theory,* 22, no. 2 (Spring 1972).

3. Louis Wirth, Preface, in Karl Mannheim, *Ideology and Utopia: An Introduction to the Sociology of Knowledge* (New York: Harcourt, Brace & World, 1936), pp. x-xxx.

4. Arthur R. Jensen, "How Much Can We Boost IQ and Scholastic Achievement?" *Harvard Educational Review,* Reprint Series no. 2, 1969, pp. 126-134.

5. For example, H. J. Eysenck, *The IQ Argument* (New York: Library Press, 1971), and Herrnstein, "IQ."

6. For a representative sampling of criticism, see the issues of the *Harvard Educational Review* that followed the Jensen article.

7. Our work in this area is reported in Herbert Gintis, "Alienation and Power: Toward a Radical Welfare Economics," Ph.D. diss., Harvard University, 1969; Gintis, "Education and the Characteristics of Worker Productivity," *American Economic Review,* 61 (May 1971): 266-279; Samuel Bowles, "Schooling and Inequality from Generation to Generation," *Journal of Political Economy* (May-June 1972); Bowles, "The Genetic Inheritance of IQ and the Intergenerational Reproduction of Economic Inequality," Harvard Institute for Economic Research, September 1972.

8. Jensen, "How Much Can We Boost IQ"; Carl Bereiter, "The Future of Individual Differences," *Harvard Educational Review,* Reprint Series no. 2, 1969, pp. 162-170; Herrnstein, "IQ"; Eysenck, *The IQ Argument.*

9. Arthur R. Jensen, "Estimation of the Limits of Heritability of Traits by Comparison of Monzygotic and Dizygotic Twins," *Proceedings of the National Academy of Science,* 58 (1967): 149-157.

10. Jensen, "How Much Can We Boost IQ"; Christopher Jencks et al., *Inequality: A Reassessment of the Effects of Family and Schooling in America* (New York: Basic Books, 1972).

11. Eysenck, *The IQ Argument,* p. 9.

12. Jerome S. Kagan, "Inadequate Evidence and Illogical Conclusions," *Harvard Educational Review,* Reprint Series no. 2, 1969, pp. 126-134; J. McV. Hunt, "Has Compensatory Education Failed? Has It Been Attempted?" *Harvard Educational Review,* Reprint Series no. 2, 1969, pp. 130-152.

13. James S. Coleman et al., *Equality of Educational Opportunity* (Washington, D.C.: U.S. Government Printing Office, 1966).

14. For example, Edward A. Ross, *Social Control* (New York: Macmillan, 1924); Louis

M. Terman, "The Conservation of Talent," *School and Society,* 19, no. 483 (March 1924); Joseph Schumpeter, *Imperialism and Social Classes* (New York: Kelley, 1951).

15. This is not meant to imply that all liberal social theorists hold the I.Q. ideology. David McClelland, *The Achieving Society* (Princeton: Van Nostrand, 1967), and Oscar Lewis, "The Culture of Poverty," *Scientific American,* 215 (October 1966): 16-25, among others, explicitly reject I.Q. as an important determinant of social stratification.

16. Jensen, "Estimation of the Limits of Heritability," p. 14.

17. Otis Dudley Duncan, "Properties and Characteristics of the Socioeconomic Index," in Albert J. Reiss, ed., *Occupations and Social Status* (New York: Free Press, 1961), p. 142.

18. Jensen, "Estimation of the Limits of Heritability," p. 19.

19. Bereiter, "The Future of Individual Differences," p. 166.

20. Herrnstein, "IQ," p. 51.

21. Jensen, "How Much Can We Boost IQ," p. 75.

22. Herrnstein, "IQ," p. 63.

23. Ibid.

24. Ibid.

25. See Peter Blau and Otis Dudley Duncan, *The American Occupational Structure* (New York: John Wiley, 1967); Otis Dudley Duncan, David L. Featherman, and Beverly Duncan, *Socioeconomic Background and Occupational Achievement: Extensions of a Basic Model,* Final Report Project No. 5-0074 (EO-191), Contract No. OE-5-85-072 (Washington, D.C.: U.S. Department of Health, Education, and Welfare, Office of Education, Bureau of Research, 1968); Bowles, "Schooling and Inequality from Generation to Generation"; and Bowles, "The Genetic Inheritance of IQ," for a more complete description. Similar calculations for other age groups yield results consistent with our three main empirical propositions.

26. Jencks, *Inequality;* Robert Hauser, Kenneth G. Lutterman, and William H. Sewell, "Socioeconomic Background and the Earnings of High School Graduates," unpublished manuscript, University of Wisconsin, August 1971; John Conlisk, "A Bit of Evidence on the Income-Education-Ability Interaction," *Journal of Human Resources,* 6 (Summer 1971): 358-362; Zvi Griliches and William M. Mason, "Education, Income, and Ability," *Journal of Political Economy,* 80, no. 3 (May-June 1972); Otis Dudley Duncan and David L. Featherman, "Psychological and Cultural Factors in the Process of Occupational Achievement," Population Studies Center, University of Michigan, 1971.

27. Bowles, "The Genetic Inheritance of IQ."

28. For a more extensive treatment of this point, using data from nine independent samples, see Gintis, "Education and the Characteristics of Worker Productivity."

29. For a more extensive demonstration of this proposition, see Bowles, "The Genetic Inheritance of IQ."

30. Duncan, "Properties and Characteristics of the Socioeconomic Index."

31. Jensen, "Estimation of the Limits of Heritability," p. 73.

32. Herrnstein, "IQ," p. 63.

33. For an explication of the social relations of production, see Andre Gorz, "Capitalist Relations of Production and the Socially Necessary Labor Force," in Arthur Lothstein, ed., *All We Are Saying . . .* (New York: G. P. Putnam's, 1970), and Herbert Gintis, "Power and Alienation," in James Weaver, ed., *Readings in Political Economy* (Boston: Allyn and Bacon, forthcoming).

34. See Bowles, "Unequal Education and the Reproduction of the Social Division of Labor," *Review of Radical Political Economy,* 3 (Fall-Winter 1971); Bowles, "Contradictions in U.S. Higher Education," in James Weaver, ed., *Readings in Political Economy* (Boston: Allyn and Bacon, forthcoming), for an explanation of the connection between the social relations of production and the stratification system.

35. On the origins and functions of the hierarchical division of labor, see Stephen Marglin, "What Do Bosses Do?" unpublished manuscript, Department of Economics, Harvard University, 1971; Richard C. Edwards, "Alienation and Inequality: Capitalist Relations of Production in a Bureaucratic Enterprise," Ph.D. diss., Harvard University, July 1972; Max Weber, *From Max Weber: Essays in Sociology* (New York: Oxford University Press, 1946); Chester I. Barnard, *The Functions of the Executive* (Cambridge: Harvard University Press, 1938). A similar hierarchy in production occurs in state socialist countries.

36. We are presently witnessing a revival of such revolts with the partial breakdown of this ideology. See Judson Gooding, "Blue Collar Blues on the Assembly Line," *Fortune,* July 1970; Gooding, "The Fraying White Collar," *Fortune,* December 1970.

37. Quoted in Norman Ware, *The Industrial Worker: 1840-1860* (New York, 1964), p. 42.

38. For contemporary discussions of the feasibility of significant alternatives to the hierarchical division of labor, see Paul Blumberg, *Industrial Democracy* (New York: Schocken Books, 1969); Carole Pateman, *Participation and Democratic Theory* (Cambridge: Cambridge University Press, 1970); Murray Bookchin, *Post-Scarcity Anarchism* (Berkeley: Ramparts Press, 1971); Gintis, "Power and Alienation."

39. Talcott Parsons, "Evolutionary Universals in Society," *American Sociological Review*, 29, no. 3 (June 1964): 507.

40. K. Davis and W. E. Moore, "Some Principles of Stratification," in R. Bendix and S. M. Lipset, eds., *Class, Status and Power* (New York: Free Press, 1966).

41. Herrnstein, "IQ," p. 51.

42. For a statement of this position, see Milton Friedman, *Capitalism and Freedom* (Chicago: University of Chicago Press, 1962).

43. Jensen reports that a panel of "experts" determined that higher status jobs "require" higher I.Q. See Jensen, "How Much Can We Boost IQ."

44. O. G. Brim et al., *American Beliefs and Attitudes about Intelligence* (New York: Russell Sage Foundation, 1969).

45. See Burton R. Clark, "The 'Cooling Out' Function in Higher Education," *American Journal of Sociology*, 65, no. 6 (May 1960); Paul Lauter and Florence Howe, "The Schools Are Rigged for Failure," *New York Review of Books*, June 20, 1970.

46. See Tables 1 and 4.

47. See Gintis, "Education and Characteristics of Worker Productivity"; Edwards, "Alienation and Inequality."

48. See Bowles, "Unequal Education and the Reproduction of the Social Division of Labor."

49. For an extensive bibliography of this research, see Herbert Gintis, "Toward a Political Economy of Education: A Radical Critique of Ivan Illich's *Deschooling Society*," *Harvard Educational Review*, 42, no. 1 (February 1972); Bowles, "Unequal Education and the Reproduction of the Social Division of Labor"; Colin Greer, *The Great School Legend* (New York: Basic Books, 1972).

50. See Frank Tracy Carleton, *Economic Influences upon Educational Progress in the U.S., 1820-1850* (Madison: University of Wisconsin Press, 1908); Theodore W. Schultz, "Capital Formation by Education," *Journal of Political Economics*, 68 (December 1960): 571-583. This ideology is discussed in its several variations in Samuel Bowles and Herbert Gintis, "The Ideology of Progressive School Reform," in Henry Rosemont and Walter Feinberg, eds., *Work, Technology, and Education: Essays in the Intellectual Foundations of Education* (Urbana: University of Illinois Press, forthcoming), and Greer, *The Great School Legend*.

51. See David Bruck, "The Schools of Lowell," honors thesis, Harvard University, 1971. In this study of cotton mill workers in Lowell in the 1840s, Hal Luft ("The Industrial Worker in Lowell," Unpublished manuscript, Harvard University, 1972) revealed no relationship whatever between worker literacy and their physical productivity. Bowles's as yet unpublished study (jointly with Alexander Field) of nineteenth-century educational expansion in Massachusetts found that the leading towns were those with cotton industries and large concentrations of foreign-born workers.

52. This is the conclusion of Robert Muchele and James Medoff ("Education and the Agrarian Order," unpublished manuscript, Harvard University, January 1972), based on a statistical study of U.S. census data. Their study sharply contradicts the interpretation of Douglas North in *The Economic Growth of the U.S., 1790-1860* (New York, 1961).

53. See William Lazonick, "The Integration of Higher Education into Agricultural Production in the U.S.," unpublished manuscript, Harvard University, 1972.

54. Bowles, "Unequal Education and the Reproduction of the Social Division of Labor," develops this argument in more detail. This perspective on the use of education is supported by a growing number of historical studies. See Bruck, "The Schools of Lowell," and Katz, *The Irony of Early School Reform*.

55. R. Callahan, *Education and the Cult of Efficiency* (Chicago: University of Chicago Press, 1962).

56. See Marvin Lazerson, *Origins of the Urban School* (Cambridge: Harvard University Press, 1971).

57. See Callahan, *Education and the Cult of Efficiency;* David K. Cohen and Marvin

Lazerson, "Education and the Corporate Order," *Socialist Revolution,* March 1972; and Lawrence Cremin, *The Transformation of the School* (New York: Alfred A. Knopf, 1964).

58. For a short review of this movement and its relation to the development of the U.S. stratification system, see Karier, "Testing for Order and Control in the Corporate Liberal State."

59. Edward C. Thorndike, "Intelligence and Its Uses," *Harper's,* 140 (January 1920).

60. Cremin, *The Transformation of the School.*

61. Karier, "Testing for Order and Control in the Corporate Liberal State."

62. George S. Counts, "The Social Composition of Boards of Education," *Review and Elementary School Journal,* Supplementary Education Monographs, no. 33 (1927); Callahan, *Education and the Cult of Efficiency.*

63. Quoted in Katz, *The Irony of Early School Reform,* p. 88.

64. See Marglin, "What Do Bosses Do?"

65. For reviews of the evidence, see Blumberg, *Industrial Democracy;* Victor H. Vroom, "Industrial Social Psychology," in G. Lindsey and E. Aaronsen, eds., *The Handbook of Social Psychology* (Reading, Mass.: Addison-Wesley, 1969); Gintis, "Power and Alienation"; and Andre Gorz, *Strategy for Labor* (Boston: Beacon Press, 1968).

66. For more on this, see Erving Goffman, *The Presentation of Self in Everyday Life* (New York: Doubleday, 1959).

67. See ibid. for a more thorough analysis.

68. See Herbert Gintis, "New Working Class and Revolutionary Youth," *Socialist Revolution,* May 1970.

69. See Edwards, "Alienation and Inequality."

70. We know of two major presentations, reviews, and overall interpretations of these studies: Goffman, *The Presentation of Self in Everyday Life,* and Claus Offe, *Leistungsprinzip und Industrielle Arbeit* (Frankfort: Europaische Verlaganstalt, 1970).

71. Goffman, *The Presentation of Self in Everyday Life,* p. 75.

72. Other studies may be cited. Gorz ("Capitalist Relations of Production and the Socially Necessary Labor Force") provides a cogent analysis of the self-presentation of technical workers. Offe's analysis *(Leistungsprinzip und Industrielle Arbeit)* includes evidence on the role of schools in codifying modes of self-presentation and reviews sociological studies of self-presentation and promotability. Finally Bensman and Rosenberg analyze the importance of conscious manipulation of self-presentation among the upwardly mobile. See J. Bensman and B. Rosenberg, "The Meaning of Work in Bureaucratic Society," in M. Stein et al., eds., *Anxiety and Identity* (New York: Free Press, 1960).

73. Goffman, *The Presentation of Self in Everyday Life,* p. 22.

74. Ibid., p. 26.

75. Norman C. Alexander and Ernest Q. Campbell, "Peer Influences on Adolescent Educational Aspirations and Attainments," *American Sociological Review,* 29 (August 1964): 568-575; Richard P. Boyle, "On Neighborhood Context and College Plans," *American Sociological Review,* 31 (October 1966): 706-707; E. Erickson, "A Study of the Normative Influence of Parents and Friends," in Wilbur Brookover et al., *Self-Concept of Ability and School Achievement,* Cooperative Research Project 2381, Office of Research and Publications, Michigan State University, 1967, vol. 3; A. Haller and C. Butterworth, "Peer Influence on Levels of Occupational and Educational Aspiration," *Social Forces,* 38 (May 1960): 289-295; William H. Sewell and Michael Armer, "Neighborhood Context and College Plans," *American Sociological Review,* 31 (April 1966): 159-168; Alan Wilson, "Residential Segregation of Social Classes and Aspirations of High School Boys," *American Sociological Review,* 24 (December 1959): 836-845.

76. See Randall D. Weiss, "The Effect of Education on the Earnings of Blacks and Whites," *Review of Economics and Statistics,* 52 (May 1970); Phillips Cutright, "Achievement, Military Service, and Earnings," Harvard University, May 1969, mimeo.

77. Marilyn Power Goldberg, "The Economic Exploitation of Women," in David M. Gordon, ed., *Problems in Political Economy* (Lexington, Mass.: D. C. Heath, 1971).

78. Ivar Berg, *Education and Jobs: The Great Training Robbery* (New York: Frederick A. Praeger, 1970).

79. For a more extended discussion, see Gintis, "Education and the Characteristics of Worker Productivity"; Gintis, "Toward a Political Economy of Education"; Bowles, "Cuban Education and the Revolutionary Ideology," *Harvard Educational Review,* 41 (November 1971).

80. Gintis, "Education and the Characteristics of Worker Productivity."

81. Gene M. Smith, "Usefulness of Peer Ratings of Personality in Educational Research," *Education and Psychological Measurements,* 1967; Smith, "Personality Correlates of Academic Performance in Three Dissimilar Populations," Proceedings of the 77th Annual Convention, American Psychological Association, 1967.

82. Peter J. Meyer, "Schooling and the Reproduction of the Social Division of Labor," honors thesis, Harvard University, March 1972. See also Edwards, "Alienation and Inequality."

83. Marshall H. Brenner, "Use of High School Data to Predict Work Performance," *Journal of Applied Psychology,* 52, no. 1 (January 1968).

84. See J. Binstock, *Survival in the American College Industry,* forthcoming, 1973.

85. Melvin L. Kohn, *Class and Conformity: A Study in Values* (Homewood, Ill.: Dorsey, 1969).

86. Ibid., p. 72.

87. Ibid., p. 163.

88. Karl Marx and Friedrich Engels, *Communist Manifesto* (New York: International Publishers, 1948).

89. John W. Gardner, *Excellence* (New York: Harper and Bros., 1961).

90. Gabriel Kolko, *Wealth and Power in America* (New York: Frederick A. Praeger, 1962); Herman Miller, *Income Distribution in the United States,* 1960 Census mimeo (Washington, D.C.: U.S. Government Printing Office, 1966).

91. Robert Lampman, *The Share of Top Wealth Holders in the National Wealth* (Princeton: Princeton University Press, 1962).

92. Richard C. Edwards, Michael Reich, and Thomas Weisskopf, *The Capitalist System* (Englewood Cliffs, N.J.: Prentice-Hall, 1972), p. 324.

93. Michael Reich, "The Economics of Racism," in David M. Gordon, ed., *Problems in Political Economy* (Lexington, Mass.: D. C. Heath, 1971).

94. William G. Spady, "Educational Mobility and Access: Growth and Paradoxes," *American Journal of Sociology,* November 1967; Blau and Duncan, *The American Occupational Structure.*

95. Blau and Duncan, *The American Occupational Structure.*

96. Parsons, "Evolutionary Universals in Society"; Davis and Moore, "Some Principles of Stratification."

97. Gardner, *Excellence.*

98. Coleman et al., *Equality of Educational Opportunity;* Frederick Mosteller and Daniel P. Moynihan, *On Equality of Educational Opportunity* (New York: Random House, 1972). Whether additional school resources are in fact irrelevant to greater academic performance is still an unsettled question. See Samuel Bowles and Henry Levin, "The Determinants of Scholastic Achievement: An Appraisal of Some Recent Evidence," *Journal of Human Resources,* 3 (Winter 1968); James Guthrie et al., *Schools and Inequality* (Cambridge: MIT Press, 1971). Available studies shed no light whatsoever on the relation between school resources and performance outside the cognitive sphere.

99. Harvey Averch et al., *"How Effective Is Schooling? A Critical Review and Synthesis of Research Findings* (Santa Monica: The RAND Corporation, 1972); David Armor, "The Evidence on Busing," *The Public Interest* (Summer 1972); T. Ribich, *Poverty and Education* (Washington, D.C.: The Brookings Institute, 1968).

100. Edward Banfield, *The Unheavenly City* (Boston: Little, Brown, 1968); Oscar Lewis, "The Culture of Poverty"; Daniel P. Moynihan, *The Negro Family: The Case for National Action* (Cambridge: MIT Press, 1967).

101. Herbert Gans, *The Urban Villagers* (New York: Macmillan, 1962); Greer, *The Great School Legend.*

102. Zvi Griliches, "Notes on the Role of Education in Production Functions and Growth Accounting," in W. Lee Hansen, ed., *Education, Income and Human Capital,* Studies in Income and Wealth, vol. 35 (New York: National Bureau of Economic Research, 1970); Weiss, "The Effect of Education on the Earnings of Blacks and Whites."

103. For example, Alexander W. Astin, "Undergraduate Achievement and Institutional 'Excellence,' " *Science,* 161 (August 1968). For a survey see Bowles, "Unequal Education and the Reproduction of the Social Division of Labor."

104. Thus Averch et al., in *How Effective Is Schooling?,* their RAND Corporation report to the President's Commission on School Finance, report: "(In our attempt) to assess the current state of knowledge regarding the determinants of educational effectiveness . . . (we

find that) educational outcomes are almost exclusively measured by cognitive achievement" (p. ix).

105. Coleman et al., *Equality of Educational Opportunity.*

106. Mosteller and Moynihan, *On Equality of Educational Opportunity,* p. 27.

107. Dan Gilbarg and David Finkelhor, *Up against the American Myth* (New York: Holt, Rinehart and Winston, 1970); Edwards, Reich, and Weisskopf, *The Capitalist System;* Gintis, "New Working Class and Revolutionary Youth"; Bowles, "Contradictions in U.S. Higher Education"; Theodore Roszak, *The Making of the Counter-Culture* (New York: Doubleday, 1969).

108. On "reproduction" and "contradiction" in the analysis of the social system, see Herbert Gintis, "Counter-Culture and Political Activism," *Telos* (Summer 1972).

109. For a more extended treatment of the contradictions of advanced U.S. capitalism, see Bowles, "Contradictions in U.S. Higher Education"; Gintis, "Counter-Culture and Political Activism."

110. For a more complete statement of their position, see Gintis, "Education and the Characteristics of Worker Productivity"; Bowles, "Contradictions in U.S. Higher Education."

111. For a more elaborate statement of this problem, see Schumpeter, *Imperialism and Social Class;* Bowles, "Contradictions in U.S. Higher Education."

112. See Jackson T. Main, *The Social Structure of Revolutionary America* (Princeton: Princeton University Press, 1965); Reich in Edwards, Reich, and Weisskopf, *The Capitalist System.*

113. See Gorz, "Capitalist Relations of Production and the Socially Necessary Labor Force."

114. The evidence is summarized in Gintis, "Power and Alienation."

115. See Therborn, reprinted in Edwards, Reich, and Weisskopf, *The Capitalist System.*

116. See Bowles, "Contradictions in U.S. Higher Education"; Gintis, "New Working Class and Revolutionary Youth"; Gintis, "Counter-Culture and Political Activism."

Samuel Bowles and Robert Gintis

The current rhetoric about schools is that they have failed, that they are dysfunctional, that they are not doing the job which they were intended to do. It is our contention that just the opposite is true—that schools *are* doing what they were intended to do, and doing it very well. They were designed to create an elite ruling class, and once that class emerged, to maintain its position in power. The myths about schools developed in order to pacify the workers and perpetuate the belief that opportunity and room at the top was available. The schools were designed as the only route towards mobility so that greater control could be exercised over the types of persons who could gain power and join the elite group. To keep the working class from rebelling, schools have functioned to lay blame for failure to rise above poverty situations upon the individuals involved, and not upon structural elements.

Schools were intended to disseminate the ideology of the status quo, and to create conformity, in an effort to stem the tides of change. That the schools have been able to do these things for so long is an indication that from this perspective they have been exceedingly functional.

If they had encouraged creativity, awareness, or higher levels of consciousness, they would have also encouraged change. If they had sought equality, a restructuring of wealth and power would have resulted. Had they really fostered such things, they would have been dysfunctional within the current structure.

chapter four

SCHOOLS AND
THE ECONOMY

From its very origins, American education had had a strong pragmatic, utilitarian emphasis. In our readings on the schools and politics, in chapter 3, we saw this emphasis as it was expressed politically. In the readings that follow we will see this emphasis at work in the relations between the schools and the American economy.

But while American education was pragmatic from the start, it was also expected to provide a classical, intellectual, even patrician education, free of pragmatic, utilitarian concerns. And there are still those today who advocate this kind of education, most especially on the higher levels, despite the fact that our schools have moved in a quite different direction. For better or worse the education that equips its students for no particular job, no particular work in the world, that is more designed for a life of contemplation and leisure than a life of job-getting, seems to be waning. Liberal arts colleges, for example, have been warned that they must expect increasing defections among college age students. The day may be approaching when this kind of education will attract increasing numbers of adults who have established themselves in their careers and who are coming back with educational purposes more compatible with the liberal arts tradition.

But as things now stand, it seems that what started out as an educational or pedagogical issue in the schools has become a problem in American political power and economics. The decline of the liberal arts in our colleges and universities is a natural outcome of the almost total victory of utilitarian education. Here and there there are still some holdouts. There are still some who speak of the "life of the mind" and "ideas for ideas' sake" but their numbers are dwindling. The story of the eventual hegemony of utilitarian education in the schools is the story of a series of rearguard actions by a dwindling number of teachers who viewed with regret this turn that American education took following the Civil War, and especially after the turn of the century.

Yet as we look at it from the perspective of one hundred-or-more years later, it is difficult to believe that our free, universal, tax-supported, public education could have done anything but become the handmaiden of the American economy. The elementary school diploma, the high school diploma, and the college diploma progressively have become tied to the dollar sign until today it can be said that one of the pillars of our economic system is American education. K through Ph.D.

But what really is the substance of this pillar? What is the relationship between our schools at all levels and the American economy? And what have been the effects on the schools of this close, symbiotic tie between schooling and economics? A popular notion has been that the schools are the royal road to reform and economic well-being. But recent studies are beginning to suggest that this may be more myth than reality. And yet it has been—and continues to be—believed by so many!

We can begin to get an idea of the real role American education has played in our economy by looking at Henry Perkinson's sketch of the downfall of America as the land of opportunity and the subsequent rise of the success ethos and the Gospel of Wealth. Perkinson describes this in *The Imperfect Panacea: American Faith in Education, 1865-1965,* and shows how the schools both contributed to and were affected by this downfall.[1]

According to the success ethos, no matter what your station in life was as a child, you could be a success in America if you were industrious, frugal, persevering, punctual and obedient. And the schools, by teaching these virtues to all, would make success available to all. It was the appearance of what we have now come to know as "equal opportunity."

But, Perkinson shows, Americans didn't really want equality when it came to wealth, success, power and status. Yet the schools were supposed to equalize. Thus Andrew Carnegie thought that the best way to deal with disproportionate wealth was through gifts from the wealthy to colleges. But with the gifts went a new purpose for colleges. It was a new ladder to climb for the would-be successful, the educational ladder by which one tested and proved oneself, not by getting into business and industry but by making it through college. Thus, Perkinson shows, where as late as 1890 few employers hired college graduates, by 1900 many had developed a decided preference for college men.

It was an important new role for the schools. It meant more and different schools were needed, and with them, Perkinson says, our first system of vocational education appeared, articulated from top to bottom and bottom to top.

Only for a time were the colleges able to resist this new vocationalism. Schooling more and more was becoming an apprenticeship for later employment. An education in America came to mean "trained minds devoted to specific lines of work," as Perkinson says. This new attitude toward education—especially higher education—emerged after the Civil War, influenced by German higher education and epitomized in the opening of Johns Hopkins University in 1867 and the University of Chicago in 1890. Research had come to American higher education, and, Perkinson claims, teaching came closer to vocationalism.

The lavishness of grants from business and industry hastened this triumph of vocationalism, according to Perkinson, and so the links of the chain of economic opportunity and education were forged. The professional education administrators emerged, what Thorstein Veblen called the "captains of erudition."

But before we had our first system of education, Perkinson points out, one last link was needed. It was the high school that deliberately prepared students for college. In 1890 it was thought that the high schools were not good enough to perform this function, and as a result a good one-half of the most qualified students (according to a moderate estimate) were denied the opportunity to go to college.

The schools blamed the colleges for this, particularly their entrance requirements and the wide diversity among them. Some kind of uniformity in admission require-

---

1. Henry Perkinson, *The Imperfect Panacea: American Faith in Education, 1865-1965* (New York: Random House, 1968).

ments was needed, and so the Carnegie point system was developed, a system still in use today, devised with great help from the Carnegie Foundation. This system made it possible for colleges to translate the studies of high school students into terms of their different admission requirements.

In his book, Perkinson describes how American schools prior to the Revolution had served to prepare students for the unexpected. It was part of a belief that men should have the opportunity to try their hand at anything they wanted. (It should be noted that this was not the belief that all men were equal.) But clearly it was impossible for this to occur in an organized, specialized industrial society, as Perkinson notes. So the schools shifted their purpose once more, from being the great equalizers of wealth and status to being the great selectors and sorters of students for their "probable destinies," as it was put.

Here was the beginning of what Michael Young dubbed "The Meritocracy."[2] It was a system in which only the most talented, the "meritorious," would rise to the top. And there was more than one ladder that could be climbed, as Perkinson notes. Not only were the most talented selected by the schools for the top jobs, but they were also selected, so it was believed, for the office jobs and for the factory jobs. And the schools selected the ladders that each student would climb.

Perkinson describes how opposition to this change in the purpose of the schools came at first from most of the educators. They wanted the schools to equalize and unify, not select and sort. But, Perkinson notes, the structure of the school system eventually defeated them, and they could only offer slogans for a liberal education. For the next fifty years most educators refused to accept what was called "career selection" as the schools' primary function. But in reality, as Perkinson shows, that is what the schools were doing.

The school system administrators, backed by the parents, wanted something more tangible from education than a liberal education—a better job, the ability to earn more money, at least one dependable outcome. And so, as early as the age of ten or twelve, children were put on separate paths as the selecting and sorting process of the schools went to work. It was the beginning of what we are all too familiar with today in our schools.

One thing this meant, Perkinson points out, is a different education for different people. Children from different groups tended to take different subjects and enroll in different programs. When children were more alike, the higher income students wound up in higher ability sections.

Furthermore, this development meant that students were now able to translate whatever educational status they achieved into organizational and corporate advantages. Supposedly this translation would occur only through the school. Thus, if you were unsuccessful in school, for whatever reason, you would be unsuccessful in life outside the school. Those of low achievement, those who had low IQs, those who just didn't like school, were the ones who suffered under this system. And they still suffer. The school's function became one of reinforcing the already existing inequalities in society, and it continues to do this, as we will see in the findings of Christopher Jencks and others. We have only recently become aware that the burden of failure thus determined by the schools falls most

2. Michael Young, *The Rise of the Meritocracy*, (Baltimore, Maryland: Pelican Books, Penguin Books, 1965).

heavily on the ethnic minorities in our society. They are the ones most likely to be sorted and selected for the lower status and lower paying jobs.

As Paul Goodman once said, for minorities the schools had become "the universal trap." It is a compulsory sorting and selecting that takes place, almost guaranteeing that minorities will wind up in unequal conditions. In 1961 Kenneth Clarke said that the schools had become "an instrument of social and economic class distinctions in American society."

Then along came "compensatory education," an attempt by the schools to preserve the sorting and selecting functions while at the same time making them less discriminatory. It was one more attempt to equalize by means of the schools. But Perkinson shows that if compensatory education was to become fully incorporated into the educational system, it would undermine the career selection process. There would be no losers and thus no winners. It is Perkinson's belief, as it is ours, that most Americans do not want their schools to stop identifying winners and losers, to stop betting on what John Holt has called the "racetrack business."

Perkinson points out that this desire to preserve selecting and sorting in the schools while at the same time trying to ameliorate its discriminatory effects resulted in the application of compensatory education among preschool children. It was appropriately labelled "Head Start." And it was supposed to give children a head start in the race to see who would be selected winner and loser. But, Perkinson somewhat ruefully concludes, it deals not at all with changing the function of the schools in allocating opportunity on what turns out to be a discriminatory basis. As we will find Jencks and others saying, the schools serve to preserve inequality in America far more than they serve to eliminate it.

A more empirical examination of the connections between education, occupation and status that resulted from the development of the American economy and the schools since the Civil War is taken by Clark. Although his figures are now somewhat dated, and his focus was almost exclusively on higher education, Burton Clark's *Educating The Expert Society*[3] was an important addition to our understanding of the chain that stretches from the social station of a student's parents to the education that student receives, and then to the future social position that student occupies. Clark concluded that "mobility through education is a core element of the twentieth-century society." He also noted that education was a "mechanism whereby social-class positions are stabilized across the generations, and is thereby a barrier to the social mobility of those who start from lower rungs."[4] This is also Perkinson's theme. The later writers in this chapter question the degree and extent to which American education has contributed to social mobility.

Clark's work was not only a pioneering study of the relationship between education and the economic interests of influential parts of American society, but it also offered detailed support for the long-held belief—amounting to a doctrine of faith for many—that schooling leads to social mobility in American society, and that this mobility is unparalleled by other societies. The case he makes seems impressive. Clark's research supported a principal tenet of American liberalism: that it is through individual achievement and mobility that social reform is to be accomplished, and that a principal means to that achievement

3. Burton Clark, *Educating the Expert Society* (Chandler, 1962).
4. *Ibid*, p. 75.

and mobility is more and more education for all. In this way, this liberal tenet holds, social justice can be promoted without having to attack such things as the distribution of income and the ownership of wealth and property.[5]

This tenet of American liberalism was at work in this country's recent "war on poverty." The Kennedy and Johnson administrations, for example, emphasized the personal deficiencies of the poor and unemployed when they proposed antipoverty programs, and these deficiencies were defined largely as educational shortcomings. Yet paradoxically these administrations said that the poor were not to blame for being poor, but did not go on to say who or what was to blame. This idea that our social, political and economic problems are the result of the failures and shortcomings of individuals is not a new idea in our society. A study of the principal reactions of Americans during the depression of the 30s, conducted by E. Wight Bakke[6] showed that the majority blamed themselves more than "the system" for their unhappy circumstances, and they regularly mentioned their lack of education. In citing this work, Ivar Berg[7] wondered to what extent the education craze that developed after World War II was a direct outgrowth of this attitude among those who grew up during the depression.

The received opinion, what Ivar Berg calls the "conventional wisdom," is that the educated person (almost always meaning the person with the longer schooling record) is a more important person than the uneducated person, especially to our economy. So wedded have we been to this idea that we have made it possible for the more educated—again almost always meaning those with the longer records of going to school, or those in the process of going to school—to avoid military service during the wars since World War II. This led a number of the teachers of these draft-deferred college students to question the justice of their grades being used to determine whether or not a student would go off to war. They thought it was as unjust to decide that a student should go to Viet Nam because he had flunked out of college as it was to decide that he should not go because he had managed not to flunk out.

Industrial and business managers, those who hire the employees, have especially supported this conventional wisdom through the "education" requirements they have placed on jobs. It was reasonable to believe that the malfunctioning of the labor market was the result of the personal failings of workers. Many managers grew up with that belief. If we could just educate workers more, train them more, then they would not be unemployed or underemployed.

A classical statement of this belief by Willard Wirtz, Secretary of Labor in the Johnson Administration, is reprinted below, followed by Paul Goodman's criticisms of the Wirtz position. You the reader can judge whether or not Goodman's criticisms are decisive. But we would also point out that in proposing that the two million teen-agers who were in the work force at the time be taken out and returned to school, to get "the kind of preparation they need for the em-

5. James D. Smith, Pennsylvania State University economist, reported at a September 1973 conference in Washingtion sponsored by the People's Policy Center that there is an elite at the very top of the American wealth pyramid, amounting to only 4.4% of the total population, who own most of the wealth of this country in the form of corporate, federal, state, local and foreign stocks and bonds.

6. E. Wight Bakke, *The Unemployed Worker* and *Citizens Without Work* (New Haven: Yale University Press, 1940).

7. Ivar Berg, *Education and Jobs: The Great Training Robbery* (Beacon, 1971), p. 2-5.

ployment which lies ahead," Secretary Wirtz was unwittingly saying that they would be better prepared for work by more schooling and not by working. The more likely reason for this proposal is that by getting these two million teen-agers out of the work force and into school, two million jobs would be opened up for other unemployed people, and the overall employment figures would, of course, drop. (And the schools would carry out one of their covert functions of keeping youths out of the labor market where they are neither wanted nor needed.) And note that in order to accomplish this return to school, Wirtz proposed extending compulsory schooling for two more years.

THE EXTENSION OF COMPULSORY SCHOOLING, 1964

Willard Wirtz

. . . In one way, to one degree or another, over 15 million people were unemployed at some time during the year last year.

And then, of course, there are figures for the various unemployment problems which show, for example, that among minority groups, unemployment is not 5 percent but about two times that. There are figures which show that among the young who are members of the work force, the unemployment figure is not 5 percent but three times that. . . .

Now . . . I should like to talk about the relationship of unemployment and education, because it seems to me that here is the most fruitful opportunity for immediate advance on the employment problem. I would like to give you a few more statistics which suggest something of the relationship of lack of education and unemployment in this country today. These statistics can be read several ways, and I will want to point that out in mentioning them.

The unemployment rate for individuals today with less than five years of school is 10.4 percent.

Those with nine to eleven years of school are 7.8 percent unemployed. Those with thirteen to fifteen years of school are 4 percent unemployed, and those with sixteen years or more of school have an unemployment rate of 1.4 percent.

I repeat that if there were more time we could go into a number of the possible explanations of this, but this salient fact stands clear. There are others that are of a related kind.

"Remarks of the Honorable W. Willard Wirtz," in Symposium on Employment, sponsored by the American Bankers Association (Washington, D.C. 1964), and reprinted with their permission.

In 1962, the educational attainment of unskilled nonfarm laborers was less than nine years. Employment for that group over the last ten-year period has declined by 3½ percent. This is a difficult figure, and I consider it quite illuminating and, therefore, I would like to be clear about spelling it out.

If you take the unskilled nonfarm labor classification, where there is an educational attainment of less than nine years, employment over the last ten years has declined by 3½ percent.

On the other hand, if you take clerical and sales workers whose educational attainment in 1962 was more than 12½ years, their employment has increased by 14 percent between 1952 and 1962.

Then if you take professional and technical workers with an educational attainment of sixteen years, employment for them during this ten-year period has increased by 62 percent.

These figures are perhaps only the statistical confirmation of what we know to be obvious in general, which is that the developments in the economy are such that there is a closer and closer incidence between education and employment and between lack of education and unemployment.

There is another factor in this situation, another set of statistics which I am not going to give because I have already talked longer than I intended to—indeed, longer than the circumstances warrant.

Another set of statistics will show a very close correlation between unemployment of an individual and the unemployment and lack of education of his father; or, summarizing the point, unemployment in this country today is becoming an inherited characteristic, and it is being inherited not through the physical genes, but through social genes of lack of education, slums, and so on and so forth.

I am not sure how much poverty we can eliminate as far as the adult generation is concerned. I know that if we are to get poverty and unemployment out of the American bloodstream, as far as I am concerned the place to start is with the educational program.

Rather than emphasizing what can be done, as far as larger employment resulting from a change in the overtime rates is concerned, I would like to suggest to you that the single largest possibility of immediate attack upon the unemployment situation would come from getting 2 million teenagers out of the work force. There are almost 3 million of them between the ages of fourteen and nineteen who are out of school and in the work force.

As far as I am concerned, this is the most fertile area for moving immediately on a fuller employment problem, because I do not think most of those 3 million out to be there. I think the number ought to be cut down by about 2 million and that those 2 million, instead of being in the work force, should be in school getting the kind of preparation they need for the employment which lies ahead.

If we could accomplish this in one way or another, it would have three effects: First, it would develop a guarantee against future unemployment by preparing these boys and girls more fully for the jobs that lie ahead; second, it would take their competition out of a work market in which they are today competing with "breadwinners" and so on; and third, it would make education the biggest industry in the country, which it ought to be.

I should like to suggest for your consideration the proposition that there ought to be, at this point, an additional two years added both to our free education system and to our requirements of compulsory education. It is not just more education of the same kind that all of these people have been getting but two years more, which in a good many cases would include advanced vocational education, as well as preparation for college.

Here is what we have done in this country: Over 100 years ago, about 150 years ago now, we started developing this idea of free education. We eventually came up with the idea of free education through high school. We made it—almost all of it—preparation for college. But that didn't matter too much because those who matriculated either went on to college or went into a work force where there was plenty of work for unskilled workers. It is not the situation today.

Then we did another thing: We provided by law in most states that boys and girls must stay in school until they are sixteen. Those two actions met the needs of that time, the need for education up to sixteen years and free education up through the high school level.

The needs, gentlemen, have continually changed in the last century and a half. The needs today are for people with more and, in some cases, a different kind of education from what has been supplied before—and the needs are for free education which would carry them through the additional, I think, two years.

. . . People get an education and jobs in this country depending upon the income of their parents. I am ashamed by the facts I find when I look at the list of high school graduates in this country, line them all up according to the incomes of their fathers, and find that, if I take those in the top 30 percent of the graduating high school class in this country—the top 30 percent measured by their fathers' income—46 percent of those boys and girls go on to college.

If I take the bottom 30 percent, measured by their parents' income, their fathers' income, 12 percent of them go on to college. It isn't fair and it is bad business.

I would like to suggest that, in the long run, we will approach the employment problem most effectively, the actual employment goal most effectively, if we attend to the basic problem of the relationship of education to employment.

We have it in connection with the training program, but we have it most basically in connection with the educational program, and I think there is a great deal to be done about getting unemployment out of the American bloodstream. I don't think that there is any reason for it as a habit.

I point out that the more we look at it, the more we find that unemployment, poverty, and ignorance all go together. We might as well hit them at one point or another. So far as I am concerned, the best way to hit them is in connection with their educational matter.

Willard Wirtz

THE CASE AGAINST COMPULSION, 1964

Paul Goodman

I.

In an address to the American Bankers Association on February 24, 1964, the Secretary of Labor proposed to *extend* compulsory schooling to the age of 18. This at a time when in New York a Kings County Grand Jury proposed *reducing* it to 15 and giving the superintendent of schools leeway to kick out the unruly. In many schools in the country policemen are stationed to keep guard over youngsters who do not want to be there. And the majority of drop-outs who were cajoled into returning to school in 1963 soon dropped out again, since nothing essential had been changed in purpose, method, or curriculum; they only suffered a new humiliation by being conned. And—*verb.sat.sap.*—older lads tend to be heavier and to carry more powerful armament. Did the Secretary of Labor think it through?

In some places, e.g., Milwaukee, the compulsory age is at present 18, on the following arrangement: if, after 16, a youngster has a job, he goes to Continuation School (Milwaukee Vocational) one day a week; if he has no job, he attends full time, till 18. How does this work out? An administrator of the school tells me, "We don't teach them anything, neither academic subjects nor a trade. They're ineducable, and there aren't any jobs for them to train for anyway. But we do try to improve their attitude. Of course, we usually only have them for about 7 months."

"Why? What happens to them?"

"Oh, they join the Army or end up in Wales"—Wales is the reform school.

Naturally I become indignant and say, "What would become of *your* attitude if I caged you in a schoolroom and didn't even attempt to teach you anything? Wouldn't it be better to go to an honest jail?" But these angry questions do not seem to flurry him at all. Obviously I am not in touch with the concrete realities of his situation.

II.

In his address, Secretary Wirtz makes the usual correlation between employment and years of schooling: "The unemployment rate for individuals today with less than five years of school is 10.4 percent. For those with nine to eleven years of school, it is 7.8 percent; for those with thirteen to fifteen years of school, 4 percent; but for those with sixteen or more years of school, the unemployment rate drops to 1.4 percent."

Paul Goodman, "A Proposal to Extend Compulsory Schooling," from *Compulsory Miseducation*, 1964, pp. 63-76, reprinted by permission of the publisher, Horizon Press, New York.

But these figures are unimpressive. As he himself implies in another context, the *prima facie* explanation of the correlation is the parents' income. By connections, manners and aspirations, middle-class children get middle-class jobs; schooling is an incidental part of it. Lower-class children used to get lower-class jobs, but just these jobs have petered out; in the present *structure* of the economy, the money and jobs do not filter down. Similarly, the docility, neatness of appearance, etc. that are useful for getting petty jobs, are not created by years of schooling but they are accurately measured by them. In my opinion, the same line of criticism strongly applies to the spectacular correlations between life-time income and years of schooling. Looking for his first job, a middle-class youth decides he wants $80 to start, and he can afford to shop around till he gets it; a poor boy must take anything and starts at $35. For obvious reasons, this initial difference will usually predetermine the whole career. Conversely, a sharp poor boy, seeing that this is the score, might choose not to bestir himself and prefer to look for a racket.

Again, Negro college graduates average in a lifetime the same salary as white high school graduates. It seems to be *not* the years of schooling but the whole context that makes the difference. Consider. If after seven or eight years, the salary increase of Negro or Puerto Rican high school graduates over those who have dropped out is perhaps $5 a week, is this worth the painful effort of years of schooling that is intrinsically worthless and spiritbreaking?

In these circumstances, it is wiser to think exactly the opposite way. It would probably help to improve the educational aspiration and educability of poor youngsters to give the money to poor families *directly,* rather than to channel it through school systems or other social agencies that drain off most of it for the same middle-class. . . .

III.

It is claimed that society needs more people who are technically trained. But informed labor people tell me that, for a job requiring skill but no great genius, a worker can be found at once, or quickly trained, to fill it. For instance, the average job in General Motors' most automated plant requires three weeks of training for those who have no education whatever. It used to require six weeks; for such jobs, automation has diminished rather than increased the need for training. In the Army and Navy, fairly complicated skills e.g., radar operation and repair, are taught in a year *on the job,* often to practical illiterates.

. . . I was struck by a recent report in the *Wall Street Journal* of firms philanthropically deciding to hire *only* drop-outs for certain categories of jobs, since the diploma made no difference in performance.

Twist it and turn it how you will, there is no logic to the proposal to extend compulsory schooling *except* as a device to keep the unemployed off the streets by putting them into concentration camps called schools. . . .

As an academic, I am appalled by this motivation for schooling. As a citizen and human being, I am appalled by this waste of youthful vitality. It is time that we stopped using the word "education" honorifically. We must ask, education how? where? for what? and under whose administration? Certainly every youth should get the best possible education, but, in my opinion, the present kind of compulsory schooling under the present administrators, far from being extended, should be sharply curtailed.

IV.

As I have been saying, by and large primary schooling is, and should be, mainly baby-sitting. It has the great mission of democratic socialization—it certainly must not be segregated by race and income; apart from this, it should be happy, interesting, not damaging. . . . But in the secondary schools, after puberty, the tone of the baby-sitting must necessarily turn to regimentation and policing, and it is at peril that we require schooling; it fits some, it hurts others. A recent study by Edgar Friedenberg concludes that spiritbreaking is the *principal* function of typical lower middle-class schools.

. . . The legal justifications for compulsory schooling have been to protect children from exploitation by parents and employers, and to ensure the basic literacy and civics necessary for a democratic electorate. It is quite a different matter to deprive adolescents of their freedom in order to alleviate the difficulties of a faulty economic and political system. Is this constitutional?

. . . At present, in most states, for 10 to 13 years every young person is obliged to sit the better part of his day in a room almost always too crowded, facing front, doing lessons predetermined by a distant administration at the state capital and that have no relation to his own intellectual, social, or animal interests, and not much relation even to his economic interests. The overcrowding precludes individuality or spontaneity, reduces the young to ciphers, and the teacher to a martinet. If a youth tries to follow his own bent, he is interrupted and even jailed. If he does not perform, he is humiliated and threatened, but he is *not allowed to fail and get out.* . . .

In his speech the Secretary referred to the admirable extension of free education from 1850 to, say, 1930. But this is again entirely misleading with regard to our present situation. To repeat, that opening of opportunity took place in an open economy, with an expanding market for skills and cultural learning. Young people took advantage of it *of their own volition;* therefore there were no blackboard jungles and endemic problems of discipline. Teachers taught those who wanted to learn; therefore there was no especial emphasis on grading. What is the present situation? The frantic competitive testing and grading means that the market for skills and learning is *not* open, it is tight. There are relatively few employers for those who score high; and almost none of the high-scorers become independent enterprisers. . . .

V.

. . . We must remember that, whatever the motive, *pouring money into the school-and-college system and into the academic social-work way of coping with problems, is strictly class legislation that confirms the inequitable structure of the economy.* . . .

VI.

In my opinion, the public buys this unexamined "education" because of the following contradiction: The Americans are guilty because these youth *are* useless in the present set-up, so they spend money on them (though they get oddly stingy at crucial moments); on the other hand, they insist that the youth work hard at something "useful"—namely useless training. One can't just let them play ball; they must compete and suffer.

I agree that we ought to spend more public money on education. And where jobs exist and there is need for technical training, the corporations ought to spend more money on apprenticeships. We are an affluent society and can afford it. And the conditions of modern life are far too complicated for independent young spirits to get going on their own. They need some preparation, though probably not as much as is supposed; but more important, they need various institutional frameworks in which they can try out and learn the ropes.

Nevertheless, I would not give a penny more to the present school administrators. The situation is this: to make the present school set-up even *tolerable,* not positively damaging—e.g., to cut the elementary class size to 20 or to provide colleges enough to diminish the frantic competition for places—will require at least *doubling* the present school budgets. I submit that this kind of money should be spent in other ways.

VII.

... Fundamentally, there is no right education except growing up into a worthwhile world. Indeed, our excessive concern with problems of education at present simply means that the grown-ups do not have such a world. The poor youth of America will *not* become equal by rising through the middle class, going to middle-class schools. By plain social justice, the Negroes and other minorities have the right to, and must get, equal opportunity to schooling with the rest, but the exaggerated expectation from the schooling is a chimera—and, I fear, will be shockingly disappointing. But also the middle-class youth will not escape their increasing exploitation and *anomie* in such schools. A decent education aims at, prepares for, a more worthwhile future, with a different community spirit, different occupations, and more real utility than attaining status and salary. ...

The dangers of the highly technological and automated future are obvious: We might become a brainwashed society of idle and frivolous consumers. We might continue in a rat race of highly competitive, unnecessary busy-work with a meaninglessly expanding Gross National Product. In either case, there might still be an out-cast group that must be suppressed. To countervail these dangers and make active, competent, and initiating citizens who can produce a community culture and a noble recreation, we need a very different education than the schooling that we have been getting. ...

On the whole, the education must be voluntary rather than compulsory, for no growth to freedom occurs except by intrinsic motivation. Therefore the educational opportunities must be various and variously administered. We must diminish rather than expand the present monolithic school system. I would suggest that, on the model of the GI-Bill, we experiment, giving the school money directly to the high-school age adolescents, for any plausible self-chosen educational proposals, such as purposeful travel or individual enterprise. This would also, of course, lead to the proliferation of experimental schools.

Unlike the present inflexible lockstep, our educational policy must allow for periodic quitting and easy return to the scholastic ladder, so that the young have time to find themselves and to study when they are themselves ready. ...

Paul Goodman

The claim that there is a direct causal link between the amount of education you have and the kind of job, income and social status you will achieve also includes the idea that this link has produced large-scale upward mobility in our society. We turn now to a more detailed series of questions and refutations of this claim.

One writer, Ivar Berg, questions whether men and women who are able to earn more than others, do so because they are more educated or more trained, or whether there are other factors involved. Does education and/or training contribute to an individual's productivity, as many who hire people claim, or does it help her get a better-paying job? If it helps her get a better-paying job, but has little or nothing to do with her productivity, is it something about the education that qualifies her for the job, or is it something that is incidental to the education but more connected to those qualities she brings to her schooling that enable her to succeed and stay on in her schooling to the point that she now "qualifies" for the better-paying job?[8]

These are some of the questions Berg raises. Instead of restricting his study of education and jobs to the pecuniary factors that economists focused on in earlier studies, Berg looks at such things as turnover in jobs, productivity, and worker dissatisfaction. No one doubts, for example, that some sort of link exists between increased education and increased productivity. But the nature of this link is not at all clear. Berg notes the wide differences in education and other characteristics among workers who are in the same job category. And he also finds that in certain areas workers with less education but more experience perform better and earn more than others.

As Berg says, the "education craze" among employers and others holds that by raising educational requirements for employment a more ambitious, disciplined work force will be recruited that will be more productive than workers who have terminated their schooling earlier. Berg's findings fail to bear out this belief, though he points out that the lack of data, often from the very employers who hold this view, must be taken into account. That is, the data are not sufficient for him to make conclusive judgments. And those employers who make such judgments cannot cite the data to support them.

What he does find does not give Berg much reason for agreeing with those who argue that educational requirements serve managers well as, for example, a screening device for either potential or actual performance. Instead, Berg finds that organizational careers are more a function of loyalty and longevity, and that educational differences tend to wash out among employees at every organizational level except that of engineers and scientists. Berg also finds that the frequency of turnover in jobs is positively related to education: the more schooling the more likely there will be turnover. Managers who raise the educational requirements for their jobs are thus likely to buy for themselves the very dissatisfactions that their expensive personnel practices are meant to discourage.

What emerges in Berg's findings is that Americans of quite diverse educational achievements perform productive functions adequately and perhaps well in all but a few professional occupations. He also finds that it is not possible to construct an occupational scale according to the intellectual abilities required by diverse occupations.

8. We hope the reader is jarred by the use of her instead of he. We think this is self-explanatory.

In sum, there is little or no evidence that increased schooling improves job performance, productivity and job satisfaction. In addition, though there seems to be some sort of connection between being educated and getting a job, it is more likely that there are factors other than education at work. Despite these critiques there has recently sprung up a new call for what is being called "career education," with former President Nixon having been in the forefront. In his wake, one superintendent[9] of public schools described career education as demanding "a major rethinking of the entire structure of education," which will insure that every youngster will have an opportunity to leave school with a salable skill. At the same time, we are told, "every youngster will have an opportunity for a new, livelier relevant academic education."

This superintendent went on to describe how education—including that over which he presides—is failing millions, noting as evidence of this failure the undereducated citizens amongst us, unemployment, poverty, alienation, segregation and soaring welfare costs. (Note the obvious implication here that somehow *education* can prevent all of these!) He also noted the low reading scores in many schools, including his own, the high dropout rates (sometimes as high as 50 percent), the high turnover in student bodies, the failure to serve students who do not speak English, the failure of 80 percent of those who go on to college to graduate, the rapid decline in jobs that the unskilled can fill (but at the same time he notes that by 1980 only 20 percent of the jobs in our society will require a four-year college degree), and the increasing demands for persons with a technical skill.

But the real concern in all of this may come at the bottom of the superintendent's list: "Too many people are coming out of schools unprepared for a job or for college. Many high school graduates go on to college because 'it is the thing to do' or because they haven't the foggiest idea of what else to do." In short, the function that, according to Perkinson, high schools were originally designed to perform, viz., determining who goes and who does not go to college, is at best being poorly performed.

Career education is offered as part of the solution to these problems. It is not supposed to be job training, we are told. Rather it is increased curriculum flexibility that will provide youngsters with the kind of experiences they need to be "effective participants in society." Graduation standards impose on all students a single curriculum "tightly designed and heavily oriented toward students who wish to go on to college." In short, what is needed is differentiated curriculum. Now lest you think this is the same thing that American education came up with in the early 1900s under the title of "vocational guidance," we are told this is not a fancy new name for vocational education. Nor is it a device for shunting off students into the "working class track," especially the low socioeconomic level students. Career education, we are told, will eliminate this kind of tracking.

It will blend under one curriculum umbrella the three traditional tracks of the college preparatory, the vocational, and the general. It gives the minority youngster a better chance to explore options available and to become aware

---

9. Dr. William Johnston is presently Superintendent of the Los Angeles City Unified School District.

of opportunities available for education and training beyond the high school or entry level of employment.[10]

This, we are assured, is not job training and it will not do away with emphasis on the traditional basic skills or academic classes. However, and here we must listen closely, "we must recognize that our society is geared to the world of work." So too, it is implied, must our schools be so geared.

Such schools will prepare young people "for everything from 'the lunch bucket' occupations to the 'attache case' professions and gives them sufficient early grounding to be able to make valid choices of their own." The present curriculum will be revised so that, beginning in kindergarten, the three Rs and other subject areas will be closely related to the many ways adults earn a living. Note carefully: *Beginning in kindergarten.*

Does this mean we begin in kindergarten to interest the child in what he or she will be doing as an adult? It is not clear what is meant by "closely relating" the three Rs to the "many ways adults earn a living." Is this a vision of the "kinder" in the "garten" beginning to think about how they are to make a living?

In the junior high, while continuing "the development of intellectual and basic skills," career education will begin to provide students with a basis for deciding about career directions. But in the senior high school the "salable skills" concept comes to the fore, and students will concentrate in specific "career clusters." This is supposed to mean that traditional college, general, and vocational tracks will be gone and in their place will be . . . a "series of ladders," in such "occupational clusters as public service, fine arts and humanities, business and office, marketing and distribution, communications and media, construction, manufacturing," and the like.

So it is a ladder (or "cluster") rather than a track, in which "a student has an option of climbing the rungs, or categories, from 'entry-skilled,' 'semi-skilled,' 'skilled,' 'technical,' 'semi-professional,' to 'professional.' " There will be flexibility and options while at the same time the student's "appreciation of the usefulness of English or mathematics is developed."

Is this consistent with Berg's findings about the relationship between jobs and schooling? Jack McCurdy, education writer for the *Los Angeles Times,* described it as vocational education being elevated to a prominent new status, but claimed that no one has yet made clear just what "career education" is.[11]

As McCurdy says, it is not very clear. We are impressed by the fact that it is not only employers who continue to believe, in the absence of supporting evidence, that the content of schooling is positively related to job performance and productivity. Faced with the fact that "too many young people are coming out of schools unprepared for a job or for college," the response of the school people is that it is the young people who are deficient and schooling can correct that deficiency.

Whether this is indeed significantly different from the old vocational guidance programs of the early 1900s remains to be seen. It might be illuminating to see what some contemporary "revisionist" historians are saying about the nature of these earlier vocational programs, and the interests they served. Was it

10. *Los Angeles Times*, Dr. William Johnston, April 9, 1972.
11. Ibid.

the interests of the students that were primarily served by these programs ("geared to the world of work"), or was it something else? We have already read Joel Spring's analysis of the role played by extracurricular activities to prepare young people for the needs of the burgeoning corporate capitalism of the early 1900s in Chapter 3, The Schools and Politics. In the following selection, Spring analyzes the role of vocational guidance and draws some of the same parallels.

EDUCATION AND THE RISE OF
THE CORPORATE STATE (PART 2)

Joel Spring

*   *   *

The birth of vocational guidance and the junior high school was a response to the specialized needs of American industry in the early 1900s. During the nineteenth century the narrow stratum of skilled workers had been trained on the job, either as apprentices to journeymen or in training programs maintained by manufacturers. As large-scale manufacturing developed, however, skills became more diverse, workers became more mobile, and the investment required to train skilled workers on the job became more and more risky. Gradually, the schools were given the responsibility of differentiating the work force in advance of graduation according to ability and vocational goals.

The early vocational guidance leaders attempted to function as human engineers who matched and shaped individual abilities to fit a particular slot in the social organism. This gave them the dual responsibility of analyzing personal talents and character and planning educational programs in terms of a future vocation. Junior high schools were designed to make educational planning and guidance possible at an early age. The original purpose of the junior high school was to divide students into separate courses of study in the hope that with proper guidance they would choose vocations early and follow a directed educational program through high school to the occupation.

There was an engineer's image of social organization in the idea of education functioning as a feeder system to the industrial complex. Certainly there was an element of frustration among early vocational guidance leaders, who were concerned about the instability of human beings and the difficulty of keeping society functioning like a well-oiled machine. Frank Parsons, often called the father of vocational guidance and founder of the first vocational bureau in Boston in 1908, wrote that a "sensible industrial system will . . . seek . . . to put men, as

Joel Spring, "Education and the Rise of the Corporate State," *Socialist Revolution,* Vol. 2, No. 2, March-April 1972, pp. 75-83.

well as timber, stone, and iron, in the places for which their natures fit them, and to polish and prepare them for efficient service with at least as much care as is bestowed upon clocks, electric dynamos, or locomotives."[1] This language reflects Parsons' own training in engineering and his involvement in economic and social reform in the 1890s.

A similar anxiety about human inefficiency permeated the work of pioneer industrial psychologist Hugo Munsterberg. Munsterberg provided the early guidance movement with vocational aptitude tests. In a book published in 1910 he complained about the absence of social barriers and economic conditions that allowed men to drift into careers for which they were not suited. In the past, he argued, the United States "could afford the limitless waste of human energy just as it felt justified in wasting the timber resources of the forest."[2] But modern conditions, Munsterberg felt, required both the conservation of resources and human talents. Society could no longer afford the social and economic waste caused by having the wrong man perform an economic or political task. Vocational guidance was to reduce inefficiency in the distribution of human resources. Thus, Eli Weaver, the pioneer of vocational guidance in New York City, envisioned the establishment of a central government vocational bureau that would function as a commodity exchange market, and to this end, between 1906 and 1910, he organized committees of teachers in the New York high schools to work with students in planning their careers. The function of the central bureau was to determine the type of training and character needed in available industrial occupations. The bureau also conducted surveys of the labor market to determine manpower shortages and surpluses. This information was used to encourage and discourage training in particular occupations depending upon the needs of the labor market. Within the schools, guidance and educational programs were to be based on information supplied by the bureau, which would also place graduates in appropriate occupations. Weaver wrote that the guidance agency would "facilitate the exchange of labor between the workers and employers as the exchange of other commodities is now assisted through the standardizing operations of other exchanges."[3]

But vocational guidance was also conceived of as a means of changing the general pattern of industrial development. Frank Parsons, a utopian reformer, believed that guidance could be one step in the direction of eliminating the profit motive from the industrial system. Parsons opened the Vocation Bureau in Boston in the last year of a life that had been devoted to campaigns for social and economic change. He once expressed the hope that someday "the humblest student of social science may drop some word, that, taking root in the brain of a man who trundles the world at his heels, shall lift the earth into Paradise."[4] The paradise that Parsons was hoping for was called "mutualism." This was a blissful state of brotherly love in which conflict and antagonism were replaced by mutual help. He believed that mutualism could only be achieved through the gradual expansion of public ownership of the means of production. To achieve this required education and industrial efficiency. Industrial efficiency made it possible to run corporate structures under public ownership, and education would "squeeze the last black drop of savage blood out of humanity's veins."[5]

Parsons' ideas reflected how much vocational guidance was a response to the development of large-scale corporate capitalism. He wrote in his book on mutualism, "Educate! Fill the children with public spirit. Enlarge the business interests of city, state, and nation. Make the railroads, monopolies, and trusts public property. . . . Educate! Educate! Teach brother-love, and practice it occasionally." Guidance into the corporate structure was one form of education designed to make the economic system run efficiently for the benefit of all. But vocational guidance was only part of a general educational plan to turn society into one large corporation of brotherly love. Another part of the plan was the creation of a guaranteed annual income that would condition men to think in terms of working for the good of society. External restraints on evil activities, such as saloons, and generous rewards for social service were to lead to internalization of these controls. The result was to be a highly organized society in which the individual was willing to sacrifice himself for the benefit of his neighbor. Performance of a job for which the individual was best suited was one way of fulfilling a social obligation. The individual in a state of mutualism, Parsons wrote, will work to the best of his abilities and without controls will consume "no more than he needs to fit him for the highest and noblest activities of which he is capable."[6]

Despite the hopes of educational reformers like Parsons, the role of the vocational guidance counselor as it emerged was part labor specialist, as well as educator and psychologist. As labor specialist the guidance counselor had to have an understanding of the job market and requirements. At the founding meeting of the Vocational Education Association in 1913 Fredrick G. Bonser of Teachers College demanded that a professional education be developed that would train the vocational counselor to know the "relationship between present and probable supply and demand, the relative wages, and the changes in methods, devices, and organization affecting the workers." Bonser also emphasized the importance of studying the physical and mental requirements of occupations.[7]

In the early stages of the guidance movement the student was often seen simply as raw material for the industrial corporation. Part of the educational duties of the counselor was that of shaping good industrial character. Parsons wrote, "Life can be moulded into any conceivable form. Draw up your specifications for a dog, or man . . . and if you will give me control of the environment, and time enough, I will clothe your dreams in flesh and blood."[8] In part this meant just the inculcation of traditional business values such as industriousness, punctuality, obediance, and orderliness. For example, as part of the guidance program at the De Kalb Township High School in Illinois the principal quoted business maxims such as, "It is none of my business what you do at night, but if dissipation affects what you do the next day, and you do half as much as I demand, you will last half as long as you hoped."[9] At the vocation bureau in Boston Parsons used interview and self-analysis sheets to determine the personality adjustments necessary for his clients. During the course of an interview Parsons would make his own character appraisal by watching the manners and habits of his subject. This appraisal would be followed by a take-home questionnaire. The instructions on the questionnaire told the client to, "Look in the glass. Watch yourself. Get your friends to . . . tell you confidentially what they think of your appearance, manners, voice. . . . Get your family and friends to help you recognize your defects." With these instructions the individual would answer questions ranging from self-reliance and industriousness to "Do you wear your finger-nails in mourning and your linen overtime?"[10]

As a psychologist the early guidance counselor used a variety of tests to determine occupational abilities. The early tests could be generally described as comparing human abilities to a machine. Historically Munsterberg believed that he was bringing together two major movements in American life, scientific management and vocational guidance. Scientific management, Munsterberg wrote in 1913 in one of his major works, *Psychology and Industrial Efficiency,* had under the direction of efficiency expert Fredrick Taylor made major advances in increasing industrial productivity. But, he argued, while the time-study approach showed how to increase the efficiency of a particular task, it did not go far enough in analyzing the physical traits best suited for the job. Working from the frame of reference of scientific management Munsterberg tried to analyze the mechanical response of man. Taylor had wanted to mechanize human action with time and motion studies. Munsterberg wanted to determine how far and in what direction any given individual could be mechanized. His tests of Boston streetcar motormen were to determine powers of sustained attention and discrimination with respect to a rapidly changing panorama. The objective was to find those who would be least likely to have an accident. Working later with the American Telephone and Telegraph Company, Munsterberg developed tests of memory, attention, and dexterity for job applicants.[11] Tests of this nature were quickly used in guidance. For instance, Jesse B. Davis, a high school principal in Michigan and early vocational guidance leader, inspired by Hugo Musterberg's streetcar and telephone tests, worked with the Michigan State Telephone Company in 1912 and 1913 to develop aptitude tests for telephone operators. These tests included the ability to remember numbers, speed, and motor accuracy.[12]

In the schools, vocational guidance acquired the role of educational guidance and evaluator of individual interests and abilities. An early model for vocational guidance was the Grand Rapids Central High School in Grand Rapids, Michigan. Its fame among guidance leaders was attested to by the fact that the first meeting of the Vocational Guidance Association was held in 1913 in Grand Rapids and the principal of the school, Jesse B. Davis, was elected the first secretary of the Association. The following year Davis became its president.

Davis not only believed that the major function of the school was to guide the student into his proper place in the corporate structure, but also that the school should be organized along the lines of a corporation. He believed that this would give the student a good introduction into the workings of the industrial community. The whole social life of the Central High School was organized to train the students for work in a corporation. Student groups were organized into a pyramid of activities. At the base were clubs, athletics, and student government. Above these activities in ascending order were a Boys and Girls Leadership Club, a Student Council, an Advisory Council, and the principal. Davis, the principal and founder of the system, believed that organization of all school activities into a social whole would demonstrate to the students the value of system and combination of effort. This type of organization he felt reflected the realities of the American industrial system. He compared his position as principal to that of a general manager and called the advisory council of teachers "a board of control." Davis stated that "the ideals upon which honest living and sound business stand, are the ideals of the public schools." While these industrial traits were being learned in the social life of the school, class work was aiding the student to choose a job. Topics in English composition were assigned in progressive steps to help the individual understand himself and the type of career he should follow. In the ninth grade students at the high school analyzed their own character and habits. In the eleventh grade they chose a career and investigated the type of preparation they would need. In the twelfth grade the students made "a special study of the vocation with respect to its social obligations, its peculiar opportunities for human service, and responsibilities . . . [to] the community." Davis believed that people should enter an occupation with the idea that "it was the best means by which they, with their ability, might serve their fellow man." This belief he placed in the historical context of the development of social interdependence.[13]

More typical of the developing role of the counselor was that suggested by Frank Parsons' successor as director of the Boston Vocation Bureau, Meyer Bloomfield. In an article in Charles Johnston's 1914 anthology, *The Modern High School,* he stated that the "vocational-guidance movement has . . . made clear one of the most important and generally neglected services which a school can render, and that is educational guidance."[14] Educational guidance involved helping the student select an educational program to match his interests, abilities, and future occupation. The tools of the counselor were aptitude tests similar to those being developed by Munsterberg, interest inventories, and character analysis. An important requirement of educational guidance was a flexible curriculum. In terms of vocational guidance the curriculum was to be subservient to the occupational goals of the student. On the one hand this meant evaluating subjects in terms of their vocational value. Bloomfield reported that this was occurring in several cities. "Such adjustments," he wrote, "and such reinterpretations of the high school scheme make for a fresh sense of values in secondary education." On the other hand this meant having a differentiated curriculum. Students would take different courses of study depending on their occupational destination. Ideally the school counselor would match the student to an occupation and then to a course of study that would prepare him for that vocation.

NOTES

1. Frank Parsons, *Our Country's Need* (Boston, 1894), p. 69.
2. Hugo Munsterberg, *American Problems* (New York, 1910), pp. 27-28.
3. Eli R. Weaver, *Wage-Earning Occupations of Boys and Girls* (Brooklyn, 1912).
4. Parsons, p. vi.
5. Frank Parsons, *The Drift of Our Time* (Chicago, 1898), p. 11.
6. Parsons, *Our Country's Need.*
7. Fredrick G. Bonser, "Necessity of Professional Training for Vocational Counseling," in *Vocational Guidance: Papers Presented at the Organization Meeting of the Vocational Association, Grand Rapids, Michigan, October 21-24, 1913,* United States Bureau of Education Bulletin no. 14, (1914), p. 38.
8. Parsons, *Our Country's Need,* p. 2.
9. P. M. Giles, "Guidance by Systematic Courses of Instruction in Vocational Opportunities and Personal Characteristics," in *Vocational Guidance, Papers Presented . . .,* pp. 57-58.
10. Frank Parsons, *Choosing a Vocation* (Boston, 1909), pp. 32-44.
11. Hugo Munsterberg, *Psychology and Industrial Efficiency* (Cambridge, 1913), pp. 36-55.
12. Jesse B. Davis, *The Saga of a Schoolmaster* (Boston, 1956), pp. 184-85.
13. Jesse B. Davis, *Vocational and Moral Guidance* (Boston, 1914), pp. 46-123; and "Vocational and Moral Guidance in the High School." *Religious Education,* February 1913, p. 646.
14. Meyer Bloomfield, "Vocational Guidance in the High School," in Charles H. Johnston, ed., *The Modern High School* (New York, 1914), p. 612

Joel Spring

The question remains: Does schooling explain why some people have higher incomes than others, and why some people have better jobs and higher social status than others? Does schooling in any way contribute to equality, especially economic equality? If it does not, is there any reason for believing that schools can achieve this goal?

The most systematic study thus far of the available evidence bearing on these questions was conducted by Christopher Jencks and associates recently, and their conclusions were published in *Inequality: A Reassessment of the Effect of Family and Schooling in America* (New York: Basic Books, 1972). In their study they found that American schools were not only failing to equalize school achievement among children, but were also failing to equalize levels of educational attainment and adult income. Jencks and his associates, in fact, concluded that we should not look to the schools to assure equal opportunity but rather take more direct steps to remove, or at least lessen, the inequality that exists in America today.

There are three questions that the Jencks study asks. 1) What is the relation between the resources of a school and the effects it has on children in that school? 2) What are the effects of the resources of a school, a child's achievement in that school, and the personal characteristics of that child on the final level of education that that child reaches? 3) What is the relation of the educational level a child reaches, his test scores, and his family background to the income and occupational status he has as an adult?

The study reinforced what the Equality of Educational Opportunity Study done by James Coleman and subsequent analyses of that study have told us. Variations in school resources do not at present have much to do with children's achievement in school, whether it be changes in funding, facilities, teachers or other students. Schools cannot now affect most of the determinants of cognitive skills.

But cognitive skills, next to family background, are the most important determinants of the number of years of schooling a child will have. Yet the Jencks study found that schools have no effect in changing the distribution of cognitive skills among students, therefore the schools' resources will have no direct influence on the amount of schooling a child receives. Ironically, the study found that it was only when they looked outside the school that they found evidence that some effect can be made on educational attainment.

As for differences in occupational status, Jencks and his colleagues were willing to attribute no more than forty to fifty percent to final educational attainment, and very little to the quality of a school. And they found that it did not help much in predicting the future income of a student if you knew what that student's family socioeconomic status and background was, his scores on tests of cognitive skill, his years of education, and his occupational status.

The Jencks study findings are by no means conclusive. Much disagreement exists as to the extent to which they provide either a basis for an indictment of the schools or for judging the effectiveness of American schooling. In their introduction to a discussion of the Jencks book, the editors of the *Harvard Educational Review* concluded:

The editors of HER share with many of our readers the predisposition to believe that the schools routinely *do* have powerful effects on the children attending them.

We would like to ask the question, what are these effects? This will involve developing ways of talking about schooling which are not now in existence in the research community. Without new questions, we fear that the current tendency to find that nothing relates to anything will continue, and that it will be misunderstood by the American public to mean that the schools are doing nothing.

In addition to recognizing that we could use more complete examination of all aspects of schooling, it is important to recognize that *Inequality* is a description of our past, rather than a delimitation of our nation's educational future. Stated differently, *Inequality* should be taken as a perspective on history, not as a pronouncement of gospel . . . given the infancy of systematic attempts to improve the schools, it is too early to assume that the schools cannot be developed so that they do succeed in reducing overall social inequality in America.[12]

If schools in America have not equalized opportunity, income, jobs and social status, what have they done? We have already encountered writers like Spring and Lichtman, who are producing reappraisals of what schools have and have not done in our society, in this case from Marxist, neo-Marxist or socialist perspectives. These opinions are a departure from the faith that most Americans still have about their schools. In the following reading, Fred Pincus carefully analyzes the question of whether the community colleges contribute toward equality. Using data available to everyone, he answers the question with a decisive "No."

12. "Perspectives on *Inequality: A Reassessment of the Effect of Family and Schooling in America,*" *Harvard Educational Review*, 43, No. 1, February 1973, pp. 37-164.

TRACKING IN COMMUNITY COLLEGES

Fred Pincus[1]

The quest for a college education has remained an unfulfilled dream for the vast majority of youth from poor and working class families. The same has been true for most young people who are members of ethnic minority groups.[2] Poor, working class and ethnic minority students are *less* likely to attend college and more likely to drop out of college than their white middle class counterparts. This has been true in private and public institutions of higher learning. (Jencks and Riesman, 1969; Crossland, 1971; Folger, et al., 1970)

Fred Pincus, "Tracking in Community Colleges," *The Insurgent Sociologist,* V, VI, No. 3, Spring 1974, pp. 17-36.

Explanations for the lack of success of these students in higher education are wide-ranging. On traditional tests of academic ability (IQ and aptitude tests) and academic achievement (grades and standardized achievement tests) middle class and white students consistently score higher than poor, working class and ethnic minority students. (Folger, 1970; Crossland, 1971) Many point to these differences in aptitude as the main cause of the class and ethnic inequalities that exist in higher education.

Although some argue that these ability differences are largely due to genetic differences in intelligence, most would agree that environmental factors are *a* major cause, if not *the* major cause of the inequalities. Some argue that the "culturally-deprived" environment in poor and ethnic communities retards the development of intellectual skills and creates low educational aspirations in students from these communities. Others argue that biased tests of ability, an irrelevant curriculum, and racist attitudes of teachers are the real causes of existing inequalities. The basic point here is that most scholars point to an entire set of economic and cultural factors that are crucial in determining a student's score on tests of academic ability and achievement, and consequently, a student's success in college.

The public community college[3] has been given the major task of providing increased opportunity for those students who have been excluded from higher education. Edmond Gleazer, President of the American Association of Community and Junior Colleges (AACJC) states that:

a much larger proportion of our population than is now doing so can benefit by education beyond high school, and that the student can best show what he can do by being allowed to try. . . . This "chance to try" is provided by the community college. (Gleazer, 1968:51)

Almost all those who are proponents of the community college stress its role in "democratizing" higher education and in providing "equal opportunity" in higher education. (E.g., Clark, 1960a; Medsker, 1960; Newman, 1971; Cross, 1971; Monroe, 1972; Carnegie Commission 1970; Yarrington, 1973.)

This paper will analyze the attempts by community colleges to "democratize" higher education. Have they succeeded or failed in providing equal opportunity for all? Before proceeding, however, it is necessary to develop a criterion for success and failure; i.e., exactly what does "equal opportunity" mean?

One view of equality conceives of higher education as a contest in which everyone should be allowed to compete. Students from all backgrounds and with a wide range of academic skills should be allowed to enter college, but only those with the appropriate kinds of academic skills should be allowed to succeed. These skills will probably not be found among most low income and ethnic minority students due to their "disadvantaged" or "deprived" backgrounds, but at least these students should be given a chance to try. For those who make it, so much the better. Those who don't can probably benefit from their limited college experience.

An alternate notion of equality in higher education looks not only to the "chance to try," but also to the "chance to succeed." Since a large part of the class and ethnic differences in educational ability and achievement are due to environmental factors, equality in higher education cannot exist until these environmental factors have been either eliminated or neutralized. In terms of the larger society, this would mean the elimination of income inequality and racism. Within the schools, it might mean having unprejudiced teachers, a more relevant curriculum, more effective tests of ability, and the like. At the very least, effective remedial programs would be necessary to "undo" some of the "damage" that has been done to low income and ethnic minority students by poverty and inadequate schooling.

The crucial point in this second conception of equality is this: as long as conditions in the larger society and/or in the schools continue to be an important cause of the unequal educational achievement between students of different social classes and between students in different ethnic groups, one cannot talk of equality. Ideally, one can talk of equality only when there is no correlation between achievement and social class, and between achievement and ethnicity. (Milner, 1972; Karabel, 1972)

This paper demonstrates that community colleges hold the "chance to try" concept of equality, and are much less concerned about the "chance to succeed." This will become evident after examining the goals that the community colleges have set for themselves. In fact, the community colleges play an important role in maintaining educational inequality and, as a result, help to reinforce the system of class and ethnic stratification that exists in the United States.

HISTORY OF COMMUNITY COLLEGES

Community colleges began to develop during the first quarter of the twentieth century, frequently as private institutions that were two-year extensions of high schools or were simply substitutes for the first two years of college. By 1922, there were over 200 community colleges in the country and most of them were private. The number of two-year institutions jumped to more than 600 by 1940.

During the decades of the 40s and 50s, community college growth slowed considerably and by 1960 there were only 656 community colleges. However, presidential commissions in the Truman and Eisenhower administrations and the 1960 Commission on National Goals recommended that community colleges be expanded. These commissions emphasized the fact that many people could benefit from two more years of education and stressed the importance of "flexibility" in the community college curriculum. Rather than simply being academic institutions, the community colleges were encouraged to develop occupational programs to meet the needs of government and industry, and to provide for the needs of millions of students who "would not otherwise receive college educations." This was the beginning of what came to be known as the "comprehensive" community college. (Monroe, 1972; Medsker and Tillery, 1971)

After 1960, the community colleges grew rapidly. By 1971, there were over 1,100 community colleges, most of them public. Between 1958 and 1973, community college enrollment increased by more than five times, from 525,000 to 2,917,000. In contrast, the number of students in all institutions of higher learning increased only two-and-one-half times, from 3,420,000 to 9,662,000. Almost all of the community college students (95 percent) are enrolled in public institutions. (USOE, 1970; Chronicle, 1974)

In the fall of 1973, 30 percent of all college enrollment was in community colleges, and all indications are that this figure will continue to increase. Over half of *all freshmen in public institutions* of higher learning are currently enrolled in community colleges, and some predict that this figure will rise to 70 percent in 1980. (Monroe, 1972; Chronicle, 1974; Carnegie Commission, 1971) In the future, most freshmen will be having their first college experience at a public comprehensive community college.

GOALS OF COMMUNITY COLLEGES

There appears to be almost universal consensus among community college administrators and planners on the basic goals of these institutions. The function of community colleges in higher education can best be understood by talking about the *public goals,* those that are discussed in school catalogues and public relations materials, and the *non-public goals,* those that are not discussed in catalogues and public relations materials but that are discussed in books, articles and reports written by educators and social scientists.

Public Goals

There are five public goals of the community colleges: 1) a comprehensive curriculum; 2) an open-door admissions policy; 3) convenient location; 4) an attempt to give students a second chance; and 5) a community orientation.

The first public goal, a *comprehensive curriculum,* refers to the broad range of programs that exist in community colleges, enabling students with different "interests and abilities" to select the program that is "best suited to their needs." The curriculum can be divided into two basic categories:

a) *Transfer* or *College-Parallel*—courses that are equivalent to the first two years at a four-year school and that will prepare students to transfer to a four-year school.

b) *Terminal Occupational*—programs lasting two years or less which provide students with the skills necessary to enter some form of employment after graduating from the community college.

In addition to these two basic curricula, there are also *remedial* or *developmental* programs designed to help students develop academic skills in which they may be deficient; *adult or continuing education programs* that help students gain their high school equivalency certificates and/or upgrade their jobs; and *general education programs* that provide courses of general interest that don't necessarily lead to any degree. This type of curriculum, then, provides something for everyone who enters community college. Diversity is the key word.

The second public goal of the community college is the *open door* principle, whereby any person who is a high school graduate or who is an adult citizen (over eighteen) is welcome to attend a community college. Thus, while other institutions of higher learning are selective in their admissions policies and expensive in cost, the community colleges will take everyone.

The *convenient location* of community college is the third public goal. Campuses should be developed in all areas of the country, but particularly in large urban areas, so that community colleges will be within commuting distance of 95 percent of the population. (Carnegie Commission, 1971)

The fourth public goal of the community college is to provide students with a *second chance* to succeed, sometimes referred to as the "salvage" function. Students who have not been successful in high school will get a second chance at a college education. This could be useful for good students who have not applied themselves in high school, and for the mediocre students who need some remedial work.

The fifth public goal is *community orientation.* The community college should offer a relevant curriculum to the members of the community in which it is located. In addition, it should serve the community by providing cultural events, expertise in solving local problems, and a meeting place for community organizations.

These, then, are the public goals of the community college that are designed to bring equal opportunity to all students in higher education. These goals are accepted by just about everyone who supports the community colleges. (Gleazer, 1968; Koos, 1970; Carnegie Commission, 1970; Medsker and Tillery, 1971; Cross, 1971; Monroe, 1972; AACJC, 1973)

Nonpublic Goals

The public goals tell only part of the community college story, however. In addition there are four nonpublic goals: 1) training a paraprofessional labor force; 2) screening; 3) cooling-out; and 4) custodial care.

Although *paraprofessional training* is publicly offered to students through the occupational tracks in the community colleges, students are not told how this training is related to the stratified labor force that they will enter. Most observers of the American economy agree that the fastest growing sector of the labor force is the category of "professional and technical workers." (e.g., U.S. Department of Labor, 1970; Berg, 1971) Institutions of higher education, in general, have the responsibility for training the vast majority of these workers, but the community colleges have the specific task of training the "technical" or "paraprofessional" part of the labor force; i.e., those middle-level workers who "assist" the professionals and who need more than a high school education but less than a college education. (Monroe, 1972; Medsker and Tillery, 1971; Carnegie Commission, 1970; Harris, 1964)

A division of labor has developed within higher education to provide American institutions with a skilled professional and paraprofessional labor force. The four-year colleges and universities will continue to train people for jobs that require a bachelor's degree—from teachers and social workers to doctors and systems analysis. The community colleges, on the other hand, will train people for jobs requiring only two years of college, including teacher's aids, X-ray technicians and computer operators. In other words, community college graduates will enter lower paying jobs that have less prestige, less job satisfaction and fewer chances for mobility. (New University Conference, 1971)

The second nonpublic goal, *screening,* refers to the community colleges' job of differentiating those students who will complete four years of college and eventually enter one of the professions, from those who will complete only two years of college. Almost half of all high school graduates attend college, and many do not have the traditionally-accepted academic skills that are necessary to successfully complete college. More and more, these "non-traditional" students are entering the community colleges. It is the job of the community college to encourage and permit bright motivated students to enter the transfer programs, and to encourage other students to enter one of the terminal programs.

> The community college may not be conscious of performing a switchman's role of sorting out individuals like freight cars in a switchyard and placing them or alleged abilities as minority spokesmen claim. . . . This sorting job is not a pleasant one since many of the persons involved feel that they have been switched onto the wrong tracks. Now that the community college has an open-door policy, the universities are relieved of much of this distasteful task of selecting between the "fit" and the "unfit." (Monroe, 1972:37; See also Roueche, 1968; Gleazer, 1968; Jencks and Riesman, 1969; Koos, 1970; Carnegie Commission, 1970; Newman, 1971; Medsker and Tillery, 1971; Cross, 1971)

Cooling Out

The third nonpublic goal, *cooling-out* students with unrealistic aspirations, is closely related to the first and second. The term "cooling-out" was originally used by Goffman (1952) to refer to the process where a swindler gets his mark (i.e., the person who has been swindled) to accept his fate and not to complain to the authorities. Burton Clark (1960b), however, applies this concept to community colleges.

Although two-thirds of the community college freshmen want to eventually transfer to a four-year school, data show that only one-third actually do transfer. (Medsker, 1960; Gleazer, 1968) Clark refers to those students who want to transfer but do not transfer as "latent terminals"—regardless of their ambitions, they are "destined" to be terminal students. These students, according to Clark, have "unrealistically high aspirations that exceed their abilities." For example, a student might want to be a doctor but cannot pass the necessary biology and chemistry courses. It is these latent terminal students that are likely to drop out of school.

Clark's solution is to cool-out these students by convincing them that they cannot succeed in the transfer program, but that they could succeed in the "appropriate" occupational program. Rather than being a doctor, the student might consider being an X-ray technician or a pharmacist's aid. This cooling-out process, it is argued, is not only good for the individual student, but also provides the larger society with another skilled person to enter the labor force. The main instrument of this process is the counselling service at the community college and the bulk of his paper is a description of a step-by-step process by which counselors can help students to "redefine" their educational goals.

In his article, Clark stresses the non-public nature of the cooling-out function of community colleges.

> One dilemma of a cooling-out role is that it must be kept reasonably away from public scrutiny and not clearly perceived or understood by prospective clientele. Should it become obvious, the organization's ability to perform it would be impaired. . . . If high school seniors and their families were to define the junior college as a place which diverts college-bound students, a probable consequence would be a turning-away from the junior college and increased pressure for admission to the four-year colleges and universities

that are otherwise protected to some degree. This would, of course, render superfluous the part now played by the junior college in the division of labor among colleges. (Clark, 1960b:575)

Many writers actually use the term "cooling-out" in discussing the goals of the community colleges. (e.g., Simon 1967; Roueche, 1968; Monroe, 1972) Most others talk about bringing people's aspirations in line with their abilities, but do not specifically mention the term "cooling-out." (e.g., Knoell and Medsker, 1964; Gleazer, 1968; Cook, et al., 1968; Koos, 1970; Carnegie Commission, 1970; Medsker and Tillery, 1971; Cross, 1971) A recent article in the *Chronicle of Higher Education* summed things up this way:

> Community colleges may be worth the money if they do nothing more than this: One student came here never having liked to read or write and never having been very good at either. Yet, he wanted to be a lawyer. After some counseling he realized the odds against him were high, so he joined the Air Force. "Apparently" says a counselor, "he's quite happy about it." (Van Dyne, 1972:3)

The fourth nonpublic goal might be referred to as *custodial care*. A certain number of community college students will lack the motivation and/or the ability to succeed in any of the community college programs.

> It has been maintained that junior colleges provide programs for low-achieving students in order to keep these young people out of the labor market, off the streets and out of trouble. (Roueche, 1968:23)

Although not all writers discuss this goal per se, they do talk about the large number of students who never receive any type of degree. In any case, custodial care is not inconsistent with the other nonpublic goals of the community college.

These, then, are the goals as discussed by spokesmen and spokeswomen for the community colleges. Although the five public goals—comprehensive curriculum, open door policy, convenient location, second chance, and community orientation—stress the importance of providing more educational opportunities to more people, the four nonpublic goals—training paraprofessionals, screening, cooling-out, and custodial care—make it clear that not everyone will end up with the same education. The bright students will transfer to a four-year school and be eligible to enter one of the professions. The students of moderate ability will be able to complete a two-year occupational program and be eligible to enter one of the paraprofessional occupations. Students of low ability might well end up leaving the community college and will be able to enter only the lesser-skilled jobs. These nonpublic goals make the community colleges an integral part of an educational system that trains people to enter a stratified labor force that serves the interests of the large corporations that dominate American society.

THE EMPIRICAL STUDY OF TRACKING IN HIGHER EDUCATION

Academic Characteristics

Students at community colleges have lower grades and score lower on standard tests of academic ability than students at four-year institutions. Cross (1968) summarizes the evidence:

> The mean score for students attending four-year colleges exceeds that of students in two-year colleges, and . . . two-year college students score higher as a group than high school graduates who do not go to college. The research demonstrating these facts is national in scope, it is unanimous in findings, and it is based on a staggering array of traditional measures of academic aptitude and achievement.

The American Council on Education national survey of freshmen in the Fall of 1972 not only replicates these differences between two- and four-year students, but they also show that freshmen at public universities have higher grade point averages and higher class ranks in high school than state college freshmen. (ACE, 1972) Thus, the brightest freshmen attend universities, the next brightest attend state colleges and the rest attend community colleges or no college at all.

Social Class

The social class background of a student is a crucial variable in determining the likelihood of that student's receiving a college education. The research in this area may be summarized as follows:

> The higher a student's social class, the more likely it is that the student will have a high grade point average in high school and a high score on a standardized test of academic ability or achievement.

> When academic ability is statistically controlled, the higher a student's social class, the more likely it will be that a student will attend college; and once entering college, the more likely it will be that a student will complete college. (Astin, 1972; Folger, 1970; Jencks, 1972; Lauter and Howe, 1970; Rothstein, 1971)

Given the way higher education is stratified, students from higher social class backgrounds with their higher grades and achievement test scores are more likely to enter universities. Students from lower social class backgrounds with their lower grades and test scores, on the other hand, are more likely to begin their higher education at a community college. (Cross, 1968; Monroe, 1972; Karabel, 1972; Hanson and Weisbrod, 1969; Windham, 1969; Birnbaum and Goldman, 1971; Trimberger, 1973)

To examine more precisely the effects of class background on college attendance, Table 1 was constructed. The table displays the median family incomes of freshmen at different types of public institutions since 1966 (the earliest available data). Four conclusions may be drawn from the data.

1. Public higher education is stratified by economic class. The median income of public university freshmen is highest, followed by state college and then by community college freshmen. In 1972, for example, the median incomes of freshmen families were $14,450 in universities, $12,180 in state colleges, and $11,000 at community colleges.

2. The pattern of stratification has remained constant since 1967. Two-year college freshmen come from families with the lowest incomes and university freshmen come from families with the highest incomes.

3. The extent of stratification and its stability can be seen by the fact that since 1967, freshmen in two- and four-year colleges have come from families whose incomes were *below* the incomes of the families of all college freshmen and even below the incomes of all families in the country (where the head of the family was old enough to have a freshman-aged child).[4] Public university freshmen, on the other hand, come from families with median incomes well *above* the family incomes of all freshmen and of all U.S. families.

4. In 1972, for the first time, the median income of all college freshmen was *lower* than the median income of all families likely to have freshman-aged children. If this difference persists, it will indicate some progress in getting persons from lower income families to enter college. However, these lower income students will be more likely to enter the two-year colleges than either the state colleges or the universities. In fact, there is no discernible trend that indicates any relative changes in the incomes of four-year colleges and university freshmen.

TABLE 1

Median Income of Families of College Freshmen at
Different Types of Public Institutions, of Families of
All College Freshmen, and of All U.S. Families with
Heads 35-44 Years of Age, 1966-1972.

Type of Family	Year						
	1966	*1967*	*1968*	*1969*	*1970*	*1971*	*1972*
Freshmen at Public 2-Year Colleges	8,600	8,760	8,900	9,520	9,900	11,000	11,000
Freshmen at Public 4-Year Colleges	8,140	9,000	9,320	10,200	11,180	11,530	12,180
Freshmen at Public Universities	9,860	12,900	11,350	12,250	13,080	13,330	14,450
All College Freshmen	9,580	9,990	10,150	10,950	11,770	12,200	12,580
All U.S. Families with heads, 35-44 years of age*	8,590	9,000	9,830	10,730	11,410	11,880	13,119

Source: American Council on Education (1967a, 1967b, 1968, 1969, 1970, 1971, 1972)
Current Population Reports (1967, 1969a, 1969b, 1970, 1971a, 1972, 1973a)
*This is an estimate of families with freshmen-aged children. See footnote 4 for details.

TABLE 2

Ethnic Composition of the U.S. Population 18-20
Years Old, of All Freshmen, and of Freshmen in
Different Types of Public Institutions in 1972, by Percent.

| | | | Ethnicity | | |
	White	Black	Spanish-American	Other	Total
U.S. Population 18-20 Years Old[6]	81.2	12.3	4.9	1.6	100.0
All Freshmen	87.3	8.7	2.1	4.0	*
Freshmen at Public 2-Year Colleges	83.8	9.1	4.2	5.5	*
Freshmen at Public 4-Year Colleges	81.6	15.0	2.0	3.5	*
Freshmen at Public Universities	95.3	3.2	0.6	3.0	*

Source: American Council on Education (1972)
    *The American Council on Education permits multiple responses on the ethnicity
question so the total percentages add up to slightly more than 100 percent.

While the stratification of public higher education is both clear and consistent in the data of Table 1, these data must be seen as an *underestimate* of the true degree of inequality that exists in higher education.

To begin with, the data in Table 1 refer only to public higher education. The family incomes of private four-year college and university freshmen are even higher than their counterparts in public institutions. In 1972, private four-year college freshmen came from families with a median income of $15,500, while private university freshmen came from families with a median income of $17,850!

Finally, the data given thus far refers only to those who *enter* college and says nothing about who finally receives a B.A. Available data indicate that even after scores on standardized tests of ability and achievement are statistically controlled, the lower a student's social class, the less likely it is that the student will complete four years of college. (Astin, 1972) Thus, if data were available showing the social class backgrounds of students receiving B.A.'s from different types of institutions, the stratification would be even more dramatically illustrated.[5]

Ethnic Composition

The two largest ethnic minority groups in America—Blacks and Spanish-Americans —are also tracked into the different institutions of public higher education. Table 2 provides the data which describe the pattern of ethnic stratification. Clearly, both Blacks and Spanish-Americans are under-represented among all college freshmen.[6]

The Spanish-American population, comprised mainly of persons from Mexican and Puerto Rican backgrounds, is almost non-existent in public universities

(0.6 percent). They are considerably underrepresented in four-year colleges (2.0 percent) and slightly underrepresented in community colleges (4.2 percent). This pattern of tracking closely corresponds to the social class tracking described in the previous section, with low-income people being underrepresented at the universities and overrepresented in the community colleges.

Blacks, too, are considerably underrepresented among public university freshmen (3.2 percent). However, they are surprisingly over-represented among state college freshmen (15.0 percent) and slightly under-represented among community college freshmen (9.1 percent). The distribution of Black freshmen in higher education follows a different pattern than generally exists among other low-income people.

The explanation of this apparently atypical pattern is to be found in the regional differences in college enrollment. In the South, where the majority of Blacks still live, there are relatively few community colleges. Consequently, only 6 percent of all Black students in this area are in public community colleges, while 55 percent are in public four-year colleges. In the far West, on the other hand, where extensive systems of community colleges exist, about 70 percent of Black students attend these two-year institutions. (Medsker and Tillery, 1971) Recent studies of Black students who attend predominantly White institutions show that they are most likely to attend community colleges and least likely to attend public universities. (Bayer, 1973; Chronicle, 1973a; Knoell, 1970)

Comparisons of enrollment changes are presently available only for Black freshmen in the 1966-1972 time period, and the data are presented in Table 3. It is difficult, however, to draw many solid conclusions from these data because they show erratic fluctuations by year and by type of institution.

Blacks were under-represented among all college freshmen during this entire period, but their position was somewhat better in 1972 than it was in 1966. However, at least part of this improvement is due to the *decrease* in the college attendance of Whites. In the Fall of 1972, the percentage of White high school graduates attending college dropped 4.7 percent from the preceding fall, while the percentage of Black high school seniors attending college increased by only 0.5 percent during this same period. (Chronicle, 1973b)

Black representation among two-year college freshmen does appear to show a modest increase since 1966. At the four-year colleges, Black representation was constant until 1971. The meaning of the large increase in 1972 is not yet clear. As far as Black representation among university freshmen is concerned, the data are fairly clear. Blacks increased their percentage of university freshmen from under 2 percent in 1966 and 1967 to slightly over 3 percent in 1968. Since then, Black representation among university freshmen has remained constant.

Preliminary data for the Fall, 1973 enrollment shows that the percentage of Black and Spanish American freshmen had fallen to 7.8 percent and 1.3 percent, respectively (Chronicle, 1974a). This might well be due to the skyrocketing inflation in 1973, but it might also be an indication that any progress that had been made in the past might be leveling off.

Transfer and Terminal Students

Approximately one-third of all community college students are enrolled in terminal programs, while the remaining two-thirds are in transfer programs.

(Medsker and Tillery, 1971) Students in the transfer programs score higher on traditional tests of academic ability and achievement than students in the terminal programs. In addition, students in the more prestigious terminal programs, called "technical" programs, score higher in academic ability and achievement than students in the less prestigious terminal programs, sometimes called "vocational programs." (Medsker and Tillery, 1971; Brue et al., 1971; Karabel, 1972)

TABLE 3

Percent of All Freshmen and Freshmen in Different
Types of Public Institutions that Were Black, 1966-1972.

| | Year | | | | | | |
Type of Freshmen	1966	1967	1968	1969	1970	1971	1972
All Freshmen	5.0	4.3	5.8	6.0	9.1	6.3	8.7
Freshmen at Public 2-Year Institutions	5.0	3.4	4.7	4.1	16.9	5.0	9.1
Freshmen at Public 4-Year Institutions	10.1	8.8	9.8	6.8	9.2	10.3	15.0
Freshmen at Public Universities	1.5	1.8	3.3	3.4	2.9	3.6	3.2

Source: American Council on Education (1967a, 1967b, 1968, 1969, 1970, 1971, 1972).

As might be expected, students in transfer and terminal programs also differ in their social class and ethnic backgrounds. A recent study of 63 community colleges shows that lower-income students are more likely than upper-income students to be in terminal programs, and less likely to be in transfer programs. For example, students from families with incomes of less than $6,000 accounted for 14 percent of all transfer students, 14 percent of the terminal-technical students, and 24 percent of the terminal-vocational students. On the other hand, students from families with incomes of more than $10,000 accounted for 36 percent of all transfer students, 28 percent of terminal-technical students, and 21 percent of terminal-vocational students. Similarly, Blacks are more likely than Whites to be in the terminal programs, and less likely to be in the transfer programs. (Cross, 1970; Coordinating Council, 1969; Brue, et al., 1971; and Jaffe and Adams, 1972)

The lowest track in the community college is the remedial or developmental programs, and most discussions of these programs refer to the "non-traditional" or "educationally disadvantaged" students who enroll in them. Although no empirical data are available to measure the social class background of the remedial students, one recent study of five remedial programs indicated an over-representation of Blacks and Mexican American students that were enrolled in the remedial courses. (Roueche and Kirk, 1972)

The data presented above clearly demonstrate the pattern of social class and ethnic tracking within public higher education, in general, and within community colleges, in particular. Despite all the talk to the contrary, community colleges do not seem to increase a student's chance of eventually getting a B.A.

Folger, et al., (1970) found after controlling for social class and academic ability, students entering community colleges were *less* likely to receive the B.A. degree than those entering four-year schools. Karabel (1972) shows that the regions of the country with the *most* well-developed community college systems have the *lowest* proportion of the age cohort completing four years or more of college. Rather than being part of the solution to class and ethnic inequality, the community colleges have become part of the problem.

COMMUNITY COLLEGE POLICY

Although community college officials have been aware of the data that have been discussed in the preceding pages, they have chosen to follow a set of policies that will inevitably lead to *more* rather than less stratification in higher education. This is particularly evident in the areas of occupational and remedial education.

Occupational Education

Almost all community college supporters are concerned with the emphasis both students and faculty place on transfer programs as opposed to occupational education. For example, a recent report of the American Association of Community and Junior Colleges (1973:146) states:

> Career education as a concept can be the vehicle through which community and junior colleges undertake a fundamental reformation of their curricula to make them more responsive to emerging needs and less dependent on their tradition of the lower division of the four-year institution.

This concern for increasing the percentage of students in terminal occupational programs stems from two basic factors—the nature of the American economy and the nature of the community college students. Most discussions of community colleges include a section on the increasing need for people in paraprofessional or middle-level occupations.

The same AACJA report encourages its member institutions to:

> consider the development of occupational education programs linked to business, industry, labor, and government a high priority. (p. 145; also see Gleazer, 1968; Medsker and Tillery, 1971; Monroe, 1972; Blocker, 1973)

The leaders of industry and government clearly agree with this analysis since they are strongly encouraging the development of occupational education. For example, the Higher Education Act of 1972 authorized $850 million to be spent on these terminal programs. Many corporations and private foundations have given written and financial support to occupational education, including North American Rockwell, the Carnegie Commission on Higher Education and the Kellogg Foundation, who also helped to sponsor the 1972 Assembly of the AACJC. Finally, it is not unusual to have an advisory board made up of members from industry and government for each different occupational program in the community college. (Karabel, 1972)

The second reason for stressing these occupational programs has to do with the nature of the community college students. As was mentioned earlier, it is commonly believed that many of these students have "unrealistically high aspirations" in wanting to transfer to a four-year school and that if they persist in this direction, they are "doomed to fail." Although these students can be "cooled-out" once they enroll in the transfer program, most community colleges would rather have them enroll in the appropriate occupational program in the first place. One way to interest entering students in the occupational programs is through effective counselling and there is almost universal agreement that counselling services must be improved.

Another way of "selling" occupational programs is through public relations campaigns to improve the image of these types of curricula. In a book published by the American Association of Community and Junior Colleges, Harris (1964) outlines an entire public relations campaign consisting of slide shows, news-spots, paraprofessional career days, and the like. He even suggests talking to high school counsellors about the establishment of a "third track" that will prepare students specifically for community colleges.

The community colleges are rather explicit in their goal of providing a paraprofessional labor force to meet the needs of government and industry. In fact, the support given to the community colleges by government and industry is largely responsible for their rapid growth since 1960.

But public education in the United States has always served these same political and economic interests (Bowles, 1973). In the nineteenth century, public schools were established to train immigrants to work in the factories of New England. In the 1920s when there was a need for a more differentiated labor force, public education responded by developing a tracking system based on a student's "ability level." Students who were defined as "bright," most of whom also happened to be White and upper-middle class, were in the upper tracks and went on to college. The "slow" students, most of whom were also immigrants and working class, had to be satisfied with vocational programs leading to semi-skilled work. The large group of "average" students, most of whom were working and lower middle class, would be able to enter skilled blue collar and lower level white collar jobs. This tracking system, which acts to perpetuate the system of class-based stratification, is still in effect today, although the growth of ethnic minority groups has added an additional factor to the stratification system (Lauter and Howe, 1970).

The community colleges are simply the next step in a tracked educational system that provides a trained labor force in an increasingly differentiated economy. The community colleges are succeeding in providing the paraprofessional part of this labor force. This explains their lack of concern about achieving social class equality in education since this was never their goal in the first place.

However, the students who end up in occupational programs are not always happy about it. "The resistance to occupational programs by many students who might profit from them has long disturbed community college leaders." (Medsker and Tillery, 1971:60) Edmund J. Gleazer, President of the AACJC (1968:71) acknowledges this desire for enrollment in the transfer programs in order to enter these "top level" jobs, and says,

In a nation which encourages aspiration and puts its faith in economic and social mobility, there is nothing wrong with this—if a person can indeed qualify for the presumably greater responsibilities at the top of the ladder and if society can use him. Realistically, however, one must face the fact of an almost infinite variety of human talent and a bewildering array of societal tasks. It is to be hoped that talents and tasks can be linked up.

What the students are not told is that their two-year terminal degree will probably be worth less money than a four-year degree. All evidence indicates that the more education a person has, the higher that person's income will be. Men with three to seven terms of college make 120 percent the income of a high school graduate, but only 80 percent the income of someone with eight or more terms of college. Some college is better than no college, but not as good as a four-year degree. (Karabel, 1972) Unfortunately, there are no studies comparing the salaries of those with two-year occupational degrees and those with four-year degrees. However, the slogans promoting paraprofessional training programs that say "earn a College Man's Salary without Attending Four Years of College" are not consistent with the available data.

Remedial Education

Since many of the students who come to the community colleges have academic deficiencies in one or more areas, remedial programs have been set up to help students overcome these deficiencies. These programs are particularly important if the lower income and ethnic minority students are to "catch up" to their White middle class counterparts since academic achievement is related both to social class and ethnicity. Although there is not much research on the effectiveness of these programs, the data that exist are not encouraging. After reviewing some of the literature, a recent study concluded

> Even with the dearth of research the evidence indicates that remedial courses and programs in two-year colleges, and in all of higher education for that matter, have largely been ineffective in remedying student deficiencies. (Roueche and Kirk, 1973:7)

The authors cite numerous studies in different areas of the country which reach the same pessimistic conclusions. Not only do many of these programs fail to provide students with the skills to succeed in the college parallel programs, they also don't provide students with the skills necessary to succeed in one of the occupational curricula.

Perhaps as a result of these failures, some writers are taking a "value-added" approach to remedial education. Even though these "high risk" students don't receive any degrees, the argument goes, they are better off than they were before. According to Monroe (1972) many of these value-added programs, sometimes referred to as "developmental programs," first:

> had the same goal as remedial courses, that is, to prepare unready students for successful participation in standard college courses. Developmental programs which were conceived with these unrealistic goals were bound to fail. . . . Since 1965, most developmental programs have had more realistic goals,

such as to prepare a student for a vocation and a better way of life than that which his parents enjoyed. (114: Also see Cross, 1971)

Thus, most attempts at remedial education have failed, and it appears that some developmental programs are becoming more "realistic" and are giving up altogether. This all leaves little hope for those low income and ethnic students who come out of poor schools in search of a social mobility through the community college. Without effective remedial programs, community college talk of "equality" is merely an illusion.

Roueche and Kirk (1973) argue that in spite of all this, some effective programs do exist. The authors then present data on "model" remedial programs at five institutions showing that the grade-point averages were higher, and the drop-out rates were lower for students enrolled in remedial programs compared with a control group of "high-risk" students not enrolled in remedial programs. By the end of the fourth semester, the grade point average for the remedial students still enrolled at the college ranged from 1.99 to 2.37, depending upon the particular institution.

Although the results of these programs are certainly better than most other programs, the progress that does exist is quite modest. From the above GPA figures, it seems safe to conclude that between one-third and one-half of those students still enrolled are doing *less* than C work. In addition, only 45 percent of the students who began the remedial program were still enrolled in the institution by the end of the fourth semester. No information is given about the type of curriculum in which the students are enrolled (transfer or terminal), and no information is given about the number of students who received the two-year degree. Finally, one of these "successful" programs was faced with a "minority student boycott" at the time of the study, although the authors present no further details. If these five programs are among the *best* that the community colleges have to offer, they simply aren't good enough.

CONCLUSION

All of the data presented in this paper are available to community college administrators and planners; and, in fact, much of the data were collected by people sympathetic to the community college movement. Yet in spite of the overwhelming evidence pointing to the rigid stratification that exists in the community colleges and among all institutions of higher learning, the educational establishment continues to talk about the important role that the community colleges are playing in democratizing higher education.

As was mentioned earlier in this paper, there are at least two different notions of "equality" and "democracy" that have been used with regard to education. The criterion used by this author has looked to the *outcomes* of the educational process and has stressed class and ethnic differences in who goes to college, what type of colleges are attended, and what type of curriculum students are enrolled in. By this criterion, equality does not exist in higher education and the evidence does not indicate much progress in this regard.

By this time, it should be clear that community college educators have a different set of concerns that can be best understood as a set of six interrelated beliefs.

228   CRACKS IN THE CLASSROOM WALL

1. *American capitalist institutions and the existing unequal distribution of wealth and power are legitimate.* Free enterprise, individualism, competition and the quest for social mobility are all acceptable values upon which to base a society.

2. *Community colleges must help to train a skilled labor force to meet the needs of government and industry.* Community colleges will train paraprofessionals, while four-year colleges and universities will train professionals.

3. *Conventional professional academic standards are legitimate.* In order to get a B.A. degree, students must be able to achieve these standards of excellence. For those who can't, more flexible standards can be used in the occupational and remedial programs.

4. *The correlations of social class and race with academic ability and achievement is an unfortunate reality.* Economically-impoverished and/or culturally different environments will prevent people from learning the skills and attitudes that will enable them to succeed in traditional academic programs, but the community colleges can't do much about that.

5. *Community colleges should strive to be meritocratic.* Some members of low-income and ethnic minorities do have the ability to compete and to enter the professions. Holding them back because of a lack of money or "biased" measures of ability would mean a loss of talent to industry and government. Therefore, more efficient sorting mechanisms should be developed and more sophisticated tracking systems should be established.

6. *Most working class and ethnic minority students can do no better than complete a two-year occupational course.* There is nothing really wrong with this since there is a need for people in these jobs and since many of these students will be better off as paraprofessionals than with no college at all.

Given these beliefs, it is not difficult to understand why community college supporters are not more concerned in their failure to enable more working class and ethnic minority students to get bachelor's degrees. One community college administrator in New York City expressed his low level of expectations this way:

Even if only a minority of them make it through, it is that many more who have been saved from going down the drain . . . I know it sounds like the Salvation Army, but when they make it, we have saved souls (Maeroff, 1973:24).

The rapid growth of the community colleges since 1960 has been caused by an increased need for skilled labor and by the demands of poor, working class and ethnic minority students for a college education. Community college development has been strongly supported by the government, the large corporations and the educational establishment. Consequently, the community colleges use standards that are defined by people at the top, have programs that benefit the people at the top, and reward students for having skills that are more accessible for people at the top.

Bowles (1973) argues that the division of labor and the American stratification system have given

rise to distinct class subcultures. The values, personality traits and expectations characteristic of each subculture are transmitted from generation to generation through class differences in family socialization and complementary differences in the type and amount of schooling ordinarily attained by children in various class positions. These class differences in schooling are maintained in large measure through the capacity of the upper class to control the basic principles of school finance, pupil evaluation, and educational objectives. (p. 56)

The social class and ethnic tracking in the community colleges and the failure of the remedial programs has more to do with who *controls* the community colleges than with who enters the "open doors."

Some community college liberals seem to throw their arms up in despair when they discuss the lack of success of working class and ethnic minority students. This feeling of despair is increased by recent studies which argue that educational inequality will exist as long as economic inequality exists (Jencks, 1972; Milner, 1972). As long as contemporary political, economic and educational institutions are accepted as legitimate, there isn't much hope for those who want to bring about educational and economic equality.

Since the community colleges and other educational institutions are closely tied to the class and ethnic division of labor in American society, the only way to significantly change the educational system is to change the class nature of society. Those that profit from the existing institutions cannot be expected to reform them so that others can share in the rewards.

NOTES

1. The author would like to thank the following persons for their comments during the various stages of the preparation of this paper: Chris Bose, Howard Ehrlich, Byron Matthews and Natalie Sokoloff.

2. In this paper, the term "ethnic" will refer to Blacks, Mexican Americans and Puerto Rico Americans. It will *not* include the so-called "White-ethnic groups."

3. In this paper, the terms "Community College," "Junior College" and "Two-Year College" will be used interchangeably.

4. The category "all U.S. families with heads 35-44 years of age" is an estimate of families with children old enough to be college freshmen. This is based on the following data: 1) 90 percent of college freshmen are 18-19 years of age; 2) the age of first marriage for men is about 23 years of age; 3) the first child usually comes within two years of marriage; 4) children will be 18 and 19 by the times their fathers are 43 and 44, respectively.

5. The only measure of social class that has been used thus far is median family income. However, the American Council on Education also has data on the median years of school completed by the student's parents. When one examines the median years of education completed by parents, the same pattern of stratification emerges—university freshmen have the most educated parents, and community college freshmen have the least educated parents.

6. Estimates of the 18-20 year-old population in 1972 were made as follows: First, the percentage of Whites, Blacks, Spanish-Americans and others were obtained from 1972 data (Current Population Reports, 1973a, 1972a). These percentages were just about identical to the corresponding figures in 1970 (U.S. Bureau of Census, 1973a, 1973b, 1973c). The only detailed data for 18-20 year olds was available for the 1970 data. It was assumed that these 1970 percentages were close estimates of the 1972 percentages and were thus used in Table 2.

BIBLIOGRAPHY

American Association of Community and Junior Colleges
    1973   "1972 Assembly Report" in Educational Opportunity for All: An
            Agenda for National Action, R. Yarrington, Ed. Washington, D.C.:
            AACJC, 141-152.
American Council on Education
    1972   The American Freshman: National Norms for Fall, 1972, ACE Re-
            search Reports, Vol. 7, No. 5.
    1971   The American Freshman: National Norms for Fall, 1971, ACE Re-
            search Reports, Vol. 6, No. 6.
    1970   National Norms for Entering College Freshman—Fall, 1970, ACE
            Research Reports, Vol. 5, No. 6.
    1969   National Norms for Entering College Freshman—Fall, 1969, ACE
            Research Reports, Vol. 4, No. 7.
    1968   National Norms for Entering College Freshman—Fall, 1968, ACE
            Research Reports, Vol. 3.
    1967a   National Norms for Entering College Freshmen—Fall, 1967, ACE
            Research Reports, Vol. 2, No. 7.
    1967b   National Norms for Entering College Freshmen—Fall, 1966, ACE
            Research Reports, Vol. 2, No. 1.
Astin, A. W.
    1972   College Dropouts: A National Profile, ACE Research Reports, Vol.
            7, No. 1.
Bayer, A. E.
    1973   "The New Student in Black Colleges," *School Review*, 81, May,
            pp. 415-426.
Berg, I.
    1971   *Education and Jobs: The Great Training Robbery*. Boston: Beacon
            Press.
Berg, E., and D. Axtell
    1971   Programs for Disadvantaged Students in California Community Col-
            leges. Oakland: Peralta Junior College District.
Birnbaum, R. and J. Goldman
    1971   The Graduates: A Follow-up Study of New York City High School
            Graduates of 1970. CUNY: Center for Social Research and Office
            for Research in Higher Education.
Blocker, C. E.
    1973   "A National Agenda for Community-Junior Colleges" in Equal Op-
            portunity for All: An Agenda of National Action, R. Yarrington,
            Ed., Washington: AACJC, pp. 125-140.
Bowles, S.
    1973   "Unequal Education and the Reproduction of the Social Division of
            Labor." in M. Carnoy, Ed. *Schooling in a Corporate Society*. New
            York: David McCay, Co., pp. 36-64.
Brue, E. J., H. B. Engen, E. J. Maxey
    1971   "How do community college transfer and occupational students
            differ?" American College Testing Program Report No. 41.
Carnegie Commission on Higher Education
    1971   *New Students and New Places: Policies for the Future Growth and
            Development of Higher Education*. New York: McGraw Hill.
    1970   *The Open Door Colleges: Policies for Community Colleges*. New
            York: McGraw Hill.
Chronicle of Higher Education
    1974   "Opening Fall Enrollment, 1972 and 1973," January 14.

1974a   "This Year's College Freshmen." February 11.
1973a   "Minority Group Students Found Under-Represented in California."
         June, 26.
1973b   "College-Going Gap Narrows Between Blacks, Whites." April 9.
1972   "9.2 Million in College, Up 2 Percent" December 18.
Clark, B. R.
1960a   *The Open Door College: A Case Study.* New York: McGraw Hill.
1960b   "The Cooling Out Function in Higher Education" *American Journal
         of Sociology* 65: pp. 569-576.
Cook, J. B., Hoss, M. A. and Vargas, R.
1968   *The Search for Independence: Orientation for the Junior College
         Student.* Belmont, Calif.: Brooks Cole Publishing Co.
Coordinating Council for Higher Education
1968   The Undergraduate Student and His Higher Education: Policies of
         California Colleges and Universities in the Next Decade. Sacramento,
         Calif.
Cross, K. P.
1971   *Beyond the Open Door.* San Francisco: Jossey Bass.
1970   "The Role of the Junior College in Providing Post-secondary Educa-
         tion for All." in *Trends in Post-secondary Education.* Washington,
         D.C.: U.S. Government Printing Office.
1968   *The Junior College Student: A Research Description.* Princeton:
         Educational Testing Service.
Crossland, F. E.
1971   *Minority Access to College.* New York: Shocken Books.
Current Population Reports
1973a   Money Income in 1972 of Families and Persons in the United States
         U.S. Department of Commerce, Series P-60, No. 87.
1973b   The Social and Economic Status of Negroes in the United States,
         1970 U.S. Department of Commerce, Series P-23.
1972a   Money Income in 1971 of Families and Persons in the United States
         U.S. Department of Commerce, Series P-60, No. 83.
1972b   Selected Characteristics of Persons and Families of Mexican, Puerto
         Rican and Other Spanish Origin: March 1972. U.S. Department of
         Commerce, Series P-20, No. 238.
1971a   Income in 1970 of Families and Persons in the United States, U.S.
         Department of Commerce, Series P-60, No. 80.
1970   Income in 1969 of Families and Persons in the United States, U.S.
         Department of Commerce, Series P-60, No. 75.
1969a   Income in 1968 of Families and Persons in the United States, U.S.
         Department of Commerce, Series P-60, No. 66.
1969b   Income in 1967 of Families in the United States, U.S. Department
         of Commerce, Series P-60, No. 59.
1967   Income in 1966 of Families and Persons in the United States, U.S.
         Department of Commerce, Series P-60, No. 53.
Folger, J. K., H. S. Astin, A. J. Bayer
1970   *Human Resources and Higher Education.* New York: Russell Sage
         Foundation.
Gleazer, E. J.
1968   *This is the Community College.* Boston: Houghton Mifflin Co.
Goffman, E.
1959   "Cooling the Mark Out: Some Aspects of Adaptation to Failure."
         Psychiatry 15 (Nov.): pp. 451-463.
Hansen, W. L. and B. A. Weisbrod.
1969   "The Distribution of Costs and Direct Benefits of Public Higher

Education: The Case of California" *Journal of Human Resources* 4: pp. 176-191.

Harris, E. C.
1964 "Technical Education in the Junior Colleges: New Programs for New Jobs." Washington, D.C.: American Association of Junior Colleges.

Herrnstein, R.
1971 "IQ" *Atlantic Monthly* (Sept.).

Jaffee, A. J. and W. Adams
1972 "Two Models of Open Enrollment." in *Universal Higher Education.* L. Wilson, Ed. Washington, D.C.: American Council on Education.

Jencks, C.
1972 *Inequality: A Reassessment of the Effect of Family and Schooling in America.* New York: Basic Books.

Jencks, C. and Riesman, D.
1969 *The Academic Revolution.* Garden City, N.Y.: Doubleday.

Jensen, A. R.
1969 "How Much Can We Boost I.Q. and Scholastic Achievement?" *Harvard Educational Review* 39 (Winter): pp. 1-123.

Karable, J.
1972 "Community Colleges and Social Stratification." *Harvard Educational Review* 4 (Nov.): pp. 521-562.

Knoell, D. M. and L. L. Medsker
1964 *Articulation Between Two-Year and Four-Year Colleges.* Berkeley: Center for the Study of Higher Education.

Koos, L. V.
1970 *The Community College Student.* Gainsville: University of Florida Press.

Lauter, P. and F. Howe
1970 *Conspiracy of the Young.* New York: World Publishing.

Maeroff, G. I.
1973 "A kind of higher education." *New York Times Magazine,* May 27: pp. 12-24.

Matson, J. E.
1973 "Student Constituencies: Real and Potential." in Educational Opportunity for All: An Agenda for National Action, R. Yarrington, Ed., Washington, D.C., AACJC, pp. 9-22.

Medsker, L. L.
1960 *The Junior College: Progress and Prospect.* New York: McGraw Hill.

Medsker, L. L. and D. Tillery.
1971 *Breaking the Access Barriers: A Profile of Two-Year Colleges.* New York: McGraw Hill.

Milner, M.
1972 *The Illusion of Equality.* San Francisco: Jossey-Bass.

Monroe, C. R.
1972 *Profile of the Community College.* San Francisco: Jossey-Bass.

Moore, W.
1970 *Against the Odds.* San Francisco: Jossey-Bass.

New University Conference
1971 *Open Up the Schools.* Chicago: NUC.

Newman, F. et al.
1971 Report on Higher Education. Washington, D.C.: U.S. Office of Education.

Rothstein, R.
1971   "Down the Up Staircase: Tracking in Schools" *This Magazine is About Schools,* Vol. 5, No. 3.
Roueche, J. E.
1968   Salvage, Redirection, or Custody: Remedial Education in the Community Junior College. Washington, D.C.: American Association of Junior Colleges.
Roueche, J. E. and R. W. Kirk
1973   *Catching Up: Remedial Education.* San Francisco: Jossey-Bass.
Simon, K. E. and W. V. Grant
1970   Digest of Educational Statistics. Washington, D.C.: U.S. Office of Education.
Simon, L. S.
1967   "The Cooling Out Function of the Junior College." *Personnel and Guidance Journal* (June): pp. 793-798.
U.S. Bureau of the Census
1973a   Census of the Population: 1970; General Population Characteristics, Final Report PC(1)-1B U.S. Summary.
1973b   Census of the Population: 1970; Subject Reports PC (2)-1E Persons of Spanish Surname.
1973c   Census of the Population: 1970; Final Report PC(2)-1E Puerto Ricans in the United States.
U.S. Office of Education
1966   Opening Fall Enrollment in Higher Education, Washington, D.C., U.S.O.E.
1970   Opening Fall Enrollment in Higher Education, Washington, D.C., U.S.O.E.
Van Dyne, L. A.
1972   "The Big City Community Colleges: Hope for the Academically Deficient" *Chronicle of Higher Education* 6 (May 30): p. 5.
Windham, D. M.
1969   State Financed Higher Education and the Distribution of Income in Florida. Ph.D. Dissertation, Florida State University.
Yarrington, R., Ed.
1973   Educational Opportunity for All: An Agenda for National Action. Washington, D.C.: AACJC.

Fred Pincus

The authors of our final selection, David K. Cohen and Marvin Lazerson, propose a framework and several unifying themes to bring together the disparate work of the preceding writers. They help us develop a new understanding of American education, and point to new ways of reforming it. Cohen and Lazerson also assert that America's schools are serving the interests of corporate capitalism, and are profoundly affected and shaped by those interests. They single out three areas of conflicts that emerged as the schools turned to serving these interests. There was the conflict between an ethos of work and the theory that education should involve play, with its own intrinsic rewards. There was the conflict between the need for the schools to socialize the young, especially the immigrant young, and the cultural differences these children brought to school. Finally, there was the conflict between a theoretical commitment of the schools to equality and social reform and the need of the economy for

selecting and sorting the meritorious for better jobs and higher social status—
the "meritocracy."

Each of these conflicts has its roots in the industrialization of this country
and, along with that, the development of its school system. Each is with us
today. Any alternative view of public education must reckon with these
conflicts.

EDUCATION AND THE
CORPORATE ORDER

David K. Cohen and Marvin Lazerson

During the last fifteen years mounting conflict over the nature and function of
schools has generated heightened concern over education and an unprecedented
awareness of school failure. Few would now proclaim, as Angelo Patri did in
1927, that "the schools of America are the temples of a living democracy."[1] A
new history of American education reflecting these social conflicts has emerged.
It focuses on the development of city school bureaucracy and professionalism,
the education of European immigrant and black children, and inequality of educational opportunity.[2] Yet, despite the broadened scope of historical research
on education, the new work remains disparate. In this paper we try to take the
next step by suggesting several unifying themes and outlining a framework for
understanding the development of education in the United States in this
century.[3]

In our view this history has to be understood in the framework of the schools'
adaptation to large scale corporate capitalism and the conflicts this engendered.
Infusing the schools with corporate values and reorganizing them in ways seen
as consistent with this new economic order has been the dominant motif. Education has been closely tied to production—schooling has been justified as a way
of increasing wealth, of improving industrial output, and of making management
more effective. The schools' role has been to socialize economically desirable
values and behavior, teach vocational skills, and provide education consistent
with students' expected occupational attainment. As a result, the schools' culture became closely identified with the ethos of the corporate workplace. Schooling came to be seen as work or the preparation for work; schools were pictured

David K. Cohen and Marvin Lazerson, "Education and the Corporate Order," *Socialist
Revolution*, Vol. 2, No. 2, Mar-April 1972, pp. 47-72. (This essay is a revised version of a
paper entitled "Education and the Industrial Order" presented to the meetings of the American Educational Research Association, 1970. Copyright 1970 by David K. Cohen and
Marvin Lazerson.)

as factories, educators as industrial managers, and students as the raw materials to be inducted into the production process. The ideology of school management was recast in the model of the business corporation, and the character of education was shaped after the image of industrial production.[4]

But the schools' adaptation to advanced corporate capitalism has not been accomplished without conflict. While the corporate society seemed to require schools that socialized students for work and evaluated their success in economic terms, the counter-argument that education should be playful and evaluated only on intrinsic and non-economic criteria has grown progressively more insistent. Industrialization drew and held a multitude of immigrants to the cities, but the public schools promulgated an essentially native version of American culture. From the outset, some newcomers reacted against schooling which barely recognized them, and sought alternative schools to legitimize and preserve their cultures. The corporate society required an academic meritocracy that selected students on the basis of ability and educated them accordingly. The great inequities in this selection system were a function of the students' presumed occupational destination and could not be squared with prevailing ideas of equality.

These conflicts still pervade the school system: schooling as work against education as play; cultural diversity against assimilation and non-recognition; academic merit against equality. These tensions are a product of the schools' adaptation to large-scale corporate capitalism, and cannot be understood apart from its evolution.[5]

THE INDUSTRIAL SYSTEM OF SCHOOLING

The leading idea of the corporate capitalist system of schooling was that education was an economic activity. Schooling was justified as a way to expand wealth by improving production. Skill and behavior training were stressed; students were selected for occupation strata based on ability, and matched to occupations through counseling and training. *Education was fashioned into an increasingly refined training and selection mechanism for the labor force.* These ideas were reflected in the formulation of a Michigan educator in 1921.

> We can picture the educational system as having a very important function as a selecting agency, a means of selecting the men of best intelligence from the deficient and mediocre. All are poured into the system at the bottom; the incapable are soon rejected or drop out after repeating various grades and pass into the ranks of unskilled labor. . . . The more intelligent who are to be clerical workers pass into the high school; the most intelligent enter the universities, whence they are selected for the professions.[6]

Such ideas had important implications for the conception and organization of schooling. If schools were the primary occupational training and selection mechanism, then the criteria of merit within schools had to conform to the criteria of ranking in the occupational structure. *The schools' effectiveness then could be judged by how well success in school predicted success at work.* The criteria for these predictions were work behavior and academic ability.

From the late nineteenth century onward, educators' concern with student behavior was justified in terms of training for work. In 1909 the Boston School

Committee described the program of instruction in an elementary school given over to "prevocational" classes—a school for children expected to become factory workers:

> Everything must conform as closely as possible to actual industrial work in real life. The product must be not only useful, but must be needed, and must be put to actual use. It must be something which may be produced in quantities. The method must be practical, and both product and method must be subjected to the same commercial tests, as far as possible, as apply to actual industry.[7]

Typically, school officials stressed that classroom activities should inculcate the values thought to make good industrial workers—respect for authority, discipline, order, cleanliness and punctuality—and the schools developed elaborate schemes for grading, reporting, and rewarding student behavior. "One great benefit of going to school, especially of attending regularly for eight or ten months each year for nine years or more," argued A. E. Winship, editor of the *Journal of Education* in 1900, "is that it establishes a habit of regularity and persistency in effort." "Indeed," Winship claimed, "the boy who leaves school and goes to work does not necessarily learn to work steadily, but often quite the reverse."[8] Going to school was better preparation for becoming a good worker than work itself!

If schooling was conceived as a preparation for work, it was only natural to organize it on the model of the factory. School superintendents saw themselves as plant managers, and proposed to treat education as a production process in which children were the raw materials.[9] It was eqully natural to evaluate schooling in terms of economic productivity. If education was work then its success or failure could be measured by income returns to schooling. This tendency to use market criteria in evaluating education flowered around the turn of the century: between 1880 and 1910 scores of studies of income returns to education appeared.[10] Superintendents, plant managers, and teachers' associations published reports that sought to show that the more education students received, the greater their later earnings would be. This was reflected in the schools' internal evaluation systems, as grades and school retention were justified as strategies for raising later earnings.

The ability criterion was no less important. The notion that adult success depended on school achievement came to have the status of religious dogma. As Ellwood Cubberley revealed in 1909, this idea is closely linked to the view that as the level of technology in production rises, workers require more education:

> Along with these changes there has come not only a tremendous increase in the quantity of our knowledge, but also a demand for a large increase in the amount of knowledge necessary to enable one to meet the changed conditions of modern life. The kind of knowledge needed, too, has fundamentally changed. The ability to read and write and cipher no longer distinguishes the educated from the uneducated man. A man must have better, broader, and a different kind of knowledge than did his parents if he is to succeed under modern conditions.[11]

The idea that knowledge is power dates back to the scientific revolution, but here Cubberley was articulating a new version. It was not simply that knowledge was power, but that technological training was the key to personal success.

These ideas were powerfully reinforced by the results of early testing research. The U.S. Army World War I tests, for example, showed a clear correlation between measured intelligence and occupational attainment.[12] This was generally presumed to prove that the occupational structure was meritocratic, allocating people to occupations on the basis of innate intelligence. Early test results also showed that people who completed more years of school had higher IQs—from which it was inferred that "on the average, the stage in the school system attained by the average individual corresponds roughly with his capacity . . . the amount of education is pretty closely related to the degree of natural intelligence."[13] These results gave an enormous boost to the notion that students who ranked high in school would later have high-ranking jobs. If people were poor, these tests seemed to prove that it was because they were stupid. It occurred to few (least of all the pioneers in testing) that people might test "stupid" because they were poor—that the tests might be biased to favor certain classes and social strata.

Whatever the merit of these inferences, they did provide a powerful thrust for educational testing. If smarter people got better jobs, then it was essential to make the ability criterion in IQ and achievement tests operational. Armed with such instruments, educators could separate students on the basis of a projection to adult status and thus tailor educational offerings to occupational expectations. The tests quickly came to be seen as the surest way to classify students and to organize schools for their work in occupational pre-selection. Cubberley maintained in his introduction to Lewis Terman's *The Measurement of Intelligence* that "the educational significance of the results to be obtained from careful measurements of intelligence of children can hardly be overestimated. Questions relating to the choice of studies, vocational guidance, schoolroom procedures, the grading of pupils, [and] promotional schemes . . . all alike acquire new meaning and significance when viewed in the light of the measurement of intelligence."[14]

Educational testing grew rapidly during the two decades after World War I. Between 1921 and 1936 more than five thousand articles on testing appeared in print; a 1939 list of mental tests reported 4,279, and six printed pages of bibliographies on testing.[15] By then almost every major school system had a full program of achievement and IQ testing and a research bureau to administer the tests and interpret the results. A new sub-profession, educational psychology, had been established, complete with separate graduate training programs, distinct departments with education schools, different degrees, and professional journals. School psychology had become a quasi-independent career line within the schools, integrated into the administrative structure from local schools to the central research bureaus. Of one hundred fifty large cities surveyed in connection with a White House Conference on vocational education, called by President Hoover in 1932, three-quarters were using intelligence tests to classify and assign their students for instruction.[16]

Occupationally diversified curriculum was the corollary of testing. Curricular differentiation began before the testing movement, but testing provided a powerful reinforcement and rationale for it. The increasing differentiation of work in an urban corporate economy, the demand of business and industrial leaders for appropriately trained and disciplined workers—and at the same time the desire to protect educational standards for non-working-class children—gave rise to diverse curricula before the theory of meritocracy was developed. Under the pressure of these forces the older curriculum had begun to give way at the turn of the century—years before the testing movement emerged—and was being replaced by a multiplicity of course offerings geared to the major strata of job categories. The National Education Association's 1910 *Report of the Committee on the Place of Industries in Public Education* summarized the rationale for educational differentiation:

1. Industry, as a controlling factor in social progress, has for education a fundamental and permanent significance.
2. Educational standards, applicable in an age of handicraft, presumably need radical change in the present day of complex and highly specialized industrial development.
3. The social aims of education and the psychological needs of childhood alike require that industrial (manual-constructive) activities form an important part of school occupations. . . .
4. The differences among children as to aptitudes, interests, economic resources, and prospective careers furnish the basis for a rational as opposed to a merely formal distinction between elementary, secondary, and higher education.[17]

The last point is important, for the inventory of differences among children clearly reveals the class character of educational differentiation. Working-class children should not only get a different sort of schooling, but also should get less. Industrial elementary schools, prevocational programs, and junior high schools all were offered as ways of assuring that working-class children would stay in school and receive appropriate training.[18] At the same time, Cleveland's school superintendent, for example, argued that working-class children would neither continue their education beyond the compulsory minimum, nor learn very much if they did stay. He proposed that their schooling be limited to the elementary years, with a curriculum that imparted basic literacy, good behavior, and rudimentary vocational skills.[19]

Later, as the high schools became less and less the preserves of children from advantaged families, curricular differentiation was necessary to maintain differences in educational opportunity within the same period of schooling. Differentiation centered more and more on curricular differences within secondary schools. At the turn of the century special business and commercial courses already had been established in the high schools; by the second decade many cities had created vocational, business, and academic curricula. The school board president in the Lynds' *Middletown* summarized the change succinctly, in the mid-1920s: "For a long time all boys were trained to be President. Then for a while we trained them all to be professional men. Now we are training boys to get jobs."[20]

The differentiation of educational offerings ran across the grain of established ideas about equality in education. As in so many things, Cubberley characterized the situation bluntly in 1909:

> Our city schools will soon be forced to give up the exceedingly democratic idea that all are equal, and our society devoid of classes . . . and to begin a specialization of educational effort along many lines in an attempt to adapt the school to the needs of these many classes. . . . Industrial and vocational training is especially significant of the changing conception of the school and the classes in society which the school is in the future expected to serve.[21]

Some educators insisted that differentiation implied no change in the reigning ideas of equal opportunity, but a greater number tried to reconcile differentiation and its implications for equality. The NEA juxtaposed "equality of opportunity as an abstraction" to the idea that education should be based on "the reality of opportunity as measured by varying needs, tastes, and abilities."[22] Although such formulations were offered to support differentiation of educational offerings along class lines, this was rarely seen as inconsistent with the idea that "education should give to all an equal chance to attain any distinction in life."[23] The reconciliation lay in the ready identification of ability with inherited social and economic status, an idea which the early testing movement reinforced. In theory, at least, there was no tension between the differentiation of school offerings and the academic meritocracy.

The appeal of the meritocratic idea extended far beyond a rationale for curricular differentiation. Educators and social reformers at the turn of the century were disturbed by the accumulation of a large, heavily immigrant industrial proletariat in the cities; they feared the prospect of class warfare, and found in educational opportunity a ready formula for remedy. Schools would provide a mechanism whereby those who were qualified could rise on the basis of ability. Even the greatest skeptics about the influence of environment on ability—E. L. Thorndike, for example—agreed that the schools should provide avenues for mobility based on selection of talent.[24] And liberals maintained that schools ought to remedy deficiencies that the environment inflicted upon children. Frank Carleton, for example, wrote in 1907 that the schools should reduce crime and dependency by providing special education for disadvantaged children. If schools compensated for environmental deficiencies, they would improve children's chances for success in later life.[25]

This faith in the transforming power of education has been the basis for compensatory education and social welfare programs since the late nineteenth century. Schooling was conceived as an engine of social reform, a mechanism whereby injustice could be remedied by distributing rewards on the basis of talent rather than inheritance. It was an idea peculiarly suited to corporate liberalism. The redistribution of social and economic status promised through schooling was neither an attack on property nor an effort to weaken the class structure. Rather than eliminating inequalities in social status or wealth, schooling would insure that these were consistent with qualification instead of birth. *The great appeal of social reform through education was that all issues of distributive social justice were translated into matters of individual ability and effort in school and marketplace.*

These developments did not occur all at once, nor was the new system of schooling monolithic. As Michael Katz has pointed out, many educators who sought to model their schools on industrial lines seemed to have little idea of how industrial corporations worked.[26] And efforts to make the curriculum correspond to the occupational structure did not mean that educators knew, or tried to find out, what labor skills were actually needed. As production utilized increasingly advanced technology, the schools slowly followed suit—just as now the old model of the schools as factories is beginning to change, as manpower needs change. But the commitment to the ability criterion, testing, guidance, and differentiated schooling has only been accentuated. While the character of work is changing, the schools' role as the primary labor training and selection mechanism continues.

TENSIONS IN THE NEW ORDER

In the course of the schools' adaptation to large-scale corporate capitalism, conflicts emerged in three areas. One centered on the system's essential educational values—extrinsically rewarded work—and the school culture this encouraged. Although the ethos of work has been dominant, the notion that education should involve play and intrinsic rewards has become increasingly prominent. A second involved the schools' role in political and cultural socialization, and the conflicts this provoked between successive groups of urban immigrants and the schools. These have been manifest in struggles over school governance and curriculum, and in the rejection of public education in favor of alternative educational institutions. Finally, tension occurred between the ideology of class structure—academic meritocracy—and the ideas of equality presumed to govern public education.

Work and Play

The tension between these two conceptions of social activity increasingly permeates advanced industrial societies; it extends from the character of productive activity to the quality of pedagogy. In education, the notion of play contains several elements. It suggests a learning environment and process that in its pure form stresses self-expression, independence, and spontaneity. Several ideas underlie this. One is the view that learning is best if it is not compelled, but occurs freely through "natural" interactions—in games, in social intercourse among children and adults, and in the reach of intermittent curiosity. Another is the assumption that the ethos of education should be arranged so as to protect children from the rigors of work—instead of instilling the disciplines of the workplace, schools should avoid routine, compelled, and occupationally oriented learning. The advocates of play in education have reflected diverse political and pedagogical viewpoints, sometimes stressing academic learning and in other cases emphasizing affective education or socialization. Some have justified play as an initial and more efficient method for producing good workers, but usually there has been hostility to extrinsic, market-oriented criteria of educational merit. Typically, the advocates of play in schooling are found in the "child-centered" wing of American education.[27]

   The idea of education as play received its first major institutional expression in the kindergarten movement at the turn of the century, and later in the nursery school movement. Upper- middle- and upper-class advocates of early childhood education opposed their notion of school as play to the more disciplined forms of schooling then current. Their young charges were to learn through games, songs, stories, and other forms of casual interaction; direct compulsion and outright discipline were to be avoided. Although they sought to harmonize this with the work ethic by claiming that play was a better preparation for work than rigid discipline and by asserting that play was the child's natural work, the advocates of kindergarten education were unable to avoid conflict with the established public schools. The kindergartens were often considered undisciplined: some educators argued that kindergarten children came to school poorly prepared, either to learn or to behave properly. While the notion that pre-school education should be playful gradually became accepted by early childhood educators, it continued to find itself in conflict with public school personnel.[28]

With the Progressive movement in education the idea of schooling as play was more widely diffused, and attempts were made to bridge the work-play conflict. Rejecting dualism in any form, John Dewey believed that work and play were part of a continuum, differing only in terms of "time-span" and the rigor of commitment to a specified goal. "In play," he argued, the "activity is its own end, instead of having an ulterior result." Play was "free, plastic," it meant keeping "alive a creative and constructive attitude." Yet Dewey could harmonize work and play only by rejecting prevailing notions of work. He contended that work in an industrial society, "especially in cities," was "anti-educational," because it took its definition from the needs of the economy, rather than individual or social needs. To offset this, schools should function with an "absence of economic pressure," allowing students to build upon individual and social experience. In school, activities "are not carried on for pecuniary gain but for their own content. Freed from extraneous associations and the pressure of wage-earning, they supply modes of experience which are intrinsically valuable; they are truly liberalizing in quality." Though Dewey would oppose the child-centeredness of later play advocates, his call for a learning process which began with the experience of the learner gave an added emphasis to intrinsic learning.[29]

Other educational reformers also juxtaposed learning from experience to learning by rote or from books. They sought to infuse the curriculum and pedagogy with spontaneity and free expression. The extreme incarnation of playful education was the child-centered school. In these schools, two commentators on the child-centered movement wrote in 1928, children "dance . . . sing . . . play house and build villages; they keep store and take care of pets; they model in clay and sand; they draw and paint, read and write, make up stories and dramatize them." Education in the child-centered classroom was designed to produce "individuality through the integration of experience." The ideal was expressed by one five-year-old who said of her painting, "It looks the way you feel inside." To the traditional notions of order, regimentation, and vocationalism, the child-centered school opposed spontaneity, freedom and self-expression.[30]

It would be wrong, however, to counterpose the movement to bring "warmth" and spontaneity into the classroom to the process of the schools' adaptation to corporate capitalism. The educational reformers often had little impact on public education. The best examples of reform were usually found in private schools for middle-class children. This more "natural" schooling process fits in nicely with the trend in middle-class child-rearing ideas, away from repression and externally imposed discipline, toward greater freedom, and happiness in learning seemed to be linked with higher levels of achievement.[31] It also fit in with the decline in the ethic of asceticism, the increase in leisure time that followed rising productivity in industry, and the promotion of a new ethic of consumption during the 1920s. Later, particularly in the period after World War II, with the growth of a large labor force engaged in social control and services, the playful style has begun to find its way into public education.

The urban school reform movement has increasingly gravitated in this direction, as Leicestershire styles of schooling emphasizing naturalness, freedom, and experiential learning, have grown in influence. Educational theoreticians have for the first time adopted a stance of conscious opposition to the notion of school as externally disciplined work. Holt, Denison, Leonard, Illich, and Friedenberg attack not only the discipline and work ethos of the public schools, but also the extrinsic rewards to which schooling is presumed to lead. They distinguish education from schooling, identifying education with freedom, natural authority, and learning-on-the-hoof; any discipline that does not arise immediately from the subject matter or the student-teacher relationship is rejected as illegitimate. They have called the entire authority structure of public education into question by rejecting the market values on which it rests. This is precisely the major change of the last decade: the polarity between work and play in education has become an overt issue of policy rather than a persistent conflict of pedagogical styles.

The source of the conflict between work and play lies in the changing character of productive activity. The increasingly technological nature of production has created a demand for a more highly trained and differentiated labor force, engaged not only in goods production, but also in the production of culture, socialization, and welfare. Among the new strata of workers, labor has become more technological, cerebral, and mobile, and has created more room for leisure. Not only must the training period of such a labor force be extended, but the kind of training must be changed. An emphasis on "creativity" replaces a pure emphasis on discipline. Play as an educational ideal becomes opposed to work, insofar as it encourages creativity.

Play is, then, closely linked to the changes in the character of urban middle- and upper-middle-income groups and the emergence of these new occupational strata as a cultural aristocracy. Schools organized to satisfy the educational values of these strata also have distinct "class" character: they often are exclusive, and more important, they represent an effort to escape or deny the ethos of the industrial system and its traditional asceticism. The free schools—like the styles of their pupils' parents—reflect not only differences in taste, but a freedom and a leisure that the distribution of wealth denies to the lower- and lower-middle-income groups.[32] Nonetheless, these new groups have become important agents of political and social change.

The development of corporate capitalism toward increasingly technological forms of production carries with it vast changes in the life styles and occupational needs of middle-income groups. If our analysis is correct, these developments carry with them values antithetical to earlier conceptions of education. The educational style of the urban upper-middle-income groups stands in increasing opposition to the central values of the established system of schooling. While the discipline of that system is still dominant, there have been enough changes to achieve an irretrievable legitimacy for play. The continued growth of the welfare-socialization-culture industries and the development of technological industrialism will only increase the pressure to treat schooling as a form of play and pleasure.

Cultural and Political Tensions

Cultural differences between urban immigrants and the schools were a second point of conflict. Industrialization attracted immigrants to the cities and held them there, producing a deluge of non-English-speaking families at the turn of the century, especially in the East. The response was twofold: efforts were made to use the schools as vehicles of intensive and rapid socialization—preparation for citizenship and work—and the movement to centralize urban school government was accelerated.

American educators had always assumed that the public school was essential to cultural unity, but at the turn of the century that idea received intensive application. Immigrants were inculcated with the values of the dominant culture through evening schools—often compulsory for the non-English-speaking—language instruction, civics, and American history, the celebration of patriotic holidays, and countless informal ways. Specially designed textbooks taught immigrants cleanliness, hard work, and how to apply for a job and naturalization papers, and informed them that rural, Protestant America epitomized the best in American life. Evening school teachers in Lawrence, Massachusetts, were told to convince the foreign-born of the efficacy of schooling: "Try to make them feel that they are coming to school not because they are obliged to, but because they wish to, because they know America means Opportunity . . . and the Opportunity now knocks at their door. . . ."[33]

Americanization programs were also established outside the schools. In the International Harvester Company plants, immigrants learned English through such lessons as:

I hear the whistle. I must hurry.
I hear the five minute whistle.
It is time to go into the shop. . . .
I change my clothes and get ready to work. . . .
I work until the whistle blows to quit.
I leave my place nice and clean.[34]

Yet if a variety of institutions sought to integrate the new-comer, the public school was almost universally considered the primary agency of assimilation. "The American school," educators and public agreed, "is the salvation of the American republic."[35]

How immigrants responded to this Americanization process is unclear. Were language instruction and the curriculum's social content points of tension? Did immigrants go to evening schools? Did particular immigrant groups relate to the public schools in different ways? The evidence is mixed. Some historians and contemporary writers report great enthusiasm for public education as a vehicle of assimilation and social mobility. Mary Antin found her first day at school "the apex of my civic pride and contentment": "To most people their first day at school is a memorable occasion. In my case the importance of the day was a hundred times magnified, on account of the years I had waited, the road I had come, and the conscious ambitions I had entertained."[36] On the other hand, there was substantial conflict at both the state and municipal levels and between immigrant nationalities over foreign language teaching in the public schools.[37] Some immigrant groups established educational institutions of their own—among Catholics usually in the form of parochial schools,[38] and among Jews as part-time educational alternatives. In the larger cities there were numerous afternoon and weekend Jewish schools—many of them apparently in wretched condition—designed to transmit religious and cultural traditions.[39]

Another source of conflict seems to have been the public schools' staff, though evidence on this is hard to come by. Teachers in immigrant neighborhoods often were antagonistic to the newcomers, and there is some evidence of resistance to accepting teaching positions in immigrant neighborhoods. Michael Gold, in his autobiographical novel *Jews without Money,* records the hostility of his teacher in a Lower East Side elementary school, calling her a "Ku Kluxer before [her] time," a woman tortured by having to teach in a predominantly Jewish school.[40] And even those teachers not explicitly hostile to immigrants rejected their unfamiliar behavior and values. Rarely were pleas for pluralism in the schools heard from professional educators.[41]

These conflicts were partly resolved by the process of ethnic succession to bureaucratic power in city school systems. Although the process occurred at different times, even by 1909 it was fairly well advanced in some of the larger cities.[42] At least in the large eastern cities, the Jews and the Irish were solidly entrenched in the teaching force by the 1920s. In addition, conflict was muted by the second-generation immigrant identification with the dominant culture; as the children of immigrants entered urban school bureaucracies they may often have rejected demands for ethnic pluralism.

The political response to the immigrants involved changes in the organization and control of urban school systems. As the Europeans inundated the cities, local schools were removed from ward and neighborhood control, and given over into the hands of central boards controlled by the established city elites. This shift away from district control and ward-oriented politicians to centralized agencies was central to the Progressive movement in politics, and it drew heavily on the Progressive ideology of reform: efficiency, expertise, and non-partisanship. But these ideas were also linked to bigotry and explicit class biases. School centralization in the interests of efficiency had the effect—and in at least some cases the intent—of removing power and influence over schooling from the hands of the poor and the culturally different.[43]

Cubberley made this explicit, in his rationale for replacing the ward system of school government with centralized school committees:

> The tendency of people of the same class or degree of success to settle in the same part of the city is a matter of common knowledge. . . .
>
> One of the important results of the change from ward representation to election from the city at large, in any city of average decency and intelligence, is that the inevitable representation from these "poor wards" is eliminated, and the board comes to partake of the best characteristics of the city as a whole.[44]

Cubberley gave the example of a city in which the board was divided between working-class and professional members, and argued that this pointed up the "constant danger" in the ward system: "The less intelligent and progressive

element would wear out the better elements and come to rule the board."[45]
When he came to suggesting the sort of people who might best serve on the new
citywide boards, Cubberley was no less forthright:

> To render such intelligent service to the school system of a city as has been
> indicated requires the selection of a peculiar type of citizen for school board
> member. . . . Men who are successful in the handling of large business under-
> takings—manufacturers, merchants, bankers, contractors, and professional
> men of large practice—would perhaps come first. . . . College graduates who
> are successful in their business or professional affairs, whatever may be their
> profession or occupation, also usually make good board members. . . .[46]

Opportunities for schooling were extended to immigrant children partly to
transform them into a stable, quiescent labor force. The school demanded
cultural homogeneity and extolled the virtues of work; work was viewed not as
a way of staying alive, but as a pattern of behavior. *Placing people in an industrial complex and making them dependent upon it—economically and psychologically—forged a link between them and the system's prosperity.* It was
toward this end that the cultural and political activities of public education
worked.

The parallels to the recent black struggle for control of education are striking. In part the current conflict represents an effort to establish a legitimate
black culture and control the instruments of its diffusion, but it is also an effort
to reconstitute more particularism in school government. Although there are
many important distinctions, because of the very different historical experiences
of European immigrants and Negro Americans, the structural features of conflict in education are strikingly similar. The schools are still essentially WASP
in their values—even with ethnic succession to teaching and administration—and
they have conceded little to racial, national, or class cultures. *Cultural diversity
is still a matter of basic struggle in education,* and groups seeking it have had to
adopt alternatives outside the public system.

Merit and Equality

In theory, the schools' relation to the social structure has been egalitarian and
reformist—to allocate status on the basis of achievement rather than inheritance,
thereby providing a remedy for injustice. Historically, however, the extent to
which the meritocracy actually worked, and the value of merit selection and its
implications for equality, have been in dispute.

At the turn of the century, the issue centered on differentiating educational
opportunities. Tension arose between the egalitarian principle that the state
should treat all citizens equally, and the meritocratic notion that equality meant
status allocated by achievement. The first implied exposure of all students to a
common curriculum, while the second involved allocating educational resources
based on expectations of students' adult status. The established egalitarian
ideology of public schooling seemed to demand the inculcation of common
values, absorption of a common heritage, and exposure to the same school experiences. The notion of schools as an industrial meritocracy implied diversification, discrimination, and hierarchy.[47] As the differentiation of school offerings
spread, a new notion of equality emerged—equal school achievement for equal

ability. Differentiation was justified as a way of organizing education to conform with social and economic realities, and this in turn was presented as a way of providing meaningful equality of educational opportunity. As the Boston school superintendent argued in 1908:

> Until very recently [the schools] have offered equal opportunity for all to receive *one kind* of education, but what will make them democratic is to provide opportunity for all to receive such education as will fit them *equally well* for their particular life work.[48]

The idea was difficult to oppose, for the advocates of equality—the unified curriculum—were identified with tradition during a ferment of progressive reform. Their defense of common learning asserted the need for broad "mental training" at a time when influential psychologists like E. L. Thorndike were calling for training for specific ends. But most important, the traditionalists seemed hostile to the educational needs of working-class and immigrant children entering the schools in large numbers.[49] The diversifiers needed only to point to evidence of massive school retardation and dropouts to make their case; the choice was diversification and vocational orientation or continued inefficiency.[50] As long as the alternatives were so limited, it is hardly surprising that differentiated educational "equality" met with such rapid acceptance.

For those who accepted this notion of equality, the success of the new system was measured by the extent to which students were actually afforded education on the basis of the announced merit criteria. From the outset critics argued that the academic meritocracy involved considerable discrimination. George Counts, for example, argued in 1922 that the differentiation of secondary educational offerings selected students on the basis of race, nationality, and class.[51] His research showed that the inherited indicia of social status played an enormous role in determining entrance to secondary school, the likelihood of remaining in school, and the curricula pursued within schools. Counts concluded that:

> ... the inequalities among individuals and classes are still perpetuated to a considerable degree in the social inheritance. While the establishment of free public high schools marked an extraordinary educational advance, it did not by any means equalize educational opportunity. Education means leisure, and leisure is an expensive luxury. In most cases today this leisure must be guaranteed the individual by the family. Thus, secondary education remains largely a matter for family initiative and concern, and reflects the inequalities of family means and ambition.[52]

He maintained that public support for secondary education could not be justified as long as the selectivity was so badly biased by students' background. Either selection should be absolutely rigorous and objective, scientifically selecting an educated elite from all classes, or the same education should be made available to all without any selection. Counts maintained that the measurement technology was inadequate to support a really scientific system, although his opposition to selectivity was political, not technological. He favored the absolute universalization of secondary education.[53]

The problem was that while Counts got his wish—secondary education rapidly became virtually universal—this was accompanied by selectivity based on the measurement technology he regarded as inadequate. Although an impressive literature grew up which raised questions about the class and ethnic bias of the tests,[54] their use to group and assign students increased. Although scores of studies of ability grouping failed to reveal any clear advantage for students in the practice, ability grouping became widespread.[55] Although—as Counts pointed out in 1922, and critics of vocational education have pointed out since—curricular differentiation really helped little in job training or placement, the spread of differentiation continued.[56] Since the 1920s evidence has accumulated that children of the poor and the working class, and those from immigrant groups, were disadvantaged by grouping, differentiation and intelligence testing. Whether educational progress was measured by curricular placement, school completion, or the tests themselves, those who were economically disadvantaged or culturally different usually came out at the bottom of the heap.[57]

The chief implication of all this was reasonably clear: the schools' methods for measuring merit—especially the tests—were seriously biased by inherited status and culture. Evenhandedness and the application of "objective measures" could not provide equal chances for school success among groups of children who arrived in school with differing class and cultural backgrounds. But educators, researchers, and reformers have generally taken different views.

Most reformers have accepted the principle of merit selection because they saw education as a vehicle for promoting social reform through individual mobility. The notion that education was a means for deferring direct (redistributive) social change by displacing it onto individual achievement has been a central element in modern American liberalism. It rests on a desire to promote social justice without attacking the distribution or ownership of property. The consequence for education has been curious—the more evidence has accumulated that school success depended upon inherited economic and social status, the more the liberal reformers insisted that the schools should compensate for environmental differences among children. Such efforts have been tried increasingly over the past four or five decades, but there is scant evidence that they work any particular advantage for the children concerned. Nonetheless, every evidence of failure seems only to reinforce the idea that more compensation is required. Because of the liberal commitment to social reform through individual achievement, the development of school reform has been perversely related to the evidence: *the more it shows that school performance is profoundly conditioned by inherited status, the more insistent the demands for compensatory schooling have grown; there never has been much mention of directly reducing the underlying status inequalities.* It is testimony to the power of liberal ideology —and the class character of school reform efforts—that evidence on the educational consequences of inequality produces efforts to improve the meritocracy, rather than efforts to reduce the inequality.

The reason for this is apparent: since the underlying function of the school system is not challenged by the educational reformers, the only thing that can be done to make it more democratic is to eliminate the barriers facing the "brighter," or more ambitious, children of minority or low-income parents. The attempt has been made over the last several decades, and especially in the 1960s, to apply the principle of merit as fairly as possible (given the class purpose of public education) so that an occupational elite can be chosen from all groups in American society while class and social stratification remains intact. Equality in education will require the elimination of the meritocratic structure, but that reform cannot take place in an educational system whose purpose is to socialize children into a stratified class society.

NOTES

1. Angelo Patri, *The Problems of Childhood* (New York, 1927), p. 10.

2. Among the recent studies are Michael Katz, *The Irony of Early School Reform: Educational Innovation in Mid-Nineteenth Century Massachusetts* (Cambridge, 1968); Marvin Lazerson, *Origins of the Urban School: Public Education in Massachusetts, 1870-1915* (Cambridge, 1971); Katz, "The Emergence of Bureaucracy in Urban Education: The Boston Case, 1850-1884," *History of Education Quarterly* 8: Summer-Fall 1968, pp. 155-88, 319-57; David Tyack, "Bureaucracy and the Common School: The Example of Portland, Oregon, 1851-1913," *American Quarterly* 19: Fall 1967, pp. 475-98; Tyack, "City Schools at the Turn of the Century: Centralization and Social Control," unpublished ms. in authors' possession; Berenice Fisher, *Industrial Education: American Ideals and Institutions* (Madison, 1967); Sol Cohen, "The Industrial Education Movement, 1906-17," *American Quarterly* 20: Spring 1968, pp. 95-110; Tyack, "Onward Christian Soldiers; Religion in the American Common School," in Paul Nash, ed., *History and Education* (New York, 1970); Timothy Smith, "Immigrant Social Aspirations and American Education, 1880-1930," *American Quarterly* 21: Fall 1969, pp. 523-43; Colin Greer, "Immigrants, Negroes, and the Public Schools," *Urban Review,* January 1969, pp. 9-12; Greer, "Public Schools: Myth of the Melting-Pot," *Saturday Review,* 15 November 1961; and the articles by David K. Cohen, Tyack, S. Cohen, Neil Sutherland, Daniel Calhoun, and Katz in *History of Education Quarterly* 9: Fall 1969.

3. For other attempts at such a framework, see Lawrence Cremin, *The Genius of American Education* (New York, 1965); Henry Perkinson, *The Imperfect Panacea* (New York, 1968); and Robert Wiebe, "The Social Functions of Public Education," *American Quarterly* 21: Summer 1969, pp. 147-64. For attempts to explain the more general revolution in organizational values in which the transformation of the schools occurred see Robert Wiebe, *The Search for Order, 1877-1920* (New York, 1967); and James Weinstein, *The Corporate Ideal in the Liberal State, 1900-1946* (Boston, 1968).

4. Raymond Callahan, *Education and the Cult of Efficiency* (Chicago, 1962).

5. Various aspects of the industrial system of schooling are discussed in Callahan, S. Cohen, and Fisher. See also Edward A. Krug, *The Shaping of the American High School* (New York, 1964), chs. 8-11; Marvin Lazerson, *Origins of the Urban School,* chs. 5-7; and Thomas Green, *Work, Leisure, and the American Schools* (New York, 1968).

6. W. B. Pillsbury, "Selection—An Unnoticed Function of Education," *Scientific Monthly* 12: January 1921, p. 71.

7. Boston, *Documents of the School Committee,* 1908, no. 7, pp. 48-53.

8. A. E. Winship, *Jukes-Edwards* (Harrisburg, Pennsylvania, 1900), p. 13.

9. Callahan, *Cult of Efficiency.*

10. A. C. Ellis, *The Money Value of Education,* Bulletin no. 22, U.S. Bureau of Education (Washington, 1917).

11. Ellwood Cubberley, *Changing Conceptions of Education* (Cambridge, 1909), pp. 18-19.

12. Robert Yerkes and C. S. Yoakum, *Army Mental Tests* (1920).

13. Pillsbury, "Selection," p. 64.

14. Cubberley in Lewis Terman, *The Measurement of Intelligence* (Boston, 1916), pp. vii-viii.

15. Florence Goodenough, *Mental Testing* (New York, 1949), pp. 89-90.

16. White House Conference on Child Health and Protection, *Vocational Guidance* (New York, 1932), pp. 25-27.

17. National Education Association, *Report of the Committee on the Place of Industries in Public Education,* 1910, pp. 6-7.

18. Frank M. Leavitt and Edith Brown, *Prevocational Education in the Public Schools* (Boston, 1915).

19. S. Cohen, "Industrial Education," pp. 105-6.
20. Robert and Helen Lynd. *Middletown* (New York, 1956 ed.). p. 194.
21. Cubberley, *Changing Conceptions*, pp. 53-57.
22. Ibid., pp. 21-22.
23. National Education Association, *Place of Industries*, p. 7.
24. E. L. Thorndike, *Educational Psychology* (New York, 1903), pp. 44-46.
25. Frank Carleton, "The School as a Factor in Industrial and Social Problems," *Education* 28, October 1907, pp. 77-79.
26. Katz, "Bureaucracy," pp. 167-68.
27. Various aspects of education as play are discussed in Cremin, *The Transformation of the School* (New York, 1961), pp. 201-24, 276-91, 309-13. On playfulness as an intellectual attribute, see Richard Hofstadter, *Anti-Intellectualism in America* (New York, 1962), pp. 29-33. The conflict between work and play is also discussed in Green, *Work, Leisure, and the American Schools*.
28. Lazerson, *Origins of the Urban School*, ch. 2; and Lazerson, "Social Reform and Early Childhood Education: Some Historical Perspectives," *Urban Education* 5, April 1970.
29. John Dewey, *Democracy and Education* (New York, 1966 edition), ch. 15, John and Evelyn Dewey, *Schools of Tomorrow* (New York, 1962 edition), details Dewey's attempt to harmonize the work-play tension.
30. Harold Rugg and Ann Shumaker, *The Child-Centered School* (Yonkers-on-the-Hudson, 1928), pp. 3, 5-6, and passim; Agnes DeLima, *Our Enemy the Child* (New York, 1926). Contrast the classrooms in Rugg and Shumaker and DeLima with Lynd, *Middletown*, pp. 188-205.
31. Bernard Wishy, *The Child and the Republic* (Philadelphia, 1968), is suggestive on nineteenth-century changes in child-rearing.
32. Education-as-play is not simply an American phenomenon. The playful style gained popular currency among the bourgeoisie in eighteenth-century Europe, and in many respects is simply the natural consequence of the emphasis on individuality and liberation common to the Enlightenment and the Romantic movement. But the idea that play is a legitimate form of activity and a suitable medium for cultural expression has its roots in the society and chivalric culture of the high Middle Ages, and in the Renaissance cult of individuality. Historically, at least, the cultivation of play is profoundly aristocratic. And in fact, striving for aristocratic culture and values always has been an important activity in the upper middle class, no less in America than in Europe.
33. Lawrence, Massachusetts, *A Syllabus for the Instruction of Non-English-Speaking Pupils in the Evening Schools* (Lawrence, 1908); Sara O'Brien, *English for Foreigners* (Boston, 1909).
34. Quoted in Gerd Korman, *Industrialization, Immigrants, and Americanizers* (Madison, 1967), pp. 144-45.
35. E. O. Vaile, "Teaching Current Events in School," National Education Association, *Proceedings and Addresses*, 1892, p. 142. See also Oscar Handlin, *John Dewey's Challenge to Education* (New York, 1959); Edward Hartmann, *The Movement to Americanize the Immigrant* (New York, 1948); Lazerson, *Origins of the Urban School*, ch. 8.
36. Mary Antin, *The Promised Land* (Boston, 1912), p. 198; Smith, "Immigrant Social Aspirations."
37. J. Fishman, *Language Loyalty in the United States* (New York, 1966), pp. 206-52; Leonard Covello, *The Heart Is the Teacher* (New York, 1958); Rudolph Vecoli, "Prelates and Peasants," *Journal of Social History*, Spring 1969, pp. 217-68.
38. Robert Cross, "Origins of Catholic Parochial Schools in America," *American Benedictine Review* 16, June 1965, pp. 194-209; Alice Masaryk, "The Bohemians in Chicago," *Charities* 13:3 December 1904.
39. Leo Honor, "Jewish Elementary Education in the United States, 1901-1950," American Jewish Historical Society, *Publications* 42: September 1952, pp. 1-42; Leibush Lehrer, "The Jewish Secular School," *Jewish Education* 7, January-March 1935, pp. 33-43; Lloyd Gartner, *Jewish Education in the United States* (New York, 1969). There are a number of autobiographical and fictional accounts of part-time Jewish schools; see e.g., Henry Roth, *Call It Sleep* (New York, 1962 edition), pp. 211-25.
40. Michael Gold, *Jews Without Money* (New York, 1965 edition), p. 22.
41. Tyack, "Onward Christian Soldiers"; and Tyack, "The Perils of Pluralism: Oregon's Compulsory Public School Bill of 1922," unpublished ms. in authors' possession.
42. U.S. Immigration Commission, "The Children of Immigrants in the Schools," *Reports* (Washington, 1911), vols. 29-33.

43. Tyack, "City Schools at the Turn of the Century."
44. Cubberley, *Public School Administration* (Cambridge, 1916), p. 93.
45. Ibid., p. 93.
46. Ibid., pp. 124-25.
47. Lazerson, *Origins of the Urban School,* ch. 7.
48. Boston, *Documents of the School Committee,* 1908, no. 7, p. 53.
49. Krug, *Shaping of the American High School,* chs. 8-9.
50. Leonard Ayres, *Laggards in Our Schools* (New York, 1909); D. Cohen, "Immigrants and the Schools," *Review of Educational Research* 40: February 1970, pp. 13-27.
51. George Counts, *The Selective Character of American Education* (Chicago, 1922).
52. Ibid., p. 148.
53. Ibid., pp. 149-56.
54. C. Brigham, "Intelligence Tests of Immigrant Groups," *Psychological Review* 37 (1930), pp. 158-65; National Society for the Study of Education, *Twenty-Seventh Yearbook* (Bloomington, Indiana, 1928).
55. U.S. Office of Education, *Cities Reporting the Use of Homogeneous Grouping and of the Winnetka Technique and the Dalton Plan,* city school leaflet 22, December 1926; see the discussion of ability grouping in National Society for the Study of Education, *Thirty-Fifth Yearbook* (Bloomington, Indiana, 1936), part 2.
56. Counts, *Selective Character.*
57. D. Cohen, "Immigrants and the Schools."

David K. Cohen and Marvin Lazerson

All of our writers, in one way or another, have questioned the principal tenets of the American faith in education, and in the chapters that follow, this questioning will continue. Historically, we thought that school was the Great Equalizer in American society and at the same time it determined who were the meritorious. This was done in the name of "merit through achievement" in the schools. It was our meritocracy. But increasingly we are discovering that our educational system, far from producing equality, has bolstered inequality as it unequitably selected and sorted the meritorious from the nonmeritorious.

Now still other writers are questioning whether the schools are even doing that; whether the schools really do in fact identify the meritorious when they select and sort. There is growing evidence that those who are identified by the schools as the meritorious and nonmeritorious are pretty well determined before their schooling begins. Thus not only are the contradictions between meritocratic selection and equality becoming more obvious, but the possibility grows that some of those who are selected are not meritorious.

If it is true that socioeconomic class bias rather than what the schools do determines who will acquire the degrees and who will not, then those who hold the high paying, high status, jobs and positions of power, as well as the social prestige that goes with them, are not necessarily the people who should receive them on the meritocratic principle.

chapter five

SCHOOLS AND SOCIALIZATION

A Woman: (kneeling before her little son as she straightens the kerchief round his neck) There! That's the third time I've had to straighten it for you. (She dusts his clothes.) That's better. Now try to behave properly and mind you start crying when you're told.
The Child: Is that where they come from?
Woman: Yes.
The Child: I'm frightened.
Woman: And so you should be, darling. Terribly frightened. That's how one grows up into a decent, god-fearing man.

Sartre, *The Flies*

Our readings and analyses thus far have argued that schools are an instrument of political and economic policy, a means for accomplishing some goals beyond schooling rather than for activities which are ends in themselves. Schools are one of the institutions which are held accountable for doing what society demands. And this may be true not only of American schools but of all schools—certainly all public schools—as we have known them. In this chapter we focus on the goals of school that are social—the social product of school, the socialization process.

The school and the family are, for our society, the primary agencies which socialize the young. Socialization is the process by which adults pass on the accumulated knowledge, values, morals and way of life of their society to new members in order to ensure continuity and stability, and recreate the relationships regarded as necessary by that society. The "reality" manipulated, controlled and defined for students of course benefits adults, and is structured to turn the young into the kind of adults desired. The young, it is argued, lack judgment and experience, and cannot know the world. Immaturity is viewed as a lack, a negative condition to be corrected by becoming an adult. Infancy and youth are not taken on their own terms, with their own values and satisfactions. The child and his education are measured against his becoming an adult quite similar to present adults. The present system of adulthood is organized around differential goals and rewards in hierarchical structures, and adults look to the schools to perpetuate this system and to stratify these not-yet-adults. Young people are to be channeled into various levels within the present divisions of labor, where they are to divide the differential spoils. In this way the schools have taken on the task of social engineering. Like the factory, the school mashes, forms and shapes its finished products and finally packages them with its own stamps of approval, as indicated by degrees and letters.

Our pattern of schooling is based upon the theoretical assumption that the child's mind at birth is a clean slate (empty head?); in John Locke's phrase, a *tabula rasa,* upon which the world is about to impress its message. As Jerome Kagan pointed out, in an address delivered to the Annual Meeting of the American Association for the Advancement of Science in December, 1972,[1] despite the widespread popularity of the thinking of Jean Piaget and Immanuel Kant, this Lockean assumption is still the dominant way of thinking about experience among American psychologists. While Kant and Piaget, each in his own way, called attention to the presence, *prior to* an experience, of mental or conceptual elements which serve to form and shape, to literally make sense of experiences, Lockean empiricism has always seen experience as a matter of an outside reality. Presumably this reality is the same for us all, and makes its imprint on a relatively passive and quiescent organism. The child or adult thus has little to do with what that experience is or the reality it is supposed to represent.

Along with this Lockean assumption there runs a deep streak of Calvinism, in our belief that we need to overcome an original, spontaneous, malevolent nature in the young by teaching them to, in Durkheim's words,

> . . . contain natural egoism, control one's passions and instincts, restrain and deprive oneself, sacrifice and subordinate one's desires to the control of one's will and confine them within proper limits . . . [to in general] exercise strong self-control.[2]

Education, in this view, is a matter of the acceptance of an obedience to political and moral authority. Each new mind is a potential threat to the existing social structure, and the pressure is on to force conformity to the status quo.

The alternative to this view of education as a process of molding the young into proper adults is to regard each child as a human being in his or her own right, with a mind patterned and programmed to unfold. William Blake argued, "Man's mind is like a garden ready planted." According to this second view, each moment of childhood is an experience, part of an ongoing process of exploration and growth toward self-actualization of a private innate potential. Moreover, "realities" are determined by the interaction of each person and his environment and by the structure of that environment.

But as long as schools continue to be linked with careers and the socialization and politicalization of the young, and while schools are expected to fit young people into slots in our economic structure, it is our contention throughout this book that no real educational alternatives are possible. A few critics of schools touch upon these issues. But more often the criticism of the schools focuses on isolated variables such as teaching methods (e.g., team teaching, "instructional models," remedial reading techniques); cognitive information and skills (new curriculum content, such as the New Math, vocational or "career" education, compensatory programs like Head Start); individual student ambition and background; the physical structure of school buildings and facilities; and scores of psychological, achievement and intelligence tests. In general, the focus has been on changing the student or teacher to fit the institution rather than on changing the institution itself.

1. Jerome Kagan address delivered to the annual meeting of the American Association for the Advancement of Science, December, 1972.
2. Emile Durkheim *Education and Sociology,* trans. S. Fox (Glencoe, Ill.: Free Press, 1956), pp. 76, 87.

Various reasons have been offered for this focus. Some critics even say that educational authorities don't understand what actually goes on in schools. Certainly more should be known about the social world of the school, the pattern of relationships, underlying and competing ideologies, myths, and other social factors involved in the school and classroom activities.

If we want any alternative style of schooling, we must examine the whole social setting of the school. What follows in this chapter are examples of this kind of examination. We begin with some answers that have been given to the question, "What is being learned in school?" This is the theme of the "hidden," "covert," "informal," or "unofficial" curriculum. It includes learning to follow rules, to participate in "sacred" rituals, to be patient, neat and punctual, to work on time schedules, to defer gratification, to pretend, to develop facades.

Our first reading is by Jules Henry, an anthropologist whose writings on the schools have received a lot of favorable and widespread attention. Henry is concerned with what teachers teach. This reading could just as well have gone in our chapter on teaching but for the principal point that Henry is making about how teachers, the classroom and the entire school, covertly and otherwise, control and manipulate the attitudes of youngsters.

ATTITUDE ORGANIZATION IN ELEMENTARY SCHOOL CLASSROOMS

Jules Henry

The word *organization* in this paper is used to stand for order and determinateness as distinguished from disorder and randomness. The emotions and attitudes of prepubertal children in our culture are not, on the whole, directed toward generalized social goals, but focused rather on the peer group and parents. From the point of view of an observer who has in mind the larger social goals, like the maintenance of stable economic relations, common front against the enemy, maintenance of positive attitudes toward popular national symbols, and so on, the emotions and attitudes of prepubertal children in our culture may be viewed as lacking order. The adult, on the other hand, is supposed to have so organized his tendencies to respond to the environment that his emotions, attitudes, and activities subserve overall social goals. While it is true that attitudes and feelings

Jules Henry, "Attitude Organization in Elementary School Classrooms," *The American Journal of Orthopsychiatry,* 27, 1957, pp. 117-33. Copyright © 1957, the American Orthopsychiatric Association, Inc. Reproduced by permission.

are bent toward social goals even from earliest infancy, (Henry and Boggs, 1952), many institutions combine to organize these attitudes and feelings so that ultimately a steady social state will be maintained. The elementary school classroom in our culture is one of the most powerful instruments in this effort, for it does not merely sustain attitudes that have been created in the home, but reinforces some, de-emphasizes others, and makes its own contribution. In this way it prepares the conditions for and contributes toward the ultimate organization of peer- and parent-directed attitudes into a dynamically interrelated attitudinal structure supportive of the culture.

This organizing process is comparable to, though not identical with, the reorganization of attitudes and resources that takes place as a society shifts from a peacetime to a wartime footing. During a period of peace in our society, adult hostility and competitiveness may be aimed at overcoming competition in business or social mobility, while love and cooperation are directed toward family and friends, and toward achieving specific social economic ends *within* the society. With the coming of war the instruments of government seek to direct hostility and competitiveness toward the enemy, while love and cooperation are directed toward the armed forces, civilian instruments of war (price controls, rationing, civilian officials, etc.), and national symbols. From the point of view of an observer *within the war machine,* the civilian attitudes at first seem random and unorganized. He wants to change them so that from *his point of view* they will seem organized. The situation is similar, though not identical with respect to the child: to an observer inside the head of even some psychotic children, attitudes and behavior may seem organized. But to the observer on the outside, whose focus is on social goals, the child seems *un-* or *dis-*organized. The prime effort of the adult world is *to make child attitudes look organized to adults.* The emphasis in this paper is on the description of the process of organizing child attitudes as it can be observed in some middle-class urban American classrooms.

THE WITCH-HUNT SYNDROME

One of the most striking characteristics of American culture since the settlement has been the phenomenon of intragroup aggression, which finds its pathological purity of expression in witch hunts (Starkey, 1949). It comes as a frightening surprise to democratic people to find themselves suddenly in terror of their neighbors; to discover that they are surrounded by persons who carry tales about others while confessing evil of themselves; to perceive a sheeplike docility settling over those whom they considered strong and autonomous. The *witch-hunt syndrome* therefore, as constituting one of the key tragedies of democracy, is selected for the elucidation of the organization of attitudes in our culture. In this witch's brew *destructive criticism* of others is the toad's horns; *docility* the body of the worm; *feelings of vulnerability* the chicken heart; *fear of internal (intragroup) hostility* the snake's fang; *confession of evil deeds* the locust's leg; and *boredom and emptiness* the dead man's eye. The witch-hunt syndrome is thus stated to be a dynamically interrelated system of feelings and actions made up of destructive criticism of others, docility, feelings of vulnerability, fear of internal aggression, confession of evil deeds, and boredom.

The witch-hunt syndrome in full panoply was observed in but one of the dozen classrooms in four schools studied in the research which I discuss here. Thus it seems a relatively rare phenomenon. But the question I set myself to answer is, How could it occur at all? What are the attitudes, present in the children, that were organized by this teacher into the syndrome? How could she do it? With what materials did she work? She did not create out of nothing the attitudes she manipulated in her "Vigilance Club" in this fourth-grade classroom in a middle-class American community. She had to have something to start with. The argument of this paper will be that the feelings and tendencies to action which this teacher organized into the witch-hunt syndrome in her class are present in an *un*organized state in other classrooms. Given a certain type of teacher, he or she will be able to develop into a highly specialized, tightly integrated system in his classroom those attitudes which are present in a differently organized state in the children in all classrooms. Let us now look at a meeting of the Vigilance Club.

1. In the extreme back of the room is a desk called the "isolation ward." A child has been placed there for disciplinary reasons. The Vigilance Club of the class is holding a meeting. . . . Officers are elected by the group. The purpose of the club is to teach children to be better citizens. The order of procedure is as follows: the president . . . bangs her gavel on the desk and . . . says, "The meeting of the Vigilance Club will come to order." Each child then takes from his or her desk a booklet whose title is *All About Me* . . . and places it on top of his desk. The vice-president calls the name of a child, gets the child's booklet, and places it on the teacher's desk. The president then calls on the child and asks, "_____, have you been a good citizen this week?" The president says, "Name some of the good things you have done," and the child tries to recall some, like opening doors for people, running errands, etc. Next the president asks the class if it remembers any good things the child has done. Each point is written in the child's booklet by the teacher. The president then . . . says to the child, "Name the bad things you have done. . . ." The child reports the wrongs he has committed during the week, and the class is asked to contribute information about his behavior. This too is written in the booklet by the teacher, who also reprimands the student, registers horror, scolds, etc. . . . When one child reports a misdemeanor of another the teacher asks for witnesses, and numerous children sometimes volunteer. . . . The child in the "isolation ward" reported some good deeds he had done; the children reported some more, and the isolated child was told he would soon be released. . . . (During this meeting some children showed obvious pleasure in confessing undesirable behavior. One child, by volunteering only good things of the students, seemed to be using the situation to overcome what seemed to the observer to be her unpopularity with the class.)[1]

Before analyzing this protocol for the attitudes present in it, it will be well to look at some events that occurred in this classroom on another day.

2. During the game of "spelling baseball" a child raised her hand and reported that Alice and John had been talking to each other. This occurred when neither child was "at bat." The teacher asked Alice if this was so, and she replied that it was, but John denied having spoken to Alice. The teacher said that John must have listened to Alice, but he denied this too. Then the

teacher asked whether there had been any witnesses, and many hands were raised. Some witnesses were seated on the far side of the room, and hence could not have seen Alice and John from their location in the room. All those testifying had "seen" Alice talking, but denied John's guilt. Alice was sent to the "bull pen," which meant that she had to sit on the floor behind the teacher's desk, and could no longer participate in the game. . . .

3. Mary raised her hand and said, "It hurts me to say this, I really wish I didn't have to do it, but I saw Linda talking." Linda was Mary's own teammate, had just spelled a word correctly, and had gone to first base. The teacher asked Linda if she had talked, and Linda said, "No, I just drew something in the air with my finger. . . ." She was sent to the "bull pen."

In these examples we see intragroup aggression; docility of the children in conforming, with no murmur of protest, to the teacher's wishes; and confession of "evil." In such a situation children develop feelings of vulnerability and fear of detection. Let us now look for these phenomena in classrooms presided over by teachers who seem to represent the more normal American type, in comfortable, middle-class, white communities: teachers who are conscientious and reasonably gentle, but creatures of their culture, and humanly weak. We begin not with internal aggression as expressed in spying and tale-bearing, but with the milder, though closely related phenomenon of carping, destructive criticism. While this occurs throughout the sample, I give here examples only from a fifth-grade classroom in the same school system.

4. Bill has given a report on tarantulas. As usual the teacher waits for volunteers to comment on the child's report.
   Mike: The talk was well illustrated, well prepared. . . .
   Bob: Bill had a piece of paper [for his notes], and teacher said he should have them on cards. . . .
Bill says he could not get any cards.
Teacher says that he should tear the paper next time if he has no cards.
   Bob: He held the paper behind him. If he had had to look at it, it wouldn't have looked very nice.

5. Betty reports on Theodore Roosevelt.
A child comments that it was very good but she looked at her notes too much. Teacher remarks that Betty had so *much* information.
   Bob: She said "calvary" [instead of "cavalry"].

6. Charlie reads a story he made up himself: "The Unknown Guest." One dark, dreary night . . . on a hill a house stood. This house was forbidden territory for Bill and Joe, but they were going in anyway. The door creaked, squealed, slammed. A voice warned them to go home. Spider webs, dirty furniture . . . Bill wanted to go home. They went upstairs. A stair cracked. They entered a room. A voice said they might as well stay and find out now; and their father came out. He laughed and they laughed, but they never forgot their adventure together.
   Teacher: Are there any words that give you the mood of the story? . . .
   Lucy: He could have made the sentences a little better. . . .
   Teacher: Let's come back to Lucy's comment. What about his sentences?
   Gert: They were too short. . . .
Charlie and Jeanne are having a discussion about the position of the word "stood."

Teacher: Wait a minute, some people are forgetting their manners. . . .

Jeff: About the room: the boys went up the stairs and one "cracked"; then they were in the room. Did they fall through the stairs or what? Teacher suggests Charlie make that a little clearer.

Lucy: If he fell through the step. . . .

Teacher: We still haven't decided about the short sentences. Perhaps they make the story more spooky and mysterious.

Gwynne: I wish he had read with more expression instead of all at one time.

Rachel: Not enough expression.

Teacher: Charlie, they want a little more expression from you. I guess we've given you enough suggestions for one time. (Charlie does not raise his head, which is bent over his desk as if studying a paper.) Charlie! I guess we've given you enough suggestions for one time, Charlie, haven't we? (Charlie half raises his head, seems to assent grudgingly.)

The striking thing about these examples is that the teacher supports the children in their carping criticism of their fellows. Her performance in this is not, however, consistent; but even where, as in Example 6, she seems at one point to try to set herself against the tide of destruction, by calling attention to the possible artistry in Charlie's short sentences, she ends up supporting the class against him, and Charlie becomes upset. Thus the teacher, by rewarding the children's tendencies to carp, reinforces them. Teachers, however, are able to make their own contributions to this tendency. The single example given below will serve as illustration:

7. Joan reads us a poem she has written about Helen Keller . . . which concludes with the couplet:

"Hellen Keller as a woman was very great;
She is really a credit to the United States."

Teacher (amusedly): Is "states" supposed to rhyme with "great"? When Joan murmurs that it is, the teacher says, "We'll call it poetic license."

From time to time one can see a teacher vigorously oppose tendencies in the children to tear each other to pieces. The following example is from the sixth grade:

8. The Parent-Teachers Association is sponsoring a school frolic, and the children have been asked to write jingles for the publicity. For many of the children the experience of writing a jingle seems painful. They are restless, bite their pencils, squirm around in their seats, speak to their neighbors, and from time to time pop up with questions like, "Does it have to rhyme, Mr. Smith?" . . . At last Mr. Smith says, "All right, let's read some of the jingles now." Child after child says he "couldn't get one"; but some have succeeded. One girl has written a very long jingle, *obviously the best in the class.* However, instead of using Friday as the frolic day she used Tuesday, and several protests were heard from the children. Mr. Smith defended her. "Well, so she made a mistake. But you are too prone to criticize. If *you* could only do so well!"

It will be observed that all the examples are taken from circumstances in which the child's self-system is most intensely involved; where his own poetry or prose is in question, or where he has worked hard to synthesize material into a report. It is precisely at the points where the ego is most exposed that the attack is most telling. The numerous instances in the sample, where the teachers, by a word of praise or a pat on the head, play a supportive role, indicate their awareness of the vulnerability of the children. Meanwhile, as I have pointed out, the teachers often fall into the trap of triggering or supporting destructive impulses in the children.

The carping criticism of one's peers is a form of intragroup aggression, which can be quite threatening and destructive. Tale-bearing, however, countenanced by some teachers more than by others, can be an overwhelming threat to autonomy. While telling on others can be organized into the patrol-monitor complex (prestige through controlling and telling), useful perhaps in maintaining order in large school populations, its operation within the classroom may have serious consequences. Let us look at a couple of examples.

9. Second grade. As teacher asked the children to clear their desks one boy raised his hand, and when called on said, "Jimmy just walked by and socked me on the head."
Teacher: Is this true?
Jimmy: He hit me first.
Teacher: Why don't you both take seats up here (in front of the room). I'm not sure people like you belong in the second grade.

10. Sixth grade special class for bright students. The children are working on their special nature study projects. Joseph passes where Ralph is working.
Ralph (to teacher): Joseph is writing too much on his birds.
Teacher: Joseph, you should write only a few things.

In our sample, telling on other children in the classroom is infrequent outside the class in which the Vigilance Club was formed. Destructive criticism is the preferred mode of attack in most classrooms. The ease with which tendencies to attack peers can be organized into telling on others, however, is illustrated by the monitor-patrol complex, and by the Vigilance Club (Example 3).

Competition

Competition is an important element in the witch-hunt syndrome. Since witch hunts involve so often obtaining the attention and approval of some powerful central figure, the examples of competitiveness that I shall cite illustrate how approval and attention seeking occur as the child attempts to beat out his peers for the nod of the teacher. It would be easy to cite examples from protocols of the merciless laughter of children at the failures or gaucheries of their classmates. I am interested, however, more in showing the all-pervading character of the phenomenon of competition, *even in its mildest forms.* The first example is from a fourth-grade music lesson:

11. The children are singing songs of Ireland and her neighbors from the book *Songs of Many Lands.* . . . Teacher plays on piano while children sing. . . . While children are singing some of them hunt in the index, find a song

belonging to one of the four countries, and raise their hands before the previous song is finished in order that they may be called on to name the next song. . . .

Here singing is subordinated, in the child, to the competitive wish to have the song he has hunted up in the index chosen by the teacher. It is merely a question of who gets to the next song in the index first, gets his hand up fast, and is called on by the teacher.

The following examples also illustrate the fact that almost any situation set by the teacher can be the occasion for release of competitive impulses:

12. The observer enters the fifth-grade classroom.

Teacher: Which one of you nice polite boys would like to take [observer's] coat and hang it up? (Observer notes: From the waving hands it would seem that all would like to claim the title.)

Teacher chooses one child . . . who takes observer's coat. . . .

Teacher: Now children, who will tell [observer] what we have been doing?

Usual forest of hands . . . and a girl is chosen to tell. . . .

Teacher conducted the arithmetic lesson mostly by asking, "Who would like to tell . . . the answer to the next problem?" This question was usually followed by the appearance of a large and *agitated* forest of hands; apparently *much competition to answer.*

Thus the teacher is a powerful agent in reinforcing competition.

It has already been pointed out that carping criticism helps to settle in the child a feeling of vulnerability and threat. In this connection it is significant that *the failure of one child is repeatedly the occasion for the success of another.* I give one illustration below from the same class as the one from which I have taken Example 12.

13. Boris had trouble reducing 12/16 to lowest terms, and could get only as far as 6/8. Much excitement. Teacher asked him quietly [note how basically decent this teacher is] if that was as far as he could reduce it. She suggested he "think." Much heaving up and down from the other children, all frantic to correct him. Boris pretty unhappy. Teacher, patient, quiet, ignoring others, and concentrating with look and voice on Boris. She says, "Is there a bigger number than 2 you can divide into the two parts of the fraction?" After a minute or two she becomes more urgent. No response from Boris. She then turns to the class and says, "Well, who can tell Boris what the number is?" Forest of hands. Teacher calls Peggy. Peggy gives 4 to be divided into 12/16, numerator and denominator.

Where Boris has failed Peggy has been triumphant; *Boris's failure has made it possible for Peggy to succeed.*

This example and also Example 6 are ones in which the discomfort of the child was *visible,* and such instances may be multiplied. They illustrate how vulnerable the children feel in the presence of the attacks of the peer group in the classroom. But since these are children who face the world with serious anxiety to begin with, the classroom situation sustains it. Let us look at some stories created by these very children, and read by them to their classmates. We have already seen one, Example 6, Charlie's story of "The Unknown Guest."

Here are *all* the stories read to their classmates by these children during an observation period.

    14. (a) Charlotte's story: "Mistaken Identity." One day last year my family and I went to the hospital to visit somebody. When we were coming out and were walking along my father hit me. I came up behind him to hit him back, but just as I was about to do it I looked back and he was behind me! I was going to hit the wrong person!

    (b) Tommy's story: "The Day Our House Was Robbed." [Observer has recorded this in the third person.] He was coming home from school one afternoon. He knew his Mom was away that afternoon. He started to go in the side door, but decided, he doesn't know why, to go round the back. He found the door open, went into the kitchen, looked into the front room where he saw a thief. Tommy "froze stiff" (chuckle of appreciation from the class), ran out, shouted, "Stop thief" as the man ran out after him. He went to a neighbor, rang the bell, called his mother at the store. The cops came, asked questions, but the man had gotten away with $99 and his mother's watch. If he had gone in the side door he would not have had a chance to see the man. Changing to the back door "may have saved my life." [Teacher's only remarks about this story were: 1) instead of having said "froze stiff," Tommy should have said, "froze stiff as something"; 2) he should have left out the word "then" in one place; 3) he could have made the story clearer; 4) he changed from the past to the present tense.]

    (c) Polly's story: "Custard the Lion." Custard the Lion was the most timid animal in Animal Town. The doctors couldn't cure him. Then they found a new medicine. It had strange effects, but Custard wanted to try it. When he did he felt very queer. (Child gives details of queer feeling.) But he soon realized he wasn't afraid of anything. [Teacher's first remark: "You didn't let us hear the last sentence."]

    (d) Dan's story: "The Boy Hero." Bill wanted to be a fireman, so he went to the firehouse. The Chief was telling him to go home when the bell clanged. While the Chief was getting into the engine, he didn't see that Bill was getting on too. (Class or teacher picks up flaw in sentence and it is reread correctly.) The Chief said O.K. as long as Bill was aboard, "But you're not to get into no mischief." (Class choruses, "Any. . . .") Everyone was out of the fire except a little girl and her doll. The firemen cannot figure out what to do, but Bill, seeing a tree near the house, climbs it over the protests of the firemen. He misses the girl on his first try, but gets her on the second. While sliding down the tree she slips and almost falls, but grabs Bill's pants, and they make it to safety. . . . (Children's remarks center on position of "clang, clang, clang" in the story. Teacher talks about how to use direct quotations, which, it seems, Dan had not used properly.)

    (e) Bertha's story: Title not recorded. The story is about Jim who was walking home past the Smith's house one night and heard a scream. Penny Smith came out and said there was a robber in the house. When the cops came they found a parrot flying around in there, and Penny's parents told her to shut the parrot up before she read mystery stories again. (This story was followed by much carping criticism, which was terminated by the teacher's telling Bertha to change the story to suit the class.)

    These stories contain elements of anxiety and even of terror. As each child finishes, the carping criticism of students and teacher then reminds him of his vulnerability. As the child sends out his cloud of fear, it returns with the leaden rain of hostility.

Docility

It comes as a somewhat shocking surprise, perhaps, to middle-class parents, to find their children described as "docile." Yet we have already seen the perfection of docility in the Vigilance Club, and we shall presently see its manifold forms in more normal classrooms.

15. First grade. The children are to act out a story called "Pig Brother," which is about an untidy boy. The teacher is telling the story. One boy said he did not like the story, so the teacher said he could leave if he did not wish to hear it again, but the boy did not leave.

16. In gym the children began to tumble, but there was much restless activity in the lines, so the teacher had all the children run around the room until they were somewhat exhausted before she continued the tumbling.

17. Second grade. The children have been shown movies of birds. The first film ended with a picture of a baby bluebird.
Teacher: Did the last bird ever look as if he would be blue?
The children did not seem to understand the "slant" of the question, and answered somewhat hesitantly, yes.
Teacher: I think he looked more like a robin, didn't he?
Children, in chorus: Yes.

Item 17 is one of a large number of instances, distributed throughout all grades, in which the children exhibit their docility largely through giving the teacher what he wants. Thus in the elementary schools of the middle class the children get an intensive eight-year-long training in hunting for the right signals and giving the teacher the response wanted. The rest of the examples of docility document this assertion.

18. Fourth grade. (a) An art lesson. Teacher holds up a picture.
Teacher: Isn't Bob getting a nice effect of moss and trees?
Ecstatic Ohs and Ahs from the children. . . .
The art lesson is over.
Teacher: How many enjoyed this?
Many hands go up.
Teacher: How many learned something?
Quite a number of hands come down.
Teacher: How many will do better next time?
Many hands go up.

(b) Children have just finished reading the story "The Sun Moon and Stars Clock."
Teacher: What was the highest point of interest—the climax?
The children tell what they think it is. Teacher is aiming to get from them what *she* considers the point of climax, but the children seem to give everything else but.
Bobby: When they capture the thieves.
Teacher: How many agree with Bobby?
Hands, hands.

19. Fifth grade. This is a lesson on "healthy thoughts," for which the children have a special book depicting, with appropriate illustrations, specific conflictful incidents among children. The teacher is supposed to discuss each incident with the children in order to help them understand how to handle their emotions.

One of the pictures is as follows: A sibling *pair* is illustrated by *three* boys: 1) One has received a ball. 2) One is imagined to react with displeasure. 3) One is imagined to react benignly and philosophically, saying, "My brother couldn't help being given the football; we'll use it together."

Teacher: Do you believe it's easier to deal with your thoughts if you own up to them, Betty?

Betty: Yes it is, if you're not cross and angry.

Teacher: Have you any experience like this in the book, Alice?

Alice tells how her brother was given a watch and she envied him and wanted one too; but her mother said she wasn't to have one until she was fifteen, but now she has one anyway.

Teacher: How could you have helped—could you have changed your thinking? How could you have handled it? What could you do with mean feelings?

Alice seems stymied. Hems and haws.

Teacher: What did Susie (a character in the book) do?

Alice: She talked to her mother.

Teacher: If you talk to someone you often then feel that "it was foolish of me to feel that way. . . ."

Tommy: He had an experience like that, he says. His cousin was given a bike and he envied it. But he wasn't "ugly" about it. He asked if he might ride it, and his cousin let him, and then, "I got one myself; and I wasn't mean, or ugly or jealous."

Before continuing it will be well to note that since the teacher does not say Alice was wrong the children assume she was right and so copy her answer.

Two boys, the dialogue team, now come to the front of the class and dramatize the football incident.

Teacher (to the class): Which boy do you think handled the problem in a better way?

Rupert: Billy did, because he didn't get angry. . . . It was better to play together than to do nothing with the football.

Teacher: That's a good answer, Rupert. Has anything similar happened to you, Joan?

Joan can think of nothing.

Sylvester: I had an experience. My brother got a hat with his initials on it because he belongs to a fraternity, and I wanted one like it and couldn't have one; and his was too big for me to wear, and it ended up that I asked him if he could get me some letters with my initials, and he did.

Betty: My girl friend got a bike that was 26-inches, mine was only 24; and I asked my sister what I should do. Then my girl friend came over and was real nice about it, and let me ride it.

Teacher approves of this, and says, Didn't it end up that they both had fun without unhappiness?

Here we note that the teacher herself has gone astray, for on the one hand her aim is to get instances from the children in which they have been yielding, and capable of resolving their own jealousy, etc.; yet, in the instance given by Betty, it was not Betty who yielded, but her friend. The child immediately following Betty imitated her since Betty had been praised by the teacher:

Matilde: My girl friend got a 26-inch bike and mine was only 24; but she only let me ride it once a month. But for my birthday my mother's getting me a new one, probably (proudly) a 28. (Many children rush in with the information that 28 doesn't exist.) Matilde replies that she'll probably have to raise the seat then for she's too big for a 26.

As we go on with this lesson, we shall continue to see how the children's need for substitute gratification and their inability to accept frustration are the real issues, which even prevent them from getting the teacher's point. We shall see how, in spite of the teacher's driving insistence on her point, the children continue to inject their conflicts into the lesson. While at the same time they gropingly try to find a way to gratify the teacher. *They* cannot give the "right" answers because of their conflicts; teacher cannot handle their conflicts, even perceive them, because *her* underlying need is to be gratified by the children! The lesson goes on:

Teacher: I notice that some of you are only happy when you get your own way. You're not thinking this through, and I want you to. Think of an experience when you didn't get what you want. Think it through.
Charlie: His ma was going to the movies and he wanted to go with her, and she wouldn't let him; and she went off to the movies, and he was mad; but then he went outside and there were some kids playing baseball, so he played baseball.
Teacher: But suppose you hadn't gotten to play baseball? You would have felt hurt because you didn't get what you wanted. We can't help feeling hurt when we are disappointed. What could you have done; how could you have handled it?
Charlie: So I can't go to the movies so I can't play baseball, so I'll do something around the house.
Teacher: Now you're beginning to think! It takes courage to take disappointments. (Turning to the class) What did we learn? The helpful way . . .
Class: is the healthy way!

Before entering the final section of this paper, we need to ask: Why are these children, whose fantasies contain so many hostile elements, so docile in the classroom; and why do they struggle so hard to gratify the teacher and try in so many ways to bring themselves to her attention (the "forest of hands")? We might, of course, start with the idea of the teacher as a parent figure, and the children as siblings competing for the teacher's favor. We could refer to the unresolved dependency needs of children of this age, which make them seek support in the teacher, who manipulates this seeking and their sibling rivalry to pit the children against each other. Other important factors, however, that are inherent in the classroom situation itself, and particularly in middle-class classrooms, ought to be taken into consideration. We have observed the children's tendency to destructively criticize each other, and the teachers' often unwitting repeated reinforcement of this tendency. We have taken note of the anxiety in the children as illustrated by the stories they tell, and observed that these very stories are subjected to a carping criticism, whose ultimate consequence would be anything but alleviation of that anxiety. Hence the classroom is a place in which the child's underlying anxiety may be heightened. In an effort to alleviate this he seeks the approval of the teacher, by giving right answers and by doing what teacher wants him to do under most circumstances. Finally, we cannot omit the teacher's need to be gratified by the attention-hungry behavior of the children.

A word is necessary about these classrooms as middle class. The novel *Blackboard Jungle* describes schoolroom behavior of lower-class children. There we see the children *against the teacher,* as representative of the middle class. But in the classes I have described we see the *children against each other,* with the teacher abetting the process. Thus, as the teacher in the middle-class schools directs the hostility of the children toward one another and away from himself, he reinforces the competitive dynamics within the middle class itself. The teacher in lower-class schools, on the other hand, appears to become the organizing stimulus for behavior that integrates the lower class, as the children unite in expressing their hostility to the teacher (Hunter, 1954).

Confession

The Vigilance Club would have been impossible without confession, and the children's pleasure in confession. But, as with the other parts of the syndrome, confessing occurs in other classrooms also; it can be elicited when the proper conditions are present, and the children can be seen to enjoy it—to vie with one another in confessing. Let us follow the lesson "healthy thoughts" a little further. We will see how confession occurs as the children seek to give the teacher *precisely* what she wants.

20.   Teacher asks if anyone else has experiences like that (of two children who have just recited), where they were mean and angry.
    Dick: He has a friend he plays baseball with, and sometimes they fight; but they get together again in a few minutes and apologize.

In this first example we note one of the important aspects of the confession element in the syndrome: the culprit must have given up his evil ways, and now be free of impurities.

In response to Dick's story, teacher says: You handled it just right. Now let's hear about someone who had a similar experience and didn't handle it just right.
    Tom: His little brother asked for the loan of his knife, but it was lost, and he got angry with his little brother for asking. (This knife story follows a sequence of several stories about knives told by other children. The exuberance of knife stories following immediately on the teacher's approval of the first one suggests that some of them are made to order and served up piping hot for teacher's gratification.)
    Teacher: Now Tom, could you have worked it out any differently? (Observer notes that Tom seems to enjoy this confession; certainly he is not abashed or ashamed.)
    Tom: Later he asked me if he could help me find it. He found it in a wastebasket, and then I let him borrow it.
    Harry: Sometimes I get angry when my friends are waiting for me and . . . (observer missed some of this) and my little sister asked if she could borrow my auto-racing set, and I hit her once or twice. (Class laughs.)

Here we see another factor so important to the flourishing of the syndrome: the audience gets pleasure through the confessor's telling about deeds the audience wishes to commit: who among Harry's listeners would not like to have hit his sister, or anyone, "once or twice"?

The teacher then goes on: What would you do now—would you hit her?
Harry: Now I'd probably get mad at first, but let her have it later.

Thus Harry has mended his ways—in teacher-directed fantasy at least—and returned to the fold.

So far we have had confession of mean and angry thoughts and violence. We shall now see confession to unacceptable fear. In all cases the teacher says what type of confession she wishes to hear, and what the resolution should be of the unacceptable behavior; and the children vie with one another to tell commensurable tales, as they derive pleasure from the total situation—through approval of the teacher, expression of their own real or fantasied deviations, and the delight of their peers. In these situations the pleasure of the peer group is seen to derive not so much from the "happy ending" the children give their stories but rather from the content of the story itself. It is interesting that no carping criticism appears; rather the entire situation is a jolly one. It seems that within unspoken limits the children permit one another to boast of "evil" behavior because of the deep pleasure obtained from hearing it. Thus impulse expression becomes a device for role maintenance in the classroom.

The lesson proceeds:

Two children enact a little skit in which they have to go to the principal to ask him something. One of them is afraid of the principal, the other is not. The moral is that the principal is the children's friend, and that one should not be shy.
Gertrude: Well, anyway, the principal isn't a lion, he's your friend; he's not going to kill you.
Teacher: That's right, the principal is a friend, he says hello and good morning to you. . . . Have you ever felt shy?
Meriam: The first year I sold Girl Scout cookies I didn't know how to approach people; and the first house I went to I didn't know the lady; and I stuttered and stammered, and didn't sell any cookies. By the second house I had thought it all out before I rang the bell, and I sold two boxes. (Triumphantly.)
Teacher: It helps to have self-confidence.
Ben now tells a story, with a happy ending, of being afraid of a principal. Then Paul tells a story, amid gales of laughter, about his being scared on a roller coaster. By this time there is so much excitement among the children that the teacher says: Wait a minute—manners!
John: He was scared to go on the Whip-the-Whirl (scornful laughter from the class); but after he went he liked it so much that he went eight times in a row. (This is well received.)
Many hands go up. Teacher waits. . . .
Michael: He was at Pleasure Park on the ferris wheel (scornful Aw from the class) and a girl kept rocking it, and I started to get green (roar of laughter).
Teacher: Now we'll have to stop.

Certain phenomena not emphasized before appear in this section. Confession is used by the authoritative figure, the teacher, to strengthen attachment to significant but potentially terrifying figures like school principals, and to polish up cultural shibboleths like "self-confidence." For the child storytellers confession becomes an opportunity for bathing in the emotional currents of the peer group, as the child stimulates the group's approval through presentation of group standards, and awakens group pleasure as the peer group responds to its own anxiety about weakness, and experiences resolution of the anxiety through the happy ending. With a perfect instinct for what is right, each child provides catharsis for his peers. By presenting himself as weak, he enables his peers to identify with him; and then, as he overcomes his weakness, he enables his companions too to feel strong.

What this lesson on healthy thoughts may have accomplished by way of creating a permanent reservoir of "healthy thoughts" is difficult to say, but that it helped create solidarity among the students, and between them and the teacher is clear from the fact that when she suddenly shifted ground to say, "Do you think you are wide enough awake for a contest in subtraction of fractions?" the children responded with a unanimous roar of "Yes," as if she had asked them whether they were ready for cookies and ice cream!

Thus in this lesson, in which all have participated more with their *unconscious* than with their conscious emotions, solidarity has been achieved. The teacher thought she was teaching the children to have healthy thoughts, but she was showing them how to gratify her. The children sensed this and struggled to gratify her, while they sought acceptance by their peers also. The essential difference between this teacher and the one who perpetrated the Vigilance Club is that though the latter tended to demolish solidarity among the children while placing the teacher in supreme command, the lesson on healthy thoughts tended to a dubious solidarity among all. *Both teachers organize some of the same elements in the children, but into different configurations, of total feeling and behavior.*

Boredom

It seems unnecessary to document the fact that children become bored in class, for much of modern thinking and curriculum arrangement is aimed at eliminating it. The shifts at 15-minute intervals from one subject to the next in the elementary school classrooms is one example of this effort. Boredom, which means emotional and intellectual separation from the environment, is an insupportable agony, particularly if the emotional vacuum created by such separation is not filled by gratifying fantasies, or if it is filled by terrifying ones. To fill this vacuum people in our culture will throw themselves into a great variety of even relatively ungratifying activities. Since in this situation, bored children attack almost any novel classroom activity with initial vigor, the witch-hunt syndrome or any modification thereof helps to overcome boredom: better to hunt than be bored. In a full and satisfying life there is no place for witch hunts. The school system that can provide a rich program for children has no need of Vigilance Clubs, or even of lessons on "healthy thoughts."

DISCUSSION AND CONCLUSIONS

In this paper I have used suggestions from communications theory in an effort to order the data obtained from direct observation of elementary school classrooms. Information, the central concept of communications theory, refers to measurable differences in states of organization. In human behavior, as seen in the classroom under discussion, we observe *qualitative shifts in state, for different teachers organize the same underlying emotional characteristics of the children to achieve different organizations of the emotions.* One teacher so organizes the children's emotions as to accomplish an intensification of the fear of intragroup aggression, while she turns the children's hostility toward one another. A different teacher may organize the emotions of the children so that a euphoria in which students and teacher are bathed in a wave of emotional gratification is achieved. The great skill in being a teacher would seem to be, therefore, a *learned* capacity to keep shifting states of order intelligently as the work demands. This does not mean the traditional classroom order, where you can hear a pin drop, but rather the kind of order in which the *emotions of the children are caught up and organized toward the achievement of a specific goal.* It is not necessary, perhaps, that even the most prominent emotions of the children, like competitiveness, for example, form part of the organized whole. Yet, on the other hand, it is difficult to see how, in the present state of our culture, competitiveness can be overlooked. It would seem, perhaps, that the important outcome to avoid is that the competitiveness should become destructive of peers, while reinforcing dependence on the teacher.

The phenomenon I have labeled "docility" occurs because of the absolute dependence for survival of the children on the teacher. That is to say success in school depends absolutely on the teacher, and self-respect, as a function of the opinion of others, in the home or among peers, is in part a function of success or failure in school. In these circumstances the child's capacity to respond automatically to the signals he gets from the teacher is bound to acquire somewhat the appearance of instinctive behavior. Although it occurs at a much higher level of integration than instinct, the child hunts for the proper signals from the teacher, and the child's responses take on instinctual quality. They *must;* otherwise, like the nestling who does not open its mouth when the mother arrives with a worm, he will never eat the ambrosia of teacher's approval, so necessary to his survival. In this situation both children and teacher easily become the instruments of their own unconscious processes, as they, like Joseph and his brethren, fall on each other's necks in a shared ecstasy of exuberant dependence. Teacher and pupil will have gratified each other, but it remains an open question whether the children will have learned what the curriculum committee planned.

We see in the organization of the components of the witch-hunt syndrome an important phase in the formation of American national character, for tendencies to docility, competitiveness, confession, intragroup aggression, and feelings of vulnerability the children may bring with them to school, are reinforced in the classroom. This means that independence and courage to challenge are observably played *down* in these classrooms. It means, on the other hand, that tendencies to own up rather than to conceal are reinforced—a development which, in proper hands, might become a useful educational instrument. It means, further, that while many teachers do stress helping others they may inadvertently develop in the children the precise opposite, and thus undermine children's feelings of security. One could come from a very secure and accepting family and yet have one's feeling of security and acceptance threatened in these classrooms. On the other hand, what seems most in evidence from the stories they make up is that the children come to school with feelings of vulnerability which are intensified in the classroom.

Meanwhile we should try to understand that all the teachers in the sample were probably trying to be good teachers,[2] and all the children were trying to be good pupils. Their unconscious needs, however, naturally dominated their behavior. The teacher who organized the Vigilance Club probably thought she was teaching her children to be upright and honest, and to perform good deeds, but her unconscious tendencies caused these worthy inclinations to seek the wrong expression. All teachers need conformity in the classroom in order that the children shall absorb a respectable amount of academic knowledge. But the teacher's (often unconscious) need for acceptance by the children, and her fear (sometimes unconscious) of her inability to control free discussion, compel her to push the children into uncritical docility at times, while they seek her approval.

The creation of stories, and their discussion by the class, are accepted principles of progressive education. But the teacher's own (at times unconscious) need to carp and criticize gets in the way of her adequately developing the creative and supportive possibilities in her charges. Thus these are not "bad," "vicious," or "stupid" teachers, but human beings, who express in their classroom behavior the very weaknesses parents display in their dealings with their children. The solution to the problem of the contradiction between the requirements of a democratic education on the one hand, and the teachers' unconscious needs on the other, is not to carp at teachers, and thus repeat the schoolroom process, but to give them some insight into how they project their personal problems into the classroom situation.

NOTES

1. In order to prevent identification of teachers and children, the names of my student observers are not used.
2. I am indebted to B. Bettelheim for this suggestion.

REFERENCES

Jules Henry and Joan Whitehorn Boggs, "Child Rearing, Culture, and the Natural World." *Psychiatry*, 15 (1952): pp. 261-271.
Evan Hunter. *The Blackboard Jungle.* (New York: Simon and Schuster, 1954).
Marion L. Starkey. *The Devil in Massachusetts.* (New York: Knopf, 1949).

Jules Henry

Edgar Z. Friedenberg's profile of the modern high school, which follows, also develops the theme of the "hidden curriculum." He points out that most of what happens and what is taught in school is related to rules, routines and rituals, and not to academic content, "subject matter," or "knowledge."

THE MODERN HIGH SCHOOL: A PROFILE

Edgar Z. Friedenberg

Not far from Los Angeles, though rather nearer to Boston, may be located the town of Milgrim, in which Milgrim High School is clearly the most costly and impressive structure. Milgrim is not a suburb. Although it is only fifty miles from a large and dishonorable city and a part of its conurbation, comparatively few Milgrimites commute to the city for work. Milgrim is an agricultural village which has outgrown its nervous system; its accustomed modes of social integration have not yet even begun to relate its present, recently acquired inhabitants to one another. So, though it is not a suburb, Milgrim is not a community either.

Milgrim's recent, fulminating growth is largely attributable to the rapid development of light industry in the outer suburbs, with a resulting demand for skilled labor. But within the past few years, further economic development has created a steady demand for labor that is not skilled. In an area that is by no means known for its racial tolerance or political liberalism, Milgrim has acquired, through no wish of its own, a sizable Negro and Puerto Rican minority. On the shabby outskirts of town, a number of groceries label themselves Spanish-American. The advanced class in Spanish at Milgrim High School makes a joyful noise —about the only one to be heard.

Estimates of the proportion of the student body at Milgrim who are, in the ethnocentric language of demography, nonwhite, vary enormously. Some students who are clearly middle class and of pinkish-gray color sometimes speak as if they themselves were a besieged minority. More responsible staff members produce estimates of from 12 to 30 per cent. Observations in the corridors and lunchrooms favor the lower figure. They also establish clearly that the nonwhites are orderly and well behaved, though somewhat more forceful in their movements and manner of speech thatn their light-skinned colleagues.

What is Milgrim High like? It is a big, expensive building, on spacious but barren grounds. Every door is at the end of a corridor; there is no reception area, no public space in which one can adjust to the transition from the outside world. Between class periods the corridors are tumultuously crowded; during them they are empty. But at both times they are guarded by teachers and students on patrol duty. Patrol duty does not consist primarily in the policing of congested throngs of moving students, or the guarding of property from damage. Its principal function is the checking of corridor passes. Between classes, no student may walk down the corridor without a form, signed by a teacher, telling where he is coming from, where he is going, and the time, to the minute, during which the pass is valid. A student caught in the corridor without such a pass is sent or taken to the office; there a detention slip is made out against him, and he is required to remain after school for two or three hours. He may

Edgar Z. Friedenberg, "The Modern High School: A Profile," *Commentary*, 36, 1963, pp. 373-80.

do his homework during this time, but he may not leave his seat or talk.

There is no physical freedom whatever at Milgrim. Except during class breaks, the lavatories are kept locked, so that a student must not only obtain a pass but find the custodian and induce him to open the facility. Indeed Miligrim High's most memorable arrangements are its corridor passes and its johns; they dominate social interaction. "Good morning, Mr. Smith," an attractive girl will say pleasantly to one of her teachers in the corridor. "Linda, do you have a pass to be in your locker after the bell rings?" is his greeting in reply. There are more classifications of washrooms than there must have been in the Confederate Navy. The common sort, marked just "Boys" and "Girls," are generally locked. Then there are some marked, "Teachers, Men" and "Teachers, Women" unlocked. Near the auditorium are two others marked simply, "Men" and "Women," which are intended primarily for the public when the auditorium is being used for some function. During the school day cardboard signs saying "Adults Only" are placed on these doors. Girding up my maturity, I used this men's room during my stay at Milgrim. Usually it was empty; but once, as soon as the door clicked behind me, a teacher who had been concealed in the cubicle began jumping up and down to peer over his partition and verify my adulthood.

He was not a voyeur; he was checking on smoking. At most public high schools, students are forbidden to smoke, and this is probably the most common source of friction with authorities. It focuses, naturally, on the washrooms which are the only place students can go where teachers are not supposed to be. Milgrim, for a time, was more liberal than most; last year its administration designated an area behind the school where seniors might smoke during their lunch period. But, as a number of students explained to me during interviews, some of these seniors had "abused the privilege" by lighting up before they got into the area, and the privilege had been withdrawn. No student, however, questioned that smoking was a privilege rather than a right.

The concept of privilege is important at Milgrim. Teachers go to the head of the chow line at lunch; whenever I would attempt quietly to stand in line the teacher on hall duty would remonstrate with me. He was right, probably; I was fouling up an entire informal social system by my ostentation. Students on hall patrol also were allowed to come to the head of the line; so were seniors. Much of the behavior that Milgrim depends on to keep it going is motivated by the reward of getting a government-surplus peanut butter or tuna fish sandwich without standing in line.

The lunchroom itself is a major learning experience, which must make quite an impression over four years time. There are two large cafeterias which are used as study halls during the periods before and after the middle of the day. The food, by and large, is good, and more tempting than the menu. The atmosphere is not quite that of a prison, because the students are permitted to talk quietly, under the frowning scrutiny of teachers standing around on duty, during their meal—they are not supposed to talk while standing in line, though this rule is only sporadically enforced. Standing in line takes about a third of their lunch period, and leaves plenty of time for them to eat what is provided them. They may not, in any case, leave the room when they have finished, any more than they could leave a class. Toward the end of the period a steel gate is swung down across the corridor, dividing the wing holding the cafeterias, guidance offices, administrative offices, and auditorium from the rest of the building. Then the first buzzer sounds, and the students sweep out of the cafeteria and press silently forward to the gate. A few minutes later a second buzzer sounds, the gate is opened, and the students file out to their classrooms.

During the meal itself the atmosphere varies in response to chance events and the personality of the teachers assigned supervisory duty; this is especially true in the corridor where the next sitting is waiting in line. The norm is a not unpleasant chatter; but about one teacher in four is an embittered martinet, snarling, whining, continually ordering the students to stand closer to the wall and threatening them with detention or suspension for real or fancied insolence. On other occasions, verbal altercations break out between students in the cafeteria or in line and the *student* hall patrolmen. In one of these that I witnessed, the accused student, a handsome, aggressive-looking young man, defended himself in the informal but explicit language of working class hostility. This roused the teacher on duty from his formal passivity. He walked over toward the boy, and silently but with a glare of contempt, beckoned him from the room with a crooked finger and led him along the corridor to the administrative office: the tall boy rigid in silent protest, the teacher, balding and stoop-shouldered in a wrinkled suit, shambling ahead of him. The youth, I later learned, was suspended for a day. At some lunch periods all this is drowned out by Mantovani-type pop records played over the public address system.

What adults generally, I think, fail to grasp even though they may actually know it, is that there is no refuge or respite from this: no coffee-break, no taking ten for a smoke, no room like the teachers' room, however poor, where the youngsters can get away from adults. High schools don't have club rooms; they have organized gym and recreation. A student cannot go to the library when he wants a book; on certain days his schedule provides a forty-five-minute library period. "Don't let anybody leave early," a guidance counselor urged during a group-testing session at Hartsburgh, an apparently more permissive school that I also visited. "There really isn't any place for them to go." Most of us are as nervous by the age of five as we will ever be, and adolescence adds to the strain; but one thing a high-school student learns is that he can expect no provision for his need to give in to his feelings, or swing out in his own style, or creep off and pull himself together.

The little things shock most. High school students—and not just, or even particularly, at Miligrim—have a prisoner's sense of time. They don't know what time it is outside. The research which occasioned my presence at Milgrim, Hartsburgh, and the other schools in my study required me to interview each of twenty-five to thirty students at each school three times. My first appointment with each student was set up by his guidance counselor; I would make the next appointment directly with the student and issue him the passes he needed to keep it. The student has no *open* time at his own disposal; he has to select the period he can miss with least loss to himself. Students well-adapted to the school usually pick study halls; poorer or more troublesome students pick the times of their most disagreeable classes; both avoid cutting classes in which the teacher is likely to respond vindictively to their absence. Most students, when asked when they would like to come for their next interview, replied, "I can come any time." When I pointed out to them that there must, after all, be some times that would be more convenient for them than others, they would say, "Well, tomorrow, fourth period" or whatever. But hardly any of them knew when this would be in clock time. High school classes emphasize the importance of punctuality by beginning at regular but uneven times like 10:43 and 11:27, which are, indeed, hard to remember; and the students did not know when this was.

How typical is all this? The elements of the composition—the passes, the tight scheduling, the reliance on threats of detention or suspension as modes of social control are nearly universal. The usurpation of any possible *area* of student initiative, physical or mental, is about as universal. Milgrim forbids boys to wear trousers that end more than six inches above the floor, and has personnel fully capable of measuring them. But most high schools have some kind of dress regulation; I know of none that accepts and relies on the tastes of students.

There are differences, to be sure, in tone; and these matter. They greatly affect the impact of the place on students. Take, for comparison and contrast, Hartsburgh High. Not fifteen miles from Milgrim, Hartsburgh is an utterly different community. It is larger, more compact, and more suburban; more of a place. Hartsburgh High is much more dominantly middle class and there are few Negroes in the high school there.

First impressions of Hartsburgh High are almost bound to be favorable. The building, like Milgrim, is new; unlike Milgrim's, it is handsome. External walls are mostly glass, which gives a feeling of light, air, and space. At Hartsburgh there is none of the snarling, overt hostility that taints the atmosphere at Milgrim. There are no raucous buzzers; no bells of any kind. Instead, there are little blinker lights arranged like the Mexican flag. The green light blinks and the period is over; the white light signals a warning; when the red light blinks it is time to be in your classroom. Dress regulations exist but are less rigorous than at Milgrim. Every Wednesday, however, is dress-up day; boys are expected to wear ties and jackets or jacket-sweaters, the girls wear dresses rather than skirts and sweaters. The reason is that on Wednesday the school day ends with an extra hour of required assembly and, as the students explain, there are often outside visitors for whom they are expected to look their best.

Students at Hartsburgh seem much more relaxed than at Milgrim. In the grounds outside the main entrance, during lunch period, there is occasional horseplay. For ten minutes during one noon hour I watched three boys enacting a mutual fantasy. One was the audience who only sat and laughed, one the aggressor, and the third—a pleasant, inarticulate varsity basketball player named Paul—was the self-appointed victim. The two protagonists were portraying in pantomime old, silent-movie type fights in slow motion. The boy I did not know would slowly swing at Paul, who would sink twisting to the ground with grimaces of anguish; then the whole sequence would be repeated with variations, though the two boys never switched roles. In my interviews with Paul I had never solved the problem arising from the fact that he was eloquent only with his arms and torso movements, which were lost on the tape recorder, and it was a real pleasure to watch him in his own medium. This was a pleasure Milgrim would never have afforded me. Similarly, in the corridors at Hartsburgh I would occasionally come upon couples holding hands or occasionally rather more, though it distressed me that they always broke guiltily apart as soon as they saw me or any adult. One of my subjects, who was waiting for his interview, was dancing a little jig by himself in the corridor when I got to him. This was all rather reassuring.

It was also contrary to policy. There is a regulation against couples holding hands and they are punished if caught by the kind of teacher who hates sexuality in the young. The air and space also, subtly, turn out to be illusions if you try to use them. Hartsburgh High is built around a large, landscaped courtyard with little walks and benches. I made the mistake of trying to conduct an interview on one of these benches. When it was over we could not get back into the building except by disturbing a class, for the doors onto this inviting oasis can only be opened from inside, and nobody ever goes there. Since the courtyard is completely enclosed by the high school building, this arrangement affords no additional protection from intruders; it merely shuts off a possible place for relaxation. The beautiful glass windows do not open enough to permit a body to squirm through and, consequently, do not open enough to ventilate the rooms, in which there are no individual controls for the fiercely effective radiators. Room temperature at Hartsburgh is a matter of high policy.

Teachers do not hide in the washrooms at Hartsburgh; but the principal recently issued a letter warning that any student caught in the vicinity of the school with "tobacco products" would be subject to suspension; students were directed to have their parents sign the letter as written acknowledgement that they were aware of the regulation and return it to school. Staff, of course, are permitted to smoke. At Hartsburgh a former teacher, promoted to assistant principal, serves as a full-time disciplinarian, but students are not dragged to his office by infuriated teachers, as sometimes happens at Milgrim. Instead, during the first period, two students from the school Citizenship Corps go quietly from classroom to classroom with a list, handing out summonses.

Along with having a less rancorous and choleric atmosphere than Milgrim, Hartsburgh seems to have more teachers who like teaching and like kids. But the fundamental pattern is still one of control, distrust, and punishment. The observable differences—and they are striking—are the results almost entirely, I believe, of *structural* and demographic factors and occur despite very similar administrative purposes. Neither principal respects adolescents at all or his staff very much. Both are preoccupied with good public relations as they understand them. Both are inflexible, highly authoritarian men. But their situations are different.

At Milgrim there is a strong district superintendent; imaginative if not particularly humane, he is oriented toward the national educational scene. He likes to have projects, particularly in research guidance. Guidance officers report through their chairman directly to him, not to the building principal; and the guidance staff is competent, tough, and completely professional. When wrangles occur over the welfare of a student they are likely to be open, with the principal and the guidance director as antagonists; both avoid such encounters if possible, and neither can count on the support of the district office; but when an outside force—like an outraged parent—precipitates a conflict, it is fought out. At Hartsburgh, the district superintendent is primarily interested in running a tight ship with no problems. To this end, he backs the authority of the principal whenever this might be challenged. The guidance office is vestigial and concerned primarily with college placement and public relations in the sense of inducing students to behave in socially acceptable ways with a minimum of fuss.

In these quite different contexts, demographic differences in the student bodies have crucial consequences. At Milgrim, the working-class students are not dominant—they have not quite enough self-confidence or nearly enough social savvy to be—but they are close enough to it to be a real threat to the nice, college-bound youngsters who set the tone in their elementary and junior high school and who expect to go on dominating the high school. These view the rapid influx of lower-status students as a rising wave that can engulf them, while the newcomers, many of whom are recent migrants or high-school transfers from the city, can remember schools in which they felt more at home.

The result is both to split and to polarize student feeling about the school, its administration, and other students. Nobody likes Milgrim High. But the middle class students feel that what has ruined it is the lower class students, and that the punitive constraint with which the school is run is necessary to keep them in line. In some cases these students approach paranoia: one girl—commenting on a mythical high school described in one of our semi-projective research instruments—said, "Well, it says here that the majority of the students are Negro—about a third" (the actual statement is "about a fifth").

The working-class students are hard-pressed; but being hard-pressed they are often fairly realistic about their position. If the Citizenship Corps that functions so smoothly and smugly at Hartsburgh was to be installed at Milgrim, those who actually turned people in and got them in trouble would pretty certainly receive some after-school instruction in the way social classes differ in values and in the propensity for non-verbal self-expression. At Milgrim, the working-class kids know where they stand and stand there. They are exceptionally easy to interview because the interviewer need not be compulsively nondirective. Once they sense that they are respected, they respond enthusiastically and with great courtesy. But they do not alter their position to give the interviewer what they think he wants, or become notably anxious at disagreeing with him. They are very concrete in handling experience and are not given to generalization. Most of them seem to have liked their elementary school, and they share the general American respect for education down to the last cliché—but then one will add, as an afterthought, not bothering even to be contemptuous, "Of course, you can't respect *this* school." They deal with their situation there in correspondingly concrete terms. Both schools had student courts last year, for example, and Hartsburgh still does, though few students not in the Citizenship Corps pay much attention to it. Student traffic corpsmen give much attention to it. Student traffic corpsmen give out tickets for corridor offenses, and these culprits are brought before an elected student judge with an administrative official of the school present as adviser. But Milgrim had a student court last year that quickly became notorious. The "hoody element" got control of it, and since most of the defendants were their buddies, they were either acquitted or discharged on pleas of insanity. The court was disbanded.

The struggle at Milgrim is therefore pretty open, though none of the protagonists see it as a struggle for freedom or could define its issues in terms of principles. The upper-status students merely assent to the way the school is run, much as middle class white Southerners assent to what the sheriff's office does, while the lower-status students move, or get pushed, from one embroilment to the next without ever quite realizing that what is happening to them is part of a general social pattern. At Hartsburgh the few lower-status students can easily be ignored rather than feared by their middle class compeers who set the tone. They are not sufficiently numerous or aggressive to threaten the middle class youngsters or their folkways; but, for the same reason, they do not force the middle class youngsters to make common cause with the administration. The administration, like forces of law and order generally in the United States, is accepted without deference as a part of the way things are and work. Americans rarely expect authority to be either intelligent or forthright; it looks out for its own interests as best it can. Reformers and troublemakers only make it nervous and therefore worse; the best thing is to take advantage of it when it can help you and at other times to go on living your own life and let it try to stop you.

This is what the Hartsburgh students usually do, and, on the whole, the results are pleasant. The youngsters, being to some degree ivy, do not constantly remind the teachers, as the Milgrim students do, that their jobs have no connection with academic scholarship. Many of the teachers, for their part act and sound like college instructors, do as competent a job, and enjoy some of the same satisfactions. The whole operation moves smoothly. But Milgrim and Hartsburgh are valid examples—though of very different aspects—of American democracy in action. And in neither could a student learn as much about civil liberty as a Missouri mule knows at birth.

What is learned in high school, or for that matter anywhere at all, depends far less on what is taught than on what one actually experiences in the place. The quality of instruction in high school varies from sheer rot to imaginative and highly skilled teaching. But classroom content is often handled at a creditable level and is not in itself the source of the major difficulty. Both at Milgrim and Hartsburgh, for example, the students felt that they were receiving competent instruction and that this was an undertaking the school tried seriously to handle. I doubt, however, that this makes up for much of the damage to which high school students are systematically subjected. What is formally taught is just not that important, compared to the constraint and petty humiliation to which the youngsters with few exceptions must submit in order to survive.

The fact that some of the instruction is excellent and a lot of it pretty good *is* important for another reason; it makes the whole process of compulsory schooling less insulting than it otherwise would be by lending it a superficial validity. Society tells the adolescent that he is sent to school in order to learn what he is taught in the classroom. No anthropologist and very few high school students would accept this as more than a rationalization; but rationalizations, to be at all effective, must be fairly plausible. Just as the draft would be intolerable if the cold war were wholly a piece of power politics or merely an effort to sustain the economy, so compulsory school attendance would be intolerable if what went on in the classrooms were totally inadequate to students' needs and irrelevant to their real intellectual concerns. Much of it is, but enough is not, to provide middle class students, at least, with an answer when their heart cries out "For Christ's sake, what am I doing here?"

But far more of what is deeply and thoroughly learned in the school is designed to keep the heart from raising awkward, heartfelt issues—if design governs in a thing so subtle. It is learned so thoroughly by attendance at schools like Milgrim or even Hartsburgh that most Americans by the time they are adult cannot really imagine that life could be organized in any other way.

First of all, they learn to assume that the state has the right to compel adolescents to spend six or seven hours a day, five days a week, thirty-six or so weeks a year, in a specific place, in charge of a particular group of persons in whose selection they have no voice, performing tasks about which they have no choice, without remuneration and subject to specialized regulations and sanctions that are applicable to no one else in the community nor to them except in this place. Whether this law is a service or a burden to the young—and, indeed, it is both, in varying degrees—is another issue altogether. As I have noted elsewhere,[1] compulsory school attendance functions as a bill of attainder against a particular age group. The student's position is that of a conscript, who is protected by certain regulations but in no case permitted to use their breach as a cause for terminating his obligation. So the first thing the young learn in school is that there are certain sanctions and restrictions that apply only to them; that they do not participate fully in the freedoms guaranteed by the state, and that *therefore, these freedoms do not really partake of the character of inalienable rights.*

Of course not. The school, as schools continually stress, acts *in loco parentis;* and children may not leave home because their parents are unsatisfactory. What I have pointed out is no more than a special consequence of the fact that students are minors, and minors do not, indeed, share all the rights and privileges— and responsibilities—of citizenship. Very well. However one puts it, we are still discussing the same issue. The high school, then, is where you really learn what it means to be a minor.

For a high school is not a parent. Parents may love their children, hate them, or like most parents, do both in a complex mixture. But they must nevertheless permit a certain intimacy and respond to their children as persons. Homes are not run by regulations, though the parents may think they are, but by a process of continuous and almost entirely unconscious emotional homeostasis, in which each member affects and accommodates to the needs, feelings, fantasy life, and character structure of the others. This may be, and often is, a terribly destructive process; I intend no defense of the family as a social institution. But children grow up in homes or the remnants of homes; are in physical fact dependent on parents, and too intimately related to them to permit their area of freedom to be precisely defined. This is not because they have no rights or are entitled to less respect than adults, but because intimacy conditions freedom and growth in ways too subtle and continuous to be defined as overt acts.

Free societies depend on their members to learn early and thoroughly that public authority is not like that of the family; that it cannot be expected—or trusted—to respond with sensitivity and intimate perception to the needs of individuals but must rely basically, though as humanely as possible, on the impartial application of general formulae. This means that it must be kept functional, specialized, and limited to matters of public policy; the meshes of the law are too coarse to be worn to the skin. Especially in an open society, where people of very different backgrounds and value systems must function together, it would seem obvious that each must understand that he may not push others further than their common undertaking demands, or impose upon them a manner of life that they feel to be alien.

After the family, the school is the first social institution an individual must deal with—the first place in which he learns to handle himself with strangers. The school establishes the pattern of his subsequent assumptions as to what relations between the individual and society are appropriate and which constitute invasions of privacy and constraints on his spirit—what the British, with exquisite precision, call "taking a liberty." But the American public school evolved as a melting pot, under the assumption that it had not merely the right but the duty to impose a common standard of genteel decency on a polyglot body of immigrants' children and thus insure their assimilation into the better life of the American dream. It accepted, also, the tacit assumption that genteel decency was as far as it could go. If America has generally been governed by the practical man's impatience with other individuals' rights, it has also accepted the practical man's determination to preserve his property by discouraging public extravagance.

With its neglect of personal privacy and individual autonomy the school incorporates a considerable measure of Galbraith's "public squalor." The plant may be expensive—for this is capital goods; but little is provided graciously, liberally, simply as an amenity, either to teachers or students, though administrative offices have begun to assume an executive look.

The first thing the student learns, then, is that as a minor, he is subject to peculiar restraints; the second is that these restraints are general, not limited either by custom or by the schools' presumed commitment to the curriculum. High school administrators are not professional educators in the sense that a physician, an attorney, or a tax accountant are professionals. They do not, that is, think of themselves as practitioners of a specialized instructional craft, who derive their authority from its requirements. They are specialists in keeping an essentially political enterprise from being strangled by conflicting community attitudes and pressures. They are problem-oriented, and the feelings and needs for growth of their captive and unenfranchised clientele are the least of their problems; for the status of the "teenager" in the community is so low that even if he rebels, the school is not blamed for the conditions against which he is rebelling. He is simply a truant or a juvenile delinquent; at worst the school has "failed to reach him." What high school personnel become specialists in, ultimately, is the *control* of large groups of students even at catastrophic expense to their opportunity to learn. These controls are not exercised primarily to facilitate instruction, and particularly, they are in no way limited to matters bearing on instruction. At several schools in our sample boys had been ordered —sometimes on the complaint of teachers—to shave off beards. One of these boys had played football for the school; he was told that, although the school had no legal authority to require him to shave, he would be barred from the banquet honoring the team unless he complied. Dress regulations are another case in point.

Of course these are petty restrictions, enforced by petty penalties. American high schools are not concentration camps. But I am not complaining about their severity; what disturbs me is what they teach their students concerning the proper relationship of the individual to society, and in this respect the fact that the restrictions and penalties are unimportant in themselves makes matters worse. Gross invasions are more easily recognized for what they are: petty restrictions are only resisted by "troublemakers." What matters in the end is that the school does not take its own business of education seriously enough to mind it.

The effects on the students are manifold. The concepts of dignity and privacy, notably deficient in American adult folkways, are not permitted to develop here. The school's assumption of custodial control of students implies that power and authority are indistinguishable. If the school's authority is not limited to matters pertaining to education, it cannot be derived from its educational responsibilities. It is a naked, empirical fact, to be accepted or controverted according to the possibilities of the moment. In such a world, power counts more than legitimacy; if you don't have power, it is naïve to think you have rights that must be respected . . . wise up. High school students experience regulation only as control, not as protection; they know, for example, that the principal will generally uphold the teacher in any conflict with a student, regardless of the merits of the case. Translated into the high school idiom, *suaviter in modo, fortiter in re* becomes "If you get caught, it's just your ass."

Students do not often resent this; that is the tragedy. All weakness tends to corrupt absolutely. Identifying, as the weak must, with the more powerful and frustrating of the forces that impinge upon them, they accept the school as the way life is and close their minds against the anxiety of perceiving alternatives. Many students like high school; others loathe and fear it. But even the latter do not object to it on principle; the school effectively obstructs their learning of the principles on which objection might be based; though these are among the principles that, we boast, distinguish us from totalitarian societies.

Yet, finally, the consequence of continuing through adolescence to submit to diffuse authority that is not derived from the task at hand—as a doctor's orders or the training regulations of an athletic coach, for example, usually are —is more serious than political incompetence or weakness of character. There is a general arrest of development. An essential part of growing up is learning that, though differences of power among men lead to brutal consequences, all men are peers; none is omnipotent, none derives his potency from magic, but only from his specific competence and function. The policeman represents the majesty of the state, but this does not mean that he can put you in jail; it means, precisely, that he cannot—at least not for long. Any person or agency responsible for handling throngs of young people—especially if he does not like them or is afraid of them—is tempted to claim diffuse authority and snare the youngster in the trailing remnants of childhood emotion which always remain to trip him. Schools succumb to this temptation, and control pupils by reinvoking the sensations of childhood punishment, which remain effective because they were originally selected, with great unconscious guile, to dramatize the child's weakness in the face of authority. "If you act like a bunch of spoiled brats, we'll treat you like a bunch of spoiled brats," is a favorite dictum of sergeants, and school personnel, when their charges begin to show an awkward capacity for independence.

Thus the high school is permitted to infantilize adolescence; in fact, it is encouraged to by the widespread hostility to "teen-agers" and the anxiety about their conduct found throughout our society. It does not allow much maturation to occur during the years when most maturation would naturally occur. Maturity, to be sure, is not conspicuously characteristic of American adult life, and would almost certainly be a threat to the economy. So perhaps in this, as in much else, the high school is simply the faithful servant of the community.

There are two important ways in which it can render such service. The first of these is through its impact on individuals; on their values, their conception of their personal worth, their patterns of anxiety, and on their mastery and ease in the world—which determine so much of what they think of as their fate. The second function of the school is Darwinian; its biases, though their impact is always on individual youngsters, operate systematically to mold entire social groups. These biases endorse and support the values and patterns of behavior of certain segments of the population, providing their members with the credentials and shibboleths needed for the next stages of their journey, while they instill in others a sense of inferiority and warn the rest of society against them as troublesome and untrustworthy. In this way the school contributes simultaneously to social mobility and to social stratification. It helps see to it that the kind of people who get ahead are the kind who will support the social system it represents, while those who might, through intent or merely by their being, subvert it, are left behind as a salutary moral lesson.

NOTES

1. See "An Ideology of School Withdrawal," June 1963.

Edgar Z. Freidenberg

The term "hidden curriculum" encompasses not only that covert content of subjects, rules, values, and attitudes, but also the less obvious elements of the teacher-student relationship. Such elements as how teachers view students and how students in turn view their teachers, are potent causal factors for social interaction in classrooms. The fact that these factors remain largely hidden from teachers and students alike makes them even more significant, for they thus go unacknowledged and uncriticized. An important part of these views are the expectations teachers and students have of one another. As Howard Becker demonstrates in the next reading, these expectations are always matters of survival for students, especially on the college level, and often sources of frustration for teachers.

MAKING THE GRADE

Howard Becker

DEFINITION OF THE SITUATION: FACULTY-STUDENT INTERACTION

The student, pursuing his academic goals in the larger community of the university, defines his situation as one in which he must do well by getting grades sufficiently high for his own purposes, however he has come to define these. He approaches his experience in each classroom with this definition in mind and searches for cues that tell him what kind of place the class is in which to pursue that objective. The realities of the situation lead him to define his classes as places in which he can get the grades he wants by performing as the teacher wants him to. The student gets his grades from the instructors for whose courses he has registered, and he earns them by working for them, by fulfilling in one way or another and at one or another level of proficiency the requirements the instructor sets for the course. In doing so, he "earns his living" as a member of the campus community. The more proficient his performance, the higher the resulting grades.

Howard Becker, "Definition of the Situation: Faculty-Student Interaction," *Making the Grade,* (New York: John Wiley & Sons, 1968), pp. 63-66, 76-79. Copyright © 1968 John Wiley & Sons. Reprinted by permission of John Wiley & Sons, Inc.

This view of classroom interaction defines the teaching situation as an exchange of rewards for performance, rather than as some kind of "educational process." Because it is so much at odds with more conventional academic conceptions of classroom interaction, we discuss, in a later section of the chapter, our reasons for not accepting those views.

The Classroom Contract

If the classroom is the workplace in which grades, the money of the college community, are exchanged for academic performance, it may be useful to extend our economic metaphor a step further and suggest that there is an agreement between teachers and students, analogous to the labor contract in the workplace, on the terms of the exchange. And there is such a contract—announced, perhaps bargained over, and fulfilled in the course of the semester as teachers and students interact in and out of the classroom. Teachers may be unaware of the terms of the contract, may not realize that their statements about how grades will be assigned are regarded by students as binding commitments. But students define their relationship with professors as one in which professors contract to reward performance in predictable ways. They devote much effort to discovering the terms of the contract and to trying to hold up their end of it, as they understand it, by appropriate academic performance.

Students decide what the terms of the contract are by observing and interpreting the words and actions of the teacher as the semester goes on. A class, for them, is not a series of isolated encounters, but rather a connected sequence of events extending over four and a half months. During that period, they engage in two simultaneous enterprises. They search for cues that, properly interpreted, will yield an understanding of what the teacher will demand in return for a given grade. At the same time, they attempt to do the things they have decided are important to get the grade they want.

Students infer the terms of the contract, in part, from the professor's general statement of what is required. He (or his assistants) may, at the beginning of the course, explain the number and kind of examinations and outside assignments required, the kind of response required in the classroom, and the contribution of each to the final grade. Some professors give little information, perhaps from laziness or forgetfulness or because they find the whole matter distasteful.

As the semester goes on, the professor's actions furnish further cues. He may praise some kinds of classroom activity and punish (if only with ridicule) others. Some students get better grades on an assignment or test than others, and students compare high-scoring papers with their own to see what kind of answers the professor prefers. When he "goes over" the test or paper in class, he may reveal further what he regards as an acceptable or superior performance. He may, for instance, explain why he will accept one answer to a question as correct but not another, and thus give the students information from which to deduce what he will accept on future examinations. All these actions give specificity to the general statements he has already made and thus define the terms of the contract more precisely.

If neither the words nor the actions of the professor or his assistants give sufficient information, students may find out the terms of the contract by interrogating other students about how the professor has acted in the past or how professors like him (others of the same rank, perhaps, or members of the same department) typically act. As we shall see later, searching for this kind of information is a common expression of the GPA perspective.

The power to define the terms of the contract lies largely in the instructor's hands. Students may argue over them or, in extreme cases, complain to a department head or dean. But they understand that, although they may make the instructor uncomfortable, they have no formal means of influencing the standards he sets for their performance. It is in such ways that the abstract idea of subjection occurs as a concrete reality in the student's daily life.

Students also believe (and their experience justifies the belief) that instructors vary greatly in the number and kind of demands they make for academic performance. Students therefore never assume that they know with certainty what an instructor wants of them; they suspect instead that every class will be different and that they can only be certain of what is expected after they have amassed a great deal of evidence, if at all.

However the terms of the contract are arrived at and communicated, the important point is that students define it as an agreement that is binding (insofar as its terms are clearly known) on the professor as well as on them: they expect him to recognize its binding character. Should he, in their view, fail to live up to his end of the bargain by ignoring or changing any provisions of the agreement, they will be angry and upset. Since they often "construct" the terms of the agreement out of an analysis of what may be offhand remarks by the instructor, he may be quite unaware that such a binding commitment has been attributed to him and may well violate it unintentionally. Indeed, he would probably refuse to agree to its terms in the first place if the bargaining were more explicit.[1]

Faculty typically have a quite different view of their bargain with students, though it too is implicit, seldom communicated directly to students. In their view, students either do or do not have the ability to learn what is being taught (however that ability is conceived or measured). Those who do not have the ability must be written off as hopeless, but (because of entrance requirements) they are presumably a small number. Among the able students, however, some do not do as well as their ability would permit because they are insufficiently "interested" or "motivated." Here is the faculty's version of the classroom bargain: every student who can do the work should be interested enough to do so and to want to do so.

In taking this view, faculty fail to give sufficient weight to the pull of other interests. They do not see, for instance, that the student may not be able to afford any more interest in their course because he needs to devote time and effort to another course that is giving him more trouble. They see even less that the student feels he may not be able to afford any further interest because he thinks that other rewards available in organizational activity and personal relationships are equally important and that academic rewards must be balanced against that competition. They do not understand, in short, that from the student's point of view true maturity consists in striking that balance in a reasonable way.

It is probably incorrect to say, as we just have, that faculty do not know these things. We could put it more precisely by saying that what they do not see is the legitimacy students accord to this competition to the interest their course should generate, the legitimacy that arises from its grounding in the students' view of maturity. In this sense, they do not understand that able students do not feel free to strike the kind of bargain faculty members propose, for to do so would be immature and unbalanced. It is likely that students willing to make such a bargain are, from the student point of view, unbalanced, for they would be students who had no other interests, who were insensitive to the attraction of other worthwhile activities possible on campus.

*   *   *

Alternative Views of the Teacher-Student Relation

We recognize that to view classes and academic work as a matter of exchange and contract, as we have in this chapter, will be considered by most educators as crass and belittling. To think of course work and the intellectual interchange of the classroom simply as the environmental context of grade-getting seems to slight the true functions of a college. Though few will deny that interaction between students and faculty has something of the economic character we have ascribed to it, few will willingly accept this as the major aspect of classroom interaction and accordingly will find students unreasonable or immature if they give it their first attention. Let us consider briefly two alternative views of the student-faculty relation commonly held by teachers and indicate why we find them inadequate.[2]

One view sees the relation of the student to his courses as one in which information and skills are transmitted to the student. He comes to class and is presented with certain materials. Readings and exercises help him to acquire the appropriate information and skills; assignments and examinations test whether he has in fact acquired what he is supposed to have acquired. This view assumes that what the instructor would like the student to learn is what the course requires him to learn. If that is true, the course requires the student to acquire information in order to get a good grade.

But things do not quite work that way. Very frequently, the assignments and requirements attached to a given course do not require the student to learn the information and skills that the instructor wishes him to learn, but rather another set of skills more closely related to the examinations and assignments actually given. Faculty members often complain that, even though their students get good enough grades on examinations, they have not really learned whatever it is the faculty member wants them to know. The difficulty is that of constructing examinations that will truly test what they are supposed to test. The English professor may want his students to acquire the ability to enjoy and analyze literature; but his examination requires them to learn names and dates. The mathematics professor may want his students to grasp and be able to use certain difficult mathematical concepts; but his examination requires them only to be able to solve certain kinds of problems, whether they understand the concepts or not. In short, even where instructors desire only to transmit information or skills to the student, the mission may not be accomplished because the instructor's actions (particularly his examinations), as the student interprets them, do not require the accumulation of the information he wants the student to have. Rather, the student may be forced by the situation, as he defines it, to learn something different in order to pass the examination and get a good grade.

Furthermore, as we have already noted, though faculty members think that all students able to do the work ought properly to be interested enough to do so, students feel that they must balance the demands of any one course against those of other courses and balance as well the demands of academic work against those emanating from other areas of college life. The student does not see his task simply as learning what he is supposed to learn, but as doing that in a context of competing demands he considers equally valid.

The second school of thought has a more ambitious view, seeing the true and important function of education as the transmission of values. In this view, information is not important; rather, the teacher wants to transform the student's way of looking at the world and judging it. In a slightly different form, the teacher asks that the student develop his personality while he is in college. The educational experience—both in the classroom and outside of it—provides an opportunity for the student to learn to know himself better and to deal with himself and the world more adequately. In this view, the student must experience an unfolding of his personality, a liberation from conventional forms of thought, if he is to have gained anything from his college experience.

Insofar as this point of view states an ideal, we have no quarrel with it here (although, it may be said, this is no simple question). However, if it supposes that students really do acquire new values or experience an unfolding of their personalities as a consequence of their academic work, it is probably incorrect and certainly ignores the effect of course work as a constraint that must be satisfactorily dealt with if one is to do well in college.

Evidence that classes are not primarily forums in which opinions are exchanged and values shaped can be found in the many studies of the effect of course work on student attitudes. Both the Jacob report[3] and the review of the relevant literature by McKeachie[4] show that classwork in college tends to have little if any effect on student attitudes and values. Furthermore, varying methods of teaching also have little effect. This makes the proposition that students are deeply influenced by their course work less credible than it might otherwise be.

The proposition suffers a more serious setback when we consider the conditions under which students take courses. The theory assumes that students wander through the university freely, taking those courses to which they are drawn by their own needs and state of maturation. The student searches out those things he is psychologically ready for and, having been exposed to them, has experiences that powerfully affect his view of himself and the world.

Such a picture of the student is grossly in error. Students do not wander around freely picking and choosing among courses. On the contrary, in most colleges their choice of courses is severely restricted by the distribution requirements for all undergraduates and by the particular requirements for various majors. To graduate from the College of Liberal Arts and Sciences of the University of Kansas, a student must accumulate 124 credit hours. Of these, it is likely that three quarters or more will be prescribed in such a fashion that they cannot be freely chosen by the student. Thus a student majoring in English will have thirty-three credit hours available for courses that can be chosen without restrictions of any kind. But this is a very generous department. In physics, there are twenty-six elective credits possible, but all of these are subject to various restrictions, since the department directs that they must be chosen from among certain courses, most of them in the natural sciences. Many other departments similarly restrict the way elective credits can be used by suggesting lists of courses from which a major in their department should choose.

Bright students may have even less freedom to choose because they can, if they wish, take double and even triple majors. This exposes them to the demands of more than one department, so that their freedom to choose courses purely on the basis of their interest in them is even smaller than that of the average student. (A few students can get permission to take unusual combinations of courses for a major essentially of their own creation. But this is uncommon.) A student who wished to go where his need for new experience led him would probably have to take many extra courses to satisfy the requirements of the college and the department in which he eventually graduated.

The view that interaction between teacher and student affects students' values and personalities fails, finally, to give sufficient weight to the organizational context within which that interaction takes place. As we have seen, the system of grades and credits provides an institutional framework that instructors can use to reward those who learn to meet academic requirements and punish those who do not. Because the GPA is a relatively objective means of distributing sanctions and because the effect of the sanctions extends into so many other arenas of campus life, students can easily define it as the chief mark of academic success and consider striving for grades by attempting to meet academic requirements as the most appropriate course of action to pursue in their dealings with instructors.

But proponents of the view we are criticizing do not believe that important changes in students can be brought about through the use of external rewards, for the rewards that lead to personality and value change are presumed to be private and personal, unconnected with any immediate social profit. If they use sanctions at all in their effort to promote personal growth in students, they are likely to make use of such devices as shaming students who do not express ideas or opinions they consider desirable. But such devices, and the ends they are designed to promote, are personal and idiosyncratic, not tied in to any campus-wide system of reward. Thus they cannot be expected to have the desired effect on students' perspectives. A student may dislike being shamed in class, but the discomfort exists only in that class and has no effect on any of his concerns or activities beyond it.

We do not argue that nothing goes on in college classes beyond the exchange of the proper performance for a grade. But we do emphasize that the exchange of performance for grades is, formally and institutionally, what the class is about. Changes in personality or values may indeed take place, but they are not directly affected by the institutionalized system of value and reward. This no doubt accounts for the hostility that partisans of personality change in college generally display toward grading systems.

NOTES

1. Similar student conceptions are described in Carl Werthman, "Delinquents in Schools: A Test for the Legitimacy of Authority," *Berkeley Journal of Sociology*, 8 (1963), pp. 39-60; and Howard S. Becker, Blanche Geer, Everett C. Hughes, and Anselm L. Strauss, *Boys in White: Student Culture in Medical School* (Chicago: University of Chicago Press, 1961), pp. 158-187.

2. For a discussion of models of the student-teacher relationship, see Blanche Geer, "Teaching," *International Encyclopedia of Social Sciences,* Vol. 15, pp. 560-565.

3. P. E. Jacob, *Changing Values in College* (New York: Harper Bros., 1957).

4. W. J. McKeachie, "Procedures and Techniques of Teaching: A Survey of Experimental Studies," in Nevitt Sanford, ed., *The American College* (New York: John Wiley & Sons, 1962), pp. 312-364.

Howard Becker

There are other, equally covert, ways in which teachers unknowingly transmit messages that students easily pick up. Most teachers fresh from departments and schools of education have little idea of the conscious and unconscious attitudes they express when they go into the classroom. Only recently have we begun to acquire systematic data that begins to lift the veil on this aspect of the hidden curriculum. A widely publicized study about the effects of teacher expectations on students by Robert Rosenthal and Lenore Jacobson appeared in 1968 under the title *Pygamalion in the Classroom.*[3] The central idea of the book, according to the authors, was that "one person's expectation for another's behavior could come to serve as a self-fulfilling prophecy."

Rosenthal and Jacobson gave each of eighteen teachers of grades one through six, in a public elementary school in a lower class community of a medium-sized city, the names of those children who, in the academic year ahead, would show dramatic intellectual growth. These predictions were allegedly based on test scores. But for each classroom the names of these special children had actually been chosen by a table of random numbers. The difference between the special and the ordinary children was thus only in the "mind" of the teacher. When the children were retested, it was found that "a significant expectancy advantage was found" for the "special" children in the first and second grades. The authors summarized their speculation as to why this happened in the following manner:

> ... we may say that by what she said, by how and when she said it, by her facial expressions, postures, and perhaps by her touch, the teacher may have communicated to the children of the experimental ["special"] group that she expected improved intellectual performance. Such communications together with possible changes in teaching techniques may have helped the child learn by changing his self-concept, his expectations of his own behavior, and his motivation, as well as his cognitive style and skills.[4]

And their conclusion was:

> As teacher-training institutions begin to teach the possibility that teachers' expectations of their pupils' performance may serve as self-fulfilling prophecies, there may be a new expectancy created. The new expectancy may be that children can learn more than had been believed possible, an expectation held by many educational theorists, though for quite different reasons (for example, Bruner, 1960). The new expectancy, at the very least, will make it more difficult when they encounter the educationally disadvantaged for teachers to think 'Well, after all, what can you expect?' ... The teacher

3. R. Rosenthal and L. Jacobson. *Pygmalion in the Classroom.* (New York: Holt, Rinehart & Winston, 1968).

4. Ibid, p. 115.

in the schoolroom may need to learn that those same prophecies within her may be fulfilled; she is no casual passer-by. Perhaps Pygmalion in the classroom is more her role.[5]

Shortly after the appearance of this study, Norma D. Feshbach published her findings on the values that teachers place on particular personality characteristics of the child. Professor Feshbach was interested in discovering whether prospective teachers show consistent preferences for particular kinds of pupils. While admitting that her study was confined to teachers in training, and thus did not say how more experienced teachers with more self-knowledge might respond in the classroom to their students, Feshbach found:

> . . . striking support for the hypothesis that student teachers prefer pupils whose behavior reflects rigidity, conformity, and orderliness or dependency, passivity, and acquiescence than pupils whose behavior is indicative of flexibility, nonconformity, and untidiness or independence, activity, and assertiveness . . . In general, it appears that student teachers perceive most positively the rigid, conforming girl and secondly, the rigid, conforming boy. The third position in the preference order is occupied by the dependent, passive girl who is closely followed by her male counterpart. The flexible boy is fifth in the ordering while the flexible girl and the independent boy vie for sixth and seventh positions. The lowest ratings are given to the independent assertive girl.[6]

Feshback found that the consistency of the ratings and the projective nature of the judgments made by these prospective teachers suggested that their judgments were primarily based on their personal attitudes and values, rather than facts about the students they were asked to evaluate. The picture that emerged from her study of the type of child that these teachers would most prefer is:

> . . . one whose behavior will facilitate expedient classroom management perhaps at the cost of other educational objectives such as spontaneity and creative problem solving . . . the pupil attributes which student teachers prefer appear to be consistent with the attributes which characterize teachers as a group.[7]

It is apparent that there is a lot more being learned in school than the academic instruction formally recognized as the main concern of the schools. There is a vast hidden curriculum consisting of behavioral norms, values, attitudes, self-conceptualizations and subcultural, informal codes and modes of interaction, all of which has a much greater impact on the lives of students than their academic instruction. The hidden curriculum involves students in the broader perspective of learning how to cope with the institutional environment, its rules (dress codes, attendance requirements), demands (neatness, testing, correct answers, papers and forms, grades), and its perceived intentions (basic economic and political lessons). In communications theory, this is called "noise," all the random fluctuations of the system which cannot be considered part of the

---

5. Ibid, p. 117.
6. Norma Feshbach, "Personality Preferences for Elementary School Pupils Varying in Personality Characteristics," *Journal of Educational Psychology*, 60, 1969, pp. 126-132.
7. Ibid, p. 83.

formal message. Good behavior and good character have thus become more important than good scholarship.

Some sociologists have pointed out that the credentialing processes in our society—whether of teachers, policemen, or any other credentialed people—ingeniously and covertly assure that these unacknowledged but nonetheless understood restraints and expectations will be internalized by the holder of the credential. It is understood, but not fully acknowledged, for example, that a teacher will avoid controversial material, or at best handle it at a distance and with kid gloves. A teacher's personal behavior must be beyond reproach, inside and outside the classroom. Teachers who are caught teaching, Friedenberg says, are usually in trouble. Thus, when Stanley Lindros read a theme to his English class at South High School in Torrance, California, which contained "controversial language," specifically "white-mother-fuckin pig," his board refused to rehire him. At the request of his students, Lindros read a story he had written about his experiences at the funeral of one of his black students in Watts, as an example in connection with assigning them the task of preparing a short story relating to a personal emotional experience. But his board found this language "coarse and vulgar" and "totally unacceptable in a tenth-grade English class." Lindros had to go all the way to the California Supreme Court in order to get his job back.[8] Clearly, educational intentions are secondary in the schools to the unwritten, unacknowledged, but understood rules of conduct.

But of all the morals and values which make up the hidden curriculum, its most salient features are the myths and rituals of production and consumption. These are, Ivan Illich says,

> . . . grounded in the belief that process inevitably produces something of value and, therefore, production necessarily produces demand. School teaches us that instruction produces learning. The existence of school produces the demand for schooling.[9]

Students are taught that if they attend school they will learn. The more time they put into it, the more they learn. The amount of learning is measured and documented by grades and certificates. Teacher and pupil become distributor and consumer. The curriculum is a

> . . . bundle of goods made according to the same process and having the same structure as other merchandise . . . a bundle of planned meanings, a package of values, a commodity whose "balanced appeal" makes it marketable to a sufficiently large number to justify the cost of production. Consumer-pupils are taught to make their desires conform to marketable values. Thus, they are made to feel guilty if they do not behave according to the predictions of consumer research by getting the grades and certificates that will place them in the job category they have been led to expect.[10]

Each subject in the curriculum comes packaged with the instruction to go on consuming one offering after another. This unlimited quantitative increase

8. *Stanley M. Lindros v. Governing Board of the Torrance Unified School District,* 9C.3d 524, Cal. Rptr., P. 2d, pp. 524-545.
9. Ivan Illich. *Deschooling Society.* (New York: Harper & Row, 1972), p. 38.
10. Ibid, p. 41.

impedes organic development. There is a well-established ritual process through which the school initiates and shapes young people to conform to a life style of consumption, and which makes the progressive consumer the economy's most important resource.

Our authors have been saying that as the institution is presently organized, school is intended to socialize young people to be motivationally oriented and technically competent to perform future adult roles. Do young people themselves have the same definition of the situation that adults do, or is their view of it different? How have students responded to the school setting, to the attempts of the school to carry out all of these functions mandated by the adult society?

Several empirical studies have been done on schools, not just as formal organizations but as small societies in themselves. The more notable of these studies were C. Wayne Gordon's *The Social System of the High School*,[11] James Coleman's *The Adolescent Society*,[12] and Willard Waller's *The Sociology of Teaching*.[13] These studies show that within the school's institutional setting, small groups or subcultures arise with conflicting aims and perspectives, such as the solitary teacher group on the one hand and the student society on the other.

These studies found that the dominant or major orientations of high school students were nonacademic and extracurricular. Peer norms regarding success in dating, athletics, and dress for the boys, and peer norms regarding dress, looks, personality and extracurricular activities for the girls were considered by students as being much more important than the school's scholastic goals. The normative basis and value scheme of the student social structure were found to be in direct opposition to and alienated from the school's formal expectations.

Two kinds of analyses of this conflict have emerged. One has been a proposal to promote recognition of scholastic achievement, thus channeling the responses of students back toward the traditionally accepted goals of the school. James Coleman noted that the outstanding student in formal academic terms had little or no way to bring glory to his school (in the way athletes do): thus, his achievements gained little reward, and were often met by ridiculing remarks from his peers, such as "curve raiser" or "grind." Colman proposed that:

> . . . rather straightforward social theory could be used in organizing the activities of high schools in such a way that their adolescent subcultures would encourage, rather than discourage, the channeling of energies into directions of learning.[14]

Coleman goes on to speculate on the effects of "scholastic fairs" composed of academic games and tournaments between schools. There could also be international fairs, a sort of "Scholastic Olympics," which, in his terms, would "generate interscholastic games and tournaments within the participating countries." In short, don't change the institution or its expectations; change and shape the student subculture. (The conceptualizations of these researchers are quite different from Joel Spring's earlier interpretation of the function of extracurricular activities.)

11. C. Wayne Gordon. *The Social System of the High School*. (Glencoe, Ill.: Free Press, 1957).

12. James Coleman. *The Adolescent Society*. (Glencoe, Ill.: Free Press, 1961).

13. Willard Waller. *The Sociology of Teaching*. (New York: John Wiley & Sons, 1932).

14. Coleman, *The Adolescent Society*, p. 16.

An alternative view has been to see students' reactions as indicative of fundamental problems with the educational structure itself.

The adolescent school society in the '50s and early '60s was studied and characterized around the dualistic polarities of academic and nonacademic norms, with the academic norms having a predetermined, preassumed superiority. The categories and typologies were defined by the investigators, not by the students being studied. Thus, the answers arrived at were shaped by the questions being asked, and the questions being asked were shaped by the nature of the answers desired.[15] The results may not have described the students at all, how they defined themselves, the kinds of questions they were asking and answering. But the results may have described how members of the adult world defined a student society. As such, they were descriptions of the dominant culture and not the subculture itself. Researchers into high school society could perhaps have organized their investigations and analyses much differently, for in the 1950s the foundations for the formation of goals antithetical to those of the schools were being laid.

Beginning in the mid-1960s with the Free Speech Movement in Berkeley growing out of the Civil Rights Movement in the South, extending to campus sit-ins, demonstrations, and riots a few years later, members of the student subculture began to be heard. They conceptualized their experience in strikingly different tones and terms from the academics, responding to the larger political and social environment from which they had come. They had begun to discover, and uncover, the replication of society's ills and weaknesses inside their schools.

The resulting new awareness, of hypocrisy and the powers of force and ideology acting upon them, of their own powerlessness and lack of control over their destinies, of the loss of communal sense, the void of deep emotional relationships, the lack of openness and sensitivity, and their insistence on the right to autonomy—all generated expressions of outrage against the system, of resentment and renunciation of all that the system held dear, including its proprieties of speech.

In his book, *Do It!,* Jerry Rubin spoke for the disenchanted students:

Schools—high schools and colleges—are the biggest obstacle to education in Amerika today.

Schools are a continuation of toilet training.

Taking an exam is just like taking a shit. You hold it in for weeks, memorizing, just waiting for the right time. Then the time comes and you sit on the toilet.

Ah!

Um!

It feels so good.

You shit it right back on schedule—for the grade. When exams are over, you got a load off your mind. You got rid of the shit you clogged you poor brain with. You can finally relax.

The paper you write your exam on is toilet paper.

Babies are zen masters, curious about everything.

15. J. Pearce. *The Crack in the Cosmic Egg.* (New York: The Julian Press, 1971), p. 61.

Adults are serious and bored.

What happened?

Brain surgery by the schools.[16]

The concerns and actions of the Free Speech Movement at Berkeley were by no means confined to that campus. This was the beginning of a new student activism, the likes of which had never been seen before in American colleges and universities. This activism was fed by: 1) growing revulsion toward the war in Viet Nam; 2) the failure of minority groups and the poor to gain redress of their grievances; 3) a growing disparity in wealth and well-being among groups in American society; 4) the unresponsiveness of colleges and universities to student demands; and 5) a new sense or a new analysis of the role education played in American society. At Columbia University, activism came to a head in the spring of 1968 when that university was forced by some of its students to face the consequences of its involvement in the larger community, and discovered how woefully unprepared it was to do this.

We turn now from an analysis of student thought and grievances to a further investigation of the educational structure itself. Still another aspect of the hidden curriculum in our schools is the textbook. Textbooks are an important means by which society carries on the socialization process. The messages which readers and texts give to schoolchildren have both a manifest and a latent function. While the narratives perform their task of increasing comprehension and understanding and of building vocabulary, the underlying message says, "This is what you should be like."

Because these books are paid for by the state and made compulsory reading for every classroom, their contents carries official approval. The production of textbooks for public schools is a multimillion dollar business. A lot is at stake for authors and publishers when a state department of education considers books for adoption. Authors and publishers have sometimes gone to great lengths to tailor their texts to the expectations of education departments and school boards. The recent controversy over the inclusion of the Biblical story of creation along-side the evolutionary account of it in science texts for the California schools is a case in point.

Children's readers bear little relation to the real world that we live in. That is the conclusion of most authors who have been taking a critical look at school texts. There are no ideological conflicts, no negative feelings, no deep social relationships or strong emotions expressed in these readers. The public school readers have been likened to bland pablum, designed to spoon-feed readers. Only one world view and one life style are presented. Alternative life styles, alternative modes of thought, alternative cultures (except from an ethnocentric point of view) are omitted. Recent criticism has stressed that the readers are also gross perpetrators of sexual as well as racial stereotyping.

Virginia Kidd examined the Harper & Row Basic Reading Program for first graders, adopted in 1969 by the State of California.[17] It was Dick and Jane of

16. Jerry Rubin. *Do It!*. (New York: Simon & Schuster, 1970), pp. 11-12.

17. As a result of direct intervention by school board members in the selection of a text on human sexuality, overriding the recommendations of the experts designated by the board to review the text, quite significant changes were made in a text before it was finally adopted by the California Board of Education. Subsequent reports indicated that few

the Scott Foresman[18] readers all over again. In this case it is Janet and Mark who:

> . . . never talk about school, paint pictures, take music lessons, write verse or wonder about a God. There are no crises; their parents do not divorce, their grandmother does not move in, they do not wear glasses, their dog never gets pregnant, they're never embarrassed or ashamed . . . They learn to behave in this way from their parents who never quarrel, espouse political ideals, engage in artistic activities, hire babysitters, get sick, display mutual affection, or—most depressing of all—speak to each other . . . Mother's chief occupation . . . is washing dishes, cooking, sewing, ironing, and wearing aprons . . . Daddy's chief occupation is coming home. Daddy is never seen wiping away Janet's tears or helping Mark clean his room; he plays ball with Mark. Mother never goes to work or drives the car; she helps Janet make a cake . . . Janet is never a potential artist, senator, scientiest. Mark never will be an actor, professor, gourmet.[19]

And . . . "Janet and Mark are inveterate consumers."

In these and other ways, school textbooks support the sexist policies of our white male-dominated society, primarily by channeling women (as they channel the poor) into occupations of lesser esteem which, therefore, offer low pay or no pay. Women are socialized to expect, and encouraged to pursue, a limited number of roles, including mother, wife, cook, housekeeper, seamstress, decorator. Outside the home women are cast in roles such as secretary, dental assistant, nurse, waitress, and teacher. According to the textbooks, there are no female lawyers, doctors, engineers, sociologists, psychiatrists, economists, business executives, athletes, architects, dentists, or politicians.

The schools, as agencies responsible for the socialization of the young into their proper roles, have attempted to carry out society's mandate. Textbooks, as already mentioned, play an important part in this effort. Teachers' expectations and the assignment of different tasks for boys and girls also plays a part. History, for example, is taught with very little discussion of the part played by women, except for the possible mention of a President's first lady and the gowns she wore, or the presentation of a picture of Betsy Ross, seamstress, sewing the flag.

An impressive documentation of this is found in the following reading.

---

school districts in the state had indicated they wanted to use the text. But it is not known whether this was a reaction to the Board's extensive excisions.

18. Virginia Kidd, "Now you See, said Mark," *This Magazine is About Schools,* Vol. 5, No. 3, Summer, 1971.

19. Ibid, pp. 59-61.

DICK AND JANE AS VICTIMS

Women on Words and Images

*   *   *

SECTION V: SUMMARY

One of the prime functions of literature and poetry is to make some sense out of the chaos in which human being live. But readers consistently duck the real issues confronting young lives. Little girls (and boys) seldom have to face grizzly bears or wolves these days. But females frequently have to overcome ridicule and discouragement over gender prejudice. The readers give girls even more to overcome by constantly belittling them.

And what are the subjects so visibly absent from these books?

Challenges and Conflicts. Absent from the readers are fathers and mothers backing their children in their quest for selfhood. Missing are fathers complimenting their daughters on their intelligence and perserverance, rather than their looks. Absent are family moments of mutual appreciation, of love between parents, and nonromantic affection between people. Glossed over are the inner and outer conflicts and moments of indecision that are inevitably part of the human condition. Ignored are one-parent families, adopted children, divorced and/or fighting parents. Missing are *realistic* stories about how to make friends in a new situation. Silent are the readers about the facts that some people remain poor and hungry and that everyone has to cope with aging. Even the wisdom and peace that can come with old age is barely alluded to.

Girls Do Not Excel. Girls are not even shown excelling in school work, something they actually do better than boys. The supposedly fragile male ego is often protected in this way at the expense of girls. The readers present a twisted view that happiness for girls lies chiefly in giving happiness to boys and men. Success, excitement, confidence, and status must be derived from association with the "powerful" sex. Even the real world, prejudiced as it is, allows girls more scope than this. In the readers, girls must take on every trait left over after boys are assigned theirs. Girls are innundated with messages that boys are doers and that girls must stand back passively if they are to remain feminine. Nothing in the readers encourages girls to persevere to complete a lengthy task from beginning to end or to tackle something difficult. Short, mindless tasks like daily domestic work do not lead to future growth or fullfillment.

Boys are Multidimensional. Boys get a potent message that they are superior human beings above household chores. They learn through countless "rites of passage" stories that they will one day become the sex upon whom the workings of the world depend. No comparable attempt is made to build up the expecta-

"Dick and Jane as Victims" in *Women on Words and Images* (Princeton, N.J., 1972), pp. 30-39. Full version available from *Women on Words and Images,* P. O. Box 2163, Princeton, N.J., 08540, for $2.00.

tions of girls, to create esteem and optimism about their future possibilities. Boys are given a perfectionistic model of the multidimensional human being. Not everybody, not even all males can be superheroes. Ironically, intermixed with the stories of hard work and use of skills are Walter Mitty and dreams-of-glory tales with magical solutions and happy windfalls. To be a boy is to be one of the lucky breed. The readers contain a stronger taboo against boys being dependent (sissies!) at *any* age than they do against *young* girls breaking out of their mold (tomboys) a little bit. Girls must abruptly rout out the so-called masculine component of themselves when they become teenagers, but boys must never give away to the so-called feminine component. This is partly carried out as we noted, by showing boys of all ages alone and away from home, courageously coping with anything that comes along. They never cry; they need no one.

Man Over Nature. There are numerous stories about men or boys subduing or conquering nature. Little is said about learning to appreciate and protect the natural environment. In a multitude of stories, males bend nature to their wills. Yet it is clear, in this new age of environmental awareness, that men and women will have to learn to live in harmony with nature rather than run roughshod over it. Can our young conquerers be re-directed once they gain maturity?

Sexism, No Respecter of Race. Indians are the race we meet most often in these stories and the readers are very ambivalent about them. Now they are courageous, marvelously skilled at meeting the challenges of the wild, and the friend of the white man. Now they are irrational, treacherous, and enemy of the white man. The terms "good Indian" and "bad Indian" are used here exclusively in the sense of what's good or bad for the white settlers, who only once in all these stories go on trial—speaking figuratively—for *their* treatment of the Indians.

But there is no ambiguity about who is the bravest sex of all. Indian males are as achievement-oriented as any palefaced male. The Indian girl, no matter how resourceful or courageous, is no better off than the rest of her sex, and when she is not changed into a shadow for trying to break out of the mold, as in one symbolic story referred to earlier in this chapter, she is subjected to similar subtle propaganda mechanisms that turn her into a domestic, condemned to live in the shadow of other people's lives. Eskimo girls don't fare any better. They are sealed up in their igloos turning hides into clothing, while the men roam the wilds with their reindeer herds or pan for gold.

After an almost total absence of blacks before the mid 1960s, an accelerated effort has been made in primers and pre-primers to integrate the lives of black and white children. They are often seen playing together in their integrated neighborhoods and schools. When blacks play an active role, it is, unsurprisingly, the male who leads; black girls along with their mothers and white sisters, are used as scenery. Only 9 blacks out of 108 biographical subjects are found in the readers—a shocking fact in the second decade of the Civil Rights Revolution.

Chinese-Americans, though statistically fewer, fare better as a group. They suffer little overt prejudice but the same sex role patterns prevail in their families. In one notable story an old grandmother's precious stone from the old country is saved by a girl so that her *brother* can go to school. As you would expect, traditional sex roles are strongly supported in stories about Mexican-Americans, along with the mystique of *machismo*.

Life in other cultures and/or in other times—Norwegian, Swiss, Hungarian, Russian, Arabian, African, Japanese, Aztec, the Middle Ages, (but notably *not* Jewish life, during Biblical days, the Diaspora, or any other time) are touched on by the readers in some of their infinite varieties. But whatever country or century is being described, when it comes to sex role stereotyping, you'll find tucked away in those faraway places and times the same old sexist plots.

Subliminal Messages. Dr. Edward Hall, in *The Silent Language*[2] finds that children are indeed assimilating the content and values of their books as they learn to read, without giving it any conscious thought. Watson and Hartley both find that by the age of eight, ninety-nine percent agreement is found among children of both sexes as to which sex does which job, what kind of person a girl or boy should be and what the role limitations and expectations are.[3] School readers must assume their responsibility in directing the subliminal learning process toward more psychologically constructive ends.

NOTES

1. As this study was going to print, the reader *I DO, DARE, AND DREAM,* (ed. John M. Franco et. al, American Book Company, Litton Educational Publishers Inc., 1970) was called to our attention as a good example of the new reader designed for Inner City use. Aside from a story about a black cowboy, the settings are urban and problems of race and environment are faced with candor and honesty. Photographs of children of many hues are excellent. But the sexism, especially in the pictures, is even worse than in the earlier readers! Overall there are six stories about girls and one biography of a woman, but nineteen stories about boys and four biographies of men. In one story about girls the stress is on a sick Papa; in a second the girl is a hostess for boys; in the third the girl narrator describes a man-run community center; and in the fourth girls babysit and coo over the accomplishments of two little boys. This reader is obviously intended as a boy's book and is a good example of aggravating one wrong in the attempt to correct another.

2. Greenwich, Conn., Fawcett Publishers, 1959.

3. Ruth Hartley, "Sex Role Pressures and the Socialization of the Male Child," *Psychological Reports* V.457, 1959, p. 268. Goodwin Watson, "Psychological Aspects of Sex Roles", *Social Psychology: Issues and Insights,* 1966, p. 427.

CHAPTER FIVE: IMPLICATIONS

There are broad social implications in the use of sex role stereotypes which are seldom considered in connection with the readers.

Children are exposed to conventional sex stereotypes long before they learn to read. The attitudes shown by friends and family, television and books are among the influences which have already begun the process of socialization. School readers have a special place in this process. They convey official approval. In many states, they have to be approved by state officials since they are bought with state money. They are used in state public schools which are attended under state compulsion until a certain age is reached. They are presented to children within a context of authority, in the classroom. Finally, every child must read them. Through the readers, society says, "This is what we would like you to be."

This expectation is presented to children at a time when most of them have not yet attained a critical perspective on themselves and their backgrounds. The official version cannot help but become the norm in childish vision. Dr. Naomi Weisstein in an article entitled "Kinder, Kuche and Kirche as Scientific Law: Psychology Constructs the Female"[1], describes numerous experiments in which both humans and animals, without outside coercion, were forced by the experimenters' expectations alone to behave in prescribed ways even when their natural abilities, desires, and moral standards would have urged otherwise. In the most shocking of these experiments, 62.5 percent of the adult subjects administered what they thought were lethal electric shocks to uncooperative "students" who acted as if they were in great pain as the shocks increased. The bizarre behavior of these subjects was apparently motivated solely by the pressure of the experimenter's demand for cooperation.[2] If adults are so vulnerable to the power of other people's expectations, how much more vulnerable must young children be!

The pressure of official expectations has a different impact on those children coming from backgrounds which differ sharply from the "approved". They are left with three choices—condemnation of themselves and their families for being atypical or abnormal, a forced conformity to societal norms, or rejection of a society to which they can never fully belong. For these children and for those who realize that the norms are unrealistic and the ideas harmful, exposure to readers can be an introduction to general disaffection with "official" American culture.

Clearly role models of one kind of another must be used in the process of socialization. For example, Margaret Mead in *Male and Female,*[3] and Eric Erikson in *Childhood and Society*[4] have shown clearly that all societies use role models to encourage self-development of their children as individuals and functioning members of the group. But when the role models remain static while society changes, they lose their value as educational devices and become instead psychological straight-jackets which constrict individual development and preparation for life. When the models deliberately build up the self-images of one group at the expense of another, they become viciously repressive. In America such practices are particularly inappropriate to the principles upon which this society supposedly was founded, and to which it still gives at least lip service. If socialization has twin goals, to rear fit individuals as well as individuals who fit, the models presented in school readers can be faulted on both counts.

Psychologists who are women are now beginning to call attention to the great damage done to both men and women by our narrowly defined role models. In a statement to the American Psychological Association in September, 1970, the Association of Women Psychologists said:

> Psychological oppression in the form of sex role socialization clearly conveys to girls from the earliest ages that their nature is to be submissive, servile, and repressed, and their role is to be servant, admirer, sex object and martyr ... the psychological consequences of goal depression in young women— the negative self-image, emotional dependence, drugged or alcoholic escape— are all too common. In addition, both men and women have come to realize the effects on men of this type of sex role stereotyping, the crippling pressure to compete, to achieve, to produce, to stifle emotion, sensitivity and gentleness, all taking their toll in psychic and physical traumas.[5]

The practice of separating all people into two arbitrarily defined molds on the basis of sex alone is the Procrustean bed of modern life. Those who do not fit are either stretched out or chopped up. We streatch our sons to fill the ideal dominant male role and fragment our daughters' personalities to make them fit the servile female role. Both processes do violence to the individual. Each damaged person depletes the human resources of the whole society. How many damaged individuals can we afford?

The society into which our children will be expected to fit is very different from that presented by the readers. In a lecture at the Princeton Adult School on October 16, 1970, Dr. Suzanne Keller, a professor of sociology at Princeton University, outlined the rapid changes which are reshaping the roles our daughters can expect to fill as adults.[6] Briefly, they can look forward to biological developments which may make family planning safer and more reliable, giving women much greater control over their own lives. They can also expect population pressures to result in small families. According to present trends, children will be born to younger parents and they will be spaced more closely together, thus giving women several decades of post-parenthood freedom in which to follow their own pursuits.

More women will find themselves on their own, either by choice or through divorce or early widowhood. The *New York Times* of Sunday, January 31, 1971, states that latest census figures show a forty-three percent increase in single adult households in the last ten years. More than half of these are headed by women.[7] Thus more women will be driven into the job market by financial or personal needs. Already forty-eight percent of women between eighteen and sixty-four years of age are working. This percentage increases every year.[8]

The high failure rate of modern marriages, which is now one in four according to *Time,* December 28, 1970,[9] will probably continue or accelerate and will produce a correspondingly expanded search for alternative living patterns, both within the context of marriage and outside it. "The trouble comes from the fact that the institution we call marriage cannot hold two full human beings— it was designed for one and a half. . ." says Cornell Political Scientist Andrew Hacker.[10] Despite our conditioning, fewer and fewer women are accepting this "half" status.

Whether or not we like these trends, we must prepare our daughters and sons to deal with them. We cannot do this by pretending changes are not happening or that they will go away if we adhere to the ideals of some past American Golden Age. The Age was never Golden, and it certainly cannot be recaptured.

The Mother of the Future will be forced to find fulfillment outside traditional motherhood for the greater part of her life. Dependence will no longer be an option for either sex, whether it is financial dependence in the case of Mother, or domestic dependence in the case of Father. Competence will be necessary for both. Men can expect to find women competing with them as equals, and as the laws of probability suggest, it will not be unusual for a man to be surpassed by a woman in fair competition.

As a nation we are developing a greater respect for the rights of minority groups and a recognition of the essentially pluralistic nature of our society. Our children must develop fexibility and tolerance towards other life styles. Publishers of current readers have responded somewhat to this imperative. Readers are now racially integrated in at least a token manner. Some previously pink faces have been literally blacked in, as we discovered in certain instances. More stories are set in urban rather than in rural surroundings. This is only a gesture, but it does represent tacit agreement by publishers with the basic principle that children are influenced psychologically and not just academically by their readers. Publishers, on their own admission, bear a heavy responsibility to refrain from damaging developing people.

However inadvertently damage has been done in the past, publishers can no longer evade responsibility for change. This report makes it clear that readers are potentially and actually very harmful to children and to the general well-being of our society.

The groundwork for a healthy adjustment to social change has to be laid in childhood. Readers are an important part of this groundwork. Changes in role models and the behavior patterns they depict can have a great impact on the changing images children have of themselves. Few but the strong can function under a constant barrage of self-doubt and social disapproval. If we wish our children to avoid the destructive conflicts in social relationships which can be traced to the effects of sex role conditioning with its dehumanizing consequences for men and women alike, then we must begin now to reform the images with which they will form themselves.

NOTES

1. In *Sisterhood is Powerful*, ed. Robin Morgan (Vintage, 1970) pp. 205-219.
2. Ibid, p. 216.
3. Dell, (New York, 1949.)
4. Norton, (New York, 1950 and 1963.)
5. From printed "Statement, Resolutions, and Motions" presented to the American Psychological Association at its convention in Miami, Florida, September, 1970 by the Association of Women Psychologists.
6. Unpublished speech entitled "The Future of the Family."
7. Sect. 2, p. 56.
8. *Women at Work,* United States Government Publication, 1969. Analyzed by Dr. Jennifer MacCleod, Princeton Adult School, November 19, 1970.
9. p. 34.
10. Ibid, p. 35.

CHAPTER SIX: RECOMMENDATIONS FOR CHANGE

The authors of this study are convinced that all readers now in use should be revised before going into new printings. In this revision top priority must be given to the eradication of harmful sex stereotypes and to the elimination of all forms of discrimination. We join those educators who have criticized publishers for attempting only token solutions to such problems. Whether readers are in fact necessary in order to teach reading, and whether they do as much harm scholastically as they do socially, are questions beyond the scope of this study. If elementary schools do continue to use readers, then steps must be taken immediately to eradicate the abuses discussed in this report.

One of the reasons often cited for the overwhelming amount of "boys' " to "girls' " material is boys' lack of reading readiness in the primary grades. Boys, we are told, will only read stories about boys, whereas girls will go along with anything. We seriously question this premise. We are convinced that if girls' stories were not so limp, so limited, so downright silly even, boys would cease to discriminate between boys' and girls' stories—there would only be "good" or "bad" stories, (it may be useful to remind ourselves that in adult literature only inferior products are labeled "a woman's book" or a "a man's book"). Harriet the Spy, and Pippi Longstocking have no trouble making friends among boys as well as girls. We cannot any longer willingly subscribe to the view that "it's the woman who pays." If boys are to be lured into better performances in the reading program at fixed ages and grades, then other means must be found, and we are sure *can* be found—means which do not demean and diminish the role of women in the world.

Future readers should reflect a sensitivity to the needs and rights of girls and boys without preference or bias. Stories in any given reader should feature girls as well as boys, women as well as men. Half the biographical content should feature women. Outstanding feminist leaders like Susan B. Anthony, Elizabeth Cady Stanton, Emmeline Pankhurst, Sojourner Truth and many other heroines of the fight for women's rights, should appear side by side with male champions of human dignity such as George Washington Carver, Mahatma Gandhi, Benjamin Franklin, Abraham Lincoln, and Martin Luther King. These women form an equally important part of human history. Biographical sections should not be segregated according to sex, nor should adventure sections and similar groupings appear under 'boy' or 'girl' headings. Animal stories should not be used as subtle vehicles for sexist ideas that would be unacceptable in the human family. Future readers should respect the claim of each of us to *all* traits we regard as human, not assign them arbitrarily according to preconceived notions of sex roles. Let the reader man and boy show emotion. Let the reader woman and girl demonstrate courage and ambition. Such a reapportionment, however, should not involve any loss of self-regard or blurring of identity for the boys pictured. Future readers should not arbitrarily bar women and girls from the rights, privileges, pursuits, and pleasures granted to men and boys, nor deny them abilities and occupations males have dominated until now. Specifically, there should be girls and mothers solving problems unassisted by boys and fathers; girls earning money and getting recognition in the form of rewards and awards; and mothers and other women functioning in positions of authority, other than the predictable ones of teachers and nurses. Some stories should feature mothers employed outside the home and independent working women. There should be girls operating machinery and constructing things; girls playing with boys on equal terms; girls in strenuous physical situations; girls travelling; girls depicted as taller, wiser, stronger or older than boys—randomly, as in the actual world. Nobody expects readers to conform to strict statistical probability, but blatant bias must be erased.

A temporary moratorium on certain abused stereotypes of females should be declared. We no longer depict Mexicans asleep under sombreros, blacks eating watermelon, or Indians scalping palefaces. The following might also disappear for a while without being missed: mother in her apron; mother baking or offering cookies; girls tirelessly engaged in playing house, dragging dolls or wheeling them in baby carriages, and having tea parties with them; girls wistfully and admiringly watching boys do anything at all. Girls must not be shown exclusively as spectators, but must appear as active participants. Males as perpetual "guests" in the home should also disappear: for example, father reading the newspaper in his armchair while mother serves him, and boys skipping out to play while the women of the house, young and old, clear tables, wash dishes, cook, sweep, wash, mend, iron, work, and work, and work. . . .

We'd like to see males participate in household chores and females in outdoor tasks, just as they often do. Boys might be shown taking music lessons and visiting art museums; girls could rough-house with dogs and boys stroke kittens. Genuine friendships between boys and girls should appear. Women should be seen working and playing together in groups. Girls might occasionally be shown as rough, unpleasing, intractable or rude, just as boys are allowed and even subtly encouraged to be. Finally, childless couples and single-parent families should be shown unpatronizingly.

There are many possible courses of action for people who will take this study seriously enough to do something about the problem. Parents, teachers, school principals and friends can review books used in classrooms, complain to publishers about offensive stories and illustrations in detail, and try to reach other teachers, principals, school boards and parent-teacher associations. They can also carry the campaign as far as official state-wide purchasing and the general public. Pressure groups can coordinate to make an impact on the situation. It is important, however, to understand that sensitivity to sex role stereotyping is a matter of consciousness-raising and can best be done by group discussion and open-ended debate. Opponents of change may need time and patience before they begin to understand.

The subject can be brought up at teachers' meetings and P.T.A. meetings. Programs to air the question can be arranged and suggestions invited on how to deal with it. Teachers can make sure that children using readers are provided with supplementary reading material that will help to counteract the message of the stereotypes. They can guide class discussions upon how the reader world compares with the real world and an ideal world.

Much can be done by small determined groups of like-minded people. Let's do it. We will know that we have succeeded when Dick can speak of his feelings of tenderness without embarrassment and Jane can reveal her career ambitions without shame or guilt.

Women on Words and Images

The foregoing analysis needs to be carried much further, to the socioeconomic material roots which support these stereotypes and make such roles necessary. Further writings from the Women's Movement have begun to do this.

The problem of racism in the schools has not been solved by court rulings. Educational inequities due to discrimination and the resulting economic consequences have been discussed in earlier chapters. Inequalities between schools in wealthy and poor areas are well known, though not credited by the Coleman Report[20] with accounting for unequal outcomes among black and white students. (For comment and criticism of this report, see S. Bowles and H. Levin, "Determinants of Scholastic Achievement," *Journal of Human Resources,* III, 1, 1968.)

The attempt to render education equal by busing students out of their segregated neighborhoods has had mixed and critical reactions, both from blacks and other minorities (some of whom do not want their children to leave the neighborhood and/or lose their cultural identity) and whites (fearful of lower standards, behavior problems, violence). There is a material basis for white opposition to busing and integration. It is not merely the issue of "bad ideas" being put into peoples' heads by racist agitators. White working class people oppose busing as

---

20. James C. Coleman, *Equality of Educational Opportunity,* U.S. Dept. of Health, Education and Welfare (Washington, D.C.: U.S. Government Printing Office, 1966).

a way of defending their material advantage over blacks. The struggle must be seen in the larger context of scarce resources, jobs, and housing. (See: "Racism and Busing in Boston," *Radical America*, Vol. 8, No. 6, Nov.-Dec. 1974, 1-32.)

There is evidence that suggests that in the more balanced classrooms interracial attitudes among students are more favorable. Sandra Koslin studied the attitudes of children in racially mixed elementary schools in a large eastern city school district.[21] Koslin and her colleagues found that classroom racial balance was related to the interracial attitudes of the children.[22] Balanced classrooms were likely to be characterized by lower levels of racial tension and less racial polarization. While the authors were not prepared to claim that there is a causal relation between classroom racial balance and interracial attitudes, their intuition was that if a school wanted to offset racial polarizing tendencies in its classrooms, faculty and administration should at least work toward a racial balance in their classrooms. And this they have the power to do within their own schools.[23]

However, schools support the racist policies of our society in at least seven ways.

Schools continue to give to all students IQ tests which have been shown to be culturally biased in favor of the white middle class majority. They then use the results of these tests as the basis for labeling black and other minority students who score poorly on them, and placing them in classes for the mentally retarded and intellectually weak. These classes turn out, of course, to be segregated.[24] Thus, schools ignore cultural differences by labeling them inherent biological defects.

Jane Mercer, in *Labeling the Mentally Retarded*[25], reports how this process occurs. She has described eight stages through which children typically pass in acquiring the status of mental retardate: 1) enrolling in the public schools (Catholic schools have no status for mental retardation, nor organizational mechanisms for labeling and processing them); 2) being assigned the status of "normal" student; 3) being retained for a grade; 4) being referred by teacher to principal for psychological evaluation; 5) being tested by the psychologist; 6) being labeled mentally retarded; 7) being placed in special education classes;

21. Sandra Koslin et al. "Classroom Racial Balance and Students' Interracial Attitudes," *Sociology of Education,* Vol. 45, Fall, 1972.

22. Ibid, p. 405.

23. Ibid, pp. 405-6.

24. But in court action in 1972 against the San Francisco Unified School District, the NAACP, in the name of black San Francisco elementary school children who were placed in EMR classes because they scored below 75 on the District's IQ tests, won an injunction against the District, restraining it from using the IQ test for purposes of determining whether to place black students in such classes. Pointing to the racial imbalance of the EMR classes, the NAACP argued that it was up to the District to show that there was a rational connection between the tests and the assignment of the students. The District did not dispute the claim that the tests were racially biased, but claimed they were the best they had available to them, that they were rationally related to the assignment of students, and that the tests were not the cause of the racial imbalance in the EMR classes. But the Court *concluded that the imbalance was indeed the result of using the IQ tests.* The Court also dismissed the argument that there was nothing better available. The Court did not, however, require the District to remove students who had been assigned to EMR classes prior to the legal action, as the plaintiffs had demanded. (Larry P., et al. v. Wilson Riles, et al., U.S. District Court, N.D. California, June 20, 1972, 343 *Federal Supplement*)

25. Jane Mercer. *Labeling the Mentally Retarded.* (Berkeley: University of California Press, 1973), pp. 96-123.

8) leaving the public school and vacating the status. Mercer noted the greater proportion of children from lower socioeconomic levels and minority groups who were being placed in classes for the mentally retarded. She found this to be the result of biased diagnoses based upon the IQ tests.

While Mercer declared the IQ tests to be racist, she concluded that the school system was not, by showing that teachers and principals referred students for testing in amounts proportionate to their component ethnicity in the school system. She said that ethnic disproportions appear only at the point in the labeling process where the IQ test is administered. In other words, her data showed that teachers were not singling out minority students to be sent for testing.

However, in looking over the data, several things become apparent. First of all, almost 30 percent of the children were put into special education classes without having first repeated a grade. There must be another path by which students get sent for testing and thereafter labeled: discussion and analysis of this path is omitted. Second, and more importantly, it appears that Mercer has included in her study those sent for testing as *gifted*. Of 747 children referred for testing by teacher and principal, 31 percent were referred as candidates for classes for the gifted. Mercer does not determine the ethnic proportions of those sent for testing as gifted; undoubtedly, these are primarily Anglo. This would mean that proportionately more minority group children were being referred for testing as retarded than her records would indicate. Mercer has absolved the teachers and the school system of being racist by stating that there is no ethnic or socioeconomic bias in the type of children referred by the teacher-principal team and tested by the school psychologist. Of course, those sent for testing as gifted were never in danger of being labeled mentally retarded. We are expected to conclude that the IQ tests are biased, but that schools are not. This conclusion is a fallacy.[26]

Another way in which schools support racist policies is in the biased textbooks that are used. If blacks are presented at all, their society is portrayed exactly like white middle class society, and not as an alternative cultural style or economic class. (See preceding discussion of textbooks.)

Third, schools within a school district are treated unequally. The Coleman Report in 1966 documented the fact that schools in black areas of a city did in fact have less money with which to operate, fewer experienced teachers of quality, and poorer school facilities. These inequities, however, were smaller than had been assumed and the Report claimed they made little difference in the outcomes of schooling. More important were class background and peer group influences, according to the Report. This was interpreted to mean that in order to provide equal opportunity and increase minority group achievements, schools would have to not only provide equal resources, but make "greater efforts" for those who come to school "educationally handicapped." But this suggests that what goes on in schools does matter. Attention was not redirected to structures external to schools.

Fourth, minorities are not included in curriculum planning and decision-making. Control of schools is not in the hands of the communities in which they lie, but rather in the hands of a centralized and authoritative bureaucracy of white conservatives, reluctant to relinquish their power of decision-making.

---

26. Ibid, pp. 110-115. (We are indebted to Peter Fonda-Bonardi for pointing this out.)

Fifth, schools attempt to channel blacks into occupations of lower esteem and income, basing their action on test scores, achievement in classes, and aspiration of the individual involved. Someone, it seems, has to perform the menial tasks in society.

Sixth, teacher orientations work against minorities. Teachers generally come from the white middle class, and have little or no understanding or conception of the reality structure of their black students. We have already seen how teacher preferences for their own kind of world tend to make them more favorable toward students who also prefer that kind of world and therefore do not create dissonance and become "behavior problems" in the classroom.

Finally, schools omit detailed discussion of the discrimination and oppression which has been experienced by minority groups and the poor. Through such omission and the ideology that anyone can "succeed" if he or she will only "try," comes the myth that failure, poverty and personal situations are the fault of the individual.

But what about all those compensatory education programs of the past several years? Millions of dollars have been expended at all levels of schooling in an attempt to compensate for the educational disadvantage of students who have been discriminated against. These programs were supposed to give these students an intense course of "bombardment" and indoctrination into the white middle class experiences, value orientation and ways of working. They were attempts to inculcate verbal skills, attitudes and descriptions of reality which these students were not getting at home and which, presumably, were lacking in their subculture. Major emphasis was put upon reading and language development in order to enable lower class children to better cope with a heavily verbal, literate school curriculum. Such skills are necessary if a child is to be able to achieve in terms of the analytical and formal school setting.

So instead of changing the structure and values of the schools, the schools went about trying to change the structure and values of these students, to make them conform to its rigid existing pattern. These students were unacceptable as they were, and the school could only see their differences as something to be erased.

By now our readings have helped make clear why the results of compensatory education were disappointing. On the preschool level, it turned out to have no lasting effect on the achievement of these children. And this was the area where most of the compensatory efforts were concentrated. Now more people are inclined to think it is the school which needs to be changed. But this is asking the schools to look to themselves for the answers to their problems, something they have avoided doing for so long. The powers that reign have assumed that their cultural modes and mores are superior in every way to those of other subcultural groups. The schools have sought to turn the blacks, Chicanos, Asians, and Indians into "little white men." Equality has never been compatible with diversity as far as our schools are concerned. It is time to forget the "melting pot" ideology and the fight against ethnic pluralism.

Differences need not be viewed, as it has been heretofor, in terms of a hierarchy of "culturally" advantaged and "culturally" deprived, but rather, as "economically" deprived or as culture conflict, wherein groups have developed from their life experience varied and mutually incompatible conceptual styles for the selection and organization of sensory data. When children whose background of experience has been in another life style come to school where a white middle class orientation prevails, totally unrelated to their conception of reality, there will be conflict. It does not automatically follow that it is right or necessary to change everyone to the white middle class orientation. This orientation has itself come under attack as a nonliberating form of education centered around formalism and literacy instead of sensory experience, and a means of confinement rather than independence.

One attempt to shape a curriculum to the needs and desires of different people was the differentiated curriculum which has been discussed by writers in our earlier chapters. But it was not the differences of the students which set the goals of the differentiated curriculum. It was the needs of society. There was a single uniform standard of success and failure, and we now know that that standard is class biased, racist, sexist, and ageist (that is, biased against the young). The differences among students, differences of class, race, sex and age, became the basis for identifying winners and losers, although the official view and widespread belief was that it was merit through school achievement that was the basis for selection.

More recently, then, the demand has been made by ethnic, class and sex minorities, and by those concerned with the preservation of human autonomy and diversity, that the schools drop their emphasis on cultural uniformity and reflect the pluralistic quality of this society. But can the schools do that and at the same time perform their traditional function of deciding the future social and economic status of the young? Can the schools preserve cultural differences and at the same time educate people for a socioeconomic system of competition that is biased against cultural differences and demands that all be educated according to a single standard? The preservation of cultural differences in the schools demands different standards for different people.

Some people think of equal educational opportunity as everyone's being able to acquire the necessary skills and knowledge to engage in the competitive economic struggle. (No one has suggested doing away with that struggle itself.) For these people the greatest shortcoming of the schools is the failure to teach the same knowledge and skills to everyone, by teaching in different ways for different people. If there is going to be a race, they reason, it is only fair that everyone start at the same place. They are telling the schools to stop attributing the failure to learn to those of different cultures, and instead get rid of their ethnocentric ways of teaching. This is the argument often heard for bilingual education, for example, and it has a strong appeal.

But if the schools change their methods of educating without changing the ends for which this educating is being done, they are apt to continue a biased selection process under the guise of preserving cultural differences. If the learning goals are themselves culturally biased, how far can you go in educating for those goals before cultural differences become obstacles to learning because the goals do not accommodate them?

We are only beginning to become aware of the nature and extent of class differences which exist. The author of our next reading points out how the manner of instruction and interaction carries with it a message about what a culture expects of its children. In McLuhan's well-known phrase, "The medium is the message."

THEM CHILDREN

Martha Ward

"TEACHING" THEM CHILDREN TO TALK

I.

> **Kathy**: Go store Mommy.
> **Mother**: Oh, you want to go to the store?
> **Kathy**: Go now.
> **Mother**: We can't go now. We have to eat dinner.
> **Kathy**: Eat dinner.

II.

> **Mother**: Sing something what Jame Brown just sing.
> What Jame Brown just sing?
> What James Brown just sing, Forry?
> **Child**: *[Sings]*
> **Mother**: What else Jame Brown sing? What else he sing? What he sing?
> **Child**: Jame Brown say "I'm black and proud."
> **Mother**: What he say?
> **Fortrel**: Black and proud! Black and proud!
> **Mother**: Jame Brown say what?
> **Child**: Black and proud!
> **Mother**: And what else he say?

The first tape (recorded by the author) was taken from a white middle-class family; the second from a Rosepoint family. As we shall see from similar conversations, there are differences in the manner in which the Rosepoint mothers and middle-class mothers perceive their role as "teacher." Sometimes this interpretation has subtle linguistic consequences. Children of both types of families acquire language and the ability to communicate within their own communities; but the pattern of their socialization is distinct. This chapter will survey instruction in the mechanics of language itself, instruction in the social context for using language, and the unconscious learning about basic postulates of the culture which result from different forms of instruction.

From *Them Children: A Study in Language Learning* by Martha Coonfield Ward. Copyright © 1971 by Holt, Rinehart and Winston, Inc. Reprinted by permission of Holt, Rinehart and Winston, Inc. pp. 44-47, 88-94.

Expansions

It has been postulated by some observers that a child approximates well-formed syntax by repeating an utterance or partial utterance of an adult or in turn having his telegraphic speech expanded into an acceptable sentence.

> There is one respect in which parental speech is not random. Quite often adults repeat the speech of small children and, in so doing, change the children's sentences into the nearest well-formed adult equivalent. Brown has called this phenomenon "expansion of child speech" (Brown 1964). It is a kind of imitation in reverse, in which the parent echoes the child and, at the same time, supplies features that are missing from the child's sentence (McNeill 1966:73).

These expansions were given much attention because they appeared so frequently in the speech of the adults and children studied by Brown and Bellugi (1964); Miller and Ervin (1964); and Braine (1963).

> The mothers of Adam and Eve responded to the speech of their children with expansions about 30 percent of the time . . . A reduced or incomplete English sentence seems to constrain the English-speaking adult to expand it into the nearest properly formed complete sentence (Brown and Bellugi 1964:144).

A middle-class American adult is seldom able to resist turning "Daddy bye-bye" into "Daddy's gone bye-bye." Frequently, a declarative intonation serves to validate the child's observation, while a rising, "Daddy's gone bye-bye?" serves as a communication check.

Typical child sentences and their expansions follow:

This ring.	This is a round ring.
Donnie all-gone.	Is Donnie all-gone?
It a bus.	Is it a bus?

(Ervin 1966:168)

No native speaker of English could confuse the mother's expansions with the baby's sentences. Not surprisingly, whole grammars of these utterances have been written in an attempt to equate the expansions with linguistic input and output.

If parental expansion of child speech contributed significantly to adult norms of grammar, the situation of the children of Rosepoint would be lamentable. In less than five percent of the total utterances recorded were reciprocal expansions clearly operative in either child's or parents' speech. The mothers occasionally enhance the pivot structures of the younger children, but not with the same frequency as would a middle-class adult. Three, four, and five morpheme sentences from older children were repeated or expanded with even less frequency. To illustrate: the middle-class mothers of Adam and Eve (Brown's subject-children) would find it difficult, if not impossible, to spend an entire day with two, three, and four year olds without expanding or repeating a single utterance of the children. To do so is a part of their native speaker's intuition.

The mothers in the present study spend entire days in this manner and suffer not at all from a thwarted instinct. That is not to say that once in a while they do not expand or repeat a child's utterance in the same way as do Adam's or Eve's mother, but rather that such responses occur infrequently and without any evident compulsion.

A closer look at Brown and Bellugi's *Adam* transcripts explains the difference. Below is reproduced a segment of Adam's first record. Adam is at this point twenty-seven months old.

Adam: See truck, Mommy.
Mother: Did you see the truck?
Adam: See truck.
Mother: No, you didn't see it. There goes one.
Adam: No I see truck.
Mother: Yes, there goes one.
Adam: There go one. See a truck. See truck Mommy. See truck. Truck. Put truck, Mommy.
Mother: Put the truck where?
Adam: Put truck window.
Mother: I think that one's too large to go in the window.

(Brown and Bellugi 1966:135).

Now note their comments on this speech sample.

The dialogue between mother and child does not read like a transcribed dialogue between two adults . . . The conversation is, in the first place, very much in the here and now. (Brown and Bellugi 1966:134.)

Whatever its shortcomings, this little recording is clearly a conversation and a dialogue, but one type specific to mother-child interaction in this subculture.

Compare with the following. The child here is thirty-six months old, eighth of eight children, and son of a factory worker.

Kenneth: Mama, look, a train.
Mother: Yeah, Kenneth, I see it.
The child's attempt at initiating this conversation is quite like Adam's method, yet the responses of the mothers differ radically.
Mother: You pissy.
Kenneth: *[He says nothing; he knows it.]*
Mother: You piss in your pant.
Kenneth: *[Smiles.]*
Mother: You shame you piss in your pant?
Kenneth: No.
Mother: You should be.
Kenneth's mother is remarking in a sweet and gentle way; it may be a turn off, but not a put down.

In the next dialogue, a tape recording of a mother and her twenty-eight-month-old son, she initiates the conversation, determines the subject matter and direction. The lack of verbal reciprocity would seem to negate this as a conversation. However, the mother is pleased with its communicative success. The conversation is typical of mother-child interaction in Rosepoint. Mark is playing with the knob on the television:
Mother: Say, Mark, quit it. Say, Mark, quit it! Say, Mark, quit it!!
[She remarks that children pretend to be deaf when they do not want to listen.]

Mother: Mark, oh Mark, come give your mother a kiss. Mark, oh Mark, come give your mother a kiss. Mark, oh Mark, come give mama a kiss.
[She gets no response at all.]
Mother: Oh, nobody to kiss me.
[She tries a new tact.]
Mother: Mark, take this belt to Cicero.
[After a long pause, Mark, attracted by her root beer, comes and sits on her lap. She shares her drink with him from the bottle.]
Mother: Mark, give me a kiss. He shame to kiss his mother in front of Joan. Mark, you shame to kiss your mama in front of Joan?[1]
[He still doesn't kiss her.]

They watch a soap opera together. Later he tries to attract her attention by biting and kissing her.

The fundamental attitude of Kenneth's and Mark's mothers in these conversations is that *children do not function to uphold their end of the conversation.* Neither mother sees any point in training herself or her child to conduct a conversation on such minutiae as trucks and trains. As the taping sessions proved, the mothers were virtual strangers in talking to their children where talk for the sake of talk was required. She responds to questions and requests with as full a measure of love as does Adam's mother. She addresses him with the complete range of affects from rage to admiration, but she will not cater to his verbal whims. Small children learning to talk are not the sort of people with whom Rosepoint adults "engage in dialogue."

If a child has something important to say, his mother will listen, and he had better listen when she decides to tell him something. But for conversation, *per se,* for the sound of a human voice, she will go visiting, make phone calls, have company, or in sheer desperation talk to an older child (eight or above). She will never find herself politely trapped, as will Adam's mother, by the verbal precocity of a three year old, with whom one cannot honestly discuss an interesting issue.

Adam's mother is committed to talking with him often, an activity which involves expanding and imitating his speech as much as possible. This technique does not necessarily teach him language since children whose parents do not expand their utterances also learn to talk. With or without indirect instruction, the child learns that "no I see truck" becomes "I don't see the truck."

Just as Kenneth and Adam learn two different dialects of English, they also learn two different sociolinguistic dialects. The verbal tricks which Adam learns from his mother will stand him in better stead at middle-class schools than the verbal tricks Kenneth learns from his mother. Kenneth has not learned how to initiate and monopolize a conversation with an adult on a topic of his choosing. Mark has never been rewarded for verbal advances; no one expects him to say more than the bare minimum. Boys growing up in Rosepoint do not fill in the bare spaces of time with talk. No one in the community takes seriously the chattering of a child. In fact, as the conversations indicate, the children hold their parent's attention longer *if they say nothing.*

Kenneth and Mark have learned to amuse themselves, to sit very still and listen to adults talk, (timed at three hours on several occasions), and to play happily with siblings and other children for days on end. Their mothers do not exist for the amusement of children.

In an experiment to determine whether expansions of a child's speech would augment grammatical development, Cazden (1965) found that simply replying to what the child had said was just as effective in stimulating speech. Expansions are, it would seem, more helpful to certain groups of parents than to any group of children.

*   *   *

The impression must not be left that the children of Rosepoint cannot speak or do not speak well. Nothing is further from the truth. In many instances they choose to remain silent. At play or particularly in the car, they chatter with abandon. Talking as a means of power or control over others is not, however, widely practiced and consequently the children do not learn to control situations verbally. As language development is rewarded only erratically, the children have few cultural incentives to speak up. As a result, the children strike the visitor as extremely pleasant and trustworthy. They can accompany adults anywhere without trouble. There are no "brats" in Rosepoint.

The size of the group to which the child belongs affects his chances for speech expression. In some communities a mother and single child, forced to rely on each other for companionship, may find verbal interaction stimulating. This is not the situation in Rosepoint where the life space is crowded with people. People are the chief resource of the child and the sounds they make are his chief stimuli. Perhaps the constant noise of the television and phonograph offers privacy and security in households whose average density is three per room.

Due to the age-grading system, unqualified love and approval are withdrawn as babies turn into children. This coincides roughly with the age at which the children begin to express themselves verbally. The outcome of the age-grading ideas may be seen in the rapid maturational advances during the first and second year of life when encouragement and acceptance are at their highest. This is followed by a period of slower growth when behavioral expectations (good conduct, quietness, helpfulness) are accelerated. The years from one or two to six, the most crucial for language learning, are the period of least adult contacts and stimulation for these children. In other ways, though, the children mature very rapidly. Their early sense of personal and corporate responsibility is evidence of this.

The Rosepoint child is at his best in peer groups. Here verbal interaction is higher than in family groups which include adults. His experience in interacting with adults has taught him the values of silence or withdrawal. When children are verbal in the presence of adults, it is because other children are nearby to provide the stimulus. Within the peer group, competition is minimized and cooperation maximized. With few toys and many young relatives, a youngster learns from and relies on other children.

The child is not expected gradually to substitute verbal pleasures for nonverbal pleasures. Much of his gratification comes from outside the medium of language. Though the mother yells at him, she also gives him a kind look and a nickel. The requirements are simple and well-defined. While in the house, he has to behave; outside, he has freedom and mobility.

Several sayings summarize local beliefs about children and their learning abilities. "What's in his head ain't in his ass" is a reference to the hardheaded quality of children. Just because they hear a command or know their duties is no guarantee of action. By the same token, this hardheadedness protects them from insult and injury. The belief that parents play little part in language learning is reinforced by the lore, "Cut his hair, cut his speech"—if the baby's hair is cut before his first birthday, his language development will be retarded.

THE SCHOOL ENVIRONMENT

The three primary influences on the development of the child are the home, peer groups, and school. As there are no public nursery schools or kindergartens in St. James Parish, and the only private one for blacks is expensive,[2] a child's first exposure to institutionalized education comes after age six. This is late in terms of language learning.

As a result of the integration crisis, the St. James Parish schools are in an unsettled and uncertain state. Though the parish is liberal by Louisiana standards, attempts to retard school integration follow the traditional southern patterns. Recently the parish voted to build two high schools—one for boys and one for girls. The implications of this strategy are obvious. Losing the elementary school in their community (even if it did not have functioning plumbing) is a severe blow to the residents of Rosepoint. Children will be bussed to a new school on the other side of the parish.

Rosepoint parents believe that most of the teachers—black or white—are authoritarian and punitive. Black children attending white schools for the first time are subjected to discriminatory practices, subtle or otherwise. Mothers who complain are treated rudely and the children punished later. One mother complained that the teachers were striking the back of children's hands hard enough to break bones. This, she felt, was wrong. The teacher should hit the palms of the children's hands, a discipline the mother understood from her own school days. The 1960 census reports median school years completed for the non-white population is 4.7. There are, in other words, four times as many people who have never attended a day of high school as have completed high school.[3]

Two aspects of the school situation have direct bearing on family life. One is a lack of communication between class and home. Parents have little notion how the school is run, what their children are taught or how to cooperate in the process. For the most part they worry whether or not the children are observing strict behavioral norms and not about the content of instruction or the child's intellectual progress. From about eleven years old on, staying in school is a touch-and-go proposition, especially for males. On the other hand, the schools show no understanding of the social problems in the parish or the subcultures with which they must cope.

The second feature is the tenuous nature of attendance. The parents will automatically accept any excuse for remaining at home: a tiny blister, no suitable shoes, missing the bus (the school is three blocks away), general malaise, or the need for help. Moreover, the teacher may send the child home on the slightest pretext—one effective way of reducing class size. At the first sign of illness or undesirable behavior—imaginary or otherwise—home goes the child. A suspected case of mumps which never materialized rated two weeks at home. Giggling in the halls rated one week. Most missed assignments or temporary irritations are good for the rest of the day. For such judgments there is no court of higher appeal. The child remains home the alloted time. Attendance patterns are significant since in some families a school day rarely passes (and for some families, never passes) in which only the preschoolers are home. On any given day a sampling of older children will be present. Some nuclei of siblings are rarely separated from each other.

THE CONFLICT OF HOME AND SCHOOL

If the *cultures* of home and school are in conflict, which captures the mind of a child? The irrelevancy of the school for most Rosepoint children is measured by the high dropout rate, the low rates of literacy, and an abiding urban and rural poverty in Louisiana.

The school creates for the Rosepoint child an environment not as much unpleasant as unnatural. For years he has been determining his own schedule for eating, sleeping, and playing. The content of his play is unsupervised and depends on the child's imagination. His yard does not contain sand boxes, swings, clay, paints, nor personnel obliged to supervise his play. At school, however, play is supervised, scheduled, and centers around objects deemed suitable for young minds. There are firm schedules for playing, napping, eating, and "learning and studying," (with the implication that learning will occur only during the time alloted for it). The authority buttressing even minimal schedules is impersonal and inflexible with an origin not in face-to-face social relationships but in an invisible bureaucracy.

Moreover, the Rosepoint home relies on verbal communication rather than on the written word as a medium. Adults do not read to children nor encourage writing. Extraverbal communication such as body movements or verbal communication such as storytelling or gossip are preferred to the printed page. The lack of money to purchase books, magazines, and newspapers partly explains this. However, access to public libraries, bookmobiles, and cheap pulp publications is seldom utilized. Perhaps the schools are at fault in not encouraging better reading habits. Yet, for children of a culture rich in in-group lore and oral traditions the written word is a pallid substitute. Whatever the reason, a child unconvinced of the need to commit his thoughts to paper is primed for trouble at school.

Another conflict arising out of the home-school discrepancy is language— specifically, "bad" language. Remember that the Rosepoint child is rewarded for linguistic creativity. At a family gathering, one two-year old girl just learning to talk said to her mother and her aunt: "Fuck you, you cow!" She was greeted with hearty laughter, a kiss, and approval. Later that month, the child's mother and aunt in speaking to a close mutual friend recounted the story with relish. They were careful, of course, to whom they related the episode, knowing that some would be shocked at this manner of addressing one's elders. But the child's growing mastery of language was not construed as a threat or insult.

In the classroom such language has an entirely different interpretation placed on it. Some educators discretely refer to it as "the M-F problem."[4] (The problem originates with the educators and not the child.) A nine-year-old girl was given a two-week suspension from classes for saying a four-letter word. This was her first recorded transgression of the language barrier. The second offense may be punished by expulsion. In such cases, the child's low grades are not a reflection of performance or intelligence, but the result of enforced absences. Children get kicked out of school for verbal infractions whether teachers and administrators are black or white. This puts the M-F problem more on the level of class than color.

That these children are not placed in competitive roles in their preschool days is a point to be emphasized. Overt peer and sibling rivalries are noticeably absent. In Rosepoint a child is exposed far more often to the values and portrayal of genuine cooperation. For another example of a society cherishing cooperation more than competition see Margaret Mead's *Coming of Age in Samoa* (1967). In the classroom, "cooperating," instead of competing, may be called cheating on a test, not trying hard enough, or not working up to potential.

The future as an idea and the preparations necessary for it motivate many of the school's policies. Getting into college, getting a job, or getting good grades are rationalizations for a given event years in advance of the event. Punishment is sometimes deferred far beyond the time span of the guilty action, cards reporting "citizenship grades" being a case in point. The moral force of the middle-class principle of delayed gratification—work now, get paid later—is inappropriate for people who have not found the pot of gold at the end of the hard work.

In the types of testing situations which determine grades or measure achievement and I.Q., the Rosepoint child is at a disadvantage. He has not received the constant drill which is characteristic of the middle-class mother and child interaction. Nor has he been trained in a specialized set of verbal skills called "correct grammar" the mastery of which is a measure of pedagogical success. He may have only limited access to that bank of childhood minutiae somehow crucial to classroom achievement.

Some as yet unanswered questions suggested by the discord between home and school cultures are:

(1) If the teachers in public schools talk like Adam's mother (in Chapter 5) rather than like Kenneth's or Mark's mother, what happens to the processes of communication?

(2) Can students learn the "language" of the teacher if the teacher does not know their "language?"

(3) What happens to students raised in a positionalized home confronted with teachers who operate on a personalized basis?

DUMB OR DEPRIVED?

It would probably not be difficult to predict the scores of these children on intelligence examinations. Which of these tests uses familiar words like "bayou," "bisque," "lagniappe," "parrain," "crayfish," "creole," or "levee"? Nor do expressions such as "making a birthday," "having a baby for Clement," "pass to the road," or "bring me ride" occur on standard achievement tests. Queries regarding directions, "north," "south," "east," or "west," may confuse a child who thinks in terms of "up the river," "down the river," "away from the river," and "to the river." Rosepoint children know the intricacies of the sugar-cane cycle but have never experienced snow. Are children who identify carrots as sweet potatoes dumb? Add to this the fact that for these children the test-taking situation is alien, the goals for such activity obscure, and the cultural expectations for performance minimal.

The notion that low scores on intelligence tests or bad grades in school indicate "cultural deprivation" is false. Individuals required to take an exam in a culture and dialect not their own will necessarily appear stupid. Tests to measure competency in the *culture* of the rural, black, and poor have not yet been invented.

THE VALUES OF THE ROSEPOINT WAY

These techniques of language socialization stem in part from the family system. In nuclear families those who have no authority over the children likewise have no responsibility and the child is left in a precarious position when one or both of his parents are absent. The strength and flexibility of the Rosepoint family lie, however, in interchangeability. If the children have a neurotic mother, an absent father, or a handicapped sibling, the family is not maimed. Its completeness is insured through the extended family. Adults who can offer maternal and paternal love are ready to assume these responsibilities. Assistance comes in the form of money, in adopting and raising each other's children, and, above all, in furnishing the emotional support often lacking in nuclear families forced on their own resources. This, for the children, is a healthy situation. The range of those people who can spank or discipline the children is increased, but then so is the range of those who will give a nickel, a car ride, some food, security, and succor.

Child-rearing techniques stem from a sense of tradition and shared belief about the proper way to raise children. This consistency is found less frequently in middle-class families who raise their children "by the book" or follow various developmental schemes. Ideas of the proper discipline are not, for example, fully shared even by members of the immediate family. Thus for Rosepoint the level of ambiguity is reduced both for the children who are exposed to the one prevailing method and for the mothers whose confidence and authority are buttressed by each other. No family or child is wholly dependent on the whims of one member.

The language component of child-rearing techniques likewise reduces ambiguity by its clarity and consistency. If a mother expects her child to be quiet, she says "be quiet" or words to that effect. Such a behavioral expectation is not considered novel or difficult for him to execute. Her tactics are straightforward. Tricking him by teasing, sarcasm, or indirect allusions is alien to her style. In the child's own home or at another's, the mother's approaches to obtaining quiet will be the same. The advantage from the child's viewpoint is the security which comes from a unified tradition of child-rearing.

An important concomitant of the linguistic socialization process is the sameness of social expectations. Unlike mobile middle-class families, Rosepoint children are not expected to enhance their parents' reputations. A mother is not known by the children she keeps. The children are free of the pressure to show off to please parents. They are expected to mind, to cooperate, and to grow up, not to be miniature Shirley Temples. If a child's speech is hesitant, his clothes dirty or torn, his manners rudimentary or behavior silly, so what—this is the natural condition of childhood. In Rosepoint everyone knows and accepts the fact that children are just like that.

NOTES

1. In the two previous conversations with Kenneth and Mark cited above, the mothers are using a form of appeal to the social oriented feeling of shame rather than to the personal oriented feelings of guilt. For more discussion of the implications of the guilt-shame complex in child-rearing, see Benedict (1946: pp. 222-223).

2. This private kindergarten costs $15.00 per month for the school year 1968-1969. An increase in this price was scheduled for the school year 1969-1970. With clothes and transportation, this is viewed as too expensive by Rosepoint families.

3. U.S. Department of Commerce, Bureau of the Census, *United States Census of Population:* 1960, Vol. I, *Characteristics of the Population,* part 20, Louisiana, Table 87, p. 220.

4. Refers to the use of obscenities in school, including "motherfucker."

Martha Ward

We have referred to different "cognitive and linguistic styles," and their dependence on appropriate cultural settings for their expression. But the differences may go deeper than styles. Recent neurological studies have suggested what is known as the "Appositional/Propositional (A-P) Hypothesis." "Appositional" and "propositional" refer to two different but complementary ways of knowing and thinking, the first a "gestalt" and "synthesizing" way, the second a "logical" and "analytic" way. And the A-P hypothesis locates the first in the right hemisphere of the brain, and the second in the left hemisphere. A tendency for a person to reply more on one hemisphere than the other may well reflect influences of early cultural exposure, according to J. E. Bogen and others. They write:

> In a culture where most individuals are exposed to intensive education of the left hemisphere potential for reading, writing, grammar, etc., we could reasonably expect a tendency for the propositional mode to dominate, even when dealing with problems for which it is less appropriate. Conversely, persons raised in a nonliterate culture emphasizing different training, in spatial skills for example, should exhibit a reverse tendency.[27]

They note that it would probably be impossible to find a culture without educational stimuli for either one or the other hemisphere. We all learn to some extent to know and think "propositionally" and "appositionally." Where differences occur is in the ratio each of us displays between the two kinds. Some of us will be high in "propositional" cognition and low in "appositional" cognition, and some will have a reverse ratio. Most importantly, these differences occur between the ratios of members of subgroups and the ratios of dominant group members in a society:

> One might suppose that in the U.S., for example, Blacks or Hopi Indians would differ from middle-class Whites in having less success in problems making greater demands upon the left hemisphere than the right. More specifically, these two minority groups can be expected to do relatively less well on verbal tests . . . whereas there are some reasons to expect that they would be better on a test emphasizing visuo-spatial recognition.[28]

27. J. E. Bogen et al. "The Other Side of the Brain IV. The A/P Ratio," *Bulletin of the Los Angeles Neurological Societies,* Vol. 37, No. 2, April 1972, p. 50.

28. Ibid, p. 50.

Rosalie A. Cohen of the University of Pittsburgh has pursued the cultural side of conceptual styles and their educational implications. She identifies two mutually incompatible conceptual styles, the "relational" and the "analytic." (A conceptual style is a set of rules by which we select and organize the data of our sense experience.) The relational style (sometimes called "self-centered" as opposed to the "stimulus-centered" character of the analytic style) requires, Cohen tells us,

. . . a descriptive mode of abstraction and is self-centered in its orientation to reality; only the global characteristics of a stimulus have meaning to its users, and these only in reference to some total context.[29]

The analytic conceptual style, on the other hand,

. . . is characterized by a formal or analytic mode of abstracting salient information from a stimulus or situation and by a stimulus-centered orientation to reality, and it is parts-specific (i.e., parts or attributes of a given stimulus have meaning in themselves).[30]

In an analysis of the ten most widely used standardized tests of intelligence and achievement in the schools, Cohen found all of them requiring the analytic style of cognitive organization, and the ability to use this style well, she found, becomes more critical at higher grade levels. Thus the person who is oriented to the relational style finds his or her work getting poorer and poorer the longer he or she remains in school.

Cohen also found many school-related learning characteristics tied to the analytic style. Things like the length and intensity of attention, preferences of optional reading material, dependence upon primary groups, and language style all are tied to the analytic mode. Her conclusion is:

. . . that not only test criteria but also the overall ideology and learning environment of the school embody requirements for many social and psychological correlates of the analytic style. This emphasis can be found, for example, in its cool, impersonal, outer-centered approach to reality organization. Analytic correlates can also be found in the requirements that the pupil learn to sit increasingly long periods of time, to concentrate alone on impersonal learning stimuli, and to observe and value organized time allotment schedules . . . So discrepant are the analytic and relational frames of references that a pupil whose preferred mode of cognitive organization is emphatically relational is unlikely to be rewarded in the school setting either socially or by grades, regardless of his native abilities and even if his information repetoire and background of experience are adequate . . . both the cognitive characteristics of [the relational] style and its sociobehavioral

---

29. Rosalie Cohen. "Conceptual Styles, Culture Conflict, and Nonverbal Tests of Intelligence," *American Anthropologist,* 71, 1969, p. 830.
    30. Ibid, pp. 829-830.

correlates have been considered deviant and disruptive in the analytically oriented learning environment of the school.[31]

Cohen tells us that the psychological literature suggests that cognitive styles are either biologically predetermined in the nature of the organism or are the result of idiosyncratic early experiences and random trials in problematic settings. These explanations, however, do not account for the dominance of relational modes among individuals from low-income situations and analytic modes among individuals from the middle class. This lack of normal distribution suggests that analytic and relational modes are the result of different social environments which stimulate, reinforce and make functional the development of one conceptual style and inhibit development of the other. She goes on to indicate a further relationship between cognitive style and what she calls "shared-function" primary groups, found primarily in low-income districts, and "formally organized primary groups," found to be typical of middle class districts. These ideal types of groups were differentiated by the manner in which critical functions were distributed within them, interaction patterns, status relationships, role expectations, individual identity, distribution of rewards and leadership. Relational styles were found to be associated with shared-function group organization and analytic styles associated with formal group organization.

In the concluding portion of her article, Cohen distinguishes culture conflict from culture difference and cultural deprivation. Culture conflict occurs when conceptual styles used between individuals and groups are incompatible, like the "analytic" school and the "relational" pupil. She then goes on to point out how the supposedly culture-free nonverbal IQ tests being used these days are not, in fact, free of a culturally-based analytic orientation. They are even more discriminatory against relational pupils. In further analyzing IQ tests, Cohen refers to two cognitive skills which she says go to make up a conceptual style. These she calls "mode of abstraction" (classification, generalization, and processing of information) and "field articulation" (selection of salient information). For the two cognitive styles she has identified, therefore, there is an analytic (formal) mode of abstraction and a relational (descriptive) mode of abstraction; and there is field independent articulation and field dependent articulation. In the analytic mode of abstraction and field articulation, analysis is centered around the parts of a stimulus or the stimulus itself. In the relational mode of abstraction and field articulation, analysis centers around the global characteristics of a stimulus or oneself. For example, pupils were asked to choose which two of three pictures were alike or went together in some way. One set of pictures consisted of a wooden chair missing one leg, a wooden table also missing one leg, and a covered armchair. Analytic responses were that the wooden chair and wooden table went together because each was missing a leg or because both were made of wood. Relational responses were that the two chairs went together because they looked good together or were both chairs. A second set of pictures consisted of a boy and a girl with hands on their hips and a third boy with arms at his sides. Analytic responses were that the boy and girl with hands on their hips went together because they had their hands on their hips. Relational responses were that the two boys went together because they looked good together or were both boys.

31. Ibid, p. 830.

CONCEPTUAL STYLES, CULTURE CONFLICT, AND NONVERBAL TESTS OF INTELLIGENCE

Rosalie A. Cohen

DEPRIVATION, CULTURE DIFFERENCE AND CULTURE CONFLICT

Once one has become aware of the stringent analytic requirements for performance in school and of the separate information-cognitive skill requirements of standardized tests, it is no longer appropriate to speak of "deprivation," "culture difference," and "culture conflict" synonymously. "Deprivation" and "culture difference" have to do with the information components of these tests and "culture conflict" with different conceptual styles and their conflicting sociobehavioral correlates.

Within the information components themselves two types of distinctions can be drawn—quantitative and qualitative. The term "deprivation" may be used to refer to the quantitative characteristics of a pupil's information repertoire and "culture difference" to its qualitative characteristics. When there is a relative lack of the number of concepts and experiences on which a pupil has to draw in order to do well in school, he may be said to be deprived. Limited experience with varied environments and limited access to books and other sources of knowledge may limit the amount of information a pupil has to use. Children from low-income environments may be deprived in this way as a result of their position in society. Institutionalized children or those from other environments that present limited stimulation or those who are sensorially limited, such as blind children, may share this disability. "Culture difference," on the other hand, involves qualitatively different kinds of things and events from those usable in school. A slum child may not know what a refrigerator is, for example, but he may know a great deal about rats. The information repertoires of such children may be sizable but different from those required by the school curriculum.

Neither the quantitative nor qualitative characteristics of a pupil's information repertoire should effectively hamper his ability to communicate with the school environment, however, because neither of them implies incompatibility with school requirements. The school curricula are relatively eclectic in the units of information that are acceptable. In addition, there is no known limit to the number of new concepts individuals can learn. It is, therefore, only when incompatibilities exist (whether or not deprivation and culture difference are also present) that "culture conflict" may be said to exist.

Relational and analytic modes of conceptual organization reflect such incompatibilities: that is, many specific kinds of response characteristics can be factored out of each style that can be demonstrated to impede the development of the

Reproduced by permission of The American Anthropological Association from *The American Anthropologist* 71, pp. 838-43, 1969.

alternate kind. Some incompatible response characteristics lie on basic levels of learned behavior, such as conditioned perceptual discrimination and sudomotor reactivity. Others are found in lexical choice and language organization and still others in a wide range of interpersonal and social process behaviors and in many derivative values and beliefs. Each context acts as separate reinforcement of the conceptual process that has been used, and each lower-order deriviative of each conceptual style suppresses its alternative. It is to selection and classification rule-sets, then, that many mutually incompatible psychological and social behaviors are tied and not to information components per se. Moreover, because of their integrity relational and analytic rule-sets can, to a great extent, both limit and determine the size and nature of an individual's information repertoire when native ability and environmental stimulation are held constant.

In addition to incompatible selection and classification rule-sets, three other areas of mutual incompatibility emerged from a semantic feature analysis of the lexicon of the hard-core poor. The additional three areas of incompatibility were in perceptions of time (as a series of discrete moments, rather than a continuum), of self in social space (in the center of it, rather than in a position relative to others who are passing together at different rates of speed through social space), and in causality (specific causality rather than multiple causality). (Cohen, Fraenkel, & Brewer 1968). Each of the above categories of thought was closely associated with relational and analytic styles along several different dimensions; that is, each reflected a number of rule components in common with its related conceptual style. For example, the analytic mode of abstraction presumes a system of linear components. Similar linear components are found in the perception of time as a continuum or in a linear projection of social space, and they underlie the notion of multiple causality. This linear component does not appear among polar-relational children on tests of cognitive style, in their characteristic language style, nor in the ordering of authority or responsibility in shared-function social groups. Certain common values and beliefs follow from such a common component. For instance, without the assumption of linearity such notions as social mobility, the value of money, improving one's performance, getting ahead, infinity, or heirarchies of any type, all of which presume the linear extension of critical elements, do not have meaning for the relational child. In essence, the requirements for formal abstraction and extraction of components to produce linear continua are not logically possible within the relational rule-set.

NONVERBAL TESTS OF INTELLIGENCE

In addition to distinguishing among "deprivation," "culture difference," and "culture conflict," the findings of these investigations also challenge the rationale for the "culture-free" nonverbal tests in current use. It has been most commonly believed that it is the information (direct experience) components of these tests that carry their culture-bound characteristics. Nonverbal tests concentrate on the ability to reason "logically." However, it is in the very nature of these logical sequences that the most culture-bound aspects of the middle-class, or "analytic," way of thinking are carried. Even more critical than either the quantitative and qualitative information components of such tests are the analytic mode of abstraction and the field-articulation requirements they embody. Figure 2, taken from the Lorge-Thorndike nonverbal battery on the ninth-grade level, may clarify this point.

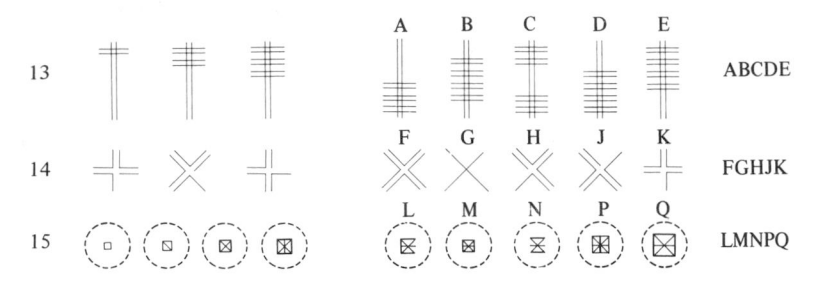

FIGURE 2. *The pupil is instructed to complete the logical sequences by choosing from the multiple choice items that are presented.*

The logical sequences in Figure 2 are most effectively solved by a parts-specific, stimulus-centered, analytic mode of abstraction. This strategy depends upon the ability of the subject to extract and relate relevant parts of the stimulus. All contextual information has been removed in advance. When an entire test battery is constructed of items like the above, as nonverbal batteries indeed are, analytic-cognitive skills have been separated explicitly from general-information components. If the essential aspect of "culture conflict" is discrepancy between cognitive modes among pupils, these tests are even more discriminatory than those formed in part to test for information growth. Even the best informed and the most widely experienced relational pupil, regardless of his native ability, would score poorly on such a test.

As a matter of fact, the most intelligent relational pupils score the worst of all. Their ability to reach higher levels of abstraction through relational pathways take them farther away from the higher levels of abstraction reached through analytic pathways. The range of dissociation of the two paths to higher levels of abstraction can be looked upon as inverted triangles, as shown in Figure 3. Highly intelligent high-relational pupils were found, in fact, to communicate best with the demands of the school on the concrete level. This was evidenced in our findings in an initial sampling of sixty-six ninth- and tenth-grade pupils of average or better intelligence (Cohen 1967) and in the markedly better scores of high-relational pupils on two achievement subtests of the Project Talent Achievement Inventory. A content analysis of the Talent battery found that the questions on only these two subtests were framed on concrete levels. Although the more intelligent high-relational pupils scored extremely poorly (15th to 20th percentiles) on the other subtests of achievement, they did extremely well (90th to 95th percentiles) on these two sets of concrete problems. It appears, therefore, that given concrete settings with intelligence held constant, high-relational pupils can compete with analytic ones. It is only when high levels of analytic abstraction are required that their ability to compete is inhibited.

Such findings suggest that in addition to the focused analytic cognitive style requirements of nonverbal tests of intelligence, the level of abstraction they require provides an additional area of difficulty for relational pupils. Since contentless figures are almost completely abstract, they tend to focus on the most extreme levels for the use of analytic cognitive skills. Therefore, not only is the

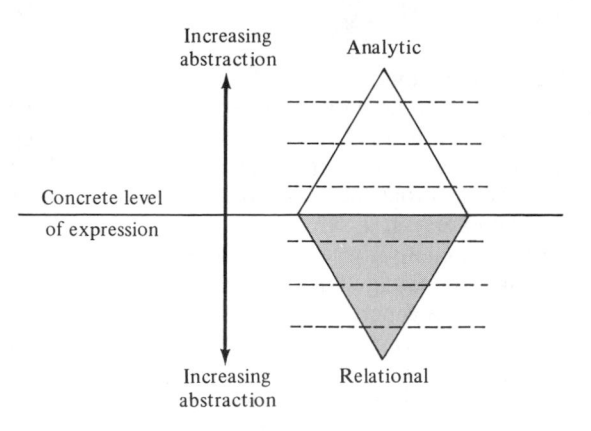

FIGURE 3. *Dissociating levels of abstraction through analytic and relational pathways.*

mode of cognitive organization required for successful performance on nonverbal tests a critical factor in the inability of relational pupils to deal with them, but the *level of abstraction* on which they focus for the demonstration of these skills intensifies the problems they present to relational pupils.

In addition to illuminating the relationship of the pupils to the tests, the two-way analysis that was followed also cast some light on the relationship of relational and analytic pupils to each other. Not only do relational and analytic pupils communicate with each other best on the concrete level, but the greatest gaps in communication occur between the most intelligent members of the two categories of pupils, as is suggested by the progressively dissociating levels of abstraction illustrated above.

Nonverbal tests of intelligence have not freed themselves, then, of their culture-bound characteristics. Instead, they have focused on one critical aspect of culture—its method of selecting and organizing relevant sense data. Traditional attempts to develop culture-free tests have eliminated their information components in the belief that it is only their substantive experience components that are culture-bound. An additional assumption has been that because they are nonverbal, they are nonstructured. The most culture-bound characteristics of these tests, however, are not their information components but the analytic-logical sequences they require. Both in the mode of abstraction these tests require and in the level of abstraction in which the items are couched, nonverbal tests of intelligence are much more discriminatory against relational pupils than are conventional instruments, which test partly for information growth. Since both the size and nature of a pupils' information repertoire and his native ability are apparently unrelated to his conceptual style, the analytic-relational opposition may be defined as a separate area of pupils performance. Pupils may be deprived or culturally different from or in culture conflict with the school. They may represent one or two or all these separate kinds of educational problem. Analytic schemata geared to the definition of learning disabilities and programs designed for one type of educational problem cannot hope to deal with the others as well.

SUMMARY

This paper has focused (1) on incompatibility in conceptual styles as a notable indicator of "culture conflict" and on the characteristics that distinguish it from "deprivation" and "culture difference" and (2) on styles of conceptual organization as culture-bound characteristics of nonverbal tests of intelligence. Evidence is also presented of the reciprocal relationships between conceptual styles and styles of primary group process.

Conceptual styles are composites of two cognitive skills—mode of abstraction and field articulation. Along with information growth, these two cognitive skills have been identified as generic components of learning. Conceptual styles are essentially integrated rule-sets for the selection and organization of sense data. Within each rule-set certain assumptions and relationships are logically possible, and others are not. They are definable without reference to specific substantive content and are not related to native ability. They can be identified in the abstract, in language selection and organization, and in attitudes about one's self and one's environment. Associated with these rule-sets, or derivative from them, are a wide variety of social and psychological characteristics in their carriers.

Although there may be more, two conceptual styles have been identified and demonstrated reliably—relational and analytic styles. Relational and analytic conceptual styles were found to be associated with shared-function and formal primary-group participation, respectively, as socialization settings. So intimate were the relationships between primary group styles and conceptual styles that among pupils with experience in both types of groups mixed and conflicting conceptual styles could be observed.

The school was defined as a highly analytic environment in all its salient characteristics and requirements. Many children, however, demonstrate a relational approach to reality organization. Relational and analytic conceptual styles were found to be not only different but mutually incompatible. That is, one approach to reality organization could effectively hinder the development of the other; each could affect its carrier's ability to participate effectively in the alternate kind of group process or to deal directly with its cognitive requirements. In practice, it was found that children who had been socialized in shared-function environments could not participate effectively in any aspect of the formal school environment even when native ability and information repertoires were adequate.

The information-cognitive skills requirements for school performance were used to distinguish among the constructs "deprivation," "culture difference," and "culture conflict." "Deprivation" and "culture difference" have to do with the quantitative and qualitative characteristics of the information repertoires of individuals. "Culture conflict" deals with conflicting styles of conceptual organization. Highly relational children in the highly analytic school are thus seen as a case of culture conflict, regardless of whether deprivation and culture difference are also present.

Attention was then directed to nonverbal methods of measuring intelligence and achievement. Nonverbal tests have been designed to reduce their culture bias by drastically reducing their information components. However, they were found instead to deal in a focused fashion with the demonstration of analytic conceptual skills. Rather than freeing themselves of their culture-bound characteristics, they have focused on one critical aspect of it—the analytic mode of selecting and organizing information. When contextual inputs have been held constant, then, nonverbal tests of intelligence are more discriminatory against relational pupils than are the conventional types, which test partly, for information growth.

A number of educational problems may be separated out of the above analysis without challenging the relevance of school curricula to future concerns among children. As in any relatively consistent environment in which there are standardized criteria for performance, in which quantity and quality of inputs are relatively standardized, in which a heterogenous population is found, particularly one in which participation is nonvoluntary, as in the school, pupils may be relatively deprived or culturally different from or in culture conflict with it. One, two, all or none of these separate kinds of phenomena may be represented. Although, as they are defined here, deprivation and culture difference may be compensated in part through individualization or variation in the input level of the settings in which pupils learn, culture conflict represents an educational problem of some magnitude. Multiple-method learning environments can be devised. However, they will not only require the development of rules of transformation from one rule-set to another, but they can also be foreseen to produce far-reaching effects on school organization, teacher training, curricula, methods, and materials, the impact of which cannot yet be predicted. Moreover, culture conflict—a transactional concept—does not yield to unimodal analysis. If this is true, procedures for more valid measurement of learning potential and the development of more appropriate learning methods and settings are dependent upon the abandonment of assumptions that there is a single method for knowing.

Although the foci of these studies arose out of practical considerations, the issues that have been explored reflect basic science concerns. If such cognitive mechanisms as styles of cognitive control act reciprocally as mediating factors between social-system characteristics and individual-response characteristics, they are seen as important keys not only to effective program development but also to basic behavioral-science research.

Rosalie A. Cohen

The following anecdote from the report by Gay and Cole on the attempt to teach the New Math to the Kpelle tribe in Liberia aptly summarizes what Cohen and others are saying about different cultures, conceptual styles and education:

A bowl of uncooked rice is being passed around the room. "How many measuring cups of rice do you think are in it?" This question was asked of a group of 60 Peace Corps volunteers in training for service as teachers in Liberia. Each volunteer made his own estimate and the results were tabulated. The estimates ranged from 6 to 20 cups and averaged slightly over 12. In fact, there were exactly 9 cups of rice in the bowl, so an average overestimate of about 35 percent was made. This result is in striking contrast to that achieved by a group of 20 illiterate adult members of the Kpelle tribe of central Liberia. When asked the same question the Kpelle adults estimated the number of cups of rice in the bowl to be slightly under 9, and underestimate of only 8 percent.

Then, to the same group of 60 Peace Corps trainees another problem was given that gave them no difficulty. Eight cards were put face-up on the table. Pasted on the cards were 2 or 5 red or green squares or triangles. The task was to sort the cards into two piles; then, after sorting them once, to sort them again in a different way; and finally, to sort them a third way. The Peace Corps volunteers scarcely hesitated in performing this task. Yet a group of 30 illiterate Kpelle adults found great difficulty in sorting the cards even once. One was unable to sort them at all, and the remainder took an average of more than 1 minute for the first sort. Ten were unable to complete a second sort, and 21 failed to make the third sort. These later sorts, if completed, frequently took as long as 2 minutes.

To the casual American observer, the inability of the Kpelle subjects to sort the cards perhaps seems incredible. In fact, it is just this kind of observation that has led men to say "Africans think like children," or to speak of the "primitive mentality." But what about the Peace Corps volunteers' performance when asked to make a simple numerical estimate? Would this not appear an inept performance to any normal Kpelle adult?[32]

It is thus clear that individuals organize their experience and understandings in such ways as are functional within their particular social context. When confronted by alternate ways of knowing, they appear inept and incompetent, when in reality their understandings serve them well in the environments within which they were learned.

As pointed out earlier, modern capitalist societies depend on the participation of members who are oriented toward the acquisition of material goods, and are conforming and obedient to those over them. Schools, we have seen, are a reflection and a tool of that ideology. They encourage and seek to develop these attitudes, not, as we have seen, through the formal curriculum or the rhetoric they use to announce their purposes, but in the covert curriculum, the institutionalized rules and regulations, the hierarchy of power and bureaucratic administration, the intensive network of adult supervision and control over the natural exhuberance of youth, the institutionalized distrust and the fear.

Highly industrialized societies have needed literate people to play their appropriate roles. The "uneducated" may very likely be inadequately "domesticated" to accept the long-term, disciplined, impersonal, extrinsically rewarding goals of a technologically advanced state. But Paulo Freire has suggested an alternative way in which literacy can be valuable to society, in a liberating rather than oppressing way. A review of Freire's books, *Pedagogy of the Oppressed*[33] and *Cultural Action for Freedom*[34] is coupled by Miriam Wasserman with a critical review of Silberman's *Crisis in the Classroom*.[35] The contrast between the liberal and the revolutionary views of not just literacy but all of education is brought out in the process.

---

32. J. Gay and M. Cole. *The New Math and an Old Culture.* (New York: Holt, Rinehart & Winston, 1967), p. 1.
33. P. Freire. *Pedagogy of the Oppressed.* (New York: The Seabury Press, 1973).
34. P. Freire. *Cultural Action for Freedom, Harvard Educational Review,* Monograph Series, No. 1, 1970.
35. Charles Silberman. *Crisis in the Classroom,* (New York: Random House, 1970).

SCHOOL MYTHOLOGY AND
THE EDUCATION OF OPPRESSION

Miriam Wasserman

We have to examine the social functions of the schools, the myths we employ to becloud those functions, and the way the myths and the functions together turn adults and children into teachers and pupils by inducing them to internalize oppression. We have to do this in order to understand why and how schools oppress, and also what a liberating and liberated education would be and what kind of people it would require and create.

An examination of a few of the many recent books about the school crisis provides a possible beginning.

The first thing is to demythicize the school crisis. It is not that schools are joyless and grim and teachers boring and unimaginative that constitutes the crisis of the schools. Nor that lower-class (black, ethnic, poor) children are academically less successful than their more well-to-do schoolmates. School was always a misery, and the teachers—themselves almost as miserable as their charges— always harsh or merely dull. And academic success has always eluded most of the poor. (The fact that formerly they dropped out of school and didn't learn to read whereas now they are counted among the school population statistics and don't learn to read is not of great significance, though it aggravates certain elements of the school crisis.)

What constitutes the crisis of the schools is that the students, no longer accepting their oppressiveness as morally and intellectually legitimate, are turning off, cutting out, and fighting back. And, in the face of drugs, truancy and rebellion, the schools are less and less able to perform their socially necessary functions.

The school crisis is a part of the crisis of society. At once a manifestation of and a contributor to the other parts of the crisis of society, the school crisis is causing considerable alarm among influential persons and institutions both inside and outside the strictly school world. While some reformers are surely genuinely concerned with the miseries of childhood—as, indeed, some human adults have been in every generation—the extent of public attention to schools and schooling is rather a measure of their breakdown as a key oppressive instrument in the perpetuation of an oppressive society. The general strategy of the reform movement is to try to make the schools less oppressive without interfering in a gross way either with the oppressiveness of the larger society or with the schools' role in supporting that oppressiveness. By this strategy, the reformers seek to stem the growing tide of drugs, rebellion, and truancy, and to restore the schools' legitimacy as socializers of the various young for the adult roles prescribed by the interaction of society's needs and their own socioeconomic origins.

Miriam Wasserman, "School Mythology and the Education of Oppression," *This Magazine is About Schools,* Vol. 5, No. 3, Summer 1971, pp. 24-36.

Concern about the children is being expressed at the highest levels. Next to the advocates of the children of the poor, the severest critics of public school systems in the past ten years have been liberal spokesmen from the professions and big business, who attack not only the schools' lamentable bureaucratic inefficiencies but also their anti-intellectualism and the crudeness of their tactics of oppression. And among the staunchest and most generous supporters of the school reform movement have been some of the nation's large foundations, which have devoted generous resources to research, development, and support of various school reform movements and proposals.

Crisis in the Classroom: The Remaking of American Education constitutes a kind of synopsis of the reform movement, its strategies and confusions, its political and educational innocence, and its role as at once a purveyor and a victim of the various myths that have until now helped to perpetuate the schools' legitimacy as an educational institution.

The book was written by a member of the Board of Editors of *Fortune* magazine, Charles Silberman, and funded at $300,000 by the Carnegie Corporation. The amount of the funding, which has been widely publicized, is an evidence of corporate concern with the school crisis. Its popularity which might be surprising in the face of its length and dullness, is probably an evidence of at least part of the adult world's desperate need to be reassured that the myths about school which justify their lives are still good coin.

Crisis in the Classroom accepts either implicitly or explicitly most of these myths:

- That public schools exist to give all children an equal opportunity to get ahead in the world.

- That education is a process through which each child's unique inner potentiality is realized.

- That our society has increasing need for men and women who have initiative, independence, and the ability to make their own decisions.

- That the function of the public schools in respect to the poor and the outcast is to bring them into the mainstream of American economic and social life.

A corollary to these myths is that the reason whole classes of children do not get ahead in the world and the reason almost all schoolchildren tend to be fearful and conformist instead of daring and independent is that somehow school people don't know how to do their job properly.

In respect to capitalist society, the analogue to the myths about school is that its most virulent malfunctions are mere squeaks and creaks in a basically sound piece of machinery. Thus Silberman writes: ". . . economic growth reduces poverty but it also produces congestion, noise, and pollution of the environment. Technological change widens the individual's range of choice and makes economic growth possible; it also dislocates workers from their jobs and neighborhoods . . . The enormous widening of choice that contemporary society makes possible also appears as something of a mixed blessing, enhancing our sense of individuality, but contributing, too, to the pervasive sense of uneasiness and malaise." The spiritual crisis of American youth "stems more from the successes of American society than from its failure." Social injustice is not being eliminated fast enough: "... improvements ... generated expectations for further improvements. . ." And so on. The war is not referred to.

Silberman's view of the relationship between a society which he thinks is failing a little bit and schools which he thinks are failing a lot is a perversion of reality. He writes: "We will not be able to create and maintain a humane society unless we create and maintain classrooms that are humane. But if we succeed in that endeavor—if we accomplish the remaking of American education —we will have gone a long way toward that larger task, toward the creation of a society in which we can answer the question 'Where art thou?' with pride rather than with dread." So does the classroom become the creator, and society the created; children and teachers the reformers, and leaders and masters the re-formed.

To overcome the crisis of the schools, and at the same time eliminate some of the squeaks and creaks in the social machinery, Silberman identifies and proposes remedies for each of four grave school problems. They are: (1) the failure of black children to acquire academic expertise; (2) the "grim, repressive, joyless atmosphere" of elementary school; (3) the unfreedom and outmoded curriculum of high school; and (4) the improper education of educators. For each of the four problems, the book explicates some common going explanations and some previous remedies which have failed. More or less exonerating all the people involved (teachers, parents, administrators, etc.), the book proposes its own one-word explanation for each problem. The word is the same in each case: Mindlessness.

Silberman believes that mindlessness is unnecessary. "The 'necessity' that makes schooling so uniform over time and across cultures is simply the 'necessity' that stems from unexamined assumptions and unquestioned behavior." He believes that the problems that stem from mindlessness can be overcome and that this is proved by the fact that in one experimental program or another they *were* overcome. Much of the bulk of *Crisis in the Classroom* is composed of examples of experimental programs which are reported to have succeeded, or at least, like expanding, affluent, capitalist America, to have only a few bugs that still need to be ironed out.

There is a kind of innocence that suffuses the entire work, from its literary style and research techniques, through its examples, to its conclusions. The writing is at once passionless and sentimental, lacking even that devotion to humanity and spiritual outrage that mark the best of the exposé books by the indignant teacher-writers of the past five years. The researchers or the writer (apparently lacking the down-to-earth sense that most school inhabitants have of what goes on in a school) cite as examples of mindlessness a number of school rules which, though horribly oppressive, have perfectly sound justification within the terms of the school system. For example, that high school students are not allowed to wander around the corridors without a pass, go home for lunch, or go to the toilet without permission. But all school inmates know that the most benign hall disturbances involve the disruption of classes in progress and that hall stickups, locker rip-offs, and stairwell rapes are occasional, although naturally not well publicized, occurrences; that high school students who go out to lunch are unlikely to come back for the afternoon session; and that while most high school students eschew the filthy toilets as places to relieve their bladders and bowels, many go there for a quick illegal cigarette and a few for a fast pill or shooting up.

As a matter of fact, reading *Crisis in the Classroom,* one wonders if in all the three years and thousands of miles of visiting schools, Silberman and his staff ever went slumming in the students' restrooms, cafeterias, and locker rooms or sat about unobtrusively and anonymously in the corners of teachers' lounges and deans' offices. For it is in these places that people shed the pretenses and the myths and reveal in their actions and words what school means and what it does.

The same innocence which informs the research for the book also informs the reporting on experimental programs. Thus the book undiscriminatingly endorses programs with profoundly contradictory aims and tendencies, e.g., the achievement-oriented CAM Academy of Chicago and the relevance-oriented John Adams High School of Portland, Oregon. Again the author admiringly quotes one rolled-up-sleeves tough, accountability principal as saying, "I don't care what you do as long as the children are reading at the norm." And then reports of the new English primary schools, which are the prototypes of his solution to elementary school oppressiveness, "while I saw 'bad' informal schools —bad from the standpoint of their students' academic achievement—I saw none that were destructive, none in which the children did not appear to be happy and engaged." Now, whipping up children to reading "norms" and undertaking that they be "happy and engaged" are not compatible aims (which does not mean that happy and engaged children do not learn to read).

The innocence in respect to the programs called experimental or innovative lies not only in a willingness to accept more or less at face value the innovators' own progress reports. More than that it lies in a common acceptance by the innovators and the author of all the going school mythology and of the validity of the program at hand as an instrument in the service of one or another of those myths (equal opportunity for all, "right to read," fullest development of individual interests and talents, and so on). For those who perpetuate myths in their own defense are often the last to lose their innocence, the last to discover that the mythic fabric is rotting off their backs.

In respect to schools, there are myths folded into myths. There are the myths which people outside the schools tell to explain what the schools are supposed to be doing. And then there are the myths which people inside the schools tell to explain to students what society is supposed to be doing. Thus the myth that society uses to becloud the children's oppression is that they are engaged in the pursuit of a meaningful education whereby they will attain their maximum potential. Meanwhile, inside the schools the children themselves are treated to myths about the society that is mythicizing their oppression on the order that all men are equal before the law, everyone has an equal chance to get ahead, etc. The two classes of myths are mutually reinforcing. But when one goes, the other goes.

The school crisis consists in their mutual disintegration. The students long ago demythicized the schools: they know they are not there to realize their inner potential, they are kept there by a combination of legal and economic coercion. Many of them have also demythicized society: they know that the policeman (court, welfare worker, etc.) isn't there to protect them, he's there to keep them in line. And some of them are beginning to synthesize these perceptions: they are beginning to understand how the myths about society are folded into the myths about schools, that is, how the myths that are told about school and the ones that are told in school serve their masters and oppress them.

I had a fine illustration of this one day when I was called to serve as a teacher of a civics class in a mainly Latino high school. A group of four or five smart and also school-smart girl students explained to me the ideological function of the schools.

I asked them, "What do you learn in this class?"

"About government."

"What about government?"

"You know, how it works. The Governor, and the President, and all things like that."

"How does it work, the government?"

"Not like it says here," referring to the thick red-white-and-blue-covered text they were carrying.

"What does it say, and how does it work differently?"

"You know, Reagan is cutting the welfare. And the cops. They hassle you. Anyway they hassle the men where we live. And all the taxes, and like that."

"And what does the book say?"

"You know, that all men are created equal, and they don't discriminate because of race, color, or — what?"

"Creed. And isn't it like that? Aren't all men equal?"

"No. Not for us it isn't. We're not equal." (I felt that they were saying that *I* might have been created equal but they weren't. And that they thought I might not understand about that.)

"Well, but you say that's not what it says in the book. But if Reagan is cutting welfare and the cops hassle poor people more than rich people, then why doesn't the book say that? Why does it say all men are created equal and all those other things about government?"

Everybody answered.

"You know, that's what they want us to think."

"The rich people want us to think like them so we'll be on their side."

"Brainwashing."

"Ideology and the Ideological Instruments of the State" by the French Marxist philosopher Louis Althusser is a theoretical development of the school function the Latino girls described as "brainwashing."

Police, army, tax collector, judge, prison, says Althusser, are among the repressive instruments of the state. Mass media, political parties, church, schools, and family are among the ideological instruments of the state. Although Althusser does not, we might define the difference by observing that the ideological instruments of the state induce us to internalize oppression. The more the ideological instruments of the state are successful, the less difficulty encountered by the repressive instruments. In neutral terms, the school as an ideological instrument serves to socialize children.

Whereas in an earlier period of capitalism, the children of the poor were socialized on the job, the reproduction of the labor force, Althusser says, now proceeds more and more outside the processes of production, with school and family serving as the major socializing agents. (In a few disappearing pockets of the economy—mainly tenant farming and migratory field work—American children continue to be socialized by the twin instruments of work-family rather than school-family.)

Poor and nonpoor families are alike expected to and usually ao act as junior partners of the school. Here in the United States, however, the school's tactics in respect to its junior partner and the parents' tactics with their children are often differentiated by the parents' socioeconomic status. Nonpoor parents rely on the symbol "the grade" to evaluate their children's relationship to the school. If the grade does not meet their expectations, they may withdraw love, pocket money, vacations, etc., or, alternatively, bestow them in greater abundance where the grade does meet their expectations. Some poor parents do this, too. But they and the schools are likely to object less to poor academic performance than to bad behavior. Schools regularly call upon the parents of children who will not accept school routines or discipline and seek to frighten or shame them into taking harsh measures against their children. In the middle class, the life style—place of residence, times of vacation, modes of recreation—often revolves around the parents' perception of their children's school needs. Poor families lack the resources or flexibility to do this. The enlisting of the family in the service of the school has come in the last few years to extend down into the preschool years. A whole new strategy of early childhood education is to train poor mothers to deal with their infants and babies in ways that will make them more amenable to school manipulation a few years hence. Thus social-worker-educator-psychologists are running a game on the poor that is being run on the middle class by the hucksters of infant reading programs, educational toys, and so on.

But within three to six years after they get into the schools, most children (probably even including the infant readers) unmask the gamesters. A part of the crisis of the schools, as we observed, consists in their perception of the schools' ideological function and their refusal to perform their expected roles, which refusal they signify in various destructive, or self-destructive, or political ways. Where their parents do not share their perception and refusal, the so-called generation gap occurs. Increasingly, however, as parents recognize, at first perhaps confusedly, that the schools oppress their children only in order to prepare them for the same life of oppression as they themselves live, they are withdrawing from the school-parent partnership. In this way they are aggravating the crisis.

The possibility that the students' dawning recognition of their subjection can be elevated into a new kind of education is suggested by the works of Paulo Freire, a sometime colleague of Ivan Illich's at the Centro Intercultural de Documentation in Cuernevaca.

Cultural Action for Freedom and *Pedagogy of the Oppressed* describe the author's techniques of using literacy training among Brazilian and Chilean peasants and urban oppressed as a way of revolutionary consciousness-raising. Seeing education as the process by which man knows and transforms himself, and his world, these beautiful writings are a contribution to the literature of both educational and revolutionary theory. In respect to the former, they offer a critique of conventional educational methods and an explanation of pedagogical techniques that are consonant with and directed to revolutionary socialist change both in the classroom and outside it. In respect to the latter, they premise that education of the oppressed must accompany social revolution; and they elaborate a humanistic theory of consciousness-raising which is in opposition to elitist vanguard strategies.

While Freire's theories and techniques derive from his work with the oppressed of South America, they can well be applied to our understanding of schooling and our work as radical teachers here. His pedagogical method, which will feel familiar to nursery school educators and followers of Sylvia Ashton-Warner, is to employ for literacy learning, material from the students' own lives as members of their particular oppressed groups. Learning to read begins with a "generative" word, from whose syllables other words can be generated. The word chosen is one which is deeply significant in the students' lives. For example, he uses *favela* in Brazil and *callampa* in Chile, each representing "the same social economic, and cultural reality of the vast numbers of slum dwellers in those countries." When decomposed into their syllables, or pieces, as the students term them, these words can be reassembled into new words. In the United States, the energetic and creative educator Caleb Gattegno, whose sense of what learning means seems to be similar to Freire's, does much the same thing in teaching reading to young children. Freire, however, carries the exploratory methodology of Gattegno, Ashton-Warner, and thousands of nursery-school and progressive educators to the next and crucial step of *conscientizacño*, "learning to perceive social, political, and economic contradictions and to take action against the oppressive elements of reality."

Learning to read by means of socially significant generative words is a revolutionary method not only because it "works," the criterion by which oppressor educators choose a pedagogy to develop in their students marketable (i.e., exploitable) skills. It is also revolutionary because it is the first step among the illiterate oppressed to self-liberation.

From two widely separated nations of the Third World, testimony has been offered of adult literacy learning as liberating.

A report from a community-development, adult-literacy project in Tanzania says, "Becoming literate as an adult in this African society is a spiritual experience in some ways related to the emergence and growth of personality. People are uplifted by it and are made aware of their power to alter their environment by individual and group action."[1]

And from Chile:

> "We asked one of the adult students, finishing the first level of literacy classes, why he hadn't learned to read and write before the agrarian reform.
>
> "Before the agrarian reform, my friend," he said, "I didn't even think. Neither did my friends.
>
> "Why?" we asked.
>
> "Because it wasn't possible. We lived under orders. We only had to carry out orders. We had nothing to say."

Both nations are somehow socialist at least in intent. What is being described is a situation in which a man who was treated, and treated himself, as a thing experiences a sense of himself as a man with the power to change himself and his world. The internal change occurs along with the social change: the situation changes and it changes the man; the man changes himself and he changes the situation. The entire process is accompanied by a feeling of elation.

The elation that accompanies learning to read by the generative word, learning to read as an act of will and for the purpose of changing oneself and controlling one's destiny, is a feeling tone that does not prevail in the classrooms of the nation. They are, indeed, as Silberman laments, "grim, joyless, repressive" places. For in the oppressive classrooms of an oppressive society, the student learns to read not by an act of will but through an act of coercion, not to change himself and control his destiny but by alienating himself and in order to submit to his destiny. And he learns to read not his own word from his own world but another's word from a mythical world. ("See Jan run." "Policemen are our friends. . . . Sometimes they scold people, but only when the people do something wrong." "A asa e da ave; the wing is of the bird.") The children of the oppressed who are silent in the face of this alien language depicting a mythical world are called by the schools "inarticulate" and "culturally deprived." But Freire calls the "inarticulateness of the culturally deprived" the "cultural silence of the oppressed." And he says that they are silent because their word has been stolen. This is so in the sense that the conditions and the internalizing of their oppression make it impossible for them to explore and express their oppression.

From learning to read by means of the generative word, which is the first step in the individual's re-creation of himself and his world, Freire's educational strategy moves to learning to solve problems by means of the generative theme. The problems are those which center about their own oppression. "I conceive the fundamental theme of our epoch," Freire writes, "to be that of *domination* —which implies its opposite, the theme of *liberation*, as the object to be achieved." But the generative theme must be the learners' own, derived with the teacher's help from their own lives, and solved, with the teacher's help, in their own words.

A footnote quotes from Malraux's *Anti-Memoirs* on this matter: "In a long conversation with Malraux, Mao-Tse-Tung declared, 'You know I've proclaimed for a long time: we must teach the masses clearly what we have received from them confusedly.' " Or, in Freire's and his students' words, "we must make words speak."

An example is given of a generative theme developed by the students quite differently from the way the group leader had thought to develop it. The students are shown a picture of a drunken man walking on the street and three young men conversing on a corner. The group leader had intended to discuss aspects of alcoholism. But the group members responded to the picture by saying that "the only one there who is productive and useful to his country is the souse who is returning home after working all day for low wages and who is worried about his family because he can't take care of their needs. He is the only worker. He is a decent worker and a souse like us." For the learners to have been able to proclaim their honest feelings about drunkenness and to articulate their view of its relation to their oppression, the "teacher" had to abdicate his intention to expound (and probably moralize) on the aspects and evils of alcoholism. (The application to drug-abuse programs for American schoolchildren is apparent.)

The analogue to the generative theme in education for freedom is problem-solving in education for oppression.

As American school people use the terms "inarticulateness" and "cultural deprivation" to describe the silence of oppressed children in the face of a mythical world encoded in alien dialects, they use the expression "deficiency in cognitive ability" to describe the children's refusal to solve the alien problems that constitute the core of our school curriculum. (Some theorists, like Arthur Jensen, ascribe the cognitive deficiency to genetic inferiority. But the liberal theorists, outraged at this explanation, ascribe it to deficient language development.) Seeking to overcome the passivity in the face of oppression that is created by that oppression, U.S. school people are experimenting with ways of stimulating problem-solving ability among the children of the poor (sometimes called "slow" or "basic" learners).

The following example shows how the process of "stealing the word of the oppressed" is carried on by means of simulation of problem-solving. The material is from a teacher's manual to a history of the United States for "slow learners," published by a leading textbook publisher and sponsored by a leading university. The intention of the method proposed in the manual is to develop the students' "willingness to answer questions," "to participate in discussions," and "to obtain permission to speak or to ask a question." The method also seeks to enhance the students' self-concept by enabling them to say, "I'm not so dumb." "I am able to learn on my own." "I can make decisions myself." The chapter under consideration is entitled "Slavery in America." The manual directs the teacher as follows:

> Parts 2 and 4 present both economic and social reasons to explain why people in the North and South held different attitudes toward slavery. By not saying "white people," the formulation excludes blacks including by implication those in the class, from the category "people." Black people in the North and the South did not hold different attitudes toward slavery. Unlike most material for basic learners, these lessons neither draw conclusions nor make generalizations. They merely present a problem. Based on the evidence offered, students make their own decisions about the fairness of slavery and the treatment of slaves. Because of contemporary racial tensions involving personal commitment to black nationalism or to white backlash movements, many students may find it difficult to examine salvery analytically. In such cases, although the materials and teaching strategies employed in the chapter encourage rational inquiry rather than irrational appeal, the teacher must also stress the value of objective historical investigation.
>
> Lead students to realize that they do not yet have enough evidence to know definitely if slaves were treated differently (i.e., some kindly and some cruelly). They should recognize however, that the two readings indicate that people had different views about how slaves were treated.
>
> Students should conclude that both are eyewitness accounts and fairly reliable, but that neither gives enough evidence on which to base a decision about the general severity of slavery.[2]

The genuine problems of oppression—in this case, How does slavery turn humans into commodities? How could or did the enslaved rebel? How do elements of nineteenth-century slavery endure in twentieth-century America? How can those still enslaved liberate themselves? etc.—are hidden by a spurious problem—were slaves treated well or badly? (This book, by the way is not exceptional. This is the conventional manner of structuring the "problem" of slavery in American history textbooks.) Having structured the problem fallaciously, the teacher (the textbook) then attempts to manipulate the students into believing that by their own thinking they will arrive at the solution. But the problem is a nonproblem, for which there is ready in the teacher's mind (implanted there by life long training and specifically reinforced by the textbook) the response that there is only a nonanswer ("objective historial investigation," "we don't have enough evidence," etc.). Those students who have learned to play the school game will know how to formulate the nonanswer and will be rewarded by being informed that they have "made some decisions for themselves, they are not so dumb." So does the oppressor steal the word of the oppressed.

In a peculiar and ironic way, this particular lesson is one that the school reformers might consider to belong to the tactic of reform called relevance. Only at the hands of the oppressor-educators, the relevant theme of oppression and liberation is washed out in a flood of secondary myths about scholarship, two sides to every questions, and so on. And the students' emerging affirmation "We are oppressed" is turned into the oppressors' affirmation "We don't treat you so badly."

By contrast, a true pedagogy of the oppressed encodes and clarifies the words and themes of the oppressed and turns them back to the students for decoding and further clarification in a process of continuous dialogue between teacher and students. This is what Freire calls *conscientizaçao*. The dialogue is accompanied by praxis: acting and reacting on the world to overcome the oppression that is being revealed—remaking one's world as one remakes oneself and one's fellow men.

Conscientizaçao and revolutionary praxis together constitute a standard by which to evaluate conventional school pedagogy and also education in noncapitalist countries and revolutionary propaganda.

Freire calls conventional school pedagogy the "banking concept of education." "In the banking concept of education," he says, "Knowledge is a gift bestowed by those who consider themselves knowledgeable upon those whom they consider to know nothing." The banking concept of education, by alienating men from their own decision-making and learning, treats them as objects; this pedagogy is appropriate for schools in a social system which treats men as objects and alienates them from their decision-making and their work. The schools therefore are not mindless, as Silberman proposes, but adapted to their function. And the joy, relevance, creativity, flexibility, freedom, humanity that the school reformers so earnestly seek to instill in the schools—while they may relieve some of their present dreariness—are not at all the same as the genuine elation of learning for liberation, just as nonproblem-solving manipulativeness is not at all the same as genuine dialogue and praxis.

In the very process of exposing and overcoming an oppressive education that turns men into oppressors and oppressed, we have to create a liberating education that will enable us to overcome oppressive institutions and the oppression within ourselves. Freire's pedagogy of dialogue and praxis can also be a guide for revolutionary consciousness-raising and socialist education.

"It is absolutely essential," Freire writes, "that the oppressed participate in the revolutionary process with an increasingly critical awareness of their role as subjects of the transformation." Again: "Scientific revolutionary humanism cannot, in the name of revolution, treat the oppressed as objects to be analyzed and . . . presented with prescriptions for behavior. To do this would be to fall into one of the myths of the oppressor ideology: the *absolutizing of ignorance*. The myth implies the ignorance of someone else . . . Those who steal the words of others develop a deep doubt in the abilities of the others. Each time they say their word without hearing the word of those whom they have forbidden to speak, they grow more accustomed to power and acquire a taste for guiding, ordering, and commanding. They can no longer live without having someone to give orders to."

Oppression is perpetuated not only by the institutions of society but also by our internalizing of the institutions via its myths. Merely the destruction of the institutions will not be sufficient to overcome the myths. Cuba's schools and China's cultural revolution evidence this. In the Movement, elitism is more than a strategy: it is the tough remaining core of the myths of the oppressor ideology. Among Movement-related teachers, the habits and attitudes of oppressor education persist.

The internalization of oppression—the capitalist cancer of the spirit—undermines the will and the ability to re-create our world. The world of oppression is not only all around us but inside us. We are beginning to understand how oppressive schools serve an oppressive society by implanting in children elements of the oppressor and the oppressed. It will not be enough to overcome the external relations of oppression. We will have to find new forms of education that will enable us to re-create ourselves in children who will refuse to be either oppressors or oppressed.

To find these forms we have need not only of a revolutionary educator like Freire, but also of the liberal school reformers like Silberman, Holt, and others. For in seeking to reform schools and education, they all cause us to question our practices as adults and teachers and to question the myths that we employ to explain them. The myths are a part of the apparatus of oppression. We have to face them and understand them in order to divest ourselves of them.

As we do this, we must engage in dialogue with our students about their and our oppression. Their emerging consciousness of how school mythology perpetuates their oppression is in many instances in advance of ours. If we can take for ourselves and give back to them clearly what we receive from them confusedly, they and we will learn from the dialogue. The area of praxis—the schools—is common to us both. Not the reformers but the actors will at some time need to re-create the schools. And this will only be done by redefining and remaking themselves and the process of education in which they are engaged.

NOTES

1. Alexander MacDonald, *Tanzania: Young Nation in a Hurry,* Hawthorn, 1966.
2. *The Americans: A History of the United States. Teacher's Manual,* by the staff of the Social Studies Curriculum Center, Carnegie-Mellon University, American Heritage Publishing Co., Holt, Rinehart & Winston, 1969.

Miriam Wasserman

It is obvious that we are still convinced that there is one right way to live, our way, and that reality comes in one package waiting to be opened and discovered, rather than in many styles formed through a variety of historical experiences and practices. We have yet to acknowledge that we do not pursue truth, we create it. And in doing this, we do not all have the same amount of power to be creative in the process of defining and organizing the world. We have all been influenced by the strength and ideology of the more powerful.

Carlos Castaneda, in his accounts of the teachings of Don Juan,[36] a Yaqui Indian sorcerer, tells us that the world of everyday life is not natural or "out there" as we believe it is. Reality is only a description, a description which has been pounded into us from birth. Everyone with whom a child comes into contact is a teacher who incessantly describes the world to him until he is able to perceive the world as it is described. From this point on, the child is a member of the group, and is capable of making all of the proper perceptual interpretations in common with others who share his membership. The fact that his reality is merely one of many descriptions and realities, is no longer a serious consideration.

Schools are expressions of the existing culture, designed to transmit it as it is.

> The function of education has never been to free the mind and the spirit of man, but to bind them; and to the end that the mind and spirit of his children should never escape, Homo sapiens has employed praise, ridicule, admonition, accusation, mutilation, and even torture to chain them to the culture pattern. Throughout most of his historic course, Homo sapiens has wanted from his children acquiescence, not originality.[37]

Jules Henry goes on to say that the function of education is to prevent the truly creative intellect from getting out of hand. Creativity occurs only after its thrust has been directed towards socially approved ends. The human being's first concern is to survive, as he sees it. New ideas provoke fear, because they might not work and his world might collapse. Thus, an individual's capacity to look at anything new is colored by his fear of change and by the existence of an internalized ideology supporting the world as it is.

We live in a society full of fears and anxieties, related basically to the material conditions of our life and to our search for absolute truths and a permanence which can be organized and controlled and which provides stability. This is within the Western tradition of philosophy. It is also within the capitalist tradition which creates isolated individuals and sees issues in isolation from larger contexts. The products of a social system such as ours (our children) mirror our fears, which are primarily fear of differences, changes, and failure, as measured by our acquisitive and competitive standards. Our children have learned too, to be afraid to show their deep emotions, passions, feelings, in the form of honest and sincere relationships. They have learned fear of subjective experience which cannot always be controlled, and they fear being open, exposed, and defenseless against potential attack. They, too, learn to live in the "then" and not in the "now."

---

36. Carlos Castaneda. *The Teachings of Don Juan, A Separate Reality, Journey to Ixtlan* (New York: Simon and Schuster, 1971), p. 2.
37. Jules Henry. *Culture Against Man* (New York: Random House, 1963), p. 286.

Impersonality, efficiency, objectivity, restraint, control—all are highly valued in our world, all hinder the spontaneous and natural development of a human being. A deluge of criticism has been loosed against these restrictive values, by philosophers, psychologists, historians, anthropologists, and sociologists, such as Carl Rogers, Abraham Maslow, Frederick Perls, R. D. Laing, Theodore Roszak, Erich Fromm, Paul Goodman, Jean-Paul Sartre, Herbert Marcuse, who have put forth the premise that a human being must feel, must experience the world and find himself through his own interpretation of those experiences, must choose his own road towards self-actualization. Now what is needed is to extend this attack on values to an attack against the material conditions which have created and supported them. Until our society exchanges its emphasis on acquisition and elite private control for emphasis on public control and real democratic political practice, the schools and the social product will look no different.

A child needs much more than to ponder over other people's experience. He/she needs his/her own experiences, numerous and varied, in order to come to terms with himself/herself and his/her own realities, which includes his/her powers, his/her potential, his/her strengths, his/her weaknesses and his/her inner being. But while the practice of life continues to revolve around competitive structures and experiences, these humanistic aims will remain inaccessible.

chapter six

WHAT IS TO BE DONE?

In the readings we have included as representative of a new analysis of American education, there has been an almost exclusive concern with organization and structure. A discussion of the contributions that individuals within the organization and structure might make to an alternative education in America has been almost totally lacking. Most of the authors of our readings thus far believe that despite any effects individuals may have on education, a much greater impact is made by the organizational structure of schools and classes, the hierarchy of roles, the authoritarian relationships dictated by the way schools are organized, and the arrangement of the schools' relationships with the rest of society.

But we see a shortcoming in such a view, particularly if our analysis is to result in an understanding of how individuals—you, our reader, among them, hopefully—might fulfill the professed commitment of our educational system to the democratic ideals of equality, justice, and liberation. An analysis that says it is organization and structure and not individuals that accounts for what happens in the schools is surely one-sided. It has the tendency to present individuals in our schools as the passive victims of large, impersonal forces. At worst it can be taken (mistakenly, we think) as saying that people are powerless to deal with "the system."

Of course these writers are not saying that individual action counts for nothing. They do, after all, address their critiques of education not to nonpersonal systems, but to individual people. And in formulating arguments backed with evidence to support their conclusions, they appeal to the thinking, deliberative processes in each of us, the very processes that are the foundation of individual choice and action.

We are confronted, then, with the question of how and where individual choice and action fits into the organizational and structural actualities of American education. On a less abstract plane, it is the question of what each of us can do to move American education toward more democratic purposes, considering both the school system's present organization and structure, and its control over what happens in our schools. But in order to answer that question we need to answer some other questions first. We need to decide whether it is "the system" we change first, or whether it is the individuals in the system that we change. There is something of a chicken-and-egg paradox here. How do we change individuals without changing the system, since it is the system that seems to play a large part in making (and keeping) those individuals what they are? On the other hand, how do we change the system without changing individuals?

A related question, often posed the same way, concerns the relationship between schools and society. The argument goes that we cannot change the schools without changing society, for the schools are inescapably reflections of their society. But then aren't all institutions reflections of society? And if we are to change society, we must also change its institutions—schools included.

We have to begin somewhere to get at this amorphous abstraction we call "society."

These paradoxes suggest that we may have incorrectly stated the questions. As Aristotle would say, let us begin again. As an alternative, let us not think of individual and system, or of school and society, as separable and opposed actualities. The "system" is of course made up of individuals and their expressions and actions. Similarly, that which we call "society" is made up in part by, and expressed, perpetuated and changed through, the actions of "schools." In such a view, when we speak of the individual and system in conflict, we should speak of one part of the system in conflict with another part. When we speak of school and society in conflict, we should speak of one part of society in conflict with another part.

But the question remains: can we achieve meaningful or radical change in organization and structure of the schools without changing other parts of society? And can we achieve such change by directing our attention to the individuals in the schools? The answer is clear to us: no single direction, no single part of the total picture, by itself, holds the promise for such change. We need to change the schools at the same time that we are changing other parts of society. And we need to change individuals associated with schools while we are changing the other structural and organizational parts of the schools. To say that we must change the system in order to get meaningful change is self-stultifying if we do not also change individuals as part of that system. It is equally self-stultifying to say we must change individuals (raise their consciousness and all that), if we do not also change the structures. We need to direct our attention to both types of change, and at more in the larger society.

Reformers of education need to draw upon, and in turn add to, the support of other parts of society, especially those parts where changes are going on in the direction of the democratic goals of equality, liberation, and justice. The various liberation groups in American society—ethnic and racial minorities, women's, gay's, men's, and perhaps most important children's liberation— represent changes going on in such basic parts of American society as the family. They also embody new ways of looking at human beings, and as William Pepper points out, there will be no meaningful changes in our schools until there are changes in our ways of looking at children.[1]

The courts have been, and continue to be, important sources of change in the schools. Court decisions regarding segregation in the schools, school financing, and students' rights, while yet to reap their full harvest, nonetheless show the power for change in the schools that legal action offers. Combined with this could be widespread advocacy for school change by legal and paralegal forces, a kind of Nader's Raiders for the schools. Such advocacy could move on several fronts, legal and otherwise, to test the constitutionality and morality of such things as compulsory school attendance and withholding from children the civil rights adults enjoy.[2] And as we will see in the readings that follow, there is the potential for change represented by both the free school movement outside the public school system and the recent alternative school movement within public schools.

1. William E. Pepper, *The Self-Managed Child; Paths to Cultural Rebirth* (San Rafael, California: Harper, 1973).
2. John Holt, *Escape From Childhood; The Needs and Rights of Children* (New York: E. P. Dutton, 1974).

We do not mean to make this sound simple or easy. We are saying that no single approach to changing our schools should be rejected automatically. At the same time we are saying that it is going to take more—much more—than a single approach. We urge you to avoid the self-delusions of individual potency that Thelma A. Olshaker, a teacher in the District of Columbia school system, recently warned new teachers about in the *Los Angeles Times*.[3] Ms. Olshaker noted that the larger segment of the faculty in a given public school is

> a group of young, zestful people who appear in September, bringing with them the great American myth that some creative, energetic teacher can change the system. By the following September they are gone, and a new group of young men and women appear, long on idealism and short on staying power.

Ms. Olshaker does not mean to put down these young new teachers. She is not prepared to say whether their methods are better or worse than those of the traditional teachers, nor does she think anyone else can determine that yet. Theirs is a different apporach, and one that any veteran of school teaching can tell you about.

> Through the school year these new teachers vociferously refute the antiquated teaching methods of the senior faculty members and the irrelevance of their subject matter. They are gung-ho on core teaching, role-playing, relevance and "rapping" with the students. They speak in student jargon, and they wear jeans. They plan trips and throw out the "outdated" books. They scorn grammar and structured lesson plans. They use newspapers and magazines and let the kids write their own curriculum. They rearrange chairs from rows to circles, and they never sit at teachers' desks.

Ms. Olshaker's concern here is not with the rightness or wrongness of their methods, but with the fact that these young teachers leave so quickly. "Why don't they sustain their energy and enthusiasm?" she asks. "Why don't they change the 'system'?"

It is her guess that they leave from "the weariness caused by the exceptional passivity of many of the students," something no education course has prepared them for, but something that the seasoned teachers have built up emotional defenses against. We would add, another reason the new teachers leave may be their monumental lack of knowledge and understanding of the way schools actually work.

In turning to our readings in this chapter on what is to be done about American schools, we suggest that you look for the ways in which the school organization and structures, which our earlier readings have exposed, are evidenced through the behavior of individuals in the schools: and in what way they are changed or departed from by individuals who, alone and in concert, seek to develop educational alternatives. When we speak of "organization and structures" we are referring especially to the values and purposes at work in the schools' actual operations, as well as the means for pursuing them.

3. *Los Angeles Times,* September 10, 1974.

The readings in this chapter give examples of two ways in which our question "What is to be done?" has been answered. The first five readings tell us what individuals, particularly individual teachers, can do. The remaining five readings tell us how groups of people have organized entire schools as alternatives to the system, both outside that system and more recently inside it.

In both cases—the efforts of individuals alone and the organization of new schools—we can see ways in which the organization and structures of schools as well as their values and purposes have been changed. Both represent individuals at work changing the system as it impinges on them. We have attempted to present accounts of efforts directed at the specific school structures which were analyzed by our earlier authors as the ones most responsible for what the schools now do, and fail to do.

We think it especially important that anyone seeking to change the schools be aware not only of these structures but also of how they are expressed and perpetuated in the actions of individuals, often unwittingly. Our first author, Stanley Charnofsky, points out that what teachers do in their schools reflects what was done to them during their own schooling. And most of these teachers are unaware that they are doing it. This is one of the major ways in which the structures of American education are perpetuated. If we eliminate the reflection we can halt the perpetuation of the old structures, and then we can change or get rid of them.

Note some of the things that Charnofsky says teachers unwittingly reflect in their practices, perhaps because they know of no alternatives. There is the classroom conformity and discipline of their own schooling; the competitiveness in such practices as grading; the impersonality of teacher-student relationships; the authority-centered teaching and curriculum; the compartmentalized learning (and living) in schools; the inflexibility of procedures and classroom and school structures; the class bias, race bias, and sex bias in teaching and the curriculum; the indoctrinating quality of most school experiences; and the subservience of learning to the purposes of others, whether teachers, adults, or state authorities. All of these practices reflect some part of the social corporate structure of the United States which our earlier authors disclosed. Change this reflection in our teachers-to-be, and you change, or begin to change, the schools.

But how can that be done when the school system structure is so organized that its products, the teachers-to-be, will almost certainly go on perpetuating the old system?

While most teachers do reflect them, a growing number do not. Our first reading represents what we would call an excursion into raising the consciousness of prospective teachers, of showing them how they unwittingly, often unconsciously, reflect the structures of their own schooling. It is but one step from that awareness to the realization that the reflecting does not *have* to go on.

EDUCATING THE POWERLESS

Stanley Charnofsky

*   *   *

What our teachers do in schools reflects what was done to them during their preparation. And most of what has been done to them violates everything that is known about communication and learning theory. Most of what they have experienced on their way to becoming teachers has occurred within several four-walled rooms, using several books as reference authorities, hearing several lecturers who are experienced authorities, and occasionally interacting with their fellow students in order to "share" ideas. In short, so it seems, our teachers pretty much learn how to teach through their formal course work. . . .

Actually, the formal course work should provide no more than a catalyst which would help to stimulate the more authentic aspects of teacher preparation. (The reference here is to all sorts of course work, and not solely to that course work officially listed in the catalogues as education courses.) No doubt, our teachers would progress without such heavy focus on formal course work—indeed, perhaps without it would be more sensitive and better able to work with children. Yet we continue to insist that the formal course work is really what does the job in preparing better teachers. *How* does course work act to desensitize large numbers of dedicated and eager teachers-to-be? Let us try a brief list and then expand upon it. . . .[1]

1. Students are assembled, for the most part, in neat rows, facing the professor. (The more adept learn, by the time they are juniors, to sleep quite well sitting up with their eyes wide open.)
2. Professors carefully avoid personal contact with their students (teachers-to-be), because their objectivity and the equity of their evaluations would otherwise suffer.
3. Many professors are quite steeped in their own subject area, but their skill at providing any incentives for their students consists primarily of *telling* them all about what they know.
4. There is a weary and dreary notion among professors that what is important to them is also going to be important to their students; and so teaching becomes a process of insisting that students master what their professors have mastered—some make it quite clear that *they* are personal role models for their students.
5. Course work for teachers-to-be is structured as if the whole of human and social evolution occurred in stratified and isolated capsules; students learn, for example, the history of the eighteenth century in one course, the art of the eighteenth century in another course, the music of the

From *Educating the Powerless* by Stanley Charnofsky, pp. 119-131. ©by Wadsworth Publishing Company, Inc., Belmont, California 94002. Reprinted by permission of the publisher.

eighteenth century in another course, and its psychology in another course (small wonder that our students leave college totally compartmentalized in their understanding of world events); they sometimes know when the American Revolution took place, but are completely frustrated about the impact of that event upon, for example, the composers or the journalists of that day, and vice versa.

6. Course work is, in most instances, temporally stifling and rigid; if, by chance, an incisive, stimulating, relevant interchange does occur, it is most often cut off at the 50-minute mark—professors rarely find time to go out on the lawn with the class to continue their argument, nor can students remain, surrounded as they are by their own inflexible schedules.

7. In college as in public schools, few examples can today be cited of courses (in all subject areas) that speak to the contributions, heritage, and present condition of American minority groups.

8. And finally, formal course work, structured as it inevitably is, convinces students that what they must all exalt and strive toward is the successful completion of other-directed, specified activities and their culminating evaluations, the grades; our teachers-to-be are so well versed in subordinating their curiosity to the assignments of their professors that they cannot help but themselves become teachers who hammer their students into conformity.

Of course, such a list could be made larger. But this short list illuminates a certain pervasive emphasis that most certainly will produce teachers who are as insensitive to their young students as their teachers were to them.

Our teachers-to-be are typically placed in a relationship with their professors which accentuates the distance between them. They are taught *at*—lectured to—for the most part, and the distance makes teacher versus learner a reality in the college classroom. *That* becomes the model for our new teachers.

A singularly distressing aspect of our teachers-to-be is that so very many of them are actually unaware of the indoctrinating nature of their experiences. They have been so nurtured in styles of authoritarian followership, so conditioned to accept routine and control and dictation that their personalities have become zippered tight. They come to accept, indeed enshrine, the "good" teacher as one who is in complete control. Just as the cycle of poverty cannot be easily broken, neither can the cycle of authoritarianism. And generations of children grow up to teach new generations all about democracy through the most undemocratic means. Small wonder they fail.

Our teachers-to-be have learned that their college teachers refused to create with them an intimacy of spirit, a communion of intellectual and emotional adventure. Thus have they learned to avoid closeness with their young students. They are sometimes exposed (in Psychological Foundations of Education courses) to discovery approaches to the mysteries of the world, but those by no means comprise the overwhelming balance of their experience.

Because of the remarkable jealousy and sense of self-preservation of each dynastic segment of academia, prospective teachers do not have a cohesive or a developmental understanding of the world in which they live. The lessons of the past do not influence their actions, because those lessons are a jigsaw puzzle of jurisdictional shrapnel, never once pulled together into a meaningful "weltanschauung." The findings of social science (indeed, some remarkable research discoveries!) have little influence on the operation of our teachers-to-be, because they see them having no influence on the way their professors have been working with them.[2]

Our teachers-to-be cannot be culturally expansive in their outlook; they have so few primary examples of teachers who have appreciated the potential diversity of American life. They have had so few teachers of their own who have not themselves been indoctrinated into a kind of antidemocratic over-simplification of the tenets of the good life. And, sadly, our teachers-to-be are woeful victims of all the overpowering stimuli in their training which cajole them into sacrificing what they are really interested in for what is *supposed* to be learned. They are wooed away from the delirium of discovery toward the doldrums of duty. And that process leaves them utterly and dismally conditioned into demanding the same kinds of behavior from their students.

When John Holt describes with insight how children fail, he is by implication also telling us how teachers fail. He is telling us how, as the principal vehicle for training teachers, formal course work has been an utter disaster; how its emphases have diverted the real notion of how one prepares to relate significantly to young learners. Teachers who are so trained emerge with totally distorted beliefs and expectations about their own students:

> Teachers and schools tend to mistake good behavior for good character. What they prize above all else is docility, suggestibility; the child who will do what he is told; or even better, the child who will do what is wanted without even having to be told. They value most in children what children least value in themselves.

Powerless children do not resist such damaging expectations from their teachers; they all too often give in to the mystery and the confusion of teachers' odd requirements. And so each generation inherits the emotional, intellectual, and spiritual debility of the one before it.

Teacher training has ignored the sensitization of students to their own feelings and to the impact their personalities have on others. The course work our teachers-to-be experience prepares them to be intolerant of cultural diversity, inflexible in their structure, overpowering in their discipline ("the strong teacher is a teacher who tolerates no nonsense"), ignorant of unusual belief systems and alien life values, and totally inured to the subverbal or feeling-level communication their students so desperately invoke.

When ample course work has been absorbed by aspiring young teachers, it is time to expose them to their practicum. Usually, this involves two semesters of mornings spent in a classroom at the secondary level, and one semester of full days or segments of days spent in the classroom at the elementary level. The university provides a supervising professor and the public school provides a master teacher.

One young woman recently described her supervised, guided student-teaching experience this way:

I cried myself to sleep every night. They weren't at all interested in my relationship with the children. They kept telling me to use pins instead of thumbtacks and kept showing me how the bulletin boards were supposed to be organized. Every evening I had reading charts to print up and my printing had to be letter perfect, just so high and just so thick. They were so worried I wouldn't learn their routine because they said the children get restless when the familiar routine is broken. This was the most uncreative five months I've ever spent in anything!

Another teacher-to-be was student teaching in a junior high school class in journalism. She described what happened to her:

Well, this teacher never even studied journalism, he was an English major. And he just didn't think much of the kids. He kept saying they were dumb and that he had to keep a tight hold on them. About half of the kids in his room were black and yet one day he brought in a study about Negro intelligence and said that it confirmed all of his beliefs and that there was no doubt in his mind about the genetic differential. And about that time there were some marches and uprisings around the city in the junior and senior high schools and our youngsters were quite restless. All he could say to me was something about what "your liberal philosophy does for you— all those kids being permitted to disrupt our institutions." The thing was, when I suggested that I would have the students write editorials about aspects of the school unrest that they felt were important, he stifled the assignment by having them finish his incomplete titles: "Public School Disruption Is Harmful because . . . ." or "Outside Agitators on the Campuses Cause. . . ."

I recently listened to a briefing of a college class of teachers-to-be about to spend a semester at a junior high school. The principal and vice principals described the school, its policies, its routines, and its disciplinary procedures. They told about how proud they were of their racial balance (about one-third Caucasian, one-third black, one-third Mexican-American). Then they described how, when school was over, the blacks all went home "over there," the whites "over there," and the Chicanos "over there," all in different directions. The principal told about the special, federally funded programs they had and all the extra equipment they were allowed because of their minority population. One of the vice principals took time to describe how the venetian blinds should be kept, and cautioned his listeners to avoid standing in front of the light because it gave the children headaches if they had to gaze at the teacher's silhouette during the lesson. The hour-and-a-half briefing was once suspended while the principal went to his office to address all the students in the school over the loudspeaker. He spoke for 14 minutes to 1700 students, all of whom were sitting in classrooms around the school, all of whom were doing exactly the same thing at that time: listening to a voice from a box. The principal told them about the PTA drive, about which home rooms were tops in recruiting, about which home rooms were winning the contest. And he told them about the vandalism at the bungalow over the weekend, "which would not be tolerated." Then he told them how proud he was of "our school" and his high hopes for its reputation as the finest junior high in the city. . . . The entire briefing had an unexpectedly premature ending when the three administrators were called away to investigate some problem in the quad during nutrition. The process of "fitting in" new members to the system had begun.

These examples do not represent isolated and unusual glimpses through the windows of our schools. When college students enter student teaching they *do* encounter such routines, such attitudes, and such insensitivity. One secondary school principal refused to permit students to student teach in the art department of his school because ". . . there are no teachers in our art department I would care to have any young teacher be exposed to. Boys are uncontrolled in some of those classes, and the leadership is quite poor." Yet, the students at that school (largely Mexican-American) were most appreciative of the specific teacher whose boys were "uncontrolled." He wore a beard and an open shirt. He was Anglo, but he spoke Spanish. He was educated, but he lived in the barrio where the children lived. He was sensitive, unstructured, nonconforming, and thoroughly loved. And no student teachers were allowed in his class.

Student eaching is the formalized, on-the-job aspect of teacher indoctrination. When student teachers conclude their time at a given school, they are rated by their master teacher and their supervisor. They are rated on such criteria as classroom management, discipline, knowledge of subject matter, ability to use methods, and a kind of superficial rapport with students. It is interesting that no one attempts to assess the deeper quality of their relationships with students, their empathy for student needs, their sensitivity toward relationships between students, their seeming alertness to principles of motivation and human learning, their spontaneity, their creativity and flexibility, their love of people, their joy or verve for life, their restlessness, their inquisitiveness and challenging nature, their resistance to dogma and to routine. . . .

When student teachers conlcude their time at any given school, they are also ready to begin the process of interviewing for a job. Often the school where they did their student teaching will get first crack at them and will choose them or not, depending upon their compatibility with the existing system. Repeatedly, a potentially imaginative and very human teacher is not selected by his training school because he is "a bit too unusual," or "he wouldn't fit in." In this way each school perpetuates its own style by stifling the potential for dissent and insuring the prevention of change. From another perspective, it can be said that each school thus continues to be static instead of dynamic, irrelevant instead of exciting.[3]

Lately, an even more unfortunate development has occurred, one which leaves the most needy schools floundering for lack of creative new talent. Young, expressive, potentially gifted teachers are beginning to interview the principals, instead of the other way around; thoughtful, restless young people are beginning to discriminate against school districts that restrict and oppress. In one sense, that could force the schools to change—at least, enough to attract capable teachers. But largely because so many of the teacher trainees wish to work in or near large population centers, and because teacher supply is catching up with demand, such districts have been able to find enough people to staff their schools. The distinct calamity is that most of those districts in large cities tend to assign most of the compliant young teachers to the ghetto areas. Thus, excellence and innovation continue to elude the schools of the center city.

Children of the poor see so few people in the schools who can speak their language or who can understand them. In the past, by the time a Negro or a Mexican-American had gone through the credentialing process of becoming a teacher, he had been indoctrinated so completely into the established mold that he was no longer a "black" or a "Chicano." Part of the training process was to make him over into an acceptable middle-class teacher, who reflected the typical ideals of the dominant culture. Student teaching for any member of the poor has always meant a rejection of the culture from which he comes, an absorption of "the way things are done," a disdain for those who don't seem to try to make it ("After all, you came from that background and look at you"), and an adoption of the ethic that hard work will pay off. But there are signs that the poor who come from minority ethnic groups are no longer willing to trade off their identity for a badge in what they now consider a society of questionable value. Through this intrepid revolution by the formerly power-less, the majority culture is being forced to take a hard look at all its educative procedures. The training process called student teaching is one of the first to need reexamination.

Closely related to the process of student teaching is the procedure of making lesson plans. Not only must student teachers make out daily lesson plans, but in many schools so must new teachers. (I recall that in my first public school teaching assignment, with a class of seventh-grade youngsters who were sup-posed to be mentally retarded, I was required to submit a weekly lesson plan to a designated senior teacher. In practice, I discovered that the children pulled the class in so many different directions that the advance plans were all but useless. I later found it expedient to make up a hypothetical plan for the entire semester, week by week, on a large cardboard poster, and by way of placating the supervisor, copying down the segment for each week as it ap-proached and turning it in to her. In all honesty, the daily activity seldom had much to do with the semester plot.)

There should be a distinction between a teacher's establishing certain goals for and with his students, and formulating daily lesson plans. There is no quarrel with the notion that the teacher will structure the environment in some given way—whether through arbitrary imposition of subject-matter drill or through his own, more personal influence. This structuring will no doubt be a product of his philosophy about children, about school, and about learning. But if his philosophy holds that children perceive the world in unique ways and that relevancy is highly personal and emergent, the external application of subject matter through lesson plans will utterly fail to relate to the student's actual needs. Yet, as it is today, lesson plans are required, and by this alone teachers-to-be are misguided about the way children are motivated to learn.

From my own vantage point, virtually every student teacher who has gone on into teaching has reacted negatively toward lesson plans. The notion of an extrinsic outline, rigidly adhered to and unilaterally composed, becomes stultifying to the creativity of the teacher. For the same reasons, leason plans inhibit the students from daring to bring up what is on the tips of their tongues. No doubt, teachers who read this have had the experience of entering a class-room at least once in their careers and asking their students "what's on your mind?" The torrent of emotion and thought that erupts is often astounding, and teachers are left amazed at what the youngsters had been holding in.

I have heard a college professor tell about how he had been leading the students in his education class through critically important areas of discussion for several weeks. On alternate days, they were visiting and observing in the public schools. While he felt that what he was discussing with them was always important, he had never thought to include open time for the students each time the class met. Finally, one bold young man told him that he was sorry if it interrupted the professor's plans, and all that, but he wanted to tell the class something very important about his school observation and see what they thought about it. The professor, later that day, exuberantly told his colleagues about the "... best class session we've had all semester! I was able to join and suggest resources and ideas so that more learning theory was discussed today than in all the other meetings combined!" Following a lesson plan would have totally failed to "catch the teachable moment," "deal with emerging, dynamic, relevant problems," and "recognize that learning is highly personal and intrinsic."

Lesson plans as general guides for the teacher and his students, composed by the teacher *with* his students, have some organizational merit; lesson plans as plots for daily activities merely add to the misguided process of indoctrination into teaching.

The concept of grading, if we really face it, is attached to the exaltation of competition as the American way; perhaps that should be amended to read, *free and open* competition. It hardly behooves the purpose of this writing to launch an indiscriminate attack on the American notion of competition, but a tacit belief that such competition is most often free and open definitely needs some investigation. Another aspect of grading which should be explored is the attendant axiom that by the processes of evaluation and comparison, some performers are bound to fail. What about that failure? Is it either necessary or healthy?

Teachers-to-be have been compared to others since (and even before) their formal schooling began. By the time they become teachers, the indoctrination into competitiveness is complete. They know only one way: to see how well each student can do in comparision with others. It is incidental that the children of the poor rarely do as well as the others. "They must learn it in school," our teachers are told. "Society is highly competitive and so our youngsters must learn to compete if they are going to make it."[4]

Oddly enough, there are signs that young people today are resisting that notion, and are seeking and finding intimacy and closeness with each other. Young people of today talk about love-ins and about going back to the noncompetitive Indian way. They talk about "being there for somebody"; about encounter or sensitivity experiences. They talk about and examine the deeper nature of man—aside from the form his so-called civilization has given him. And yet, their resistance is isolated and specific, and the majority of our population appears to continue in the quest for dominance.

Dominance over what? It is highly probable that, appealed to on a deeper level of feeling, most Americans would not exalt the ranking process of human beings, the process which sets up certain arbitrary criteria of "superior" and others equally arbitrary of "inferior." As standards of living for most Americans go up and the "good life" is experienced, it is likely that there is less and less need for the affluent (of spirit as well as possessions) to perpetuate an artificial hierarchy. Yet, instead of being sensitive to that deeper growth and maturity

WHAT IS TO BE DONE?   347

in our population, to that "coming-of-age-in-America," our schools continue to operate as if we live in a frontier era. They continue to operate in a framework of laissez-faire competition, while the society, at least in its deeper processes, moves toward an organized "cooperacy." We are saying that the schools by their function of grading contend that they reflect society's—that is, industry's—desires. "Corporations want to know who the *best* students are." We are also saying that, being on the forefront of knowledge, our schools should be sensitive to the subtleties of progress, and should indeed *lead* society into new dimensions of humanness.

As it is today, competition is not free and open. Since all Americans are not equally blessed, the competition we reverently cling to as the American way is shamefully undemocratic in its application to Americans who are culturally different. In most instances, the poor find themselves without the tools needed to compete equally (and no one allows for that), and find themselves failing. That revered competition is a major contributor to the perpetuation of powerlessness among many Americans. It is only when Americans who are powerful have been willing to give up some of their power (cooperation!), to be deliberately noncompetitive, that powerless Americans have begun to feel adequate and to move into emotional and personal health.

Grading implies success, and it implies failure. When one is constantly compared with someone else, it is either favorably or unfavorably, as a success or as a failure. Do we set up arbitrary ways for children to fail who otherwise might grow up with many feelings of adequacy and accomplishment? Are we not told that the world is hard and cruel and judgmental? (Of course our schools help to keep it that way!) If so, then our children will certainly encounter much failure after leaving school. Why can they not build margins of good feelings in school so that failure in the hard and callous world will not destroy them? Why can they not have so many experiences that reinforce their concepts of their own abilities and their own goodness that they *will* believe in themselves—the potential criticism of others be hanged!

And yet, a note of optimism. . . . Some colleges and universities have experimented boldly with the whole concept of the letter grade as an indication of achievement. At one institution, an experiment was initiated where, at the discretion of the student, he could enroll in any or all of his classes on a "pass—no credit" basis. Note that it is not pass-fail, which leaves a negative evaluation on the student's record. In pass—no credit, a student either achieves the desired goal (the teacher's or his own, depending on the operating philosophy in the classroom) or he does not. If he does not, then he may want to re-try his study in a certain area, or he may decide to avoid it. In any case, the negative imputation of the "fail" grade is removed.

A final point about grading has an ironic twist to it. It is the thought of Arthur Combs, and is quoted here because it seems to me that it shows unusual candidness and insight:

It is indeed a shame if, with all the richness of the American language, we are reduced to evaluating a student's promise in terms of A, B, C, D, or F! The college placement office is keenly aware that this is by no means enough and so requires much fuller descriptions of students to supply to prospective employers. As a consequence, the placement office, whose contact with the student may be for no more than ten minutes, knows him better than the college which has lived with him for four or five years!

Whether competition and evaluation will become anachronistic as our society grows in its sentivity and its humanity, is a moot point. But certainly, as Combs makes so clear, even within the existing structure, our approach to the evaluation of one human being by another can be so much more personalized and so much less mechanistic, so much deeper as a vehicle in utlimately enhancing the person being evaluated, and so much less an obvious criticism.

Our teachers have been indoctrinated with the belief that assignments of work at home after school will somehow add to the diligence, devotion, training, and knowledge of students. Sadly, it has worked so that very close to the opposite has occurred.

Homework has been an influential factor in negatively reinforcing school activities. Children who are frustrated at the blandness and dullness of their school routines find such an influence following them even into their homes and bedrooms. They resent their schools and they resent their homework and both become less pertinent to their real feelings and their deeper motivations.

A youngster from a family that lives in a culturally different style, perhaps a culturally rural life pattern, finds the typical approach to homework stultifying and prejudicial. Very likely he will not have an "isolated and quiet place to study," a "well-lighted, clean, flat-surfaced, distraction-free cubicle." Nor is the homework content such that he can (or would want to) share it with or get help from his family.

Work of an intellectually challenging nature could very well be an enhancing takehome experience for children of the poor. And, carefully and wisely created, such assignments might indeed offer an opportunity to involve an entire family in educational activity—the whole family zestfully digging in, being nourished. Obviously, such activities would necessitate much prethought, much learning on the teacher's part about his students and their life styles, much careful examination, and, let's hope, some insight into the family living of his youngsters.

Now homework is the leftovers, drill time. Homework is the punishment— more if you are a slow worker in class, less if you are fast. Most teachers are trained to accept and follow, and few have ever thought about the entire concept of homework and what it is that homework might accomplish.

In this writing there has most certainly been a negative tone about education as it is. But I hope if the reader is as sensitive as one might imagine, he will see, even to this point, all kinds of wild shafts of light which knife through the darkness and give promise of a better day. And if through the system as it currently exists, with all its oppressive qualities, some young people have managed to emerge creative and challenging and pestiferous, there must be a certain amount of flexibility—at least enough for the aggressive to take advantage of.

And certainly, to those teachers who have indeed struggled all these years to be facilitators for their youngsters, who have lived and loved their pupils' lives and loves, who have felt the tragedy it has been to be different in America's schools—to those teachers perhaps this writing is a compliment. Perhaps they will find an "aha" or a "Eureka" as they read these words.

*   *   *

NOTES

1. We must keep in mind that as these criticisms are written, they are being responded to. There is evidence that significant change is coming about in many institutions around the country. The model of a teacher "product" herein described will be, I hope, well on the road to extinction by the time these words are read.

2. The University of Pittsburgh Teacher Training Model, for one, is a striking exception to this condition. Their program of individualizing the teacher instruction pattern, and providing an environment which they hope will be the kind the teacher would create with students, is an example of enlightenment in teacher education.

3. It is interesting that political leaders more and more are castigating teachers, administrators, and schools for disproportionately hiring so-called "liberal" teachers, especially at the college level. They claim that this amounts to indoctrination into a liberal philosophy. If any message is at all apparent from this present writing, it is that the exact opposite is true. Regardless of political bent, most teachers, when it comes to education and their relationship with students, are unbelievably reserved and conservative, "up-tight" and conforming, static and nonexperimental, obedient and institutionally patriotic.

4. Jack R. Gibb, former Resident Fellow at the Western Behavioral Science Institute in California, in a speech to secondary school administrators in 1969, challenged such a notion. He said that such a point of view, with its attendant concepts of leadership and aggresiveness, "prepares the child for life, but for a life that's leaving us, for a world that was, for a society of the past." He went on to call for more "team building" and "cooperative problem-solving" in our schools.

Stanley Charnofsky

A recent study of teacher credentialing revealed that over the past decade only a little more than 70 percent of the teachers who receive credentials become immediately employed. Of the 30 percent who do not, some 13 percent are simply not accounted for. No one knows what becomes of them. Furthermore, about 12 percent of all teachers leave the schools at the end of each school year.

No one has yet been able to offer a convincing reason why the teaching profession fails so drastically in holding teachers, especially good teachers. Radical reform of teacher credentialing might be one way to counteract this failure. But while admitting this possibility, we also realize that there are powerful reasons why the teaching profession in this society both attracts so many and repels so many once they have entered it. (The Office of Education reported in 1973 that there were nearly as many students in college who were saying they intended to go into teaching as the number of teachers throughout the United States: 1.5 million and 2 million respectively.)

Another notable characteristic of the teaching profession is the predominance of women teachers in the public schools. It is clear that this predominance is connected to the comparatively low status the occupation of teaching has in this society, despite our pious avowals of its nobility and importance and that great rush into teaching discovered by the Office of Education. We know that a principal reason why women came to predominate in the teaching profession was that they were expected by their society to accept less pay, and to be more tractable than men. And they went along with it. (Another example of how in their actions individual teachers reflected the traditional structures of schools and their society!) It was—and continues to be—part of the ethos of our society that women should not expect pay that is equal to men's.

But for women to come into the schools in such numbers there had to be changes in the school organization. Prior to 1830 most teachers were men.

What happened that made it possible for more and more women to become public schoolteachers was directly the result of what was happening in American society, its industrialization. The schools—including the individuals in them—reflected that industrialization in many ways. Most important for female teachers was the homogeneous grouping of children, the end of the one-room school and the beginning of placing children in grades according to age level, to facilitate the standardization and regimentation of the growing numbers of children who were flocking to the public schools. With homogeneous grouping, schools found they could better control students. Women could not be teachers in the heterogeneous one-room school because, it was thought, only men could maintain the necessary control. (A common nightmare teachers-to-be invariably report is that of finding themselves in a classroom that is out of their control.) It is easy to see why homogeneous grouping continues to this day.

Illustrating how the practices of individuals in the schools reflect and perpetuate the structures of the schools and of the larger society, Patricia Cayo Sexton describes the predominance of women in teaching against the background of the status of women in all of our institutions:

> Sex stereotypes permeate all social institutions, indeed all human activity. They are found in a most pernicious form in the job market. Women have a *place* in the working world, different from what it once was—but not much. They have, in brief, an inferior place, a status shared by most disadvantaged minorities. They serve, but rarely direct. They are "helpers." Seldom are they found at or near the summit, in major executive posts. When they do occupy these lofty posts, they often direct housekeeping activities. They are in shortest supply in enterprises that deal with things rather than people, power rather than service . . . In all these places, women are usually servants rather than masters. They do not control a single major institution. They come closest in the home and school, and they are much closer in some institutions than in others. But in *all* of them, the bosses at the top are men.[4]

In the following reading, Adria Reich tells how women came to dominate the lower levels of public education. She also is saying, in her concluding proposal, that the reflection by female teachers of feminine subservience—sexism— does not *have* to continue.

---

4. Patricia Cayo Sexton, *The Feminized Male* (New York: Vintage, 1969), pp. 23-24.

TEACHING IS A GOOD
PROFESSION . . . FOR A WOMAN

Adria Reich

Why do women become teachers? Channeling from Mother, guidance counselors, teachers; a lack of other options; social concern, a desire to work with people; feelings of academic inadequacy; a B.A. and no typing skills. Emerging from this mixture of positive, but mostly negative reasons comes the decision to be a teacher. Given the options, it's a choice that makes sense.

Teaching is one of the only jobs available to women with a "mere" B.A. that does not put us directly at the service of a man. It is one of the only jobs in which women are more than adornment. Responding to impersonal bells all day may be horrible, but bells are clearly preferable to a boss telling you to hurry up with his coffee. Teaching from a prescribed curriculum guide may be constraining, but it is certainly preferable to typing words you had no part in writing. And once a teacher is in the classroom, behind a closed door, she does have some discretion over what goes on.

In other words, teaching, because it is a profession (albeit low status) does offer some job control, some prestige; and, the teaching profession, because it is predominately women, avoids some of the blatant sexism common to other jobs.

"IF WOMEN HAD NOT BEEN CHEAPER . . ."

It is true that sentimental reasons are often given for the almost exclusive employment of women in the common schools; but the effective reason is economy . . . If women had not been cheaper than men they would not have replaced 9/10 of the men in American public schools.

Charles Elliot,
President of Harvard

The process which eventually led to women standing in front of a classroom began over a century ago in America. Between 1840 and 1860, the percentage of men teaching school in Massachusetts went from 60% to 14%. Although crude, Elliot's statement that this was an economy measure seems essentially correct. The feminization of the teaching profession coincided with several important changes in the economic and social character of America.

Growth of American business and industrialization was creating new job opportunities for men; the increase in the number of immigrants expanded the population that primary schools had to serve, without expanding the tax base.

Adria Reich, "Teaching is a Good Profession . . . For A Woman," *The Red Pencil,* Vol. III, No. 2, Jan., 1972, pp. 4-5

Obviously something had to be done to expand the number of teachers without increasing the funds available to the schools. The school boards saw the solution in (1) feminizing and expanding the primary school teaching force; and (2) decreasing the number of masters (always men) needed for those well-to-do students pursuing further education, by creating centralized high schools.

In other words, women were hired because it seemed natural for them to work with little children and because they would be cheap . . . not because those doing the hiring believed that women were capable of doing important work, making important decisions. Hence, there have always been more women in the primary schools than in the secondary schools, and there have always been very few women in administrative positions.

The current statistics are reflective of these trends. In 1967, 85% of primary school teachers were women, 68% of the profession as a whole. In secondary schools, men held a bare majority. Women are 25% of elementary, 4% of junior high, and 10% of senior high principals. In both elementary and secondary schools, the percentage has declined since 1950. According to the NEA, there are at most a handful of women superintendents in the country. Furthermore, women in 1960 constituted only 10% of school board members. More than half of all school boards have no women members.

This is more than interesting background; these statistics have very real consequences for women teaching in the public schools. They indicate that while women are in the majority in most schools, we don't have the power that derives from numbers, because we are underrepresented in the decision-making positions. Ironically, the imbalance between women and men teachers is used to justify the opposite imbalance (more men than women) in the authority positions. The logic goes someting like this: we need more men in the schools. In order to bring in and retain men, they have to be given some incentive. Men have families to support; men have to be able to move up, both in salary and prestige.

All of us have heard this argument. It might be used as an explanation of why a woman did not get to be class adviser (which may carry with it several hundred dollars) or why a woman was not chosen to be part of a curriculum workshop (which often means release time and extra pay). Or we might simply have overheard such conversations in teachers' rooms. It is hard for a woman to respond in that situation—hard to sort out our own interests and anger, our view of what the best learning situation would be for the kids, and the interests of the administration in proposing the change in ratios.

On a certain level it does seem important to have integrated teaching staffs (especially in the elementary schools where imbalance is greatest). If any type of sex equality is to be achieved in America, people have to see that working with children is not simply women's work. And children should see that men as well as women can be responsive, sympathetic, capable of tenderness, that these are human qualities, not just male or female qualities.

"A FEMININE ENVIRONMENT IS HARMFUL FOR BOYS"

These, however, are not usually the reasons the educational authorities and administrators favor male advancements. They tend to take basic sex roles in society as given and desirable. Men are (and should be) aggressive, bold, inventive, energetic, strong. Women are (and should be) passive, shy, gentle, sweet, and kind. By this logic, if boys are to grow into healthy adult men, they need "real men" around them, providing a model for them. And, conversely, it is harmful for boys to attend school in a predominately feminine environment where they will be weakened, made effete.

If women teachers create such a narrow, "prissy" environment, why aren't the administrators similarly concerned about what will become of the girl students? Why is there no worry about how girls will relate to all these "masculine" new teachers? The assumption underlying all of this seems to be that it's the boy students who count. They will be the future leaders, the men who will build our tomorrow, while the primary function for girls will be as wives and mothers.

In reality, of course, as any of us who have worked in sex-integrated faculties can attest, there are both male and female teachers who limit the interest, potential creativity and strengths of both boys and girls by stressing obedience to all the minute regulations of the school, neatness, and punctuality. And there are both male and female teachers who react against those standards and try to help their students question and analyze. If the first type of teacher predominates over the second, we need to look beyond sex-imbalance or feminization for an explanation.

Those fearing the "feminization" of boys in school are forgetting the important point that schools educate both girls and boys for social roles and for jobs in the labor force. All children are being channeled into a bureaucratic and corporate America. Workers are expected to perform narrow, impersonal tasks, to meet regulations someone else fixes. The behaviors and values traditionally associated with "real men" may have no place in this society. When you look for basic causes for the problems of schools, you have to look at the demands of the society, not particular sex ratio.

Certainly, increasing the number of male teachers will not change these realities. In fact, if the only way to bring more men into the schools is to create more hierarchies and hence more chances for promotion, (both the State Dept. of Education and the Mass. Teachers Association have made proposals calling for team leaders, master teachers, etc.) the schools will become an even more efficient training ground for the corporate bureaucracy than they are now. Students will see their teachers jockeying for position, competing for advancement.

"WHY CAN'T YOU BE MORE LIKE ONE OF THE GUYS?"

Women teachers can't afford to ignore these proposals, or the assumptions and fears that underly them. As the unemployment rate (especially among college graduates) grows, so does the "teacher surplus." Women are no longer facing just the question of promotions, but rather of who gets hired, retained, and finally given tenure. It seems almost the reverse of the situation in the 1840s and '50s when the expanding industrial and commercial opportunities lured men away from teaching. As men find their way back into the schools, where does that leave us?

Everywhere we go to apply for teaching positions we are made to feel guilty that there are so many of us—young women teachers, with lots of ideas, and often with little or no experience. Sometimes they are even honest with us; they tell us that if a man comes along with the same qualifications, he'll almost certainly get the job. After all, these are "tough kids," of it's a "tough school," or the kids could use a man to relate to. If we're married they seem suspicious we might have a baby; if we are single, they wonder when we'll get married and quit.

And even if we get a job, it is harder for us to hold on to it. In trying to integrate into the life of the school, women face built-in (structural) difficulties. Because the teachers' rooms are usually sex-segregated, and often the tables in the lunchroom are, we don't get to have a smoke with or joke with the "people who count"—the coaches, the Union representatives, the Department Chairmen. We can never be "one of the guys."

Furthermore, for the most part, the "guys" don't feel comfortable around us. They don't know what to make of a young, intelligent, agressive woman (which is what you have to be to get the job in the first place!). Sometimes we can overcome this discomfort, by getting to know the few women they do accept, by working for the Union and having beers before Union meetings, by smiling sweetly at the right times. But it's hard—much harder than for a new male teacher. And, of course, hanging over us always, is the threat that they will have no trouble replacing us with someone who does fit in better.

There have been attempts by women in the school systems in this area to do something about this situation. In cases where there is clear discrimination, women are trying legal actions. Most school systems have laws requiring a woman to stop teaching by her fifth or sixth month of pregnancy and forbidding her to return to her position until a year from the first September after the baby is born. (All without any compensation, of course). In Newton, a case has been filed by a woman who gave birth in August, and a male teacher at the same school, whose wife gave birth the same month. As a man, he, of course, faces no restrictions on his return to work. [Supreme Court in January, 1974 declared this unconstitutional—Ed.]

Women in several liberal high schools (Lincoln-Sudbury, Newton South) have succeeded in getting the schools to set up nursery programs, to which they can bring their children. By approaching a school system in pairs, some women have managed to convince administrators to hire two part-time people for one job. In several suburban systems (Weston, Brookline, Newton) women teachers have begun to find new ways to talk to each other and female students by offering women's courses, mini courses or discussion groups.

But for most women teachers for whom none of these special actions are possible or appropriate, the best immediate step is to get together with other teachers facing a similar situation. Several groups of women teachers who met at a workshop at the Teacher Center (a drop-in storefront for teachers) have begun meeting regularly to support each other, to talk about teaching, and particularly the problems of being a woman teacher. In the short run, such discussions make it easier to survive in the schools; in the long run they may lead to some programs for action.

Adria Reich

Gloria Channon had been teaching in the New York City schools for twelve years when she wrote *Homework*. She could not think of doing anything other than teach, in part for practical reasons, but also because she thought it "socially useful, potentially creative, soul-fulfilling" work. But then she began to question whether it was that, and her answer seemed more and more often to be no.

One year she kept a log of what was happening in her classroom, and thought she was seeing it through the eyes of the children. But she wasn't. She was seeing it through the sight of the child she had been:

> . . . timid, shy, conforming, a good student for whom school was a fantasy world. School was the place where the wise and powerful, recognizing my secret dreams and my WORTH, would benignly honor and reward me.
>
> When I came to the classroom as teacher, as one of the adults, I discovered that I was not the wise and powerful person that my teachers had seemed to be. My child's view of the school world had betrayed me. I judged with bitterness the adults around me. I once, after a half-dozen years' experience, wrote my judgment out. (pp. 5-6)

Channon's judgment is an unusually candid and insightful view of school-teachers by a schoolteacher. As people who "appear" regularly before others, teachers are generally an unobserved and uncriticized group. A teacher who speaks the way Channon does in what follows cannot expect to experience the acceptance of many of her colleagues. But her account of the change in her consciousness shows how with that change comes inescapably a change in action. Note how it is a *willing* reflection of the school's and society's structures that often characterizes a teacher's actions, and how at such times pointing at the "system" as the culprit can be a cop-out. It is a reminder that we must deal with both individuals and structures if we are to achieve the kind of schools our rhetoric has falsely claimed we have.

HOMEWORK: REQUIRED READING
FOR TEACHERS AND PARENTS

Gloria Channon

*   *   *

In her relationships with her supervisors, the teacher is distrusting, critical, hypersensitive, suspicious, hostile. She cannot talk easily with them. She either toadies or becomes aggressively defensive. She is destroyed by the slightest criticism. She is insatiable in her quest for reassurance and praise. Sometimes she asserts her superior qualities so stridently that her listeners, equally sensitive and threatened, tune her out. She does not really believe in her own ideas and talents.

She is constantly backing down or preparing her exits. She is always burning her bridges before her or hitting back first. She is afraid to assert her rights, to insist on her dignity and worth as a person, to demand respect. Should she, rarely, be treated with dignity and respect, she is enveloped in tension and can find release only in retreat and denial.

Her school is an island in the community, as insulated and isolated as were the British colonials in India. Within the school the pattern of isolation persists. She is alone in her room, surrounded by hostile natives, out of touch with her peers. Outside the classroom, she joins small cliques. If she is manipulative and domineering, her clique will contain two or three weak copies of her who give her strength and gain their own in the aura and illusion of her pseudostrength.

The teacher loves to gossip. She loves to complain. She is jealous of her accomplishments, afraid to share her techniques or her professional secrets. She jockeys for position. She is sarcastic, easily hurt. Sometimes she will not talk to another member of the staff for months or years. She expects new members to approach her first and they, in turn, are hurt when she does not make the first gesture.

If she is threatened by outsiders, whether parent, civil rights group, or supervisors, she will form strong talking alliances with others on the staff. The alliances rarely lead to action. She passes the buck. No single indignity is ever important enough to make an issue of. Her shoptalk is of monsters and geniuses. She is of course responsible only for the latter.

She will, infrequently, praise another teacher. But this is a self-serving device. Either she identifies with the praiseworthy one or, with becoming modesty, claims a part in the development of the praised person, or she finds praise a socially acceptable technique for ranking out a third person (the auditor) by indirection.

She has no interest in ideas. She pretends to an interest in methods, but only because she seeks panaceas. She confuses improvements in working conditions with radical educational innovations. She is often but not always prejudiced. She tends to be conservative-Democrat in her politics and in New York City was antiunion until the short strike of 1967 showed how safe it was to be in favor of it.

She has very little patience for the classical masochists on the staff, the victims, the losers, the ones who bear the brunt of administrative criticism and persecution, the ones who are loaded down with the dirty jobs: permanent morning duty or audiovisual aids or books-and-supplies or, until the union contract changed the practice, the roughest classes.

She is quite interested in talk about furniture or clothes or shopping. She diets at noon according to every fad and gorges herself at night, fodder for the next day's lunchtime conversation. She is critical of the men on the staff and associates with them as little as possible. She may work in a school for years and not know by name people whose classes are on a different floor or who do not share her lunchroom. She rarely drinks. When she does, she often will regale her listeners with mildly scandalous anecdotes about her students or their families. She is, usually, quite Victorian in her judgments of her students' and their families' morals, while finding some malicious pleasure in their real or imagined improprieties. She often finds it necessary to take tranquilizers or barbiturates.

But she is not lazy. She works like a dog. She fills out reading cards and duplicate office records, book inventories, lunch lists, class photo lists, state census forms, report cards, reports by the hundred. She used to correct standardized tests, although her supervisors often would not let her correct those of her own class (in which she had some interest) because, of course, she is not to be trusted. She writes lengthy anecdotal records and case-history forms for the guidance counselors. But she will not write a letter of protest or even sign a petition. Teachers conform, within limits, on the side of the majority, because they fear the social consequences of saying no.

Although she complains and suffers, the teacher feels quite at home with an authoritarian principal. A weak principal upsets her. She does not know where she stands. She begins to join small negative groups of her peers. The tension is enormous. When everyone is suffering at the hands of some comma-counting dictator, she does not feel personally persecuted and will accept the most denigrating contempt as only her fair share of the injustice. But when the weak man is inconsistent, she is in torment. She crawls and whines and curries favor ruthlessly. When the ax shaves the neck (it never really decapitates regulars—only substitutes) of a colleague, she feels the strong relief and pleasure that people feel in battle or on highways when somebody else—*not me!*—gets killed.

The children are the enemy and she fears them. She cannot be aggressive and angry with supervisors or fellow teachers, so the children are fair game. Of course she has ways of working with them: she is not always in a rage. She uses fear, seduction, guilt, concern, and love. She uses threats and sarcasm and rejection.

She cannot abide the children who are most like her. If she is passive, dependent, guilt-ridden, lacking confidence, she will be infuriated by the passive, failure-prone, meek, fearful child. If she is "strong," willful, assertive, rigid, she will be enraged by the willful, assertive kids who stand up to her, who question her wisdom or sincerity or authority. She will bully the weakest child in the hope that the strongest child will be intimidated. She will encourage the class to scapegoat a classmate, in the hope that the class will not scapegoat her. She is concerned with forms and masks. How can children respect you if you are open and honest with them? How can you control a class in June, the month of heat and relaxation and letdown, if you tell the children what you knew in mid-May: who will be held over? Let the anxious ones sweat it out.

You must have rationalizations for your failures—administration or race or parents or last year's teacher or books-and-supplies. You must have rationalizations for your lack of imagination and energy: "busywork." Busywork copying four lines of a math problem when the answer is one number which can be worked out in one's head; training in being careful and thorough, in penmanship, in thinking, in anything but what it is: training in sterility and conformity, while the teacher catches up on clerical work. And above all, you must train the children well: books and knowledge are not a reward, they are a punishment. Arts and crafts are the rewards for a good day. Gym is the reward, Never the WORD!

I have a vision of the New York City school system today. At the top: tough, authoritarian, political Irish Catholics who send their children to parochial school and despise the teachers and the children who don't have the guts or the money to get out. In the middle: teachers and school supervisors, who have come from lower-class white minorities, many of them (like the Italians and the Jews) strongly marked by cultural masochism. And at the bottom: the children. Is it so different elsewhere?

In general, the system is certainly one of the most secure and protected of all the secure and protected government jobs. It is, to judge by its personnel, quite adequately paid and vacationed and pensioned.

But it is a medieval serfdom and the serfs are willing and compliant participants. They complain and dissipate their energies in complaining. They hate and dissipate their hatred in suffering, in provoking guilt, in destroying the children around them. Then they stand over the corpses weeping, weeping at the terrible system, this devil machine, this THING that did it, that did it to THEM, that did not let them succeed. They drive with a passionate overpowering drive toward failure and in this, at least and overwhelmingly, they succeed.

And don't tell me they don't fail with the middle-class children too, only the failure is one of mind and imagination and openness and courage, not the paper skills of math concepts and reading levels.

Saul Alinsky, the organizer, says a democracy lacking in popular participation dies of paralysis. But participation requires strength and courage and faith and love. The school system, lacking these, dies of paralysis every day.

Maybe what the teachers of the immigrants of fity years ago had was not better children in a more mobile society. The babies out of Italy with the evil eye and the garlic charm around the neck were surely as "disadvantaged," culturally and economically, as the Puerto Rican or Negro children today. Maybe what the teachers had then was more courage, more self-respect, and a fair share of faith in their jobs and themselves and their children.

When I showed these pages to other teachers, they invariably remarked, "It's so true—about them." At first I was amused by thier insistence on excluding themselves. But that was precisely my own reaction too. I was so sure that I was not one of the teachers I had described. It became uncomfortably clear that I could not condemn other teachers for their blindness as long as I too was blind. And when I returned to the log, reluctantly I began to discover how much a part of the world of teachers I was.

*   *   *

Gloria Channon

Things like discipline, order, control, and—in a muted background—freedom (but always coupled with "responsibility"), receive an inordinate amount of concern from teachers. The anxiety about these matters testifies to the deep wish and need that the teacher as the keeper of order and control brings to the classroom. Order and control are given to teachers by their schools and their society, and it is up to them to keep them. One of the worst things that can be said of you in an evaluation of your teaching is that you failed to "keep control" (control as evidenced by your students doing what is expected of them). There is strong reinforcement for such ideas, and for the wishes and needs of prospective teachers, in teacher training.

Gloria Channon tells us that from the beginning she resented the cool authoritarian atmosphere of many classrooms. She tended to be permissive, but largely because she did not know how to be anything else. And she justified it with a "loose and sentimental psychology." But when she ran a relatively tight or closed classroom she was still uncomfortable. What she was discovering was how deeply she had internalized the authoritarian values of our society. Her experience is a warning that the changes we seek in individuals that will facilitate changes in our schools must be deep and strong before they can truly be reflected in new classroom structures. Just overcoming the reflection of the old structures is a big task. But it is only the first step. Something has to be there to take its place.

In desperation, Channon tells us, she determined to explore the possibilities of a freer classroom for her fifth grade.

HOMEWORK *(continued)*

Gloria Channon

*   *   *

I was confronted by twenty-two children, all but three of them black or Puerto Rican. They had come to me from middle-income co-ops, from low-income housing, and from the transient population of the tenements. Some could not read at all; almost half had been held over on grade at some time in the past. Some had very little English at their command. And some had severe enough physical or emotional problems as to require extensive help, which was not of course available.

I did not have a clear plan for what I wanted to do. To my supervisors I described it as "an attempt to meet the challenge of the heterogeneous class," jargon which was less threatening to them than a more accurate description would have been. They had not heard of the English schools experiments in any case, and they were under pressure to produce such results as were measurable on reading tests. Beyond that goal, they had little interest. They were convinced, though, that the "experimental school" that they were running, if given enough time, would prove a success. What a teacher did behind closed doors was a matter of her "teaching style" and the supervisor's concern was only to hope that it would be successful, no matter what it was.

Within these limitations I was determined to work. School opening had been delayed by the short strike of 1967. But the children arrived, in spite of the delay, with their September manners, quiet, observant, taking the measure of their new teacher. They found desks for themselves, into which they proudly stuffed the evidence of their good intentions, new notebooks and pencils and rulers and crayons.

I tried to explain my hopes for the class, saying that I would let them choose what they wanted to study as much as possible. But they found the idea incomprehensible, or, if not that, then incredible. I laid out what materials I had on tables and shelves and in unlocked closets: my own set of Cuisinaire Number Rods, some toys and games, books, scales, whatnot—everything except art supplies. I justified the exclusion of the latter on the grounds that "art" was always the escape activity in school: "If you are good now, you may paint or draw later." I was sure that the children would never choose the academic options if art were a choice. Although I was aware of my prejudices, I was also aware of the supervisor's. In a test-oriented school, I lacked the courage to put this matter to a test. There would be opportunities later on for the children to "have art," as a gift if not an option.

I invited the children to wander about the room to investigate the materials. They were still in the throes of first-week-of-school good manners. Most of the children sat at their desks playing with the Cuisinaire Rods, building airy towers and squat enclosed forts, or, surprisingly, using them as they would crayons, to lay out a flat picture of a house with a pitched roof and chimney. Only a few walked around, and they did not open closet doors nor poke around on shelves. They walked almost on tiptoe, like intruders not sure how to extricate themselves from an embarrassing situation. Maybe they did not understand the reason for the invitation and did not trust it. They did not know what was expected and played it safe. Or else they settled for the first attraction, plunging into the doing right away.

I noted in my log that José, fresh from parochial school, sat quietly looking around, doing nothing. Only in rereading this entry did I realize that even I, recording the event, equated "looking around" with doing nothing.

In those first days, most of the children saw freedom as "freedom to play." Number rods became toys. Spring scales became weapons, from which clumsy objects could be launched with gratifying noise. The numbers on the scales were ignored. Balance beams, which I previously had made for another class, held the same destructive fascination that toy makers capitalize on: the beams were loaded with infinite patience until they reached the reckless moment when the whole thing came crashing down. When I insisted that the children record their observations and experiments, trying to legitimize their activity, the most avid balancers lost all interest. Seashells became improvised templates to be used in the dull inaccurate pattern drawings they rarely seemed to tire of or go beyond.

I never came to terms that year, or in the years following, with their need to play and with their seeming inability to play constructively and creatively. I did not (and do not) know how to make use of their playing. I did not trust them enough to wait while they exhausted the possibilities of the materials out of their needs and experience. Often the materials were lost or destroyed long before they had explored them fully. And I could not wait to see if they would go further with the materials by themselves. I was not able to help them find new meanings in the materials, not beyond the prosaic academic tasks I tried to impose too soon upon them.

Their play, indeed, became for me not an expression of freedom but an obstacle to it. So from the beginning I began defining freedom for them, only half aware that definition was, automatically, denial.

Thus, not believing in what I wanted as a teacher most desperately to believe, I decided that we must inch our way to freedom. Certain times of the day would be set aside as free time. When the children took me literally, choosing to play or talk even in this limited free time, I backed down further. Like colonials or slaves, they were not ready for freedom. Therefore clearly defined and carefully structured tasks must be provided for them. I did not dare experiment with real freedom of choice and action although it was a long time before I could admit this to myself. The admission was not a liberating one. It served instead more to help me excuse my limitations and tolerate the limitations under which teachers work than it did to strengthen my resolve to go forward to freedom.

The children too were in strange territory. They clung to their turf. The idea of moving from one place to another to work at specific jobs was acceptable. But the notion that there need not be a home base from which they departed, a desk which was theirs, seemed to make them uncomfortable. They wanted a defined place to go when they entered the room, when they finished a job, when they were acting as a group. They wanted to pick their nieghbors if they could and to stay with them.

Even the business of lining up was difficult. Standard procedure is to line up according to size. A vote showed that the majority of the children did not like lining up by size. But when we practiced complete freedom in lining up, the result was weeks of bickering and bullying. The worst problems were solved by rotating the job of line leader. Eventually they got bored with arguing about position and came to accept the random lineup. But what a long and noisy time it was! And when a new child joined the class, or when another teacher or an aide was in charge, there was always an outbreak of disorder, as children tried to explain the system to people unfamiliar with it and unwilling to accept it.

As to their ideas about appropriate classroom behavior, when I asked for them, they suggested staying in your seat, raising your hand if you wanted to talk or get something or take a drink. At least in the beginning they did not trust my words but voiced, with the brilliant intuition of children, the message of my emotions.

Not that they stayed in their seats or raised their hands. Within days, the stark advice appeared in my log: Isolate George, Julio, Walter, Carl.

There will always be a George, a Julio, a Walter, a Carl. They have not been school broken. They have problems with reading and math. They have problems with being people. They are bored, foolish, hypertense, restless, angry. They do not know what to do with themselves, but they do not want you to tell them what to do. I was convinced that even these children would see the new freedom in the classroom as a great gift which they had always wanted, in whose absence school was an intolerable burden and punishment. What I really wanted was for them to be civilized and constructive and cooperative—to be good.

They were not about to see things in my terms. For some of the children, the "good" ones, freedom to choose was part of some game whose rules and limits had simply not yet been defined. They tested uneasily to find out what the limits were. For some, freedom meant that now they would be able to draw all day, and of course they were quickly set straight on that score. But the boys who needed isolation had always had "freedom" in school, because they had always behaved according to their own internal needs.

They had never really enjoyed the freedom. They had always, accurately, seen it as a rejection. You let me do what I want because you can't control me. You can't make me BE GOOD. This can only mean that you find me uncontrollably BAD. Therefore freedom is bad. In the past they had made deals, bargaining, consciously or not, with their teachers. If you let me do this, I will be good (i.e., quiet) for x number of minutes. If you do not let me do that, I will have a tantrum or will curse or throw chairs or get in a fight. Each year they had to discover, by trial and error, what the acceptable terms were.

And each year, in the first months of exploratory turmoil, George, Julio, Walter, Carl remember wistfully that last year they were "good." They accuse you of incompetence and indifference because you have not yet discovered how to make them be good. They want to be good but they are convinced that they have no control over their own behavior. They can only maneuver and bargain and malfunction until *you* finally discover the formula (of fear or seduction) that will impose upon them the behavior that they insist they value highly. They believe in original sin, and everything they do seems to reinforce their belief in their innate wickedness. Their actions seem to plead for you to produce some miraculous redemption in whose permanence they do not really have any faith at all.

Now and then we had a class discussion of behavior. For teachers, such classroom discussions are often a form of self-indulgence which is highly approved by guidance counselors. In the course of the discussion children supposedly will discover profoundly useful insights into their motivation and behavior. To some extent this happens. But I discovered, in retrospect, that my choice of the "teachable moment" was determined more by my needs than by the children's. When the class had affronted me beyond bearing, it was almost enjoyable to set the hour's duties aside and "have a discussion."

The children, predictably, would parrot all the expected rules and rituals of behavior as though they had just discovered them. Asked for help in determining what the consequences of disruption should be, they would come up with the harshest of punishments: hit him with a ruler, send him to Mr. Whoever-had the meanest-reputation-in-the-school, stand him in the corner leaning on his fingertips, don't let him sit all day, call his mother so she'll give him a beating.

At first I concluded that they had been exposed to all kinds of sadism in the past. But their descriptions were tinged to some extent by fantasy. Usually the most disruptive children had the most punitive suggestions. They were also the ones most likely to describe appropriate behavior in impossibly repressive terms.

However enjoyable it initially was for me as the suffering adult to listen to their breast beating, sooner or later I would be oppressed by the tenor of the discussions.

In one such discussion, they as usual defined good behavior in the most puritanical school terms: always busy, always quiet, always still. Anything else, by definition, was bad. So I asked them if they could think of any good ways to be bad. After all, sometimes you needed some release from an unbearable task or tension.

They settled on three possibilities to start with.

You could stop working, do nothing at all, daydream.

You could walk to the sink, wash up, clean the sink, take a drink.

You could go and look out of the window for a while.

Windows in classrooms are designed so that the child at his low desk can see little of the world outside. This is surely deliberate. How rarely children, or teachers for that matter, seem to be aware of windows. It is as if, upon entering the school, one sets the environment securely and firmly aside, not only symbolically but intellectually and physically. One concentrates all one's attention inward, inside the walls. It is part of the jail psychology that one develops in the schools. Activity and excitement are provided, if at all, by the life in the corridors, almost never by the streets outside.

It was literally years before I even became aware of the wall that windows are. Windows were there to have pictures pasted on or to be raised or lowered the mandatory six inches. That I developed, at home, a strong resistance to drawing curtains and pulling down shades, even at night, had for me no connection with the fact that I worked in a spiritually blind room every day. When an astute if insensitive architect in New York City went the logical step to designing a school without any windows, I was outraged but for no sensible reason I could think of at the time.

Looking out of windows was, at any rate, institutionalized in our room as a good way to be bad.

Within a day or two I noticed that Walter was unusually restless. He wasn't fighting or throwing things, but he was walking, walking, walking. He made frequent trips to the sink. With sidelong glances, he made long detours to the window, where he would drape himself dramatically on the sill, nose pointed to the glass but eyes seeking me out.

He knew. Time and again I would tell him, impatiently, to sit down, to stop wandering. He was testing me, but he knew I would fail. Finally, one day, he confronted me angrily with my failure.

All I could do was admit he was right. The new rules and ways were unfamiliar to me too. After years of teaching I too had learned to internalize the school definitions of good/bad. He must try to be patient with me when I failed and to remind me when I forgot. I in turn would try to be patient with him. He was not to be placated so easily. The science teacher was due in and he was all primed for battle. I told him that he was angry with me, after all, and not with the science teacher, at least not yet. If he could set aside his anger during science, he was quite welcome to resume the business of being mad at me when I returned to the room. He managed to suppress most of a smile of satisfaction, and after science he graciously and pointedly declined to be angry.

Time and again the children and I were to go through such incidents and time and again we failed one another. I was all too willing to attribute their failure to their years of authoritarian schooling. It was not until I returned to the log after the school year had ended that I even began to be aware of the degree to which I was, subtly or stridently, denying the freedom that I was so sure I wanted and that, at the time, I was so sure the children were not ready for.

Gloria Channon

Gloria Channon continues her account of what happened to her, the sometimes painful self-discoveries that she went through, as she tried to undo that deep internalization of the unliberated and authoritarian values of her society and of the schools she found herself in. She was struggling against being one more reflection of these structures, and we know of no teacher who goes through this without difficult and painful moments. Yet they are moments of great learning, especially if they are seized as opportunities for personal change rather than times for cynical and defeated finger pointing at "the system."

It is clear from what Channon and others like her have experienced that the system just would not work without the cooperation—willing and otherwise—of teachers, administrators, *and* students. Channon shows us what kind of persons the system works best with. "You can choose to be free," she says she wants to tell all young teachers. We may think the system is slow to change, but look at how she describes the slowness to change in teachers. The two are connected, of course. But in their connection, the system and the individual do not collapse into one another. They need one another, and both are susceptible to change. (Remember: the individual is part of the system.) The revolution always remains incomplete, and is eventually betrayed, if only *one* of these is changed.

HOMEWORK *(continued)*

Gloria Channon

THE TEACHER—AGAIN

I had returned to the log, "to the notes written in anger and contempt and concern, to try to discover what I, *a teacher,* am." But the log is not enough.

I have used the term *authoritarian* to describe the kind of education I oppose. The structure of the school system is authoritarian and so is its intent. But most teachers would insist, with accuracy, that they are authoritarian neither by intent nor disposition. They are right, of course, or else we would not have so many problems with disruptive and rebellious children. If the majority of teachers were authoritarian we would not need policemen in the halls of our schools.

Why is it, then, that the only subject we continue to teach successfully is failure? More importantly, what happens to us when we fail? For our children's failure is in a larger sense our own. If they cannot tolerate it, if it is destructive for them, then is it no less intolerable and destructive to us?

We are always being handed ready-made excuses for the failure, and we need them—to relieve us of our burden of guilt and helplessness. For example, there is Robert Coles, one of the most humane writers on the subject of education. Coles uses the term *culture shock* to explain why children, in the third and fourth grades, suddenly seem to come to a complete halt. They slow down the already slow rate of progress, they lose interest in school, sooner or later they give up and drop out.

According to Coles, the ghetto and its dreadful promises come into focus for the child. The child knows now, Coles says, that there is no hope for him, no place to go, and he withdraws from the suddenly perceived irrelevance of school.

Be this as it may, something has been happening inside the school itself. In the first grade or the second the child has been trying to learn to read, usually by the sight method, and to some limited extent his working environment has been humane. There are breaks in the routine. Milk snacks and cookies are still provided, as is informal playtime. Most teachers still use art activities as a major part of the curriculum. There is still an emphasis on talk, music, acting, games.

But in third grade the curriculum gets whipped into shape. Children sit at their desks for hours. Notebooks and textbooks become the main focus of their activity. Lessons are formally organized into spelling, penmanship, reading, composition, math. Silence and good behavior are at a premium now as never before. The restless child graduates from being seen as immature (and therefore to some degree tolerated) to being judged as disruptive and as having emotional problems.

Besides this difference in the climate of the classroom, the gaps in learning loom unmanageably large. The child who has not mastered all the intricacies of the numbers through twenty is now expected to learn all kinds of difficult concepts about fractions and multiplication and place values and "exchanging." The odds and ends of sight words that he was expected to have memorized are now clearly insufficient for his needs. What phonic tricks he may have been taught (initial consonants, rhyming words) will not serve him. His nonstandard dialect or native Spanish create problems that his teachers do not recognize. His third-grade books free themselves from the simple redundant syntax of the first two readers and present him with a language full of unfamiliar words and idioms and unfamiliar content and undecipherable syntactic relationships.

The double burden of an increasingly restrictive school environment and an increasingly incomprehensible curriculum prove too much. Failure becomes his daily companion to a degree unnoticed by the adults who teach him.

Instead the teachers point to the environment outside. Teachers and others say the middle-class parents instill in their children a belief in the value of education. Middle-class children can postpone gratification. They work for long-range goals. They know they must study hard so that they can get into college. But do they? Sure, in many families there is the assumption that the child is collegebound. So the children come to put college on their agenda in the same way and with the same resignation that all children put junior high and high school on their agenda. It is simply something they will have to go through.

The real pressure for grades and competition for place, the real work-for-long-range-goals, does not begin until the middle of junior high, when the children recognize that this semester's grades will be counted in one's average for college. Until then, the pressures are more selective and immediate.

The elitism of special classes, the honors and attention and rewards reaped from unusually good work, the sighs and reproaches and deprivations that accompany the failure, that are seen as a betrayal by the parents, these are what goad the children to work. Even failure has its compensations in the middle classes, up to a point. I heard a mother talking on a bus in Queens one day. Her voice was that strange and irritating combination of complaint coated over with self-congratulation. Her high school son had fallen behind in some course or other and had been signed up for special tutorials in the summer. (There's another area for research: the number of middle-class kids who have had private tutoring.) Naturally it was unthinkable that the rest of the family take its Florida vacation as planned. Perhaps he would be lonely. Perhaps he was not to be trusted. But he had further extracted from his sacrificing family the promise of scuba-diving gear AND scuba-diving lessons upon successful completion of his make-up class.

There are, even for the not so bright middle-class kids, the professional and scholastic options: teaching, accountancy, journalism, banking, merchandising, and the scores of small colleges which flood our mailboxes with their thinly veiled promises of low standards, easy work, and a giddy social life. The middle classes do not need open enrollment. They have it already.

I go back again to the child I was. Did I have long-range goals? Did I expect to go to college? Not at all. My family, like most immigrant and ghetto families, valued education for its promise of better jobs than they could get. But neither my parents nor the community at large expected us to go to college. We were poor Italians in a rural community. The school, happily, was indifferent. If you could do college-preparatory work you were assigned to the college-preparatory courses. What you did with your diploma afterwards was no concern of the school. When I got a job in the library after the school day, the WASP ladies used to talk in front of me about how unusual and marvelous it was that *an Italian* should be found shelving books. I read Richard Halliburton and never dreamed in realities.

All I knew, if I thought of the future at all, was that I did not want to be a school teacher. I didn't have the slightest idea what other professions might be open to women, but of this I was sure, teaching was out. I see with a pang of recognition the young black mothers dreaming of going back to school to learn to be nurses. For them, too, teaching is never a viable option.

*   *   *

The profession of teaching, however, seems to be one tailor-made for masochists. It has most of the prerequisites: our father figures are often gratifyingly sadistic. We are asked to perform with all the nobility and dedication of spirit that martyrs love to indulge in. We are guaranteed failure and humiliation and punishment by the nature of our tasks and the rules of the game. We are given the opportunity within the structure to moan to our hearts' content. Most important of all, we are given victims for our sacrifice. The only negatives in the profession, from the masochist's point of view, are the reasonably adequate salary and the more than adequate vacations and the

job security. But we manage to find hobgoblins to threaten even these: from
the community that will fire us to the proliferation of requirements for
licensing and salary raises, which doom us to spend our spare hours in stuffy,
dull graduate school classrooms, doing penance for our sins of leisure.

There are a lot of good qualities in masochists. They can work like drones;
they are possessed of inhuman amounts of patience; they can endure the unspeakable long after everybody else has fled in despair. But their virtues also
contain the seeds of their destruction. They support institutions that should
be, if not destroyed, then certainly radically reformed. They tolerate the
destruction of the children because they do not know how to fight. In the
end, oppressed by their burden of guilt, they rid themselves of it, in self-defense,
by participating actively in the destruction of the children.

I know. I've been down that road. Now like an alcoholic on the wagon,
I can recognize, with a not very commendable mixture of malice and pity, my
fellow drunk anywhere. I talk to young teachers who have come to the schools
all full of ideals and hopes and energy. They are beautiful. (All young healthy
masochists are beautiful. Peace Corps people are beautiful. Young people in
communes are beautiful.) I listen to the words begin to turn sour on their
lips and I want to shake them and say, "Wait, wait, you don't have to travel
that road. You can choose to be free."

I don't mean to make a parlor game of it. It is much too important for
that. I see the young teachers betraying their own best feelings about children
and the classroom, helpless victims not only of the system but of themselves.
I hear them reject the free classroom because they "can't stand the noise," or
accept all the sociological explanations in the same spirit that Noah took the
news about the flood: *Sauve qui peut* and I can't save everybody. I watch
them fall into the standards and jargon and rituals of the approved classroom
or caught in the trap of rage at the authority above whom they cannot resist
and at the children below who persist in resisting them. I see them turn the
gift of love into the dreary obligations of duty. And when the children
reject them, I watch as love dies, to be replaced by the poison trees of hate
and fear.

How do you teach a young adult the difference between guilt and love,
between giving and sacrificing, between impotent rage and productive,
channeled anger? How can you teach them to forgive themselves and in that
act to forgive all others? You don't, no more than you teach children anything
at all. You just go on explaining things over and over, in this form and that,
in the hopes that some day their need and your lesson will coincide and they
will suddenly understand.

One of the less fashionable but still current explanations for the failure
of the schools is that there is a culture clash in the schools, between the values
and mores of the ghetto and those of the middle classes. But with surprisingly
few exceptions, the teachers in our schools were the products of lower-class
immigrant culture, just one or two generations back.

America is no longer the land of the immigrants. It is the land of the
second and third and fourth generation American. But consider what the
immigrants brought with them to this country. The Italians brought their
peasant culture of close-knit families, submissive women, dominating men.
The Jews brought their closed urban ghetto culture, highly defensive and exclusive. Within their protected places they had learned to nurture a faith in

their own superiority to help them withstand the hostile dismembering world outside. The blacks faced with an even harsher world were never permitted the sustaining gift of pride. Their norms have served them poorly, permitting them only survival, and in a sense insuring that they would never be able to rise above that grim level.

For them as for us, the children of the immigrants, the old emotional patterns no longer serve. Our tribal cultures just will not do in megalopolis. Concern for individual-family-tribal-ethnic survival is changed by some wretched alchemy in the open-for-whites society into a narrow and paralyzing conformity.

Emotions that were necessary and comfortable in the Old World are not or should not be necessary in the New. They are, needless to say, not comfortable at all. But we are stuck with them and we don't know it. As we move further and further from the spiritual and material world that produced the emotions, we are oppressed with feelings of anxiety and of loss. The emotions remain but they grow twisted and deformed in an alien environment. A kind but inaccurate simile would be to compare the feelings with a cactus plant set out in a landscape of rich soil and greenery and much rain. In the midst of abundance it must sicken and die.

It is strange that America has served to emasculate its immigrant men and to enhance the guilt-provoking martyrdom of its women. Now the young are trying to escape the pattern. Their parents and grandparents had to suffer in one way or another to achieve their version of the American dream, paying the price of dull jobs and unfulfilled pleasures, even now paying the most gratifying price of all: the rejection of them by the children for whom they gave everything.

But the young do not have such an easy way to psychic survival, not in a world of affluence. So they have grown up with a huge undischarged debt to their own parents and therefore the world. For many it has become unbearable enough so that they have willingly declared bankruptcy. I leave your values, your world, your debts and obligations, your life witout joy. Some of them manage to escape. But too many carry their innocent burden of guilt with them and find in escape only self-destruction. For all their longing to love and be loved, they have never really been allowed to learn how. Maybe that is why there is so much emphasis on the external identifications of style—that's how you can tell that I am one of the lovable ones, that's so I'll be able to recognize you. And they find their enemies: the pigs and the greasers.

The police and the working-class kids (or their elders) still are trying to make it. For them the Old World patterns of emotion still work. But the New World is closing in on them too. The young and their enemies sense in one another threats to their own survival. Their confrontations are really an externalization of the internal conflict between the two sides of the coin. I am still suffering and sacrificing to achieve what you testify is worthless. I don't want to believe you. I cannot afford to believe you, or else what is it all about? And on the other side, the flower children so carefully repress their rage and aggression and so wantonly invite the still accessible rage and aggression of their other, secret selves, whom they have labeled (with a hatred they did not know they were capable of displaying) the pigs and the greasers.

What can we do, we teachers and policemen and flower children and workers, when we are, so many of us, galloping masochists in a society that no longer requires such emotions for its stability and survival? A society, indeed, that needs for its survival people who will refuse to suffer? The tragedy is that destiny truly devours us. It is so hard for us to see what is going on and to understand it and to change ourselves first and then our world. So instead we keep changing the world so that it meets the twisted specifications of our emotions. With safe jobs and our houses bulging with driftwood lamps and matching bedroom sets and stuffed and yielding furniture, how will we suffer now? We manage, for humans are nothing if not inventive. We are pledged to inaction, whether it is the helplessness of "You can't fight City Hall" or the elaborate intellectualizations about the mythical powers of the military-industrial complex or the secret all-powerful manipulative Establishment. Not that these do not exist in some way in objective reality. But it is generations of timidity and helpless self-negating paralysis that have bolstered them. We attribute to them great power and strength when the truth is we have given them the gift of our unused power and unrecognized strength.

How many times have we voted for a candidate we did not like because our real choice had "no chance of winning"? How else explain the "liberals" who will compromise themselves into an about-face rather than fight? Or in the schools again, how else understand why teachers complain most vociferously about the not-so-petty indignities inflicted upon them but, in a showdown, can never find a good enough reason to stand and make a fight? No issue is ever important enough. They are always saving their big guns for a really important issue, they say, while their guns are water pistols, rusting away from disuse.

Thus in our lives we either destroy one another inside the safe walls of home or we create a hostile world outside that is clamoring to destroy us: a punishing world of miserable subways, traffic jams, overcrowding, injustice, air and water pollution, indifferent bureaucracies, unresponsive leaders, war. Our paralysis permits our exploitation. We create and nourish our exploiters.

The enemy grows more numerous and stronger every day, as we narrow our world down to the smallest of insular families. In the vacuum of our impotence, the enemy does indeed multiply, thereby giving the truth to our lies and delusions.

We teach our children not the middle-class values (whatever they are), but our Old World values deformed and misshapen into a reasonable facsimile of what we think middle-class values should be. But more and more our public faces come to be the private faces of our masochistic women. We teach our sons that fighting is bad before we ever let them learn that they can fight to protect themselves, or that they are worthy of defending. We teach them that tears are not manly, but neither is healthy aggressiveness. That is the brute's way. Indeed for many of us the very word aggressiveness has come to have only *bad* connotations. We teach them that they must yield and give of themselves unstintingly as we do, but they know by our example that we keep careful records of indebtedness and obligation that can never be erased. (My father: "I may forgive but I'll never forget.") So they learn that giving is never disinterested, it is always accompanied by the gift of guilt, the product of self-sacrifice and self-denial. It is never the natural outcome of an abundance of joy.

Violence is bad. Anger is bad because it can only lead to violence. Anger must be hidden, denied, suppressed. Self-assertion is bad because it will only lead to confrontations and rejections that will lead to anger, which will of course end in violence. It is no wonder that Buber's philosophy has made so small a mark on the world. It is the glorious rejection of the world of denial and impotence.

We teach our children to be nice and proper and to share and to love-love-love certain selected people. We teach them to hide their feelings in words. We supply them with a vocabulary that becomes more euphemistic and meaningless with each passing year. The attraction of sensitivity-training-institutes-of-joy is surely that of a safe protected place where we can play at having real feelings.

I watched a family at the beach one day. The mother, enjoying surcease from her punishing domestic tasks, was sunbathing. Father was very involved in being father, American style, playing with his children. The children had started to build a sand castle, sloppy and poorly conceived and soul-satisfying. Father came over and helped them create an architectural triumph beyond their puny skills, with much directing and correcting and patient smoothing and shaping. When it was finally done, they sat back on their heels to admire it. The little girl, a three-year-old, toddled over to it and gave the valued monument a whack. The five-year-old boy, basking with his father in the glorious outcome of their shared labor, became enraged, as who would not? He started after the girl but father intervened. Mustn't hit. She's only a little girl. It doesn't matter. *It's only an old pile of sand anyway.*

The boy stormed off, kicking up sand and complaining, but staying well away from sister and castle. By and by he distracted himself. But he was playing alone. Father could not bear the reproach and rejection implied by his isolation.

He called him over, and the little girl too, to the now abandoned castle. It's only a pile of sand. We don't like it. Let's bust it. Boom. Let's bust it down.

And the three of them began the terrible game of pseudorage, pseudodestruction, venting the bloodless remnants of their anger and disappointment on a castle now designated as worthless, in a joyless ritual game of pretense.

So that is how it is done. I thought. How sad and terrifying. As the failure-ridden children of the schools have shown us, the hardest lessons to unlearn are the ones we learned unconsciously. The schools, like our parents and our television sets, are the transmitters of culture. But what if a large part of that culture is no longer worth transmitting? What if it has reached that critical point, as our society seems to have done? Do we continue teaching the same paralyzing lessons over and over again? And do we watch as our world is more and more polarized, not between rich and poor or black and white or young and old but between autism and sadism, between violence and withdrawal? Is the civility we desire worth the price of the funeral?

Or do we dare risk life?

Do we, trained to endure the unspeakable, have within us the strength for one more sacrifice, the only one worthwhile? Can we, parents and teachers, set our children free of us?

We judge the turmoil and disruption in our schools and streets as destructive and dangerous. Maybe some of it is. But most of it is not. We condemn it and fear it where we should be nurturing it and performing tribal fertility rites around it. This is the life-force which is exploding from our dry, long-buried, long-dormant seed, the life-force that threatens us with salvation.

Sometimes I think that the only fit motto for our schools is "Abandon

Hope, all ye who enter here." It should be "Unless ye become as little children—." Maybe the free classroom will be one of the doors leading into the kingdom of Man.

Gloria Channon

Miriam Wasserman is one teacher who has fought the good fight against reflecting the traditional, undemocratic structures of American education. As a writer, teacher, and political activist she has demonstrated how, both alone and in concert with others, the individual can expose those parts of American schooling that keep it the way it is, and do something about it.[5]

As her writings attest, Wasserman has been able to achieve that level of insight into herself and American schools that one can truly describe as "radical." By "radical" here we mean that it is antiestablishment, that it is incorporated in the life style of the individual, that it seeks the roots of institutions and values, and that is more often politically left than anything else. We think this is the direction we must go if we are to achieve the kind of change toward democratic purposes in American schools that we have been discussing throughout this book.

Miriam Wasserman shows us how you can take a radical approach in a classroom even if you are a substitute. Some might argue that subbing offers an ever better opportunity than regular teaching for doing the sort of thing Wasserman describes here.

5. See Miriam Wasserman, *The School Fix; NYC, USA,* Outerbridge & Dientsfrey, 1970. and *Demystifying School,* Praeger, 1974.

THE RADICAL SUBSTITUTE

Miriam Wasserman

One role in which a radical teacher has the possibility of exercising some influence on students is the role of the substitute.

Generally the school and the substitute herself look on her task as simply holding the lid on. And a lot of conventional advice to substitutes consists of clever techniques for sitting on the lid without getting your ass blown up. But the substitute who doesn't want to sit in that hot seat may not be quite sure, bird of flight that she is, what she can do.

Actually, an experience from my own school days convinces me that a

Miriam Wasserman, "The Radical Substitute," *No More Teachers' Dirty Looks,* No. 3, 1970, Bay Area Radical Teachers Organizing Committee.

substitute can sometimes have an influence on students astronomically out of proportion to the amount of time she spends with them (if she is willing to come on as herself and forego the ego gratification of observing the effects of her influence). I studied Latin for four years, taking what pleasure I did from the fact that translating was a difficult puzzle which I was able to solve neatly. My teacher was thorough, I believe a good Latin scholar, and hard working, and I liked to earn her approval. One day, in my fourth year class we had a substitute (an ugly old lady with a grating voice) for whom Vergil was a poet. She just read the *Aeneid* and talked with us about it as one reads and talks about poetry one loves. And in that one hour I found out that the puzzles I'd been doing for four years were literature and the Romans were people. For what it is worth to teachers who, like most teachers, want to be remembered by their students, I remember to this day, thirty-five years later, the substitute's name and face and voice.

The Latin substitute had an advantage over our regular teacher: she didn't have to prepare us to do brilliantly in Latin examinations and competitions, and she didn't have to cope with us every day, give us grades, and generally be responsible for us. Not having that day-to-day responsibility, she was free, sort of in the way a grandparent can be more free with kids than the parents can.

This is a freedom that many substitutes have, and the question is what are some ways that a radical teacher can take advantage of that freedom. The question is particularly pertinent if you are substituting in a so-called bad or tough school. From the point of view of your relations with the authorities, you are not too bad off in a tough school. They know that even the regulars have a hard time keeping order: a substitute can excusably do even worse. Often, if you merely survive the day without rushing hysterically into the office or without some catastrophic fight, you're a success. In a lot of tough schools, if a substitute manages to stay out of sight, they're only too happy and won't bug him or her.

But how do you survive the day, not only without hysterics and catastrophe but as a radical?

Two years ago, when the insanity in New York's insane schools was at a manic pitch, I went as a substitute into a couple of the most insane junior high schools of all. The schools were so manic that they couldn't get substitutes, and none of the regular staff could understand how I could last a day, apparently placidly, and then come back for more. There were huge lunchroom brawls, involving scores of kids and taking the whole male staff to quell (the following year things got worse and they had to get cops for that job). Almost every day, sometimes more than once a day, some kid would turn out all the interior corridor lights during change of class, and the corridor would become a mass of shrieking, rushing bodies. Everybody threw paper, pencils, software out of windows; some people threw books and clothing; and once in awhile somebody would throw furniture into the street or yard. Throwing furniture around the room was normal. Kids played tag in the classroom, ducking under desks, into lockers and closets, etc. In the music room they dragged out all the instruments and bammed around on them. Lots of teachers would never give an order unaccompanied by a smack on the legs, shoulders, etc., usually with a yardstick or some other weapon (despite the fact that in New York schools corporal punishment is illegal).

In this situation it was out of the question for most regular teachers, no less substitutes, to hold the attention of a whole class for a whole hour. I did not try ever. But I also didn't want to stand around stupidly and uselessly. So I'd come into each class as if I was a real teacher, write some assignment or other on the board, take attendance, hand out some papers or exercise sheets or something like that. Usually two or three, up to a half dozen, kids would do the work. Every once in awhile, for reasons or nonreasons I never did figure out, a whole class would do the school thing, and I'd have a real class, which would give us all a quiet hour although not necessarily a fruitful one. But most of the time they'd form in little knots of three or four or five kids. Then I'd go up to one such little group and either get in on what they were doing or get them in on my thing. If they rejected me (which would be maybe half the time), I'd move on. Once a little group and I would get going on something, if the rest of the class was hysterical, fighting, throwing things, blowing our ears with their transistors, I'd just move out for a minute and say, "look we're not bothering you, so would you please quit bothering us. We can't hear a thing with all this going on." I'd use a tough, but not a teachery tone, and generally they'd respond to that—for five or ten minutes anyway. With classes that I came back to, often a kid would undertake to perform the task of keeping people out of each other's hair.

The test of the success of a group's activity would be when, during the course of the hour, the other kids would one by one start coming over to see what was going on and either watch or get in on it. A couple of times, by the end of the hour, the nucleus group had grown to include the whole class. Two such times that I remember were when the nucleus group was discussing a real gut issue.

The first time, it was I who had introduced the topic. For a year or two, Random House published a semi-weekly school newspaper, which had relevant urban topics and excellent photos. (It eventually flopped because the teachers preferred *My Weekly Reader*.) I had a stack of old copies of that which I'd carry around with me when I went on a job. Conventional advice to substitutes is to carry around on the job a packet of "interesting materials," in the form of printed or dittoed sheets, stencils or ditto masters, materials for the kids to read or for the teacher to read to them. The radical teacher will adapt this to her interests and subject matter specialty. One thing that I personally had some success with in "English" classes was some exercises in which the kids were to turn standard-dialect sentences into Negro-dialect sentences. Standing the teacher-learner relationship and the right-wrong relationship on their heads is not only radical, it's fun. One issue had a story about dope-taking, addiction, pushing, etc. I started to talk with a group of two or three boys about the story. They knew why people take drugs (to escape their problems, show off, etc.), what drugs are addictive, where the pushers are to be found, the terrible fate of addicts, etc. (It's a laugh that they're trying to put in drug-prevention programs with middle-class straight teachers teaching those hip kids about drugs.) I just let the kids talk, maybe asked a couple of questions (serious questions, not teacher questions). They were so turned on to being allowed to be themselves in school that they went on to talk about sex next, revealing, despite undoubted practical experience, some fantastic ignorance and superstition. ("Is it true your prick could come off if you let it stay in a girl's cunt too long?"). I wasn't exactly a political radical that day, but maybe a couple of kids found out that a teacher can be a serious listener and a resource person from whom you can get serious information. Anyway, one kid kept coming back into my classes all day, each time claiming he was his brother, until finally near the end of the afternoon, another teacher or maybe a dean came and yanked him out to go to his real class with a real teacher.

The next time a group grew into the class was even better, I believe because the topic came from the kids. It was in I.S. 201, just then the center of the whole city's fury, and it was the day after the M. L. King funeral. A group of girls in a domestic science class started a play, being ladies talking about King, the funeral, peace, nonviolence, etc. They acceded to my request that I be an audience, even started again from the beginning after they had seated me. The play quickly became a discussion in which they revealed the fears and anxieties aroused in them by the murder, the subsequent rioting in Harlem, and violence in general, I suspect including the violence and general disorder of the school. They kept referring to King as a man of peace, trying to make peace all over the whole world, "even in Africa." In order to point out the resistance rather than simply the nonviolent element in King's philosophy, I asked permission to be in the play "for just one question." They gave it. Other kids started to gather around and wanted to contribute. At first the original cast wouldn't let in outsiders, saying they couldn't talk because they weren't "in the play." I asked if they couldn't be in the play, and they said, "No, 'cause she was running around." Eventually you could earn entrance into the play by sitting around quietly and listening for a bit. By the end of the hour the entire class was either "in the play," or listening.

What we had then was an organic group, not a coerced one created by the teacher. It grew out of a common pressing concern, whose consideration was initiated by one or two natural leaders and which took a form which, when the anxieties became too great, could mask the participant's personal involvement. (They were using a bowl of artificial flowers as pretend grown-ups' refreshment, although of course some of them had M&M's, etc. in their pocketbooks and pockets, and from time to time as feelings would begin to rise precipitously, the "hostess" would jump up and pass the artificial flowers around with little simpering ladylike murmurs and smiles.) At the end of the hour there was a kind of relaxation in the room which suggested that some gratifying catharsis had occurred.

I don't know that I contributed much to the process. Possibly the following: (1) I didn't try to take over the class, so at least I didn't prevent it from happening. (2) I perhaps gave the proceedings legitimacy by attending them myself. (3) I may have helped the nucleus grow by asking if other people couldn't be in the play. But I'm not sure this wouldn't have happened anyway. On the other hand, I am pretty sure that if I had ordered that everybody be let in it, I would have smothered the whole thing. (4) Maybe somebody got the political message that King was murdered not for his nonviolence but for his resistance.

I think with more experience, I could have developed the technique of helping a concerned nucleus grow and then leading the students to new insights. I would of course like to see some other teachers try it. I'm beginning to believe that that's one of the most important legitimate functions a teacher can perform, maybe the only one.

Miriam Wasserman

If you think that in order to develop an awareness of how teachers can reflect traditional undemocratic values of most schooling you have to be an experienced, mature, highly intellectual person, our next series of readings will tell you otherwise.

The schoolboys of Barbiana, ranging in age from thirteen to sixteen, wrote their *Letter to a Teacher* as a full-year project in a school in a community of about twenty farmhouses, in the Tuscany hills outside Florence. The school was begun by Don Lorenzo Milani when he discovered the children on the farms were without schooling. Most had either flunked out or were bitterly discouraged by the teaching they had received. He gathered about him ten boys, then expanded the class to twenty, and gave them a full schedule of eight hours' work, six or seven days a week. The "I" in their letter is a composite of eight authors who were assisted by other classmates on Sundays. The "you" they address stands for the kind of teacher they had all known in their schools. In their dedication they say the book is not written for teachers, but for parents. "It is a call for them to organize." In a quite important other sense then, it *is* a book for teachers.

A steady and passionate concern runs through their letter about how and why students are flunked, especially students from poverty backgrounds:

> You won't remember me or my name. You have flunked so many of us.
>
> On the other hand I have often had thoughts about you; and the other teachers, and about that institution which you call "school" and about the kids that you flunk.
>
> You flunk us right out into the fields and factories and there you forget us. (p. 3)

The boys admit that it is harder to run a school with the poor students around. They see that the temptation to get rid of them is at times strong. But if they are lost, school is no longer school, they point out. School becomes a hospital which tends to the healthy and rejects the sick.

> It becomes just a device to strengthen the existing differences to a point of no return.
>
> And are you ready to take such a position? If not, get them back to school, insist, start from scratch all over again, even if you are called crazy.
>
> Better to be called crazy than to be an instrument of racism. (p. 14)

The discrimination is documented by them in several places in their letter, much to the disbelief of the teachers they showed it to. They showed how more students from peasant backgrounds were flunked than those from non-peasant backgrounds, and more from "isolated houses" (houses without water, electricity and other communal resources) than from houses in towns. In both cases the majority from these backgrounds failed, a story that is repeated even in the highly industrialized and urbanized schools of this society.

One teacher who resisted their documentation most fiercely insisted she knew nothing about her students' backgrounds when she graded them. When a test is worth a 4, she said, she marked it with a 4. The boys comment:

She could not understand, poor soul, that this is exactly the charge against her. Nothing is more unjust than to share equally among unequals. (p. 48)

And they have more to say about equality, stupidity, poverty—and flunking. They conlcude with the comment: "You want us crushed. Go ahead, do it, but at least don't pretend to be honest. Big deal, to be honest when the Code is written by you and cut to your measurements."

LETTER TO A TEACHER

Schoolboys of Barbiana

*   *   *

BORN DIFFERENT?

The Stupid and The Lazy

You tell us that you fail only the stupid and the lazy.

Then you claim that God causes the stupid and the lazy to be born in the houses of the poor. But God would never spite the poor in this way. More likely, the spiteful one is you.

Defense of the Race

It was a Fascist who defended the theory of "differences by birth" at the Constituent Assembly: "The Honorable Mastroianni, referring to the word 'compulsory,' points out that certain children have an organic incapacity to attend schools."

And a principal of an intermediate school has written: "The Constitution cannot, unfortunately, guarantee to all children the same mental development or the same scholastic aptitude. But he will never admit it about his own child. Will he fail to make him finish the intermediate? Will he send him out to dig in the fields? I have been told that in the China of Mao such things are happening. But is it true?

Even the rich have difficult offspring. But they push them ahead.

From *Letter to a Teacher* by Schoolboys of Barbiana, translated by Rossi and Cole (pp. 53-57). Reprinted by permission of Random House.

Others' Children

Children born to others do appear stupid at times. Never our own. When we live close to them we realize that they are not stupid. Nor are they lazy. Or, at least, we feel that it might be a question of time, that they may snap out of it, that we must find a remedy.

Then, it is more honest to say that all children are born equal; if, later, they are not equal, it is our fault and we have to find the remedy.

Removing the Obstacles

This is exactly what the Constitution says, in reference to Gianni:

"All citizens are equal before the law, without distinction as to race, language, or personal and social conditions.

"It is the duty of the Republic to remove the obstacles created by economic or social conditions which, limiting the freedom and equality of citizens, prevent the full development of the human personality and the full participation of all workers in the political, economic and social organization of the country" (Article 3).

IT WAS UP TO YOU

Unloader of Barrels

One of your colleagues (a sweet young bride who managed to fail ten out of twenty-eight kids in first intermediate—both she and her husband Communists, and quite militant) used this argument with us: "I did not chase them away, I just failed them. If their parents don't see to it that they return, that's their worry."

Gianni's Father

But Gianni's father went to work as a blacksmith at age twelve and did not even finish the fourth grade.

When he was nineteen he joined the Partisans. He did not quite grasp what he was doing. But he understood far better than any of you. He was looking forward to a world with more justice, where Gianni at least could be equal to all. Gianni, who was not even born.

This is the way Article 3 sounds in his ears: "It is the duty of Mrs. Spadolini [a teacher] to remove all obstacles . . ."

And he pays you, too—quite well. He gets 300 lire per hour, and out of it he pays you 4,300.

He'd be willing to give you even more if you would work a respectable number of hours. He works 2150 hours a year, while you work 522 (I don't count the examination hours; they are not teaching hours.)

Substitution

But Gianni's father cannot by himself remove the obstacles that weigh him down. He has no idea how to discipline a boy going through the intermediate grades: how long the boy should sit at his desk, or whether it is good for him to have some distractions. Is it true that studying causes headaches and that his eyes "begin to trill," as Gianni says?

If Gianni's father knew how to manage everything by himself, he would not have to send Gianni to you for schooling. It is up to you to supply Gianni with both education and training. They are two faces of the same problem.

If you lead him forward, Gianni will be able to work with you in a different way and will be a more competent father tomorrow. But for today, Gianni's father is what he is. What he was allowed by the rich to be.

Tutoring

That poor man—if he knew what was going on he would pick up his weapon and be a Partisan again. There are teachers who tutor for money in their free time. So, instead of removing the obstacles, they work to deepen the differences among students.

In the morning—during regular school hours—we pay them to give the same schooling to all. Later on in the day they get money from richer people to school their young gentlemen differently. Then, in June, at our expense, they preside at the trial and judge the differences.

The Little Civil Servant

If some little civil servant did his paper work quickly and well at home, for a good price, but at his desk did the same job slowly and badly, you would have him locked up.

Consider further that should he whisper to clients, "In this office your documents will be given to you late and all messed up. Let me suggest that you find someone who can do them better at home for a little extra"—he would be locked up.

But no one locks up that teacher whom I heard say to a mother: "The boy's not going to make it on his own. Get him a tutor." That's what he said, word for word. I have witnesses. I could bring him to court.

To court? To see a judge whose wife herself makes a bit extra by tutoring? Anyway, the Italian Penal Code, for some reason, does not list such a crime.

Schoolboys of Barbiana

The "Gianni" they refer to was a fourteen-year-old student, "inattentive, allergic to reading," whose teachers had declared him delinquent. The boys admit they were not totally wrong, "but that was no excuse for sweeping him out of their way." Because the boys of Barbiana ignored his failing marks and put each person in the right grade for his age, Gianni came to them, and then he experienced the "first satisfaction" he had ever had in his unhappy school career.

The boys of Barbiana display a political astuteness as they look at the teacher and the role he plays in the selecting and sorting process that inevitably means some lose out. They note that teachers can blame fate for the fact that some must lose: "To read history as keyed to fate is so restful." But to read it as keyed to politics is quite another matter. Selecting and sorting then can be seen as a "well-calculated scheme to assure that the Giannis are left out." Their denunciation of the teacher's role in this is scathing:

> The apolitical teacher becomes one of the 411,000 useful idiots armed by their boss with a grade book and report cards. Reserve troops charged with stopping 1,031,000 Giannis a year, just in case the sway of fashion is not sufficient to divert them. One million, thirty-one thousand children *respinti* [rejected] each year. *Respinti* is a technical word used in your so-called school. But it is also a word used in military science. *Respinti* before reaching draft age. It is not by chance that exams are a Prussian invention. (p. 61)

And the boys add in one of many footnotes that they use to document their charges and explain their references to their readers: "It is commonly said that the military mania of the Germans comes from the Prussians."

LETTER TO A TEACHER *(continued)*

Schoolboys of Barbiana

*   *   *

FOR WHOSE SAKE ARE YOU TEACHING?

Good Faith

The good faith of teachers is a different matter entirely.

You teachers are paid by the government. You have the children right there in front of you. You have studied your history. You teach it. You should be able to see more clearly.

Of course, you see only selected children. And you got your culture from books. And the books were written by men in the Establishment. They are the only ones who can write. But you should have been able to read between the lines. How can you possibly say you are acting in good faith?

From *Letter to a Teacher* by Schoolboys of Barbiana, translated by Rossi and Cole, pp. 71-73. Reprinted by permission of Random House.

The Nazis

I try to understand you. You look so civilized. Not a hint of the criminal in you. Perhaps, though, something of the Nazi criminal. That superhonest, loyal citizen who checked the number of soap boxes. He would take great care not to make mistakes in figures (four, less than four), but he does not question whether the soap is made from human fat.

Even More Timid than I

For whose sake are you doing it? What do you gain by making school hateful and by throwing the Giannis out into the streets?

I can show you that you are more timid than I ever was. Are you afraid of Pierino's parents? Or afraid of your colleagues in the upper schools? Or the superintendent?

If you are so worried about your career there is a solution: cheat a little bit on your pupils' tests by correcting a few mistakes while you are walking up and down between the desks.

For the Good Name of the School

Or perhaps you don't fear something so obvious and so simple. Perhaps you fear your own conscience instead. Then your conscience is built wrong.

"I would consider promotion of this child injurious to the good name of the school," wrote a principal in his report. But *who* is the school? We are the school. To serve it is to serve us.

For the Good of the Child

"After all, it's for the child's own good. We must not forget that these pupils stand at the threshold of high school!" pompously cried the headmaster of a little country school.

It was immediately clear that only three of the thirty children in the class would go on to the upper grades: Maria, the daughter of the drygoods merchant; Anna, the teacher's daughter; and Pierino, of course. But even if more of the children went on, what difference would it make?

That headmaster has forgotten to change the record on his phonograph. He hasn't yet noticed the growth of the school population. A living reality of 680,000 children in the first grade. All of them poor. The rich, a minority.

It's not a question of a classless school, as he calls it. His is a one-class school, at the service of those who have the money to push ahead.

For Justice

"To pass a bad student is unfair to the good ones," said a sweet little teaching soul.

Why not call Pierino aside to say to him, as Our Lord said in the parable about the vine trimmers: "I am passing you, because you have learned. You are twice blessed: you pass, and also you have learned. I am going to pass Gianni to encourage him, but he has the misfortune not to have learned."

For Society

Another teacher is convinced that she has a responsibility toward Society. "Today I pass him into third grade (intermediate), and tomorrow he turns up as an M.D.!"

Equality

Career, culture, family, the good name of the school: you are using tiny sets of scales for grading your students. They really are petty. Too small to fill the life of a teacher.

Some among you have understood, but cannot find a way out. Always in fear of the sacred word. And yet, there is no choice. Nothing but politics can fill the life of a man of today.

In Africa, in Asia, in Latin America, in southern Italy, in the hills, in the fields, even in the cities, millions of children are waiting to be made equal. Shy, like me; stupid, like Sandro; lazy, like Gianni. The best of humanity.

Schoolboys of Barbiana

The boys of Barbiana are saying what our authors have said: school success and failure result more from factors outside the school than from what the school does or does not do. But the schools are nonetheless involved, in nothing less than a coverup. In the meritocratic formula, it is the child who is held to be the principal—if not sole—cause of his or her failure or success, not society, not socioeconomic status, and most certainly not the school. (Though the school is willing to share in the glory of its successes, it seldom shares the blame for its failures. You never read about *them* in the alumni reports!) According to this formula the schools and the rest of society can say to you, "We gave you the chance to show what you could do and you showed us you can't do it. You just don't have the aptitude."

In this way, schools—and that means teachers too—convert society's failures into individual failures. As the Barbiana schoolboys point out, teachers hide behind things like "aptitude," "ability," "IQ," and all the tests that supposedly measure these individual powers. Theirs is a damning indictment of the willing cooperation of teachers in perpetuating a system of competition and inequality while covering up their cooperation with rhetoric of merit and equality. It is quite clear to them that teachers use society "out there" as an excuse for these practices, practices that enable schools, through their cooperating teachers, to serve the purposes of everyone else but the students.

LETTER TO A TEACHER *(continued)*

Schoolboys of Barbiana

*   *   *

Aptitudes

You can't hide any more behind the racist theory of aptitude tests.

Every child has enough "aptitude" to reach the third grade of the intermediate and to get by in all subjects.

It is so convenient to tell a boy, "You are not cut out for this subject." The boy will accept this; he is just as lazy as his teacher. But he knows that his teacher does not consider him an Equal.

It is not good policy to tell another child, "You are clearly cut out for this subject." When he has too much fondness for just *one* subject, he should be forbidden to study it. Call his case "specialized," or "unbalanced." There is so much time, later on, to lock oneself up in a specialized field.

By Piecework

If all of you knew that, by any means possible, you had to move every child ahead in every subject, you would sharpen up your wits to find a way for all of them to function well.

I'd have you paid by piecework. So much for each child who learns one subject. Or, even better, a fine for each child who does not learn a subject.

Then your eyes would always be on Gianni. You would search out in his inattentive stare the intelligence that God has put in him, as in all children. You would fight for the child who needs you most, neglecting the gifted one, as they do in any family. You would wake up at night thinking about him and would try to invent new ways to teach him—ways that would fit his needs. You would go to fetch him from home if he did not show up for class.

You would never give yourself any peace, for the school that lets the Giannis drop out is not fit to be called a school.

You are the Ones from the Middle Ages

On extreme provocation at our school we even use the rod.

Now don't play squeamish. Forget all those pedagogical theories. If you need a whip I can give you one, but throw away that pen lying on top of your record book. That pen leaves its mark all through the year. The mark of a whip disappears by the next day.

From *Letter to a Teacher* by Schoolboys of Barbiana, translated by Rossi and Cole, pp. 76-78. Reprinted by permission of Random House.

Because of that nice "modern" pen of yours, Gianni will never in his life be able to read a book. He can't write a decent letter. That is cruel punishment, way out of proportion.

Mathematics

The math teacher is the only one who might have some reason to complain if he can't ever fail a pupil. The second- or third-grade lessons are useless to someone who has not learned the material in first grade.

But mathematics is just one subject among many. The three hours a week of math that a boy can't master should not cause him to lose all the twenty-three other hours in which he could do well.

Less is Enough

We could start a discussion here on the question of mathematics, similar to the one the Assembly had on Latin.

How much math does anyone have to know for his immediate needs at home and at work? Or in order to read the newspaper? In other words, just how much mathematics will a nonspecialized man of culture remember?

The ordinary math taught in the eight-year program, except for numerical expressions and algebra.

There is still the problem of making the word "algebra" a meaningful part of the language. But that could be done in one lesson during the year.

Schoolboys of Barbiana

But all of this implicit and explicit faith that the schools can be changed, whether by individual or collective action, by direct assault on the schools or through changes in the rest of society, may be without much support. A recently published study of the education of teachers by Donald J. McCarty, Dean of the University of Wisconsin's School of Education, and associates—fifteen people connected with education and the education of teachers—has one persistent message: schools are not going to change. As McCarty puts it:

> There is almost a desperate defeatism in these pages. Liberal arts professors are detached from the concerns of teacher education, tight budgets inhibit significant educational reform, the public likes the schools the way they are, leadership from state departments and the federal government is often confusing and disruptive rather than constructive, and teaching is a pseudoprofession, resting on experience and apprenticeship rather than ideas.[6]

McCarty does not believe that this will please either the reactionaries who want to dissolve teacher education, or the radicals who consider the education of teachers to be beyond repair. "Teacher education," he says, "has suffered

---

6. Donald J. McCarty & Associates, *New Perspectives on Teacher Education* (San Francisco: Jossey-Bass, 1973), p. 2.

greatly from what the philosophers describe as inflated ideals; the antidote is not to declare the process useless but to make the necessary improvements."

Perhaps our proposals for change in the schools, including our belief that the schools can be changed meaningfully, also suffer from inflated ideals. But with McCarty, we would rather deflate them than throw them away. Others, however, have decided that there is little hope for the public school. In significant numbers in the 60s, young people and adults turned their backs on the public school and joined what came to be known as the New School or Free School Movement. Some would date its beginnings with the appearance of A. S. Neill's *Summerhill* in 1960. It was a revolt, but not against outdated curricula or ineffective teaching methods, which were the concerns of the late 50s and early 60s. As Bonnie Barrett Stretch pointed out in 1970,

> The revolt today is against the institution itself, against the implicit assumption that learning must be imposed on children by adults, that learning is not something one does by and for oneself, but something designated by a teacher. Schools operating on this assumption tned to hold children in a prolonged state of dependency, to keep them from discovering their own capacities for learning, and to encourage a sense of impotence and lack of worth. The search is for alternatives to this kind of institution.[7]

We turn now to look at what happened in this revolt. In our next reading, Allen Graubard, who was associated with this revolt from its beginning, describes the schools that sprang up outside the public school system. While "free" and "alternative" are sometimes used interchangeably to describe these schools, for the most part the new schools created outside the public system have been called "free" schools. The new schools that have been created inside the public system in more recent years, and about which we will be reading later, are more often called "alternative" schools, and many people in these schools insist that they be distinguished from the free schools.

Even though the free schools have been outside the public system, and the people associated with them generally have refused to have anything to do with public schools, there are those—and Graubard is among them—who have wondered what role these free schools might play in effecting change in the public school system. Graubard describes the free schools and considers their possible influence on public schools.

---

7. Bonnie Barrett Stretch, "The Rise of the 'Free School,'" *Saturday Review*, June 20, 1970.

THE FREE SCHOOL MOVEMENT

Allen Graubard

About nine of every ten American school children attend the public schools. The great majority of the remaining ten per cent satisfy the compulsory school attendance laws in parochial schools, although this number has declined sharply over the past few years. A small number of children are educated in private "prep" schools, which are often small, expensive, and elite. The economic troubles of the past few years have been an important factor in the decline in both the number and enrollments of these nonpublic schools.

Yet, while the customary American private school education has begun to decline, a very special kind of private school has appeared and grown astonishingly in numbers. These schools have received increasing attention from the media and from people interested in educational reform. They are most frequently called "free schools," though they are also known as "new schools" or "alternative schools." In five years the number of these free schools has grown from around 25 to perhaps 600; around 200 have been founded in the past year alone. These schools are usually very small: in absolute numbers of participants—students, parents, and staff—the phenomenon is very limited, but their public impact and symbolic significance are relatively great.

This essay presents some objective data about free schools along with a discussion of the various educational and social change concepts which underlie them. Particular emphasis is given to the extent to which differences of social class, ethnicity, and political perspective contribute to the variation of styles within the broad free school movement. My purpose is to give an overview of the movement, to analyze its significance, and to speculate about its future, especially in relation to reform within the public school system.

The basic theoretical concept is, naturally, freedom. The literature of radical school reform associated with free schools vehemently opposes the compulsory and authoritarian aspects of traditional public and private schools. This literature attacks the emotional and intellectual effects of conventional pedagogy and projects a radical theory in which freedom is the central virtue. The most uncompromising form of both the attack and the theoretical alternative is found in A. S. Neill's *Summerhill*. The small number of free schools which existed in the U.S. before the current wave began are almost all explicitly Summerhillian schools. In recent years, the writings of Paul Goodman, John Holt, Edgar Z. Friedenberg, George Leonard, Neil Postman and Charles Weingartner, George Dennison, Herbert Kohl, Jonathan Kozol, and others have popularized the general notion surrounding free schools: that children are naturally curious and motivated to learn by their own interests and desires. The most important condition for nurturing this natural interest is freedom supported by adults who enrich the environment and offer help. In contrast, coercion and regimentation only in-

Graubard, Allen, "The Free School Movement," *Harvard Educational Review*, 42, August 1972. Copyright © 1972 by President and Fellows of Harvard College.

hibit emotional and intellectual development. It follows that almost all of the major characteristics of public school organization and method are opposed— the large classes, the teacher with absolute power to administer a state-directed curriculum to rigidly defined age groups, the emphasis on discipline and obedience, the constant invidious evaluation and the motivation by competition, the ability tracking, and so forth.[1]

We can see in this central concept of freedom two distinct ideological sources for an alternative school movement, one political and one pedagogical (or more broadly, cultural). These sources are in real tension, sometimes even contradiction. By the *political* source, I mean the spirit behind the first "freedom" schools—those in Mississippi, in 1964—when groups of people sought control of the oppressive educational processes to which they and their children were being subjected. This spirit is seen in the movement for community control. It views the public schools and most professional educators with great hostility, and it articulately opposes indoctrination in the content and method of the public schools. This spirit has been most extensively expressed in black communities' struggle for control of public schools. But over the past few years some minority community groups have turned their anger and energy toward starting their own alternative schools, despairing of the possibilities of working inside the system.

These schools emphasize control by the local community, black (or brown or red) consciousness in the curriculum, and the schools' participation in the political and social struggle for equality; the pedagogical idea of allowing each child the freedom to unfold his or her individuality is not given so dominant a position as in most middle-class free schools. So, in many of the black community schools, there is a good deal of structure and organization, including, sometimes, required classes, well-organized compulsory activities run by the teacher, intensive drilling in basic skills—items which contradict in varying degrees the more strictly pedagogical concept of freedom.

If one looks back about six or seven years, one can see the two strands in the earliest days of the free school wave—there were a few Summerhillian schools (e.g., Lewis-Wadhams in New York State, founded in 1963) and a few black community schools starting in the ghettos (e.g., Roxbury Community School, 1966).

Each kind of school is an alternative, articulating a profound opposition to the methods and results of the public schools (this is not true of most private schools); each is a "free" school. But one trend emphasizes the role of the school in the community's struggle for freedom and equality (the freedom of the "Freedom now!" cry of the civil rights movement), while the other represents the strongest possible claim for the individual child's freedom from coercive approaches to learning and social development as expressed by the organization and techniques of most public schools.

The complex differences and possible tensions between these two sources of freedom make it difficult to specify clearly what is a free school and what is not. All of the institutions reasonably inlcuded in the class oppose the public schools; but the political and pedagogical sources of this opposition are expressed in varied ways across the range of new schools. (See the typology of free schools below.) Moreover, these tensions exist *within* schools and even within individuals, providing a constant source of serious discussion. (For example, Jonathan Kozol's recent acerbic criticisms of counter-cultural, apolitical free schools [*Free Schools,* 1972] were the occasion for renewed intense debate among free school people.)

FREE SCHOOLS: SOME DATA AND A TYPOLOGY

The complicated problem of definition should be kept in mind in approaching the data that follows. How "free" must a school be for it to count as a "free school" pedagogically? And if a black school is militant and community-controlled, but has rather traditional pedagogy and methods, is it a "free school"? For most of the schools, identification is not a problem. But there are fairly significant grey areas which have occasioned some subjective judgments in gathering the data. Consequently, the data, though it looks precise, being numbers and percentages, should be taken softly, and it is offered in this spirit. It was gathered between March and August, 1971, by the New Schools Directory Project,[2] a group of free school people who wanted to compile an accurate and detailed directory of existing alternative schools, since no real data seemed available and a good deal of dubious information was being widely quoted as fact (e.g., that the average life of the schools is 18 months or that there were 1600-2000 new schools).

*   *   *

Rough as the methods were, I think we missed only a few of the free schools then in existence. (Some 200 schools opened in September 1971, and most of these were not included in the survey.) My own check of the data indicates that the range of accuracy was 80-90 percent.

The survey limited itself to "outside-the-system" schools. Free school-type programs within the public school system have proliferated rapidly, with important implications for the free school movement. But the concern of the survey was with the grass roots movement that had begun outside of the state-controlled system.

The number of free schools has increased dramatically during the past five years, especially in contrast to the decline of parochial and traditional private school education . . . .

A few very progressive or Summerhillian schools (less than five) were founded every year during the early 1960s. Then, in 1966 and 1967, the real rise of free schools began, simultaneous with the growth of a widespread movement for social change and an increasingly radical critique of American institutions. Around 20 free schools were founded in 1967 and 1968. Over 60 were founded in 1969. By 1970, the number was around 150, and, as mentioned before, the number of new free schools begun during 1971-72 is substantially greater.

A considerable number of free schools close after one or two or three years of existence. Although the existing data does not present an entirely accurate picture, my sense is that the oft-quoted figure of an eighteen month average lifespan is very wrong. Since most of the schools are less than two years old, it is difficult to get a meaningful figure, but it seems that at most one out of five new schools closes before the end of its second year, and perhaps not more than one out of ten.

Given the difficulties of starting schools, this dramatic rise in the number of parents, students, and teachers who are willing to make the enormous commitment needed to start their own school is significant far beyond the actual numbers. It is obvious that if there were a free-choice tuition voucher plan or the widespread possibility of alternatives inside the public school system, the number of new free schools and participants would be much greater than at present.

Clearly, the data is heavily dependent on the kind of definitional problem described above. We tended toward a relatively strict conception of "free school"; that is, we wanted the selection to reflect as much as possible the sense of being part of a conscious movement to create schools very different from the normal public and private schools. This selection process was often quite difficult—almost arbitrary at times. For example, we excluded Shady Hill School in Cambridge and Miquon School in Philadelphia, two well-known and established "progressive" schools, but included Miquon Upper School, a free high school started by Miquon last year. Such decisions are obviously complex; in general, we tried to avoid inflating the figures by including schools which, though progressive, are not really participants in this new wave of radical school reform.

The following figures are based on the survey of 346 schools. Lacking complete information from every school, the percentage figures given are often based on smaller numbers. Also, it should be clear that figures such as enrollment statistics change constantly. No systematic attempt was made to find schools opening in September, 1971, though some are included. There are other institutions and projects which are clearly related to the free school impulse—community-control day care centers and pre-schools, after-school "liberation" high schools, community-based "free universities," but these have not been included. The survey was limited to full-time schools for kindergarten through high school.

Distribution by State

. . . Thirty-nine states have at least one free school. It should be noted that four states—California, New York, Massachusetts, and Illinois—have fifty-two per cent of the total surveyed. California alone has twenty-seven per cent. There appear to be several particular areas of free school concentration—the San

---

TABLE 1

Enrollment and Student Characteristics*

Total enrollment: 11,500-13,000
Total number of schools: 350-400

Elementary	51%		
High School	29%		
Elementary-high	20%		
Day	91%		
Boarding (and day-boarding)	9%		

Student characteristics:

Male	53%	White	77%
Female	47%	Spanish surname	4%
		Black	16%
		Other	3%

*For all figures, read "approximately."

Francisco Bay area, the Chicago area, the Boston area, Madison-Milwaukee, and Minneapolis-St. Paul. There is good reason to think that cosmopolitan urban areas, especially those with high concentrations of university and college-associated people, generate the critical masses of people who share the philosophy of free schools and have the willingness and capability to commit the necessary time, energy, and resources to such efforts.

Staff Characteristics

The data on staff are especially vague (See Table 2). In most free schools there are part-time and volunteer teachers, as well as parents, who participate in teaching and other staff activities. In many schools some of the volunteers are part-time teachers share community governance and policy-making with full-time staff. It is impossible to ascertain precisely either the number of volunteers or the time that part-time and volunteer staff put in. What can be said is that free schools generally emphasize the importance of individual attention and small intimate groups, and the staff-student ratios bear this out. A rough estimate which included all volunteers and part-time staff would be about 1:3, while a figure which involved only full-time staff would be 1:7.

TABLE 2

Staff* Characteristics

Number of staff: 2,600

Ethnic characteristics of staff:

| 85% white | 11% black | 4% other |

Age distribution:

Under 20 years of age:	6%
20-29	: 63%
30-39	: 20%
Over 40	: 10%

*Exclusive of volunteers.

Black teachers are concentrated almost completely in the relatively small number of black community schools and street academies. It is obvious that free school teachers are a considerably younger group than teachers in general. As compared to the national mean age for teachers of thirty-seven years, almost seventy percent of free school teachers are below thirty, and it is safe to say that at least eighty-five percent are below the national mean age.

This age distribution suggests some fairly obvious speculations. First, a significant part of the free school movement is related to the youth and student movement of the 1960s, both political and cultural. Second, many schools are started by young parents of very young children, and some of them become the teachers. Finally, the financial situation of most free schools makes it difficult for older people with families to participate, given their need for job security and dependable income. Young people, mobile and without encumbering family responsibilities, constitute the most obvious pool for very low paid and volunteer staff.

School Size and Finances

The data on school size and finances are especially interesting and revealing. A discussion of these figures will serve as a basis for a detailed typology of the free schools.

Most urban Americans think of schools as institutions housed in large expensive buildings, containing anywhere from a few hundred students (elementary) to two, three, or four thousand students (high schools). In contrast, the average size for the free schools in this survey is approximately thirty-three students. Approximately two-thirds of the schools have an enrollment of less than forty. . . .

The fact that two-thirds have enrollments of under forty can be explained mainly as a conscious commitment to a special kind of intimate community. Many free school people value the idea that everyone in the school knows everyone else fairly well; that staff people can truly relate to each other and to all the children, thus avoiding the impersonality associated with mass education institutions. Many free schools refuse to expand beyond thirty or forty, fearing that some of the essential qualities of the free school atmosphere would be lost. Some schools have actually decided to reduce enrollment from around thirty down to twenty because the people involved felt that even thirty was too large a group.

All of the schools with enrollments of around 100 and up deviate from the mean for specific reasons. Some, like Peninsula School in California (230 children) or Shady Lane School in Pittsburgh (101) are fairly established progressive schools that have stayed sufficiently experimental and innovative to justify inclusion in the study. Others are predominantly black or integrated community schools, which emphasize community participation, service in the larger community, and parent involvement in governance. These schools place a much lower priority on a warm, intimate, personal atmosphere than do the more numerous and smaller white, progressive, middle-class, and often isolated free schools.[3]

The data on school finances needs especially careful interpretation since free schools do not, in general, keep very accurate, detailed, or complete financial records. Since resources come from very diverse sources—tuition paid on a sliding scale (and often irregularly), small contributions, a very few large contributions from individuals and foundations, bake sales, rummage sales, donated equipment, and even, in the case of one school, panhandling—accurate accounting is not often available.

The main source of income, as one would expect for nonpublic schools, is tuition. Eighty-one percent of the schools charge tuition, with almost all of them stating that they give scholarships. Since the great majority of these schools use a sliding scale for tuition, the concept of "scholarship" is quite hazy. Most schools ask people to pay what they feel they can afford, hoping there will be enough high tuition payers to balance the people who can afford little. This is important since most free schools do not want to see themselves as "elite" private schools providing a special form of education for those who can afford it. Tuition for most traditional private schools ranges from $1500 to $4000 per year, while a sampling of schools in the survey shows that the normal range for free schools would be $0 to about $1200 per year. It is impossible to determine the average paid tuition, as we were unable to get accurate data concerning how many paid what.

Almost all the schools which do not charge tuition are true community schools and street academies serving poor and minority groups. There is no tuition because the people starting the schools intended to involve groups who can not afford it. The founders wanted to provide true alternatives to the public system rather than private schools that are alternatives only for those who can afford them (and a few scholarship cases). A good example of the tuition-free school is the Children's Community Workshop School in Manhattan. An elementary school with around 125 students, it is completely integrated racially and by class, and is parent controlled, with many poor black and Puerto-Rican parents involved. The school has been supported (with a large, well-paid staff) by contributions from foundations, but financial hardships during the past year have threatened its survival. However, the local school board has voted to grant the Workshop School "public" status, and stability may be achieved with public money.

Other tuition-free community schools include Highland Park Free School, Roxbury Community School and the New School for Children, and three schools forming the Roxbury Federation of Community Free Schools. Over the past couple of years, they have managed to obtain substantial foundation help, including a $500,000 grant from the Ford Foundation, and thus to stay in operation without charging parents. Some dropout-oriented free high schools also do not charge tuition: Genesis II in Springfield, Mass., Independent Learning Center in Milwaukee, Independence High School in Newark, Freedom House in Madison, Wisc., City Hill School and Northside Street Academy in Minneapolis, and Harlem Prep in New York. Funding sources for such schools are diverse: local, state, and federal programs for delinquency prevention, Model Cities and other poverty agencies, church groups, foundations, and corporations. But such funding is difficult to find and very chancy. For example, the Providence Free School began with the hope of being a tuition-less community school supported by individual contributions and foundation help. By the second year they were forced to charge tuition in order to stay in existence.

The data on free school expenditures are very revealing. . . .

The mean and median [of per pupil expenditure] are somewhere in the $500 to $600 range, closer to $600 per year. The curve, however, is far from the normal bell-shaped distribution that would be expected for the public schools in any given state. Instead we find a relatively even distribution all along the spectrum. Rather than a rapid tapering off at the high and low extremes, one finds a distinctive peak in the highest range (over $1000), with nineteen percent of the schools in this category. At the other extreme, although the curve does taper off slightly, twenty-nine percent of the schools report per capita expenditures below $300 and twelve percent report below $100.

It is hard to compare these figures to public school data. For free schools, rent is a major expense, while public school figures, as usually reported, do not contain an equivalent charge. Even so, we do know that the public schools show much greater expenses in general (as do traditional private schools). For example, at the top of the public school scale, localities like Beverly Hills spend $2000 per student per year while urban averages usually fall in the $1000 to $1500 range (if some category equivalent to rent were added in, these figures would be even higher).

Although there are some public school districts in the $500 to $1000 category, there is no parallel in the traditional public and private school experience to the fact that more than a quarter of the free schools work on less than $300 per student and more than one out of ten report less than $100. Moreover, these new schools value individual attention to student needs and desires—i.e., teacher-student ratios on the order of 1:5 to 1:10, versus the 1:25 or so that generally obtains in public schools. This consideration makes the contrast in per capita expenditure figures even more extraordinary.

Of course, many free school teachers work for very little money, often for room and board or less. In addition, many free schools use volunteers from local communities and nearby colleges and universities. Parents often take major roles in the classroom and especially in administration, fund raising, and building maintenance. Students, parents, and staff donate or scrounge up much of the material. Thus, the financial figures as represented on the graph systematically understate the resources used by free schools. If one could assign true value to the work of the teachers, the time of the volunteers and parents, the homes often used for classrooms, the gasoline and cars volunteered, the out-of-pocket unreimbursed expenses of volunteers, and the donated materials, the cash value of resources invested in the schools would be much higher than the actual money figures.

Still, the survival of most free schools depends on the fact that many people, often highly qualified and capable of holding teaching positions in public schools and elsewhere at $9,000-$15,000, are willing to work, for at least one or two years, at salaries in the $2,000-$5,000 range or even lower. Also, of course, there are often more than enough willing and able volunteers.

It should be noted that, with very few exceptions, free school workers are not voluntary ascetics. Their salaries are low because there is no money. The very few schools that have obtained large foundation grants or government help have tried to pay salaries comparable to the public schools, and the poorer schools wish they could. Ideally, free schools would have well-paid teachers and still maintain their low teacher-student ratio without exceeding public school expenditure levels. They would accomplish this by their use of volunteers, community resources, and inexpensive facilities, and by eliminating vandalism by hostile students, massive testing and grading programs and expensive standardized textbooks, and practically the whole full-time public school administrative apparatus.

Types of Free Schools

Within the summary data presented above it is important to distinguish among several different types of free schools: The "classical" free school, the parent-teacher cooperative elementary school, the free high school, and the community elementary school.

The *"classical" free school* is the Summerhillian-influenced community, usually quite small and enrolling students of all ages. Many of these are boarding schools that aim to be truly self-sufficient, intimate, even therapeutic whole communities. As the Summerhill Ranch School in Mendocino, California, wrote in its brochure:

> Educationally, this school can be described as 24-hour life tutorial, where students and staff learn in accordance with their own interests . . . our emotional developments remain primary. Self-awareness, individuality and personal responsibility to oneself and to others here are most important. We have not the rewards and punishments nor the competitiveness of public schools. Many of us regain self-confidence and awareness here, both of which aid us in dealing with the impersonal real world.

These schools are almost exclusively white and middle-class in their constituency, and, when boarding schools, they are naturally quite expensive. They emphasize the emotional and expressive aspects of the personality rather than the formal academic curriculum or job preparation. Development replaces achievement as the primary purpose. Collective decision-making often plays a central role in school activities.

A second type, which overlaps the first, is the *parent-teacher cooperative elementary school.* These schools are formed by parents, especially young, white, liberal, middle-class parents who do not want their children subjected to the regimentation of the normal public schools. They read John Holt's books and Joseph Featherstone's articles on the open classroom as it has developed in the British Infant Schools. Some parents call others; they organize a meeting and decide to start a free elementary school. They find sympathetic teachers who are willing to sacrifice financial reward for the satisfaction of the job. Often one or more of the parents will be full-time teachers in the school. A parent board officially controls the school and participates regularly in school activities, though the staff handles much of the day-to-day operation. Tuition is paid on a sliding scale and usually some minority students are admitted free or almost free; but in general, these schools do not really appeal to poor-minority parents, and in any case, they are not intended to confront the problems of ghetto families and their children.

These parent cooperatives differ from the relatively new, very progressive elementary schools which are on the fringe of the free school development, such as Shady Lane in Pittsburgh and Fayerweather Street School in Cambridge. Like the older progressive schools, these schools, though rather libertarian in pedagogy, are well-organized, well-equipped, fairly expensive, and rather professional about staffing. In contrast, parent cooperatives tend to have looser organization, less equipment, and fewer "professional" teachers.

Another type, the *free high school,* includes several variants, again determined by the social class constituency and the way the political and the pedagogical aspects of the "freedom" idea interact. They are high school counterparts to the Summerhillian schools, oriented toward the white middle class and hip youth counterculture. In contrast with the types mentioned above, prospective students usually provide the initial impetus, along with some committed adults who are potential staff. Deeply disenchanted with the public schools, these young people want to be involved honestly in the planning and governance of their own school. Several of these middle-class high schools project a politically radical perspective in their rhetoric, curriculum, and other activities. This does not mean that all the young people in such schools are activists, but that some of the originators and staff are, and that activism is in the atmosphere. These schools often participate in anti-war and civil rights activities, and the classes often focus on the Vietnam War, draft resistance, women's liberation, and the legal rights and difficulties of youth.

In the past couple of years, several white working-class high schools have formed, a development with no parallel in the earlier progressive education movement. These schools involve mainly drop-outs and potential drop-outs who feel very hostile to their public high schools. Whereas the middle-class high schools can charge tuition, working-class schools do not have this option, for neither the students nor their parents have the money. Moreover, their parents do not usually find the political and pedagogical style of such schools familiar or appealing. The permissiveness of the free school is often congenial to progressive middle-class parents, but has much less appeal to working-class parents who suspect that such experimental schools will not serve the needs of their children. (Neither do the public schools, of course, but parents persist in the hope that the American dream of working hard, getting skills and credentials, and making it in the world will somehow come true for their children.)

These working-class schools differ from their middle-class counterparts by directing a much greater focus on vocational help and remedial work and by exhibiting a real concern with thinking through what it means to be of the working class. For example, "Self Worth and Competency of Working Class Youth" is the name of a summer course at the Group School in Cambridge. According to the course description, "Self Worth" was

> originally conceived with two express purposes in mind. Because of the obvious lack of information relating to the working class struggle in American history, both in elementary and high school curriculum, it was felt that an objective labor history course was necessary as a foundation for viewing working class competency and self worth. Once a basic historical foundation was laid, it was hoped that the class could begin to tackle the more personally related questions of 'how does it feel to be a kid without a history?' or 'if I as a working-class youth have never learned about my history, whose culture have I adopted?' (from the Group School summer course brochure).

The working-class schools—with their constituency of public school "drop-outs" and "push-outs"—thus directly confront the tracking function of the public schools which "prepare" these students for the lower rungs of the social and job hierarchy. In contrast, students in middle-class free schools have been slated for college and high career achievement. For them, the free high school is a way to get off, for a while at least, the beaten path to college and beyond.

Another variant of the high schools for drop-outs, more established and larger than the white working class schools, are the street academies for poor minority youth. The most famous of these is Harlem Prep, with over 400 students, but there are such places in most large cities. They are organized by adults, often with the support of community groups (e.g., the local Urban

League). They seek to reawaken motivation in young people who have been completely turned off by school. While there is an atmosphere of discipline, the students do not perceive it as the same sort of discipline they experienced in the public schools. Instead, street academy discipline comes from having staff who can relate well with the students, and from the idea of black people "getting it together."

The street academies have a sense of participation, though far from the Summerhillian image of community, participatory democracy, and almost unlimited individual choice. The pedagogy with its emphasis on skills is more conventional, and the strong commitment to getting the young people into colleges differs from the mood of the dominant free high school culture.

The *community elementary schools*, as noted above, tend to be much larger and more highly organized than the average free school. More than the middle-class groups, the people who start community schools see the struggle for community control of the public schools as a vital goal; for them the politics of control are more important than the pedagogical emphasis of middle-class reform groups. These community schools put great stress on skills and on cultural consciousness and pride. Low-income parents, wary of romantic "freedom and spontaneity" rhetoric, often seem to support the more traditional classroom approaches, including strict discipline. Nevertheless, there is still a good deal of pedagogical innovation and libertarian atmosphere in these community schools. The implication here is that when the parents and community people feel they are in control, they are most open to "experimentation" than when it—like all the other school stuff they know—is imposed by the system which has been failing their children for years. For example, most of these schools share an aversion to fostering individual competition by means of grades; instead, they stress giving each child a sense of his or her own worth and capacities. In these schools, as in the public community controlled schools such as CCED School in Boston or Morgan Community School in Washington, D.C., one finds variations of the open classroom.

FREE SCHOOLS AND SOCIAL CHANGE

The classification above describes ideal types. Many of the schools, of course, combine aspects of different types. For example, the New Community School, a high school in Oakland, has a large white middle-class group, but provides a strong Black Studies program for its large minority of poor black students. Behind the different schools stand a variety of conceptions, not only of education but also of social change and how educational reform relates to more general political and social issues.

Within the Summerhillian tradition there is a definite "apolitical" quality. The school-community deliberately looks inward, sometimes consciously disengaging itself from the larger community and its affairs; the public schools are simply ignored. This perspective makes a minimal political demand on the larger society: to be left alone by the authorities—for instance, health and fire officials who don't like "hippie schools"—so that those who share the philosophy can "do their own thing."

A more social change-oriented expression of this apolitical perspective conceives of the free schools as exemplars and models of what good schools could be like, moving others, even in the public schools, to change. Another more radical rationale conceives of the growth of these free schools as a kind of strategy to attack and weaken the public school system as more and more people withdraw from it to start their own free schools. Throughout, one underlying view of social change is that the libertarian pedagogy and the schools based upon it will develop children who are joyful, cooperative, and peaceful, neither racist nor sexist nor repressed—and the more people like this, the greater the progress toward solving social ills and building a humane, just society.

This view is more often implicit than explicit. For most middle-class elementary schools, whether staff-run or parent-cooperative, the emphasis is on a small group providing for themselves the kind of education they want for their children. They don't like the kind of education offered in the public schools—at least for their own children—but they don't see that they can or should do much to change the public schools, and they refrain from a political analysis of the role of those schools. The following excerpt from a brochure expresses a fairly common situation:

> My wife and I started the school, with the help-support of a few parents dedicated to the no-pressure idea, in fear and trembling since it was beyond our ability, and is not our responsibility—we pay taxes for suitable schools. Fed up with the degrading and humiliating experience of our children in "the system" we determined to at least have a "school" for them—others joined us from a small newspaper ad.

Speaking of tuition, these school organizers write:

> Sometimes we have felt rather crass. We charge at about the "going rate" for the area. This rules out many who are sold on the principles of free education. Our justification goes like this: this is not our responsibility—if the system listened and acted in accord with the desires of people, there would now be available voluntary participation schools to which we would send our children.

Schools like this can afford only a limited number of scholarship students. Many of the parents—including those just quoted—would be completely satisfied if there were a voucher system or easily available "open classroom-free school" options within the existing public school system.

The more politically oriented middle-class free schools would not be so easily satisfied. There we find strong elements of counter-cultural and counter-institutional feeling, as well as a real and justifiable fear that the system will attempt to coopt educational innovations and water down their efforts. The dream of the counter-institutional "greening of America" perspective is that the dominant institutions will collapse as more and more people go off and build their own good places, self-sufficient and uncompromised by the taint of corruption in the dominant institutions. In a more immediate sense, this vision sees free school education as a way of breaking down the socialization function that most public schools serve. That is, simply being what they are, free schools accomplish a worthwhile moral and political goal by helping some children escape the "brainwashing" of the public school system.

For example, students of the Exploring Family School in San Diego wrote about the role of the public school as they see it:

. . . after graduation from school the students go out into the world trained to fit into society. Our economic system must create men and women to fit its capitalistic needs. The system has to have men and women who have the same values, who feel free and independent, but who will nevertheless do what is expected of them, people who can easily be controlled.

So stark a political analysis would make many people in free schools rather uncomfortable. They are against indoctrination, and they do not want to think that there is a hint of this in their own schools which are committed to the freedom of the child to learn and think and see in his or her own way, shaped as little as possible by adults. The Exploring Family School is mainly white and middle class, K-12, with as libertarian a pedagogy as any. But many of the people involved share a radical political perspective, and this makes the school somewhat atypical. More than most, the school attempts to relate to sympathetic public school teachers and gets involved in community political activity.

This approach is more typical of the community school, of course. For black community schools, there is little ambivalence in setting forth a strong political analysis and reflecting it in the spirit and curriculum of the school. Whereas most brochures of middle-class schools emphasize the pedagogical flaws of public schools, e.g. unnecessary regimentation, too large classes, and insufficient scope for creative and emotional development, the minority group community schools concentrate on the political inadequacies. The Nairobi Community School in East Palo Alto writes in its brochure:

> The destruction of our minds is planned, programmed. The racist school boards, teachers, administrators conspired to waste our precious youth, who knew they would force the change, plan, learn how to make the radical complete breakaway from systems of white control, manipulation and destruction. We went through the stages of seeking solutions, such as at tempting a futile integration and sneaking into white neighborhoods to attend their schools of white supremacy, only to experience—death at an early age.

The white middle-class schools are clear in theory on what they are *not* going to do (be authoritarian, repressive, etc.) but they often have very serious problems deciding what they *are* going to do. This is less a problem for the black community schools. For example, the curriculum at Nairobi High includes African history, black current events, and Black U.S. history, as well as physics, math, algebra, science, communications, reading, art, music, and French. It is designed to "produce black problem solvers, to produce young black community scholars, who recognize our slave condition and the necessity of breaking these chains on our minds, to heal these scars on our backs and souls." This type of curriculum and this clear sense of purpose typify the new black community schools.

Clearly, minority groups that see themselves struggling to end racial and economic oppression will insist on fighting a school system that they see as part of the process of oppression. They see themselves engaged in political struggle, and they want the community schools they run to prepare their young people for participation in this struggle. From this perspective, the pedagogical free school ideas of not structuring, pressuring, or inculcating social and political beliefs will seem neither relevant nor serious. Whereas A. S. Neill claimed that Summerhill students did not know his own political or religious beliefs, it would be odd for black community school people to avoid projecting their belief in the black revolution or black consciousness. To see this as "laying a trip on the kids" would be to press some of the pedagogical concepts to a dubious extreme.

The political strand in the education reform movement insists on the essentially political nature of the educational system. In particular, it stresses the way the groups in control of the major institutions of society use the school system and other institutions to help maintain the status quo. (This assertion need not evoke a plot; it is true about institutions in any social order.) From this point of view, the very concept of educational reform presents ambiguities. Black and other minority communities either start their own community schools outside the system or try to exert enough political power to get control of the public schools in their communities. They want to make schools major instruments in the struggle for freedom and equality. But many of the problems of the schools are not the product of the schools alone. The value of liberal education, the chance for getting jobs which are intrinsically satisfying and financially rewarding, the sense of growing up in a stable, sustaining social community— these conditions are not readily available to poor and minority youth. Neither community control of schools, nor a really effective alternative school like Harlem Prep, nor the new white working class high schools can change the basic discouraging social reality that most "lower class" or "disadvantaged" young people encounter. From the political perspective, although these community free schools can often do good things for some young people who were "failed" and unhappy in the public schools, they have only been able to work with a very small number—and they have not been able to "save" all of these.

So, from this perspective, truly liberating educational reform that works for all children can only come with major social, political, economic, and cultural transformations that eliminate not only bad educational conditions but also the roots of those conditions in other institutions.

If these premises are true, then we can expect that serious efforts will be made to coopt the growing discontent with public school education as most clearly and completely expressed by the free schools. Silberman's *Crisis in the Classroom* has been accepted, so to speak, in important areas of the educational establishment, with the result that there is increasing support for public alternative schools and programs. One obvious danger is that, as with many reforms, such reform will blunt and buy off discontent before it can bring about the larger changes which are its goals. Free-type schools supported by the system could be used to siphon off "malcontents," "troublemakers," and activists— among students and parents—and thus ease the spreading troubles in the public schools. Or public alternatives will be closely controlled by the current managers of the school system, so that experiments that are too abrasive and too "radical" can be toned down by threatening to withdraw financial support. (We have already observed this phenomenon in some of the public alternative school projects.)

A similar fear is voiced from the more pedagogical and cultural sectors of the free school movement, but since the demands there are not so extensive, many could be more easily met by a set of open classroom public alternatives or, especially, by a tuition voucher plan.

Looking Ahead

Alternatives inside the public sector supported by local, state, or federal aid, are sure to spread in the very near future. (A recent column by Albert Shanker in the weekly propaganda slot the teachers' union buys in the *New York Sunday Times* confirmed this assertion. Shanker attacks the claims of success for alternative schools—in a misleading and dishonest manner. But his tone is very defensive, as if against a growing trend he opposes.) Many parent groups are organizing to ask the school authorities for alternative public schools committed to libertarian methods. For example, the Cambridge School Committee recently approved such a proposal from the Committee for an Alternative Public School, a group of parents who organized and negotiated for almost two years to get an inside-the-system *free* school. The number of teachers, parents, and students who want such schools is growing, even though most Americans would still say that they basically approve the traditional style of the average public school. As noted, the number of free schools continues to increase rapidly. But contrary to the predictions of some free education activists, this development will not mushroom into thousands of schools and hundreds of thousands of students. As the difficulties of running free schools and scrounging even for meager resources become more widely known, enthusiasm will diminish. And as pressure for reform builds up on the public school system, it will seem more realistic as a strategy to get an alternative public school established, even at the cost of some compromise with the system, than to establsih another small and fragile free school that might easily fail after a couple of years. Even now, some schools that started outside the system are trying to figure out ways of being accepted as public schools in some form, without giving up their essential spirit or autonomy. This has happened in the case of the Children's Community Workshop School. For many free school people with a political perspective, the possibility of free schools being alternative public schools will be very attractive, despite the constant danger of being coopted and controlled. As part of public systems, reformers will be able to gain more visibility and influence for their innovations. Also, public financial support will enable schools serving poorer communities to achieve the stability needed to attract parents to what might at first seem a dubious experiment.

Some free schools will prefer to maintain their independence so as to ensure freedom from the pressures and compromises inevitably imposed by involvement in the public system. This stance includes both politically and pedagogically oriented school reformers, since it is obvious that there are free schools expressing both strands that would be too "far out" for any state system to tolerate.

Within a few years the free school movement has emerged as a significant phenomenon, if not for its actual numbers, then for its symbolic significance as representative of the spreading popularity of radical reform ideas. There have been other movements of radical progressive reform; movements that do not seem to have accomplished the serious changes of the sort they initially envisioned. We can hope that the new wave of radical school reform will find ways to avoid repeating this melancholy history.

NOTES

1. Clearly, these ideas overlap with aspects of the progressive education movement of the early 1900s, which spawned a number of experimental "progressive" schools. But in this current revival of the progressive school reform spirit, we find more emphasis on *participation* in the "freedom" notion—the idea that parents and students should have a much greater part in all aspects of educational institutions. This clearly implies a negative attitude toward professional educators and teachers, whose authority stems from a dubious though certified claim of expertise.

2. Funded by HEW.

3. In this category are Michael Community School in Milwaukee, formerly a Catholic school, now a community school moving rapidly to libertarian methods (290 students), the New School for Children, a black community school in Roxbury, Mass. (140 students), and East Harlem Block Schools, a group of mainly black and Puerto Rican elementary schools in New York (a total of 220 students in four sites). A related category is that of predominantly black street academies for high school people, such as C.A.M. Academy in Chicago (250 students) and Harlem Prep (500 students). A very special category is that of experimental demonstration schools run by colleges which, after some serious hesitation, were included in the study—Margaret Sibley School for Educational Research and Demonstration, Plattsburgh, N.Y. (275 students), run as part of the state university system, and Webster College School, St. Louis (150 students), are examples.

Allen Graubard

From the perspective of some "free schoolers" the success of any alternative school rests ultimately on the extent to which major social, economic, political and cultural transformations occur in the larger society. And they also warn about the ever-present threat of co-optation of alternatives by the system, of alternatives both inside and outside that system. (Perhaps the way to deal with that threat is to expect it to happen, and when it does go on and develop a new alternative to the co-optation.)

We have already argued that change in the schools alone would not be likely to result in very meaningful, certainly not radical, change. We have also argued, however, that this can be self-stultifying if it means we have to wait for other changes before we can plan and implement change in the schools. There are changes going on "out there"—we have pointed to the various liberation movements as most promising, perhaps—and these changes can be reflected in the classroom.

Any serious philosophy for alternative education in America will have to include, or be a part of, a political and social philosophy. While "free schoolers" have done much in a pedagogical and curricular way to free up the education of young people, they have seldom—if ever—developed anything like a full-blown political and social philosophy. (They haven't even developed an educational philosophy, in large part deliberately, because in their revolt they also rejected philosophies and philosophizing as part of the problem they were struggling with. Neither the free school movement nor the more recent alternative public school movement has produced its John Dewey yet.)

In more recent years, the public schools have become the object of research and analysis by people with parallel political orientations. Many of them are represented among our authors. Our next two readings describe the early organizing efforts of a radical, socialist-oriented group of people who have combined their political orientation with a commitment to working within the public school system.

There are several similar groups of people in various parts of the country. Among their publications are *The Red Pencil* (Cambridge, Mass.), *Outside The Net* (Lansing, Mich.), *This Magazine* (Toronto), *EdCentric* (Eugene, Ore.), and the publication from which the next two readings have been taken, *No More Teachers' Dirty Looks* (San Francisco). These selections tell us about the "BARTOC Story," the story of the formation of the Bay Area Radical Teachers Organizing Committee

THE BARTOC STORY

Linda and Jane

We had a lot in common when we decided to start a radical teachers' group. We were both new to San Francisco, both were living with men who had been quite active in left wing politics, and both felt hesitant about trying to get into the heavy movement scene of the Bay Area. The women's movement was not yet strong, and we couldn't help but feel isolated and politically irrelevant. What we wanted was a way to connect our jobs—teaching—with our socialist politics, so we decided we'd try to form a socialist teachers' group.

Our first step was to issue a statement, "A Call To Radical Teachers," along with a notice of our first meeting, to all of the movement and underground papers in the city. We invited a teachers' group of the Berkeley International Socialist Club, and we passed the news to others by word of mouth. About forty people showed up at the first meeting.

We had two raps prepared: one of us presented our theoretical position, and the other gave a tentative program for projects, which included a newspaper, workshops, lesson plans, and research topics. There were a lot of questions. Some free school people questioned our goal of creating change by working in the public schools, but there were enough enthusiastic responses that we made plans to meet again in two weeks.

After the second meeting we began to run into problems. We felt increasingly bogged down by two different types of people. The first type were those who told endless anecdotes without making any cogent political points. These people were grossly insensitive to others: their stories would go on for as long as 30 or 40 minutes, and never had anything to do with the topic under discussion. Although we realized that their story-telling obviously filled a need, the majority of the group became irritated because it kept us from doing other work. We were anxious to talk with all teachers who needed support and advice about

Linda and Jane, "The BARTOC Story" *No More Teachers' Dirty Looks,* Vol. II, No. 2, 1971, pp. 4-7.

their teaching situation, but we could not function as a therapy or encounter group.

The other type posed a different sort of problem. They wanted to push us towards a rigid, predefined political line. For example, members of one sectarian political faction did not consider teachers to be part of the "revolutionary working class" because teachers "do not produce surplus value." A member of another political group kept insisting that more psychologists were needed in the schools in order to treat the "disrupters." We could never get across our belief that most "disrupters" were not aberrant but normal in their reactions to a repressive and boring educational system, and that what was needed was a political direction to their anger, not more psychiatrists. He told us that psychiatry was the only answer.

In response to both these groups, we found ourselves repeating the same arguments with no positive results and most of our energy was being used up in senseless debate. In spite of our desire to make ourselves available to all teachers in trouble, we found open meetings were a disaster. Most of those who were not interested in doing political work dropped out anyway, but we also made a conscious decision to organize ourselves into a collective all of whose members shared some sort of socialist perspective.

Once the basis of a common politics was spelled out, the group (there were 13 of us) decided to publish a newspaper as a way of reaching teachers throughout the Bay Area and the country. Our meetings were devoted largely to discussions of the politics underlying each article. In this way the writing of the articles and the formulation and development of our politics went hand in hand.

Then and now we were concerned, not with all new ideas in education, but with new ideas in the context of building a socialist movement in this country. For example, if we published an article on a new reading method, we would discuss why children have trouble learning to read in a system that stresses grades and competition, and we would evaluate the new method to determine if it helped break down student alienation.

While our newspaper is a central focus, we have offered over the past two years various workshops for elementary and secondary teachers: a workshop on socialist teaching methods; a workshop for students and teachers; a women's group; and a summer workshop which produced the lesson plans in the third issue of "No More Teachers' Dirty Looks." Some of the workshops were very successful for a while. Many teachers were involved in them on a regular basis, and we, in BARTOC, found them invaluable for exploring new ideas and teaching techniques. But after about a year and a half, interest in these unfocused discussions began to falter. We discovered that the workshops which were most successful were those that had a main project, such as a written account of what went on. With this in mind, we are planning a workship on "Current Issues In Education" this summer. We hope to publish a series of leaflets based on this workshop.

We've encountered one serious organizational problem since we decided to become a collective two years ago. At that time two people joined BARTOC who were also members of a Marxist-Leninist collective that considered itself to have "the correct line" about the revolution. They saw themselves primarily as organizers. Consequently many of us in BARTOC suspected that their motives in joining us were to organize us to their way of thinking, and not to learn more about how students and teachers can help build a socialist movement. Besides feeling manipulated, some of us found their strict brand of Marxism was more of a dogma than a creative tool for understanding the world. The members of the Leninist group were asked to leave after long hours of discussion. Not all of us in BARTOC agreed with the decision at the time, and it was a difficult decision to ask them to leave, but once they had left, we were once again able to work and grow together.

"THE CORRECT LINE"

Today, one year later, we are still publishing "No More Teachers' Dirty Looks" and have subscribers in every state of the union. Recently a few of our members helped form a Rank and File Caucus which is challenging the undemocratic nature of the San Francisco American Federation of Teachers.

By necessity, BARTOC has become the sort of political group whose members do most of their day-to-day political work individually, or with one or two allies outside of BARTOC. This is necessary because none of us live together and none of us teach in the same school. Getting together is often a problem. Yet we always meet at least once a week to discuss our political work with each other, to criticize each others' activities, and to give support and encouragement when needed.

Linda and Jane

THE POLITICS OF TEACHERS' LIVES

Linda and Jane

There's a certain confusion in being BARTOC. While everyone understands vaguely what it means to be a "radical teacher," we find ourselves lumped in at one moment with the Weathermen, at another with Herbert Kohl, and at a third we discover that someone has us crawling around with our eyes closed feeling and touching one another.

We're really like none of those, but rather than attempt to deal with the problem through alterations of our name that would show we're socialists—

Linda and Jane, "The Politics of Teachers' Lives," *No More Teachers' Dirty Looks,* Vol. II, No. 1, 1971, pp. 3-8.

BASTOC–or socialist revolutionaries–BATSROC–we'll try to explain what we are and how we got to be that way.

When BARTOC started, most of us were suffering from a divided consciousness. Each of us identified in some way with the Movement, confused and fragmented as it was, and through the Movement we saw the war, racism, and poverty as problems, specifically as problems with political solutions.

However, the Movement told us very little about our lives as teachers or about our situations in the schools. Schools were places where students were socialized and prepared for lives as workers. Teachers were cops or sellouts who should quit or lead their students in attempts to close the schools.

That was the general Movement perspective and we accepted most of it. But most of the detailed information we had about schools and teaching came from distinctly nonmovement and nonpolitical sources, from Holt and Kohl and Goodman, and others. They described what happened in the schools in a way that helped us understand our own experiences and that projected a vision of education with which we could identify. But they tended to ignore the social origins of school problems, such as racism, and to see problems and solutions in psychological or humanistic or individualistic terms. Seeing only the childrens' problems and their own successes, they, like the Movement, generally ignored the lives of teachers.

EDUCATION IS POLITICS

Part of what we have tried to do as BARTOC is to put the understanding that Holt and Kohl and the others provide in the broader political context that we brought with us from the Movement. We began with the assumptions that what happens in our lives as teachers–the frustration, the weariness, the anxiety– is a function of the same process that distorts the lives of the children, and that, like the children's school lives, our school lives have political meaning and make political sense.

To make political sense of what happens in the schools means to us trying to understand the function that schools serve in our society. We are not willing to accept that the schools are repressive because principals are crazy, because superintendents are irrational or stupid, because teachers are old-fashioned, or because some greedy, evil genius is hatching plots in Washington or Sacramento. We believe the schools as they now operate provide almost the best possible preparation for life and work in a capitalistic economic system, and that whatever humanity and life do appear in schools signify their failure to perform that function.

On one level, everyone understands that. Principals and teachers tell students, and students even tell each other, that you have to stay in school to get a job. Often they even understand that it won't be math or history or woodshop that will help them get that job, but the piece of paper awarded for lasting through it all.

For example, almost all of us have had to survive a series of education courses that nearly everyone agreed were boring and meaningless to our future lives as teachers. We took those courses and stuck with them only because they were required for certification.

But while it is almost universally understood that school is job preparation and that it offers little or nothing of value in and of itself, there is little sense of the connection between the school system and the social system. Schools offer little or nothing of value because they are preparing students for jobs in a society where work offers little or nothing of value in and of itself.

CORPORATIONS AND EDUCATION

As a part of job preparation, students are taught to think of work as unpleasant and to accept deferred, extrinsic rewards for sticking with it. They are prepared to accept the regimentation and stratification that they will find in the corporations that will provide most of them with jobs. The entire world of the schools is organized to reflect the world of the corporations and its values.

At the core of the school world, as of the corporate world, are clear hierarchies, with administrators above teachers and teachers above students, with college-bound students above vocational-track students, and with custodians, cooks, and secretaries somewhere in between. Interpersonal relations tend to be competitive within levels of the hierarchy, and authoritarian, repressive, or paternalistic from each level to the levels below. The racial and sexual discrimination and stereotyping, expressing other dimensions of the organizational hierarchy, and the competitiveness and individualism valued in the business world all reproduce themselves in schools. Even the greater freedom of suburban schools and of colleges only mirrors the greater freedom of the roles which their graduates will assume as they move into the corporate world.

In other words, it is nonsense to examine the schools as if they were somehow not connected with what happens in the larger society. They are not only connected with it, they serve the specific function of creating the stratified work force or proletariat of future generations.

TEACHERS AND THE MOVEMENT

Much of our understanding of the political meaning of education we shared with other groups within the Movement. Where we differed is that we did not see teachers as cops who might magically or accidentally be transformed into radicals. We saw in our own experience as teachers the basis for a socialist revolutionary perspective that identifies teachers as members of a diversified proletariat, of which students and workers are also a part.

The Movement denied teachers that status. Past socialist movements defined the proletariat as industrial workers, and the Movement accepted that strict definition, even though the proletariat changed as capitalism changed.

Our socialist perspective emphasizes that teachers, as well as factory workers, have to live by selling their labor-power to others. Where the factory worker is dependent on the corporation, the teacher is dependent on the state—a state whose function is to preserve corporate capitalism.

But within the proletariat, groups are divided from each other by the different positions they occupy in a hierarchy of income and authority. Whites are divided from blacks; men from women; welfare workers from people on welfare; teachers from their students; and teachers from the parents of their students.

In the schools we have to overcome what divides us from our students and their parents by creating a movement based on what we have in common—our ultimate powerlessness and our common experience of helpless humiliation at the hands of others higher up.

PUBLIC SCHOOLS OR FREE SCHOOLS?

When BARTOC began, we took the position that teachers should go into the public schools because by far the greatest number of children and teachers were there. Also, we were committed to free public education and opposed the use of supposedly democratic, public institutions for the socialization of children into the nondemocratic hierarchy of the corporate state. More broadly, we advocated socialism and were not interested in alternative schools that could exist doing their own thing in a generally repressive society.

Our basic commitment to the public school remains, but the experience of two teachers—described elsewhere in this issue—has forced us to examine again our ideas about alternative schools.

The two teachers wound up in alternative schools for very different reasons: one because she could find no other job; the other, through out-of-school relationships with her students and former students with whom she shared a commitment to a political movement and a vision of the limitations of the public schools.

From these two different starting points their experiences have been quite different except that both have had to face the same problem. Like those of us in public schools they found that working without a conscious, shared political understanding and the common values derived from it, actions tend to be framed in bourgeois terms and understood in terms of bourgeois values.

For example, a teacher in the public schools who refuses to send his or her students to the dean may find that action understood as fear or weakness or not-caring. In a free school, parents with no consciously shared political perspective may reject all rules and all authority in reaction to their own experience of the rules in capitalist society as oppressive. Or tutors in a political free school may act without consciousness of the values they express or the social meaning of those values, and reproduce in their classes much of the repressiveness of public schools.

In all those situations and in others like them, we first have to work with others to understand the political meaning of the actions and attitudes involved. We have to do that not out of some abstract desire to know, but as socialists who want to create a society in which people can work together to determine their lives.

Secondly, we have to challenge existing social relations and present alternatives.

*   *   *

Yet any action in itself will lose its meaning unless it is made and understood in the context of creating a socialist movement. The formation of BARTOC and the publication of *No More Teachers' Dirty Looks* both express our perception of our individual impotence, of our interdependence, and of our faith in collective power. Isolated and alone, individual teachers or small groups like BARTOC can do nothing. With others who share our needs and our understanding we can hope to change the schools and the society. Our primary objective as BARTOC is to take part in the development of a new socialist movement that will make those changes.

Linda and Jane

A major theme running throughout our analysis is the lack of diversity that has been a part of the structure of the schools from their beginning. This was the result in part of the use of the schools to socialize a polyglot population, but it was also the result of the bureaucratization of the schools (anything that is standardized is thereby easier to direct and control). The homogenization of educational standards, curricula, and teaching is a principal target of those who are in various stages of rebelling against the school as an institution.

But among those still working within the schools there has been a growing concern for more diversity and choice in public schools. Alternative public schools—about which we will learn more shortly—have come into existence primarily because parents and their children, and sometimes a few teachers, want to have available a variety of options, within schools and between schools.[8]

For some time the voucher system of education has been under consideration. Its backers claim its use would result in a public school system that would be much more responsive to the diverse educational needs of young people. Its opponents see it resulting in the end of public education as we know it. (That's why they oppose it, they say.) The public school system is monopolistic, controlled by legislators, school boards, and professional educators, but not by parents, teachers, and students. And nearly half of all the students in public schools are under the control of less than 4 percent of the school boards. The voucher system of education would make parent and student choice the principal controlling factor in public schools. It would involve a publicly accountable agency that would issue vouchers to parents, who could then take their children to any school that abided by the rules of the voucher system. The parents, of course, would take their vouchers to the schools of their choice, and the schools would turn their vouchers in for cash.

The Office of Economic Opportunity tried for some time to promote the voucher system, with the assistance of the Center for the Study of Public Policy in Cambridge. In December 1970 the Center issued a proposal for a voucher system and together with OEO began looking for communities willing to test it. The Alum Rock, California, school district near San José agreed to conduct such a test. They found that the voucher system has one major restriction which seriously limits its effect on the public school monopoly. For under the Alum Rock plan, parents can choose only from among the participating public schools. The opportunity for people outside the public school monopoly to provide alternatives—the principal feature that attracts many voucher proponents—is thus missing.

This significant hamstringing of the voucher idea is part of the reason for the opposition it has received from professional educators, especially teachers and their organizations like the National Education Association and the American

---

8. Mario Fantini, *Public Schools of Choice* (New York: Simon & Schuster, 1973).

Federation of Teachers. The most often heard criticism is that the voucher system would mean the end of public education. And in a sense that could be true. Parents—under a full-blown, nonrestrictive voucher system—would be able to choose from any school, public or private, that would agree to abide by the voucher rules. That would certainly blur the distinction between public and private. And in that sense we would not talk much about a *public* school system. But voucher proponents point out that the distinction is already blurred, and has been for some time.

Opponents of vouchers also claim that the system would wind up being the same old story of the affluent getting the better schools and the poor taking what is left over. But there is difficulty in seeing why this condition would be any worse than it now is, and why, indeed, it would not be ameliorated under a voucher system. As voucher proponents point out, the "better" public schools are now available to the affluent more than to the poor because these schools are located in the neighborhoods of the affluent. A voucher system would require that every participating school must accept any applicant so long as it had vacant places. If it had more applicants than places, it would have to fill at least half of these by picking applicants randomly, and fill the other half in such a way as not to discriminate against ethnic minorities. Still, some teachers and their organizations see segregation, by race and by income, as the only outcome.

What about church-state separation? Wouldn't a voucher system mean public support for religious schools? Proponents of vouchers do not insist that religious schools be included. On the other hand, they do not believe these schools do any worse than public schools in serving their children.

But nothing seems to change the thinking of opponents of the voucher system. Despite repeated denials and counter-arguments by such voucher proponents as Christopher Jencks, the opposition among teachers and their professional associations is adamant. And when all of their arguments seem to have been answered, and their opposition continues unabated, we are left to wonder what is the real reason for their opposition.

There is one thing that we can be pretty sure a voucher system would do, which would be opposed by a lot of teachers and the organizations dedicated to the promotion of their interests. A voucher system would very likely initiate and support a variety of educational options that are not part of the present public education monopoly. Professional educators, including teachers, have a vested interest in that monopoly. This monopoly has been created and maintained through education codes, school boards, and state credentialing. The OEO voucher proposal would require participating schools to meet only the existing state requirements for *private* schools. And these requirements are less stringent, less excluding, and less restrictive than requirements for public schools.

Through these requirements, backed by law, the monopoly in public education is maintained. The voucher system is a direct threat to that monopoly. And any large-scale, alternative system of education ultimately would threaten it, a point that Eric Davin makes below. It is not surprising, therefore, that alternative *public* schools are beginning to receive criticism from teachers and their organizations.

Alternative public schools have grown steadily since the mid-60s. The promise they hold for the improvement of public education has yet to be assessed. In many respects they resemble the efforts of progressive education proponents of the '20s and '30s. They are home-grown, and in their initial stages at least, they seldom involve professional educators. They stress parent involvement, and control of the school by parents, students and teachers. (Alternative schools-within-schools differ in this respect, and some of their supporters consider that a source of strength for them. They don't have the hassles that always go with democratic or town meeting types of operation.)

It is too early to say how well these new schools are doing. Although many "alternative schoolers" insist their schools are "open" schools but definitely not "free" schools, they often resemble the latter in their early stages. Like the "free schoolers" before them, the "alternative schoolers" are united in what they are opposed to in public schools. But when it comes to deciding what they want in their new school they find themselves in continuing conflict. And, too, the parental participation often falls short of what is hoped for. Sometimes staff members find it difficult to live with parental involvement. Many times the parents themselves cannot find the time or wherewithal to keep up their participation.

The alternative schools teeter from crisis to crisis, to be sure, but then the president of one of the famous "Seven Sisters" women's colleges once described her college that way. And, for reasons not yet entirely known, the alternative schools always have a better second year.

We can provide some figures and facts about these alternative public schools. The National Consortium for Options in Public Education, based at Indiana University, recently conducted a survey of alternative public schools and we reprint their findings.

DIRECTORY OF OPTIONAL ALTERNATIVE PUBLIC SCHOOLS

NCOPE

Since the National Consortium for options in Public Education was first formed, an effort has been underway to identify optional alternative public schools in operation in the United States and in other parts of the world. At first this was a rather informal effort involving little more than keeping files on alternative schools that came to our attention through correspondence, through contacts at alternative school conferences, and through random mention in various publications. As interest in public school alternatives began to increase, our

"Directory of Optional Alternative Public Schools," NCOPE, *Changing Schools; An Occasional Newsletter on Alternative Public Schools,* No. 008, pp. 2-6.

files were supplemented with a number of state and regional directories, and a few directories that provided "selected samples" of the kinds of options being developed in the public schools.

By September, 1972, a fairly systematic effort was underway not only to identify alternative schools, but also to verify the fact that they were in fact public school options. Using a make-shift staff of volunteer workers, and hampered by a lack of external funds, a national directory slowly began to take shape. A master file of listings of alternative schools was developed, and requests for information on alternative schools were sent out to all parts of the country. Once a contact person and a mailing address were obtained, a survey questionnaire was mailed to verify whether the listing was a public school alternative.

PROBLEMS

While the above procedure appears quite simple, the task of obtaining an accurate listing proved extremely difficult due to three reasons:

1. The Band-Wagon Effect

In developing an accurate listing of alternative public schools we had to contend with what we came to call the "Band-Wagon" effect, for "faddish" educators began to use the term *alternative* to describe anything and everything that they happened to be doing. One state directory even included "Operation Doghouse, a program whereby students planned, built and sold doghouses." Such inclusions helped to alert the surveyors that things that were called alternatives were often not what they hoped to appear.

2. Rapid Growth

The rapid and continuing growth of alternative public school likewise renders any directory almost immediately out of date. Twice the NCOPE Directory was postponed because an influx of information on new schools arrived before we could go to press. Thus *Changing Schools* will continue to report supplements to the NCOPE Directory.

3. Confusion Over Definition

Lacking a clear, precise definition of what is and what isn't an alternative school, many regional and state listings included schools and programs that were clearly not alternative schools. Earlier lists included vocational schools, work-study programs and, a wide assortment of "innovative" programs that were very worthwhile but did not offer students freedom of educational choice.

DIRECTORY DEFINITION

An alternative public school has been defined in the NCOPE Directory as any school within a community that provides alternative learning experiences to the conventional school programs and that is available by choice to every family within its community at no extra cost. Since alternative public schools usually develop as responses to particular educational needs within their communities, there is no single model or group of models that would encompass their diverse nature. However, the majority of alternative public schools fit into the following types or into combinations of these types.

Open Schools*—with learning activities individualized and organized around interest centers within the classroom or building. While the concept of open education is not new, there has been a revival of interest in it beginning with the development of informal infant schools in Great Britain following World War II.

Schools Without Walls*—with learning activities throughout the community and with much interaction between school and community. Philadelphia's Parkway Program, which opened in 1969, was the first and probably most well-known of these.

Learning Centers—with a concentration of learning resources in one location available to all of the students in the community. This would include magnet schools, educational parks, career education centers, vocational and technical high schools, etc.

Continuation Schools—with provisions for students whose education in the conventional schools has been (or might be) interrupted. This would include dropout centers, re-entry programs, pregnancy-maternity centers, evening and adult high schools, street academies, etc.

Multi-Cultural Schools—with emphasis on cultural pluralism and ethnic and racial awareness and usually serving a multi-cultural student body. Bilingual schools with optional enrollment would be included here.

Free Schools—with emphasis on greater freedom for students and teachers. This is usually applied to nonpublic alternative schools, but a few are available by choice within public school systems.

Schools-Within-Schools—with a small number of students and teachers involved by choice in a different kind of learning program. This would include minischools and satellite schools. A satellite school is a school at another location which maintains administrative ties to the parent school. The schools-within-schools would usually belong to one or more of the six types above.

Not all alternative public schools would fall into these types. We have identified optional alternative public schools where all learning activities are based on behavior modification (Grand Rapids, Michigan) and others that are nongraded continuous-progress schools (Minneapolis, Minnesota). In addition to the above, many alternative public schools operate as voluntary integration models within their communities.

---

*Both of these terms (open schools and schools with walls) are also used for architectural concepts in school building. We do not so use them here. The terms refer to concepts for organizing learning activities that may be used in a diverse array of physical facilities.

DIRECTORY LISTINGS

Of the 600 plus schools NCOPE has identified during the past two years as somehow claiming to be an alternative public school, only 464 have been included in this listing. The 464 alternative schools are found in 35 different states and five countries, but 75% of the schools are found in eight states, with the alternatives in California, Washington, and New York totalling over 40%.

The Directory has attempted to include for each listing the name of the school, the school address, type of school, grade levels, and number of students.

*   *   *

DIRECTORY OMISSIONS

A word should be added about the schools that are not included in the Directory. Only public school alternatives have been listed. A large number of special function schools have not been included in the Directory because they serve students who are assigned or referred without freedom of choice. Many of these schools are for students who have been labeled delinquent or disruptive. While such schools may be desirable in some communities, they should not be confused—regardless of what they are called, with optional alternative public schools. Other school districts have developed policies of open enrollment, so that students in a community may choose to attend any school regardless of geographic proximity. (An example of this is East Lansing, Michigan, where a policy of open enrollment has been instituted at the elementary level.) Such open enrollment schools have also been omitted due to space limitations. When a community has several optional alternative public schools available, the conventional school, of course, becomes one of the options, but for the purposes of the NCOPE Directory such conventional school options have not been included.

SURVEY OF ALTERNATIVE SCHOOLS

Of the 464 alternative public schools listed in the Directory, a survey questionnaire was returned by 276 schools. Of the schools polled 79% were secondary, 19% were elementary, and 2% were K-12. The most dramatic insight gained in the survey was the steady growth in the number of alternative public schools since the mid-60s.

The survey found a fairly equal distribution of types of alternative public schools. Open Schools, Schools-Without-Walls, Learning Centers and Continuation Centers each totalling approximately 20% of the schools surveyed. Multi-Cultural Schools, Free Schools, and Schools-Within-Schools combined for another 20%.

The size of the schools surveyed ranged from less than 50 students to over 1,000 with most schools having between 50 and 150.

The survey and Directory both help to verify the existence of a new trend in American education. The list of 464 schools is certainly a modest appraisal of the number of alternative schools in operation in the fall of 1973. Due to our limitations, no comprehensive search of public education was undertaken, rather we relied entirely on identifying schools that came to our attention. One might also suppose a large number of new schools are opening their doors this fall, and there are hundreds of other groups now planning and developing new alternative public schools.

Some predict there are over 1,000 alternative public schools now in operation, but only continued effort on our part—and on yours will verify this estimate.

NCOPE

Still, the doubt persists. Are these truly alternative? And alternative to what? Is turning schools over to their students, parents and staff any guarantee that anything much different from American public education of the past 100 years will emerge? And what about the school system of which these schools must remain a part? Won't its celebrated ability at co-opting affect these schools as well? As long as it is through the public system that these schools are funded and receive their standing as schools, won't that control work effectively to keep the options within the bounds that all options have been kept within heretofor?

These are the questions Eric Davin raises about alternative public schools. It should be noted that Davin begins on a note of rejecting these schools in favor of nonpublic free schools. But in the end he comes back to Allen Graubard's concern: the role that the free schools might play in effecting change in the public schools.

ON COMBATTING LIBERALISM

Eric Davin

There is a certain middle-class segment of the Free School Movement which has been enthralled by *Changing Schools*, a beautifully printed newsletter issued by the National Consortium on Options in Public Education at the School of Education, Indiana University, *New Schools Switchboard* from Baltimore quoted almost a full page in one of their issues. *New Ways in Education* from Los Angeles offers reprints to their subscribers. The people who put out the *Education Exploration Center Newsletter* in Minneapolis are eagerly looking forward to working with *Changing Schools* on a national conference scheduled for October. A Harvard sponsored alternative school I recently worked for subscribes to *only Changing Schools* and visiting strangers who drop by my house

Eric Davin, "On Combatting Liberalism," *New Schools Exchange Newsletter,* pp. 5-7.

looking for information wave copies of it at me. This is not to say that the newsletter itself is widely known or that it is a wildly successful profit-making publication. Rather, that its influence is disproportionate to its significance. Still, it is a symbol of what I have called the "cycle of reform."

There is a cycle of ideology which, in times of optimism, speaks of problems from an environmentalist perspective. In times of retrenchment, problems are phrased in terms of hereditarianism. There is a cycle of finances which commits significant sums of money and energy to projects at their start, but, with meager results and declining enthusiasm, money and energy are progressively withdrawn. And, there is the cycle of personnel. In 1962, James Wilson wrote *The Amateur Democrat* in which he detailed how amateurs are the ones who usually lead political reform efforts. But, it is not only in politics where amateurs open up the windows to fresh winds—*all* true reform efforts, in politics, education or any other field, are the creations of un-tutored and unprofessional *amateurs*. As the reform movement gains momentum and scores successes, a peculiar form of senility sets in. The "revolution" devours its children and professionals replace the enthusiastic beginners. Methods and means of handing down knowledge and skills—usually illusory—are codefied and "legitimized." Then, the reform movement becomes an antique institution no longer speaking to the needs of the people who find themselves trapped within it. This is the cycle of reform. This, too, is now the problem the free school movement must face.

It is obvious in reading *Changing Schools* that they and I mean completely different things when we speak of free schools. To them, it is merely another "alternative" easily compatible with the public structure. To me, free school means amateur parent, amateur student, amateur teacher. Being unapologetically amateur, it is, at this point, outside the public school system. If it is inside the system, it may be an "alternative," "open school," "school without walls," or whatever—but it can never be that small, struggling, shared, face-to-face experience of parents, kids and learners called a "free school."

There is nothing mystical in my insistence that a Free School *at the present time* must of necessity and almost by definition be outside the public school system. It is simply a belief that, as Kozol says: "The school that flies the flag must in the end serve the flag." It is a belief that those who control the public schools may introduce "alternatives"—but only as a means of retaining their control over restless students. A recent article in the *Nation's Schools*, a trade magazine of principals and superintendents (and, seemingly, a favorite of *Changing Schools* staff—see Issue #4, front page), says: "The best way to deal with the vocal minority is to get them involved in setting up an alternative structure."

A recent nation-wide study of 925 School Committee members conducted by the Massachusetts Teachers Association and reported in the January, 1973 issue of their journal reported that 48% of the members were from three occupations: Businessmen from middle or upper management in corporations, lawyers or physicians. Housewives, who constituted 15% of the sample, were predominantly wives of businessmen, lawyers or physicians. The study covered rural, suburban, urban, wealthy, middle class and poor communities. In its conclusion, the study said: "If we assume that school board members pursue the ordinary amount of self-interest behavior, then the actions of the typical school board member are not apt to be harmonious with the needs of public school children. The *conflicts we are witnessing in education are caused by differences in points of view between people on either side of a vast socio-economic gulf.*"

If this study and its conclusions are accurate, and I believe they are, then it explains why a free school must be "independent" and why the kind of educational reform advocated by liberals like those at Indiana University, despite their persuasive rhetoric about brave new horizons, presents no perceptible change in either direction or goals from the present educational structure. It'll make the Darkies down on de ol' plantation a bit happier, but it won't change the fact that Massuh still has slaves.

As far as I can determine, Bob Barr & Co. don't *know* why there is a "Crisis in the Classroom"—or they just don't want to *think* about *why*. They present no reasons for student unrest and parental dis-affiliation. It is not as if we find only the symptoms/free schools here and there as particular local responses to unique local problems. They are nation-wide and affect every strata of society. Shouldn't we know what is causing the problem in order to correctly prepare our response? *Changing Schools* prefers to operate in a social and educational vacuum . . . as if a hungry child presents *only* an educational problem instead of nutritional and economic ones as well. All problems, they believe, can be solved if only we produce enough professional educators to handle them. Next, they will be producing *professional* "amateurs" to teach in "Free Schools." And, why not? Indiana U, is already the third largest teacher-factory in the nation. If they don't do it, who will? *Noblesse oblige!*

Why is it that we see this sudden interest among the professional educators for establishing "alternatives"? Perhaps it is because anyone who is even slightly aware of what is happening in American education knows that the only life to be found is in the Free Schools. Let me quote from *Changing Schools*: "We tried it all—team teaching, multi-media instruction, nongraded classes, programmed instruction, small classes, large classes, new methods, new courses, new curricula, modular scheduling, behavioral objectives, individualized instruction, remedial reading, and even compensatory education." And, still, the Darkies were restless. Nothing worked. Until they discovered "alternatives."

Lo, while the professionals have been working their butts off for the past few decades rearranging deck chairs on the Titanic, an entirely nonprofessional, yet effective method of education was found by uneducated Black parents, amateur unknowns and freaks. Where the professionals failed—the people succeeded. Where the professionals educated to domesticate—the people educated to liberate.

Educational history has repeatedly seen this process of amateur reform among the people replaced by professional "legitimization" by the ones-who-rule. Anything that moves in the lower classes is fair game. Montessori developed her famous method specifically for the working class kids of Rome. Montessori schools are now almost totally the preserve of the middle and upper classes. The child-centered schools of the early Twentieth Century in Greenwich Village, such as the Play School, were designed specifically for the working class and immigrant kids of New York. The artists and intellectuals of the Village flooded the schools. Sesame Street was designed for the inner-city child. Now we can see Sesame Street kits selling for $20 a throw in the stores—and guess who buys them so their kids will get even *more* out of the show? The Progressive Education Association was founded by total unknowns and nonprofessionals. It quickly evolved into the official organization of the triumphant liberal professionals. The descent of the liberals upon the free schools is part of the historical pattern.

This is where I'm coming from. The schools are the way they are by design—not by accident and not by a one hundred-fifty year fit of what Charles Silberman calls "mindlessness." *School is war upon the poor and that's the way the liberals of the ruling class want it.* Schools are used by those on top to stay on top. Inasmuch as the majority of us accept schools as the "natural order of things"—they have succeeded in their purpose. Like all institutions, schools serve the status quo. As such, they are no different than the other prison-institutions: the family, the church, the military, the courts, the media, the prisons themselves. Their purpose is to socialize us into our proper roles in life.

The Schoolboys of Barbiana were perceptive when they said: "We may seem to be implying the existence of some master who manipulates you. Someone who has cut the schools to measure. Does he really exist? Is there a handful of men gathered around a table, holding all strings in their hands: banks, business, political machines, the press, fashions? We don't know . . . If we claim this we feel our book takes on a certain mystery-story tone. If we don't, we seem to play the simpleton . . . It is like arguing that so many little gears have fallen into place by chance. Out sprang an armored car able to make war by itself, with no driver."

However, it is not a group of men around a table who cut the schools to measure, but an underground river of cultural and psychological values which pulls us all into its current. This society—indeed, all societies—has always been and continues to be based upon class inequality. What the liberal reformers of the "Progressive Era" did was simply to replace what that inequality was *ostensibly* based upon—but they did not touch the inequality itself.

Liberals couldn't accept the blatancy of class inequality based upon inherited social and economic status. This was not only an embarrassment to the ideals this country was founded upon, but, more importantly, it was too obvious and vulnerable as a wall of privilege. What they did, therefore, was to *ostensibly* change the basis of inequality from birth to talent/ability/ambition/intelligence. They created a society governed by an elite chosen from *all* the classes—*but,* there was *still* an elite and *still* the Great Unwashed. They created the Meritocracy. They created the schools as we know them and used them as an excuse for not dealing simply and *directly* with the political, economic and social inequalities of our society.

It is more difficult to build up the resentment, the frustration, the hatred of class inequality needed for a true class consciousness when the best of the poor, the most aggressive, the most ambitious, the natural leaders of the poor, are welcomed into the ruling ranks as the returning prodigal sons. Again, the Schoolboys are right-on: "If the poor would band together at the university, they could make a difference. But, no. Instead, they are received like brothers by the rich and soon are rewarded with all their defects. The final outcome: 100 per cent daddy's boys."

Even more important in this process, however, is the psychological emasculation of the poor who don't make it, instead of being blatantly forced out of the path to upward mobility, the poor are "cooled out." While they may get to college, they know full well that it is an alien environment. Seldom is a working class student actually flunked out. Rather, the student gets the message and transfers to an "easier" school or program, or drops out into the job market, the army or the first prospective husband who comes along. And the student will always afterward believe that he *could* have made it—*if* he had had what it takes. He believes he had a real chance and that his children *will* have a real chance at making it.

However, his actions are not totally his own. His entire environment has motivated him to strive for some things rather than others—to accept some things while not expecting others. There is a class culture of which he is inextricably a part, a class culture which society studiously nurtures, and this class culture motivates the ruling class to succeed and the lower class to fail—and to accept their failure. Of course, the important part this propaganda of culture plays in determining "college chances" is never acknowledged by society, for the myth of unlimited opportunity for all plays an integral role in maintaining the psychological, political, social and economic status quo. If the "eased out" students realized the system was rigged against them, they would not accept so easily the unequal distribution of social rewards and privileges based upon "credentials." Most importantly, therefore, the schools must discourage the working class student from making those first radical psychological decisions upon which all true class consciousness must be based.

In our society, one's *self* respect usually results from the fact that others respect you. Others give respect based upon external, material possessions—cars, clothes, homes, degrees, women, men—whatever. If one is poor, one does not have the possessions, the respect of others dependent upon possessions, nor, consequently, self-respect. Thus, one attempts to "make it" as others do. The moment he does so, he is lost. Concentration on sports, fashion, style, sex, possessions, does not leave energy and time enough for the difficult struggle of "consciousness raising" and the political organizing necessary to actually change one's condition. It creates a condition of psychological acceptance of things as they are . . . a condition of "every man for himself and the Devil take the hindmost." One must make a radical psychological decision to say "No" to the propaganda of culture before one can really challenge one's condition in any meaningful way. But, the schools militate against the likelihood of making this decision by encouraging the struggle of all against all—and liberal ideology discourages class consciousness and unity by holding up the meritocratic society in which any *one* can make it—but your brothers and sisters must be abandoned. Thus, by putting the emphasis upon *individual mobility*, the liberals maintained *class immobility* and could continue to enjoy the benefits of privilege.

Anyone seriously and honestly interested in "changing schools" must ask the real purpose of schools, especially when faced with the success of someone like Paoli Freire. Freire has demonstrated with *entire villages* of adults in both Brazil and Chile that basic literacy can be taught to total illiterates in 40 hours of instruction. If this is true, what are the kids doing in school from 9 to 5, nine months a year, for nine, ten, twelve years? Learning to read? Then why is it that according to statistics of the School Department itself, 50% of all Cambridge children cannot read up to their grade level? Could it be that kids aren't sent to school to learn to read and write, but to undergo psychological and cultural indoctrination and the instilling of certain behavioral traits? One is firmly forced to the conclusion that exposure to the propaganda of culture is the main reason kids are in school.

Upper class schools have always been characterized by a certain element of playfulness, independence and flexibility which has been absent in schools designed for the mass of the people. The people were destined for the worker-slots of our corporate-industrial society, therefore, they had to learn to be punctual, to be consistent, to obey rules, regulations and authority figures, to be neat, to be silent and to learn their place. These, then, are the things we learn in school—and we learn our lessons well. We are hooked into the American

Dream at an early age and our "habit" allows the liberal ruling class to hold on to their privileges and property while insuring a modicum of social justice to salve the conscience.

We thus come to the present condition of liberal education reform symbolized by *Changing Schools*. The more people withdraw their allegiance from the system and evidence mounts that school and, consequently, societal success depends upon inherited position, the more liberals say the schools should compensate. Thus, we have the proliferation of remedial programs like Head Start and Follow Through (Son of Head Start) and public "alternatives." And, as there is no real evidence that compensatory programs help the children involved or that public "alternatives" change the function and purpose of schooling, we shall see more of the same. And never, never must we question the basic societal reasons for these problems nor try to deal *directly* with them.

In a lead article by Mike Hickey in *Changing Schools #3*, it is stated: "The system of public education in Seattle—indeed, in any city today—does reasonably well what it was designed to do, namely, to provide an educational program aimed at meeting the needs of the majority of its students." An examination of schools today and of the historical record shows that schools were *never* meant to "meet the needs of the majority of its students"—unless those needs happened to coincide with the needs of an industrial-capitalist society. Whether *Changing Schools* presents arguments like this in innocence or not is irrelevant. It still serves the purpose of de-radicalizing educational protest. For this reason, they must be rejected. We must know clearly who our enemies are and we must have the courage to declare them so.

Changing Schools would have us direct our energies towards their kind of public alternatives—yet from personal experience I know the Boston alternatives they hold up for emulation to be phantoms of change and from what Herbert Kohl and others have said about the Federally force-fed alternatives in Berkeley, they, too, are not what they claim to be. The type of alternatives liberals champion usually bring with them the hierarchical structure and bureaucratic style of the public schools—and that is the main enemy.

Changing Schools would also have us abandon free schools as, they say, free schools are only here for the blink of an eye. In the above quoted article by Mike Hickey, he makes the statement: ". . . the educational life-span of these private alternatives (are) less than a year." In honesty, most opponents of free schools give us a little longer quoting Harvey Haber's completely imaginary life-span of "18 months."

Yet, Allen Graubard, director of the New Schools Directory Project (the most accurate national directory to date) has stated that *most* free schools haven't even been in existence for two years yet, so it is difficult to give an accurate survival-estimate. However, he would guess that perhaps only one in five free schools and possibly only one in ten, have actually folded. The decentralization of the Movement and the lack of accurate information works against us when it keeps us from realizing that, contrary to the seemingly gleeful statements of public school liberals, independent free schools *can* grow, thrive and survive as strong and viable bodies.

As strong and viable bodies, free schools serve, as no other educational structure can, to show us what it means to live and learn in an environment of freedom. In doing this, the best free schools also serve as catalysts for changing the public schools . . . and change them we must.

The public schools, whether "alternative" or not, shall continue to fail until school, as we know it, ceases to exist. Justice and lives for our children worth living requires the elimination of the channeling function of these schools. Yet, nowhere does *Changing Schools* help us here. They are articulate and seductive in their reasoning about "alternatives to suit everyone," but are their offerings *really* alternatives? Nowhere do they ask the only question worth asking: What is the class structure and function of the schools? One is required, therefore, to question their committment to "changing" the "schools." Yet, they are absolutely right in one respect. There must be a committment by *someone* to changing public schools. It is in this role that free schools can find their most legitimate purpose.

Free schools will never serve more than a fraction of the kids who need schools of freedom. Therefore, public schools *must* be changed. To use a rough analogy, free schools can serve as guerilla sanctuaries where those committed to real change in the public schools can learn, gain strength and inspiration from, and prepare to set out once more on the larger struggle.

I do not oppose educational liberals *because* they focus on public schools. No, I object to the *way* in which they focus on public schools. I agree that public monies should be spent on free schools, but if one must also accept "accountability," as *Changing Schools* phrases it, it is better to go it alone. Free schools are only accountable to the people who run them—the parents, the kids, the teachers. The kind of alternatives the liberals want are accountable to the *existing* structure of professionals, administrators and bureaucrats—to the ruling class.

The uniqueness of free schools which the professional cannot duplicate (and why, at this point, a public free school is a contradiction in terms) is the "decentralized" power and control of resources. It is a home-grown affair with no outside interference. And, it is *that* which free schools have a responsibility to bring to public schools.

We should not say it cannot be done. Already, there are signs of success. The Central School, in Cambridge, is a free school committed to changing the public schools. It deliberately does not go beyond age six so that the children and their now-radicalized parents are forced back into the public system where they serve as catalysts for change. Already, parent councils in two public elementary schools have chosen new headmasters (principals) to fill vacancies with the Superintendent merely rubber-stamping their choices. The new Alternative Public School was nurtured into existence by the Central School and has built-in parent participation. And, parent councils to run each local school will be a major issue in the next School Committee election in November. This— because of advocates for the people and a strong and enduring free school committed to changing the public schools of the city.

This is the direction in which we should head. A commitment to change public schools, yes, but a commitment which brings with it the passionate belief in the people's right to control their own lives . . . a commitment which cannot be detoured from its demand for a massive decentralization of power and resources. Any other struggle, any other "alternative," is not worthy of the name.

Eric Davin

How can you tell in what ways, and to what extent, a school embodies the organization and structures that are antithetical to the pursuit of the democratic ideals of equality, justice, and liberation? To bring it down to the everyday practices of schools, here is a checklist we have adapted in order to help you check out a school. Anthony Barton prepared this continuum originally as a way of measuring the continuum or spread of a school ranging from the conventional, authoritarian, straight school to the unconventional, non-authoritarian, open, free, or alternative school. It doesn't tell you whether a school is good or bad unless you say which of these practices are good and which are bad. Try using this checklist on the next school you find yourself in. How many items on the checklist apply to it? Look back over the list after you have checked the applicable items. What do you see?

____ A notice on the wall prohibiting something.

____ A system of bells or speakers with which it is possible to interrupt the work of many people simultaneously.

____ A classroom with a chalkboard, a set of chairs with built-in book racks, and a tidy floor.

____ A bulletin board with a timetable pinned to it.

____ A set of thirty or more identical books, or a row of thirty or more private lockers too small to hold a guitar.

____ A computer terminal dispensing programmed instruction.

____ A system whereby meals are prepared by those other than students and staff.

____ An understanding that the school is run by the staff, who respect the wishes of the students.

____ A room which students enter only with permission from a member of the staff.

____ A library in which as many books as possible are numbered and catalogued.

____ A locked storeroom from which an appointed member of the staff dispenses stationery or other materials.

____ A janitor who sweeps the floors regularly.

____ A cold wall which is hard to touch and painted a pastel shade.

____ An asphalt playground.

____ A daily assembly.

____ Organized competitive games.

____ A telephone which students use only with permission of a member of the staff.

____ A large television set used by whole classes to watch educational TV.

____ A stage with lighting, flats and curtains.

____ A carpeted resource center or library with audiovisual equipment in carrels with headphones for students to use quietly.

____ A swimming pool.

____ Supervised visits to places outside the school by large numbers of students.

___ A room which members of the staff use only with the permission of a student.

___ A garden or grounds with mowed lawns and trim paths.

___ Still and movie cameras which students are told how to use.

___ A precision instrument, such as a telescope or a machine tool, which students use under supervision.

___ Still and movie cameras which students use without instruction.

___ A resource center or library in which students are free to use projectors and record players and to make a noise and a mess.

___ A copying machine free for the use of students and staff.

___ A hobbies room open to all and equipped with benches, power tools and materials.

___ A flexible area with an overhead grid carrying power and communications, which is used for informal drama, movie-making, discussions and dances.

___ A number of mobile chairs, tables, cameras, spotlamps, mirrors, and "hospital" screens.

___ An open storeroom from which people take what they need when they need it.

___ A warm wall painted a bold color, into which your fingers sink.

___ Unsupervised visits to places outside the school by small numbers of students.

___ A large surface (such as walls and ceilings) on which people paint murals and slogans and graffiti.

___ Unrestricted use of a telephone, or unrestricted use of all the audio-visual equipment in the school.

___ An informal cooking area where students fry eggs and brew cocoa when they feel like it.

___ An understanding that decisions affecting the community are made by students and staff together.

___ A room serving no particular purpose.

___ A school vehicle which students drive.

___ A bin filled with free learning materials.

___ A pile of junk, or a room which is never tidy.

___ Spontaneous noncompetitive games.

___ Trees which are climbed.

___ Space in which people run.

___ Water with which people play.

___ Mud in which people roll.

___ Long grass in which people roll.

___ Sky.

We found Anthony Barton's checklist in the *de schooling primer no. 7,* a publication of the Zephyros Education Exchange, 1201 Stanyan St., San Francisco 94117.

CONCLUSION

People of strikingly different political persuasions throughout the world agree that the purpose of education—always identified with schooling—is to serve the ends of society. Whether it is emerging Third World nations, communist and socialist nations, black nationalists, conservatives or liberals, all join the middle class industrialized nations in bending their schools—and the children in them— to the service of society. They may differ as to which segments of society and for which ends the schools are to serve. But no one—not China, not Cuba, and certainly not Russia—questions this role of the schools. And for all of his alleged radical ideas in education, John Dewey never questioned this identification of the basic purpose of education/schooling.

It hasn't been questioned because the purpose is an integral part of the industrial development of a nation, and few have questioned the value of that. Formal education as we know it today—that is, schooling—is a creature of middle class industrial society. That is what our authors have been saying throughout this book. In William Pepper's words:

> Despite the occasional loftiness of its rhetoric, American education primarily serves the interests of society and attempts to fulfill the purposes of the state. In doing so it follows the long historical line of formal educational systems which in various ways have been committed to molding subservient individuals in accord with the needs of an outside institution—usually the state or the church. Our children, like us and all who have gone before, are subject to pressures to adopt societally sanctioned attitudes, aspirations, and modes of behavior. The pressures and training for mass conformity may not be as explicit in the modern world as Margaret Mead has found them in primitive cultures, as they existed in ancient Sparta, or as they were fulfilled under the theocracy of the Hebrews, but they are just as real for our young. If anything, they are more insidiously pervasive and dishonest because they hold out the promise of being something else; open, free, and child-centered.[9]

As Pepper points out, there is hardly a country in the world today that does not compel its children to attend school at least until the age of fifteen. And if compulsory school attendance was challenged as unconstitutional in our courts today, it would likely be ruled that overriding social purposes demand that the state require the attendance in school of all its young people.

A number of society's purposes are served by this compulsory attendance. We have devoted separate chapters to the more pervasive purposes: political, economic, social. As Pepper says, by keeping them in schools we keep the young away from the unpredictable learning experiences which always pose a threat to the established order.

> Not only does schooling afford an opportunity to train and produce manpower for the various functions of the economy—previously blue-collar industrial workers, and now increasingly white-collar service-oriented employees—but it also allows the state to assert its perspectives of the world, people, and ideas through the media of the academic disciplines . . .

---

9. Pepper, *The Self-Managed Child*, p.105.

Formal education from the earliest ages provides a marvelous opportunity to shield our young from real-life experiences which might undercut or bring into question the official interpretations of the past, used constantly to justify the present and prepare the next generation for more of the same.[10]

But now some people—Pepper among them—are pointing out that America is in a "post-industrial" age. We no longer are building an economy (though we seem to have to spend a lot of time keeping the thing healthy). We no longer are a nation in need of people who embody the industrial/frontier values of thrift, hard work, industry, self-denial, and all the rest of those necessities that we made into virtues. Our schools from their very beginning were expected to foster these virtues, and foster them they did (at considerable expense to other human virtues). And they are still basically organized and structured for that purpose. They are anachronisms in this respect.

We come then to the conclusion that in our society the future of schools as the means of meeting our educational needs is indeed dim. We are acutely aware of the fact that, in all of our encouraging our readers to learn how schools operate in order to bring them around to foster the democratic ideals that our rhetoric has always said they are serving, we may be urging on them an exercise in futility. A kind of washing of the garbage before throwing it out. However, we do not rule out that in order for American education to serve the democratic ideals of justice, equality, and liberation we will have to end, or at least seriously attenuate, school attendance. The more we pursue radical change of schools the more it will become obvious that we have reached the limit to what schools can do.

In short, we believe that our call to change schooling in this society will ultimately lead to the development of alternatives to schooling as a means of dealing with our educational needs. It is our belief that there already exist in this society more potent and more successful means of teaching the young than formal schooling; that these are going on all around us—the media are perfect examples—and that by the time a youngster enters formal schooling, he or she has been highly "educated" by the many conditioning, training, and indoctrinating forces in our society. Many questions can be raised about the purposes of these forces. That they are not recognized as supplements and substitutes for schooling, and thus do not receive the formal recognition as part of our educational system, perhaps should be more cause for alarm than what happens (and doesn't happen) in our schools. (Not the least cause for alarm is the fact that so many of these forces, like our schools, are serving the purposes of the state and other special interests in society rather than the interests of those who learn from them.)

We may well be at that point where schools provide the least amount of learning in our society. A new method is called for, tied to a new idea of what the educational needs of our citizens are—especially our young citizens. We do not see our analysis as antithetical to that eventuality. We would like to think that it will only be through such an analysis, or one similar to it, that significant numbers of people will begin to see the new and seriously attentuated role of

10. Ibid., pp. 105-106.

formal learning (as exemplified in institutional learning), and the wider and more flexible learning arrangements possible in our social relationships (such as more humane ideas of young people and their nurture.)

It has been pointed out that being in a crisis situation is not all bad; that a crisis also carries within it the possibility for change, for new directions. There is no institution in American society that is not now being challenged for its human worth. Periods of great human achievement have always been preceded by periods of great unrest and turmoil. Something like this may now be going on in our educational arrangements. Perhaps the best attitude here is to remain skeptical, to avoid positions of certitude when our knowledge is not adequate to justify it; to test the claims that are made in formal education—and there are many—with constant critical scrutiny. That alone could win you the title of "radical." Not many people like to have their balloons popped.

It is not easy to persist with questions in the face of pressures to go along. But to go along without question, to agree in the face of your own doubts, is to become part of the problem. Whatever final decisions you come to concerning the many issues in education today, you may perform one of your most effective acts by deciding on the basis of your own thoughts and feelings.

If some one idea, some insight, some point in the writings of the authors we have assembled here has contributed to your decision to try anew, to take a different direction, then our purpose in putting this book together will have been achieved. For it is in what our readers do after they have read this book that we will find its worth.